BORLAND PRESS

Borland® C++ 4.0 Programming for Windows™

Paul Yao

New York

Borland® C++ 4.0 Programming for Windows™

Published in the United States by Random House, Inc., New York, and simultaneously in Canada by Random House of Canada, Limited.

Manufactured in the United States of America

First Edition

0 9 8 7 6 5 4 3 2 1

ISBN 0-679-75146-7

New York Toronto London Sydney Auckland

Foreword

This is a serious programmer's book, as a quick glance at the extensive code listings will demonstrate. But it's a lot more than the sum of the listings, as the concepts and mindset of Windows are also covered in detail.

No one ever said that traditional Windows programming was easy—at least no one sane! The full power of Windows lies in its complexity, which is conventionally accessed through C function calls to the Windows Application Program Interface (API). We at Borland feel that our ObjectWindows library greatly simplifies the task of dealing with the API by successfully encapsulating many complex features, but programmers still need to know how Windows is wired together, to create well-behaved applications that follow the Windows user interface standard.

We're extremely pleased to welcome well-known Windows expert, Paul Yao, to this task, as an official Borland Press author. Paul brings to this project a depth of understanding of Windows programming that few can approach, let alone rival. Borland C++ 4.0 and ObjectWindows 2.0 give you the tools to master Windows, while Paul gives you the skills and insights to use those tools effectively.

Paul's intent is twofold—to show the concepts behind the full range of Windows features—text, graphics, menus, dialog boxes, scroll bars, and custom controls—and to show you how these features can be implemented quickly and efficiently with OWL 2.0. You'll also find useful discussions of memory management, resources, and dynamic link libraries.

If you want to increase your knowledge of Windows as a programming environment (and these days, who doesn't?), I think you'll find this book a very useful adjunct to your programming efforts.

PKahn

Philippe Kahn
CEO, Borland International

Contents

13 Windowing 357

14 Dialog Boxes 409

PART FIVE

Message Driven Input 443

15 Keyboard Input 445

To my mother, Mary Grace Yao

Acknowledgments

Thanks to the developers who have attended my Windows programming workshops at corporations around the United States. Your unceasing quest to "get it right," and your tough questions keep me on my toes. Thanks also to the development team at Abacus Research AG in St. Gallen, Switzerland for their timely comments, hospitality, and proving that bunnies do exist.

At Borland International, thanks to Glenn Cochran for a thorough technical review of the first edition, and to Peter Eden and Eric Swenson for your help in understanding the design of OWL 1.0. Thanks to Thomas Cromwell for a technical review of this edition. Thanks to Nan Borreson and the rest of her department for getting me the software—and other support—when I needed it.

Much of what I know about Microsoft Windows—and its various API—is due to help from members of the development teams of Windows 1, 2, 3. Thanks to the developers and marketers who gave generously of their time and energies to help me get it right: Peter Belew, John Butler, Mark Cligget, Clark Cyr, Rick Dill, Marlin Eller, Ron Gery, Bob Gunderson, Paul Klinger, Scott MacGregor, Ed Mills, Walt Moore, Gabe Newell, Chris Peters, John Pollock, Rao Remala, Lin Shaw, Charles Simonyi, Tandy Trower, Manny Vellon, David Weise and Steve Wood. Thanks to the Windows "New Technology" developers Dave Cutler and Lou Perazzoli for a better understanding of how the NT Executive does its portable magic.

Elsewhere at Microsoft, thanks to those who helped and supported in the creation of this book. First, a special thank you to David Durant, who is and always will be my first Windows programming instructor. Thanks to Jim Cash for helping solve the puzzle of making Windows programming comprehensible and to Paul Klemond, a crackerjack Windows application developer who helped me solve quite a few Windows programming riddles.

Thanks to the staff at ISD-The Paul Yao Company for their support during the first and subsequent editions of this book. Thanks to ISD's best coach, mentor, and friend, Bill Bergman.

At Random House Electronic Publishing, I'd like to thank my publisher, Kenzi Sugihara. Thanks also to Stephen Guty, my editor, for his long hours and painstaking efforts. Thanks to Stephen Gambino for his editing help and to Karl Barndt of Electric Ink, Ltd.

And finally, a special word of thanks to Nancy and Helen Brocard of Pogacha Restaurant in Bellevue, Washington, the official caterer for this book.

Preface

This book is for experienced C++ programmers who wish to learn about writing Windows programs using Borland's ObjectWindows Library (**OWL**) 2.0 class library. If you know C but haven't gotten up to speed on C++ yet, I'd recommend learning C++ before attempting to tackle a new programming environment (Windows) *and* a new class library (OWL). On the other hand, if you are an experienced Windows programmer and are just starting to learn C++, this book will map your knowledge of Windows programming to the specifics of OWL 2.0.

The first edition of this book was a spin-off of *Peter Norton's Windows 3.0 Power Programming Techniques*, a book I wrote to help C programmers explore the intricacies of the Windows API. The earlier edition covered OWL 1.0, but emphasized the Windows API. Borland's update to OWL, version 2.0, more completely encapsulates the native Windows API. The growth of OWL has caused me to shift the emphasis of this book towards the work done for you by OWL. However, a solid understanding of the native Windows API (**WinAPI**) is still required to get the most from OWL, so that is still the primary focus of this new edition.

The fundamentals of Windows programming remain the same no matter what language you use. For this reason, the overall structure of this book is identical to the C version. Significant portions have been rewritten, however, to reflect support for the Win32 API and the enhancements that are new to OWL 2.0. In particular, these portions of this book are completely new:

- Chapters 2, 3, 4, and 5 have been completely rewritten. This reflects the fact that a minimum Windows program in C differs substantially from a similar OWL 2.0 program in C++. I have placed more emphasis on the "big picture" architecture of Windows, while covering significant details of the OWL Application (**`TApplication`**) class and the frame window (**`TFrameWindow`**) class.
- All sample programs have been completely rewritten. To reflect the growing importance of the Win32 API, make-files to build Win16 as well as Win32 programs are provided. Some programs, like the toolbar and status line demo in Chapter 13 (GADGETS) have no equivalent in the C book. Order a machine readable version of all the sample programs by calling 1-800-942-3535 (see last page of the book for more details).

To get started programming with OWL 2.0, you'll need version 4.0 of the Borland C++ compiler. For hardware, you'll need a minimum 386 computer with 4 megabytes of RAM, 75 megabytes of hard disk space for the compiler. (You can manage with 50 meg in a pinch.) A faster CPU, more RAM and more disk space is nice, but you probably already knew that.

Version 4.0 of the compiler comes equipped with several debuggers, including a 16-bit version in the Integrated Development Environment (**IDE**), a 32-bit version in the 32-bit IDE, a 16-bit Turbo Debugger for Windows (**TDW**) and 32-bit TDW. When debugging with TDW, you might want to consider the following additional (but optional) hardware to give TDW its own output device:

- On computers equipped with an AT-style bus, an MDA card and a monochrome monitor. A Hercules monochrome graphics card can be substituted for the MDA card.
- On computers equipped with an MCA-style bus, an 8514/a adapter and an 8514 (or equivalent) monitor.

Intertwined with the discussion of OWL 2.0 and Windows programming in this book, I place special emphasis on the architecture and inner workings of Windows. I interviewed members of the Windows development team—both past and present—to learn their design goals, problems, and worries while they were building the various versions of this operating system. For this version of the book, I also spent time talking with the OWL developers to insure that I fully understood the design of this class library.

This book is divided into six sections. Part I provides a brief history of Windows and describes the three challenges that new programmers face: event-driven programming, graphical output, and mastering built-in user-interface objects. I provide some suggestions based on work I have been doing for the past seven years—at conferences, in classrooms, through books and magazine articles—teaching the basics of Windows programming.

Part II dissects a minimum Windows program, and explores several fundamental topics in Windows programming. The purpose of this section is to help you understand the basic structure that all OWL programs share. As you'll see, the foundation of every OWL program are two pieces: an application object and a frame window object.

Part III introduces you to Windows' Graphics Device Interface (GDI). Your programs will use GDI to send output to the display screen and to the printer. Chapter 6 describes basic concepts in graphic programming, such as drawing coordinates, clipping, the role of GDI's **device context**, and the role of the very important `WM_PAINT` message. Subsequent chapters cover the details of drawing pixels, markers, lines, filled areas, and finally text.

Part IV covers the three key user-interface objects: menus, windows, and dialog boxes. This section covers the internal WinAPI operation, as well as the ways that OWL 2.0 extends these capabilities and in general, simplifies your life.

Part V describes the ways a program gets user input. All implementations of Windows—Windows 3.1, Windows NT, and even the future CHICAGO—are event-driven operating systems. It's not surprising that input—in the form of mouse and keyboard messages—arrives as event-generated messages. As always, the emphasis is on the inner workings of the system: how input is received by the physical hardware, passed through the various device drivers and system components, and finally delivered to an

OWL program.

Part VI covers operating system considerations. This includes two basic areas: memory and dynamic linking. The Win32 API promises to send segmented memory packing. The C++ **new** operator provides hope that dynamic memory allocation will get easier over time. In spite of these developments, however, the Windows API has numerous capabilities that can help you fine-tune your program's memory use. If you plan to implement your software for the currently dominant installed base of Win16 computers, you'll want to know about every trick I describe. If you have the luxury of not worrying about memory, you'll want to consider this material as background reading to help you in your debugging efforts.

PART ONE

An Introduction to Windows

1

An Introduction to Windows

Unless you've been programming in another graphical user interface (GUI) system, learning to program for Windows takes a lot of time and effort. It takes time because Windows has a large, quirky programming interface. Depending on how you count them, there are between 750 and 1250 function calls in the various Windows APIs. You probably won't call every single function, but wading through the documentation to find the ones you *do* need takes time.

Learning Windows programming requires quite a bit of effort because Windows—like other GUI environments—uses programming models that are new to most programmers. The use of **printf** to create character output, for example, has been replaced with a large library of graphic-output primitives. The friendly, sequential, almost batch ordering of program instructions has been replaced with many, disjoint minisequences. And the user interface—while "friendly" enough in its own right—has a programming interface that needs taming before it will serve you and your users.

One question that every Windows programmer should think about is why Windows has gotten so much attention from **users**. The most important thing—certainly the most obvious thing—that Windows provides is a **standard user-interface**. A "Windows-compatible" application, after all, is one that—to an experienced Windows user—behaves in a predictable way. This makes it easy to learn new programs, and easy to remember how to accomplish common tasks like editing, printing, and getting help.

To get a better idea for how this standardization simplifies things for users, consider a simple command—the one to exit an application. Table 1.1 shows some of the variety in the exit command among non-Windows applications.

Table 1.1 Exit Commands

Application	*Command To Exit*
dBASE III	Type "quit" at dot command prompt
Lotus 1-2-3 for MS-DOS	/ W(orksheet) Q(uit) Y(es)
UNIX "vi" editor	:q!
Taito's Arkanoid II	Hit [F10] Key

If you stop for a moment and think about applications that you use daily, you'll find that you can think of other, different exit commands. These differences arise because of the different styles of user-interface, and because these programs were written without regard for user-interface standards.

Windows applications share a common exit command, which makes it easy for a user who knows how to exit *one* Windows application to exit *any* Windows application. And that's just one example of the hundreds I could list for you. The important thing is that—after the initial shock of learning their first Windows application—users find that Windows makes it easier for them to be productive with computers. That's good for software developers because when users figure out how valuable software can be, they want even more software!

Since the user-interface is such an important part of Windows, a programmer who is new to Windows should spend some time every day using a Windows application. For example, get into the habit of using a Windows word-processor to write your design documents or your status reports. Figure your taxes using a Windows spreadsheet, or put together a database using a Windows-compatible database application. The time you spend learning the subtle nuances of the Windows user-interface will help you make better decisions when you create Windows software.

A History of Windows

All GUI systems trace their roots back to the work done at Xerox. In 1970, Xerox created the Palo Alto Research Center (PARC). Its charter was to create a new architecture for the way information is handled. Among its other accomplishments, PARC is credited with the development of laser printing, local area networks, graphical user interfaces, and advances in object-oriented programming.

The researchers at PARC built several versions of a machine they dubbed "Alto." Over the years, several hundred of these internal research machines were built and were in widespread use. Built on the research with Alto, Xerox created a commercial GUI system: the Star 8010 workstation. Xerox introduced the Star in April 1981, four months before the IBM PC was made public. This multitasking system came equipped with a mouse and a bitmapped graphical display on which were displayed icons, windows, and proportionally spaced text. Although its high price kept it from becoming a commercial success, the Star marks an important milestone as the first commercially available GUI system.

The story is told that Steve Jobs, a co-founder of Apple Computer, was taken on a tour of Xerox PARC in 1979 or so. He was so impressed by the various Alto systems that he saw, that he returned to Apple and pushed for development of a similar system. Apple introduced its first GUI system in 1983: the Apple Lisa. Apple followed the Lisa with its second GUI system, the Apple Macintosh. For its announcement, Apple bought time during the Super Bowl in January 1984 and aired a commercial that introduced the Macintosh as the computer to save the world from the nightmare of Big Brother described in George Orwell's novel *1984*. The importance of the Apple Macintosh is that it was the first commercially successful GUI system.

Microsoft started working on Windows in the spring of 1983. Eight years had passed since Microsoft's founders, Bill Gates and Paul Allen, wrote a BASIC interpreter for the world's first computer kit, the MITS Altair. And two years had passed since IBM introduced its personal computer, which came bundled with two Microsoft products: DOS and BASIC. Microsoft was just getting ready to ship version 2.0 of DOS, with its support for a hierarchical file system to support the hard disk of another new product, IBM's PC/XT computer.

At that time, there was talk at Microsoft of building a GUI system for the IBM personal computers, but no firm plans had been put in place. The primary reason was that the typical PC in those days had two floppy drives, 64K of RAM, and an 8088 CPU. For a GUI system to have acceptable performance, it was felt that more powerful hardware was needed. Hard disks would have to be available to provide fast access, and more memory would be needed to accommodate both the sophisticated code and the memory-hungry graphic data that such systems require. But something happened to spur Microsoft into GUI development.

In February 1983, VisiCorp, makers of the (then) popular spreadsheet VisiCalc, announced a GUI product for the IBM PC. Dubbed "VisiOn," it provided the motivation for Microsoft to begin working on its own GUI system. After all, if VisiOn caught on, it presented the possibility of taking software developers off the MS-DOS standard. And one thing was clear very early on at Microsoft: Software standards and compatibility would always be critical to the success of the microcomputer industry.

A team of developers that became known as the "Interactive Systems Group," or ISG, was assembled at Microsoft. Among the members of the team was a Xerox PARC alumnus, Scott MacGregor. Another Windows developer, Neil Konzen, had worked on porting Microsoft's spreadsheet, Multiplan, to the Macintosh. When the first version of Windows was introduced in November 1985, it had features that reflected the influence of Xerox PARC and the Apple Macintosh. But Windows itself was home-grown Microsoft.

Version 1.01 of Windows started shipping in November 1985. As depicted in Figure 1.1, the first version of Windows provided automatic tiling of program windows. It was felt that the automatic arrangement of windows minimized the amount of work required of the user. This first version also supported overlapping or "popup" windows, which served primarily for the creation of dialog boxes. Windows 1 sported a "three-slice toaster," which provided access to the system menu. Some of the developers joked that this was actually a tiny vent that served to cool the screen lest it become overheated from the speed of the graphics.

The first version of Windows was built to run on a two-floppy-drive IBM PC with 256K RAM and an Intel 8088 CPU. This, incidentally, was the configuration used by ISG team members themselves during the earliest days of Windows development. Only later were tools available that developers today take for granted: hard disks and high-speed local area networks with file and print servers. And while this slowed development somewhat, Microsoft knew that this was the equipment that application developers would someday use to create software that would run under Windows. Developing in this environment, then, helped to stress test Windows' suitability for application development.

The next major revision of Windows was version 2, which started shipping in September 1987. Windows 2, shown in Figure 1.2, featured overlapping windows. The primary reason for the change from automatic tiling was feedback Microsoft had received from end users who did not appreciate the benefits of tiled windows, but who felt rather that tiling got in the way.

Besides a new user interface, one of the key improvements introduced in Windows 2 was better use of memory in the form of support for expanded memory—memory made available according to the **Expanded Memory Specification (EMS)**. EMS describes a

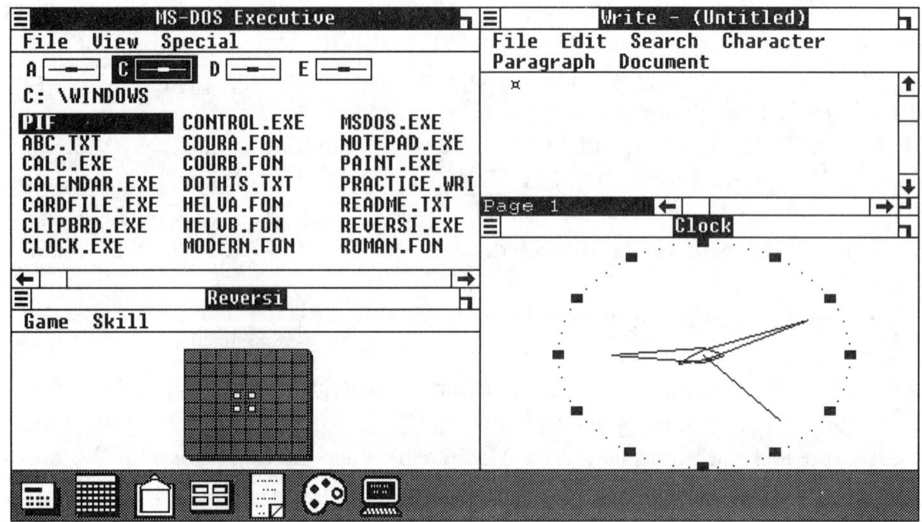

Figure 1.1 Windows version 1.01

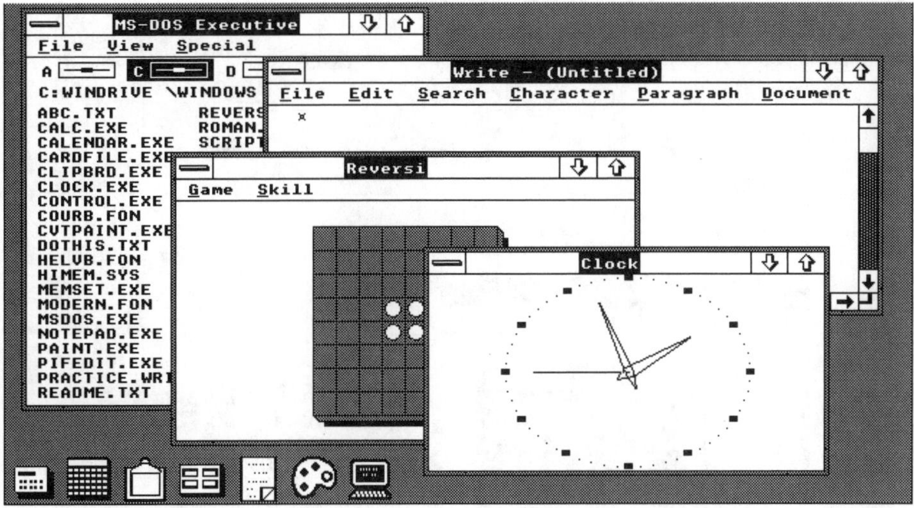

Figure 1.2 Windows version 2

bank switching technique that allows additional memory to be available, although bank-switched memory is not *simultaneously* available. EMS under Windows 2 allowed more Windows programs to reside in memory at the same time, since each program was given a private EMS bank. EMS helped relieve the memory crunch that Windows 1 users had experienced, but didn't completely solve the memory shortage problem since Windows 2 only ran in Real Mode. Even on the powerful Intel 80286 and 80386 chips, for compatibility reasons, Intel gave these chips the same one-megabyte address space as its less powerful siblings, the 8088 and 8086.

With much fanfare, Microsoft announced version 3 of Windows on May 22, 1990, and started shipping shrink-wrapped packages immediately. Within six weeks, Microsoft had shipped 500,000 copies of the new version, breaking every record for the sale of any software product in a six-week period. From a sales standpoint, industry watchers worldwide have found Windows 3 to be a smashing success.

Figure 1.3 shows the new Windows 3 user interface, created to give Windows a new look for the 1990s. It features a proportional system font, to give Windows a more refined look and to make text easier to read. Three-dimensional shadowing, color icons, and redesigned applications combine to make Windows more appealing to the average user. Windows 3 also has better support for running DOS applications, which prompted many MS-DOS users to use Windows as a task-switcher between their DOS applications.

From a programming point of view, Microsoft provided an even richer set of capabilities in the user interface: Support for owner-draw menus, owner-draw listboxes, and owner-draw buttons gives programmers the capability to customize Windows more than ever before. Menus in the new Windows can be nested as deeply as programmers can make them, and tear-off menus give programmers the freedom to place menus anywhere they

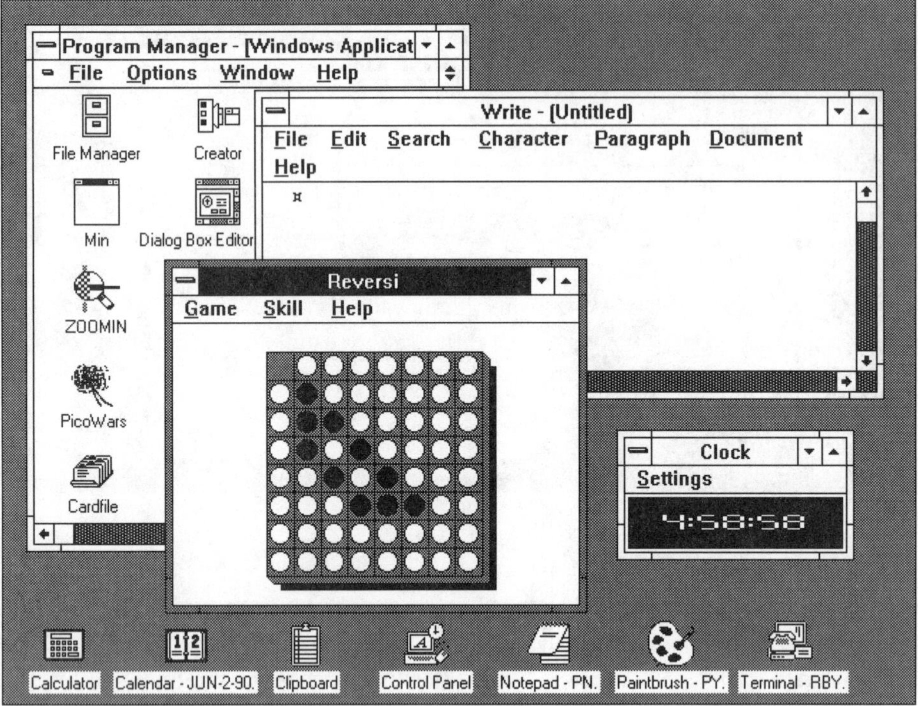

Figure 1.3 Windows version 3

please. The MS-DOS Executive, which was so familiar to users of earlier versions, was fired and replaced by a set of programs that manage programs and files: the **Program Manager**, the **Task List,** and the **File Manager**.

Internally, the most significant feature of Windows 3 is support for extended memory. Under Windows 3, Windows programs can access up to 16 megabytes of RAM. And when an 80386 or higher CPU is present, Windows uses the memory management features of these chips to provide virtual memory. In its 386-Enhanced mode, virtual memory up to four times the installed physical memory is available. For example, with 16 megabytes of physical memory (and enough room in the page file) Windows provides a 64-megabyte address space!

Windows 3 also has better network support than earlier versions, making it easy to connect network file servers and print servers. It supports a device-independent bitmap format that provides a standard for sharing color bitmaps among devices; and on devices that support more than 256 colors, applications are even given access to the hardware color palette. This means that support for picture-perfect images, such as those that a multimedia system might use, is now available in Windows. Another new feature is a built-in, sophisticated help facility that you can use to provide hypertext help to the users of your programs.

Windows NT

It seems that every company that develops a GUI system has gone on to build "new and improved" versions. Xerox first built the Alto, then went on to create the Star. Apple started with its Lisa and later built the Macintosh. After Windows, Microsoft joined forces with IBM to create the OS/2 Presentation Manager.

One goal of OS/2 was to provide a migration path for existing Windows applications. While some Windows applications *did* make the move to OS/2, many did not. The reason? Although the Presentation Manager is architecturally very similar to Windows, it provides a completely new API. Every function name is different. For example, Presentation Manager has `WinCreateWindow` to replace Windows' `CreateWindow`. Parameters to similar functions are in a different order or are missing. Presentation Manager introduced a completely new set of symbolic constants. If a Windows developer was thinking of porting code to a new operating system, the work required to move to OS/2 was about the same as moving to any other GUI environment: Macintosh, X-Windows, etc.

Windows NT represents Microsoft's admission that it made a mistake with OS/2. Although there are warts on the Windows API, enough application software has been written to make them *our* warts. While the Windows 32-bit API cures some of the ills of Windows, in general, it represents an API that is based on and derived from the 16-bit API of Windows 3.1. The new API was created with portability in mind, and retains the same function names, symbolic constants, and data structures as the old API.

One change that does occur between the two APIs is that every 16-bit element has been made 32 bits wide. While this may sound like a radical change, it's not. As you'll see, every Windows data type is defined using portable types. In other words, instead of using `short int` or `long`, there are uppercase types like `HWND` and `HDC`.

The two APIs are so similar that it's pretty easy to write Windows programs that will compile in either environment. In fact, every program in this book can be compiled as a Win16 program or a Win32 program. For details, refer to the discussion on development tools in Chapter 2.

Operating Systems and Application Programming Interfaces

When programmers talk about developing an application to run on an operating system, there is normally no distinction made between the **operating system** (**OS**) and the **Application Programming Interface** or **API**. An API is a set of rules to access some set of services. The rules include function calls, data types, and any special concerns in getting at the services. Put together, these rules make up a contract between the applications which use a service and a service provider.

An operating system is a product that you purchase. It might be delivered on tape, on floppy, on a CD-ROM, or come preinstalled on a system. You buy an operating system because it supports an API needed to run some set of application programs. Because some operating systems support multiple APIs, the distinction between an operating system and the APIs which are supported is an important one to make. Table 1.2 lists various operating systems and the APIs that each supports.

Table 1.2 Operating Systems and APIs Supported

Operating System	*API(s) Supported*
MS-DOS	MS-DOS
Windows 3.1	MS-DOS, Win16
Windows 3.1 w/Win32s	MS-DOS, Win16, Win32s
OS/2 2.0	MS-DOS, Win16, OS/2 character, OS/2 Presentation Manager
Windows NT	MS-DOS, Win16, Win32, POSIX, OS/2 character based*

* The support provided by Windows NT for OS/2 character based applications is limited to the Intel-86 platform.

The Win16 and Win32 APIs

The Win16 API was the primary programming interface for Windows version 1.x thru version 3.x. Win16 is built around the 16-bit architecture of the Intel-86 family of microprocessors. The 16-bit members of this family trace their roots to the 1978 introduction of the Intel 8088. In silicon technology terms, this is a pretty old architecture. As of this writing, the vast majority of the installed base of Windows only support this API, and the vast majority of shipping applications are Win16 applications. Since the introduction of Windows in 1985, the Win16 API has had a good ten years of life. Nevertheless, it's only a matter of time before Win16 goes away.

Microsoft has designated the Win32 API as the successor to the Win16 API. The primary goal of Win32 is upward compatibility with Win16. Another goal is portability to non-Intel platforms. A clear sign that Win32 is the wave of the future, however, is that Microsoft has set a stake in the ground and announced that the Win16 API has been frozen, and that with the release of version 3.1 of Windows, all future API enhancements will only be available via the Win32 API.

So how do the two APIs differ? The most obvious difference is that Win16 function calls and data structures use 16-bit values, while the corresponding Win32 functions and data structures take 32-bit values. The creators of the Win16 API anticipated this widening, however, by providing a set of data types that make this change almost invisible. Win16 code that uses the portable data types ports easily to Win32.

Since Win32 was designed to be portable to other processor platforms, another difference is that Win32 doesn't have the Win16 functions that access Intel-86 specific features. Nonportable functions like **AllocSelector**, **GlobalDosAlloc**, and **ValidateCodeSegments** are gone. Non-Intel platforms, after all, don't reference memory using selectors, don't run MS-DOS, and don't divide their address space into segments. These low-level structures rarely represent a porting problem.

Reasons to develop for the Win16 API include the following: if (a) a large percentage of your users run Windows 3.0, or (b) a large percentage of your users run Windows 3.1 on an 80286-based system, then Win16 makes sense. Also, (c) installation programs should use Win16, since it runs on all Windows platforms. Such an installation program will at least be able to tell a user what is needed to complete the installation. Another type of program that will continue to run in Win16 is (d) programs that rely heavily on third-party, Win16 dynamic link libraries (DLLs).

The Win32 API was created to exploit the 32-bit addressing and 32-bit registers of today's 32-bit processors. This API was designed to be portable and, is available running under Windows NT on the following processor platforms:

- Intel x-86 (32-bit 80386 and greater)
- MIPS R4000
- DEC Alpha
- Motorola PowerPC
- Intergraph

The presence of *two* Windows APIs might worry you. If you have existing Win16 code, you might wonder how much work is involved in porting to Win32. If you haven't started writing code yet, you might wonder whether you should start with Win16 API or jump directly to Win32 coding. How compatible are the two APIs? Which one makes the most sense?

Although it's an important decision, the choice is not as drastic as it may at first sound. The two APIs are very compatible. Of the dozen or so porting efforts I have heard about, most took days to complete[1] . This is compared to the months (or years) it might take to port a Win16 program to the Macintosh or to the OS/2 Presentation Manager.

For the near term—1994 and 1995—the installed base of Windows 3.x might compel you to develop for Win16. To encourage you to develop for Win32, however, Microsoft has created an add-on for Windows 3.1 that—it hopes—will convince you to move into the world of 32-bit Windows programming. That add-on is called "Win32s." (The "s" stands for "subset.")

---

[1] The one exception was a program that used native C data types—int, char, short, etc.—instead of the uppercase types—HWND, HDC, HBRUSH, etc.—defined for the API. The lesson is clear: To enhance portability, use uppercase types instead of native C types.

Win32s

From a technical viewpoint, Win32 is clearly superior to Win16. But its lower installed base makes it a hard sell to developers. Systems able to support Win32 include those running the 250,000 copies of Windows NT that had shipped by the end of 1993. Win16, on the other hand, could run on those Windows NT systems, as well as on the 40,000,000 copies of Windows 3.x that had shipped. It seems like no contest.

To level the playing field, Microsoft has released a royalty-free add-on to Windows 3.1 called Win32s. It doesn't work with Windows 3.0, and it won't run on 80286 systems. But it does provide a way for programs written to Win32 to get access to systems that make up the larger market share. The "s" in Win32s stands for "subset," since only a subset of the Win32 API is supported. While this sounds like a problem, in fact it represents a superset of the support provided by Win16. The reason is that Win32s is a thin layer on top of the regular Win16 libraries.

Win32s, then, supports almost all the functions supported by Win16. The 16-bit Win16 libraries are **thunked**[2] to provide Win32 support, so that if the Win16 libraries provided you the support you needed, then via Win32s you would get the same support. In addition, there are extra capabilities provided by Win32s, including: (1) 32-bit unsegmented memory access, (2) structured exception handling, (3) a complete set of file i/o APIs, and (4) support for critical sections. There is more Win32s information with your copy of Borland C++ version 4.0.

What does all this mean to you as a Windows programmer? As you begin using the Borland C++ compiler and the OWL libraries to create your Windows programs, you can feel confident that your software will have a long life.

Whichever API you choose to work with, it's a simple matter to convert your code for the other API. To simplify the matter even more, the OWL libraries hide some of the nasty, low-level intricacies of the two APIs from you. On occasion, you'll encounter minor differences between the two APIs—but these are the exceptions rather than the rule.

Now that you know where Windows has come from, and have an idea about where it's going, the time has come to discuss the major obstacles that you will encounter as you learn to program in Windows. It is important to be aware of the required effort, because it is easy to look at Windows' flexible user interface and conclude (incorrectly) that the programming interface is just as easy to work with.

In fact, the challenge to Windows programmers is to understand the fundamental principles and models embodied in its architecture. Once you understand the "Windows-way" of thinking, you'll find that Windows programming is as easy to tackle as any other type of programming that you have done. Incidentally, if you have programmed with any other GUI system, such as the Apple Macintosh, the OS/2 Presentation Manager, or the various

---

[2] A "thunk" is a thin layer of translation code sitting between a caller and a called function. In this case, it sits between the 16-bit, segmented memory world of Win16 and the 32-bit, unsegmented memory world of Win32. An issue for application developers is whether the benefits of Win32 outweigh the inevitable performance cost of the thunking layer.

X-Windows systems, you'll find much that is familiar in Windows. Let's consider, then, the challenges that lie ahead and some strategies for dealing with these challenges.

The Windows Programming Challenges

Consider the following scenario. It is Friday afternoon, and on your way out of the office you run into your boss. He has good news: The proposal that you made for the Windows development project has been approved. This means that you, and the crack team of programmers who work for you, are going to get to build your company's first Windows program. One of the first things you'll have to do is make sure that everyone on your team is up to speed on Windows. What challenges will be faced by the programmers who work for you who have no previous Windows programming experience?

Assuming that a programmer is proficient in C++, the three primary challenges are understanding event-driven programming, controlling graphical output, and using the various user-interface objects like windows, menus, dialog boxes, etc. Incidentally, if a programmer has been exposed to one or more of these areas, it makes it easier to learn Windows programming.

Before I discuss each of these areas in detail, one suggestion I'd like to repeat is that you—and the members of your development team—become full-time users of at least one Windows application. There are subtleties in the Windows user interface that only become evident when you have spent time as an *end user*. For example, the way the keyboard and mouse work together, the ways that menus and accelerator keys operate, and the operation of the various types of dialog box controls. If you become a full-time Windows user, it will help you to become a better Windows programmer. At the very least, try to find one Windows program that you can use on a daily basis: It might be a word processing program, a drawing package, terminal emulation software, or even a game.

Let's take a look at the three challenges that every new Windows programmer faces, starting with event-driven programming.

Challenge 1: Event-Driven Programming

Most programmers are used to writing code that runs in a sequential, procedure-driven manner. Such a program has a well-defined beginning, middle, and end. Consider, for example, a program that displays a series of data entry screens for the creation of some written document, which might be an airplane ticket or a company purchase order. The flowchart in Figure 1.4 depicts the strict sequence in which such a program might operate.

For the sake of this discussion, let's say that this flowchart represents a program used by travel agents to issue airplane tickets. The first entry screen accepts passenger information: name, address, etc. The second screen allows the input of flight information and provides fares and scheduling information. And finally, the third screen accepts payment information based on the fares in the previous screen. Each data entry screen must be cor-

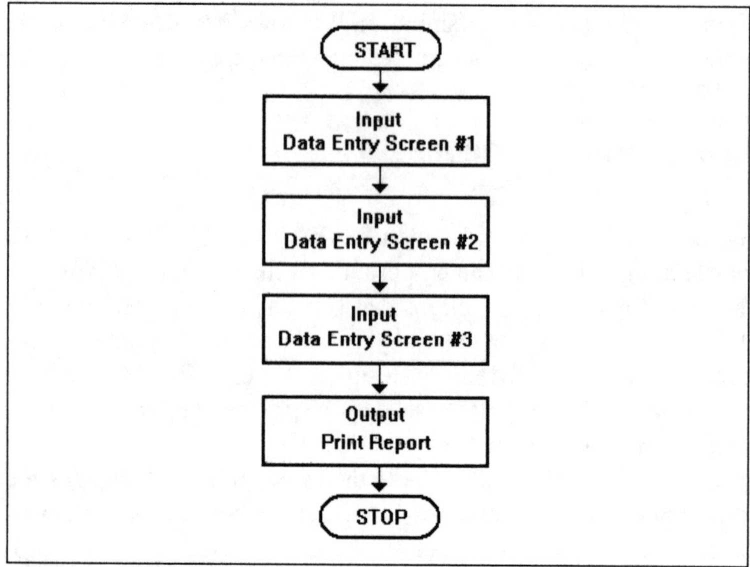

Figure 1.4 A sequence-driven program

rectly filled in before the travel agent can proceed to the next step, and all three screens must have correct information to issue a ticket.

At first glance, this seems like a reasonable way for such a program to proceed. After all, the job of the computer program is not only to issue tickets, but to make sure that correct passenger information has been received and that the payment provided agrees with the currently available fares. There are limitations to this approach, however, that are a direct result of this sequence-driven orientation.

For example, since the program dictates the sequence of operation, a travel agent cannot get to the second screen—for fare and flight information—without first entering complete passenger information. While a travel agency might like this feature, since it allows them to avoid giving away free information, the net result is the creation of unnecessary steps.

While the program ensures that all required information has been entered, it doesn't take into account real-world exceptions. For example, if a travel agent were to sell a group of tickets—perhaps to a family that is going on vacation—the travel agent must traverse all three screens for every ticket that is issued. Once again, the program does its job of ensuring that all the necessary information has been collected, but at a cost to the travel agent in the form of the additional work required.

An event-driven program, on the other hand, allows a travel agent to enter the data in whatever order seems appropriate. Perhaps an agent would choose the same order that the sequence-driven program dictated. However, an agent would be free to perform the necessary tasks in a sequence that fit the requirements of different customers. Figure 1.5 gives a rough idea of how an event-driven approach might change the traditional, sequence-driven program that we described earlier.

And yet, this is only one aspect of the way that an event-driven program differs from a sequence-driven program. An event-driven operating system like Windows goes even further so that, for example, within the data entry screens, the travel agent would have a tremendous amount of flexibility in the order in which fields were entered.

A sequence-driven program is built on an awkwardly arranged set of **modes**. A mode is a state of a program in which user actions are interpreted in a specific way and produce a specific set of results. In a reaction against sequence-driven programs, some GUI programmers may tell you that modes are bad. Unfortunately, this is an oversimplification.

A primary problem having to do with modes occurs when the user cannot easily move from one mode to another. In our sequence-driven ticketing program, for example, each of the four steps is a mode. But since the program dictates that the user traverse the modes in a strict sequence, the user is prevented from structuring his use of the program to meet the various demands that are made.

Another problem with modes occurs in programs that rely on the user to remember the current mode. Instead, a program should provide visual clues to help the user identify the program's current mode. In Windows, there are many user-interface objects that support this. The shape of the mouse cursor, for example, can indicate when a drawing package is in rectangle drawing mode and when it is in text drawing mode. You will see that modal dialog boxes are a very common way to retrieve input from the user that is required to complete a command.

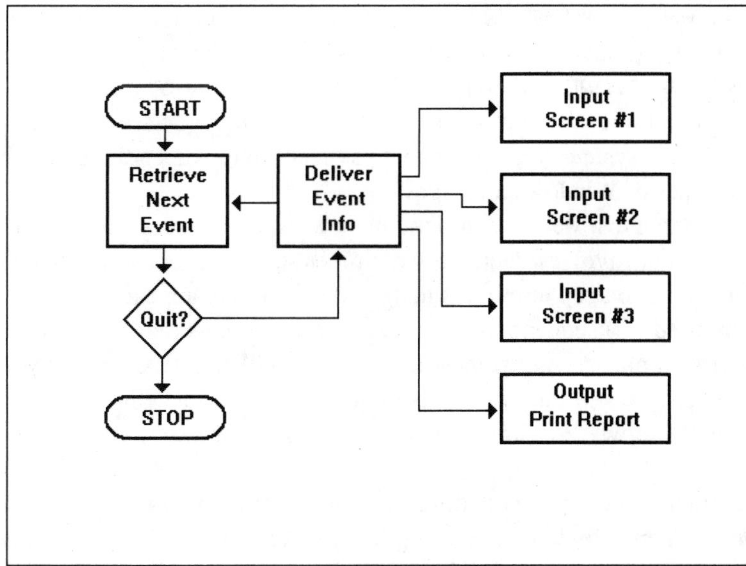

Figure 1.5 An event-driven program

The modes in a program should be carefully designed to prevent data loss when the user accidentally fumbles into a mode. A story often told about modes involves a text editor called Bravo, which was built at Xerox PARC in the 1970s. In this editor, regular keyboard keys are used for commands. For example, the letter "i" puts the program into insert mode, "d" is used for delete mode, etc. One user wanted to place the word "edit" in a document, but forget to first enter insert mode. The editor interpreted these keystrokes as

E (verything)	select everything in the document.
D (elete)	delete it.
I (nsert)	enter insert mode.
T	type the letter "t."

Oops. The entire contents of the document were replaced by the letter "t." When designing the user interface of a program, you should be aware of the modes that are created, and build in the necessary safeguards to help users avoid such unpleasant surprises.

From a programming point of view, modal programs are easier to implement than modeless programs. The code that supports each mode can be written and debugged in relative isolation from the other parts of the program. And yet, Windows makes it easier to create modeless programs because all interaction with the outside world—all events—are funneled to a program in a modeless manner. All events of interest generate messages.

What is a message? It is information about some change in the user interface, such as a window getting moved, or a keyboard key being pressed. Messages notify a program that a timer has gone off. Messages are used for data-sharing operations.

From a programming point of view, a message is a value that, for ease of reading, is assigned a symbolic constant that starts with the letters `WM_` (short for "Window Message"). For example, the **`WM_LBUTTONDOWN`** message tells a program that the user has pushed the left mouse button. Another message, which gets sent after the left mouse button has been released, is **`WM_LBUTTONUP`**. Throughout this book, we'll introduce messages in the context of the different topics that are covered. But if you're eager to see all the different types of messages in the system, you may want to skip ahead to Appendix A, which summarizes the various types of Windows messages.

Messages are very important to a Windows programmer. Most of the work that you will do as a Windows programmer involves deciding which messages to process and which messages to ignore. One thing to keep in mind is that messages do not appear in any predefined order. If you are used to a sequentially oriented program, things may seem disorganized and chaotic at first. It may seem that messages fly at you like bullets. To help you understand the flow of messages in the system, Borland provides you with a program called WinSight. Figure 1.6 shows WinSight listening to the messages of the Windows Calculator program.

Windows' message orientation is best suited for programs that require a high level of interaction with the user. Therefore, language compilers, which tend to have very little interaction with the user, gain little from running as Windows programs. But games and text editors that a programmer might use are well suited for Windows, since both require

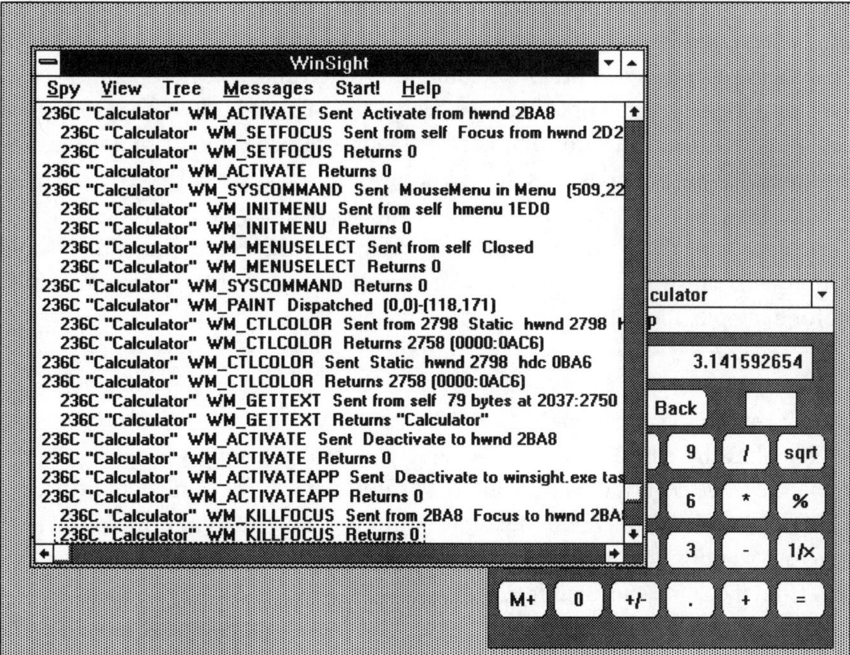

Figure 1.6 WinSight listening to messages belonging to the Calculator program

a high level of user interaction. Spreadsheets and data entry programs are also good candidates for interactive, event-driven applications.

An event-driven operating system like Windows puts a high priority on allowing the user to intervene at any point in a process. A sequence-driven program, on the other hand, puts a high priority on dictating the sequence in which a job must be performed. In a sequence-driven program, it is all too tempting for the programmer to create arbitrary rules about the order in which steps should be taken. While it is possible to create sequence-driven programs in Windows, the extra effort it requires virtually guarantees that such restrictions will only be put in place where they are actually needed.

Messages and Program Scheduling

There is a close relationship between messages and processor scheduling. After all, the presence of a message represents a request for processor time. What this actually means depends on the specific implementation of Windows. All implementations of Windows are multitasking, which simply means that multiple programs can run simultaneously. But there are two basic mechanisms used to share the processor in the various Windows systems.

Windows 3.x uses a scheduling system that dates back to the first version of Windows. In this system, scheduling is **nonpreemptive**. Windows programs are not interrupted by the operating system; instead, each program voluntarily interrupts its own operation to let other programs run. This system works because such programs are built to be very hungry for messages, and so each program constantly polls the operating system for messages. As long as all programs follow the rules, this multitasking system is just as effective as a more standard, preemptive scheduling system. The one weakness in this system, however, is that some program might not follow the rules. For example, a program could become "busy," or it could simply just crash. When the following line of code is executed in a Windows 3.x program, for example, the entire user-interface hangs:

```
while (1);
```

Clearly, this makes the entire system vulnerable to a problem in any single program. Fortunately, the presence of Windows' local boot facility lets a user punish an offending program quickly and easily. But clearly developers of programs for Windows 3.x have to be careful to avoid hanging the system. It's interesting to note that OS/2, which uses this model, suffers from the same shortcoming.

For the sake of compatibility, Windows NT programs are also message-driven. But the message delivery mechanism works alongside a more robust multitasking system that is based on **threads**. A thread is the unit of scheduling under Windows NT (and under OS/2). Threads are sometimes called lightweight processes, since they allow the independent scheduling of a process without the overhead associated with a process. When a program runs under Windows NT, a process is created and the process is given a thread. That thread is scheduled independently of other threads in the system. While a message waiting for a specific thread does give the thread a priority boost, the scheduling system of Windows NT cannot be upset by the "infinite-loop" that causes the Windows 3.x scheduler to come to a screeching halt.

Messages provide a program with input, but that's only half the story. The other half involves the output that a program produces. And output in Windows means just one thing: graphical output. This is the second challenge that new Windows programmers must face, and our next topic of discussion.

Challenge 2: Graphical Output

All output created by Windows programs is graphical. Figure 1.7 shows a sample of some of the lines, filled figures, and text that GDI can draw. Programmers who are used to working in a character-oriented environment will find that graphical output requires a new way of thinking. As you might expect, graphical output means that geometric figures can be drawn—lines, circles, boxes, etc. In addition, text itself is treated as a graphical object. This makes it easier, for example, to freely mix text and geometric figures. Paradoxically, while graphical output systems make the output of geometric shapes easier, they also tend to make the output of text harder.

Geometric shapes are easier because your program does not have to calculate each pixel. By simply calling the `Rectangle` routine, for example, GDI draws a filled rectangle for you. Text output is harder, because GDI's graphical orientation requires that you deal with text as a graphical object. Text is positioned using pixel coordinates rather than character cell coordinates.

Device-Independent Graphics

GDI provides device-independent graphics. This means a Windows program can draw on any device using the same set of calls. For example, the `Rectangle` routine is called to draw rectangles on the display screen as well as on printers. GDI works hard so that, from the point of view of a program, all devices look similar. This includes devices that only know how to turn pixels on and off—like the CGA display card—as well as very smart devices that know how to do complex graphics, like PostScript printers. Each device has a device driver that is responsible for doing the actual drawing. For devices that require assistance, GDI provides **software simulations** that use the low-level capabilities of a device to provide high-level functionality.

GDI knows about four types of devices: the display screen, hard-copy devices (like printers and plotters), bitmaps, and metafiles. Two of these are physical devices: the display screen and hard-copy devices. The other two, bitmaps and metafiles, are pseudodevices. A pseudodevice provides a means to store a picture in RAM or on disk, as well as a standard way to share graphical images between applications.

When drawing on the display screen, GDI provides window-oriented graphics. Window-oriented graphics means several things. Each window is treated like a separate drawing sur-

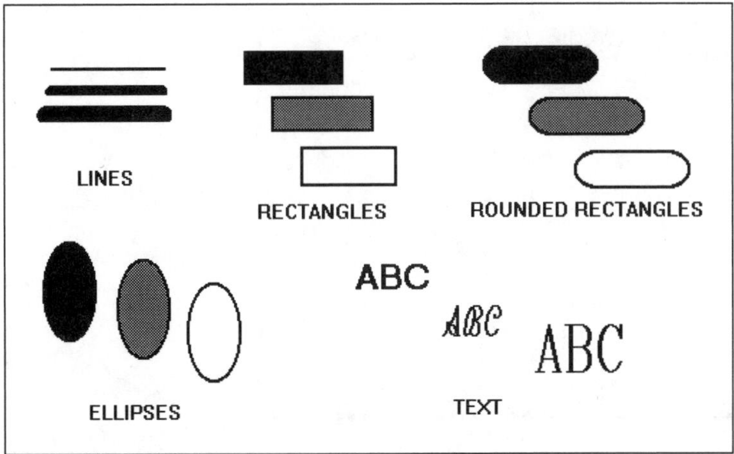

Figure 1.7 A sample of GDI's lines, filled figures, and text

face. When a program draws in a window, the default drawing coordinates are set up so that the origin (0,0) is in the upper-left corner of the window's client area (see Figure 1.8).

Window-oriented graphics also means that drawings are automatically clipped to a window. Clipping means that the drawing done for each window is limited to the window's border. Even if a window tried to draw beyond its own border, it would not be able to. A window is automatically protected from the wayward pixels that other windows might send its way. This protection mechanism works both ways, so that when you draw, you don't have to worry about accidentally overwriting another program's window.

Challenge 3: User-Interface Objects

Windows has built-in support for a number of user-interface objects: windows, icons, menus, dialog boxes, etc. Built-in support means that the amount of effort required to create and maintain these objects is fairly minimal. In particular, if you were to write your own code to support these objects, it would require a vast amount of effort on your part. And the results would probably not be as flexible nor as robust as the user-interface objects that Windows provides.

Taking advantage of these user-interface objects requires you to understand how each is implemented. As we look at the different types of user-interface objects, we'll provide some insights into the design and implementation of each. In many cases, this will mean a discussion of the messages that are associated with a given user-interface object. In other cases, this means delving into the various Windows library routines that control each type of object.

Among user-interface objects, the most important is the window. Any program that wishes to interact with the user must have a window, since a window receives mouse and

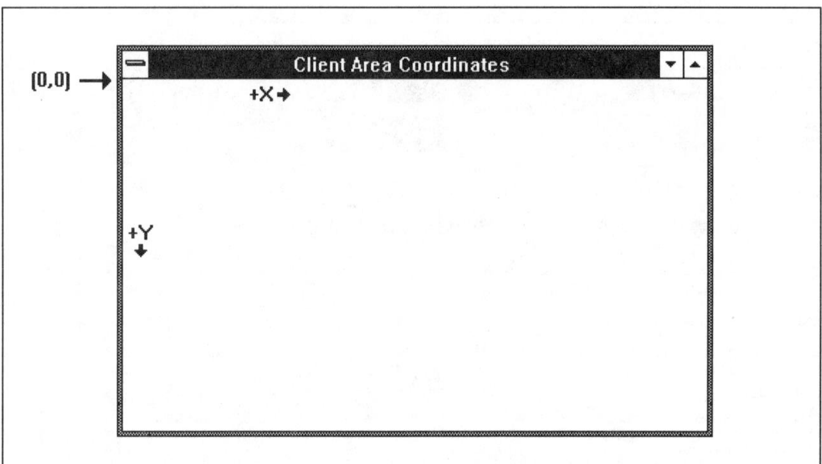

Figure 1.8 Default origin in client-area coordinates

keyboard input and displays a program's output. All other user-interface objects, like menus, scroll bars, and cursors, play supporting roles for this leading character.

The Window

The window is the most important part of the user interface. From the perspective of a user, a window provides a view of some data object inside the computer. But it is more than that, since to a user, a window *is* an application. When the user starts to run an application, a window is expected to appear. A user closes a window to shut down an application. To decide the specific application to be worked with, a user selects the application's window. Figure 1.9 shows the standard parts of a typical program's main window.

To programmers, a window represents several things. It serves to organize the other user-interface objects together and directs the flow of messages in the system. A window provides a display area that can be used to communicate with the user. Input is channeled to a window and thereby directed to the program. Applications also use windows to subdivide other windows. For example, dialog boxes are implemented as a collection of small windows inside a larger window.

Every window is created from a **window class**. A window class provides a template from which to create windows. Associated with every window class—and therefore with every window—is a special type of subroutine called a **window procedure**. The job of a window procedure is to process messages. In a message-oriented operating system like Windows, you can imagine that this is an important task. In fact, most of the work that you will do as a Windows programmer will involve deciding how to handle one message or

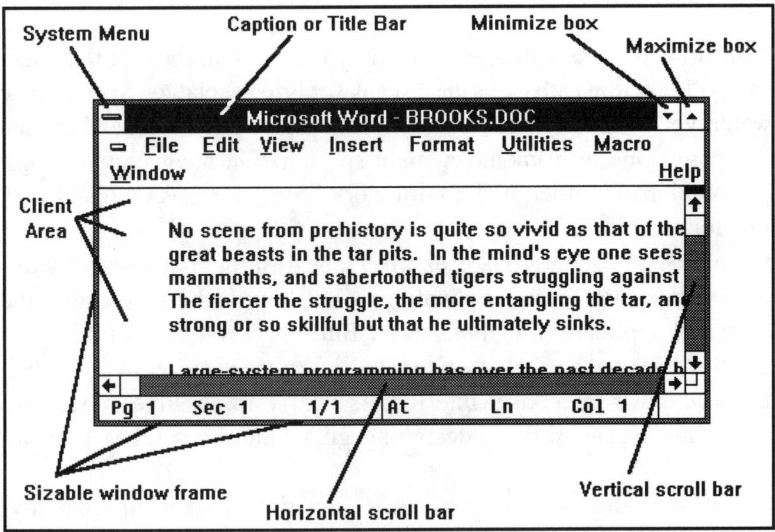

Figure 1.9 The standard parts of a window

another that is received in a window procedure. It receives the mouse and keyboard input that is directed to a window, which arrives in the form of messages. It receives notifications about other events of interest, such as changes in the size and location of a window. One of the first areas that we're going to explore, starting with the next few chapters, is the way that messages arrive at and are processed by window procedures.

Meeting the Challenges of Windows Programming

At the beginning of this chapter, I said that learning Windows takes time and effort. Now that you have a better idea of what the challenges are, it's time to discuss strategies for learning Windows. Some will probably be familiar to you, and some will probably be new.

Attend a Class

Before encountering Windows, I spent years teaching myself to use different programming tools. When I started to work with Windows, however, I realized that this was going to be different. So I attended a class with David Durant, the industry's first Windows programming instructor. That class helped orient me toward working with Windows, and saved me countless hours of frustration. For some developers, attending a class is the most efficient way to learn to program for Windows. Several organizations teach Windows programming. For information on the training services provided by my company, please refer to the information on the last page of this book.

Specialize

Attending a class will help you get oriented, but how do you deal with the fact that there are over 750 Windows API function calls? The easiest answer is to specialize. Specializing works particularly well if you are part of a development team, since different members can specialize in different parts. One team member might specialize in menus and dialogs, while another focuses on graphic output, and a third works out the issues involved with building dynamic link libraries.

An area that is worth time and attention is **user-interface design**. Windows provides the building blocks to create interactive applications—but how to best assemble the pieces? In a well-designed application, it looks easy. But when you start building an application, it quickly becomes apparent that a poor user-interface is easier to build than a merely workable one. And a great user-interface is nearly impossible. There are always compromises to make, and skill in designing great interfaces takes years to develop.

An important part of specializing in an area is to experiment with building toy-applications to test your knowledge. Only by trying all the different options in a few function calls will you develop a sense for what is possible. As you write the code, make sure you keep the best examples of what you create in a safe place. A library of sample code is a valuable resource that serves as an archive for the things that you learn. For ideas on potential areas of speciality, refer to the table of contents.

Review Sample Code

Any sample code that you or your coworkers write is an important resource. But don't forget about the other sources of sample code. The Borland C++ 4.0 compiler, for example, comes with 59 different sample OWL programs. For your convenience, these are described briefly in Appendix I, along with the 30 different sample programs in this book. Another place to find sample source code is online, either on Compuserve or on the Internet.

Get Connected Electronically

If you've never connected to a usenet news group or logged into a programming forum on Compuserve, you're in for a treat. You can lurk in the shadows and listen to discussions between other developers who are struggling with the same issues you are. Or, you can ask a question to help solve a thorny problem. As you spend time writing code, you'll find that you're able to answer others' questions and flex your own expertise. Getting connected electronically enables you to learn about important industry events, new tools, and other changes that affect you.

Join a User's Group

An excellent source of information on Windows programming is user groups. For example, I live in Seattle and a special interest group (SIG) of the Washington Software Association (WSA) meets monthly to discuss topics of interest to Windows programmers. I'll drop in occasionally to give a talk or to listen to someone sharing insights into the development process.

Become a Regular Windows User

My final suggestion is the first suggestion I made at the beginning of this chapter: Get comfortable with the mouse; learn to use the keyboard interface to menus and dialogs; explore how a good user-interface works. To be a great Windows programmer, it helps to be an experienced Windows user.

In summary, the three major conceptual hurdles to learning Windows programming are: event-driven programming, creating graphic output, and using the built-in user interface objects. These three areas are the focus of parts 2, 3 and 4 of this book.

The next few chapters discuss Windows' event-driven nature in the context of a minimum Windows program built using the OWL class library. While a smaller, three line minimum program was possible, I have carefully chosen the elements in this program to reflect what I feel is a good starting point for every other program in this book. As I describe each part of this program, I'll describe how each fits into the overall architecture of Windows itself.

PART TWO

A Minimum OWL 2.0 Program

2

Foundations

To help you deal with Windows' size and complexity, I'm going to introduce you to the foundations of Windows programming from two different angles. I'll start with the 10,000 foot view to address the Windows API—and the way OWL encapsulates this API—by looking at the major components, the behavior of these components, and their common characteristics.

Then, since your major concern is probably writing code, I'll introduce the source code to MIN, a minimum Windows program that uses OWL. You can easily type in the source code to this tiny program and compile it to create your first working Windows and OWL program. In this chapter and the ones which follow, I'll spend quite a bit of time discussing MIN, since it is the starting point for every program in this book. When you thoroughly understand every line in MIN, you will have grasped the essence of Windows and OWL programming.

Windows System Architecture

Windows programs use three libraries: KERNEL, USER and GDI[1]. Figure 2.1 shows these libraries along with the major parts of Windows 3.x. A comparable diagram for Windows NT appears in Figure 2.2. To understand the various Windows APIs, it helps to understand the personality of each of these three libraries. You'll find common qualities among functions from the same library, so getting a sense for each library will help in your coding

[1] Under Windows 3.x, the file names are KRNL286.EXE or KRNL386.EXE, USER.EXE, and GDI.EXE. Under Windows NT, the file names are KERNEL32.DLL, USER32.DLL and GDI32.DLL. In spite of these cosmetic differences, the structure and behavior of the two operating systems are identical.

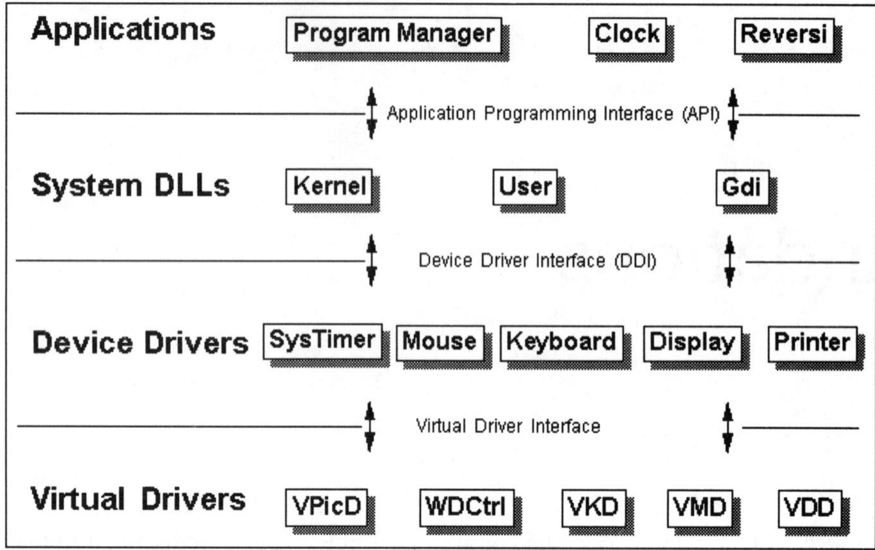

Figure 2.1 Major Components of Windows 3.x

efforts. For example, GDI's drawing functions are low-level primitives, while quite a number of USER functions are made up of calls to other USER functions. The practical impli-

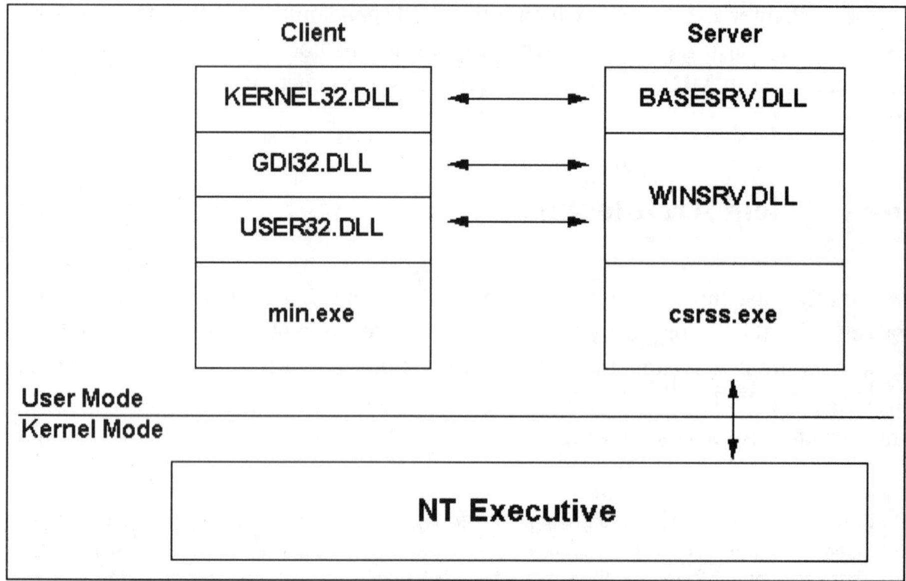

Figure 2.2 Major Win32 Components of Windows NT

cation is that there are usually several ways to do the same operation in USER, while GDI functions tend to be atomic. As you get into building Windows software, you'll see more and more of these types of patterns.

Each component creates and manages a set of system objects: KERNEL creates memory, USER—the **user-interface** component—creates windows, and GDI—the **Graphics Device Interface**—creates pens and brushes for drawing. When any component creates an object, a numeric ID—known as a **handle**—is issued. To use an object, you must pass this handle to the appropriate Windows API function.

There are a few practical things to keep in mind when working with handles. A handle is meaningful only to the system component that issued the handle. If USER provides you a handle to a window that it creates, you cannot pass that handle to GDI and expect it to have any meaning. Also, you'll find that OWL objects wrapped around Windows API objects always allow you access to the system object handle. This is useful for when you need to bypass OWL and access an object with a direct call to the Windows API. As we explore the OWL libraries, I'll point out the important relationships between OWL objects and the Windows system objects (what I call **WinAPI objects**).

KERNEL

The Windows KERNEL is responsible for low-level support for file i/o, memory, program loading, dynamic linking, and chores that belong to a traditional operating system. Although the accompanying diagram shows the three system libraries on an equal level, in fact the KERNEL supports both USER and GDI when they need its services. In Windows 3.x, three interchangeable versions are available to tailor support for 8088 CPUs (KERNEL.EXE for Real Mode), for 80286 CPUs (KRNL286.EXE for Standard Mode), and for 80386 CPUs (KRNL386.EXE for Enhanced Mode).

Under Windows NT, the KERNEL32.DLL component is a very thin layer that redirects most calls to the NT Executive. A complete discussion of the NT Executive is beyond the scope of this book. However, it's worth mentioning that the low-level support provided by the NT Executive is what allows Windows NT to be able to support the many different programming APIs that it does.

The KERNEL manages the following system objects: modules (the image of an executable file in RAM), dynamic link libraries (a special case of modules), memory, and files. Under Windows NT, other objects created and managed by the NT Executive include processes, threads, synchronization objects, and shared memory sections.

The two most important KERNEL objects are memory and files. As with other system objects, handles are used to identify allocated memory. In particular, the local and global heap allocation functions (**`LocalAlloc`** and **`GlobalAlloc`**) both return memory handles. While your use of the C++ **`new`** operator will spare you the need to call these functions, there are a few times—such as when you access the Windows Clipboard—during which calls to the native API allocators are necessary.

In general, whenever you call a WinAPI function that issues a handle, the function notifies you of failure by returning an invalid handle value. For *almost* every system object, the value of an invalid handle is ZERO. For example, here's a code snippet—using native WinAPI calls—that allocates memory, then checks for success:

```
HGLOBAL hmem = GlobalAlloc (GMEM_MOVEABLE, 500);
if (hmem)   // If not equal to zero...
    { /* success. */ }
else
    ( /* failure. */ }
```

The one exception to this rule is for **file handles**. When a file open request fails, the value (-1) is returned. Why? It's mostly a matter of history. Both Win32 and Win16 use this value to maintain compatibility between the two APIs. The older API, Win16, used this value because it was the invalid file value of MS-DOS and the earliest implementations of Win16 relied on MS-DOS for file i/o. MS-DOS inherited the use of this value from Digital Research's CP/M operating system, since the first version of MS-DOS was written as a CP/M clone. It's ironic that Win32—the programming API for the 1990s—uses a critical value initially used by a 1970's era operating system. Perhaps it reflects the importance of compatibility. So remember, when checking for file open failure, always check for a value of -1:

```
HFILE hfile = OpenFile(lpszName, &of, OF_READ);
if (hfile != (HFILE)-1)
    { /* success */ }
else
    { /* failure */ }
```

You could, if you'd like, use the Win32 symbolic constant **`INVALID_HANDLE_VALUE`**. (The name hides the fact it applies *only* to file handles.) But this is one instance when I don't mind hard-coding a numeric constant.

USER

The USER module handles the creation and management of user-interface objects, including windows, menus, dialog boxes, dialog box controls, carets, cursors, and icons. Although user-interface is traditionally among the less important concerns[2] for software developers, Windows gives USER a central role. For example, application scheduling—something that might seem the proper task of KERNEL—is the domain of USER. Under Windows 3.x, application scheduling is *entirely* USER's domain. The reason is that mouse and keyboard activity create **messages**, and these serve as the Windows 3.1 time-slice. Under Windows NT, USER32 shares this job with the NT Executive which has a sophis-

---

[2] Less important, for example, than performance, optimal memory use, algorithms, error handling, and efficient operation in general.

ticated preemptive scheduler. When USER32 receives user input—that is, when messages are generated—it calls the Executive to boost the recipient's priority. In this way, USER32 plays a role in application scheduling in a way that is way out of proportion to the importance ordinarily put on user-interface concerns. This orientation helps make both Windows 3.x and Windows NT very responsive to user input.

The most important user-interface object is the window. Its importance is reflected by the fact that—of all the class hierarchies in OWL—the one that wraps around the WinAPI window—`TWindow`—has the most number of derived classes. Another indication of the importance of the window in the native Windows API is that messages, the unit of system scheduling, are always targetted to a specific window[3]. And the fact that other user-interface objects aren't even allowed to appear until connected to a window clearly indicates how this single system object dominates the user-interface scene.

GDI

GDI, the Graphics Device Interface, is the artist in the family. When pixels light up a display screen or output appears in a page created by a Windows application, you are witnessing the work of this artist. Naturally, GDI's graphic device drivers help make this happen, but GDI gets called by applications whenever they want to create any sort of visual output. Even USER, which manages the internal operation of the user-interface, relies on GDI to draw windows, menus, dialog boxes, and all other user-interface objects.

GDI is the oldest component of Windows. Even before work began on the first version of Windows in early 1983, work was underway at Microsoft for a device-independent graphic library. The plan was to bundle the library with a language product, such as a BASIC compiler or perhaps a FORTRAN compiler. Although GDI was made part of Windows, it was kept separate from the other components in case Windows didn't sell. For Star Trek fans, this is like the saucer section of a Federation star ship that can separate from the rest of the ship during emergencies. If Windows hadn't become a hit, Microsoft might have separated GDI from Windows to make it available for other uses.

The most important GDI object is the **device context**, known more commonly as the **DC**. I don't particularly care for this name, since I'm not sure what a "context" is. I prefer "device connection," which suggests more clearly the role of this system object[4]. Before you create output on a GDI device, you must first gain access to a DC. Drawing on the display screen, for example, is only possible with a DC for the display screen. Sending pages of output to a printer with GDI requires a printer DC.

---

[3] While this is true of the native Windows API, the OWL classes modify the message flow somewhat to allow unhandled messages to be diverted from one **TEventHandler**-derived object to its base class handlers.

[4] The term "device connection" has the added benefit that it allows the use of the initials "D.C." to still be used.

➤ *A Note on Win32s*

The Win16 API meets the Win32 API under Win32s. As suggested by Figure 2.3, when a Win32 program is run using Win32s, a set of libraries is provided that match the Windows NT library names. These three libraries—KERNEL32.DLL, USER32.DLL and GDI32.DLL—do not contain all the support of their Windows NT cousins. Instead, they provide a thin layer that converts the 32-bit Win32 parameters to the 16-bit equivalents that are defined for the Win32 API. This "thunking" layer calls the 16-bit libraries to get real work done. Another way to think about Win32s, then, is that it's the 32-bit version of the Win16 API.

What happens when a Win32 program running on Win32s calls a function not supported by Win16? The call simply fails. Within the Win32s layer, unsupported functions are stubbed to fail gracefully. Of course, it's up to your application to recognize function failure and find another way to get the work done. This means that you can create a single Win32 executable program that is binary compatible between Windows 3.1 (running Win32s), Windows NT, and whatever future versions of Windows support the Win32 API.

The OWL 2.0 Libraries

One way to look at the OWL class library is as a set of wrappers around the C-oriented Windows API libraries. It's a little more complicated than that, however, since OWL builds on the low-level capabilities of Windows to provide a new way to approach Win-

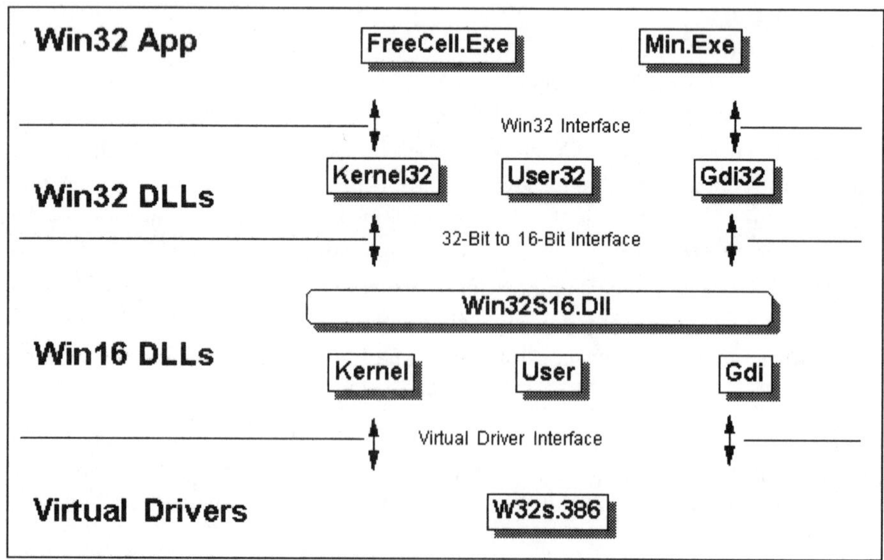

Figure 2.3 Win32s Components within Windows 3.1

dows programming. Once you're familiar with OWL, it will make your Windows programming efforts much easier than coding in straight C.

In some cases, OWL adds capabilities not found in the native API—such as support for toolbars, message windows, and the document/view architecture to name just a few. In other cases, OWL provides a fairly thin layer between your C++ program and the native Windows API. For example, OWL implements most drawing calls as straight inline calls to the GDI drawing function. In only a few cases you'll bypass OWL and call the native Windows API functions directly.

To learn how to use the OWL library, you should rely on the sample programs—both the ones in this book and the ones that Borland ships along with its compiler. If you don't want to type in all the programs in this book, you can order a machine-readable version of the code for a nominal fee. Please refer to the inside back cover of the book for more details. Appendix I provides a cross reference between the OWL class libraries and the sample source programs—both in this book and those with the compiler—that use the various classes.

Another very important resource is the class library source code. If you installed the compiler using the default settings, you would find the library source code in \BC4\SOURCE\OWL and the include files in \BC4\INCLUDE\OWL. Since quite a bit of important class information is in the include files (inline functions, for example), you'll want to spend time perusing the source code in both directories. To help you quickly locate source files, you'll want to learn to use the GREP.EXE program that Borland provides with its compiler. This is an MS-DOS command line program that can quickly search a lot of files for a specific string. For example, to find all references to the string TWindow—the name of the OWL class that wraps around the native WinAPI window—change to the desired directory under an MS-DOS command prompt and type the following command:

```
C> grep TWindow *.cpp
```

I personally like to redirect the output of this utility to a file, since it's often longer than a single line:

```
C> grep TWindow *.cpp > \out.dat
```

You can also invoke this utility well within the IDE from the tools menu.

Another resource that is invaluable in working with the OWL library is familiarity with the native Windows API. Since OWL is a wrapper around Windows, the more you know about Windows the easier it will be to use OWL. You'll notice that the basic orientation of this book is to discuss the internal operation of different parts of the system, then discuss the native API, and conclude with a discussion of the way the OWL libraries make a particular capability available. This "bottom-up" approach should help you gain a solid foundation with both the native Windows API and with the OWL library.

For your convenience, I've reprinted the ObjectWindows hierarchy diagram as Appendix K of this book. An abbreviated version of that diagram appears in the upper half of Fig-

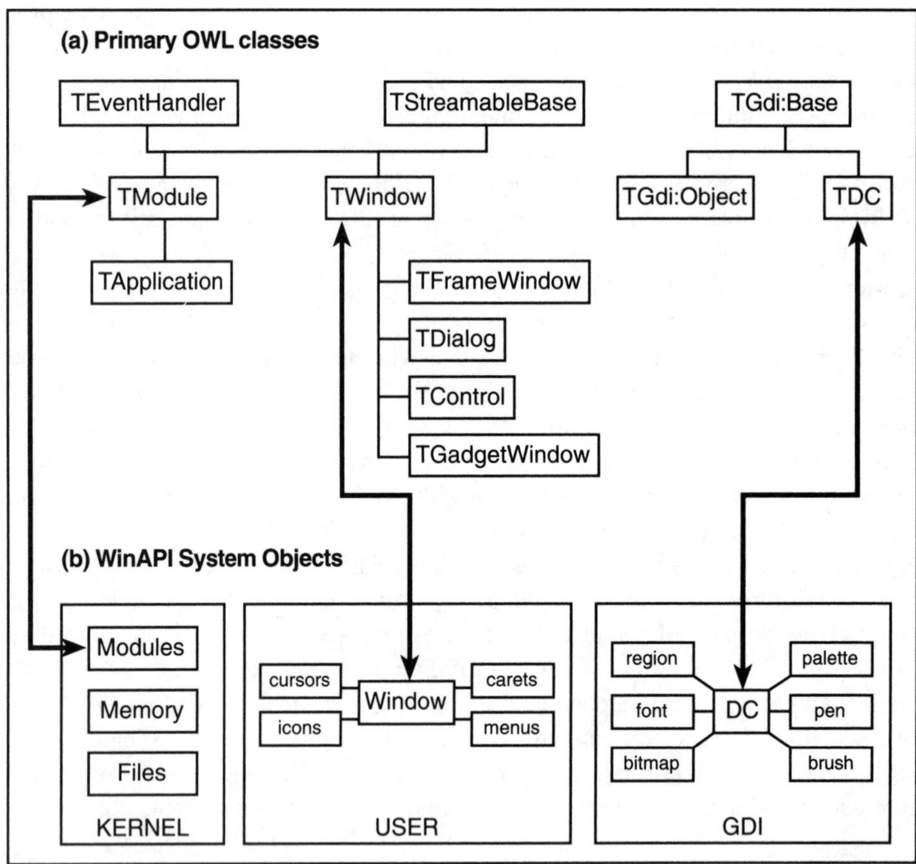

Figure 2.4 Relationship between OWL classes and WinAPI system objects

ure 2.4. The lower half of this same figure shows the various objects created by the native Windows API. Lines connect OWL classes to the corresponding WinAPI system objects.

This class hierarchy has three important base classes: **`TEventHandler`**, **`TStreamableBase`**, and **`TGdiBase`**. All the classes that inherit from **`TEventHandler`** have the ability to tap into Windows' message delivery mechanism. Some, like **`TWindow`**, directly correspond with the WinAPI way of doing things. For other classes, like **`TModule`** and **`TApplication`**, this message delivery mechanism represents broader support than that provided by the native API. Also, notice that GDI objects—according to the OWL way of looking at the world—aren't part of this message delivery hierarchy.

Classes that inherit from **`TStreamableBase`** have built-in support for the type of persistence that you find in regular C++ streams. Thus, you can save the state of an application off to disk when a user shuts down an application and restore that state the next time the application starts up. A fairly involved streams example is included with the OWL compiler in the \bc4\examples\classlib\pstream subdirectory. Please refer to that code example for more details on taking advantage of this capability. Almost all of the classes that inherit from **`TEventHandler`** and **`TStreamableBase`** support user-interface functionality. That is, these classes primarily provide support for Windows' USER library.

Support for Windows' GDI library is provided by the OWL classes that inherit from the **`TGdiBase`** base class. This set of classes, then, provides the means of accessing GDI drawing capabilities. Since the primary GDI system object is the DC, it stands to reason that the most important OWL class for GDI support is **`TDC`**. If you take a look at the class declaration for **`TDC`**, you'll find that the entire WinAPI programming interface for GDI is provided as part of the 1500 lines of the file \bc4\include\owl\dc.h.

As mentioned earlier, the Windows API is big. And the OWL library, which is large enough to wrap around the Windows API is a pretty big library as well. Putting the rich functionality to work for you will require a bit of effort, so let's get started with a look at a minimum Windows program that's built on top of the OWL 2.0 class library.

A Minimum OWL 2.0 Program

This section introduces a minimum Windows program, MIN.EXE. MIN serves as the basis for every other program in this book. Figure 2.5 shows the window that MIN creates. The window can be moved, resized, closed, *minimized* (made into an icon), or *maximized* (enlarged to fill the screen). In other words, to an experienced Windows user, the window created by this program does all of the "right" things. MIN has a menu, which is typical for a Windows program, and also a custom icon that is displayed when MIN is minimized.

The five files in the minimum OWL program are listed in Table 2.1, along with the program build files. Four of the program files are textfiles (MIN.CPP, MIN.H, MIN.RC and MIN.DEF) and appear in this listing which accompanies this discussion. One contains a graphic image—MIN.ICO—and is shown in Figure 2.6 inside Borland's Resource Workshop editor. This file contains the icon that is displayed when MIN is minimized.

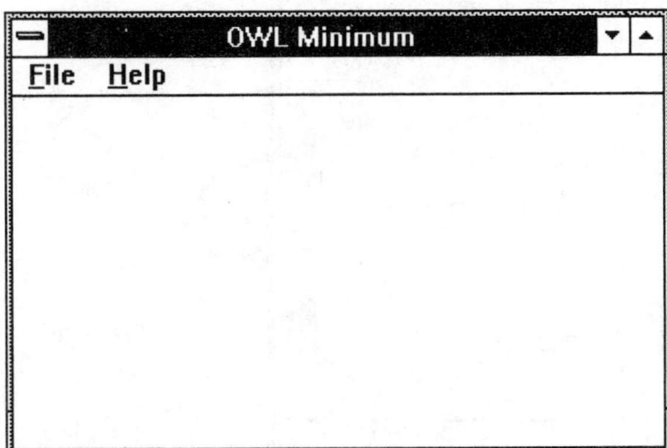

Figure 2.5 The window created by our minimum Windows program

Table 2.1 Files That Make Up the Minimum Windows Program

Program Files	
MIN.CPP	C++ source file.
MIN.H	Include file.
MIN.RC	Resource file, for user-interface data objects.
MIN.ICO	Icon file, a resource.
MIN.DEF	Module definition file; used by linker.
Program Build Files	
MIN.IDE	Integrated development environment setup
DYNA16.MAK and DYNA16.LNK	Win16 make files for using OWL DLLs
DYNA32.MAK and DYNA32.LNK	Win32 make files for using OWL32 DLLs
STATIC16.MAK and STATIC16.LNK	Win16 make file for static use of OWL
STATIC32.MAK and STATIC32.LNK	Win32 make file for static use of OWL32

When you build MIN, you have several choices available to you. First, you'll want to decide whether to use the Borland Integrated Development Environment (IDE), which is a

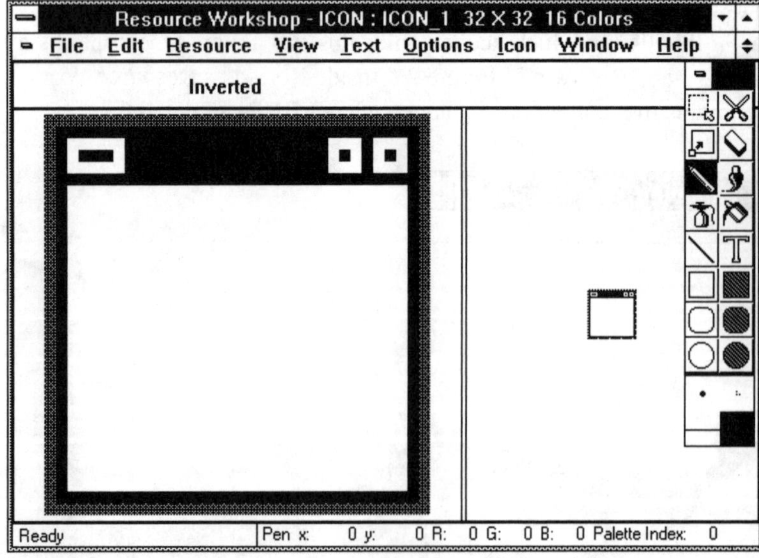

Figure 2.6 The icon of our minimum Windows program

multipurpose Windows-compatible editor / compiler / linker / debugger. I understand that its editor does a pretty good emulation of the BRIEF editor. The other alternative is to use the MS-DOS command line compilers. This is the choice I personally prefer, just because I'm hooked on a text editor that I've used for years.

If you're using the MS-DOS command prompt compilers, your next choice is between the four sets of program build files. If you're using the Borland IDE, the same choices are available from within the IDE, but they're a little hard to find at first. First, open a project file by selecting the Project.Open Project... menu item. In the project menu, use the right mouse button (not the left-button that you're used to from using other Windows programs). When the menu appears, select the TargetExpert... menu item. Figure 2.7 shows the Target Expert window.

One pair of MAKE files is for creating Win32 applications; the other is for creating Win16 applications. Once you decide which to create, you'll want to decide whether to statically link to the standard OWL libraries or to use the DLL versions of the standard OWL libraries. You can change your mind any time later, but you'll have to make a final decision before shipping your application to your users. In general, if you use the DLL version, your own program executable files will be smaller but you have to ship the Borland DLL files with your software. If you use the static version, your program executable files will be larger but can run without external DLLs.

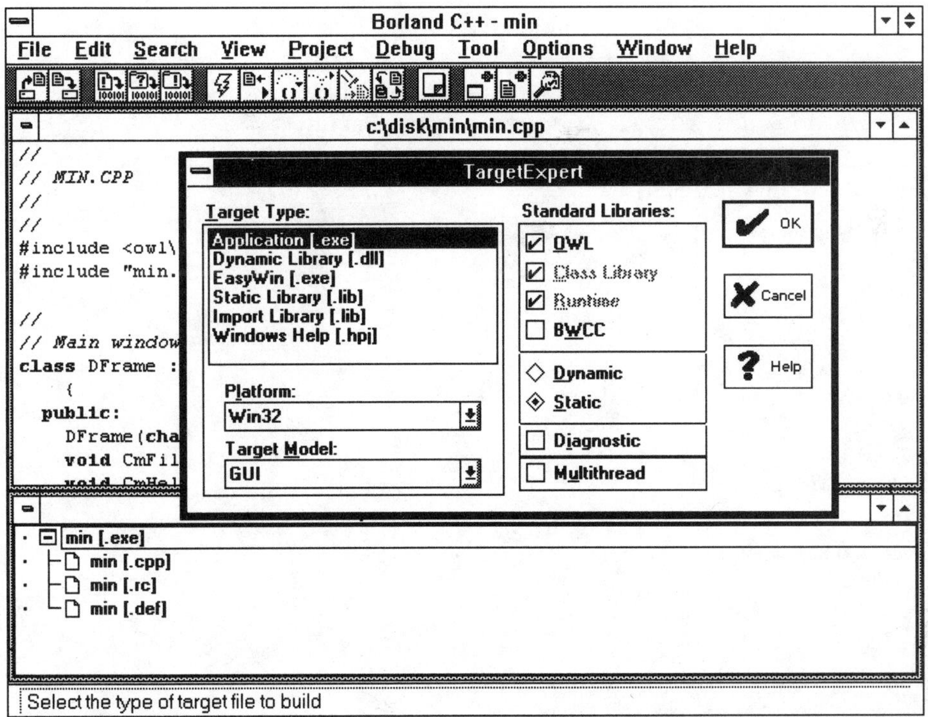

Figure 2.7 The Target Expert window inside the Borland Integrated Development Environment (IDE).

MIN.CPP

```
//
// MIN.CPP     A Minimum OWL 2.0 Program. MIN displays a window, has
//             a menu, a custom icon, and a message box.
//
#include <owl\owlpch.h>
#include "min.h"

//
// Main window
class DFrame : public TFrameWindow
    {
  public:
    DFrame(char * title);
    void CmFileExit();
    void CmHelpAbout();

  DECLARE_RESPONSE_TABLE (DFrame);
    };

DEFINE_RESPONSE_TABLE1 (DFrame, TFrameWindow)
  EV_COMMAND(CM_FILEEXIT, CmFileExit),
  EV_COMMAND(CM_HELPABOUT, CmHelpAbout),
END_RESPONSE_TABLE;

DFrame::DFrame(char * title) : TFrameWindow(0, title)
    {
    }

void DFrame::CmFileExit()
    {
    CloseWindow(0); // Cause application to terminate
    }

void DFrame::CmHelpAbout()
    {
    MessageBox("   Minimum OWL 2.0 Program\n\n"
               "'Borland C++ 4.0 Programming\n"
               "  for Windows', by Paul Yao", Title);
    }

//
// Application object
class DApp : public TApplication
    {
  public:
    DApp();
    void InitMainWindow();
    };

DApp::DApp() : TApplication()
    {
    }

void DApp::InitMainWindow()
    {
    SetMainWindow (new DFrame("OWL Minimum"));
    MainWindow->AssignMenu("MAIN");
    MainWindow->SetIcon(this, "SNAPSHOT");
    }
```

```
//
// Application main entry point.
OwlMain(int, char **)
    {
    return DApp().Run();
    }
```

MIN.H

```
#define CM_FILEEXIT 100
#define CM_HELPABOUT 200
```

MIN.RC

```
#include "min.h"

snapshot icon min.ico

main menu
    BEGIN
    POPUP "&File"
        {
        MENUITEM "E&xit", CM_FILEEXIT
        }
    POPUP "&Help"
        {
        MENUITEM "&About...", CM_HELPABOUT
        }
    END
```

MIN.DEF

```
EXETYPE WINDOWS

CODE MOVEABLE DISCARDABLE
DATA MULTIPLE MOVEABLE

HEAPSIZE   512
STACKSIZE 8192
```

DYNA16.MAK

```
#  MAKE file for Win16 API using dynamic BIDS,
#  OWL and C-runtime libraries.
#
#     C> make -fstatic16.mak
#

.AUTODEPEND
CC = -c -H -H"owl\owlpch.h" -ml -R -vi -WS -X-
```

```
CD = -D_RTLDLL;_BIDSDLL;_OWLDLL;_OWLPCH;
INC = -I\BC4\INCLUDE
LIB = -L\BC4\LIB

min.exe :  min.obj min.res
  tlink -c -C -Twe $(LIB) @dyna16.lnk
  brc min.res min.exe

min.obj :  min.cpp
  bcc $(CC) $(CD) min.cpp

min.res :  min.rc min.ico min.h
  brc $(INC) -31 -R min.rc
```

DYNA16.LNK

```
\bc4\lib\c0wl.obj+
min.obj
min,min
\bc4\lib\bidsi.lib+
\bc4\lib\owlwi.lib+
\bc4\lib\import.lib+
\bc4\lib\crtldll.lib
min.def
```

DYNA32.MAK

```
#  MAKE file for Win32 API using dynamic BIDS,
#  OWL and C-runtime libraries.
#
#    C> make -fdyna32.mak
#

.AUTODEPEND
CC = -c -H -H\""owl\owlpch.h\"" -p- -R -vi -W -X-
CD = -D_RTLDLL;_BIDSDLL;_OWLDLL;_OWLPCH;
INC = -I\BC4\INCLUDE
LIB = -L\BC4\LIB

min.exe :  min.obj min.res
  tlink32 -aa -c -Tpe $(LIB) @dyna32.lnk
  brc32 min.res min.exe

min.obj :  min.cpp
  bcc32 $(CC) $(CD) min.cpp

min.res :  min.rc min.ico min.h
  brc32 $(INC) -w32 -R min.rc
```

DYNA32.LNK

```
\bc4\lib\c0w32.obj+
min.obj
```

```
min,min
\bc4\lib\bidsfi.lib+
\bc4\lib\owlwfi.lib+
\bc4\lib\import32.lib+
\bc4\lib\cw32i.lib
min.def
```

STATIC16.MAK

```
#  MAKE file for Win16 API using static BIDS,
#  OWL and C-runtime libraries.
#
#    C> make -fstatic16.mak
#

.AUTODEPEND
CC = -c -H -H"owl\owlpch.h" -ml -R -vi -WS -X-
CD = -D_OWLPCH;
INC = -I\BC4\INCLUDE
LIB = -L\BC4\LIB

min.exe :  min.obj min.res
  tlink -c -C -Twe $(LIB) @static16.lnk
  brc min.res min.exe

min.obj :  min.cpp
  bcc $(CC) $(CD) min.cpp

min.res :  min.rc min.ico min.h
  brc $(INC) -31 -R min.rc
```

STATIC16.LNK

```
\bc4\lib\c0wl.obj+
min.obj
min,min
\bc4\lib\bidsl.lib+
\bc4\lib\owlwl.lib+
\bc4\lib\import.lib+
\bc4\lib\mathwl.lib+
\bc4\lib\cwl.lib
min.def
```

STATIC32.MAK

```
#  MAKE file for Win32 API using static BIDS,
#  OWL and C-runtime libraries.
#
#    C> make -fstatic32.mak
#

.AUTODEPEND
CC = -c -H -H\""owl\owlpch.h\"" -p- -R -vi -W -X-
```

```
CD = -D_OWLPCH;
INC = -I\BC4\INCLUDE
LIB = -L\BC4\LIB

min.exe :  min.obj min.res
  tlink32 -aa -c -Tpe $(LIB) @static32.lnk
  brc32 min.res min.exe

min.obj  :  min.cpp
  bcc32 $(CC) $(CD) min.cpp

min.res  :  min.rc min.ico min.h
  brc32 $(INC) -w32 -R min.rc
```

STATIC32.LNK

```
\bc4\lib\c0w32.obj+
min.obj
min,min
\bc4\lib\bidsf.lib+
\bc4\lib\owlwf.lib+
\bc4\lib\import32.lib+
\bc4\lib\cw32.lib
min.def
```

You may be surprised at the size of our minimum program. With about 66 lines of source code, MIN.CPP may be the longest *minimum* program you have ever encountered. The size reflects the amount of work that a program must do to tap into the Windows and OWL libraries. But once a program has made the necessary connections, Windows and OWL work together to do a substantial amount of work for you.

For example, Windows provides default support for the different parts of our window. Consider the system menu, with its seven commands: *Restore*, *Move*, *Size*, *Minimize*, *Maximize*, *Close*, and *Switch To*. Windows does all the right things to make these commands operational, with only a minimum of effort required of our program. The OWL libraries, in turn, are structured so that the messages generated by these menu selections are delivered to the correct place to make the right things happen.

Each *part* of this minimum program is required to allow the OWL objects to interact properly with Windows. The *structure* of this program is extensible so that, when we create more sophisticated programs later in this book, we can use MIN as the starting point. The structure of this program is important because it embodies the structure of every Windows program built using the OWL libraries.

Because you may be eager to compile and run this program, we'll start by talking about the tools that you'll need to build Windows programs. You are already familiar with some tools, such as the Borland C++ Compiler and the Linker. You'll need to pay special attention to the compiler switches in order to generate Windows-compatible code. As for the linker, it needs a special input file: the **module definition(.DEF) file**. Other tools that we'll describe are specific to the Windows development environment, such as the Resource Compiler and the Resource Workshop.

After we describe the development tools, we're going to take a minor detour in the next chapter to talk about some of the conventions that have been adopted for Windows programming. This includes the **Hungarian Naming Convention**, which is used to name data structures and variables. And, we'll introduce the various include files that you'll need to take advantage of the Windows and OWL libraries: WINDOWS.H and OWLPCH.H to name just two. These files contain the required symbolic constants, data structures, function prototypes, and C++ class definitions.

Subsequent chapters will look at the code from our minimum Windows program. We'll start with a look at the application object, as defined by the `TApplication` class. An instance of this class is created in `WinMain`, the function which serves as the entry point for every Windows program. `WinMain` typically creates an application object, and then starts it running in an (almost) endless loop to retrieve hardware-related **messages**. A message is a unit of input to a Windows program, as well as the "time-slice" that makes Windows' nonpreemptive multitasking system work.

In Chapter 5, we're going to review `TWindow` and `TFrameWindow`, the two classes which are the ancestors of MIN's window class object. The three member functions of MIN's window object seem to do very little, and yet they play an important role in every Windows program. We'll look at the way that MIN uses the `TWindow` and `TFrameWindow` classes to connect a window to the Windows libraries.

We'll conclude this section of the book with an in-depth look at the different types of messages that you'll encounter in your Windows programming career. As you'll see, about 250 different messages are defined in WINDOWS.H. We create eight categories in our "Taxonomy of Messages."

Let's begin with a look at the development tools that are used to build our minimum Windows program.

The Mechanics of Compiling and Linking MIN.EXE

When you write Windows programs, you use development tools that you are familiar with from other environments: a language compiler and a linker. Other tools are specific to the Windows environment, like the **Resource Compiler** and the **Resource Workshop**. These tools are used to create user-interface objects and merge them into a program's executable file. Almost every Windows program that you write will require the use of resources. In Chapters 11 and 14, for example, you'll see how resources are used to create menus and dialog boxes. MIN contains just two resources: a menu and an icon.

➤ *Note to Apple Macintosh Programmers*

Windows resources are similar to Macintosh resources. Unlike a Macintosh program, however, a Windows program cannot alter the disk-image of its resources. In other words, Windows resources contain read-only data.

The Resource File

MIN.RC lists the resources to be merged into MIN.EXE. To the Windows memory manager, a resource is a read-only data object. By separating a program's read-only data from its read-write data, a Windows program helps the Windows memory manager optimize the way memory is used. Since almost all user-interface objects are stored as resources, every Windows program (knowingly or not) helps optimize memory use. Table 2.2 lists the eight types of predefined resources. For this set, there are Windows functions which create and control these objects. If you use large blocks of read-only data, you can create custom resource types to further optimize memory use (a technique described in Chapter 18).

Resources are normally read into memory when needed, although you can make a resource `PRELOAD` so it will be resident at program startup. When read into memory, a resource usually resides in a `DISCARDABLE` memory block. Such memory can be purged if the Windows memory manager requires it.

Table 2.2 Windows' Predefined Resources

Resource Type	*Covered In Depth*
Accelerator table	Chapter 11
Bitmaps	
Cursors	Chapter 16
Dialog box template	Chapter 14
Fonts	Chapter 10
Icons	
Menu template	Chapter 11
String table	Chapter 18

Our minimum Windows program has one type of resource: an icon. To create your own icons, use the Borland Resource Workshop.

I created our icon from a snapshot of MIN taken while it was running. I created the snapshot using a built-in capability of Windows. When you strike the [PrtSc] (print screen) key,

Windows puts a snapshot of the *entire screen* onto the clipboard. When you strike [Alt] + [PrtSc], Windows limits the snapshot to the currently active window.

I used the [Alt] + [PrtSc] combination to capture a snapshot of MIN.EXE. Then I pasted it into the Resource Workshop. After a bit of cleanup, I had a ready-to-use icon. Next, I saved the icon to its own file and made entries into MIN.RC, indicating our name for the resource, the resource type, and the resource file name.

When our program is built, the resource compiler copies the icon resource into MIN.EXE. This is done so that every Windows program is a stand-alone executable file, with a minimum dependence on external files.

Hint The Windows screen-capture capability will be very useful in creating documentation for your Windows programs. In fact, I used this method to create all of the screen shots for this book. I used a monochrome VGA display driver and an HP LaserJet II printer.

The Linker and the Module Definition File

In addition to the .OBJ and .LIB files, the linker gets input from a **module definition file** (.DEF) when creating Windows programs. The role of a module definition file is to describe the structure and organization of a program. You can think of the .DEF file as a set of linker switches. Let's review each statement in our module definition file, MIN.DEF.

This statement tells the linker to create a Windows program:

```
EXETYPE WINDOWS
```

This statement is optional, since the **`/Twe`** switch already tells the linker to create a Windows program. Nevertheless, I like to use this switch in preparation for a future version of the linker which may create OS/2 programs. At that time, I'll substitute `OS2` for `WINDOWS`.

The `CODE` statement sets the default memory disposition for code segments in a Windows program:

```
CODE MOVEABLE DISCARDABLE
```

As I will discuss in Chapter 18, the use of the **`SEGMENTS`** statement allows you to specify the memory disposition for individual code segments. For now, the `CODE` statement by itself will work fine. `MOVEABLE` (versus `FIXED`) allows a segment to be relocated. The `DISCARDABLE` declaration means that, when memory is low, the code segment can be purged from system memory. The dynamic link mechanism allows code to be moved around in memory, as well as removed from memory, in a manner that is completely transparent to your program.

The DATA statement is similar to the CODE statement, except that it sets the memory disposition of a program's data segment:

```
DATA MULTIPLE MOVEABLE
```

MOVEABLE allows the data segment to move in memory. (When a message is delivered to a program, the data segment is locked in place to avoid unexpected results. This is only a concern in Real Mode Windows, but since the Borland compiler only creates protected mode applications, this isn't a concern for you.) The MULTIPLE declaration is the standard for Windows programs. It allows several copies of a single program to run at the same time.

STACKSIZE sets the size of a program's stack:

```
STACKSIZE 8192
```

The stack has three uses: storing of local variables, passing parameters to called functions, and saving return addresses to allow "anonymous calling." Windows programs must have a minimum stack size of 5K. (If a smaller amount is specified, the Windows loader automatically allocates a 5K stack.) Of this, 2K is meant for your program's use. The other 3K is for Windows' use. When a program calls a Windows library routine, the arguments to the routine are passed on the program's stack. Use a higher value for programs with a lot of local variables or recursive operations.

The HEAPSIZE statement sets the initial size of a program's local heap. Our minimum program uses the following value:

```
HEAPSIZE 512
```

The local heap is one of two places from which dynamic memory allocation can occur. (The other place is the system's global heap.) The local heap is private to a program, and resides in the program's data segment. The HEAPSIZE statement sets the initial size of the local heap. A heap can grow beyond its initial size, limited only by the restriction that, running in Win16, a segment cannot be larger than 64K.

At this point, you have enough information to type in and create a minimum Windows program. I suggest you pause now and do so. It will give you an opportunity to check that your development environment is properly set up. It will also give you the chance to become familiar with this program before we delve into its inner workings.

In the next chapter, we're going to address some of the coding conventions of the Windows programming world, and the conventions used in the OWL class library.

3

Windows and OWL Programming Conventions

Of all the things for a programmer to be concerned with, you'd probably put the creation of variable names near the bottom of the list. And yet, creating variable names is a task that every programmer must perform. I'm going to introduce you to **Hungarian Naming**, a practice that permeates Windows programs. If you're like me, you may be puzzled by your first encounter with Hungarian. But over time, I have become so convinced of its value that I'm going to talk about it first.

After I've covered the issues relating to Hungarian Naming, I'll talk about the various include files that your programs will need. You may have already noticed that one of the first lines in our Windows program is

```
#include <owl\owlpch.h>
```

This causes the most basic OWL class declarations to be loaded, and WINDOWS. H as well.

WINDOWS.H is a very large—150K—data file which describes all the elements you'll need to connect to Windows. If you're like me, you might want to print out this important file and thumb through it. It contains the bare-bones definition of the Windows API as your program will see it.

I'll once again discuss **handles**, a data type you will encounter often in your Windows programming career. Handles have been referred to as "magic numbers," "magic cookies," and "claim check numbers." Whichever term you prefer, handles identify objects created by one part of the system or another. A handle is a number, but the meaning of the number is only known to the part of the system that created the object and issued the handle.

Finally, I'll touch on an issue that will concern you when you look at older Windows code: **casting**. While it used to be required in the earliest days of Windows programming, developments in language compilers have made this an obsolete practice. In fact, as I'll explain, the use of casts can be downright dangerous and can introduce hard-to-find errors into your code.

Let's get started with a look at Hungarian Naming.

Hungarian Naming

Hungarian Naming is a convention for creating names of variables and functions. It is widely used by Windows programmers because it makes code easier to read and easier to maintain. Hungarian Naming, or Hungarian for short, gets its name from the nationality of the original developer, Charles Simonyi. The name is also a tongue-in-cheek description for the convention because programmers often find Hungarian to be initially confusing. Simonyi developed this naming convention as part of his doctoral dissertation on programmer productivity. It became widely used at Xerox PARC, where Simonyi was working when he developed this practice. It was adopted at Microsoft after Simonyi began working there, and has since become a standard of sorts among Windows programmers.

Creating *useful* variable names can be a real challenge. Should they be short and sweet? Short variable names are easy to type, but they can make your code hard to understand. You know what I mean if you've tried reading BASIC programs with very short variable names. What can you tell about the variables `A` and `B` in these lines of BASIC code? Not very much from the names alone.

```
20    LET B=10
30    FOR A=1 to 10
40    LET B=B+A
50    NEXT A
```

If short names are cryptic, perhaps we can create useful variable names by making them long anddescriptive.Isthereanydoubtabouthowavariablecalled **`loopindex`**isused?Andyet, this approach can lead to variable names that are long and unwieldy. Consider the names in this list:

```
countofcharacters
numberoffiles
temporaryfilename
windowhandle
pointertoarrayofcharacters
```

While such names may make code more readable, they put a burden on the programmer who has to type them. The use of long names also increases the chance that one will be mistyped.

Hungarian takes a middle road between these two extremes. In Hungarian, variable names are created by putting a short prefix in front of a longer, more descriptive name. The prefix describes the *type of data* referenced by the variable. In some cases, a prefix also describes the *way a variable is used.* For convenience, a prefix can be used alone as a variable name.

Here are some examples of Hungarian:

```
char ch;              // 'ch' = character.
char achFile[128];    // 'a'  = array; 'ch' = character
char far * lpszName;  // 'lp' = long (far) pointer.
                      // 'sz' = null (zero) terminated string.
int cbName;           // 'cb' = count of bytes.
TWindow * ptwMain;    // 'p'  = pointer.
                         'tw' = Owl Twindow object
```

Note that prefixes are lowercase, and long names combine uppercase and lowercase. The first variable, **ch**, is the prefix for character data. It is an example of a prefix used as a variable name. The prefix for **achFile** has two parts: a means this is an array, and ch tells us the type of data in the array, characters. The prefix for **lpszFirstName** also has two parts: **lp** means long pointer, and **sz** describes the data pointed to, a null-terminated string. The variable **cbName** contains the prefix **cb** to tell us that the variable contains a count of bytes. There are two parts to the Hungarian prefix for the last one in this list, **ptwMain**: The **p** stands for pointer; the **tw** means that the pointer refers to the OWL **TWindow** class.

Understanding Hungarian helps us read and understand lines of code like this:

```
LPSTR      lpszName;
LPSTR      lpsz;
int        cbName;

for (lpsz = lpszName, cbName=0;
     lpsz != '\0';
     lpsz++, cbName++);
```

The prefix **cb** tells us that the variable **cbName** *must* contain a count of bytes. Since that's the case, it is pretty clear that the purpose of this code is to calculate the number of characters in the null-terminated string referenced by the pointer **lpszName**. Incidentally, the use of a Hungarian prefix by itself is quite common for "temporary" variables, which is what **lpsz** is used for.

In addition to helping you read code, Hungarian helps you avoid silly (but very common) programming errors. As you become familiar with Hungarian, you will come to recognize that

```
lpszName = achFile;
```

is a valid statement, while the following is not:

```
lpszName = cbName;
```

After all, it makes sense to assign the address of an array to a pointer. But it does not make sense to assign a count of bytes to a pointer.

The trick to learning Hungarian is to learn the prefixes. Here is a list of the more common prefixes used in Windows programming:

Prefix	*Data Type*
`a`	Array (compound type)
`ch`	Character
`cb`	Count of bytes
`dw`	Unsigned long, (WINDOWS.H typedef: DWORD)
`h`	Handle—16-bit identifier
`hdc`	Handle to a device context
`hwnd`	Handle to a window
`i`	Index (compound)
`l`	Long integer, (WINDOWS.H typedef: LONG)
`lp`	Long (or far) pointer (compound type)
`n`	Integer
`np`	Near (or short) pointer (compound type)
`pt`	An *x,y* point (WINDOWS.H typedef: POINT)
`r`	A Rectangle structure (WINDOWS.H typedef: RECT)
`sz`	Null-terminated string
`w`	Unsigned integer, (WINDOWS.H typedef: WORD)

Notice that some of these prefixes are "compound types." This means they are used as prefixes to other prefixes. The following code fragment shows how two compound prefixes, `a` and `i`, define variables that can be used together:

```
char     ch;
int      ich;              /* Index a character array. */
char     achName[64];      /*  Character array. */
...
ch = achName[ich];
```

It is worth noting that there is no "official" list of prefixes. Since any given programming project is bound to have its own unique data types, prefixes can be created to reflect those types. In general, however, the usefulness of Hungarian comes from having a relatively small number of types and from agreement by the members of a development team on the meaning of each type.

Hungarian is also used for function names. There are several "dialects" that we have encountered. One combines a verb and a noun to describe a function. For example, three

Windows library routines are **CreateWindow**, **DrawText**, and **LoadIcon**. Within the Windows libraries, you can see other dialects: Some library routines consist of a noun by itself, such as **DialogBox**. For routines that convert from one type to another, the form XtoY is common. For example, the Windows library routine **DPtoLP** converts device points into logical points.

A special routine encountered in OWL programs is the message handler. Windows sends messages to your program when an event of interest occurs. For example, the `WM_PAINT` message tells you to repaint a window. A `WM_LBUTTONDOWN` message lets you know that the left mouse button has been pushed. All messages get sent to a window procedure. OWL sends these messages on to message handlers which you have defined. The name of a message handler is derived from the name of the message. For example, an `EvPaint` member function handles a `WM_PAINT` message, and an `EvLButtonDown` member function handles a `WM_LBUTTONDOWN` message.

If you choose to adopt Hungarian naming, it will help you write code that is easier to read and easier to maintain. Even if you don't adopt this convention, a familiarity with Hungarian will help you read sample code from this book and from other sources. It will also help you read and make sense of definitions that you encounter in the Windows include file, WINDOWS.H.

OWL Naming Conventions

Borland's OWL libraries roughly follow Hungarian naming, with a few variations. Although this difference can sometimes be confusing, we find it helps distinguish the OWL parts of a program from the strictly Windows parts of a program.

The OWL libraries use an uppercase prefix to identify a class name: `T`, which stands for "type." Here are some of the classes defined in OWL:

```
TApplication
TControl
TDialog
TWindow
TFrameWindow
```

OWL class member functions follow the Hungarian convention of mixing uppercase and lowercase letters. You'll notice, however, that OWL strays from strict Hungarian in names given to class data members.

Throughout this book, we've adopted Hungarian for class data members, since it helps distinguish OWL data members from our own. Also, to avoid confusion with OWL class names, the sample programs in this book use the prefix **D** at the start of all the derived types. MIN, for example, defines the **DApp** and **DFrame** classes that inherit from OWL's **TApplication** and **TFrameWindow** classes. And class names that do not inherit from OWL classes use no prefix at all.

Handles

A handle is an identifier. Handles are 16-bit unsigned integers. In the same way that MS-DOS issues file handles when a file is opened, Windows issues handles to identify objects. Keep in mind that the only use of a handle is as an identifier. It is just a number that has no meaning outside the context for which it was issued. You cannot, for example, cast a handle to a pointer and do any useful work with it. Quite a few Windows library routines return handles. When such routines fail, they return a "null handle" (that is, `handle == NULL`).

▼ **Warning!** Be careful—while a NULL value indicates an invalid handle from Windows, an invalid *file* handle has a value of –1.

The two most important types of handles to a Windows programmer are **window handles** and **device context handles.**

A window handle identifies a window. Each window in the system has a unique handle. All window manipulation routines use a window handle as a parameter. Once you have a window's handle, you can move it, size it, make it invisible, and in general do anything you want with it.

Device context handles are used for controlling graphics output. All GDI drawing routines take a handle to a device context as the first parameter. When you wish to use the GDI graphics library to draw in a window or send output to a printer, you must first get a handle to a device context for the desired device.

Handles are used to identify other objects as well. User-interface objects have handles: menus, icons, and cursors. Drawing objects are identified by handles: pens, brushes, fonts, regions, and bitmaps. Even memory that is dynamically allocated is identified using a handle.

Let's take a look at the include file which every OWL program will reference: OWLCORE.H.

The OWL Include Files

The OWL include files are arranged quite simply: Most classes have their own include (.H) file, although in some cases several related classes are defined together. Whenever you use a class, then, you add a reference to the class include file. To keep this from getting too awkward, one include file—**`owlcore.h`**—references a set of classes that most applications will use, including: **`TModule`**, **`TApplication`**, **`TDC`**, **`TMenu`**, **`TWindow`**, **`TMDIFrame`**, and **`TDecoratedMDIFrame`**.

Another include file, **owlpch.h**, includes **owlcore.h** if the precompiled header option has been requested from the compiler. (**pch** stands for "precompiled header".) The precompiled header option lets the compiler cache header file symbols so it can run faster. I recommend that you always compile with this option.

Here's a complete list of the include files that **owlcore.h** references (both directly and indirectly):

Include File	*Description*
owldefs.h	Basic macros for OWL class, data, and function modifiers. Also, this file includes the next six files in this list.
windows.h	The main Windows API library include file. Described in the next section, this file contains type definitions, symbolic constants, and data structures needed to connect to the Windows API.
shellapi.h	Another Windows API include file for shell-level operations like drag and drop support, the registration file API, searching for, and running executable files.
systypes.h	Declaration of basic integer data types used by OWL libraries.
cstring.h	Declaration of string and stream classes.
checks.h	Declaration of some debugging and diagnostic classes.
except.h	Declaration of exception handling classes.
version.h	Defines Owl version number constant.
module.h	Declaration of TModule class.
applicat.h	Declaration of TApplication class.
dc.h	Declaration of TDC class, and various descendents including TWindowDC, TScreenDC, TClientDC, and TPaintDC among others. Also contains inline functions for the entire GDI programming interface.
menu.h	Declaration of TMenu and related menu classes.
window.h	Declaration of TWindow class, which encapsulates the Windows API window.
mdi.h	Declaration of classes which support the multiple document interface (MDI), including TMDIClient and TMDIFrame.
mdichild.h	Declaration of TMDIChild class.
decmdifr.h	Declaration of TDecoratedMDIFrame class, which is a decorated (supports gadgets like control bars and message bars) window frame that supports the MDI user-interface.
dialog.h	Declaration of the TDialog class which wraps around a WinAPI dialog box.
control.h	Declaration of the TControl class which wraps around a WinAPI dialog box control.

The Windows Include File

While C and C++ language libraries come with many small include files (STDIO.H, STRING.H, etc.), the Windows libraries come with a single, large (162K) include file: `WINDOWS.H`. This file needs to be referenced—directly or indirectly—by every source file that accesses the Windows API because of the definitions it contains. There are three basic types of definitions in WINDOWS.H: symbolic constants, data types, and library function prototypes. Let's take a moment to look at each of these in some detail.

Symbolic Constants

In general, it's a bad practice to place "magic numbers" like 15 and 400 into a program. It makes your code hard to read. You should use symbolic constants instead. By convention, symbolic constants are written in uppercase to distinguish them from variable names. In C, the **`#define`** preprocessor statement creates symbolic constants:

```
#define MAXOPENFILES 15
```

Because WINDOWS.H is used for both C and C++ programs, only **`define`** statements are used instead of C++'s more advanced **`const`** statement.

In either language, symbolic constants improve the readability of a program and make program maintenance easier. Instead of hunting through a mountain of source code when numeric values change, only the single line of code that defines the value must be updated.

There are about 1,500 symbolic constants in WINDOWS.H. To help you sort them out, Hungarian Naming is used. For example, the symbols for window messages start with the prefix `WM_` (as in **`WM_CREATE`** and **`WM_DESTROY`**). If a constant is only used with a single library function, the Hungarian prefix is derived from the function name. For example, you can only use the **`CW_USEDEFAULT`** constant with the **`CreateWindow`** function.

Data Type Definitions

Quite a few data types are defined in WINDOWS.H. Some of them are little more than a convenient way to refer to commonly used C types. For example, the following statement appears in WINDOWS.H:

```
typedef char far * LPSTR;
```

This definition makes it easy to define a far pointer to a character string, since

```
LPSTR lpszName;
```

is equivalent to

```
char far * lpszName;
```

Here is a list of commonly used data types:

WINDOWS.H Name	*C Definition*
BOOL	int
BYTE	unsigned char
DWORD	unsigned long
HANDLE	unsigned int
HDC	unsigned int
HWND	unsigned int
LONG	long
LPSTR	char far *
NPSTR	char near *
WORD	unsigned int

Three types are defined as *unsigned int*: **HANDLE**, **HDC**, and **HWND**. Each defines a **handle**. Earlier in this chapter, we introduced handles as the method for identifying objects in Windows. The use of handles allows the complexity of an object to be hidden from your program. (In other words, Windows has data encapsulation!) Objects and object handles are very important to Windows programmers. When your program creates a window, for example, a handle is issued to identify the window: the HWND data type.

In addition to simple data types, WINDOWS.H holds a number of structure definitions. You might imagine that a rectangle structure would be useful in an environment that creates rectangular windows. You'd be right. Here is the rectangle data structure from WINDOWS.H:

```
typedef struct tagRECT
  {
    int    left;
    int    top;
    int    right;
    int    bottom;
} RECT;
```

Since Windows allows the user to select objects with a mouse pointer, you might expect to find a data structure to record the location of the mouse pointer. Again, you'd be right on target. Here's the `POINT` data structure:

```
typedef struct tagPOINT
  {
    int     y;
    int     y;
  } POINT;
```

Function Prototypes

An important feature of C++ is the ability to create **function prototypes**. Prototypes provide a means by which the compiler can perform some critical error checking for you. A function prototype tells the compiler how a routine should be called. Consider this prototype from WINDOWS.H:

```
BOOL WINAPI TextOut(HDC, int, int, LPSTR, int);
```

This declaration tells the compiler that the routine *must* be called with five parameters. A compiler error is generated if the function is called with too few (or too many) parameters. If you think about it, this capability alone makes the use of prototypes a recommended practice. How many times have you written a function, later added a parameter to the function definition, and then forgotten to change a line of code that calls the function? By doing so, you introduced a bug into your program. (Of course, this type of bug waits to appear until you demo your work to your boss.) A prototype lets the compiler complain about this type of problem so that you can find and correct it early.

A prototype tells the compiler about the expected *type* of each argument. When a type mismatch is encountered, a compiler error is generated. Consider this call to `TextOut`. It is clear that the fourth parameter is incorrect:

```
TextOut (hDC, 10, 20, 30, 2);
```

Based on the prototype from WINDOWS.H, the fourth parameter should be a far pointer to a character string (`char far *`). When the compiler encounters the value of 30, it complains because the type is incorrect. Correcting this particular problem might require us to place quotes around the number, as in

```
TextOut (hDC, 10, 20, "30", 2);
```

Using prototypes, a C or C++ compiler can also check for the correct use of a function's return value. That is, it checks for type-mismatch errors. The prototype for **`TextOut`**, for example, defines the return value as **`BOOL`** in WINDOWS.H. This code causes the C compiler to complain:

```
char far * lpch;
lpch = TextOut (hDC, 10, 10, "Hello", 5);
```

Every Windows function has a prototype in WINDOWS.H, so that the compiler can check your calls. Prototyping is useful for Windows library functions. Fortunately, it is also a requirement of any C++ code you write. Sometimes, developers combine C and C++ code. This is especially true when there is a large body of C code that is already in place. If you find yourself mixing C and C++ code, we recommend that you create prototypes for your C code, even if the compiler doesn't require it. This will save you a lot of grief.

The availability of function prototypes has made one practice obsolete: casting. And yet, a lot of code was written before function prototypes were available. For this reason, you need to be on the lookout for older Windows programs that may reflect an overuse of explicit casting.

An Outdated Practice: Casting

One of the best ways to learn any new programming environment is to look at someone else's code. You need to be careful, though, not to be misled by an outdated practice that you might come across in some older Windows programming: **casting of pointers.** This is outdated because newer compilers support function prototypes, which allow the compiler to automatically generate the correct code.

A moment ago, we looked at the function prototype for the **`TextOut`** function:

```
BOOL WINAPI TextOut(HDC, int, int, LPSTR, int);
```

The earliest Windows programmers had to write code like the following:

```
TextOut (hDC, 10, 10, (LPSTR)"Hello World", 12);
```

Notice the cast to **`LPSTR`**. This forces the creation of a *far pointer*. It used to be that, in a small-model or medium-model program, the expression "`Hello World`" would cause a near pointer to be generated. But the function requires a far pointer, so a cast was required.

At first glance, this casting seems harmless enough. The only problem seems to be that a lot of extra keystrokes are wasted. However, there is a real danger to casting. If you were to follow the old-fashioned practice of casting every pointer, you might hide certain problems that the compiler would otherwise detect for you. Consider the following line of code:

```
TextOut (hDC, 10, 10, (LPSTR)30, 2);
```

Perhaps the programmer had meant to use the string `30` as the fourth parameter. Without the cast, the compiler notifies us of the type-mismatch error. But a cast forces the value to the correct type, hiding the error from the compiler. The cast tells the compiler, in effect, "I know what I'm doing. Please don't ask any questions."

The message should be clear: Avoid casting. It negates the compiler's automatic checking, and can hide problems from you.

This is not to say that casts are never needed. For example, they are often needed when working with Windows' dynamic memory allocation routines. These routines are prototyped to return character pointers. If you assign the return value to any other type, the compiler complains. The **GlobalLock** routine, for example, is defined as returning a `LPSTR(char far *)`:

```
LPSTR WINAPI GlobalLock(HANDLE);
```

The following lines of code cause the compiler to complain:

```
int far * lpint;   /* Define an integer pointer. */
lpint = GlobalLock(hMem);   /* Compiler whines.   */
```

The second line of code would be required if we had stored an array of integers in the block of memory referenced by the handle **hMem**. Even though the compiler complains, this line of code creates a correct result. However, it's a good practice to reserve compiler complaints for things that really matter. The cast in the following line of code produces the same result, except that the compiler is now happy that there is no type-mismatch error:

```
lpint = (LPINT)GlobalLock(hMem);
```

(Of course, you'll use **LPINT** instead of **int far ***, because it helps make your code more portable.)

So you see, there are times when casting is necessary. In general, however, the compiler will let you know when the time is right. The rule still stands: Avoid casting. Then, when the compiler complains, you can look at the offending code and determine whether or not a cast will fix your problem.

Messages

Before you started writing object-oriented C++ code, you probably were used to a sequential, procedure-driven manner of coding. Windows borrows heavily from the world of object-oriented programming. However, you should take care not to be confused by the term "message." In the context of a C++ program, it really means "a call to an object's member function." In the context of Windows programming, it refers to something a little different.

Windows messages are generated in response to some change in the user interface, such as a window getting moved or the user striking a key on the keyboard. Messages are used to notify a program that a timer has gone off. Messages are also used for data sharing operations, which means the clipboard and the Dynamic Data Exchange (DDE).

From a programming point of view, a message is a numeric value that, for ease of reading, is given a parameter name that starts with `WM_`, like `WM_LBUTTONDOWN`. The `WM_LBUTTONDOWN` message means that the left button on the mouse has been pushed down. Another message will get sent when the left mouse button is released: `WM_LBUTTONUP`.

As you might guess, Windows messages are very important to a Windows programmer. Most of a Windows programmer's work involves deciding which messages to process and which messages to ignore. As with C++ messages, there is no predefined order to Windows messages.

To a certain extent, this is simply an implementation issue. Conceptually, a C++ message and a Windows message are the same. The only difference is that each C++ function handles one and only one message. On the other hand, a single function in a Windows program—known as a window procedure—handles all the messages sent to one type of window. When you start to work with a C++ class library, you learn about the public functions (messages) in the different classes. In the same way, learning to work with Windows' windows, you need to learn about the public messages that you'll get sent. To help you get started, we've included a "Taxonomy of Messages" at the end of Chapter 5 and also in Appendix A.

Now that we've reviewed some of the basic conventions of Windows and C++ programming, it's time to take a closer look at MIN's source code. We're going to start by looking at the parts which make up MIN's application object class, which inherits from OWL's **`TApplication`** class.

4

The Application Object

If you're fairly new to C++ programming, the idea of an **application object** may seem puzzling at first. After all, the *operating system* creates the application—why create an ***application object***? Certainly you don't want—nor expect—to see a second copy of your application! In fact, it's quite common for a class library[1] to have an application object that serves as a framework for the other pieces within an application.

From a design perspective, the application object is a container for everything that makes up the application. For example, OWL's application class has member functions for accessing an application's executable file, the application startup code, the application termination code, and application-level error handling[2]. And, as you'll see shortly, OWL's **`TApplication`** class also supports the connection to the application's message queue, which is a Windows program's primary connection to user input.

From a practical point of view, application object data members are of interest to every part of an application. For example, OWL's **`TApplication`** class has data members for the four parameters passed to a Windows' application's **`WinMain`** entry point, since they are needed in many different parts of an OWL program. In terms of C programming, a (very) loose way to think of an application object's data members is that they are like a C program's global variables: Both have a scope that encompasses the entire application. C++ application object data members and C global variables are treated with great reverence, and the smart programmer avoids creating them at all.

In this chapter, I'll start by explaining the application object in MIN, the program introduced in the last chapter. Next, I'll explore the capabilities of the OWL's **`TModule`** and

---

1 For example, MacApp on the Macintosh has a **`TApplication`** class for this purpose; in Microsoft's MFC class library, this role is served by the **`CWinApp`** class.

2 Some are inherited from **`TModule`** and others are placeholders for your use, so you'll want to look in both <owl\applicat.h> as well as <owl\module.h> for the complete class declaration.

TApplication classes, from which MIN's **DApp** application class is derived. Finally, I'll drill down until we hit the core of what makes up any Windows application—the message processing that's managed by **TApplication**'s innermost core.

MIN's DApp Application Class

Here is the code for MIN's **DApp** application class:

```
// Application object
class DApp : public TApplication
    {
  public:
    DApp();
    void InitMainWindow();
    };

DApp::DApp() : TApplication()
    {
    }

void DApp::InitMainWindow()
    {
    SetMainWindow (new DFrame("OWL Minimum"));

    MainWindow->AssignMenu("MAIN");
    MainWindow->SetIcon(this, "SNAPSHOT");
     }
```

DApp overrides a single **TApplication** member function, **InitMainWindow**. Although a Windows application can have many different windows, one window earns the title "main window." To users this means the window with the application menu and the one that contains the application's data. To the OWL libraries, this window is tightly coupled to the application object such that when the main window is closed, the application terminates.

Within **DApp::InitMainWindow**, a **TFrameWindow** derived window is created, and a pointer to that window is passed to **TApplication::SetMainWindow** to mark it as the main window. This function stores the pointer to a **TFrameWindow** in the **MainWindow** data member. You might be tempted to set the value directly:

```
// Don't set MainWindow like this.
MainWindow = new DFrame ("OWL Minimum");
```

but **TApplication::SetMainWindow** does some other useful things, so it's a mistake to do it yourself.

The next two functions called, **AssignMenu** and **SetIcon**, are **TFrameWindow** function members. These functions connect user-interface objects from MIN's resource file, MIN.RC, to our application's main window. That's a topic for the next chapter, where I'll describe the role played by an application's main window.

Right now, let's take a look at the code that gets MIN up and running—its entry point.

MIN's Entry Point

A C program's normal entry point is declared like this:

```
int main (int argc, char *argv[])
```

The entry point for OWL programs varies from this a bit:

```
int OwlMain (int argc, char *argv[])
```

The two parameters provide what most C programmers expect: a count of parameters and a pointer to an array of character string pointers. But why the different name? As you'll see shortly, the *real* entry point to a Windows program is **WinMain**, and it takes four parameters—not the two shown here. Before taking a look into that entry point, though, let's look at MIN's tiny **OwlMain** function:

```
// Application main entry point.
OwlMain(int, char **)
    {
    return DApp().Run();
    }
```

This function creates a **DApp** application object, then calls **TApplication::Run()** to engage the application object machinery. As we peel back the layers that make up **DApp**'s base classes, you'll see that **TApplication::Run** is really **TApplication**'s main function. For example, it calls MIN's derived application initialization function, **DApp::InitMainWindow**, as part of its startup before connecting to the Windows system's message delivery mechanism.

As a side note, this tiny code fragment shows some interesting aspects of C++ programming that might puzzle you if you're new to C++. In the function definition, for example, parameter *types* are given without the parameter *name*. This is not legal in C, but is useful in C++ to avoid getting a "parameter not used" warning message.

Another somewhat puzzling C++ construct is the creation of an *unnamed* local variable of type **DApp** in this function. An alternative—but more verbose—way to do the same thing is:

```
OwlMain(int, char **)
    {
DApp MinApp;
    return MinApp.Run();
    }
```

You'd do this to have a name for your temporary application object if, for example, you wanted to access its data or function members. Another verbose alternative, using the C++ **new** and **delete** operators, is:

```
OwlMain(int, char **)
    {
    DApp * pMinApp;
    int iRetVal;

    pMinApp = new DApp();
    iRetVal = pMinApp->Run();
    delete pMinApp;

    return iRetVal;
    }
```

In the interest of saving keystrokes, MIN's version of **OwlMain** is the best one, even if it's somewhat cryptic.

Since most Windows applications start up the same way, you can rely OWL's application object to start an application correctly most of the time. But because you'll needed to tweak the OWL default application class from time to time, it's worth spending some time drilling through the OWL layer until we hit the encapsulated WinAPI. That's what I'll do for the rest of this chapter, starting with a look at the entry point common to all Windows program, **WinMain**.

The WinMain Entry Point

If you look at Windows programs that don't use OWL, you'll find neither **main** nor **OwlMain**. Instead, the entry point for a Windows program is **WinMain**[3]. In an OWL program, you can use either **OwlMain** or **WinMain**, but **OwlMain** makes for less typing so it's the one I use. The OWL libraries contain a **WinMain** function, which does some initialization and then calls your **OwlMain**. **WinMain** is declared:

```
int PASCAL WinMain (HINSTANCE hInstance,
                    HINSTANCE hPrevInstance,
                    LPSTR lpszCmdLine,
                    int  nCmdShow)
```

When a program starts running, Windows gives it information about who it is and who it is related to. The **hInstance** parameter says who a program is. Think of it, if you'd like, as a program's name. Windows gives each program in the system a unique name. Of course, the name is not "Joe" or "Fred," but an integer (the type for which **HINSTANCE** is defined in WINDOWS.H).

[3] To convince yourself that this is the case, take a peek at \bc4\source\owl\winmain.cpp, which shows this declaration and the call to your OwlMain.

Windows tells a program its name because certain Windows library routines require this as a parameter. This allows Windows to know "who is calling." This parameter is important enough to be stored as a data member of **`TApplication`**. But its use in an OWL program is rare because the OWL classes handle the chores associated with this parameter. If you search the OWL source code, you'll see the importance of this parameter—it's needed to load resources from your program's executable file, including menus, icons, cursors, dialog box templates, bitmaps, etc.

In a program written to the Win16 API, the second parameter, **`hPrevInstance`**, tells a program who it is related to. If it isn't related to any currently running program, the value of **`hPrevInstance`** is **`NULL`**. How does Windows decide if two programs are related? By name. In the same way that two people with the same last name are (often) related, two programs are related if either (1) the file names are the same, or (2) the **module names** are the same.

Under Win32 API, **`hPrevInstance`** is always **`NULL`**. The original idea of this parameter was to make it easy for two copies of a program to share things. But the ability to share can create some problems. For example, when two programs share object, there is the issue of who should do the cleanup and when—an issue sometimes referred to as one of **object ownership**. Sharing can also get in the way of security and robustness. If it's too easy, then accidental—or malicious—mishaps can also occur too easily. For these reasons, in a program written to the Win32 API, this second parameter is always **`NULL`**, and programs that wish to share things simply have to work a little harder.

The third parameter to **`WinMain`**, **`lpszCmdLine`**, gives the command line arguments for a program. There are a number of ways that command line arguments get created. The simplest involves putting the arguments after the program name in the Properties dialog box of the Program Manager. Like the **`argv`** parameter in the usual C or C++ program entry point

```
main (int argc, char **argv)
```

the **`lpszCmdLine`** parameter allows a program to read its command line for arguments like file names, option switches, etc. Unlike **`argv`**, however, **`lpszCmdLine`** points to a single character string and not to an array of character pointers.

The final parameter, **`nCmdShow`**, tells a program what to do with its main window when it first starts. Should it be minimized? Should it be displayed full screen? When we talk about the **`TWindow`** and **`TFrameWindow`** classes in the next chapter, you'll see that this parameter is passed by an application's main window object to the **`ShowWindowWinAPI`** routine.

With an understanding of the four WinMain parameters under our belt, we're ready to look at the guts of the two classes on which MIN's application class is built: **`TModule`** and **`TApplication`**. Let's start with **`TModule`**.

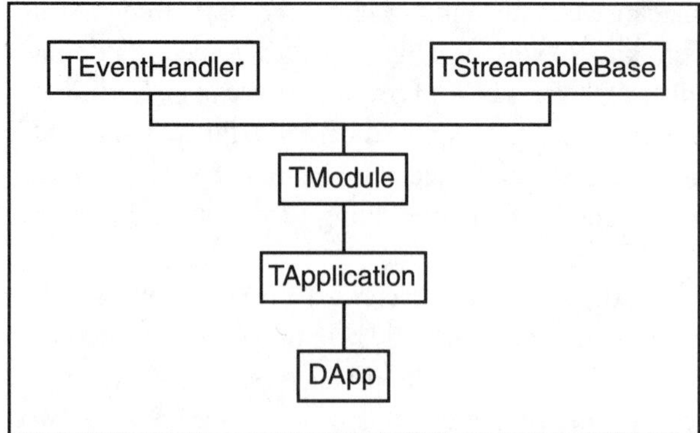

Figure 4.1 The relationship of MIN's DApp application class to the OWL class hierarchy

The TModule Class

A **module** is the RAM image of a disk-based executable file. Windows knows about two kinds of modules: **applications** and **dynamic link libraries (DLLs)**. Among the differences between them is that an application gets scheduled while a DLL does not. An application owns resources and is active, while a DLL can't own things and remains a passive service provider to applications and to other DLLs. Among the similarities between the two types of modules, both applications and DLLs share a common file format. And to optimize memory use, the KERNEL keeps a single copy of a module present in RAM even when the module is accessed by multiple users. For example, two copies of NOTEPAD only require a single copy of its code and resources to be present in RAM. The same is true for DLLs: A single copy of KERNEL, USER and GDI serve all WinAPI applications.

The **`TModule`** class reflects the way the OWL class library represents a Windows module (see Figure 4.1). When creating either type of module with OWL, you start by creating a **`TModule`** Object. Let's take a closer look at the **`TModule`** class. As defined in MODULE.H, here are **`TModule`**'s data members:

Type	*Name*	*Description*
`char *`	**`Name`**	Module name. Normally the executable file name without an extension. This member is protected, but settable and readable at runtime with member functions. To define a different name at program link time, make an entry in the module definition (.DEF) file. Applications use the NAME keyword for a new module name; DLLs use the LIBRARY keyword for a new module name.

Type	*Name*	*Description*
HINSTANCE	**Hinstance**	Protected data member that identifies the module instance to the Windows KERNEL. Get and set using class member functions.
int	**ShouldFree**	A private flag set by the constructor to let the destructor know whether to clean up (**FreeLibrary**) the DLL.
char *	**lpCmdLine**	Command line entered to start application. You should use **argc** and **argv** from **OwlMain**, since this parameter is present for OWL 1.0 compatibility.
Tstatus	**Status**	Error handler. Present for backward compatibility with OWL 1.0.

The primary use of the **TModule** class by itself is for run-time loading[4] of dynamic link libraries. As a base class for **TApplication**, it's interesting for the fact that it serves as a wrapper for several KERNEL functions. Most of the wrapped KERNEL functions load **resources**—read-only data objects mostly for user-interface definitions—from a module's executable file. Here's a list of the more interesting **TModule** member functions[5]:

Function Name	*Description*
TModule()	Three constructors. One loads a DLL by name, a second is for DLLs that have been loaded by some other mechanism (such as a call to the WinAPI **LoadLibrary** function), and a third is for use by the **TApplication** class.
~Tmodule()	Destructor calls WinAPI **FreeLibrary** function if needed.
GetModuleFileName()	Fetch the fully qualified path of the executable file (KERNEL).
FindResource()	Search for resource location in an executable file (KERNEL).
LoadResource()	Allocate memory for a resource found with FindResource (KERNEL).

---

[4] I use the term run-time loading of a DLL as opposed to link-time loading. Most of the time, a DLL is link-time loaded—which means that the linker takes care of putting information into an executable file so that the KERNEL's dynamic link/loader can make the right connections. A less common—but extremely useful—capability is run-time loading, which means your program specifies the DLL file name and asks the KERNEL to load it for you. For details, see Chapter 19.

[5] For a complete list, run help (winhelp.exe) and search through the ObjectWindows library help (in owl.hlp). Or, look at module.h, which provides the complete C++ class declaration. For KERNEL functions, the best reference is the help file that contains the Windows API Reference (bwinapi.hlp).

`LockResource()`[6]	Obtain a pointer to a RAM-resident copy of a resource (KERNEL).
`LoadAccelerators()`	Load an accelerator table resource from an executable file (KERNEL).
`LoadBitmap()`	Load a bitmap resource from an executable file (KERNEL).
`LoadCursor()`	Load a cursor resource from an executable file (KERNEL).
`LoadIcon()`	Load an icon resource from an executable file (KERNEL).
`LoadMenu()`	Load a menu resource from an executable file (KERNEL).
`LoadString()`	Load a string resource from an executable file (KERNEL).

There are functions other than those listed here, but I have omitted them because their inclusion in OWL 2.0 is for backward compatibility with OWL 1.0 or for backward compatibility with Win16. You should avoid such functions, since their use will limit the useful life of your program. A look at **`module.h`** will give you an idea of the functions to avoid. Comments describe functions and data members defined for compatibility with OWL 1.0. For compatibility with Win32, pay attention to the places where conditional compilation is controlled by the **`__WIN32__`** symbolic constant.

Most of the interesting application-level activity is performed by a class that is derived from **`TModule`**, namely the **`TApplication`** class. We're going to explore this class next.

The TApplication Class

OWL's **`TApplication`** class is the immediate base class for DApp, MIN's Application class. **`TApplication`** handles the things a typical Windows application does: It initializes, creates a main window, and queries the system for messages. Let's take a close look at **`TApplication`** to help you see the work it—along with the Windows library functions—does for you.

`TApplication`'s important data members, as defined in APPLICAT.H, are as follows:

---

[6] This member function isn't in the copy of module.h that ships with Borland C++ 4.0. However, it belongs there—see Appendix H for a list of the patches I recommend making to the OWL include files.

Type	*Name*	*Description*
`TFrameWindow *`	**`MainWindow`**	Pointer to a **`TFrameWindow`** window (or a class derived from this class). When this window is destroyed, the application terminates.
`TDocManager *`	**`DocManager`**	Pointer to the application's document manager for controlling the opening and closing of different document types and connecting file data to the appropriate viewer window class.
`BOOL`	**`BWCCOn`**	Private. Flags whether to use Borland custom control library.
`TModule *`	**`BWCCModule`**	Private. Connection to Borland custom control library.
`BOOL`	**`Ctl3dOn`**	Private. Flags whether to use 3-D dialog box control library.
`TModule *`	**`Ctl3dModule`**	Private. Connection to 3-D dialog box control library.
`HACCEL`	**`HAccTable`**	OWL 1.0 keyboard accelerator table handle (obsolete).

All of the data members listed here (aside from the obsolete OWL 1.0 data member, which is included to help you avoid wasting time with it) deal with global, application level issues. If the two boolean flags are FALSE, then all dialog boxes in an application will use Windows' standard, built-in dialog box controls. When your application uses controls from either control library, call the corresponding enable function in the application object to allow it to perform the required library initialization.

The most important data member is **`MainWindow`**, since the main window is the primary connection between **`TApplication`** and your application's user interface. If you don't create a main window, OWL's default behavior is to create one for you. From a user's point of view, a main window provides the main connection to an application—when the main window is closed, the user expects the application to terminate.

Another important data member is **`DocManager`**, which is a pointer to a **`TDocManager`** object. You aren't required to create a document manager object, but when building applications that manage different types of data and which provide different views into each different type, a document manager can be very helpful. For details on samples programs illustrating the use of the document manager/viewer classes, see Appendix I.

The other side to **`Tapplication`**, of course, is the class member functions. Here's a list of the most interesting ones:

Function Name	*Description*
PUBLIC:	
TApplication()	Two constructors, depending on the entry point used. A default constructor[7], for use when the application object is created from **OwlMain**. A second constructor is for when the old-style **WinMain** entry point is used.
~TApplication()	The destructor does some cleanup.
CanClose()	Query whether the application can close. This unifies a query that in non-OWL Windows programs requires two messages (**WM_CLOSE** and **WM_QUERYENDSESSION**). Allows an application to protect a user's data from loss.
Run()	Starts and operates an OWL application.
MessageLoop()	An (almost) infinite loop that runs for duration of application's life.
PumpWaitingMessages()	Get next message from application and system message queues.
ProcessAppMsg()	Most messages are handled by window objects, but this function handles application-level messages like keyboard accelerators.
PROTECTED:	
InitApplication()	Override this function for first instance initialization. Win32 doesn't recognize different instances, so this only works in Win16 programs.
InitInstance()	Override this function for every instance initialization. Call base class function, though, since it performs important startup work.
InitMainWindow()	Override this function to set a **TFrameWindow** as your application's main window.
TermInstance()	Override this function for application-level cleanup.
IdleAction()	Override this function to do low-priority, background processing.

The life of **TApplication** centers around its **Run** member function. Here are its essential parts:

```
TApplication::Run()
    {
    // First instance initialization.
    if (!hPrevInstance)
```

[7] In case you're new to C++, a default constructor is one that doesn't require any parameters.

```
    InitApplication();
// Each instance initialization.
// Calls TApplication::InitMainWindow();
InitInstance();

// Message loop for duration of application's life.
MessageLoop();

// Application cleanup.
TermInstance();
}
```

Of the four **TApplication** member functions in this code fragment, only one is worth overriding in derived classes: **InitInstance**. It's needed for application level initialization that requires the presence of a WinAPI window. For example, if you create a dialog box control (**TControl**) window—such as a listbox—you cannot initialize the contents until the actual WinAPI system object has been created. This distinction between OWL objects and WinAPI objects requires you to think about initialization as a two-step process: first create the OWL object, then later initialize the WinAPI object[8].

The essential elements of **InitInstance** function appear here:

```
TApplication::InitInstance()
    {
    InitMainWindow();

    if (MainWindow)
        {
        MainWindow->SetFlag(wfMainWindow);
        MainWindow->Create();
        MainWindow->Show(nCmdShow);
        }
    else
        // Error.
        THROW ( TXInvalidMainWindow() );
    }
```

The first function that **InitInstance** calls, **InitMainWindow**, is a prime candidate for overriding. It creates a **TFrameWindow** object, then calls **TApplication::SetMainWindow** to establish this as the application's one and only main window.

If a main window is provided, then **TFrameWindow** member functions are called to initialize this window. First, a bit is set in the frame window object so that this window will shut down the application when the window is destroyed. Next, the **TFrameWindow::Create** function is called to create the WinAPI window. Finally, the WinAPI window is made visible with a call to **TFrameWindow::Show**, which is little more than a wrapper around the WinAPI **ShowWindow** function. The parameter that gets passed, **nCmdShow**, is a value passed to the **WinMain** entry point. It describes how the window should appear: minimized, maximized, or normal. With all the work that it does, be sure to call the base class **TApplication::InitInstance** if your derived classes override it.

[8] A program that uses this approach is GADGETS in Chapter 13.

I dismiss the other three functions called by **TApplication::Run** as not worth overriding for a variety of reasons. **InitApplication** truly belongs to the world of Win16 programming, since WinMain's **hPrevInstance** parameter is always zero in Win32 programs. If you need to distinguish between the first and subsequent instances of a program, you'll have to try other tricks[9]. The **MessageLoop** function isn't worth overriding because it contains a fairly robust message loop. You're welcome to write your own if you need to, but I suspect that won't be very often. The timing of calls to **TermInstance** coincides with calls to an application object destructor, so this function seems redundant in the class. However, if you allocate anything in the various initialization function, then freeing those in this member function certainly makes sense.

Although you probably won't ever override the message loop, it plays a very key role in the delivery of WinAPI messages to your OWL objects. For this reason, a good understanding can be helpful. Here are the essential parts of this function, boiled down from the original OWL source code:

```
TApplication::MessageLoop()
    {
    while (!BreakMessageLoop)
        {
        if (!IdleAction()
            ::WaitMessage()
        if (PumpWaitingMessages())
            idleCount = 0;
        }
    }
```

This function is an (almost) infinite loop that keeps spinning until the **BreakMessageLoop** flag turns FALSE. As you'll see shortly, this happens when a **WM_QUIT** window message is received. That message, in turn, gets sent when an application's main window is destroyed[10]. Proper termination from this loop is critical, for without it, an application gets left in memory long after the user has dismissed its window.

Within the almost-infinite message loop, two functions are called. The first one, **IdleAction**, lets Win16 programs get processing time when the system is idle. The STARS program in Chapter 7 provides an example of this type of background scheduling in action. Without this mechanism, there would be no way for a Win16 program to get processing time without receiving a message. (In the next section, I'll describe why this is so difficult.) The idle time function gets called when *there are no messages for any application in the system*. This means that the user isn't doing anything. It's a good time for applications to

---

[9] For example, call **FindWindow** on your application's main window to see if one has already been created, which works 99% of the time. It will fail if two copies of an application are started very quickly, which can be accomplished with a simple batch command file. Bullet-proof protection requires the use of a named Win32 synchronization object.

[10] To convince yourself of this fact, see the source file to **TWindow**. The **EvDestroy** member function calls the **PostQuitMessage** when the "wfMainWindow" flag is set for a window being destroyed.

do background chores: repaginating files, saving dirty buffers, continuing lengthy sorts, etc.. The key thing to remember for any background chore is that you only do a little bit of work during each cycle. When nothing else is happening in the system, you get lots of cycles.

Win32 programs can also use this mechanism, which means it works for code that must be portable between the two APIs. For a program that only needs to support the Win32 API, however, **threads** provide a more robust way to do background work. I'll touch on threads in the next section.

The second function called from `TApplication::MessageLoop` is `PumpWaitingMessages`. This function connects to Windows' message delivery mechanism. Before delving into the specifics of this function, let's look at the roles messages play in the various WinAPI compatible operating systems.

Messages: Input Mechanism and Multitasking Time-Slice

From the very first version of Windows, multitasking has played an important role in this operating system family. From Windows version 1.x thru Windows version 3.x, however, multitasking has not followed the traditional model. Instead of the **preemptive** approach, which is typical of the vast majority of multitasking operating systems, the early versions of Windows adopted a **nonpreemptive** scheduling model. Switching between different tasks is performed using a system akin to the token-passing[11] approach used by some network hardware. In this nonpreemptive multitasking system, programs are not interrupted by the operating system, but instead a program runs in response to a message, then interrupts itself to allow other programs to run.

Windows programs rely on **messages** to receive input from the user and from user-interface objects. Some messages are hardware related, and tell a program that the user has pointed with the mouse or typed a keystroke. Other messages come from user-interface objects like windows, menus, and scroll bars. To access the flow of messages, a program calls specific WinAPI message-retrieval functions. When a call is made to one of these functions, either a message is returned immediately, or the call blocks within the function until a message is available. In this way, the nonpreemptive multitasking switcher is embedded within the message delivery mechanism.

Since user-input arrives in the form of messages, this design accomplishes the goal of making operating systems that are very responsive to users. Windows programs are written to be very hungry for the tokens—**messages**—provided by the operating system. When a program isn't busy processing a message, it extends a hand to the operating system in hopes of receiving yet another tasty token. This works quite well, and in general users cannot tell the difference between the behavior of this multitasking system and one based on

---

[11] It's not truly a token passing system, since the flow of "tokens" (messages) is one way from the operating system to programs and not from one program to another. But the idea of token-passing is familiar to many readers—particularly those who are familiar with the operation of token-passing networks.

the preemptive model. It works well, that is, as long as every program cooperates in staying hungry.

It's possible, however, for an application to choke on a message, with perhaps a longer—but equally intrusive—code fragment like the following:

```
while (1);
```

Prior to Windows version 3.1, the remedy was awful—the entire system had to be rebooted with a push of the [Ctrl] + [Alt] + [Delete] keys. Starting with Windows 3.1, the **local reboot** mechanism responds to the reboot keystrokes to allow a user to terminate the choking program. After such a crashed program has terminated, message passing continues. While the user loses data held by the offending program, at least the loss doesn't affect other programs.

Starting with Windows NT, the message-based multitasking system has been enhanced with support for **preemptive multitasking**. Input still arrives as messages, but multiple messages can be simultaneously delivered to multiple applications. Each application must still be written as hungry for messages, but overall no single application can hold the entire system hostage. The system feature that enhances the message delivery mechanism is support for **threads**.

Threads are the units of scheduling in preemptive Windows systems. A traditional operating system schedules processes, while preemptive Windows schedules threads. In the Windows family of operating systems, the term **process** refers to the system's unit of ownership. A process owns system objects like memory, open file handles, windows, and threads. One way to understand the role of threads in preemptive Windows systems is to consider that nonpreemptive Windows (version 3.1 and earlier) systems behave like they have a single thread of execution that is shared by all applications. Under preemptive Windows (Windows NT and later) systems, each program starts running in a process that has its own independently scheduled thread.

Under preemptive Windows, it's much harder for one application to crash the system[12]. And yet, Windows applications still have to be written very hungry—that is, very responsive—to messages. Since messages represent user-input, an application that ignores messages ignores the user. Ignoring a user too long is like ignoring your boss for too long—eventually, you get fired.

When considering how to best take advantage of threads under preemptive Windows, it helps to make a distinction between **foreground threads** and **background threads**. A foreground thread is one that has created user-interface objects. For such a thread, a message queue is created for handling messages sent to the user-interface objects owned by the threads. A background thread, on the other hand, is one that doesn't have any user-interface objects associated with it, but rather works to manage nonuser-interface related data. The

[12] Much harder, but unfortunately it's still possible for a single application to crash the system—much like Luke Skywalker in Star Wars when he flew into the Death Star and caused its demise.

ability to have background threads helps make preemptive Windows robust, responsive, and efficient. When accessing any part of the user-interface API, however, foreground threads must be as responsive and hungry for messages as a nonthreaded application running in nonpreemptive Windows.

From this discussion, it is clear that a message serves a larger purpose than its namesake in the real world; that is, it does more than just communicate something. To a Windows program, messages are the unit of processing. They have the effect of creating time-slices during which a program runs. To get a clearer understanding about the dual role that messages play, let's take a closer look at the message delivery system.

A Windows program receives messages in one of two ways. The first way is by reading message buffers. Windows doesn't allow us direct access to its internal buffers, but rather reads a buffer for us when our program calls one of two Windows library routines: **`GetMessage`** or **`PeekMessage`**. (There are subtle differences between these two functions, but for purposes of this discussion assume they behave the same.)

Two system buffers get read: the hardware event queue and the application message queue. The **hardware event queue** holds system-wide mouse and keyboard events. The **application message queue** holds application-specific messages. Each program has a message queue. To be more precise, preemptive Windows gives each foreground thread its own message queue. Background threads have no message queue, although a thread that doesn't have a message queue automatically gets one when it starts to make calls to the user-interface API. Nonpreemptive Windows provides a message queue for each copy of each program that runs. If it finds a message for a program, **`GetMessage`** pulls the message into the program.

If **`GetMessage`** doesn't find messages for a program, it puts the program to sleep. At such times, the scheduler takes over and transfers control to another program that does have messages waiting for it. The **`GetMessage`** routine, then, serves to make the message-driven multitasking system work.

The second way a program receives messages is by a direct call to one of its window procedures. In C++ terms, a window procedure has a member function for every message of interest to a class of windows. A window procedure is called as if it were a subroutine of Windows itself. In fact, you can think of a window procedure as an installable extension to Windows. Messages delivered by this mechanism don't wait in a message queue, but are processed immediately when a call is made.

Let's pause a moment and consider the implications of these two approaches. The first method, in which **`GetMessage`** (or **`PeekMessage`**) reads message buffers for us, is called **pull-model processing**. The name describes the active role our program plays in pulling a message from a buffer. The second method is called **push-model processing**. The name describes the passive role our program plays in waiting to be called and letting Windows *push* a message into a window procedure.

Figure 4.2 illustrates the two paths a message can take in the Windows API to get to an application. The buffered pull-model method passes through the application object, where it is dispatched to the correct window object. To place a message into an application's mes-

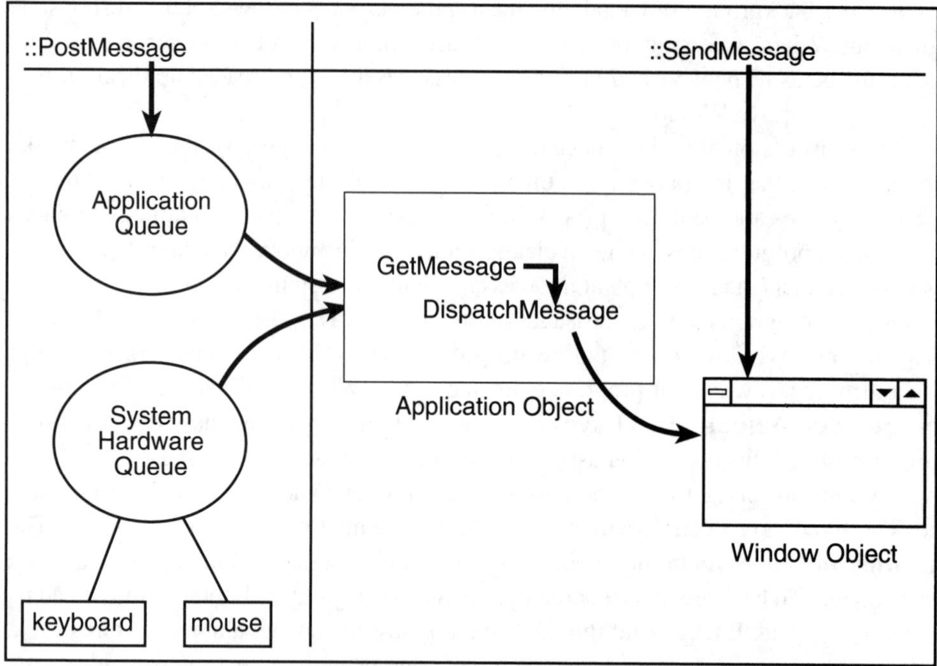

Figure 4.2 Windows message traffic

sage queue, the WinAPI's **PostMessage** function is called. These types of messages are like postcards that you write and drop into a mailbox. You're not terribly concerned about when the message arrives, only that it arrives sometime in the future. Timing is not important, therefore, nor is there a return value associated with a posted message. Such messages are used for notifications.

The second path for a message to take is direct from the caller to the window object. This unbuffered, push-model method bypasses the application object and goes directly from the caller to the window object. The WinAPI function associated with this type of message transmission is the **SendMessage** function. If **PostMessage** is like a postcard, **SendMessage** is like making a telephone call. It's a direct connection from the caller to the called object. And like a direct telephone call, the function that is called can respond to the caller, in this case by means of the return value.

It's no wonder that the send method was the first one implemented in Windows: The earliest model of a windows program was a subroutine library. In the earliest implementations, which date back to the 1983 to 1985 time frame, the entire operating system had a single stack that was shared by every application. The message mechanism consisted of a predefined set of 10 messages, which couldn't be extended without breaking every application in existence.

In early 1985, about a year before Windows 1.x started shipping, pull-model processing was added to Windows. At that time, every application was given its own stack, along with the ability to "own" things like memory and files. This change allowed for the creation of new messages, since instead of ten different message functions, a single message function—the **window procedure**—was defined to be able to process many different types of message.

When pull-model processing was added to Windows, each application also got its own message loop. Since the message loop is the connection between an application and the system, this addition allowed each application to decide how it wanted to handle input. If it liked, it could handle all input through a single message loop. Or, it could create secondary message loops for certain special cases. Two such special cases occur when a menu is active and when a modal dialog box is active. In both cases, input is treated in a slightly different manner from normal.

When menus are active, for example, mouse and keyboard input is reserved solely for the use of the menu system. Unfortunately, this creates the problem that keyboard commands—accelerators—are disabled when menus are visible. The KEYCMD2 program in Chapter 12 shows how to fix the problem this can create for users who may wonder why they can read accelerators keys in the text of a menu but not access the keyboard command.

There are two types of dialog boxes: modal and modeless. The difference between them is simply that a modal dialog box has its own message loop while a modeless dialog box shares the application's main message loop. As you'll see in Chapter 14 when I discuss both types of dialog boxes, modeless dialog boxes require a change to your application's main message loop. The modal dialog box, on the other hand, has some unique characteristics because it has its own, hidden message loop.

The key benefit of having two paths for input, then, is that applications get to decide how input will be handled. After a look at a minimum message loop that every Windows program must have, I'll discuss the message loop created for you by OWL's **`TApplication`** class.

The Standard Message Loop

Every Windows program has a message loop allowing it to poll for messages. In this way, a program stays in touch with the supply of messages so vital to its proper operation. This is what a standard message loop in a Windows program looks like:

```
while (GetMessage(&msg, 0, 0, 0))
        {
        TranslateMessage(&msg);     /* Keyboard input.    */
        DispatchMessage(&msg);
        }
```

This loop runs during the life of the program. Each iteration represents the receipt of a single message from a message buffer. Except for the **`WM_QUIT`** message, each message causes **`GetMessage`** to return a value of **`TRUE`**. On receipt of **`WM_QUIT`**, a program drops out of its message loop and terminates. When we discuss MIN's window object in Chapter 5, you'll see how code in the **`TWindow`** class sends a **`WM_QUIT`** message when the application's main window is destroyed. Without this message, a program won't terminate properly and the memory it occupies will be lost forever.

Let's look at each routine in this tiny message loop. A moment ago, we introduced the idea that **GetMessage** pulls messages into our program from system buffers—the hardware event queue and an application message queue. We can request **GetMessage** to filter messages by providing filter information in the second, third, and fourth parameters. Since we're interested in *all* messages, however, filtering is disabled by setting these to zero.

The most interesting parameter to us is the first parameter, a pointer to a structure that **GetMessage** fills with message data. Notice that a pointer to this structure is the sole parameter to the other routines in our message loop.

The **TApplication**'s member function, **PumpWaitingMessages()**, defines a local variable to hold message data as follows:

```
MSG msg;
```

For the definition of **MSG**, look in WINDOWS.H to find the following:

```
typedef struct tagMSG
  {
    HWND hwnd;
    UINT message;
    WPARAM wParam;
    LPARAM lParam;
    DWORD time;
    POINT pt;
  } MSG;
```

Let's look at each of the six elements in this structure:

- **hwnd**, an unsigned integer, contains a window handle. Every window in the system is given a unique handle. Like the instance handle we describe earlier, the window handle is simply an id given a window. The reason a window handle is associated with a message is that every message is directed at one window or another.
- **message**, another unsigned integer, contains the *type* of message, encoded as a 16-bit value in the Win16 API, and a 32-bit value in the Win32 API. Starting on page 93, we'll take a look at all the different types of messages in Windows.
- **wParam** and **lParam** contain message data. The meaning depends on the type of message. For example, the menu command message uses wParam to identify the menu item that has been selected. Mouse messages pack the location of the mouse pointer into **lParam**.
- The last two items, **time** and **pt**, are rarely used by Windows programs. Both describe the state of the system when the message was put into the message queue: **time** holds the time, and **pt** holds the location of the mouse pointer.

TranslateMessage is the second function called in a typical message loop. This routine calls on the Windows keyboard driver to convert raw keystroke messages (**WM_KEYDOWN**) into cooked ASCII values, which are placed in the application message queue as **WM_CHAR** messages. This makes it easy for our program to tell the difference between "A" and "a" without having to get involved with the state of the shift key.

TranslateMessage also provides support for international keyboards. A British shopkeeper, for example, would probably use the £ symbol to quote you the special price of £35. If the shopkeeper used a Windows word processor to send you a note with this information, the word processor would call **TranslateMessage** to convert the keystroke to the proper symbol. As part of this translation process, **TranslateMessage** makes diacritics available; it allows Windows programs to display French words like *Voilà*, Spanish phrases like "*Hablo español,*" and German city names like *München*.

The final routine in this loop, **DispatchMessage**, takes message data from the **MSG** structure and uses it to call the correct window procedure. It *pushes* the message into the window procedure for processing.

The OWL Message Loop

The **PumpWaitingMessages** function is a slightly more specialized message pump than the one that appears in a normal Windows program. But the two versions do roughly the same thing—each receives WinAPI messages from the operating system for processing by an application's windows. Here are its critical parts:

```
TApplication::PumpWaitingMessages()
    {
    MSG msg;

    while (::PeekMessage(&msg,0,0,PM_REMOVE))
        {
        // Check for termination message.
        if (msg.message == WM_QUIT)
            {
            BreakMessageLoop = TRUE;
            // Make sure all loops exit.
            ::PostQuitMessage();
            break;
            }

        // Give Tapplication a chance to see message.
        if (!ProcessAppMsg())
            {
            // Otherwise, 'normal' message processing.
            ::TranslateMessage();
            ::DispatchMessage();
            }
    }
```

One thing you'll notice while examining the OWL source files is that the use of the global scope operator (**::**) often means that a native WinAPI function is being called. That's certainly the case here.

This **PumpWaitingMessages** function gets its name from the fact that it pumps messages out of the waiting message queues and into the various OWL objects that process the messages. This message pump doesn't pay any attention to the contents of each message, but instead leaves that chore to the message recipient.

While this looks quite a bit more involved than the standard message loop, many of the components are the same. Messages are retrieved with a call to **PeekMessage**, keyboard support is provided by **TranslateMessage**, and messages are sent to the proper window procedure by **DispatchMessage**. As mentioned earlier, **ProcessAppMsg** provides support for modeless dialog boxes, accelerators, and MDI windows. Notice that OWL's message loop requires special processing for the WM_QUIT message, since **PeekMessage** doesn't respond to this message in the same way that **GetMessage** does.

At this point, our walk through MIN's application object is complete. Along the way, we have explored some of the fundamentals of Windows' messaging architecture. But our journey is not over yet. We still have one more object to explore: our program's window object. This is the subject of our next chapter.

5

OWL's Window Classes

Almost half of the classes in OWL deal with one type of window or another[1], so understanding OWL's window support classes is clearly important. In the OWL class hierarchy, window-related classes start with **TWindow** and include all the classes derived from **TWindow**. Some are for dialog box frames (the **TDialog** branch); some are for dialog box controls (the **TControl** branch), and a third set are for an application's main window, represented by the **TFrameWindow** branch.

To help you get a handle on the foundation provided by MIN, I'll start with a look at MIN's use of OWL's frame window class. After covering the basics of using OWL window classes, I'll drill through to its WinAPI roots to explain OWL's support for windows and the window message processing. Along the way, you'll learn about **TEventHandler**, **TWindow** and **TFrameWindow**, the base classes for **DFrame**, MIN's frame window class. Finally, I'll provide a taxonomy of WinAPI messages, so you can see all the different kinds of messages that a window might want to handle.

MIN's Frame Window Class

MIN's frame window class is defined:

```
// Main window
class DFrame : public TFrameWindow
    {
  public:
    DFrame(char * title);
    void CmFileExit();
    void CmHelpAbout();
```

[1] Of the 128 classes in OWL, 55 are derived from **TWindow**, the primary WinAPI window wrapper.

```
    DECLARE_RESPONSE_TABLE (DFrame);
      };

  DEFINE_RESPONSE_TABLE1 (DFrame, TFrameWindow)
    EV_COMMAND(CM_FILEEXIT, CmFileExit),
    EV_COMMAND(CM_HELPABOUT, CmHelpAbout),
  END_RESPONSE_TABLE;

  DFrame::DFrame(char * title) : TFrameWindow(0, title)
      {
      }

  void DFrame::CmFileExit()
      {
      CloseWindow(0); // Cause application to terminate
      }

  void DFrame::CmHelpAbout()
      {
      MessageBox("    Minimum OWL 2.0 Program\n\n"
                 "'Borland C++ 4.0 Programming\n"
                 "   for Windows', by Paul Yao", Title);
      }
```

The term "frame window" is an OWL term meaning an application's main window. This is the window that holds all of a program's user-interface elements. MIN's main window is created inside the **InitMainWindow** member of **DApp**, MIN's application object, by the following lines of code:

```
SetMainWindow (new DFrame("OWL Minimum")};
MainWindow->AssignMenu("MAIN");
MainWindow->SetIcon(this, "SNAPSHOT");
```

This code fragment creates a **DFrame** window object, which in turn creates the WinAPI window object. After being created, two user-interface elements are connected to the window: a menu and an icon. These elements are read from MIN's executable file, MIN.EXE, where they have been stored as read-only resources. These resources were created with the following entries in MIN.RC, MIN's resource script file:

```
snapshot icon min.ico

main menu
    BEGIN
    POPUP "&File"
        {
        MENUITEM "E&xit", CM_FILEEXIT
        }
    POPUP "&Help"
        {
        MENUITEM "&About...", CM_HELPABOUT
        }
    END
```

Once the icon is connected to MIN's window, it's self-operating. The same holds true for the menu—this Windows system object appears when the user clicks the mouse or strikes a menu summoning key. The only thing that's needed is a function to call when a user has selected a menu item. That is the reason for **DFrame**'s two member functions. (The constructor is just a placeholder.) When the user clicks the **File.Exit** menu item, the **CmFileExit** function gets called which closes the main window and terminates the application. When the user selects the **Help.About...** menu item, the **CmHelpAbout** function is called which displays a message box with application information.

The specifics of these two menu selections are less important than what they demonstrate about Windows programs, which are set up to handle messages that are sent to its windows. With an OWL Windows program, this means having a set of **message response** member functions, with one for each message to be processed. With more than 200 messages in the Windows API, it's clear that picking the right messages to process is important. Table 5.1 shows what I consider the top Windows API messages that Windows programmers—whether using OWL or native C—have to be concerned with.

Some of the functions in Table 5.1 start with the letters "Ev," such as **EvChar**, **EvMove** and **EvSize**. These represent raw WinAPI messages that—with the exception of some

Table 5.1 The 11 Most Important WinAPI Messages and Related TWindow Function

WinAPI Message	*OWL Handler*	*Description*
WM_COMMAND	<class specific>	Three types of user-interface objects send this message: (a) menus, (b) keyboard accelerators, and (c) dialog box controls. The default **TWindow** handler is called **EvCommand**, but this handler splits messages out to individual response table handlers. This is why, for example, MIN has two **DFrame** member functions—one for each menu item.
WM_CHAR	**EvChar**	This message means that keyboard input corresponding to printable character input has been received. For more details, see Chapter 15.
WM_CREATE	**SetupWindow**	Initialize window-specific objects. You'll initialize the window object data in the class constructor, of course, but override this function for initialization that requires the presence of a WinAPI window. The default **TWindow** handler is **EvCreate**, but **TWindow** uses this so you should rely on **SetupWindow**—but be sure to call the base class member.

(continued)

Table 5.1 The 11 Most Important WinAPI Messages and Related `TWindow` Function *(Continued)*

WinAPI Message	*OWL Handler*	*Description*
WM_DESTROY	**CleanupWindow**	Handles cleanup after a window has been destroyed. The default **TWindow** handler is **EvDestroy**, which calls this member function. Don't steal **WM_DESTROY** handling from **TWindow**, since it performs application termination for main windows.
WM_KEYDOWN	**EvKeyDown**	The user has pressed a key on the keyboard. Respond to this event for nonprintable keys such as function keys and arrow keys. Respond to **WM_CHAR** for printable characters. See Chapter 15 for details.
WM_LBUTTONDOWN	**EvLButtonDown**	The user has clicked the left mouse button. See Chapter 16 for details.
WM_LBUTTONUP	**EvLButtonUp**	The user has released the left mouse button. See Chapter 16 for details.
WM_MOUSEMOVE	**EvMouseMove**	The mouse has moved over a window's client area. See Chapter 16 for details.
WM_MOVE	**EvMove**	The client area of a window has moved.
WM_PAINT	**Paint**	A window's client area has been damaged and needsredrawing.Thedefault **TWindow**handler for this message is **EvPaint**, but the base classes handle some of the WinAPI messiness, so it's better to only override the **Paint** member. See Chapter 6 for more details.
WM_SIZE	**EvSize**	A window's client area has changed size.

minor parameter repackaging—are received without any OWL intervention[2]. The functions without this prefix correspond to WinAPI messages for which OWL has done a little bit of preprocessing for you. In general, where possible, let OWL preprocess messages for you.

As you'll see in all the sample programs in this book, a major part of writing a Windows program consists of deciding what messages—what input—a window is going to handle.

---

[2] Actually, OWL *does* package up the parameters in a message-specific way, but it does no processing per se, which is why I say these messages are free from OWL's intervention.

In OWL, responding to a message means writing a message response function for a window class, then adding a reference to the class's response table.

For example, if we modified MIN's **DFrame** window class to handle the **WM_LBUTTONDOWN** message, you'd first need to create a member function defined like this:

```
// Display mouse location in window caption.
void DFrame::EvLButtonDown(UINT /*modkeys*/, TPoint& pt)
    {
    char ach[120];
    wsprintf (ach, "Mouse At (%d,%d)", pt.x, pt.y);
    SetCaption(ach);
    }
```

A couple of things might puzzle you. First, how did I pick the function name? Also, how did I know what parameters to provide? The answer to both questions is that each message has a function *name* and *parameters* that are part of how a particular message response function must be created. To find out what these are, refer to the OWL help file by searching for the string "EV_WM_xxx". For your convenience, Appendix J of this book also has this information.

But a message response function by itself isn't connected to the message delivery mechanism. For that to happen, two things are required. First, the function must be part of the class declaration. Next, an entry must be made in the response table. Here's the new class declaration with an entry for this function:

```
// Main window
class DFrame : public TFrameWindow
    {
  public:
    DFrame(char * title);
    void CmFileExit();
    void CmHelpAbout();
    void EvLButtonDown (UINT modKeys, TPoint& pt);

  DECLARE_RESPONSE_TABLE (DFrame);
    };
```

That part's obvious, since a function doesn't "belong" to a class unless it's part of the class declaration. The second requirement is that an entry is required in the class's response table. Here's **DFrame**'s new response table that includes an entry for the **WM_LBUTTONDOWN** handling.

```
DEFINE_RESPONSE_TABLE1 (DFrame, TFrameWindow)
  EV_COMMAND(CM_FILEEXIT, CmFileExit),
  EV_COMMAND(CM_HELPABOUT, CmHelpAbout),
  EV_WM_LBUTTONDOWN,
END_RESPONSE_TABLE;
```

If this seems too easy to be true, it might help to know that the "EV_WM_LBUTTONDOWN" is a macro that gets expanded to form the connection between the TWindow message delivery mechanism and our function.

At this point, you have enough of the nuts-and-bolts of OWL programming to start modifying MIN and getting some code up and running. If your primary interest is just getting your code to work, now is a good time to skip ahead to the next chapter, which gets into using GDI to draw. On the other hand, if you want to understand more about how this message response table works, the next few sections get into their internal operation. It's pretty complex, and the good news is that OWL hides the messiness from you in a robust, easy-to-code manner.

TEventHandler

The **TEventHandler** class is OWL's postal carrier, since it takes invidual letters (messages) and delivers them to the proper mailbox (message response function). In the last chapter, I talked about the application object and how it receives messages and sends them to the correct window object. This is done using a window-oriented message delivery mechanism provided by Windows. Once it has received a message, a window object calls **TEventHandler** functions to deliver the message to the correct **TWindow** member function for processing. This class has three member functions:

Function Name	*Description*
Find()	Search for a message response function in the current **TWindow** response table.
SearchEntries()	Low-level routine for walking a message response function searching for a match to a message. **Find()** calls this routine to do its work.
Dispatch()	Once the correct message response function has been found, call it using message-specific parameters.

None of these function names appear in MIN, but that's because the required code is added to your window class by the various response table macros. These macros make **TEventHandler**'s delivery mechanism available to MIN's **DFrame** window class. MIN's **DECLARE_RESPONSE_TABLE** macro expands like this:

```
// DECLARE_RESPONSE_TABLE (DFrame);
  private:
    static TResponseTableEntry<DFrame> __RTFAR __entries[];
    typedef TResponseTableEntry<DFrame>::PMF TMyPMF;
    typedef DFrame                           TMyClass;
  public:
    BOOL Find (TEventInfo&, TEqualOperator = 0);
```

Since this macro is placed inside the squiggle braces of **DFrame**'s declaration, these lines add code and data members to **DFrame**. In particular, a private array named **__entries[]** is declared and a public function **Find**, which has as its sole task searching through the **__entries[]** array. The two **typedef** statements declare types used in the body of the **Find** function to conform to C++ type-checking.

If you're puzzled by the "**<DFrame>**" in this declaration, it's **template** notation. This is a pretty advanced C++ capability that allows the declaration of new types much like the C language **typedef** statement. It's more powerful than **typedef**, however, since it allows entire classes—both data and function members—to be created from a class template definition. Fortunately, you don't need to fully understand **templates** to build a response table.

The **DFrame::Find** function and the **__entries[]** response table are defined by these macros:

```
DEFINE_RESPONSE_TABLE1 (DFrame, TFrameWindow)
  EV_COMMAND(CM_FILEEXIT, CmFileExit),
  EV_COMMAND(CM_HELPABOUT, CmHelpAbout),
END_RESPONSE_TABLE;
```

The macro creates the following **Find** function definition:

```
BOOL DFrame::Find(TEventInfo& eventInfo, TEqualOperator equal)
    {
    eventInfo.Object = (GENERIC *)this;
    return SearchEntries ((TGenericTableEntry __RTFAR *)__entries,
                          eventInfo, equal) ||
                          TFrameWindow::Find(eventInfo, equal);
    }
```

When a message arrives for a **DFrame** window, the window object calls **DFrame::Find** to search for a message response function. This function calls the **TEventHandler::SearchEntries** helper function, which scans the table for a match. If a match is found, the search routine plugs a pointer to the response table entry into **eventInfo**. Otherwise, it calls **TFrameWindow::Find** to see whether its base class window object wants to handle the message. Once again, a match causes the function to get called. Otherwise, the window object sends the message to a default handler.

The response table that gets created looks like this:

```
TResponseTableEntry<DFrame> __RTFAR DFrame::__entries[] =
    {
        // Array element [0]
        { 0,
          CM_FILEEXIT,
          (TAnyDispatcher)::v_Dispatch,
          (TMyPMF)v_Sig(&TMyClass)::CmFileExit)
        }

        // Array element [1]
        { 0,
```

```
        CM_HELPABOUT,
        (TAnyDispatcher)::v_Dispatch,
        (TMyPMF)v_Sig(&TMyClass)::CmHelpAbout)
      }

      // Array element [2]
      { 0,
        0,
        0,
        0
      }
    };
```

Each element in this array is a structure of type **`TResponseTableEntry`**[3]**:**

```
struct TResponseTableEntry
    {
    union {
        UINT        Msg;
        UINT        NotifyCode;
        }
    UINT            Id;
    TAnyDispatcher Dispatcher;
    PMF             Pmf;
    };
```

This structure holds two integers and two function pointers. For most message response entries, the **`Msg`** value serves as the table index. For **`WM_COMMAND`** messages, however, the **`Id`** value is used. This seems an odd exception, and yet because every menu and every dialog box control uses it to communicate useful information, this message is overused. This "sub-message" switching, then, helps simplify an otherwise messy situation.

The previous example shows the response table entry for **`WM_COMMAND`** messages. To give you a more complete idea of how **`TEventHandler`** works, here is the response table entry for a **`WM_LBUTTONDOWN`** message:

```
{ WM_LBUTTONDOWN,
  0,
  (TAnyDispatcher)::v_U_POINT_Dispatch,
  (TMyPMF)v_U_POINT_Sig(&TMyClass)::EvLButtonDown)
}
```

The third and fourth members of a **`TResponseTableEntry`** structure contain function pointers. The first, **`v_U_POINT_Dispatch`**, is an OWL library function that calls the class-specific message response function, **`::EvLButtonDown`**. *Two* function pointers are needed to handle the fact that different messages require different parameters[4]. In

[3] I've taken the liberty of removing elements from the original definition. For example, the original is actually a C++ template. What's shown, however, corresponds to the data layout of response data entries.

fact, to handle the 250 messages defined in the Windows API, 25 different parameter packages are required.

Here, for example, is the declaration MIN uses to process a menu command message:

```
void CmFileExit();
```

The declaration for a message response function for a left-mouse button message, on the other hand, looks like this:

```
void EvLButtonDown(UINT modkeys, TPoint& point);
```

OWL handles the parameter packaging for you, requiring only that the proper parameters be defined for each message response function.

This tiny, but important, class allows OWL to smooth over some of the rough edges in the Windows API. The biggest benefit is its support for inheritance. Without it, Windows programmers working in C++ can use inheritance for every class member function *except* where message handling is concerned. With it, the inheritance of message response functions is fast, efficient and—perhaps most important—trivial to write code for.

The message dispatching that **TEventHandler** provides is important to the operation of the Windows user interface. Its primary reason for existence, however, is to support the classes that wrap WinAPI windows with a type-safe, flexible C++ exterior. Foremost among these classes is **TWindow**, to which we now turn.

TWindow

TWindow is OWL's largest class, with the largest include file, the largest source file and the most number of derived classes. In spite of its size, the functionality that **TWindow** provides can be summarized in three categories: First, it encapsulates the Windows user-interface API; next, it funnels messages to the proper message response function; and finally, it provides the primary base class for all of OWL's window functions.

The most important attribute of **TWindow** is that it encapsulates the windowing API of Windows' USER module. This means that if you want to create a window—the WinAPI system object—you do so by creating an OWL **TWindow** (or derived class) object first. This class creates a WinAPI window object for you. To manipulate the WinAPI object—that is, to move, resize, maximize, minimize, show or hide a window—you call a **TWindow** member function.

TWindow plays an important role in message handling. **TWindow** member functions form a funnel that captures a window's messages. Then, as described in the previous section,

---

[4] For a complete list of the function prototypes for message response functions, see Appendix J. A partial list showing the more commonly used messages appears on the inside back cover of this book.

TWindow member functions call **TEventHandler** functions to search message response tables and dispatch to the correct message response function. In some cases, this means **TWindow** message response functions, since it handles some messages itself. Along the way, **TWindow** member functions hide some of the Win16/Win32 message delivery differences, and connect each WinAPI window message to the correct OWL window object.

A third role that **TWindow** plays is default message processing. If a derived class doesn't handle a message, **TWindow** ultimately gets a crack at handling it. You'll want to study up on what **TWindow** does, then, to minimize the code that you have to write yourself. Ultimately, if no OWL object handles a particular message, then **TWindow** sends that message to the WinAPI default handler, the **DefWindowProc**[5]. The following list describes the WinAPI messages that **TWindow** handles for you, along with some notes about each:

WinAPI Message	*Description*
WM_CLOSE	Requests a window to close itself and cleanup. Don't respond to this message, but instead override **CanClose**—which gets called by **TWindow**'s message response function for **WM_CLOSE**.
WM_COMMAND	Notification message used by menu items and dialog box controls. In response to this message, **TWindow** searches a message response table for the appropriate menu or dialog box control response function.
WM_COMPAREITEM	This is an owner-draw message. **TWindow** sends owner-draw messages for dialog box controls to the corresponding OWL **TControl** object.
WM_CREATE	Notifies you that a WinAPI window has been created, so it's a good time for initialization. **TWindow** calls its **SetupWindow** member function, which you should override for doing window-related initialization. The **SetupWindow** call is the first chance you have to access the WinAPI window handle.
WM_CTLCOLORBTN (Win32)	Calls WinAPI's **DefWindowProc** to set control color.
WM_CTLCOLORDLG (Win32)	Calls WinAPI's **DefWindowProc** to set control color.
WM_CTLCOLOREDIT (Win32)	Calls WinAPI's **DefWindowProc** to set control color.

[5] Microsoft makes the source code to this Windows API function publicly available. The source code to **DefWindowProc** is reprinted in Appendix B of this book for your convenience.

WinAPI Message	*Description*
WM_CTLCOLORLISTBOX (Win32)	Calls WinAPI's **DefWindowProc** to set control color.
WM_CTLCOLORMSGBOX (Win32)	Calls WinAPI's **DefWindowProc** to set control color.
WM_CTLCOLORSCROLLBAR (Win32)	Calls WinAPI's **DefWindowProc** to set control color.
WM_CTLCOLORSTATIC (Win32)	Calls WinAPI's **DefWindowProc** to set control color.
WM_DELETEITEM	This is an owner-draw message. **TWindow** sends owner-draw messages for dialog box controls to the corresponding OWL **TControl** object.
WM_DESTROY	Notification that a WinAPI window has died, so it's a goodtimetodocleanup. **TWindow**callsits **Cleanup-Window**memberfunction,whichyoushouldoverride to do an WinAPI windowing cleanup before WinAPI window handle becomes invalid. If a window is the application's main window, then when it is destroyed, posta **WM_QUIT**messagetoterminatetheapplication.
WM_DRAWITEM	This is an owner-draw message. **TWindow** sends owner-draw messages for dialog box controls to the corresponding OWL **TControl** object.
WM_ERASEBKGND	Request to erase a window background. **TWindow** handles it. This message is closely related to the **WM_PAINT** message (although **WM_PAINT** is far more important).
WM_HSCROLL	Message means that the user has clicked on the horizontal scroll bar. **TWindow**responds by notifying its **TScroller** object (if it has one) to scroll.
WM_KILLFOCUS	Notifies a window that it has lost keyboard focus. **TWindow** calls **HoldFocusHWnd**, which frame windows override to remember who last had the (keyboard) focus.
WM_LBUTTONDOWN	Notification that the user has clicked the left mouse button in a window's client area. **TWindow** supports auto-scrollingwhena **TScroller**objectisattached to a window and the user clicks and drags the mouse.

(continued)

WinAPI Message	*Description*
WM_MEASUREITEM	This is an owner-draw message. **TWindow** sends owner-draw messages for dialog box controls to the corresponding OWL **TControl** object.
WM_MOVE	This message gets received when a window moves. In response, **TWindow** records the new location in the **Attr** data member.
WM_NCDESTROY	The last message a window sees when it gets destroyed. **TWindow** sets the value of the window handle member (**HWindow**) to zero.
WM_PAINT	This is a very important message (see Chapter 6) that tells a window to redraw its contents. **TWindow** responds in the required way and calls the **Begin-Paint** / **EndPaint** functions. Don't override this function, but rather override the **Paint** member which **TWindow** calls for paint handling.
WM_QUERYENDSESSION	The Windows system sends this message to every application's top-level window when the user tries shutting down the system. Shutdown is allowed only if every application says it's OK. **TWindow** calls **CanClose** to ask if it's OK to terminate, so you can override this function—either in your application object or in your main window object—to answer Yes (true) or No (false).
WM_SETCURSOR	This message represents a request from the Windows API to change the mouse cursor. **TWindow** requests the correct cursor.
WM_SIZE	This message means that a window's client area size has changed. **TWindow** responds by recording the new size in the **Attr** data member.
WM_SYSCOLORCHANGE	This means that the user has changed a color from the Windows Control Panel. This message means that anyone who is sensitive to system color settings should update his color settings. **TWindow** sends this message to every child window in the application.
WM_VSCROLL	This message means that the user has clicked on a vertical scroll bar. **TWindow** responds by notifying its **TScroller** object (if it has one) to scroll.

Here are the data members which have been defined for **TWindow**. I've only included the ones which seemed truly useful—either directly or for what it says about **TWindow**.

Type	*Name*	*Description*
PUBLIC:		

HWND	**HWindow**	A WinAPI window handle, which you'll need to access if you ever makes direct calls to any of the USER WinAPI calls which require a window handle. To convert between a **TWindow&** and a window handle, use the **HWND** operator. For example, here's how to get a WinAPI handle to the main window in an application object member function.
		`HWND hwndMain =`
		`HWND(*MainWindow);`

char far *	**Title**	The window caption. Set by calling **SetCaption**.
TWindow *	**Parent**	Points to a window's parent window object.

TWindowAttr	**Attr**	A structure containing parameters passed to the WinAPI window creation routine, **CreateWindow**. The window location (X,Y) and size (W,H) are kept up to date. Here's the structure:
		`struct TWindowAttr {`
		`    DWORD Style;`
		`    DWORD ExStyle;`
		`    int X, Y, W, H;`
		`    TResId Menu;`
		`    int Id;`
		`    char far * Param;`
		`    TResId AccelTable;`
		`    }`

TScroller *	**Scroller**	A scroller object, which tracks vertical and horizontal scrolling for you.
PROTECTED:		
HCURSOR	**HCursor**	A window-specific cursor. Set this by calling the **SetCursor** member function.

(continued)

Type	*Name*	*Description*
DWORD	**BkgndColor**	Window background color. **TWindow** fills the window with this color on receipt of the **WM_ERASEBKGND** message. Call **Set-BkgndColor** to set.
PRIVATE:		
TApplication *	**TApplication**	For access to application object's data and member functions, call **GetApplica-tion** to retrieve an application object pointer.

TWindow Member Functions

An important distinction to make in a class library is to distinguish between **interfaces** and **implementation**. In a base class, an interface is a place holder for derived classes to override. A base class implementation, on the other hand, provides useful services that are available when called from derived classes. While the distinction between these two types can sometimes be murky—when, for example, you override a function and then call back to the base class function—nontheless, it's a useful distinction to make. The two lists of functions in this section show **TWindow** implementation—under the title "Commonly Called Member Functions"—and **TWindow** interfaces—under the title "Commonly Overridden Member Functions."

Commonly Called TWindow *Member Functions*

Since every windowing function of the WinAPI is encapsulted by **TWindow**, the list of functions that you can call is quite long. For a complete list, refer to the Win16/Win32 API Programmer's Reference help database. If you look at the Functions and Overviews section, the section on "Windows" gives you a complete list. **TWindow** adds useful functions, in addition to the native WinAPI functions, some of which are listed below:

Function	*Description*
CloseWindow()	Requests a window to close. First, **TWindow** checks that it's OK to close by calling **CanClose**. If the answer is "yes," then the window is destroyed.
GetApplication()	Retrieves pointer to application object. Useful to gain access to member functions and data in application object.
GetClientRect()	Query size of client area, which is size of drawing space in a Windows application.

Function	*Description*
`Invalidate()`	Declare part of a window invalid, such that the window receives a **`WM_PAINT`** message to redraw.
`MoveWindow()`	A WinAPI function that changes location and/or size of a window.
`SetBkgndColor()`	Set a window's background color.
`SetCaption()`	Call to change a window's caption, and the **`Title`** member of **`TWindow`**.
`SetCursor()`	Connect a new mouse cursor to a window.
`Show()`	Make window visible/invisible.

Commonly Overridden `TWindow` *Member Functions*

A few of **`TWindow`** member functions are prime candidates for overriding. In some cases, be sure to call the base function member.

Function	*Description*
`CanClose()`	Override in main window to monitor user requests to close a window. If a window holding unsaved data is about to be closed, you'd display a YESNOCANCEL message box asking the user whether to (a) YES—save the data and close the window, (b) NO—don't save the data but close the window, or (c) CANCEL—don't save the data and forget about closing the window.
`CleanupWindow()`	Termination and cleanup handling for a window object.
`Paint()`	Redraw the contents of a window's client area in response to a **`WM_PAINT`** message. Since **`TWindow`** default handling of this message does the right thing, simply override **`Paint`** for window drawing.
`SetupWindow()`	Window initialization. This function gets called after a WinAPI window has been created, so it's a good time to perform whatever initialization requires you to access the WinAPI window object. Be sure to call the base class member when you override.

By itself, **`TWindow`** doesn't add a lot to the functionality of the Windows API. It represents a repackaging of the user-interface API rather than an addition of many more capabilities. The classes derived from **`TWindow`** represent OWL's enhancements to the Windows API. One of them, the **`TFrameWindow`** class, is the subject of the next section.

TFrameWindow

Every OWL application will have an application object. That by itself gives it membership in the Windows system. If it wants to connect to the Windows user-interface, however, it needs a window. The windows designed to play this role are those created from **`TFrameWindow`** and its derived classes.

The Windows API provides the support for most of the things associated with an application's main window: a menu, caption bar, sizeable border, and an icon for when the window is minimized. Much of what you find in **`TFrameWindow`**, then, is that it provides a way to connect to these capabilities.

What **`TFrameWindow`** does add, however, are some refinements that help smooth over the rough edges of a normal WinAPI window. In particular, support for a child window created inside another window is an area that isn't handled well by the native Windows API. **`TFrameWindow`** simplifies support for things like dialog box controls within an application's main window, saving and restoring the keyboard focus to the correct child window, and properly resizing a client window when one is present. It also allows an application's main window to have some of the same privileges as the application object itself, such as idle-time processing and the ability to listen in to the application's main message loop.

Since window objects are primarily message processing objects, let's start with a look at the messages that **`TFrameWindow`** handles for you—or for the classes you derive from it.

WinAPI Message	*Description*
`WM_PAINT`	This message is a request from the windowing system to redraw the contents of a damaged (or newly created) window. The frame window calls a Paint member for drawing, or—if the window is iconic—drawing the icon.
`WM_ERASEBKGND`	This message is a request to erase the background before painting. **`TFrameWindow`** sends this on to the default handler for proper processing.
`WM_QUERYDRAGICON`	This message asks a window for an icon handle to be used while the window is dragged.
`WM_INITMENUPOPUP`	This message requests menu initialization. **`TFrameWindow`** responds by enabling and disabling menu items.
`WM_SETFOCUS`	This message tells a window that it will be receiving keyboard input. **`TFrameWindow`** sets the focus to its child window that last had the focus.
`WM_SIZE`	This message tells a window that its client area has changed size. If it has a client window, **`TFrameWindow`** responds to this message by changing the size of its client window to fit within its client area.

WinAPI Message	*Description*
WM_PARENTNOTIFY	This message tells a window that one of its child windows has been created, destroyed, or has been clicked with the mouse. **TWindow** enhances this support by also sending this message when a child window changes size. **TFrameWindow** responds in several ways. If the client window is being closed, the application itself is shutdown. If the client window is changing size, the frame window adjusts its own size accordingly.

Of course, a complete picture of the messages that **TFrameWindow** handles requires you to also look at the messages handled by **TWindow**.

Some interesting features of **TFrameWindow** can also be learned by looking at its data members, which are presented here:

Type	*Name*	*Description*
PUBLIC:		
BOOL	**KeyboardHandling**	Flag to decide whether to enhance application object's message loop to support the keyboard interface to dialog box controls. You'll want this if, for example, you're using dialog box controls in your application's main window. Setting this flag to TRUE allows the [Tab] key to move between controls. Enable by calling **EnableKBHandler()** memberfunction.
PROTECTED:		
HWND	**HWndRestoreFocus**	When a frame window contains several child windows, this field identifies the window which has the focus so it can be restored when, for example, an application becomes inactive then becomes activated again.
TWindow *	**ClientWnd**	The optional OWL window object that handles client window operation. MIN, for example, doesn't create a client window although other sample programs in this book—such as GADGETS in Chapter 13—do. Set and query this member by calling **SetClientWindow** and **GetClientWindow**.

(continued)

Type	*Name*	*Description*
PRIVATE:		
TModule *	**IconModule**	The module handle for the icon displayed when the frame window is minimized.
TResId	**IconResId**	The icon resource ID for the icon displayed when the frame window is minimized.
TPoint	**MinimizedPos**	The minimized location of a frame window.

You can of course also call the **TWindow** member functions for a **TFrameWindow** window, which means the entire windowing API is available for your use. Here, however, are the implementation functions provided by **TFrameWindow** for your use:

Commonly Called TFrameWindow *Member Functions*

Function	*Description*
AssignMenu()	Identify the resource ID of the menu to use for the frame window.
EnableKBHandler()	Call to add call to **IsDialogMessage** WinAPI function to application message loop. This enables the keyboard interface to dialog box controls within the frame window, which mostly means the use of the [Tab] key between controls.
GetClientWindow()	Returns a **TWindow *** to the frame's current client window.
SetClientWindow()	Assign a new **TWindow *** derived object as the frame's client window.
SetIcon()	Identify the module object and the resource ID of the icon to use when the window is minimized.
SetMenu()	Connect a WinAPI menu to a frame window object.

The other set of interesting class functions are, of course, the interface functions. Override these functions to fine-tune the operation of **TFrameWindow**-derived classes:

Commonly Overridden TFrameWindow *Member Functions*

Function	*Description*
PreProcessMsg()	The application message loop calls this function for top-level windows to allow some preprocessing of message loop messages. These are mostly used to massage keyboard input, such as allowing keyboard acclerators to work. If you override, be sure to call base class function.

Function	*Description*
IdleAction()	Called by application object when the message loop is idle. The application class has a similar member function with the same name. Idea is to allow "background" processing to occur.
SetupWindow()	Associated with **WM_CREATE** initialization. Override this function to do any initialization work for a window that can only be done after the WinAPI window has been created.

At this point, you understand the basics of using two key OWL window objects to create Windows programs. There's one crucial topic, however, that hasn't yet been covered: proper program termination. While this might seem to be the job of an application object, in fact proper program termination in Windows is usually tied to the life of a program's main window. Let's see how an OWL window object should handle this important task.

Program Termination

An important issue for every Windows program is proper termination. Proper termination is necessary to allow the cleanup and reclamation of memory and other resources used by a program. In our discussion of the application object, we introduced the `WM_QUIT` message. When the message loop detects this message, it causes the "infinite message loop" (and our program) to terminate. Let's see how the `WM_QUIT` message gets into our message queue.

Program termination usually occurs when the program's main window is closed. A user can close a window in any number of ways. Two of the more common ways are by selecting the Close item on the system menu or by striking the [Alt] + [F4] key combination. Each of these actions causes a stream of messages to be sent to our window procedure. Here is a list of messages that are sent to our window procedure when MIN's window is closed using the [Alt] + [F4] key combination:

Message	*Comment*
`WM_SYSKEYDOWN`	[Alt] key was struck
`WM_SYSKEYDOWN`	[F4] key was struck
`WM_SYSCOMMAND`	System Command generated
`WM_CLOSE`	Window is told to close
`WM_NCACTIVATE`	Turn off titlebar (nonclient area) highlight
`WM_ACTIVATE`	Window is becoming inactive

Message	*Comment*
WM_ACTIVATEAPP	Application is becoming inactive
WM_KILLFOCUS	Window is losing the keyboard
WM_DESTROY	Window has been destroyed
WM_NCDESTROY	Time to cleanup nonclient area data

The first thing to be said about this stream of messages is that the default window procedure handles the bulk of the work to make the "right things" happen. For example, it takes the first two messages, which are raw keystroke messages, and translates them into the third message: a system command. The system command message is handled by the default window procedure to implement system level commands.

A system command is a generic request for some action to occur (move a window, size a window, etc.). A window object usually does not process these messages. Instead, it looks for more specific messages to respond to. In this case, that message is WM_CLOSE, a request to close our window.

The **TWindow** class has a member function to handle this message: EvClose. For an application's main window, this function calls **TWindow::CloseWindow**, which is the generic window-closing function for **TWindow** and derived classes. This function first asks if it's OK to close the window. It does so by calling one of two different member functions named **CanClose**. If dealing with an application's main window, the application object's **CanClose** function is called. If dealing with any other window, it calls the window object's **CanClose** function. For both application object and window object, this member function returns one of two values: TRUE (nonzero) to allow the window to close, or FALSE (zero) to prevent the window from closing.

The default action of **TApplication::CanClose** is to call the main window's CanClose function. For this reason, we think it makes sense to think of this member function only in terms of its window object incarnation. The application object's version makes it easy to request application shutdown from any part of an application.

A typical **CanClose** member function might check for an unsaved file in our window. If one exists, our window object might display a message box like that shown in Figure 5.1 to warn the user of the possible loss of data. A **CanClose** member function makes sure that no harmful results will come from closing the window. In the sample message box, **CanClose** would return a TRUE (OK to close) message if the user clicked "Yes" or "No" On the other hand, if the user clicked "Cancel," **CanClose** would return FALSE to prevent the window from closing.

TWindows handles the WM_QUERYENDSESSION message, in its **EvQueryEndSession** member function. Windows sends this message to the main window of every program when the user goes to shut down the system. Essentially, a vote is taken. A unanimous reply is needed to allow Windows to terminate. Once again, **CanClose** is called to ensure against loss of user data. First, the application's **CanClose** is called, which in turn calls the main window's **CanClose** member function.

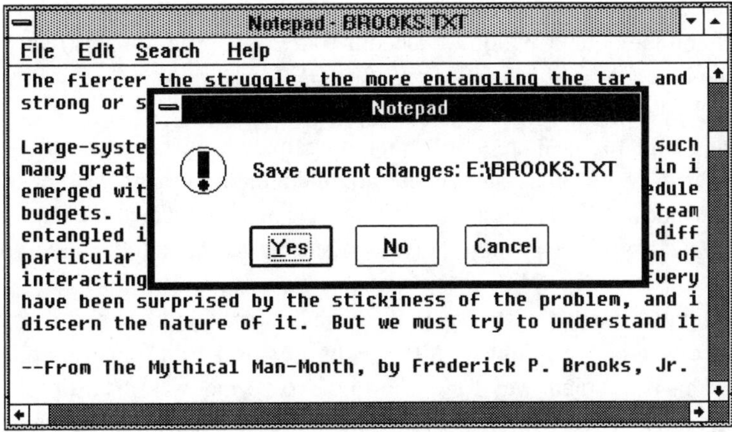

Figure 5.1 Protecting the user from loss of data

When **CanClose** says it's OK to close, the **Destroy** member function is called. This is a **TWindows** member function which cleans up the MDI document windows which have been created. Next it calls the MS-Windows routine **DestroyWindow**. This routine completely and irrevocably eliminates a window. It sends a "death certificate," in the form of a `WM_DESTROY` message.

Once again, **TWindows** has a member function to handle this important message. Its **EvDestroy** member function does the job. If it's an application's main window, it calls the Windows **PostQuitMessage** routine, which puts a `WM_QUIT` message onto an application's message queue. It is this message, you will recall, that is responsible for terminating an application's message loop so that the program itself can terminate.

As you can see, most of program termination is taken care of for us by the OWL libraries. Of course, we can intervene at any point simply by overriding the base class member functions. Another component that helps out is Windows' own default window procedure. Let's focus our attention on this important workhorse.

Default Message Handling

As we discussed in Chapter 1, the chief reason for the attractiveness of Windows comes from the consistent "look and feel" of the Windows user interface. Even the most casual Windows user notices the remarkable uniformity between programs. For example, menus work the same between two otherwise unrelated programs, and windows in different programs respond in the same way to the same actions.

Deep in the bowels of Windows, it is the work of the default window handler that accounts for this high degree of uniformity. The flood of messages that a window object diverts to the default handler is the cause of the similarities between programs. While a C program will rely heavily on the default window procedure, an OWL program gets many of these services from the base OWL objects. But even the OWL programs rely, to some degree, on the work done by the default window procedure.

While this work is being done for us, there is still something that we must do. A window object plays the role of traffic cop for messages. After all, the default message handler is never called directly by Windows. Instead, our window objects always receive messages first. To keep the user interface working properly, OWL passes messages on to the default window procedure.

There may, in fact, be times when we wish to vary the behavior of a window away from the default behavior. For example, we might wish to prevent the user from picking up a window by the titlebar. (This is a typical way for a user to move a window.) It is a simple matter to trap the messages associated with this action, and prevent them from arriving at the default window handler. For the most part, however, we'll allow the default window procedure to do its work for us, so that our program can participate in the consistency that makes Windows so usable.

In looking at the different parts of our minimum Windows program, we have talked a lot about the flow of messages through the system. We have also identified a few messages that are important. In order for you to fully understand how the message pipeline can work to your advantage, it will help you to know the types of messages that flow through these pipes. For this reason, we're going to conclude this chapter with an in-depth look at the types of messages in Windows.

A Taxonomy of Messages

There are about 250 predefined messages in Windows. Fortunately, you do not have to be familiar with every single one of them, because most have very specialized uses. For example, a large number of messages are specific to one type of window. Other messages are used for very special purposes, like sharing data or implementing the **Multiple Document Interface** (MDI) standard. Still other messages float through our message pipeline but are never documented for our use. These are internal messages that Windows creates for its own purposes.

To help you come to terms with messages, we'll divide the messages into eight categories. These categories are intended as a framework in which to begin understanding messages. But this won't be the last you hear about messages. Almost every chapter in this book will provide details on the messages that apply to the different parts of Windows. So let's get started on our look at Windows messages.

Messages have names. Message names are defined in WINDOWS.H like this:

```
#define WM_COMMAND 0x0111
```

The WM_ Hungarian prefix tells us that a symbol is a "window message." In spoken language, the prefix is ignored, so that programmers often refer to WM_COMMAND as a "command message." These symbolic names stand in for the raw numeric value of a message: a 16-bit unsigned integer. Besides the WM_ prefix, there are other Hungarian prefixes for messages: EM_, BM_, DM_, LB_, and CB_ (like EM_GETSEL, BM_GETCHECK, etc.). These are private messages, which don't concern us at this moment, except that they show that you can create your *own* private messages as you need them.

A useful tool for learning about messages is WinSight. Borland provides this utility with version 3.0 and later of the Borland C++ compiler. It's provided to help you eavesdrop on the message traffic for a window—even if you didn't write the program! When you use WinSight, you will be surprised at the number of messages encountered. For example, Figure 5.2 shows the messages generated by the simple action of making a menu selection. Even without knowing what specific messages do, you can tell that this is a lot of messages. A little experimentation with WinSight will demonstrate that this is typical for other user actions as well.

Why so many messages? Some messages are for Windows' internal use, to synchronize events in different parts of the system. These messages are passed along to the default win-

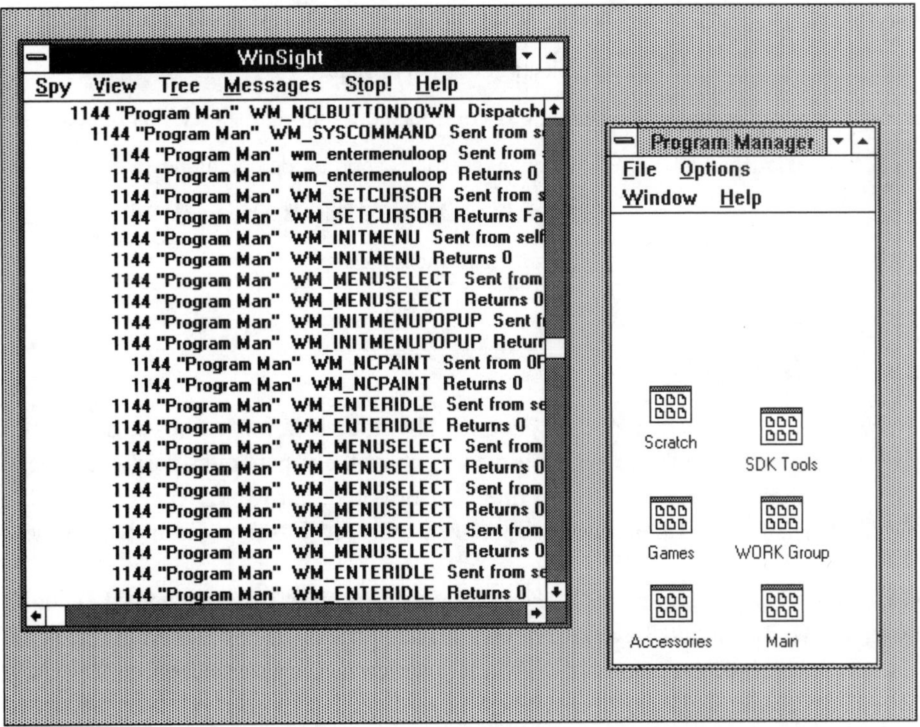

Figure 5.2 WinSight showing messages generated by making a menu selection

dow procedure, which we introduced a short time ago. Other messages notify the window procedure of actions taken by the user. Messages guarantee that a window procedure will always have the latest information about what the user is doing. Once you understand the type of messages that are generated, messages ultimately mean less work on your part to keep in touch with a lot of information. It's like having a daily paper delivered to your door: "All the Messages Fit to Print."

Table 5.2 shows the eight categories of messages. As we review each category, we'll list the specific messages that are in the category. Since some of the categories are quite specialized, we'll limit our discussion to a brief introduction and omit a list of specific messages. All messages from all categories are listed in Appendix A, in case you're curious about what it is that we're omitting. Let's start with our first message category: hardware messages.

Table 5.2 The Eight Types of Messages

Type	*Description*
Hardware	Mouse and keyboard input
Window Maintenance	Notification, request for action, query
User-Interface Maintenance	Menu, mouse pointer, scroll bar, dialog boxes, MDI
Termination	Application or system shutdown
Private	Dialog box controls: edit, button, list box, combobox
System Resource Notification	Color changes, fonts, spooler, device modes
Data Sharing	Clipboard and Dynamic Data Exchange (DDE)
Internal System	Undocumented messages

Hardware Messages

A window procedure receives messages generated by three different pieces of hardware: the keyboard, the mouse, and the system timer. Each of these generates hardware interrupts. Since Windows' scheduling is not interrupt-oriented, hardware events have to be buffered. This ensures that hardware events are processed in the order in which they occur.

For example, when you strike the "H" key, an interrupt notifies the system that keyboard input is ready. The Windows keyboard device driver retrieves this input and creates an entry into the **hardware event queue**. When its turn comes, messages bearing "H" key information are delivered to the proper window procedure. The mouse and timer messages are handled in a similar fashion. Table 5.3 shows the 29 messages that are generated in response to hardware activity.

Table 5.3 Hardware Messages

Mouse Messages: In a window's client area	
`WM_LBUTTONDBLCLK`	Left button double-click
`WM_LBUTTONDOWN`	Left button down
`WM_LBUTTONUP`	Left button up
`WM_MBUTTONDBLCLK`	Middle button double-click
`WM_MBUTTONDOWN`	Middle button down
`WM_MBUTTONUP`	Middle button up
`WM_MOUSEMOVE`	Mouse move
`WM_RBUTTONDBLCLK`	Right button double-click
`WM_RBUTTONDOWN`	Right button down
`WM_RBUTTONUP`	Right button up
Mouse Messages: In a window's nonclient area	
`WM_NCLBUTTONDBLCLK`	Left button double-click
`WM_NCLBUTTONDOWN`	Left button down
`WM_NCLBUTTONUP`	Left button up
`WM_NCMBUTTONDBLCLK`	Middle button double-click
`WM_NCMBUTTONDOWN`	Middle button down
`WM_NCMBUTTONUP`	Middle button up
`WM_NCMOUSEMOVE`	Mouse move
`WM_NCRBUTTONDBLCLK`	Right button double-click
`WM_NCRBUTTONDOWN`	Right button down
`WM_NCRBUTTONUP`	Right button up
Keyboard Messages	
`WM_CHAR`	Character input
`WM_DEADCHAR`	Dead-character (umlaut, accent, etc.)

(continued)

Table 5.3 Hardware Messages *(Continued)*

Keyboard Messages	WM_KEYDOWN	Key has been depressed
	WM_KEYUP	Key has been released
	WM_SYSCHAR	System character input
	WM_SYSDEADCHAR	System dead-character
	WM_SYSKEYDOWN	System key has been depressed
	WM_SYSKEYUP	System key has been released
Timer Message		
	WM_TIMER	Timer has gone off.

➤ ***Caution:***

Like mouse and keyboard messages, timer messages are queued. This means that Windows timers are not exact. This is necessary since an interrupt-driven timer message would conflict with the nonpreemptive nature of Windows. The usefulness of a timer is that it lets you know that a minimum amount of time has passed.

With mouse messages, a distinction is made between the mouse messages generated in a window's client area and those generated in the nonclient area. (Remember: The nonclient area of a window includes its border, system menu, titlebar, menu, etc.) In general, an application only pays attention to client area mouse messages and lets the default window procedure process nonclient area mouse messages.

While we're on the subject of mouse messages, the `WM_MOUSEMOVE` message deserves some special attention. The `WM_MOUSEMOVE` message is handled in a special way to keep the hardware event queue from overflowing. After all, if you move the mouse quickly, you can easily create hundreds of mouse interrupts. To minimize the disruption this might cause, Windows keeps only *one* mouse move message at a time. When a new mouse move message arrives, Windows checks if one already exists. If so, the old message is updated with the new location information. A new entry is made only if a mouse move message isn't already present.

There are two basic types of keyboard messages: regular and system. In general, you can ignore system keyboard messages, which have names like `WM_SYSCHAR` and `WM_SYSKEYDOWN`. The default window procedure turns these into the proper system command. The regular keyboard messages are intended for application use. We'll discuss the details of all keyboard messages in Chapter 15, when we talk about getting input from the user.

Window Maintenance Messages

This group has 27 messages. It seems that this is the trickiest group of messages, mostly because it takes a long time to learn the subtle nuances of each. Unfortunately, the names of the messages do not help very much.

To begin with, there are three types of window maintenance messages: notification, request for action, and queries. Table 5.4 lists all the window maintenance messages, sorted into these three types.

Table 5.4 Window Maintenance Messages

Window Messages: Notification		
	`WM_ACTIVATE`	Window is active.
	`WM_ACTIVATEAPP`	Application is active.
	`WM_CREATE`	Window has been created.
	`WM_DESTROY`	Window has been destroyed.
	`WM_ENABLE`	Input to the window has been enabled.
	`WM_KILLFOCUS`	Window has lost keyboard control.
	`WM_MOUSEACTIVATE`	Notifies a window that it is going to become active because of a mouse click.
	`WM_MOVE`	Window has been moved.
	`WM_SETFOCUS`	Window has gained keyboard control.
	`WM_SIZE`	Window has changed size.
Window Messages: Request for action		
	`WM_CLOSE`	Close (destroy) window
	`WM_ERASEBKGND`	Erase background
	`WM_ICONERASEBKGND`	Erase background of iconic window
	`WM_NCACTIVATE`	Change title bar to show active state
	`WM_NCCREATE`	Create nonclient area data

(continued)

Table 5.4 Window Maintenance Messages *(Continued)*

Window Messages: Request for action		
	`WM_NCDESTROY`	Destroy nonclient area data
	`WM_NCPAINT`	Redraw nonclient area
	`WM_PAINT`	Redraw client area
	`WM_PAINTICON`	Redraw iconic window client area
	`WM_SETREDRAW`	Inhibit redrawing of window
	`WM_SETTEXT`	Change window text
	`WM_SHOWWINDOW`	Change window visibility
Window Messages: Query		
	`WM_GETMINMAXINFO`	What are min/max sizes for window?
	`WM_GETTEXT`	What is the window text?
	`WM_GETTEXTLENGTH`	What is the length of the window text?
	`WM_NCCALCSIZE`	How big should the client area be?
	`WM_QUERYNEWPALETTE`	Do you have a new palette?
	`WM_QUERYOPEN`	Can iconic window be opened?

A notification message tells a window procedure that the state of a window has changed. Nothing is required from the window procedure to perform the action implied by the message name. The `WM_MOVE` message, for example, is *not* a request for your program to move anything. Instead, it is an after-the-fact message to tell you that your window has already been moved. It is worth noting that nothing in the message tells us how our window was moved. Maybe the user moved a window with the mouse. Or perhaps another program moved our window. Whichever is the case, notification messages are one-way communication to a window procedure.

A request for action message requires that some action take place. Without the action, a hole is created in the user interface. For example, the `WM_PAINT` message is sent to a window procedure when a window has been damaged and needs to be redrawn. If the window procedure doesn't repair the window, it stays broken. For the most part, the default window procedure provides the needed minimum action. There are times, however, when you must intercept and process one of these messages yourself—as is the case with the WM_PAINT message we brought up a moment ago. When you do, be sure that you mimic the actions of the default handler. Finding out what this means is simpler than you might think: Just look at the source code to **DefWindowProc**.

For your convenience, we have duplicated a listing of **DefWindowProc** in Appendix B of this book for version 3.0 of the Software Development Kit. Check with your software dealer for the latest version of the Software Development Kit, since the listing we provide in the appendix of this book is subject to revision.

A query message requires an answer. This is used for two-way communication between Windows and your program. Like the request for action messages, you can rely on the default window procedure to give a reasonable answer for most cases. You may decide to intercept one if you want to change the default answer. For example, you will get a WM_QUERYOPEN message when the user tries to open a minimized window. If you want a program to run only in an iconic state, you simply answer FALSE instead of the default answer of TRUE.

User-Interface Messages

This group contains messages for the other user-interface objects, including the application menu, mouse pointer, scroll bar, dialog boxes, and dialog box controls. It also includes a group of messages used to support the Multiple Document Interface (MDI). See Table 5.5. This is a user-interface convention that was first seen in Microsoft's Excel spreadsheet program. Since then, it has become something of a standard, so that Windows now includes built-in support for MDI. The use of MDI is beyond the scope of this book, but we'll cover the other types of messages elsewhere: menu messages in Chapter 11, mouse pointer messages in Chapter 16, scroll bar messages in Chapter 20, and dialog box messages in Chapter 14.

Table 5.5 User Interface Messages

Menu Messages	
WM_COMMAND	Menu item has been selected.
WM_INITMENU	Initialize menu bar menu.
WM_INITMENUPOPUP	Initialize popup menu.
WM_MENUCHAR	Mnemonic key used to select menu.
WM_MENUSELECT	User is browsing through menus.
System Commands: System Menu, Min/Max Buttons, Titlebar, etc.	
WM_SYSCOMMAND	A system command has been selected.

(continued)

Table 5.5 User Interface Messages *(Continued)*

Mouse Pointer Messages	
WM_NCHITTEST	Query: Where is mouse on the window?
WM_SETCURSOR	Request: Change pointer to correct shape.
Scroll Bar Messages	
WM_HSCROLL	Horizontal scrollbar has been clicked.
WM_VSCROLL	Vertical scrollbar has been clicked.
Dialog Box and Dialog Box Contrl Messages	
WM_COMMAND	Control communicating with Dialog Box.
WM_COMPAREITEM	Sent to the parent of an owner-draw dialog box control, asking to compare two items for the purpose of sorting.
WM_CTLCOLOR	Control asking for colors to be set.
WM_DELETEITEM	Notification to an owner-draw listbox or an owner-draw combobox that an item has been deleted.
WM_DRAWITEM	Request to the parent of an owner-draw control, or owner-draw menu, to draw.
WM_GETDLGCODE	Query control: Want keyboard input?
WM_GETFONT	Query control: What font are you using?
WM_INITDIALOG	Initialize dialog.
WM_MEASUREITEM	Request to the parent of an owner-draw control or an owner-draw item to provide the dimensions of the item that is going to be drawn.
WM_SETFONT	Request to control: Use this font.
Multiple Document Interface Messages	
WM_CHILDACTIVATE	Notifies a parent window that a child is active.
WM_MDIACTIVATE	Notifies an MDI child window that it is either gaining or losing activation.
WM_MDICASCADE	Request to arrange the open MDI child windows in a cascading, stair-step fashion.

(continued)

Table 5.5 User Interface Messages *(Continued)*

WM_MDICREATE	Requests an MDI client window to create an MDI child window.
Multiple Document Interface Messages	
WM_MDIDESTROY	Request to an MDI client window to destroy an MDI child window.
WM_MDIGETACTIVE	Query an MDI client window for the currently active MDI child window.
WM_MDIICONARRANGE	Request to arrange the iconic MDI child windows in an orderly fashion.
WM_MDIMAXIMIZE	Request to maximize, or zoom, an MDI child window so that it occupies all of its parent's client area.
WM_MDINEXT	Request to activate the next MDI child window.
WM_MDIRESTORE	Request to restore an MDI child window to its previous state≈iconic, normal, or zoomed.
WM_MDISETMENU	Adjusts the menu on an MDI frame window.
WM_MDITILE	Request to arrange the open MDI child windows in a tiled fashion in the MDI parent's client window.

Termination Messages

This is the smallest group of messages. See Table 5.6. But these messages are very important, since they are used to control the termination of a Windows program (WM_QUIT), as well as the termination processing for the system (WM_QUERYENDSESSION and WM_ENDSESSION). We covered the WM_QUIT message earlier.

Table 5.6 Termination Messages

Application and System Termination	
WM_QUIT	Request that a program should terminate.
WM_QUERYENDSESSION	A Query: Ready for system shutdown?
WM_ENDSESSION	Notification of results of shutdown query.

Private Messages

Private window messages are for use with a specific window class. The predefined private messages in WINDOWS.H are used with the following window classes: edit, button, listbox, and combobox.

The use of private messages by predefined window types is a pretty good clue that we can use this technique for our own windows. Why would you want to do this? You might find that existing messages do not provide the required functionality. It is a simple matter to define your own private message types and use them for communicating between different windows that you create. Even though 250 message types have already been defined, message variables are unsigned integers, which means that there is room for 65,535 different message types. When you define a private message, you should use the range starting at `WM_USER`, which is defined in WINDOWS.H as follows:

```
#define WM_USER      0x0400
```

If we wrote a window procedure for windows that display numbers, we might control how numbers appear with the following private messages (`PM_` is Hungarian for "private message"):

```
#define PM_DECIMAL     WM_USER + 0
#define PM_BINARY      WM_USER + 1
#define PM_HEX         WM_USER + 2
#define PM_OCTAL       WM_USER + 3
#define PM_NODECIMAL   WM_USER + 4
#define PM_DOLLARS     WM_USER + 5
#define PM_WITHCOMMAS WM_USER + 6
```

Other parts of our program (or other programs that we write) can control the number display window simply by sending messages.

System Resource Notification

There are eight system resource notification messages. See Table 5.7. These are sent to the top-level window of every program when a change has been made to a system resource. For example, when fonts are added or removed from the system, a `WM_FONTCHANGE` message is distributed. When the user changes the system colors or the system time from the Control Panel program, the `WM_SYSCOLORCHANGE` or `WM_TIMECHANGE` messages are sent out. The typical response to a notification is to record the change.

Of course, not every change is of interest to every program. For example, a clock program would probably check the new time when it receives a `WM_TIMECHANGE` message. But if it didn't use different fonts, it would probably ignore the `WM_FONTCHANGE` message.

Table 5.7 System Resource Notification Messages

System Resources Notification Messages	
WM_COMPACTING	Notification that system memory is low, and that the Memory Manager is trying to free up some memory.
WM_DEVMODECHANGE	Printer setup has changed.
WM_FONTCHANGE	Installed fonts in the system have changed.
WM_PALETTECHANGED	Hardware color palette has changed.
WM_SPOOLERSTATUS	Job has been removed from spooler queue.
WM_SYSCOLORCHANGE	One or more system colors has changed.
WM_TIMECHANGE	System time has changed.
WM_WININICHANGE	Initialization file, WIN.INI, changed.

Because most programs use the system colors, just about every program will respond to the WM_SYSCOLORCHANGE message. This is a notification that one or more system colors have changed. Ordinarily, system colors are changed by the Control Panel program under the direction of the user. When a change has been made, the Control Panel sends WM_SYSCOLORCHANGE. On receipt of this message, programs that use system colors respond by redrawing with the new colors.

Data Sharing Messages

Data sharing plays an important role in Windows. So it's not surprising that there are messages that are used in data sharing. Both data sharing mechanisms, the clipboard and Dynamic Data Exchange (DDE), make extensive use of messages. A full discussion of data sharing is beyond the scope of this book; however, Windows' data sharing messages are listed in Table 5.8.

Table 5.8 Data sharing Messages

Clipboard Messages	
WM_ASKCBFORMATNAME	Asks for the name of a Clipboard format.
WM_CHANGECBCHAIN	Notification of a change in the viewing chain.
WM_DESTROYCLIPBOARD	Clipboard contents are being destroyed.
WM_DRAWCLIPBOARD	Clipboard contents have changed.

(continued)

Table 5.8 Data sharing Messages *(Continued)*

Clipboard Messages	
WM_HSCROLLCLIPBOARD	Horizonal scrolling of owner draw clipboard item.
WM_PAINTCLIPBOARD	Requests drawing of an owner draw clipboard item.
WM_RENDERALLFORMATS	Request to provide the data for all clipboard formats that have been promised.
WM_RENDERFORMAT	Request to provide data for a single clipboard format that has been promised.
WM_SIZECLIPBOARD	Notification to the owner of owner draw clipboard data that the size of the Clipboard viewer window has changed.
WM_VSCROLLCLIPBOARD	Vertical scrolling of an owner draw clipboard item.
Dynamic Data Exchange(DDE) Messages	
WM_DDE_ACK	Acknowledgment.
WM_DDE_ADVISE	Request from a DDE client to establish a permanent data link.
WM_DDE_DATA	Send a data item from a DDE server to a DDE client.
WM_DDE_EXECUTE	Request a DDE server to execute a series of commands.
WM_DDE_INITIATE	Logon to a DDE server.
WM_DDE_POKE	Request by a client for a server to update a specific data item.
WM_DDE_REQUEST	One-time request by a DDE client for a piece of information.
WM_DDE_TERMINATE	Logoff from a DDE server.
WM_DDE_UNADVISE	Terminate a permanent data link that was initiated with the WM_DDE_ADVISE message.

Internal System Messages

A large group of messages are defined in WINDOWS.H but not described in any documentation. These are internal system messages, the last group of messages we are going to discuss. Windows uses these messages for its own purposes. This is the same idea as private messages, with the exception that private messages are meant for only one class of window. Internal messages are encountered in the context of every window class.

If we don't know the reason for a message, why is it sent to a window procedure? Like other message types, if a window procedure does not process it, the message is passed on to the default message handler. The default message handler does the right thing with this group of messages.

Since you have the source code to the default message handler, you might think that you could reverse-engineer some of these messages and use them for your own purpose. You can do this, but be careful. A future version of Windows may change the way internal messages are used, or eliminate some altogether! It has been our experience that "undocumented goodies" are interesting to look at, but dangerous to include in software that is intended for general distribution.

PART THREE

Introduction to the Graphics Device Interface

6

Overview of GDI

For the next few chapters, the focus is on creating graphical output. This, of course, means that the focus will be on using Windows' **Graphics Device Interface** (**GDI**) library. In the same way that OWL's **`TWindow`** class encapsulates the WinAPI *windowing* interface, OWL's **`TDC`** class encapsulates the WinAPI *graphical output* interface. As each topic is covered, you'll find sample programs to give a more complete idea of how to incorporate graphic output into your own programs.

This chapter covers the basic capabilities of GDI, starting with a discussion of the types of drawing that GDI can do and the types of devices GDI supports. After discussing the basics of drawing coordinates and drawing objects, I'll introduce the **device context** (**DC**)—the WinAPI data structure that represents a connection to a device. This structure contains GDI's drawing attribute information. The contents of this structure help you get, for example, black vs. blue text, thin vs. thick lines, and colored vs. hatched areas. In short, you control the appearance of graphic output by manipulating the contents of a DC. After discussing the role that GDI's clipping plays in providing support for the system's windowing capabilities, I'll introduce you to the **`WM_PAINT`** message, which is arguably one of the most important messages a window object will respond to. It is only by responding properly to this message, after all, that a window object can maintain any sensible output in its window. Finally, I'll touch on how the OWL libraries wrap GDI's capabilities for you in its **`TDC`** class. Let's roll up our sleeves, then, and take a look at Windows' pixel-powered graphic output engine.

An Overview of the Graphics Device Interface

GDI is Windows' graphic output library. GDI handles graphic output for the display screen as well as hard-copy devices like printers and plotters. GDI creates every line, letter, and mark displayed by a Windows program. Windows itself uses GDI to draw the user interface: Windows, icons, menus, dialog boxes, etc. are all drawn by calling GDI functions.

Figure 6.1 shows some of the types of graphic objects that GDI can draw: lines, filled figures, and text of different shapes and sizes. This chapter and the chapters that follow introduce the basic concepts and programming techniques needed to take advantage of the capabilities that GDI has to offer.

GDI Devices

GDI can draw on many different types of devices: display screens, laser printers, dot-matrix printers, plotters, etc. For GDI to work with a specific device, it depends on a special piece of software: a **device driver**. A GDI device driver converts drawing requests into the specific actions needed to draw on a specific device. For example, when a Windows program draws a picture of the space shuttle on a VGA display, GDI calls the VGA device driver to turn on the correct pixels. And when a program generates output on an HP LaserJet printer, GDI calls another device driver for help: the HP printer driver. In addition to performing this work, a device driver provides GDI with a set of **device capability bits**. These are flags that let GDI know about a device's built-in drawing ability. There are five sets of flags: a set each for curves, lines, polygons, bitmaps, and text. These flags tell GDI when to give a high-level drawing request directly to a device and when it must convert such requests into an equivalent group of low-level drawing requests.

At a minimum, a GDI device must be able to do two things: turn on pixels and draw solid lines. For a device with these minimum capabilities, GDI (with the help of a device driver) is able to do the rest. GDI has a set of built-in **software simulations** that take a high-level drawing request, like "draw a filled polygon," and convert it into a series of line and pixel operations. The software simulations are one reason that GDI is referred to as a **device-independent** graphics library. For devices with capabilities beyond the minimum,

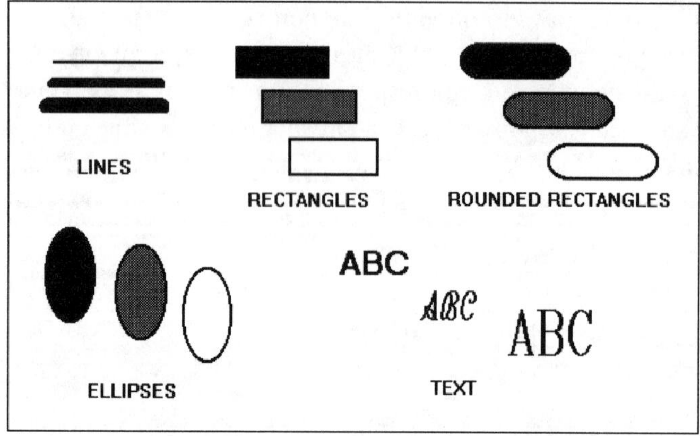

Figure 6.1 A sample of GDI lines, filled figures, and text

such as a PostScript printer, GDI uses the capability bits to determine when to send a high-level drawing request directly to the device driver.

In addition to physical devices like video screens and printers, GDI supports logical or **pseudodevices**. Pseudodevices are used for picture storage. Unlike physical devices, which display pictures using dedicated hardware, pseudodevices capture a picture in RAM or on disk. GDI supports two types of pseudodevices: **bitmaps** and **metafiles**.

In Windows, bitmaps are always rectangular. A bitmap stores a picture in memory in the same way that a display adapter uses memory to hold graphic images. For this reason, bitmaps provide a fast way to make a copy of a picture. Bitmaps are also used to store images that must be drawn quickly onto the screen. For example, Windows uses bitmaps to store icons and cursors, as well as the tiny symbols used to draw system menus, minimize/maximize icons, parts of a scroll bar, and even the check mark inside menus.

Another use of bitmaps is to store scanned images, such as company logos. A scanned image is created by running a paper copy of a logo through a device called a **scanner**. A scanner digitizes an image, making it suitable for storage in a bitmap. Figure 6.2 shows a bitmap created using a scanner and then placed into a PageMaker document.

Metafiles are created by GDI's record-and-playback facility. A metafile is cheaper than a bitmap, in terms of memory use, but is slower in terms of drawing time.

A metafile is like a cassette tape. To create a metafile, you place the tape into GDI's cassette deck and push the "Record" button. GDI calls are recorded onto the metafile until you press the "Stop" button. Once a metafile has been created, it can be stored on disk, or passed to another program. For example, the clipboard is often used to pass GDI metafiles between programs. And when an OLE object is passed from an OLE server application to an OLE container application, a metafile is often provided so the container application can

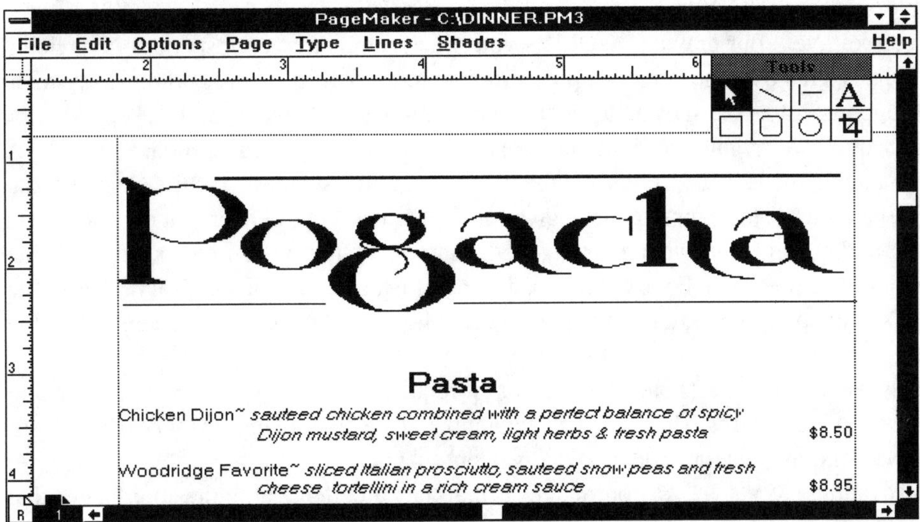

Figure 6.2 A scanned image in a Pagemaker document

draw the object the way the server application expects it to appear. To recreate the drawing, GDI is given the metafile "tape" and told to replay its contents.

As you get started with GDI programming, you'll probably concentrate most of your efforts on learning to draw on physical devices. After all, there are a number of subtle issues that you need to learn about before you can make effective use of display screens and printers. When you are comfortable drawing on these devices, you will then be ready to begin exploring the ways that the pseudodevices can be used to enhance your program's graphic output.

With the variety of devices and pseudodevices that GDI supports, you might be concerned that this somehow translates into a complicated and hard-to-use graphics library. After all, some graphics libraries provide two sets of routines: one for display screens and one for printers. If GDI were like that, you might have *four* different sets of drawing routines to worry about: one each for displays, printers, bitmaps, and metafiles.

But GDI is not like that: GDI has one set of routines for all devices. The **`SetPixel`** routine, for example, draws a single pixel on all devices that GDI supports. The **`Polyline`** routine draws a series of connected lines on any GDI-supported device or pseudodevice. We're going to focus our attention on writing output to the display screen. Nevertheless, you'll find that it applies to all of the different devices that GDI supports.

Drawing Coordinates

Before you can use GDI to create any output, you need to understand how GDI interprets drawing coordinates. GDI gives you quite a bit of control over drawing coordinates. For example, you can ask GDI to use inches, millimeters, or hybrid units that you specify. For the most control over your drawing, GDI lets you specify units that correspond to a device's native pixels. GDI uses the term **mapping mode** to refer to the different coordinate systems that it supports. Table 6.1 shows the eight mapping modes available in GDI

In this chapter, we're going to limit ourselves to GDI's default mapping mode: `MM_TEXT`. In this mapping mode, a unit refers to a pixel—that is, to the smallest "picture element" that a device can draw. This mapping mode gives us the greatest control over graphic output and avoids rounding errors that other mapping modes can create. It is often used for programs that require absolute precision. For example, Aldus PageMaker, a page layout program, uses the `MM_TEXT` mapping mode to ensure that objects aligned on the display screen match the alignment on the printer.

One drawback to `MM_TEXT`, however, is that it requires additional effort to avoid writing device-specific programs. That's the key advantage to the other mapping modes: They provide a way to draw in a more device-independent manner..

An advantage of `MM_TEXT` coordinates is that they are identical to the coordinates that are used for mouse input. This coordinate system is called **client area coordinates**. In cli-

Table 6.1 GDI Mapping Modes

Mapping Mode Name	*1 Logical Unit*	*Inches*	*Millimeters*
`MM_TEXT`	1 pixel	—	—
`MM_HIMETRIC`	0.01 mm	0.000394	0.01
`MM_TWIPS`	1/1440 inches	0.000694	0.0176
`MM_HIENGLISH`	0.001 inches	0.001	0.0254
`MM_LOMETRIC`	0.1 mm	0.00394	0.1
`MM_LOENGLISH`	0.01 inches	0.01	0.254
`MM_ISOTROPIC`	} Scaling based on ratio between two device context		
`MM_ANISOTROPIC`	} attribute values: window and viewport extents		

ent area coordinates, the origin (0,0) is located at the upper-left corner of the client area. Unlike the familiar Cartesian coordinate system, the value of *y* increases as we move *downward*. Figure 6.3 shows the location of the origin and the directions in which *x* and *y* values increase.

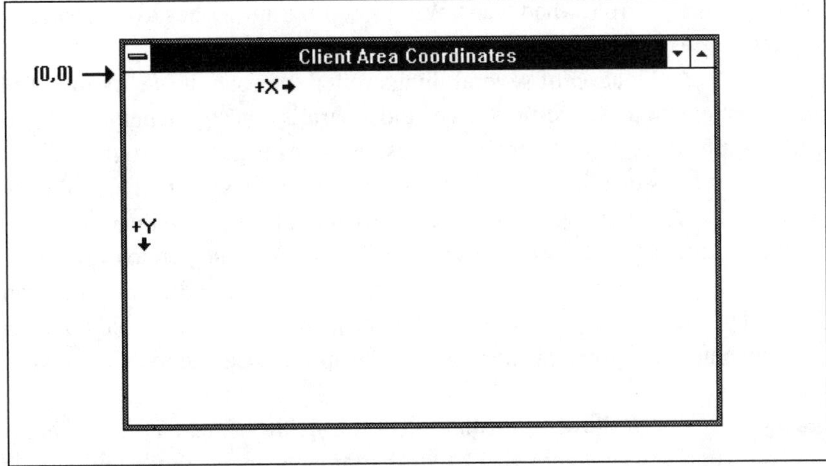

Figure 6.3 GDI's default coordinate system

Logical Drawing Objects

One of the means that GDI uses to achieve device independence is through the use of logical drawing objects. A logical drawing object describes how output should appear: It is a high-level, device-independent *request*. GDI supports the following logical drawing objects: pens (to draw lines), brushes (to fill areas), fonts (to display text), and logical colors (to describe color).

When a logical drawing object is created, it can be used on any device. But the results may differ from one device to another, since devices have different capabilities. For example, a red pen might draw a red line on a 16-color VGA display but draw a black line on a monochrome dot-matrix printer. It's the device driver's job to interpret a logical drawing object in a way that makes sense given a specific device's capabilities.

As we introduce each type of GDI drawing primitive, we'll describe the use of different logical drawing objects, and provide sample code to show how to use them.

The Device Context

To get an idea of how GDI works with different types of devices, let's take a look at a GDI drawing routine: **TextOut**. This routine displays a single line of text on any GDI-supported device. This line of code writes the word "Hello":

```
TextOut (hdc, 10, 10, "Hello", 5);
```

Notice the first parameter: **hdc**. This is a commonly used Hungarian prefix for an important GDI data type: a **handle to a device context.** Recall what we have already said about handles: They are 16-bit unsigned integers used to identify objects. The object identified by this handle plays a key role whenever a Windows program wishes to draw on any device: It is a **device context** (or DC, for short).

A device context is a combination of several things rolled into one. It is a toolbox full of drawing tools, a connection to a specific device, and a permission slip to help GDI control the use of different devices by different programs. GDI never gives a program direct access to a device context. Instead, it provides a handle to identify a specific DC. Like the **TextOut** routine, every GDI drawing routine takes a DC handle as its first parameter.

As a toolbox, the DC is a set of **drawing attributes** that include one pen to draw lines, one brush to fill areas, and one font to display text. At any time while drawing, you can change the tools in a DC to give you, for example, red lines, green areas, and bold text. Put together, drawing attributes give you total control over the appearance and location of your program's output.

Every DC is a toolbox with 27 drawing attributes. By storing these in the DC, GDI hides complexity from you. There is a slight drawback to this approach, but we think you'll agree in the long run that it makes GDI easier to work with.

The drawback is that, until you become familiar with what they do for you, hidden attributes can be confusing. For example, consider the **TextOut** routine. We'll add some comments to explain the parameters:

```
TextOut (hdc,      /*  Handle to DC.        */
         10,       /*  X-location of text.  */
         10,       /*  Y-location of text.  */
         "Hello",  /*  Text to display.     */
         5);       /*  Text length.         */
```

From this code, can you tell what color the letters will be? Will they be red, blue, or black? And what type of font will be used—will it be 14-point bold Times New Roman, or 24-point italicized Arial? Because this information is part of the DC, you can't answer these questions by simply reading this line of code.

When the **TextOut** routine draws, it plucks the drawing attributes it needs from the DC. These attributes determine the appearance and location of the displayed text (including text color and font). As we introduce the different GDI drawing routines, we'll describe the DC attributes that each set of routines depends upon.

By hiding their drawing attributes in a DC, GDI routines can get by with a minimum number of parameters. In practical terms, this means less typing for you when you write code that calls GDI. After all, drawing attributes tend to stay the same from one call to the next. To get an idea of the work that might be required in a world without a DC, consider what the **TextOut** function might look like:

```
/* Mythical TextOut in a world without a DC. */
TextOut (10,          /*  X-location of text.     */
         10,          /*  Y-location of text.     */
         "Hello",     /*  Text to display.        */
         5,           /*  Length of text.         */
         coFore,      /*  Foreground text color.  */
         coBack,      /*  Background text color.  */
         hClip,       /*  Clipping Region.        */
         hPalette,    /*  Color Palette.          */
         hFont,       /*  Text Font.              */
         iSpace,      /*  Intercharacter spacing.*/
         mmMapMode,   /*  Mapping mode.           */
         xyViewExt,   /*  Viewport extent.        */
         xyViewOrg,   /*  Viewport origin.        */
         xyWinExt,    /*  Window extent.          */
         xyWinOrg);   /*  Window origin.          */
```

Even without knowing the meaning of each drawing attribute, you can tell that 15 is a lot more than the five parameters that **TextOut** actually needs. In a world without DCs, you'd have a lot of work to say "Hello."

What's in a DC? Table 6.2 lists all the drawing attributes in a DC. For your convenience, we have indicated the type of primitive that uses each attribute.

Table 6.2 Drawing Attributes in a DC

Drawing Attribute	*Default Value*	*Lines*	*Filled Areas*	*Text*	*Raster*	*Comments*
Arc Direction	Counterclock wise	x				Win32 only
Background color	White	x	x	x		Styled pen, hatch brush, text
Background mode	`OPAQUE`	x	x	x		On/off switch
Brush handle	White brush		x		x	Filled areas
Brush origin	(0,0)		x		x	Hatch and dithered brushes
Clipping region handle	Entire surface	x	x	x	x	
Color Adjustment					x	Win32 only
Color palette handle	Default palette	x	x	x		
Current pen position	(0,0)	x				For `LineTo` routine
Drawing mode	`R2_COPYPEN`	x	x			Boolean mixing
Font handle	System font			x		
Font Mapper Flag	Yes			x		Use device specific fonts?
Graphics Mode	Win16 mode	x	x	x	x	Use world transform and other Win32 enhancements?
Intercharacter spacing	0			x		
Mapping mode	`MM_TEXT`	x	x	x	x	One unit = 1 pixel
Miter Limit	10.0	x				For paths, ratio of line width to join width
Pen handle	Black pen	x	x			
Polygon-filling mode	Alternate		x			For `Polygon` routine

(continued)

Table 6.2 Drawing Attributes in a DC *(Continued)*

Drawing Attribute	*Default Value*	*Lines*	*Filled Areas*	*Text*	*Raster*	*Comments*
Stretching mode	Black on white				x	For `StretchBlt` routine
Text alignment	Left and top			x		
Text color	Black		x	x		Foreground color for text and for monochrome pattern brushes
Text justification	0,0			x		Break extra and character extra
Viewport extent	(1,1)	x	x	x	x	Coordinate mapping
Viewport origin	(0,0)	x	x	x	x	Coordinate mapping
Window extent	(1,1)	x	x	x	x	Coordinate mapping
Window origin	(0,0)	x	x	x	x	Coordinate mapping
World Transform	Off	x	x	x	x	Coordinate transform that enables rotation

Not every drawing attribute in the DC is used by every drawing routine. For example, the text color is never used to draw lines. Instead, each drawing routine takes the attributes it needs from the DC. Let's look at the other roles played by the DC.

The second role of a DC is that it connects a program to a specific drawing surface. For example, a program that wants to draw on the system display must gain access to a DC for the system display (we'll describe how this is done in a moment). To draw on a printer, or on a pseudodevice like a bitmap, a program obtains a DC to connect to each of these drawing surfaces.

The connection that the DC provides is a logical connection and not a physical one. Windows, after all, is a multitasking system. If programs had direct access to the physical device, it would cause confusion both for the user and for the Windows programs. As each program fought to maintain control of a given device, the result would be mixed up graphical nonsense.

To understand what we mean by a physical connection, consider the way an MS-DOS program like Quattro Pro works. When it draws on the display, it writes directly to the memory buffers on the video adapter board. It directly manipulates the hardware registers to cause the hardware to perform the necessary tricks to display the desired spreadsheet or graph. To support this capability, it requires a private device driver so that it can tell the difference between the CGA, VGA, and 8514/a display cards. Lotus 1-2-3 is able to do this because MS-DOS is a single-tasking operating system. There isn't any danger that other programs might be disrupted.

But Windows is multitasking, so programs cannot access a physical output device without disrupting other programs. Instead, a Windows program must use the logical connection represented by the DC. All Windows programs use this approach, so that GDI can resolve the conflicts that might otherwise disrupt the system when two programs access the same device. This introduces the third role of a DC: its role as a permission slip.

To avoid conflicts on shared devices, a DC is a permission slip that a program must have before it can draw on any device. The permission system works in one of two ways, depending on the type of device. On hard-copy devices, the process is known as **spooling**. On video display devices, the permission system is called **clipping**.

On printers and plotters, GDI borrows a technique from mainframe computers: Output is spooled to disk. The Windows spooler, also known as the Print Manager, plays the role of a traffic cop to direct the flow of output to hard-copy devices. Otherwise, the output of one program might get mixed in with the pages of another. For spooled output, the DC helps GDI keep different print jobs separate.

On the display screen, Windows takes a different approach to separate the output from different programs. The method is called **clipping**. Clipping involves the creation of imaginary fences around a program's drawing area. To paraphrase an old saying: "Good clipping fences make good Windows programs."

My next-door neighbor has a fence around his yard that prevents his dog from running away. The dog can go where he wants inside the yard, but cannot stray into my yard. The fences that GDI creates provide the same type of boundary enforcement. When a program wants to draw in a window, it gets a DC from the Window Manager that has a built-in fence around the window's client area. Inside the fence, a program is free to draw what it wants. But the fence prevents the program from letting its drawing stray.

An example might clarify exactly what we mean by clipping. Figure 6.4 shows two programs sharing the display screen: NOTEPAD and CLOCK. Before either program draws, a fence is built to prevent the program from drawing outside its client area.

The NOTEPAD program's fence forms a rectangle. Notice that the fence prevents NOTEPAD from drawing on the face of the CLOCK. It also prevents NOTEPAD from drawing on the nonclient area of its own window. After all, like most Windows programs, NOTEPAD doesn't maintain the nonclient area of its window; it leaves that work to Windows.

The clipping for CLOCK is a little more complex. But we know that the clipping works because CLOCK's sweeping second hand doesn't brush NOTEPAD away. Instead, the clock hands appear to go "behind" the NOTEPAD window. Figure 6.5 shows the shape of the fence that prevents NOTEPAD from drawing outside its client area.

You might imagine that CLOCK has its work cut out for it to avoid drawing on NOTEPAD. In fact, CLOCK doesn't even know that NOTEPAD is present. The DC that CLOCK gets from the Window Manager is the key to this magic. When CLOCK calls different GDI

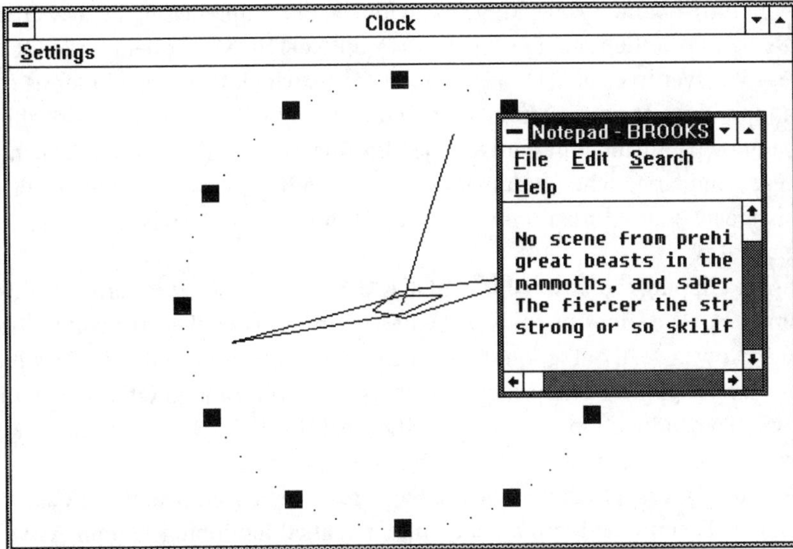

Figure 6.4 Output from Clock and Notepad are kept separate through clipping

drawing routines, the DC handle lets GDI check the location of the fence to make sure that no drawing is done out of bounds. Hence, there is very little work that CLOCK must do; GDI does it all.

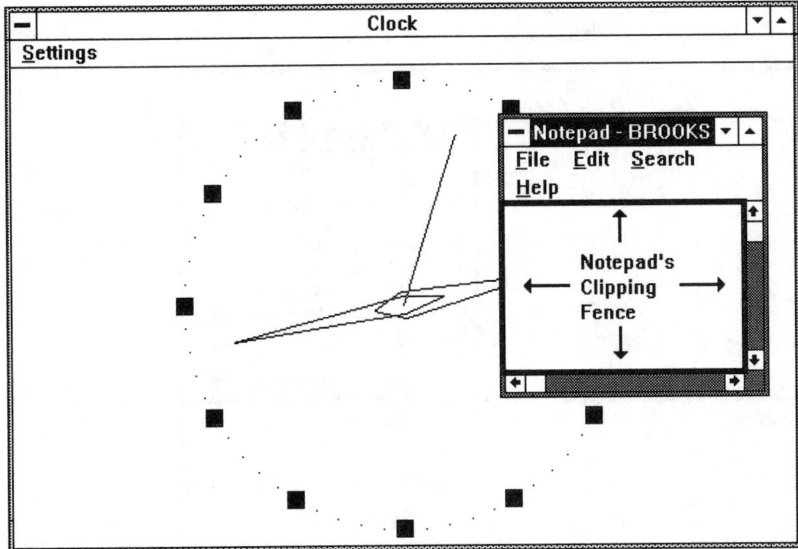

Figure 6.5 The shape of the fence around Notepad's client area

How does GDI perform boundary checking? Let's look at the simpler case: the way GDI clips NOTEPAD's output to the rectangle that makes up NOTEPAD's client area. GDI works with the device driver to establish a rectangular fence, which is defined in terms of four coordinates: top side, left side, bottom side, and right side. The boundaries of this fence are part of a drawing attribute in the DC: the **clipping region**. Every GDI drawing routine checks these boundaries when it draws. As you can tell by looking at the NOTEPAD window, this means that words might be chopped in half. But this is necessary to make windowing a reality.

The more complex clipping we observe in CLOCK can be understood in terms of this simpler case. Namely, GDI defines clipping for CLOCK in terms of the four rectangles shown in Figure 6.6. Now instead of the four boundaries for one rectangle, GDI works with 16 boundaries for four rectangles. The principle is the same, even though GDI does four times as much work. To handle clipping like this, GDI treats each drawing operation like four separate drawing operations, with one for each clipping rectangle.

This complex clipping gives us a clue to how GDI stores clipping information. A set of one or more rectangles is combined into a data structure called a clipping region. As we mentioned earlier, a clipping region is an attribute that is part of the DC. This means that clipping can be performed on any GDI device. A clipping region might contain the entire drawing surface. Or, as we have seen, it might contain a set of one or more rectangles.

While clipping can be done on any device, clipping on the display screen is special. The reason is that Windows provides the clipping information to keep one program from accidentally overwriting another program's output. The part of Windows that takes care of display screen clipping is the part of Windows responsible for creating windows: the Window Manager.

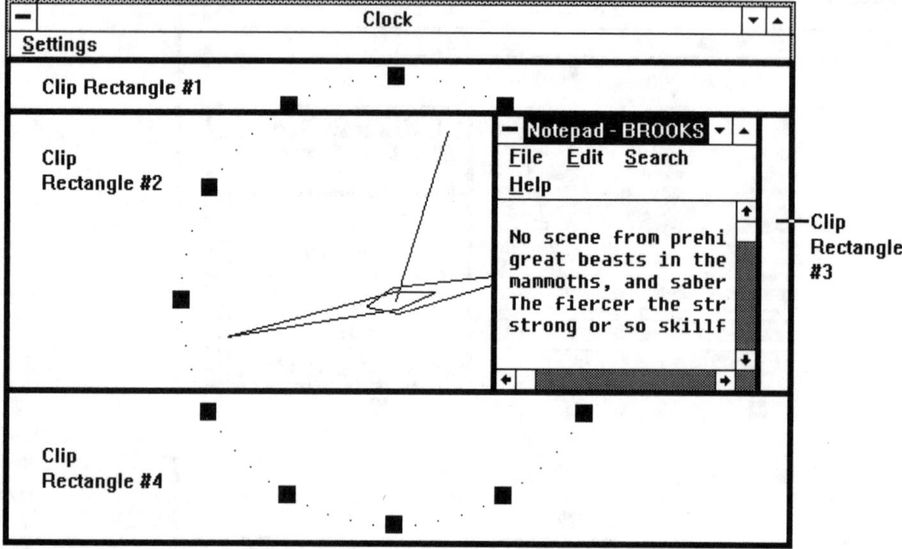

Figure 6.6 The four clip rectangles for Clock

Clipping and the Window Manager

From our discussion of the interaction between NOTEPAD and CLOCK, it is clear that GDI's ability to perform clipping is what makes windowing possible. It lets programs share the display screen without requiring programs to worry about stepping on each other's toes.

Although GDI routines provide the clipping service, GDI itself does not set window boundaries. That job belongs to the Window Manager. When we introduced the Window Manager in Chapter 1, we said it was responsible for the user interface. Since the user interface resides on the display screen, the Window Manager builds and maintains all the display screen "fences."

The Window Manager owns a set of DCs for drawing on the system display. When a program wants to draw in a window, it borrows one of these DCs. Before it lends a DC to a program, the Window Manager installs a clipping region. There are three different Window Manager routines that a program can use to borrow a DC. For each of them, a different clipping region is installed in the DC. These routines are shown in Table 6.3, along with the routine that is used to return the DC to the Window Manager. When a program borrows a DC from the Window Manager, it must be careful to return the DC when it is finished.

Table 6.3 WinAPI Routines to Borrow and Return System Display DCs

Borrowing Routine	*Returning Routine*	*Description*
`BeginPaint`	**`EndPaint`**	Clip to invalid part of client area
`GetDC`	**`ReleaseDC`**	Clip to entire client area
`GetWindowDC`	**`ReleaseDC`**	Clip to entire window (client and nonclient areas)

Figure 6.7 gives an example of how clipping is set for each of these three routines.

The first routine, **`BeginPaint`**, allows a program to respond to requests by the Window Manager to draw in a window or repair damage that has been done to part of a window. The Window Manager sends the **`WM_PAINT`** message to let a program know that a window needs to be repaired. This message plays a central role in the maintenance of a window's client area.

The second routine, **`GetDC`**, allows a program to draw in the client area of a window. The clipping fence keeps output in the client area, even if another program's window is lying on top of the client area, as we saw in the CLOCK-NOTEPAD example. This routine is used for most drawing *outside* the **`WM_PAINT`** message. For example, in response to a **`WM_CHAR`** message, we might wish to echo the character typed.

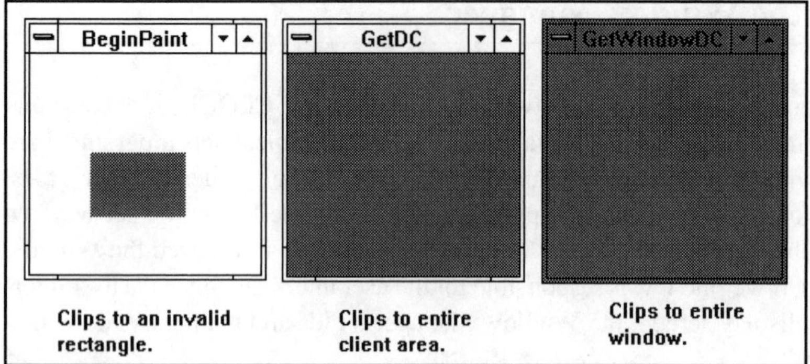

Figure 6.7 Three ways that the Window Manager sets clipping

The third routine, **GetWindowDC**, sets clipping to allow drawing anywhere in a window, including the nonclient area. This routine is called by the Window Manager itself to draw the nonclient parts of a window. After all, a Windows program typically does not do this work itself, but lets the default window procedure take care of it.

From this conceptual discussion—and the accompanying figure—you perhaps now have a sense that there's some connection between a device context, some WinAPI functions, and the clipping area into which drawing can occur. To show you exactly what that connection means, it might help to look at some code. Before looking at an OWL program that draws, however, I should start by describing the support that OWL provides for drawing with GDI.

OWL's Support for GDI Drawing

The OWL classes that have been built around GDI make up a class hierarchy that is separate from the windowing classes discussed in earlier chapters. In general, these classes make up a very thin layer over the native WinAPI drawing calls. This is not to say that OWL doesn't make things easier. It's just that OWL doesn't add any new capabilities to what GDI does for you.

The layout of OWL's GDI classes illustrates the structure of GDI system objects. In particular, there are three basic types of OWL GDI classes: (a) the classes (derived from **TDC**), which wrap around the various types of GDI device contexts, (b) the DC attribute objects, which include class derived from **TGDIObject** (except for **TBitmap**), and (c) the bitmap storage objects, which consist of the remaining classes—**TIcon**, **TCursor**, **TDib** and **TBitmap**[1]. The use of objects in the second and third groups will be covered in the

[1] Conceptually, these classes could get their own base virtual class, named something like **TBitmapObject**. In fact, at the WinAPI implementation level, only two have any real similarities: **TCursor** and **TIcon**.

remaining chapters on using GDI. For now, it makes sense to delve into the most important group—the device context classes.

The OWL class hierarchy shows the different kinds of DCs that GDI supports. Here is a list of these types, along with details about each:

OWL Class	*Corresponding WinAPI Function*	*Description*
TClientDC	**GetDC(HWindow)**	Draw in a window's client area in response to any message except **WM_PAINT**. See **TPaintDC**.
TDesktopDC	**GetWindowDC** and **GetDesktopWindow**	Draw on the desktop window.
TDibDC	**CreateDC("DIB", ...)**	Use GDI functions to draw into a device independent bitmap (DIB) bitmap.
TIC	**CreateIC**	Create an information context, for use when querying about a device but not for drawing. It was intended as a cheaper alternative to a DC, but for most devices the two objects are the same.
TMemoryDC	**CreateCompatibleDC**	Create a DC for **TBitmap** bitmaps.
TMetaFileDC	**CreateMetaFile**	Create a metafile for storing a sequence of GDI drawing calls.
TPaintDC	**BeginPaint**	Draw in a window's client area in response to a **WM_PAINT** message. See **TClientDC**.
TPrintDC	**CreateDC(<driver>, ...)**	Creates a connection for sending output to a printer.
TPrintPreviewDC	n/a	Creates a mechanism for mapping between a display screen and a printer.
TScreenDC	**GetWindowDC(0)**	Draw anywhere on the display screen, including over other windows. Fun, but neither useful nor polite.
TWindowDC	**GetWindowDC(HWindow)**	Draw anywhere in a window—includes both client area and nonclient area.

This table includes the corresponding WinAPI function so that you can refer to the WinAPI help files or documentation for more details. In general, accessing a particular device involves creating the corresponding DC object, and then drawing away. When a DC is created, it has a default set of drawing attributes so you don't even need to set these up yourself (although in most cases you will).

For drawing in a window, two DC classes are generally used: **TClientDC** and **TPaintDC**. The rules for using these are quite strict and seem fairly arbitrary: When drawing in response to a **WM_PAINT** message, always use **TPaintDC**. All other times, use **TClientDC**. Fortunately, the **TWindow** class captures **WM_PAINT** for you, then creates a **TPaintDC** and passes a reference to it in a call to **TWindow::Paint**. Handling this message correctly, then, involves having your window class override this single function.

The **WM_PAINT** message is an important, yet quirky message. To give you an idea of the quirks that are involved, the next section has a program named WM_PAINT.EXE to show how this message doesn't produce the results that are sometimes expected. Before discussing this program, though, I'd like to cover some of the basics of the **WM_PAINT** message itself.

The WM_PAINT Message

Windows' event-driven architecture means that a Windows program is structured as a set of window objects, where each object handles a set of messages[2]. The role of some messages is obvious from its name: **WM_MOUSEMOVE** relates mouse movement information, **WM_CHAR** tells about character input, **WM_CREATE** and **WM_DESTROY** notify you when a window has been created or destroyed. These are easy to understand because each relates to things that most programmers have experience with.

The **WM_PAINT** message is different. Put simply, it tells a window that some portion of it has been damaged. How does a window get damaged? Like a bull in a china shop, the user creates holes while tromping across the display screen: Windows are moved, resized, opened, and closed. Dialog boxes are brought up and dismissed, and data gets scrolled inside different windows. Each window must repair any damages caused by the user. How? On receipt of this message, a window object will redraw the portion of its client area that has been damaged.

This message is puzzling to many first-time Windows programmers because most operating systems[3] buffer an output area—like a window—for you. For example, multiple dif-

---

[2] The subject of window objects and message response functions has already been covered in previous chapters.

[3] To programmers experienced with event-driven, GUI environments, however, this is not a new concept, and this message is definitely not puzzling. If you have experience with systems like the Apple Macintosh, OS/2 Presentation Manager, DRG's GEM, or Motif, then you are familiar with the role of **WM_PAINT**.

ferent MS-DOS programs can run in multiple MS-DOS boxes under Windows. None has to rewrite the output buffer, since the operating system takes care of this for you. So why must a Windows program redraw its output area?

While it is *possible* for an operating system like Windows to buffer output for you, it's a matter of history that Windows doesn't. Windows was born in a time of relative RAM-scarcity when a typical Windows computer had a maximum of 1-megabyte of memory. Buffering output for each application requires lots of RAM—a single 640 by 480 monochrome bitmap, for example, takes up 37.5K. A 16-color version of the same bitmap consumes 150K. Multiply that by three or four applications in the system, and you've eaten up your entire address space.

In fact, there are cases when Windows is able to anticipate that an object—such as a dialog box or a menu—will overwrite a portion of a window for a brief period of time. In such cases—for the sake of performance—Windows takes a snapshot of the area about to be overwritten. When the short-term guest goes away, Windows redraws the damaged part of the window *without* generating a **WM_PAINT** message.

This type of help, however, is the exception rather than the rule. The rule is a window object must be able to respond at any time to a request from Windows—in the form of a **WM_PAINT** message—asking it to repair the damaged part of its client area.

The easiest way to deal with this situation is to override the **TWindow::Paint** member function and redraw every object within a window. This may mean that you're redrawing undamaged parts of your window along with the damaged parts, but—until you start drawing several *hundred* objects—the overhead associated with this is actually quite small.

Windows' Window Manager treats the **TPaintDC**-type DC in a special way. It *only* allows drawing to occur in the damaged part of a window. This is done using the clipping capability described earlier in this chapter. This is done for two reasons: performance and user-perception. The performance reason is based on the fact that video RAM is very slow, so the fewer pixels touched, the faster the drawing. The user-perception reason is that if a program touches every pixel in the client area, it can cause the window's contents to blink. Although it sounds silly, it's in fact very annoying to a user to have a window that's blinking on and off like a Times Square neon sigh. Windows' conservative drawing policy, then, helps your program run faster and minimizes screen blink.

To get a better idea for the effect of a conservative **WM_PAINT** policy, consider the program in Figure 6.8. The client area contains four sets of patterns: a black rectangle and several hatched 'L'-shaped areas. When this program started running, the client area was the size of the black rectangle. Then the window was resized three times. Each of the four different kinds of areas was drawn in response to a different **WM_PAINT** message. Here's the code to the program; further explanation will continue after the listing.

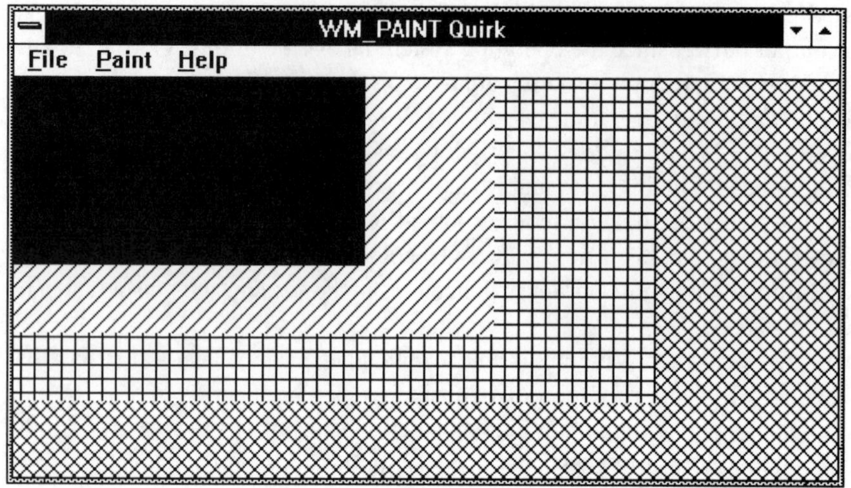

Figure 6.8 A quirk caused by the Window Manager's conservative paint policy

WM_PAINT.CPP

```
//
// WM_PAINT.CPP  Demonstrates how the all-important WM_PAINT message
//               message draws in a conservative - and sometimes
//               unexpected - way.
//
#include <owl\owlpch.h>
#include "wm_paint.h"

//
// Brush List Class

const int MaxBrush = 3;
const int MinBrush = 0;

class BrushList
    {
  public:
    BrushList (BOOL bColor);
    ~BrushList();
    BOOL   IsColor() {return bColor;}
    TBrush Next();

  private:
    BOOL     bColor;
    int      iCurrent;
    TBrush * tbr[4];
    };

BrushList::BrushList(BOOL bColor)
    {
    if (bColor)
        {   // Create color brushes
```

```
        tbr[0] = new TBrush(TColor::LtBlue);
        tbr[1] = new TBrush(TColor::LtRed);
        tbr[2] = new TBrush(TColor::LtGreen);
        tbr[3] = new TBrush(TColor::Black);
        }
    else
        {   // Create hatch brushes
        tbr[0] = new TBrush(TColor::Black);
        tbr[1] = new TBrush(TColor::Black,HS_BDIAGONAL);
        tbr[2] = new TBrush(TColor::Black,HS_CROSS);
        tbr[3] = new TBrush(TColor::Black,HS_DIAGCROSS);
        }

    iCurrent = 0;
    BrushList::bColor = bColor;
    }

BrushList::~BrushList()
    {
    delete tbr[0];
    delete tbr[1];
    delete tbr[2];
    delete tbr[3];
    }

TBrush BrushList::Next()
    {
    // Increment (or roll) index
    iCurrent = (iCurrent == MaxBrush) ? MinBrush : iCurrent + 1;

    // Give out next brush in list.
    return *tbr[iCurrent];
    }

//
// Main window
class DFrame : public TFrameWindow
    {
  public:
    DFrame(char * title);
    ~DFrame();
    void EvInitMenu(HMENU);
    void CmFileExit();
    void CmPaintColor();
    void CmPaintMono();
    void CmHelpAbout();
    void Paint (TDC&, BOOL, TRect&);

  private:
    BrushList * ClientBrushes;

  DECLARE_RESPONSE_TABLE (DFrame);
    };

DEFINE_RESPONSE_TABLE1 (DFrame, TFrameWindow)
  EV_WM_INITMENU,
  EV_COMMAND(CM_FILEEXIT, CmFileExit),
  EV_COMMAND(CM_PAINT_COLOR, CmPaintColor),
  EV_COMMAND(CM_PAINT_MONO, CmPaintMono),
  EV_COMMAND(CM_HELPABOUT, CmHelpAbout),
END_RESPONSE_TABLE;
```

```
void DFrame::EvInitMenu(HMENU menu)
    {
    WORD wState;

    // Set/clear checkmark for Paint.Color menu item
    wState = (ClientBrushes->IsColor()) ? MF_CHECKED : MF_UNCHECKED;
    ::CheckMenuItem (menu, CM_PAINT_COLOR, wState);

    // Set/clear checkmark for Paint.Monochrome menu item
    wState = (ClientBrushes->IsColor()) ? MF_UNCHECKED : MF_CHECKED;
    ::CheckMenuItem (menu, CM_PAINT_MONO, wState);
    }

DFrame::DFrame(char * title) : TFrameWindow(0, title)
    {
    ClientBrushes = new BrushList (TRUE);
    }

DFrame::~DFrame()
    {
    delete ClientBrushes;
    }

void DFrame::CmFileExit()
    {
    CloseWindow(0); // Cause application to terminate
    }

void DFrame::CmPaintColor()
    {
    delete ClientBrushes;
    ClientBrushes = new BrushList (TRUE);
    }

void DFrame::CmPaintMono()
    {
    delete ClientBrushes;
    ClientBrushes = new BrushList (FALSE);
    }

void DFrame::CmHelpAbout()
  {
  MessageBox("WM_PAINT Drawing Demonstration\n\n"
             "'Borland C++ 4.0 Programming\n"
             "  for Windows', by Paul Yao", Title);
  }

void DFrame::Paint (TDC& dc, BOOL, TRect&)
    {
    // Get window's client rectangle coordinates.
    TRect trClient = GetClientRect();

    // Select next brush for drawing.
    dc.SelectObject(ClientBrushes->Next());

    // Try filling entire client area with selected brush.
    dc.PatBlt(0, 0, trClient.right, trClient.bottom, PATCOPY);
    }

//
// Application object
class DApp : public TApplication
```

```
    {
  public:
    DApp() : TApplication() {}
    void InitMainWindow();
    };

void DApp::InitMainWindow()
    {
    SetMainWindow (new DFrame("WM_PAINT Quirk"));
    MainWindow->AssignMenu("MAIN");
    MainWindow->SetIcon(this, "SNAPSHOT");
    }

//
// Application main entry point.
OwlMain(int, char **)
    {
    return DApp().Run();
    }
```

WM_PAINT.H

```
#define CM_FILEEXIT     100
#define CM_PAINT_COLOR  200
#define CM_PAINT_MONO   201
#define CM_HELPABOUT    300
```

WM_PAINT.RC

```
#include "wm_paint.h"

snapshot icon wm_paint.ico

main MENU
{
 POPUP "&File"
 {
  MENUITEM "E&xit", CM_FILEEXIT
 }

 POPUP "&Paint"
 {
  MENUITEM "&Color", CM_PAINT_COLOR
  MENUITEM "&Monochrome", CM_PAINT_MONO
 }

 POPUP "&Help"
 {
  MENUITEM "&About...", CM_HELPABOUT
 }

}
```

WM_PAINT.DEF

```
EXETYPE WINDOWS

CODE MOVEABLE DISCARDABLE
DATA MULTIPLE MOVEABLE

HEAPSIZE   512
STACKSIZE 8192
```

DYNA16.MAK

```
#  MAKE file for Win16 API using dynamic BIDS,
#  OWL and C-runtime libraries.
#
#    C> make -fstatic16.mak
#

.AUTODEPEND
CC = -c -H -H"owl\owlpch.h" -ml -R -vi -WS -X-
CD = -D_RTLDLL;_BIDSDLL;_OWLDLL;_OWLPCH;
INC = -I\BC4\INCLUDE
LIB = -L\BC4\LIB

wm_paint.exe :  wm_paint.obj wm_paint.res
  tlink -c -C -Twe $(LIB) @dyna16.lnk
  brc wm_paint.res wm_paint.exe
wm_paint.obj :  wm_paint.cpp
  bcc $(CC) $(CD) wm_paint.cpp

wm_paint.res :  wm_paint.rc wm_paint.ico wm_paint.h
  brc $(INC) -31 -R wm_paint.rc
```

DYNA16.LNK

```
\bc4\lib\c0wl.obj+
wm_paint.obj
wm_paint,wm_paint
\bc4\lib\bidsi.lib+
\bc4\lib\owlwi.lib+
\bc4\lib\import.lib+
\bc4\lib\crtldll.lib
wm_paint.def
```

DYNA32.MAK

```
#  MAKE file for Win32 API using dynamic BIDS,
#  OWL and C-runtime libraries.
#
#    C> make -fdyna32.mak
#
```

```
.AUTODEPEND
CC = -c -H -H\""owl\owlpch.h\"" -p- -R -vi -W -X-
CD = -D_RTLDLL;_BIDSDLL;_OWLDLL;_OWLPCH;
INC = -I\BC4\INCLUDE
LIB = -L\BC4\LIB

wm_paint.exe :  wm_paint.obj wm_paint.res
  tlink32 -aa -c -Tpe $(LIB) @dyna32.lnk
  brc32 wm_paint.res wm_paint.exe

wm_paint.obj :  wm_paint.cpp
  bcc32 $(CC) $(CD) wm_paint.cpp

wm_paint.res :  wm_paint.rc wm_paint.ico wm_paint.h
  brc32 $(INC) -w32 -R wm_paint.rc
```

DYNA32.LNK

```
\bc4\lib\c0w32.obj+
wm_paint.obj
wm_paint,wm_paint
\bc4\lib\bidsfi.lib+
\bc4\lib\owlwfi.lib+
\bc4\lib\import32.lib+
\bc4\lib\cw32i.lib
wm_paint.def
```

This program creates a list of four GDI brushes—in OWL terms, four **TBrush** objects. The brushes are put in an array within a **BrushList** type object. Each time a **WM_PAINT** message is received, the program tries to fill its client area with a different brush. In this code fragment, the call to **GetClientRect** gets the coordinates for the client area. The call to **SelectObject** connects the "next" brush to the DC provided to the **DFrame::Paint** member by **TWindow::EvPaint**. The call to **PatBlt** simply requests GDI to fill the client area with the selected brush color.

```
void DFrame::Paint (TDC& dc, BOOL, TRect&)
    {
    // Get window's client rectangle coordinates.
    TRect trClient = GetClientRect();

    // Select next brush for drawing.
    dc.SelectObject(ClientBrushes->Next());

    // Try filling entire client area with selected brush.
    dc.PatBlt(0, 0, trClient.right, trClient.bottom, PATCOPY);
    }
```

The program is called "WM_PAINT Quirk" because it shows the result of the Window Manager's conservative paint policy. The paint policy is simple: When part of a window has been damaged, a **WM_PAINT** message requests that the window be repaired. The conservative part of the policy is that drawing can only occur in the damaged part of the window.

In a sense, this program is not typical of the ones you write. After all, if you are trying to fill a window with a single color, you probably *don't* want the type of pattern in the illustration. What this *does* reflect, however, is a problem that can occur when a lag occurs between the current contents of a window and the internal state of a program.

What you see in Figure 6.8, then, is the result of resizing the window three times. Each of the three successive L's was caused by a different **WM_PAINT** message. If you stop to think about it, it makes sense that redrawing only occurs for pixels that had not been drawn before. This is what I mean by a "conservative paint policy." Type in and experiment with this program to get a better idea for the types of user actions which cause a **WM_PAINT** message[4]. To help you get started, here's a list of user-actions, an indication about whether it results in a **WM_PAINT** message, and a brief explanation..

User Action	*WM_Paint?*	*Explanation*
Start an application	Yes	Need to draw window at application startup
Terminate an application	No	Only applications left on the screen are told to paint. The terminating application does not get a request to paint.
Move a window	No	Unless part of the window had been lying outside the display screen, no paint message is needed when a window is moved. Instead, GDI's **BitBlt** function is called to move the pixels from one part of the screen to another. However, if another window was underneath the window being moved, it would be told to repair itself.
Make a window larger	Yes	The "damaged" part of the window corresponds to the new area being exposed.
Make a window smaller	No	Although part of the client area gets clipped away, what's left doesn't have to be drawn again since it's presumably still valid.
Maximize a window	Yes	The contents of the client area are copied to the upper left corner of the maximized window area, and a paint request is placed for the L shaped area that is newly exposed.

[4] All programs in this book are available in machine-readable form. Please consult the information on the last page of this book.

User Action	*WM_Paint?*	*Explanation*
Minimize a window	No	New pixels are not exposed, so there's no reason to paint—except that in OWL the **TWindow** object gets a **WM_PAINT** for drawing the application's icon.
Display then hide a menu	No	The Window Manager takes a snapshot of the area below a menu, then restores that area when the menu disappears.
Display then hide a dialog box	No	As with menus, the Window Manager takes a snapshot* before a dialog box visits on top of another window. If the dialog box gets moved when it's visible, however, the Window Manager revokes this privilege and *will* generate a paint message when it disappears.

* Using the CS_SAVEBITS window class style bits. I refer to this feature as the "in-law" bit, since it's set in hopes that the visitor—presumably your in-laws—don't stay long. My in-laws are nice, though.

It's important to keep in mind that the **WM_PAINT** message means "Your window *has* been damaged. You must repaint now." There is no easy way for an application to find out that a window *will* be damaged. Developers sometimes wonder about that in hopes of preventing damage before it occurs. Instead of pursuing this fruitless path, you're better off building your window objects to respond to requests to paint in the way that Windows—and OWL—expect.

Much of this introduction to GDI has been fairly high-level and conceptual. For the next few chapters, I'll focus on a particular set of GDI drawing functions with the idea of giving each area fairly in-depth coverage. These next few chapters set the pace for the rest of the book, in which I'll provide the theoretical discussion of what the system does, then back it up with some interesting code examples. In the next chapter, I'm going to start very simply with a discussion of drawing pixels and a type of drawing object that GDI doesn't natively support, namely markers.

7

Pixels and Markers

The fundamental unit of drawing in a graphical environment is a **pixel**, a term which refers to the individual dots on a display screen or on a printed page. To get started with GDI drawing, this chapter introduces pixel drawing with GDI's **`SetPixel`** and **`SetPixelV`** functions. Pixels have two attributes: color and location. The first program in this chapter, STARS, selects random colors and random locations to draw pixels that produce an effect like stars twinkling in the night sky. The second program, MARKERS, gets more serious about location. It accepts mouse input to draw **markers**. Support for markers is something that Microsoft apparently intended for Windows, but it somehow never got implemented. A marker is a symbol that highlights a specific point. While MARKERS just draws markers in response to mouse clicks, it shows a set of drawing routines that you can use for your own graphic applications.

Figure 7.1 is a snapshot of STARS running. In operation, tiny stars appear in random colors and at random locations. Although the primary purpose of STARS is to show pixel drawing, it also shows how to do background processing by overriding the OWL class idle time functions. Here are the source files to STARS.

STARS.CPP

```
//
// STARS.CPP   Demonstrates drawing in a window for:
//             (1) WM_PAINT for refreshing a dirty window,
//             (2) WM_ERASEBKGND for window erasing, and
//             (3) Non-WM_PAINT drawing.
//             Also shows idle time processing (pseudo-
//             threads for Win16), and enumerating a device's
//             colors.
//
```

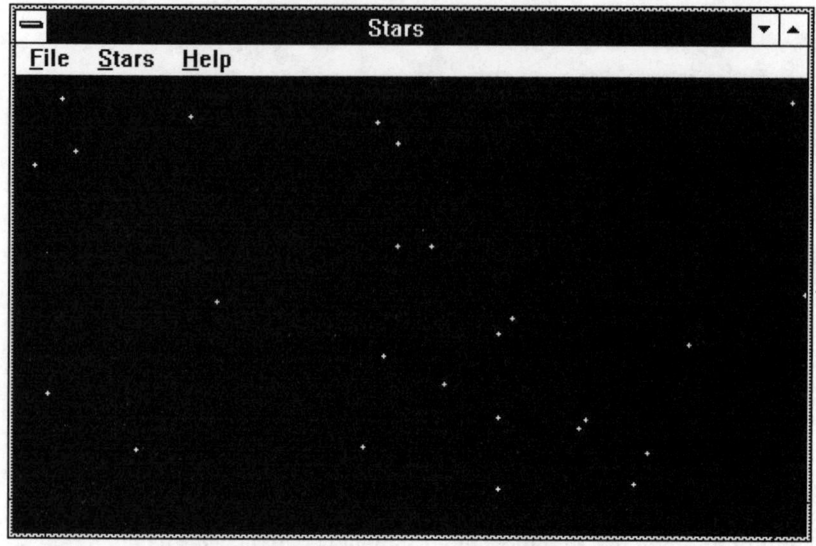

Figure 7.1 Random stars drawn by `SetPixel`

```
#include <owl\owlpch.h>
#include <classlib\arrays.h>
#include "stars.h"

DEFINE_RESPONSE_TABLE1 (DFrame, TFrameWindow)
  EV_WM_ERASEBKGND,
  EV_WM_INITMENU,
  EV_WM_SIZE,
  EV_COMMAND(CM_FILEEXIT, CmFileExit),
  EV_COMMAND(CM_TWINKLE, CmStarTwinkle),
  EV_COMMAND(CM_SLOW, CmStarSlow),
  EV_COMMAND(CM_MODERATE, CmStarModerate),
  EV_COMMAND(CM_FAST, CmStarFast),
  EV_COMMAND(CM_TINY, CmStarTiny),
  EV_COMMAND(CM_AVERAGE, CmStarAverage),
  EV_COMMAND(CM_LARGE, CmStarLarge),
  EV_COMMAND(CM_HELPABOUT, CmHelpAbout),
END_RESPONSE_TABLE;

DFrame::DFrame(char * title) : TFrameWindow(0, title)
    {
    bTwinkle = TRUE;
    cxWidth  = GetSystemMetrics(SM_CXFULLSCREEN);
    cyHeight = GetSystemMetrics(SM_CYFULLSCREEN);
    PaceCount = 0;
    Pace = CM_SLOW;
    Size = CM_TINY;
    crBackground = TColor::Black;
    }
```

```
    {
    delete [] NightSky;
    }

void DFrame::SetupWindow()
    {
    TFrameWindow::SetupWindow();     // Create WinAPI window

    NightSky = new STAR[STARCOUNT]; // Allocate star buffer

    randomize();  // Start random number generator

    // Build list of available device colors by asking
    // for list of all device pens. Color information
    // comes along as well.
    TClientDC dc(HWindow);

    // Build array of available colors. Actual list work
    // is done in ObjEnumProc. This function gets called
    // by dc.EnumObjects via the "thunk" created by the
    // call to WinAPI's MakeProcInstance function.
    ColorCount = dc.GetDeviceCaps(NUMCOLORS);

    // If device is monochrome, make all colors white.
    if (ColorCount == 2)
        {
        AvailableColors.Add(COLORREF(TColor::White));
        AvailableColors.Add(COLORREF(TColor::White));
        }
    else
        {
        ColorCount = 9;

        AvailableColors.Add(COLORREF(TColor::LtGray));
        AvailableColors.Add(COLORREF(TColor::Gray));
        AvailableColors.Add(COLORREF(TColor::LtRed));
        AvailableColors.Add(COLORREF(TColor::LtGreen));
        AvailableColors.Add(COLORREF(TColor::LtYellow));
        AvailableColors.Add(COLORREF(TColor::LtBlue));
        AvailableColors.Add(COLORREF(TColor::LtMagenta));
        AvailableColors.Add(COLORREF(TColor::LtCyan));
        AvailableColors.Add(COLORREF(TColor::White));
        }
    }

void DFrame::CmFileExit()
    {
    CloseWindow(0); // Cause application to terminate
    }

void DFrame::CmStarTwinkle() { bTwinkle = !bTwinkle; }
void DFrame::CmStarSlow()     { Pace = CM_SLOW;      }
void DFrame::CmStarModerate(){ Pace = CM_MODERATE; }
void DFrame::CmStarFast()     { Pace = CM_FAST;      }
```

```
void DFrame::CmStarTiny()    { Size = CM_TINY;    Invalidate();}
void DFrame::CmStarAverage() { Size = CM_AVERAGE; Invalidate();}
void DFrame::CmStarLarge()   { Size = CM_LARGE;   Invalidate();}

void DFrame::CmHelpAbout()
    {
    MessageBox("Random Stars in Random Colors\n\n"
               "'Borland C++ 4.0 Programming\n"
               "   for Windows' by Paul Yao\n", Title);
    }

BOOL DFrame::EvEraseBkgnd (HDC hdc)
    {
    // Make window background BLACK.
    PatBlt(hdc, 0, 0, cxWidth, cyHeight, BLACKNESS);
    return TRUE;
    }

void DFrame::EvInitMenu (HMENU menu)
    {
    WORD wState;

    // Set / clear Stars.Twinkle menu item
    wState = (bTwinkle) ? MF_CHECKED : MF_UNCHECKED;
    ::CheckMenuItem (menu, CM_TWINKLE, wState);

    // Set / clear Stars.Slow menu item
    wState = (Pace == CM_SLOW) ? MF_CHECKED : MF_UNCHECKED;
    ::CheckMenuItem (menu, CM_SLOW, wState);

    // Set / clear Stars.Moderate menu item
    wState = (Pace == CM_MODERATE) ? MF_CHECKED : MF_UNCHECKED;
    ::CheckMenuItem (menu, CM_MODERATE, wState);

    // Set / clear Stars.Fast menu item
    wState = (Pace == CM_FAST) ? MF_CHECKED : MF_UNCHECKED;
    ::CheckMenuItem (menu, CM_FAST, wState);

    // Set / clear Stars.Tiny menu item
    wState = (Size == CM_TINY) ? MF_CHECKED : MF_UNCHECKED;
    ::CheckMenuItem (menu, CM_TINY, wState);

    // Set / clear Stars.Average menu item
    wState = (Size == CM_AVERAGE) ? MF_CHECKED : MF_UNCHECKED;
    ::CheckMenuItem (menu, CM_AVERAGE, wState);

    // Set / clear Stars.Large menu item
    wState = (Size == CM_LARGE) ? MF_CHECKED : MF_UNCHECKED;
    ::CheckMenuItem (menu, CM_LARGE, wState);
    }

void DFrame::EvSize (UINT sizeType, TSize& size)
    {
    TFrameWindow::EvSize(sizeType, size);
```

```
    cxWidth  = size.cx;

    cyHeight = size.cy;

    // Force a complete redraw when size changes.
    Invalidate();
    }

BOOL DFrame::IdleAction (long /* lCount */)
    {
    // Very important!  Return FALSE if you don't need
    // idle time; otherwise, power management software
    // can't save your laptop battery power.
    if (!bTwinkle)
        return FALSE;

    int Draw;

    switch (Pace) {
        case CM_SLOW:     Draw = PACESLOW;     break;
        case CM_MODERATE: Draw = PACEMODERATE; break;
        case CM_FAST:     Draw = PACEFAST;     break;
        }

    // At the right time, we draw.
    if (++PaceCount < Draw)
        return TRUE;

    // Fetch a DC for drawing anywhere in our client area.
    TClientDC dc(HWindow);

    // Under Windows 3.x, the clip box gets set to null
    // when windows are getting moved. To prevent problems,
    // abandon drawing during window movement.
    TRect tr;
    if (dc.GetClipBox(tr) == NULLREGION)
        return TRUE;

    // Erase old star
    int i = random (STARCOUNT);
    DrawStar (dc, NightSky[i].ptLocation, crBackground);

    // Calculate new location
    NightSky[i].ptLocation.x = random (cxWidth);
    NightSky[i].ptLocation.y = random (cyHeight);

    // Calculate new color
    NightSky[i].color = AvailableColors[random(ColorCount)];

    // Draw new star
    DrawStar (dc, NightSky[i].ptLocation, NightSky[i].color);

    PaceCount = 0; // Reset flag.
```

```
    // TRUE means we want more idle time
    return TRUE;
    }

void DFrame::Paint (TDC& dc, BOOL, TRect&)
    {
    // Draw individual stars.
    for (int i = 0; i < STARCOUNT; i++)
        {
        DrawStar (dc, NightSky[i].ptLocation, NightSky[i].color);
        }
    }

void DFrame::DrawStar (TDC& dc, TPoint& pt, COLORREF color)
    {
#if defined (__WIN32__)
    // Add SetPixelV to DC.H before this code
    // will compile properly. See Appendix H.

    // Win32 on Windows NT
    if (! (GetVersion() & 0x80000000L))
        {
        // Draw one pixel for all cases.
        dc.SetPixelV(pt.x, pt.y, color);
        if (Size == CM_TINY) return;

        // Draw two more for average & large
        dc.SetPixelV(pt.x+1, pt.y, color);
        dc.SetPixelV(pt.x, pt.y+1, color);
        if (Size == CM_AVERAGE) return;

        // Only draw two more pixels for large stars.
        dc.SetPixelV(pt.x-1, pt.y, color);
        dc.SetPixelV(pt.x, pt.y-1, color);
        }
    else
        // Win32s API on Windows 3.1...
#endif
        // ...also Win16 API support
        {
        // Draw one pixel for all cases.
        dc.SetPixel (pt, color);
        if (Size == CM_TINY) return;

        // Draw two more for average & large
        dc.SetPixel (pt.x+1, pt.y, color);
        dc.SetPixel (pt.x, pt.y+1, color);
        if (Size == CM_AVERAGE) return;

        // Only draw two more pixels for large stars.
        dc.SetPixel (pt.x-1, pt.y, color);
        dc.SetPixel (pt.x, pt.y-1, color);
        }
    }
```

```
DApp::DApp() : TApplication()
    }

void DApp::InitMainWindow()
    {
    SetMainWindow (new DFrame("Stars"));
    MainWindow->AssignMenu("MAIN");
    MainWindow->SetIcon(this, "SNAPSHOT");
    }

//
// Application main entry point.
OwlMain(int, char **)
    {
    return DApp().Run();
    }
```

STARS.H

```
#define CM_FILEEXIT 100        // File Popup Menu ID

#define CM_STARTWINKLE  200
#define CM_STARSLOW     201    // Star Popup Menu IDs
#define CM_STARMODERATE 202
#define CM_STARFAST    203
#define CM_STARTINY     204
#define CM_STARAVERAGE205
#define CM_STARLARGE   206

#define CM_HELPABOUT    300    // Help Popup Menu ID

typedef struct tagSTAR
    {
    TPoint   ptLocation;
    COLORREF color;
    } STAR, far * LPSTAR;

extern "C" {
int CALLBACK ObjEnumProc(LPVOID lpObject, LPARAM lpData);
};
```

STARS.RC

```
#include "stars.h"

snapshot icon stars.ico

main MENU
{
```

```
POPUP "&File"
  {
  MENUITEM "E&xit", CM_FILEEXIT
  }

POPUP "&Stars"
  {
  MENUITEM "&Twinkle",  CM_STARTWINKLE
  MENUITEM SEPARATOR
  MENUITEM "&Slow",     CM_STARSLOW
  MENUITEM "&Moderate", CM_STARMODERATE
  MENUITEM "&Fast",     CM_STARFAST
  MENUITEM SEPARATOR
  MENUITEM "&Tiny",     CM_STARTINY
  MENUITEM "&Average",  CM_STARAVERAGE
  MENUITEM "&Large",    CM_STARLARGE
  }

POPUP "&Help"
  {
  MENUITEM "&About...", CM_HELPABOUT
  }
}
```

STARS.DEF

```
EXETYPE WINDOWS

CODE MOVEABLE DISCARDABLE
DATA MULTIPLE MOVEABLE

HEAPSIZE   512
STACKSIZE 8192
```

DYNA16.MAK

```
#  MAKE file for Win16 API using dynamic BIDS,
#  OWL and C-runtime libraries.
#
#     C> make -fstatic16.mak
#

.AUTODEPEND
CC = -c -H -H"owl\owlpch.h" -ml -R -vi -WS -X-
CD = -D_RTLDLL;_BIDSDLL;_OWLDLL;_OWLPCH;
INC = -I\BC4\INCLUDE
LIB = -L\BC4\LIB

stars.exe :  stars.obj stars.res
  tlink -c -C -Twe $(LIB) @dyna16.lnk
  brc stars.res stars.exe

stars.obj :  stars.cpp
  bcc $(CC) $(CD) stars.cpp

stars.res :  stars.rc stars.ico stars.h
  brc $(INC) -31 -R stars.rc
```

DYNA16.LNK

```
\bc4\lib\c0wl.obj+
stars.obj
stars,stars
\bc4\lib\bidsi.lib+
\bc4\lib\owlwi.lib+
\bc4\lib\import.lib+
\bc4\lib\crtldll.lib
stars.def
```

DYNA32.MAK

```
#  MAKE file for Win32 API using dynamic BIDS,
#  OWL and C-runtime libraries.
#
#    C> make -fdyna32.mak
#

.AUTODEPEND
CC = -c -H -H\""owl\owlpch.h\"" -p- -R -vi -W -X-
CD = -D_RTLDLL;_BIDSDLL;_OWLDLL;_OWLPCH;
INC = -I\BC4\INCLUDE
LIB = -L\BC4\LIB

stars.exe :  stars.obj stars.res
  tlink32 -aa -c -Tpe $(LIB) @dyna32.lnk
  brc32 stars.res stars.exe

stars.obj :  stars.cpp
  bcc32 $(CC) $(CD) stars.cpp

stars.res :  stars.rc stars.ico stars.h
  brc32 $(INC) -w32 -R stars.rc
```

DYNA32.LNK

```
\bc4\lib\c0w32.obj+
stars.obj
stars,stars
\bc4\lib\bidsfi.lib+
\bc4\lib\owlwfi.lib+
\bc4\lib\import32.lib+
\bc4\lib\cw32i.lib
stars.def
```

Ordinarily, when you look at a Windows program to study how it draws, you start by looking at how it handles the **`WM_PAINT`** message. For an OWL program, that means you look for a window class function to override **`TWindow::Paint()`**. You can also look for **`EvEraseBkgnd()`**, the function for handling **`WM_ERASEBKGND`**. As discussed in the last chapter, **`WM_PAINT`** deals with making repairs to a damaged window. A related message is **`WM_ERASEBKGND`**, which is often sent before a paint message to insure the client area is clear of debris from previous occupants. STARS has both, but the really interesting drawing occurs in **IdleAction()**.

Both the **TApplication** and **TWindow** classes contain an **IdleAction()** function. As discussed in Chapter 4, **IdleAction()** is called when there aren't any messages for any application. In other words, not only is *your* message queue empty, but *every* message queue in the system is empty. This is a good time for background processing, which for STARS means it's the time to draw.

The behavior of this function relies on menu settings made by the user. The three different user-settable program options are shown in the STARS menu in Figure 7.2. Star twinkling can be turned on or off, the twinkling speed set, and star sizes—ranging from tiny (1 pixel), to average (3 pixels) on up to large (5 pixels)—selected. These three options are represented by the following **DFrame** data members: **bTwinkle**, **Pace**, and **Size**.

One of the first things that **IdleAction()** does is to check whether twinkling is on. If it's turned off, this function returns **FALSE** to the caller. As noted in the program comments, this is important because—when idle time is not used—our message loop notifies the Windows system libraries that our program is now truly idle[1]. It's very important to do this, or Windows can't know when to start the timer for the Power Management support provided by some hardware. While this seems like a trivial issue, the recent explosive growth of the portable computer market means that issues like battery conservation are becoming more important to the average computer user.

After the various flags and counters are checked, this routine creates a **TClientDC** object to use for drawing in STAR's client area. You will almost always create this object as a local object, and almost never create an instance of it using the **new** operator[2]. Within the Win16 API, when you create this type of DC object, you are borrowing one of *five* DCs that the Window Manager creates for the shared use of all windows in the system. You shouldn't "borrow" a DC for long periods of time, just like you don't borrow video tapes from the video store for many months. In both cases, there are penalties to pay if you do. When all five Window Manager DCs are loaned out, the penalty is quite severe—the system hangs[3].

Star twinkling is simply a matter of generating a few random numbers, for which the Borland run-time library provides the following functions: **randomize()** turns the generator on, and **random()** produces random integers. First, a random star in the **NightSky[]** array is selected and that star is erased. Then, a random location is selected along

---

[1] Within the message loop, this is represented by the call to the **WaitMessage** WinAPI.

[2] The point is to never hold a window DC for longer than the duration of a single message. An exception is for windows created with the **CS_OWNDC** class style bit, something that Microsoft's EXCEL does quite extensively. This bit allows a window to have a private DC that is separate from the Window Manager's cache of DCs.

[3] Under preemptive versions of Windows, the penalty is not so harsh: More DCs are created. Given the interest in creating portable code, however, it makes sense to continue following the rules established under nonpreemptive Windows.

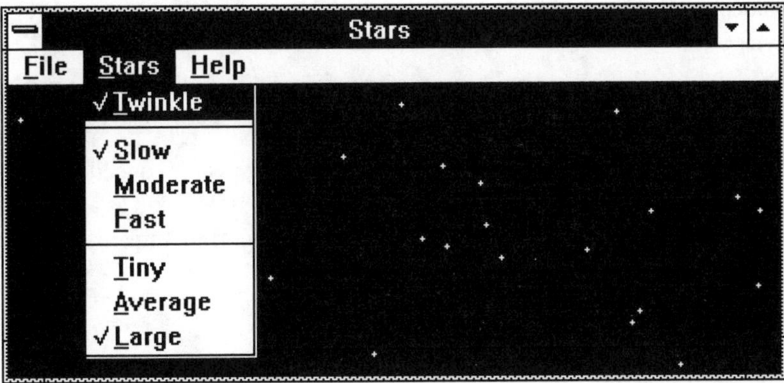

Figure 7.2 STARS menu

with a random color from the display screen's available colors. The **DrawStar()** function actually illuminates the specific pixels to make stars appear and disappear.

From a GDI perspective, the most important parts of **DrawStar()** involve calls to **SetPixel()** and **SetPixelV()**. These routines take the same number and type of parameters, and produce the same result. The difference is that **SetPixel()** returns the RGB value for the color used, while **SetPixelV()** returns a boolean value saying whether the function was successful or not. This becomes an issue with Windows NT, where calls to **SetPixelV()** are quite a bit faster than calls to **SetPixel()**. Ordinarily, drawing calls in Windows NT get batched before being sent to the Win32 subsystem, which minimizes process context switches and speeds up drawing. **SetPixel()**, with its requirement for a return value, causes a performance hit because batching is disabled.

DrawStar() handles these differences by calling **SetPixel()** for Win16 and Win32s programs in Windows 3.1, and **SetPixelV()** for Windows NT. Unfortunately, this latter routine is not supported by Win32s. The OWL libraries themselves don't mention **SetPixelV()**, but because of its performance advantage under Windows NT, I have added it to the OWL include files. See Appendix H for details on patching the OWL include files.

The OWL libraries provide two versions of **SetPixel()**[4], as you can tell by taking a look in the ObjectWindows Library Help file. In both cases, you provide the location of the pixel to be illuminated and the color to use. Specify the location with either an (x,y) integer pair, or put these two values into a **TPoint** type variable. In OWL, color values are expressed using the **TColor** class.

A quick look at the OWL Help file shows there are nine different constructors for this data type. A very simple way to store color information is to make copies of the predefined

---

[4] Everything mentioned here regarding **SetPixel** applies equally to **SetPixelV**.

TColor's static values. For example, here's how to create a **TColor** variable and initialize its value to gray.

```
TColor tc = TColor::Gray;
```

At the level of Windows's GDI interface, the OWL color constructors are reduced to three different ways to define a color value: as an RGB triplet, as a palette index, and as a palette-relative RBG value. Let's take a closer look at how color—and other drawing attributes—is specified to GDI.

Requesting GDI Color Information

Asking GDI for something is a lot like ordering at a restaurant. For example, what do you get when you ask for a burger? To know the answer to this question, you first have to know what's on the menu. At a fast-food restaurant, for example, you might get a meal wrapped in paper. At a vegetarian restaurant, you might get a garden burger made with soybeans. And at a sushi restaurant, you'll probably get directions to another place to eat.

The point is this: When you eat out, you look at the menu *before* you order. The same holds true for GDI: Before drawing, you find out what's on the menu—that is, what drawing attributes are available. Unfortunately, with GDI there isn't just one place to look. To help simplify this process for you, here's a list showing some of the things you can ask before drawing:

Drawing Attribute	*How to Query*
Brushes	**EnumObjects (hdc, OBJ_BRUSH,...)** **GetDeviceCaps (hdc, NUMBRUSHES)**
Colors	**GetDeviceCaps (hdc, NUMCOLORS)**
Fonts	**GetDeviceCaps (hdc, NUMFONTS)** **EnumFontFamilies(hdc,...)**
Pens	**EnumObjects (hdc, OBJ_PEN,...)** **GetDeviceCaps (hdc, NUMPENS)**
Printer Page Size	**Escape (hdc, GETPHYSPAGESIZE,...)**
Screen Size	**GetSystemMetrics (SM_CXFULLSCREEN)** **GetSystemMetrics (SM_CYFULLSCREEN)**
Window Size	**GetClientRect (HWND, TRect&)**

These are not OWL functions, but are instead native WinAPI function calls. I did this for two reasons: first, to remind you to look at the Windows API help file, since it contains a wealth of information that will help you use the OWL libraries; second, to show how similar WinAPI functions are to OWL functions. For example, to call **GetDeviceCaps**, remove the first **hdc** parameter and treat it as a **TDC** class member function. Here is how STARS calls this function to get the number of available colors:

```
ColorCount = dc.GetDeviceCaps(NUMCOLORS);
```

STARS changes its drawing based on the results of this call. If it finds a device that only supports two colors—a monochrome device, in other words—all stars are drawn in white. Otherwise, it uses a set of nine colors that are predefined by OWL. When you write a program that uses color, always be sure to think about monochrome devices and how you will treat them.

There are other ways to pick colors. For example, you could call the WinAPI's **GetSysColor** function. This function returns RGB triplets for the system's user-interface colors. These colors are defined by the user in the Windows Control Panel, so you'll want to become familiar with these colors to make sure that your application fits with what users expect. If color selection is really important to your application, you might consider calling the color picker dialog box to let your user pick colors for you. This is a common dialog box provided as part of Windows and covered in more detail in Chapter 14.

Color selection, then, should take user preference into account, but you still need to find a way to specify color information to GDI. Although OWL has its own set of **TColor** constructors, these ultimately call one of the three provided by GDI: RGB triplets, palette indices, and palette RGB values.

RGB Triplet

An RGB triplet gets its name from its three parts: a red value, a green value, and a blue value. An RGB triplet is always an unsigned long integer, that is a four-byte-wide, 32-bit value. Three of the bytes hold the red, green, and blue intensity of the color you are looking for. With one byte per color, that means there are 256 intensities for each color, and over 16 million unique combinations.

The **RGB** macro in WINDOWS.H provides the easiest means for creating an RGB triplet. The syntax for this macro is

```
rgbColor = RGB (bRed, bGreen, bBlue)
```

where `bRed`, `bGreen`, and `bBlue` are integers between 0 and 255. The **RGB** macro packs the intensity of all three colors into a single unsigned long integer.

Although you can specify over 16 million different RGB combinations, the actual color that is produced will depend on the device. For example, the 16-color EGA adapter will map the RGB values to the nearest available physical color. When we talk about pens, we'll talk about how GDI **dithers** to simulate many more colors on a device. But for pixels, the only colors that are available are the physical, or "pure," colors. Two RGB triplets have guaranteed results: RGB (0,0,0) is always black, and RGB (255,255,255) is always white.

A second way to specify color is with a palette index. A palette is a table of RGB triplets. Therefore, at first glance, a palette index is another way to specify an RGB triplet.

Palette Index

But unlike RGB triplets, palettes allow a program to specify the exact physical color that should be represented. For example, the VGA and 8514/a display adapters have hardware that supports 262,144 different colors. But only 256 of these colors are available at any one moment. The device driver selects a palette that is distributed evenly across the color range. But this isn't good enough for some uses. Palettes allow a program to select the exact colors to be used in the 256 available slots.

On devices that support GDI palettes, a program can actually change the hardware registers of a device to represent the exact set of colors that are required. For example, if a program wants to display a color bitmap of a woodland scene, it might need 150 shades of green to show all the subtle nuances in the grasses, trees, and shrubs. Or a color bitmap of skiers on a snow-covered mountain might require 100 shades of white, 50 shades of hot-pink and orange, and 10 shades of blue. Palettes allow a program to show images like these on a display screen with near picture-perfect representation.

Like RGB triplets, palette indices are unsigned long integers. The only difference is that a flag is set in the fourth, unused byte to indicate that the value is a palette index and not an actual RGB triplet. The **PALETTEINDEX** macro selects a palette index value. For example, to select color number 137, you would use the following:

```
PALETTEINDEX (137);
```

Palette-Relative RGB Index

The third and final way to specify color is with a palette-relative RGB index. Like an RGB triplet, this allows you to specify a red, green, and blue portion of a color. But a palette-relative RGB color is never dithered. Instead, GDI finds the nearest pure color in the existing palette, and uses it. The **PALETTERGB** macro creates this type of color reference:

```
PALETTERGB (0, 128, 255);
```

Creating Markers

Our second GDI program introduces a type of drawing primitive that is not native to GDI: **markers**. The most obvious use of a marker is on a graph, like the one in Figure 7.3. Each "+" symbol is a marker. In this example, each marker represents a population value for a given year.

At first glance, you might wonder why markers are special. After all, from the chart it is clear that GDI can display text. What's the difference between a marker and a text character?

As you'll see in Chapter 10, GDI text routines make it easy to work with different sizes and styles of text on a variety of devices. This very flexibility makes it difficult to guarantee that a specific letter will be centered on a specific location.

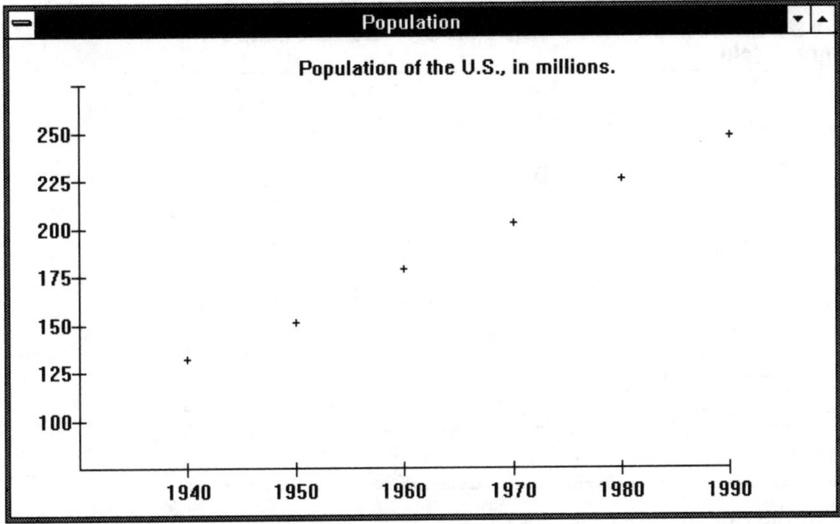

Figure 7.3 Markers highlight points in a graph

For example, if you used GDI letters to mark the location of buried treasure on a map, you introduce a margin of error. The location of the cross-hairs on the letter X, for example, will move depending on the font you are using.

Markers overcome this limitation since a marker is guaranteed to be centered over an exact location. That's the reason that markers are used for graphs. In the chapters that follow, we use markers to help explain all of the GDI drawing routines.

One way to mark a location is with the **`SetPixel`** routine that we introduced in the preceding section. But a single pixel is often hard to see. For this reason, we create our "+" marker by drawing lines.

When we introduce other GDI drawing primitives, we're going to use markers to show the relationship between the coordinates we specify when we call a drawing primitive and the resulting output. This will help clarify GDI's "inclusive-exclusive" drawing approach, and help you see how GDI creates lines, filled areas, and text output.

Figure 7.4 shows a sample of the output produced by our marker program, MARKERS.CPP. This program uses mouse input to place markers.

Here are the source files to MARKERS:

MARKERS.CPP

```
//
// MARKERS.CPP  Shows a new type of drawing object
//              created by drawing lines.
//

#include <owl\owlpch.h>
```

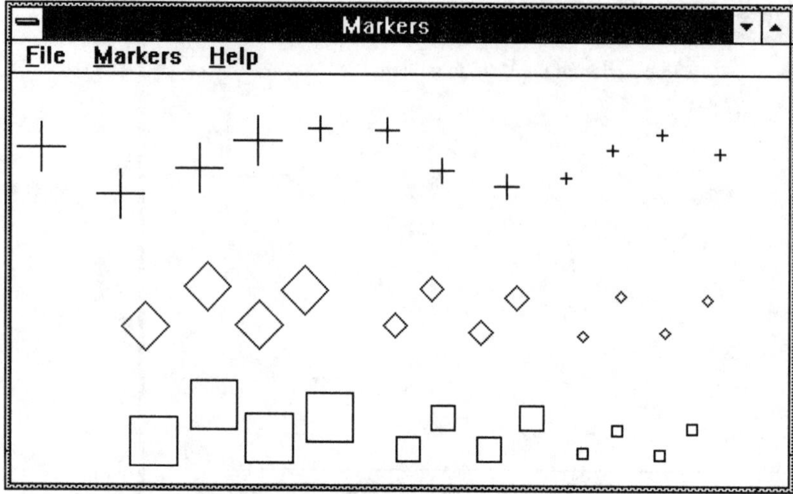

Figure 7.4 Sample output of MARKERS

```
#include "markers.h"
#include "cls_mark.h"

//
// Main window
class DFrame : public TFrameWindow
    {
  public:
    DFrame(char * title);
    ~DFrame();
    void CmFileExit();
    void CmCross();
    void CmSquare();
    void CmDiamond();
    void CmSmall();
    void CmMedium();
    void CmLarge();
    void CmErase();
    void CmHelpAbout();
    void EvInitMenu (HMENU menu);
    void EvLButtonDblClk(UINT modkeys, TPoint & point);
    void EvLButtonDown(UINT modkeys, TPoint & point);

    void Paint (TDC&, BOOL, TRect&);
    void DrawMarker (TDC&, DMarkerPoint&);

  private:
    int           cMarkers;
    int           Size;
    int           Shape;
    DMarkerPoint * ptMarks;

  DECLARE_RESPONSE_TABLE (DFrame);
    };

DEFINE_RESPONSE_TABLE1 (DFrame, TFrameWindow)
```

```
  EV_COMMAND(CM_FILEEXIT,  CmFileExit),
  EV_COMMAND(CM_CROSS,     CmCross),
  EV_COMMAND(CM_SQUARE,    CmSquare),
  EV_COMMAND(CM_DIAMOND,   CmDiamond),
  EV_COMMAND(CM_SMALL,     CmSmall),
  EV_COMMAND(CM_MEDIUM,    CmMedium),
  EV_COMMAND(CM_LARGE,     CmLarge),
  EV_COMMAND(CM_ERASE,     CmErase),
  EV_COMMAND(CM_HELPABOUT, CmHelpAbout),
  EV_WM_INITMENU,
  EV_WM_LBUTTONDOWN,
  EV_WM_LBUTTONDBLCLK,
END_RESPONSE_TABLE;

DFrame::DFrame(char * title) : TFrameWindow(0, title)
    {
    ptMarks = new DMarkerPoint[MAXMARKERS];
    cMarkers = 0;
    Size =  SIZE_SMALL;
    Shape = CM_CROSS;
    }

DFrame::~DFrame()
    {
    delete [] ptMarks;
    }

void DFrame::CmFileExit()
  {
  CloseWindow(0); // Cause application to terminate
  }

void DFrame::CmCross()   { Shape = CM_CROSS;    }
void DFrame::CmSquare()  { Shape = CM_SQUARE;   }
void DFrame::CmDiamond() { Shape = CM_DIAMOND;  }
void DFrame::CmSmall()   { Size  = SIZE_SMALL;  }
void DFrame::CmMedium()  { Size  = SIZE_MEDIUM; }
void DFrame::CmLarge()   { Size  = SIZE_LARGE;  }

void DFrame::CmErase()
    {
    // To erase, set marker count to zero.
    cMarkers = 0;

    // Declare window dirty (to force WM_PAINT msg).
    Invalidate();
    }

void DFrame::CmHelpAbout()
    {
    MessageBox("Use mouse to draw markers.\n\n"
               "'Borland C++ 4.0 Programming\n"
               "  for Windows', by Paul Yao", Title);
    }

void DFrame::EvInitMenu (HMENU menu)
    {
    WORD wState;

    // Set/check Markers.Cross menu item.
    wState = (Shape == CM_CROSS) ? MF_CHECKED : MF_UNCHECKED;
    ::CheckMenuItem (menu, CM_CROSS, wState);
```

```
    // Set/check Marker.Square menu item.
    wState = (Shape == CM_SQUARE) ? MF_CHECKED : MF_UNCHECKED;
    ::CheckMenuItem (menu, CM_SQUARE, wState);

    // Set/check Marker.Diamond menu item.
    wState = (Shape == CM_DIAMOND) ? MF_CHECKED : MF_UNCHECKED;
    ::CheckMenuItem (menu, CM_DIAMOND, wState);

    // Set/check Marker.Small menu item.
    wState = (Size == SIZE_SMALL) ? MF_CHECKED : MF_UNCHECKED;
    ::CheckMenuItem (menu, CM_SMALL, wState);

    // Set/check Marker.Medium menu item.
    wState = (Size == SIZE_MEDIUM) ? MF_CHECKED : MF_UNCHECKED;
    ::CheckMenuItem (menu, CM_MEDIUM, wState);

    // Set/check Marker.Large menu item.
    wState = (Size == SIZE_LARGE) ? MF_CHECKED : MF_UNCHECKED;
    ::CheckMenuItem (menu, CM_LARGE, wState);
    }

void DFrame::EvLButtonDblClk(UINT modkeys, TPoint & point)
    {
    // OwlWindows always get double-click mouse
    // messages. Since we aren't interested in these,
    // call the single-click mouse message routine.
    EvLButtonDown(modkeys, point);
    }

void DFrame::EvLButtonDown(UINT /* modkeys */, TPoint & point)
    {
    if (cMarkers == MAXMARKERS)
        {
        ::MessageBeep (MB_ICONEXCLAMATION);
        return;
        }

    // Store marker info.
    ptMarks[cMarkers].point = point;
    ptMarks[cMarkers].Size  = DFrame::Size;
    ptMarks[cMarkers].Shape = DFrame::Shape;

    // Fetch a non-WM_PAINT DC and draw
    TClientDC dc(HWindow);
    DrawMarker (dc, ptMarks[cMarkers]);

    // Count of markers in array.
    cMarkers++;
    }

void DFrame::Paint (TDC& dc, BOOL, TRect&)
    {
    for (int i = 0; i < cMarkers; i++)
        DrawMarker (dc, ptMarks[i]);
    }

void DFrame::DrawMarker (TDC& dc, DMarkerPoint& pt)
    {
    switch (pt.Shape) {
       case CM_DIAMOND:
            Marker::Diamond(dc, pt.point, pt.Size);
```

```
            break;
        case CM_SQUARE:
            Marker::Square (dc, pt.point, pt.Size);
            break;
        case CM_CROSS:
            Marker::Cross (dc, pt.point,  pt.Size);
            break;
        }
    }

//
// Application object
class DApp : public TApplication
    {
  public:
    DApp() : TApplication() {}
    void InitMainWindow()
        {
        SetMainWindow (new DFrame("Markers"));
        MainWindow->AssignMenu("MAIN");
        MainWindow->SetIcon(this, "SNAPSHOT");
        }
    };

//
// Application main entry point.
OwlMain(int, char **)
    {
    return DApp().Run();
    }
```

MARKERS.H

```
#define CM_FILEEXIT  100
#define CM_CROSS     200
#define CM_SQUARE    201
#define CM_DIAMOND   202
#define CM_SMALL     203
#define CM_MEDIUM    204
#define CM_LARGE     205
#define CM_ERASE     206
#define CM_HELPABOUT 300

const int MAXMARKERS = 250;

// Marker pixel widths.
const int SIZE_SMALL = 7;
const int SIZE_MEDIUM = 15;
const int SIZE_LARGE  = 29;

struct DMarkerPoint
    {
    int    Size;
    int    Shape;
    TPoint point;
    };
```

CLS_MARK.CPP

```
//
// CLS_MARK.CPP  Here are some routines you can use when
//               you need to make graphical marks in your
//               drawings.
//
#include <owl\owldefs.h>
#include <owl\dc.h>
#include <owl\point.h>
#include <owl\color.h>
#include "cls_mark.h"

void
Marker::Cross (TDC &dc, TPoint& pt, int Size, HPEN hpen, int rop)
    {
    Cross (HDC(dc), pt, Size, hpen, rop);
    }

void
Marker::Cross (HDC hdc, TPoint& pt, int Size, HPEN hpen, int rop)
    {
    // Request raster operation to invert pixels
    int ropOld = SetROP2(hdc, rop);

    // Pen to draw markers with.
    if (hpen == 0)
        hpen = (HPEN)GetStockObject(BLACK_PEN);
    HANDLE h = SelectObject (hdc, hpen);

    // Calculate distance from center point.
    int cxyWidth = Size / 2;

    // Draw "cross-hairs" marker.
    //  . . . . . . .
    //  . . . o . . .
    //  . . . o . . .
    //  . o o x o o .
    //  . . . o . . .
    //  . . . o . . .
    //  . . . . . . .
    MoveToEx(hdc, pt.x - cxyWidth, pt.y, 0);  // Horizontal line
    LineTo(hdc, pt.x + cxyWidth, pt.y);
    MoveToEx(hdc, pt.x, pt.y - cxyWidth, 0);  // Top spur
    LineTo(hdc, pt.x, pt.y);
    MoveToEx(hdc, pt.x, pt.y + cxyWidth, 0);  // Bottom spur
    LineTo(hdc, pt.x, pt.y);

    // Restore DC to the way we found it.
    SetROP2 (hdc, ropOld);
    SelectObject (hdc, h);
    }

void
Marker::Diamond  (TDC& dc, TPoint& pt, int Size, HPEN hpen, int rop)
    {
    Diamond (HDC(dc), pt, Size, hpen, rop);
    }

void
Marker::Diamond  (HDC hdc, TPoint& pt, int Size, HPEN hpen, int rop)
    {
```

```
    // Request raster operation to invert pixels
    int ropOld = SetROP2(hdc, rop);

    // Pen to draw markers with.
    if (hpen == 0)
        hpen = (HPEN)GetStockObject(BLACK_PEN);
    HANDLE h = SelectObject (hdc, hpen);

    // Calculate distance from center point.
    int cxyWidth = Size / 2;

    // Draw a diamond marker.
    //  . . . . . . .
    //  . . . o . . .
    //  . . o . o . .
    //  . o . x . o .
    //  . . o . o . .
    //  . . . o . . .
    //  . . . . . . .

    // Build array of points.
    TPoint apt[5];
    apt[0].x = pt.x;             apt[0].y = pt.y - cxyWidth;
    apt[1].x = pt.x + cxyWidth;  apt[1].y = pt.y;
    apt[2].x = pt.x;             apt[2].y = pt.y + cxyWidth;
    apt[3].x = pt.x - cxyWidth;  apt[3].y = pt.y;
    apt[4].x = pt.x;             apt[4].y = pt.y - cxyWidth;

    // Draw it.
    Polyline(hdc, apt, 5);

    // Restore DC to the way we found it.
    SetROP2 (hdc, ropOld);
    SelectObject (hdc, h);
    }

void
Marker::Square (TDC& dc, TPoint &pt, int Size, HPEN hpen, int rop)
    {
    Square (HDC(dc), pt, Size, hpen, rop);
    }

void
Marker::Square (HDC hdc, TPoint &pt, int Size, HPEN hpen, int rop)
    {
    // Request raster operation to invert pixels
    int ropOld = SetROP2(hdc, rop);

    // Pen to draw markers with.
    if (hpen == 0)
        hpen = (HPEN)GetStockObject(BLACK_PEN);
    HANDLE h = SelectObject (hdc, hpen);

    // Calculate distance from center point.
    int cxyWidth = Size / 2;

    // Draw a square marker.
    //  . . . . . . .
    //  . o o o o o .
    //  . o . . . o .
    //  . o . x . o .
```

```
    //  . o . . . . o .
    //  . o o o o o o .
    //  . . . . . . . .
    MoveToEx(hdc, pt.x - cxyWidth, pt.y - cxyWidth, 0);
    LineTo(hdc, pt.x + cxyWidth, pt.y - cxyWidth);
    LineTo(hdc, pt.x + cxyWidth, pt.y + cxyWidth);
    LineTo(hdc, pt.x - cxyWidth, pt.y + cxyWidth);
    LineTo(hdc, pt.x - cxyWidth, pt.y - cxyWidth);

    // Restore DC to the way we found it.
    SetROP2 (hdc, ropOld);
    SelectObject (hdc, h);
    }
```

CLS_MARK.H

```
//
// Marker Class
class Marker
    {
  public:
    static void Cross (TDC&, TPoint&, int Size,
                       HPEN hpen = 0, int rop = R2_NOT);
    static void Cross (HDC, TPoint&, int Size,
                       HPEN hpen = 0, int rop = R2_NOT);
    static void Diamond (TDC&, TPoint&, int Size,
                         HPEN hpen = 0, int rop = R2_NOT);
    static void Diamond (HDC, TPoint&, int Size,
                         HPEN hpen = 0, int rop = R2_NOT);
    static void Square (TDC&, TPoint&, int Size,
                        HPEN hpen = 0, int rop = R2_NOT);
    static void Square (HDC, TPoint&, int Size,
                        HPEN hpen = 0, int rop = R2_NOT);
    };
```

MARKERS.RC

```
#include "markers.h"

snapshot icon markers.ico

main menu
    {
    POPUP "&File"
        {
        MENUITEM "E&xit", CM_FILEEXIT
        }
    POPUP "&Markers"
        {
        MENUITEM "&Cross",   CM_CROSS
        MENUITEM "&Square",  CM_SQUARE
        MENUITEM "&Diamond", CM_DIAMOND
        MENUITEM SEPARATOR
        MENUITEM "&Small",  CM_SMALL
        MENUITEM "&Medium", CM_MEDIUM
        MENUITEM "&Large",  CM_LARGE
```

```
        MENUITEM SEPARATOR
        MENUITEM "&Erase", CM_ERASE
        }
    POPUP "&Help"
        {
        MENUITEM "&About...", CM_HELPABOUT
        }
    }
```

MARKERS.DEF

```
EXETYPE WINDOWS

CODE MOVEABLE DISCARDABLE
DATA MULTIPLE MOVEABLE

HEAPSIZE   512
STACKSIZE 8192
```

DYNA16.MAK

```
#  MAKE file for Win16 API using dynamic BIDS,
#  OWL and C-runtime libraries.
#
#    C> make -fstatic16.mak
#

.AUTODEPEND
CC = -c -H -H"owl\owlpch.h" -ml -R -vi -WS -X-
CD = -D_RTLDLL;_BIDSDLL;_OWLDLL;_OWLPCH;
INC = -I\BC4\INCLUDE
LIB = -L\BC4\LIB

markers.exe :  cls_mark.obj markers.obj markers.res
  tlink -c -C -Twe $(LIB) @dyna16.lnk
  brc markers.res markers.exe

cls_mark.obj :  cls_mark.cpp
  bcc $(CC) $(CD) cls_mark.cpp

markers.obj :  markers.cpp
  bcc $(CC) $(CD) markers.cpp

markers.res :  markers.rc markers.ico markers.h
  brc $(INC) -31 -R markers.rc
```

DYNA16.LNK

```
\bc4\lib\c0wl.obj+
markers.obj+cls_mark.obj
markers,markers
\bc4\lib\bidsi.lib+
```

```
\bc4\lib\owlwi.lib+
\bc4\lib\import.lib+
\bc4\lib\crtldll.lib
markers.def
```

DYNA32.MAK

```
#  MAKE file for Win32 API using dynamic BIDS,
#  OWL and C-runtime libraries.
#
#     C> make -fdyna32.mak
#

.AUTODEPEND
CC = -c -H -H\""owl\owlpch.h\"" -p- -R -vi -W -X-
CD = -D_RTLDLL;_BIDSDLL;_OWLDLL;_OWLPCH;
INC = -I\BC4\INCLUDE
LIB = -L\BC4\LIB

markers.exe :  markers.obj cls_mark.obj markers.res
  tlink32 -aa -c -Tpe $(LIB) @dyna32.lnk
  brc32 markers.res markers.exe

markers.obj :  markers.cpp
  bcc32 $(CC) $(CD) markers.cpp

cls_mark.obj :  cls_mark.cpp
  bcc32 $(CC) $(CD) cls_mark.cpp

markers.res :  markers.rc markers.ico markers.h
  brc32 $(INC) -w32 -R markers.rc
```

DYNA32.LNK

```
\bc4\lib\c0w32.obj+
markers.obj+cls_mark.obj
markers,markers
\bc4\lib\bidsfi.lib+
\bc4\lib\owlwfi.lib+
\bc4\lib\import32.lib+
\bc4\lib\cw32i.lib
markers.def
```

The messages processed by MARKER's **DFrame** window are quite ordinary for a Windows program. Markers are drawn where the user clicks the left mouse button, which we receive as **WM_LBUTTONDOWN** messages. In OWL terminology, this means we have a **EvLButtonDown** response function, and it collects marker information in the marker information array.

One thing worth mentioning about the OWL libraries is that the receipt of double-click mouse messages is enabled by default. This is a problem because this feature can convert two successive mouse messages into a **WM_LBUTTONDOWN** and a **WM_LBUTTONDBLCLK** message. To the user, it appears that the second mouse click has been ignored. To hide this annoying feature from users, MARKER's **DFrame** window grabs the double-click message and calls the single-click mouse function. Forgetting to cover yourself against this problem means that users with quick mouse-click fingers will complain.

Like the other programs in this book, MARKERS is built on the foundation of MIN. As shown in the accompanying figure, this program can draw three different markers—a cross, a square, and a diamond—in three different sizes. These choices are available in MARKER's menu, shown in Figure 7.5.

The marker drawing functions themselves are in the file CLS_MARK.CPP. There are comments and diagrams in the code to clarify how each object is drawn. I took great care in writing this code to insure that these markers met the requirement that they draw symbols centered over the requested location.

If you glance through these routines, you'll notice the use of WinAPI data types and function calls instead of the corresponding OWL types. For example, this line of code appears:

```
HANDLE h = SelectObject (hdc, hpen);
```

instead of the OWL equivalent

```
dc.SelectObject (tpen);
```

I used the native WinAPI to select a new pen into a DC, then restore the old pen at the end of the routine. This is not easy with OWL objects. Leaving the DC unchanged is important for utility routines like these. Otherwise, the caller has to worry about restoring the state of the DC after calling our routine. When writing your own general purpose utility routines, you may need to bypass OWL in favor of what WinAPI can do for you.

One of the first calls in each marker function sets the raster operation (**ROP**):

```
int ropOld = SetROP2 (hdc, rop);
```

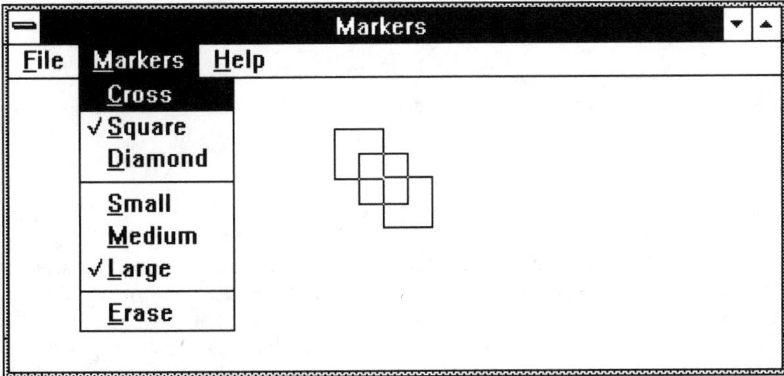

Figure 7.5 MARKERS menu

The raster operation defines the use of boolean operators in a drawing operation. For example, the default DC value of **rop** is **R2_COPYPEN**, which means that the source overwrites the destination. A problem this creates for markers is that a black marker drawn in a black area disappears. The default marker rop is **R2_NOT**, which means that markers are drawn by inverting the destination pixels without regard for color. Raster operations will be more fully explained in the next chapter.

Markers themselves are drawn by drawing lines. Earlier editions of this book called **SetPixel** multiple times to draw the markers, but this became clumsy for the variable size marker drawing supported by the current program. Also, as explained earlier, the overhead associated with drawing pixels under Windows NT[5] made it clear that creating markers with lines was the best way to go.

As you'll see in the next chapter, lines are drawn using an inclusive/exclusive approach. In other words, a lines starting pixel is *included* and its ending pixel *excluded.* This approach allows complex lines to be drawn from multiple calls *without* touching any pixel more than once. This is a necessity for proper support of raster operations. If, for example, GDI used inclusive/inclusive drawing, then the corner where two lines met would get touched *twice*—which would be disastrous for our markers. Since the default marker ROP is **R2_NOT**, pixels at corners would first be inverted, then inverted again—which changes them back to their original state. This would create missing corners on markers.

I originally created markers to help illustrate the inclusive/exclusive characteristic of GDI's line and figure drawing routines. You'll see these markers again—in the next chapter, then again in an example of owner draw menus. For now, it's time to proceed with a discussion of GDI's line drawing capabilities—the subject of the next chapter.

---

[5] Explained earlier in this chapter. **SetPixel** requires a return value, so batching of drawing requests is disabled and each pixel drawn requires 2 process context switches. Even **SetPixelV**, which doesn't have this property, nevertheless fills up the drawing queue with one instruction per call. Since the queue is of limited size (default 10 drawing calls), it's more efficient to draw markers using lines. For details on Windows NT operation, refer to the **GdiSetBatchLimit** function in the Win32 help database.

8

Drawing Lines

Before we begin to draw lines with GDI routines, let's stop to consider: *What exactly is a line, anyway*? A line is a geometric figure created by joining a set of points. Lines are considered **open figures**, meaning that our interest is in the line itself, and not the area around the line. In the next chapter, we're going to look at **closed figures**, in which a line plus the area it surrounds make up a single geometric figure.

A GDI line is a geometric figure drawn by a GDI line drawing routine. Every GDI line has a starting point and an ending point. GDI draws lines using what graphics programmers refer to as an **inclusive/exclusive algorithm**. That is, the starting point is *included* in the line, but the ending point is *excluded*.

Figure 8.1 shows a zoomed-in version of a GDI line, with square markers to highlight the end points. In this figure, the starting point is on the left and the ending point is on the

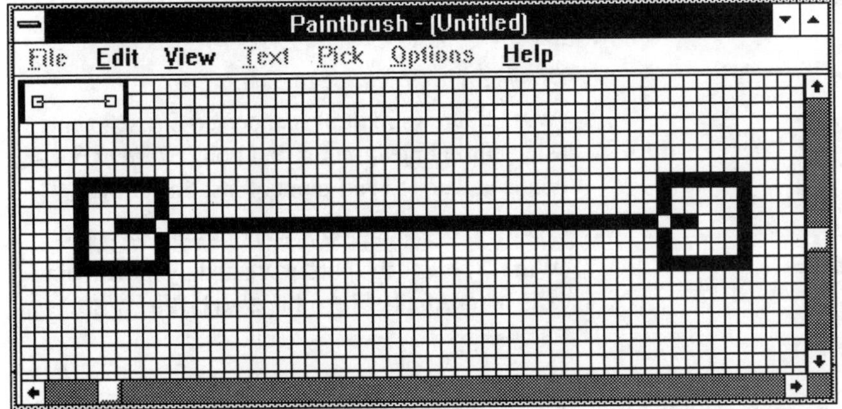

Figure 8.1 Paintbrush Zoom-In showing GDI's inclusive/exclusive line drawing.

right. If you look closely, you'll notice that the center pixel of the starting point (left side) is *included* in the line. The center pixel of the ending point (right side), on the other hand, is *not* included in the line.

Although inclusive/exclusive drawing may seem odd at first, it lets you draw complex figures by making many simple line drawing calls. Each new figure picks up where the other left off. And as we'll see in Chapter 16, when we create dragable objects for the mouse pointer, this is especially important when using different drawing modes.

All of GDI's line drawing routines use inclusive/exclusive drawing. Let's tour the available routines, to see what GDI can do for us. In the process, we'll review the DC attributes that affect line drawing.

Line Drawing Primitives

GDI has thirteen line drawing routines:

Function	*Description*
`AngleArc`	(Win32) Draws an arc of specified radius using a start and stop angle.
`Arc/ArcTo`	Draws an arc from a bounding rectangle and (x,y) start and stop coordinates. (ArcTo is a Win32 function)
`MoveTo/LineTo`	Draws straight lines.
`MoveToEx`	(Windows 3.1/Win32) More Windows NT-friendly version of **`MoveTo`**.
`PolyBezier/PolyBezierTo`	(Win32) Draws sets of bezier curves.
`PolyDraw`	(Win32) Draws sets of bezier curves and straight lines.
`Polyline`	Draws multiple line segments.
`PolylineTo`	(Win32) Draws multiple connected line segments using current position for first point. Current position is updated to end-point of last line drawn.
`PolyPolyline`	(Win32) Draws multiple disjoint polylines.
`StrokePath`	(Win32) Draws the border created by the drawing calls bracketed between the **`BeginPath/EndPath`** calls.

Several function names include "To." These routines draw using the current position value in the DC as a starting point, then update the current position value to the line's end-point. To give you a sense for what each of these routines does, I'll touch on some of the highlights.

A simple way to draw straight lines is to call **MoveTo** and **LineTo**.

MoveTo doesn't actually draw lines. Instead, it stores a pair of *x* and *y* values in the **current position**. The second routine, **LineTo**, uses this value as a starting point for a line. The **LineTo** function itself provides the ending point as a parameter. Here is how you use these routines to draw a line from point X1,Y1 to point X2,Y2:

```
dc.MoveTo (X1, Y1);
dc.LineTo (X2, Y2);
```

After the **LineTo** function has drawn a line, it updates the value of the current position in the DC to reflect the end point of the line. You can connect a series of points by making calls like the following:

```
dc.MoveTo (X1, Y1);
dc.LineTo (X2, Y2);
dc.LineTo (X3, Y3);
dc.LineTo (X4, Y4);
```

When these routines are called in this way, they produce the same result as our next routine, the **Polyline** function. You might wonder why GDI has this kind of redundancy.

It is partly a question of convenience. You will find that **MoveTo/LineTo** requires less work, since each takes an *x,y* value as a parameter. The **Polyline** function, on the other hand, requires the *x,y* values to be stored in an array of points.

Although it requires its parameters in a special format, the **Polyline** routine is the obvious choice when performance is important. The speed advantage is a direct result of the overhead incurred when a function is called. One **Polyline** call will draw many lines. Using **MoveTo/LineTo**, many calls would be required to draw the same lines.

Like the **MoveTo/LineTo** pair, **Polyline** draws straight lines. Unlike this pair, however, **Polyline** does not use the current position value in the DC. Instead, it relies solely on an array of **points** that are passed as a parameter. If we store the points (x1, y1), (x2, y2), (x3, y3), and (x4, y4) in an array like this

```
POINTS pt[] = {x1, y1, x2, y2, x3, y3, x4, y4};
```

the following call to **Polyline** connects the points:

```
dc.Polyline (pt, 4);
```

If, on the other hand, to involve the current position in drawing a polyline—when you were developing for Win32—call **PolylineTo**. The **PolyPolyline** lets you pack multiple **Polyline** calls into a single call. If you are drawing thousands of lines, this function eliminates the overhead otherwise incurred for individual calls to **Polyline**. As a Win32 function, of course, it isn't available under Windows 3.1—even with the Win32s extender.

The **Arc** function draws a curved line. The parameters to **Arc** define three boundaries: a bounding box, a starting point, and an ending point (see Figure 8.2). If the starting point

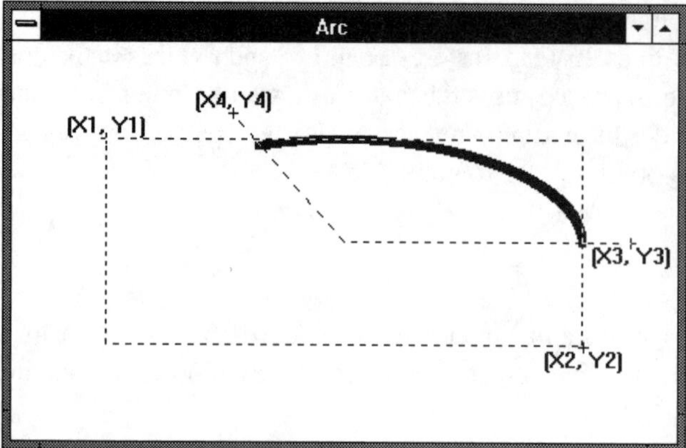

Figure 8.2 The ARC function

and the ending point are the same, the **Arc** function draws a complete ellipse (or a circle, if the bounding box is a square). Otherwise, **Arc** draws a portion of an ellipse.

With the other line drawing functions, the relationship of starting point to ending point was important, since GDI uses inclusive/exclusive drawing. This is also true for arcs. In addition, Win16 arcs are always drawn in a counterclockwise direction. Figure 8.3 shows how two different Win16 curves are drawn if the starting and ending points are swapped. Win32 introduces a new DC attribute—**arc direction**—that lets you choose between counterclockwise or clockwise arc drawing.

The **AngleArc** function draws a line segment and an arc (a semicircle). An example is shown in Figure 8.4. The line segment is drawn from the current position to the beginning of the arc. When this function is done, it sets the current position to the end point of the arc. In the illustration, the current position was set to the beginning of the arc to prevent a line segment from being drawn. To draw pie wedges with this function, just set the cur-

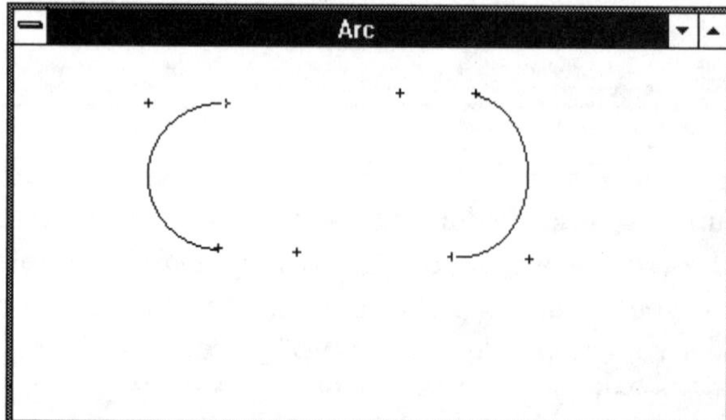

Figure 8.3 Arcs are drawn counterclockwise

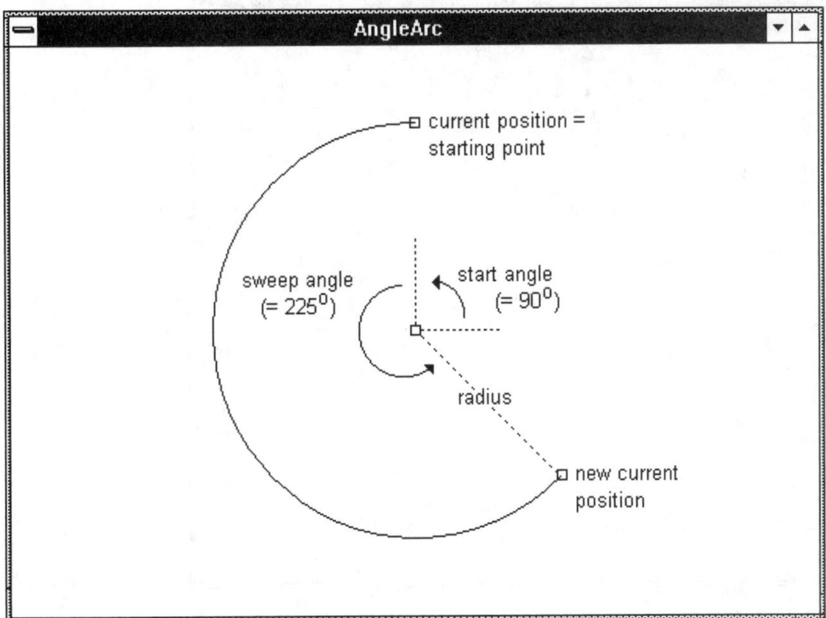

Figure 8.4 The AngleArc Function

rent position to the center point. When called, **`AngleArc`** draws one side of the pie and the outer boundary.

Another curve drawing function is **`PolyBezier`**. As shown in Figure 8.5, four control points are required to draw this function: The first and fourth points are endpoints. The second and third points are used to define the amount of curve. The first half of the curve is drawn tangent to the line connecting points 1 and 2. The second half of the curve is tangent to the line connecting points 3 and 4. (The straight lines are not part of the curve.)

A second bezier could be drawn with just *three* more points, since the endpoint of the first bezier would get used as the starting point for the second bezier. One of the nice features of bezier curves is to the user, there is a pretty clear relationship between the four control points and the curve that is drawn. Also, it's pretty easy to draw multiple beziers and have them run very smoothly into each other. To get a better feeling for how beziers work, you can run the Paintbrush program and experiment with its bezier drawing tool.

Paths provide a way to combine multiple GDI drawing functions into a single object. For example, the **`StrokePath`** function lets you combine two or more line-drawing functions together. Doing anything with paths start with defining a path between a **`BeginPath`** and **`Endpath`** bracket, like this:

```
dc.BeginPath();
dc.PolyBezier(&ptMarks[0], 13);
dc.Polyline (&ptMarks[13], 11);
dc.PolyBezier(&ptMarks[24], 7);
dc.EndPath();
```

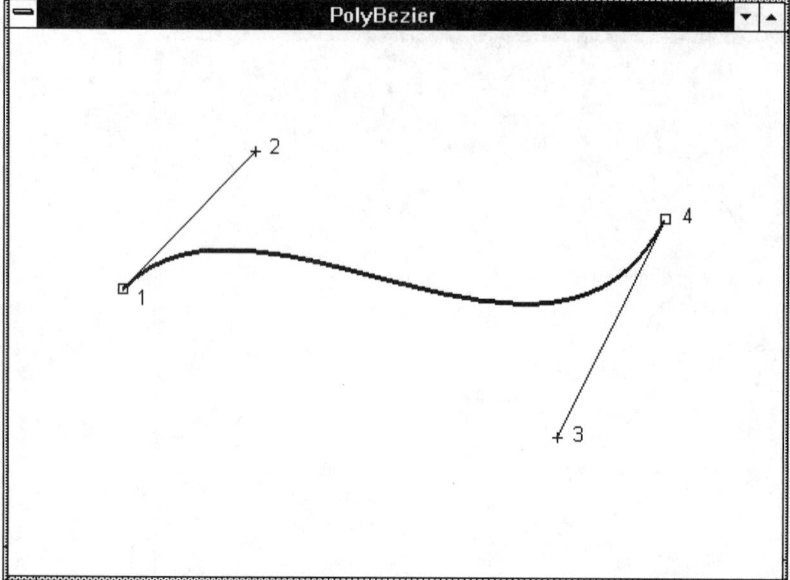

Figure 8.5 The PolyBezier Function

After you define a path bracket, the DC holds the data ready to go at a moment's notice. To draw this as a path, call the `StrokePath` function, as shown here:

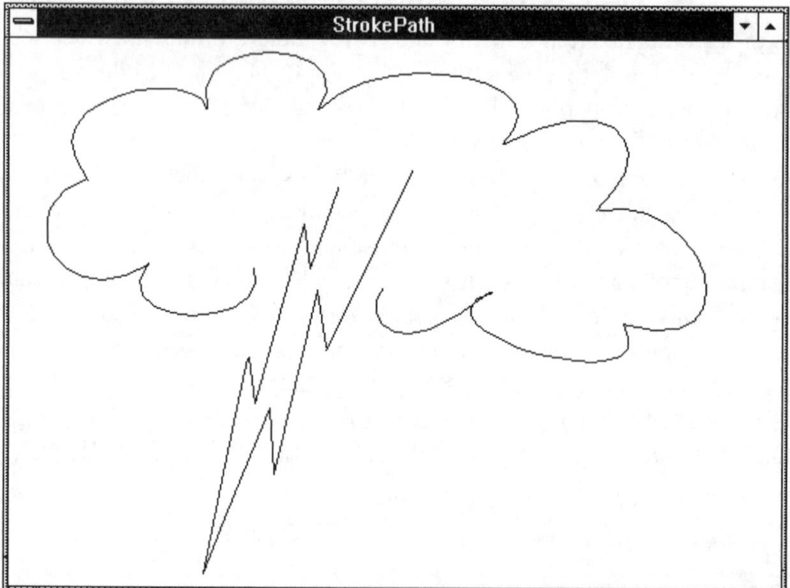

Figure 8.6 The StrokePath Function

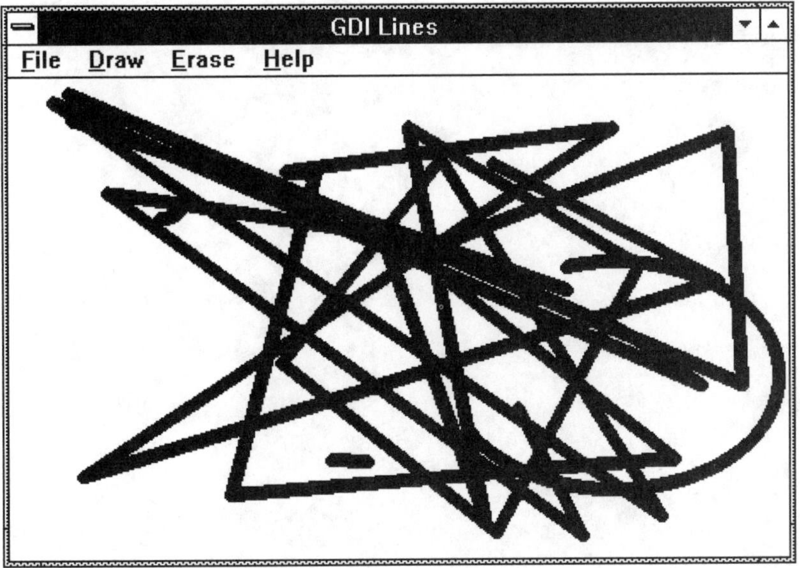

Figure 8.7 Random GDI Lines

```
dc.StrokePath();
```

Figure 8.6 shows an example of a **PolyBezier** and a **Polyline** combined together as a stroked path in a storm cloud.

Figure 8.7 shows an example of the output of LINES, a program that draws random GDI lines using randomly selected colors. A complete listing of LINES appears below.

LINES.CPP

```
//
// LINES.CPP   Randomly select pen and function to draw to show
//             some of the GDI line drawing capabilities. Also
//             shows background processing based on a timer tick.
//
#include <owl\owlpch.h>
#include <owl\point.h>
#include <classlib\arrays.h>
#include "lines.h"

const int ERASESEED     = 5;
const int MAXPOINTS     = 50;
const int MAXPENS       = 16;

// The Win32 API has 5 line drawing functions. Win16 has 2.
#if defined(__WIN32__)
```

```
const int MAXFUNCTIONS = 5;
#else
const int MAXFUNCTIONS = 2;
#endif

//
// An array of color references. We'll use this
// to build a list of available device colors.
class ColorArray : public TArrayAsVector<COLORREF>
    {
  public:
    ColorArray(int max = MAXPENS) : TArrayAsVector<COLORREF>(max) {}

    BOOL operator ==(COLORREF cr)
        { return (*this == cr); }
    };

//
// Main window
class DFrame : public TFrameWindow
    {
  public:
    DFrame(char * title);
    ~DFrame();
    void CmFileExit();
    void CmDrawArc();
    void CmDrawAngleArc();
    void CmDrawPolyline();
    void CmDrawPolyBezier();
    void CmDrawPolyDraw();
    void CmEraseNever();
    void CmEraseSometimes();
    void CmEraseAlways();
    void CmHelpAbout();
    void EvInitMenu (HMENU menu);
    void EvSize (UINT sizeType, TSize& size);
    void EvTimer (UINT);
    void SetupWindow();
    void MenuCheckMark(HMENU menu, int id, BOOL bCheck);
  private:
    enum Operations {Never, Sometimes, Always };
    enum Shapes { ARC, POLYLINE, ANGLEARC, POLYBEZIER, POLYDRAW };

    BOOL       bArc;
    BOOL       bAngleArc;
    BOOL       bPolyline;
    BOOL       bPolyBezier;
    BOOL       bPolyDraw;
    ColorArray AvailableColors;
    int        cxWidth;
    int        cyHeight;
    Operations opErase;
    int        PenCount;
    TPen     * aptpen[MAXPENS];
    BYTE       abTypes[MAXPOINTS];
    TPoint     ptDraw[MAXPOINTS];

  DECLARE_RESPONSE_TABLE (DFrame);
    friend int CALLBACK ObjEnumProc(LPVOID lpObject, LPARAM lpData);
```

```
    };

DEFINE_RESPONSE_TABLE1 (DFrame, TFrameWindow)
  EV_WM_INITMENU,
  EV_WM_SIZE,
  EV_WM_TIMER,
  EV_COMMAND(CM_FILEEXIT,   CmFileExit),
  EV_COMMAND(CM_ARC,        CmDrawArc),
  EV_COMMAND(CM_POLYLINE,   CmDrawPolyline),

#if defined(__WIN32__)
  EV_COMMAND(CM_ANGLEARC,   CmDrawAngleArc),
  EV_COMMAND(CM_POLYBEZIER, CmDrawPolyBezier),
  EV_COMMAND(CM_POLYDRAW,   CmDrawPolyDraw),
#endif

  EV_COMMAND(CM_NEVER,     CmEraseNever),
  EV_COMMAND(CM_SOMETIMES, CmEraseSometimes),
  EV_COMMAND(CM_ALWAYS,    CmEraseAlways),
  EV_COMMAND(CM_HELPABOUT, CmHelpAbout),
END_RESPONSE_TABLE;

DFrame::DFrame(char * title) : TFrameWindow(0, title)
    {
    // Initial window size = (0,0), but a WM_SIZE message
    // comes at window creation time to update size info.
    cxWidth = cyHeight = 0;

    // At startup, draw only polylines
    bArc        = FALSE;
    bPolyline   = TRUE;
    bAngleArc   = FALSE;
    bPolyBezier = FALSE;
    bPolyDraw   = FALSE;

    // At startup, always erase
    opErase = Always;
    }

DFrame::~DFrame()
    {
    // Important!!!  Be sure to delete any pens created!!!
    // Neither Win16 (nor OWL) does it for you.
    for (int i=0; i < PenCount; i++)
       delete aptpen[i];
    }

void DFrame::CmFileExit()
    {
    CloseWindow(0); // Cause application to terminate
    }

void DFrame::CmDrawArc()          {  bArc        = ! bArc;        }
void DFrame::CmDrawPolyline()     {  bPolyline   = ! bPolyline;   }


// These three functions are defined in Win32 and not in Win16.
// Hiding them makes OWL disable the related menu items.
#if defined (__WIN32__)
void DFrame::CmDrawAngleArc()     {  bAngleArc   = ! bAngleArc;   }
void DFrame::CmDrawPolyBezier()   {  bPolyBezier = ! bPolyBezier; }
void DFrame::CmDrawPolyDraw()     {  bPolyDraw   = ! bPolyDraw;   }
```

```
#endif

void DFrame::CmEraseNever()       { opErase = Never;     }
void DFrame::CmEraseSometimes()   { opErase = Sometimes; }
void DFrame::CmEraseAlways()      { opErase = Always;    }

void DFrame::CmHelpAbout()
    {
    MessageBox("GDI Line Drawing Demonstration\n\n"
               "'Borland C++ 4.0 Programming\n"
               "   for Windows', by Paul Yao", Title);
    }

void DFrame::EvInitMenu (HMENU menu)
    {
    MenuCheckMark(menu, CM_ARC,        bArc);
    MenuCheckMark(menu, CM_POLYLINE,   bPolyline);
    MenuCheckMark(menu, CM_ANGLEARC,   bAngleArc);
    MenuCheckMark(menu, CM_POLYBEZIER, bPolyBezier);
    MenuCheckMark(menu, CM_POLYDRAW,   bPolyDraw);

    MenuCheckMark(menu, CM_ALWAYS,    (opErase == Always)    );
    MenuCheckMark(menu, CM_SOMETIMES, (opErase == Sometimes) );
    MenuCheckMark(menu, CM_NEVER,     (opErase == Never)     );
    }

void DFrame::EvSize (UINT sizeType, TSize& size)
    {
    TFrameWindow::EvSize(sizeType, size);

    cxWidth  = size.cx;
    cyHeight = size.cy;
    }

void DFrame::EvTimer (UINT)
    {
    int cFunc = 0;
    int Enabled[MAXFUNCTIONS];

    // Count number of enabled drawing functions.
    if (bArc)        { Enabled[cFunc++] = ARC;        }
    if (bPolyline)   { Enabled[cFunc++] = POLYLINE;   }
    if (bAngleArc)   { Enabled[cFunc++] = ANGLEARC;   }
    if (bPolyBezier) { Enabled[cFunc++] = POLYBEZIER; }
    if (bPolyDraw)   { Enabled[cFunc++] = POLYDRAW;   }

    // Grab a DC
    TClientDC dc(HWindow);

    // Erase background -- either always, sometimes or never.
    BOOL bErase = (opErase == Always);
    bErase = (bErase ||
             (opErase == Sometimes) &&
             (random(ERASESEED) == 0));

    if (bErase)
        {
        dc.PatBlt(0, 0, cxWidth, cyHeight, WHITENESS);
        }

    // Don't do anything if no functions are enabled.
    if (cFunc == 0)
```

```
        return;

    // Select a random pen.
    dc.SelectObject(*aptpen[random(PenCount)]);

    // Select random number of points to draw
    int cPoints = random(MAXPOINTS);

    // Fill array with random points
    for (int i = 0; i < cPoints; i++)
        {
        ptDraw[i].x = random(cxWidth);
        ptDraw[i].y = random(cyHeight);
        }

    // Select a random function
    switch (Enabled[random (cFunc)])
        {
        case ARC:
            if (bArc)
                {
                for (int iArc = 0; iArc < cPoints; iArc +=4)
                    {
                    dc.Arc(ptDraw[iArc].x,   ptDraw[iArc].y,
                           ptDraw[iArc+1].x, ptDraw[iArc+1].y,
                           ptDraw[iArc+2].x, ptDraw[iArc+2].y,
                           ptDraw[iArc+3].x, ptDraw[iArc+3].y);
                    dc.SelectObject(*aptpen[random(PenCount)]);
                    }
                }
            break;
        case POLYLINE:
            if (bPolyline)
                dc.Polyline(ptDraw, cPoints);
            break;
#if defined(__WIN32__)
        case ANGLEARC:
            if (bAngleArc)
                {
                FLOAT flStartAngle, flSweepAngle;
                for (int iArc = 0; iArc < cPoints; iArc += 2)
                    {
                    flStartAngle = random(360);
                    flSweepAngle = random(360);
                    dc.MoveTo (ptDraw[iArc].x, ptDraw[iArc].y);
                    dc.AngleArc(ptDraw[iArc].x, ptDraw[iArc].y,
                                (DWORD)ptDraw[iArc+1].x / 5,
                                flStartAngle, flSweepAngle);
                    }
                }

            break;
        case POLYBEZIER:
            if (bPolyBezier)
                dc.PolyBezier(ptDraw, cPoints);
            break;
        case POLYDRAW:
            if (bPolyDraw)
                {
                // Set up abTypes array to decide whether
                // to draw (a) LineTo, or (b) BezierTo
                int iType = 0;
```

```
                abTypes[0] = PT_MOVETO;
                for (iType = 1; iType < cPoints;)
                    {
                    if (random(2))
                        {
                        abTypes[iType++] = PT_LINETO;
                        }
                    else
                        {
                        // Check for room in array.
                        if (iType <= cPoints - 3)
                            {
                            abTypes[iType++] = PT_BEZIERTO;
                            abTypes[iType++] = PT_BEZIERTO;
                            abTypes[iType++] = PT_BEZIERTO;
                            }
                        else
                            {
                            // Not enough room in array -
                            // pick LineTo
                            while (iType < cPoints)
                                abTypes[iType++] = PT_LINETO;
                            }
                        }
                    }
                dc.PolyDraw(ptDraw, abTypes, cPoints);
                }
            break;
#endif
        }
    }

void DFrame::SetupWindow()
    {
    TFrameWindow::SetupWindow();

    // Ask for regular timer messages.
    SetTimer(1, 100, 0);

    // Start random number generator.
    randomize();

    // Build list of available device colors by asking
    // for list of all device pens. Color information
    // comes along as well.
    TClientDC dc(HWindow);

    // Calculate number of pens to create.
    PenCount = dc.GetDeviceCaps(NUMCOLORS);
    if (PenCount > MAXPENS) PenCount = MAXPENS;

    // Create list of colors in system.
    TProcInstance itEnumProc((FARPROC)ObjEnumProc);
    dc.EnumObjects(OBJ_PEN, (GOBJENUMPROC)FARPROC(itEnumProc), this);

    // Create array of pens.
    int cxyWidth;
    for (int i=0; i < PenCount; i++)
        {
        cxyWidth = random(3);
        if (i == PenCount / 2) cxyWidth = 8;
        aptpen[i] = new TPen(AvailableColors[i], cxyWidth);
```

```
        }
    }

void DFrame::MenuCheckMark(HMENU menu, int id, BOOL bCheck)
    {
    WORD wState;
    wState = (bCheck) ? MF_CHECKED : MF_UNCHECKED;
    ::CheckMenuItem (menu, id, wState);
    }

int CALLBACK ObjEnumProc(LPVOID lpObject , LPARAM lpData)
    {
    LOGPEN far * lpPen = (LOGPEN far *)lpObject;
    DFrame * lpDF = (DFrame *)lpData;

    // Add colors to list if they aren't there already.
    if (INT_MAX == lpDF->AvailableColors.Find(lpPen->lopnColor))
        {
        lpDF->AvailableColors.Add(lpPen->lopnColor);
        }
    return 1;
    }

//
// Application object
class DApp : public TApplication
    {
  public:
    DApp() : TApplication()
        {
        }
    void InitMainWindow()
        {
        SetMainWindow (new DFrame("GDI Lines"));
        MainWindow->AssignMenu("MAIN");
        MainWindow->SetIcon(this, "SNAPSHOT");
        }
    };

//
// Application main entry point.
OwlMain(int, char **)
    {
    return DApp().Run();
    }
```

LINES.H

```
#define CM_FILEEXIT    100

#define CM_ARC         200
#define CM_ANGLEARC    201
#define CM_POLYLINE    202
#define CM_POLYBEZIER  203
#define CM_POLYDRAW    204

#define CM_NEVER       300
#define CM_SOMETIMES   301
#define CM_ALWAYS      302
```

```
#define CM_HELPABOUT   400

// Declare C language callback for
// enumerating GDI drawing objects.
extern "C" {
int CALLBACK ObjEnumProc(LPVOID lpObject, LPARAM lpData);
};
```

LINES.RC

```
#include "lines.h"

snapshot icon lines.ico

main MENU
    BEGIN
    POPUP "&File"
        {
        MENUITEM "E&xit", CM_FILEEXIT
        }
    POPUP "&Draw"
        {
        MENUITEM "&Arc",         CM_ARC
        MENUITEM "&Polyline",    CM_POLYLINE
        MENUITEM "An&gleArc",    CM_ANGLEARC
        MENUITEM "Poly&Bezier",  CM_POLYBEZIER
        MENUITEM "Poly&Draw",    CM_POLYDRAW
        }
    POPUP "&Erase"
        {
        MENUITEM "&Always",      CM_ALWAYS
        MENUITEM "&Sometimes",   CM_SOMETIMES
        MENUITEM "&Never",       CM_NEVER
        }
    POPUP "&Help"
        {
        MENUITEM "&About...", CM_HELPABOUT
        }
    END
```

LINES.DEF

```
EXETYPE WINDOWS

CODE MOVEABLE DISCARDABLE
DATA MULTIPLE MOVEABLE

HEAPSIZE   512
STACKSIZE 8192
```

DYNA16.MAK

```
#  MAKE file for Win16 API using dynamic BIDS,
#  OWL and C-runtime libraries.
#
#    C> make -fstatic16.mak
#

.AUTODEPEND
CC = -c -H -H"owl\owlpch.h" -ml -R -vi -WS -X-
CD = -D_RTLDLL;_BIDSDLL;_OWLDLL;_OWLPCH;
INC = -I\BC4\INCLUDE
LIB = -L\BC4\LIB

lines.exe :  lines.obj lines.res
  tlink -c -C -Twe $(LIB) @dyna16.lnk
  brc lines.res lines.exe

lines.obj :  lines.cpp
  bcc $(CC) $(CD) lines.cpp

lines.res :  lines.rc lines.ico lines.h
  brc $(INC) -31 -R lines.rc
```

DYNA16.LNK

```
\bc4\lib\c0wl.obj+
lines.obj
lines,lines
\bc4\lib\bidsi.lib+
\bc4\lib\owlwi.lib+
\bc4\lib\import.lib+
\bc4\lib\crtldll.lib
lines.def
```

DYNA32.MAK

```
#  MAKE file for Win32 API using dynamic BIDS,
#  OWL and C-runtime libraries.
#
#    C> make -fdyna32.mak
#

.AUTODEPEND
CC = -c -H -H\""owl\owlpch.h\"" -p- -R -vi -W -X-
CD = -D_RTLDLL;_BIDSDLL;_OWLDLL;_OWLPCH;
INC = -I\BC4\INCLUDE
LIB = -L\BC4\LIB

lines.exe :  lines.obj lines.res
  tlink32 -aa -c -Tpe $(LIB) @dyna32.lnk
  brc32 lines.res lines.exe

lines.obj :  lines.cpp
  bcc32 $(CC) $(CD) lines.cpp
```

```
lines.res :  lines.rc lines.ico lines.h
  brc32 $(INC) -w32 -R lines.rc
```

DYNA32.LNK

```
\bc4\lib\c0w32.obj+
lines.obj
lines,lines
\bc4\lib\bidsfi.lib+
\bc4\lib\owlwfi.lib+
\bc4\lib\import32.lib+
\bc4\lib\cw32i.lib
lines.def
```

Now that we've looked at GDI's line drawing routines, let's examine the DC attributes that deal with lines.

DC Attributes

Five DC attributes are used by GDI to draw lines:

Drawing Attribute	*Comments*
Arc Direction	(Win32) Determines whether arcs are drawn in a clockwise or counterclockwise direction (default = counterclockwise).
Background color	Second color for nonsolid pens
Background mode	Turns on/off background color
Current position	(*x*,*y*) position for `LineTo` routine
Drawing mode	Boolean drawing operation
Miter Limit	(Win32) Determines how far a pointy (mitered) corner can extend beyond the limit of the corner. (Only affects geometric pens created with the `PS_JOIN_MITER` join style—See `ExtCreatePen` Win32 function.)
Pen	Line color, width, and style

Without a doubt, the most important attribute is the pen, which determines the appearance of the line in terms of color, width, and style (or pattern, such as solid or dotted). The term **styled lines** is often used for lines with a nonsolid style: dotted, dashed, etc.

The second most important attribute is the **drawing mode**, which lets us specify a Boolean operator to use in a drawing operation. More on that later.

Of the other three attributes, two affect *styled* lines, but not solid lines: background color and background mode. GDI uses the background color for the spaces between the lines—that is, between the foreground dashes or dots. The background mode toggles whether the background part of a styled line should be filled in or left alone. Keep in mind while using these two attributes that they also affect filled areas—when a hatched brush is used—and text.

The background color is set using the **SetBkColor** routine, defined as follows:

```
dc.SetBkColor (crColor)
```

- `crColor` is a color reference value; it is (a) an RGB triplet, (b) a palette index, or (c) a palette-relative RGB value.

The following line of code sets the background color to blue:

```
dc.SetBkColor (RGB(0, 0, 0xFF));
```

To set the background mode, you call the **SetBkMode** routine, whose syntax is

```
dc.SetBkMode (nBkMode)
```

- `nBkMode` is the on/off switch: Set to `OPAQUE` to enable background color, and to `TRANSPARENT` to disable background color.

The final attribute, the current position, is a DC attribute that we discussed in relation to the **MoveTo/LineTo** routines. It is an *x,y* value that is used by these routines as part of their drawing: **MoveTo** sets the current position; **LineTo** uses it as the starting point for the line to draw. **LineTo** updates the current position to the end point of the line it draws.

Let's take a close look at pens, and the way they are created and manipulated.

About Pens

A pen is a DC drawing attribute that describes how lines are drawn. Pens have three qualities: color, width, and style. If you'd like, you can think of each of these qualities as a drawing attribute in its own right. In the world of graphics programming, when drawing attributes are grouped in this way, the group is called an **attribute bundle**. Attribute bundles are convenient because they let you refer to several drawing attributes at the same time.

The Win16 version of GDI is very flexible in the way it lets you share pens: Pens can be shared between programs and between devices. GDI has a set of stock pens that any program can use, or a program can create a set of custom pens and let different devices share them. The net effect of this sharing is that GDI minimizes the amount of memory needed to store drawing attributes. GDI is thrifty with memory because earlier versions of Windows had to run in only 640K of RAM.

Besides pens, the other freely shareable objects under Win16 include DCs, brushes, fonts, bitmaps, regions, and palettes. In spite of the benefits to sharing that were just discussed, a serious drawback involves ownership. What happens if a GDI object never gets cleaned up? What happens if it gets cleaned up too soon? On the one hand, memory can get wasted. On the other hand, you introduce bugs when an object gets cleaned up while someone is still using it.

This problem is addressed under the Win32 version of GDI by making all drawing objects *private* to each process. This solves the ownership issue: When a process needs a GDI object, it creates one. When it's done using it, it destroys it. If a process terminates without doing clean up, GDI32 eliminates leftover objects with no risk of damage to any program. The Win16 version of GDI never had this freedom.

The various OWL classes that wrap around these GDI drawing objects handle the required initialization and cleanup. The built-in constructor/destructor mechanism of C++ lends itself naturally to the needs of GDI. To make it work, though, you must be sure to destroy any object that you create. To make sure that GDI objects get cleaned up, experienced Windows programmers always write cleanup code immediately after writing allocation code. In OWL terms, right after you type the code to allocate, say, a pen

```
tpenBlue = new TPen (TColor::Blue);
```

you think about when it makes sense to delete the pen and for that event type the following cleanup code:

```
delete tpenBlue;
```

Getting into the habit of matching allocation routines to cleanup routines is a good practice anyway. With the Win16 version of GDI, it's critical.

Pens and Device Independence

How can pens be used for different devices? The term **logical pen** describes how this is possible. A pen is a request to a device to create lines with a particular appearance. When GDI is ready to draw on a specific device, it makes a request to the device to **realize** a pen. Only at this time does the device driver create the data structures needed to draw lines with the desired qualities. This aspect is hidden in the GDI device-driver interface, but it allows a program to share pens between devices.

Creating and Using Pens

When Windows starts up, GDI creates a set of pens that can be shared by all programs. These are known as **stock pens**. GDI has three stock pens: one black, one white, and one null (invisible ink) pen. The null pen is a placeholder, since every DC must contain a valid pen. The other two pens draw solid lines with a width of one pixel.

Pens are identified by a handle. To get the handle of a stock pen, you could call the WinAPI **GetStockObject** routine, as shown here:

```
HPEN hpen;

hpen = GetStockObject (BLACK_PEN);   /* or */
hpen = GetStockObject (WHITE_PEN);   /* or */
hpen = GetStockObject (NULL_PEN);
```

Using the OWL libraries, you'll create a pen by calling one of the many OWL **TPen** constructors. If you got a stock object directly from GDI, you'd use the first constructor to wrap a **TPen** around it:

```
TPen (HPEN, TAutoDelete)
TPen (TColor, width, style)
TPen (LOGPEN far*)
TPen (TPen&)
TPen (penStyle, width, TBrush&, styleCount, style)
TPen (penStyle, width, LOGBRUSH&, styleCount, style)
```

Another way to access GDI's stock pens is to call the second constructor in this list. If you request a black or white pen with a width of 1-pixel, it returns a **TPen** wrapped around a stock pen handle. (The null pen is not supported by OWL.) If the pen you request *doesn't* match a stock pen, OWL calls one of the various GDI pen creation routines to create one for you. Once you have a pen, you call **SelectObject** to install the pen into a DC. This code creates a blue pen and connects it to a DC:

```
tpenBlue = TPen(TColor::Blue);// def-width=1, def style=PS_SOLID
dc.SelectObject(tpen);
```

After a pen has been selected into a DC, it is used for all subsequently drawn lines. This includes lines drawn with **MoveTo/LineTo**, **Polyline**, and the other GDI drawing routines.

It's easy to create custom pens if you need them. GDI provides three routines for this purpose: **CreatePen**, **CreatePenIndirect**, and **ExtCreatePen** (Win32). Let's take a look at each of these GDI routines and the associated OWL **TPen** constructor.

The only difference between the first two routines is the way the parameters are specified. The syntax for **CreatePen** is:

```
hpen = CreatePen (nPenStyle, nWidth, crColor);
```

- `nPenStyle` selects a pen style from the flags shown in Figure 8.8.
- `nWidth` sets the pen width.

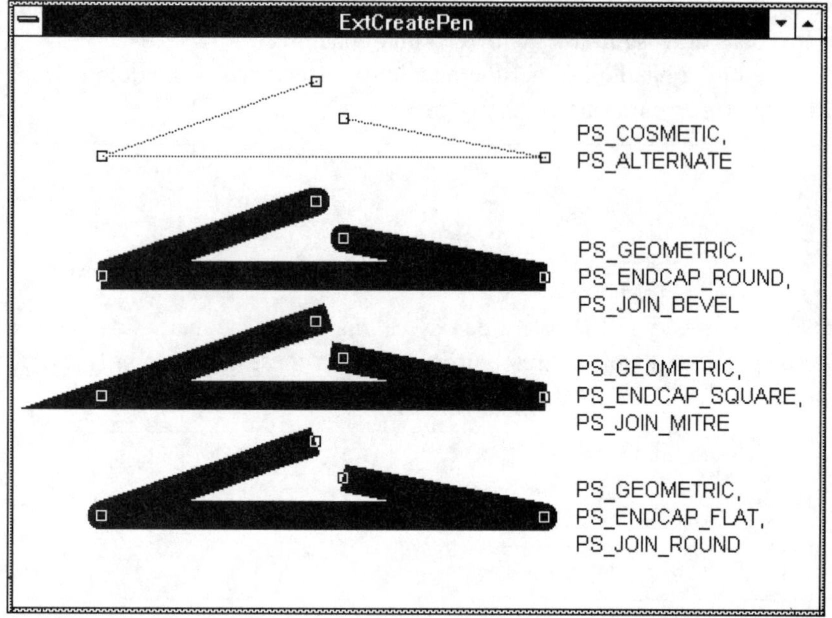

Figure 8.8 ExtCreatePen penstyles showing one cosmetic line, and three geometric lines.

- `crColor` is a color reference; as before, it is (a) an RGB triplet—or an OWL `TColor` value, (b) a color palette index, or (c) a palette-relative RGB value.

So to create a red pen that draws lines two units wide, you say

```
hpen = CreatePen (PS_SOLID, 2, RGB (255, 0, 0));
```

The corresponding OWL constructor is declared:

```
TPen (TColor color, int width=1, int style=PS_SOLID)
```

which means that the equivalent OWL statement to the above **`CreatePen`** call is

```
TPen tpenRed = (TColor::Red, 2)
```

The syntax for GDI's **`CreatePenIndirect`** is

```
LOGPEN logpen;
hpen = CreatePenIndirect (&logpen)
```

`LOGPEN` is defined in WINDOWS.H as

```
typedef struct tagLOGPEN
  {
    WORD  lopnStyle;
    POINT lopnWidth;
    DWORD lopnColor;
  } LOGPEN;
```

The OWL constructor that wraps **CreatePenIndirect** is of course the one that uses the **LOGPEN** structure to describe the desired pen:

```
TPen (const LOGPEN far* logpen)
```

One difference between **CreatePen** and **CreatePenIndirect** is that the **LOGPEN** structure uses a **POINT** structure to hold the pen width. As you may recall, the **POINT** structure has two members, one for an *x* value and one for a *y* value. To create the same red pen as above, you say

```
LOGPEN logpen;
logpen.lopnStyle = PS_SOLID;
logpen.lopnWidth.x = 2;
logpen.lopnColor = RGB (255, 0, 0));
hpen = CreatePenIndirect (&logpen)
```

GDI's third pen creating routine, **ExtCreatePen**, is a Win32-specific routine. With it, the Win32 API shows some refinements over the Win16 line drawing capability. This function gives you control over how the ends of lines are drawn, over how the joins between lines are drawn, over how a line is filled, and over the appearance of styled lines. Figure 8.9 shows some of the variations in endcap styles and in join styles. Win16 pens only draw rounded encaps and round joins. This function is defined:

```
LOGBRUSH logbrush
hpen = ExtCreatePen (DWORD dwStyle, DWORD dwWidth, LOGBRUSH * logbrush,
                     DWORD dwStyleCount, DWORD * lpStyle)
```

- **dwStyle** selects a pen style, which is a combination of a style from figure 8.9, OR'ed ('|' operator) with one from each of the following sets of style values:

  —Line scaling: **PS_GEOMETRIC** or **PS_COSMETIC**

  —End caps: **PS_ENDCAP_ROUND**, **PS_ENDCAP_SQUARE**, **PS_ENDCAP_FLAG**

  —Joins: **PS_JOIN_BEVEL**, **PS_JOIN_MITER**, **PS_JOIN_ROUND**
- **dwWidth** is the pen width, which must be one (1) for cosmetic pens.
- **logbrush** points to a **LOGBRUSH** structure, which GDI uses to define brush attributes—a style, color, and hatch pattern.
- **dwStyleCount** defines the number of style values in the **lpStyle** array.

- **lpStyle** points to an array of values for custom styles. If you don't like the dash and dot patterns in the predefined styles, use this field to create your own.

This figure also shows a difference between cosmetic (**PS_COSMETIC**) lines and geometric (**PS_GEOMETRIC**) lines: Cosmetic lines are always one pixel wide. Geometric lines, on the other hand, can be wider than one pixel and scale when the coordinate transformation changes. You'd use cosmetic lines to draw lines that aren't part of a drawing but rather are intended to highlight parts of a drawing—such as elevation marks on a map. Geometric lines scale, on the other hand, so that as you zoom in on them, they would grow larger. On a blueprint of a building, for example, you'd expect to have the walls grow wider as you zoom in to examine some part in greater detail.

Not shown in the accompanying figure is how **ExtCreatePen** lets you create pens with more complex patterns than Win16 pens. In particular, you specify the color with a **brush**—a drawing object used to fill interiors, which I'll discuss in the next chapter. Unlike Win16 pens, you can create hatched brushes and you can create brushes from bitmaps. **ExtCreatePen** can use either type of brush to define a pen.

OWL provides two constructors which call GDI's **ExtCreatePen** function:

```
TPen (penStyle, width, LOGBRUSH&, styleCount, style)
TPen (penStyle, width, TBrush&, styleCount, style)
```

The parameters to the first constructor exactly match those you pass to **ExtCreatePen**, so it's slightly more efficient than the second one. The second one lets you define the pen's pattern with an OWL brush in place of a **LOGBRUSH** structure, so it might be convenient when you're creating pens and brushes together.

Aside from the new styles defined for **ExtCreatePen**, both the Win16 and Win32 versions of GDI support seven pen styles, as illustrated in Figure 8.9. The last style, **PS_INSIDEFRAME**, provides the same results as the **PS_SOLID** style with two important differences: color, and use in filled figures. This is the only line style that uses dithered colors. All other pens are only available in solid colors.

In the context of filled figures, the **PS_INSIDEFRAME** style has some unique features. As you'll see when we discuss filled figures, a pen with the style **PS_INSIDEFRAME**

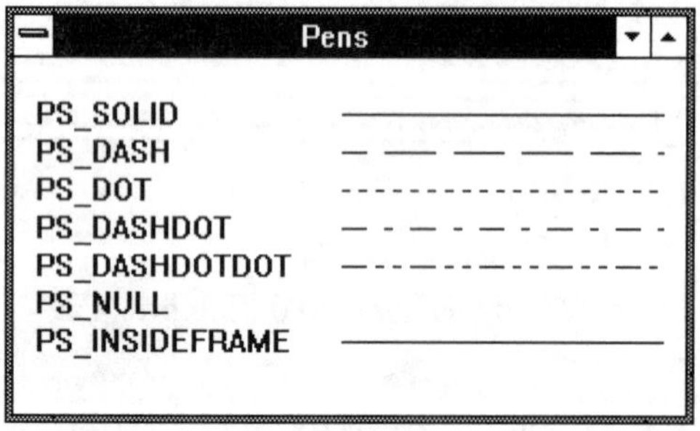

Figure 8.9 GDI's seven pen styles

draws on the inside of the boundaries. Other pens are centered on the boundary so that half is inside the border and half is outside.

You specify the width of a pen in logical units. This corresponds to the units of the current mapping mode in the *x*-axis. Since we are using the **MM_TEXT** mapping mode, our units are pixels. If you specify a pen width of zero, then regardless of the mapping mode, you will get a pen that is exactly one pixel wide.

Like pixel colors, pen colors are defined using one of three methods: an RGB triplet, a palette index value, or a palette-relative RGB triplet. Whichever you choose, pens are ordinarily created from solid colors. The exception is pens with the **PS_INSIDEFRAME** style. The color of such a pen can include dithered colors.

Dithered colors are created by combining two or more colors. In the real world, color mixing is nothing new. If you go to buy paint, for example, the store clerk might mix a little bit of black into a can of white paint to create a shade of gray.

GDI creates dithered colors by combining two (or more) colors in a regular pattern to create the illusion of hundreds of colors on 16-color devices, like EGA and VGA display adapters. On monochrome devices, like the Hercules and CGA display adapters, dozens of shades of gray can be created using this technique. Dithering works so well that, without the aid of a special program like MAGNIFY, it is often hard to tell a dithered color from a pure color.

Because dithered colors require a little more work from a device driver, only one pen style supports dithering: **PS_INSIDEFRAME**. Usually, dithering is reserved for brushes—a subject we'll cover when we discuss the creation of filled figures.

We're now going to investigate the last DC drawing attribute that affects lines: the drawing mode. In the process, we'll give you a preview of our mouse input program from Chapter 16.

Drawing Modes and Lines

A **drawing mode** is a Boolean operation that directs GDI how to draw pixels, lines, and filled figures. The drawing mode, sometimes called a raster operation, or "ROP" for short, determines how source pixels will interact with destination pixels.

With lines, a drawing mode describes how pens interact with pixels already present on the display surface. In the physical world, a ballpoint pen overwrites whatever surface it touches. While some drawing modes produce this effect, drawing modes provide a much richer set of effects than are available with a ballpoint pen. You already saw one program that uses ROPs: The MARKERS program in the last chapter. This program used the **R2_NOT** raster operation to ensure that a marker is visible, no matter where it's drawn.

Another use of drawing modes lets us draw shapes that seem to "float" on the display screen. This is the technique used for the mouse cursor, which wanders everywhere with-

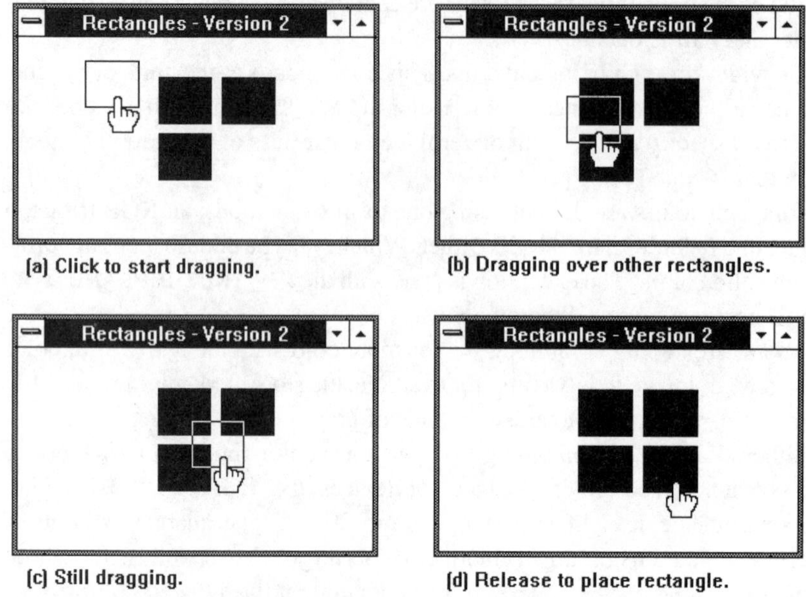

(a) Click to start dragging.

(b) Dragging over other rectangles.

(c) Still dragging.

(d) Release to place rectangle.

Figure 8.10 One use of drawing modes: dragable objects

out leaving a trail of dirty pixels. In Chapter 16, we'll write a program that uses drawing modes to drag objects across the display. Figure 8.10 illustrates object dragging.

It may seem strange that we want to perform Boolean algebra on graphic output. And yet, in a digital computer, every piece of data is encoded as a number. RGB triplets, for example, are numbers that describe colors. In the depths of graphics devices like the EGA display, numbers make up the pixels of a graphic image.

Drawing modes take advantage of this to allow the application of Boolean operations. And since a computer's CPU uses Boolean algebra as part of its day-to-day operation, it is a simple matter to apply Boolean operations to graphic images.

Figure 8.11 shows the 16 raster operations that GDI supports, along with the lines that are created with a white and with a black pen against a white and a black background. Notice how every drawing mode is different. If you'd like, you can inhibit output with the **R2_NOP** mode, or guarantee that something will be drawn using the **R2_NOT** mode. Notice that two of the modes, **R2_BLACK** and **R2_WHITE**, ignore the pen color.

One thing to keep in mind about drawing attributes is that they affect more than just lines: They affect the output of pixels (**SetPixel** routine) and filled geometric figures (the GDI primitives in the next chapter). GDI doesn't use drawing modes when drawing text, however. The reason has to do with performance. Even though raster operations are implemented at the level of the device driver and are quite fast, they slow down the output of text and so are not used by GDI's text drawing routines.

To find out the current setting of the drawing mode, you call the **GetROP2** routine. To set a new drawing mode value in the DC, you call the **SetROP2** routine, as in

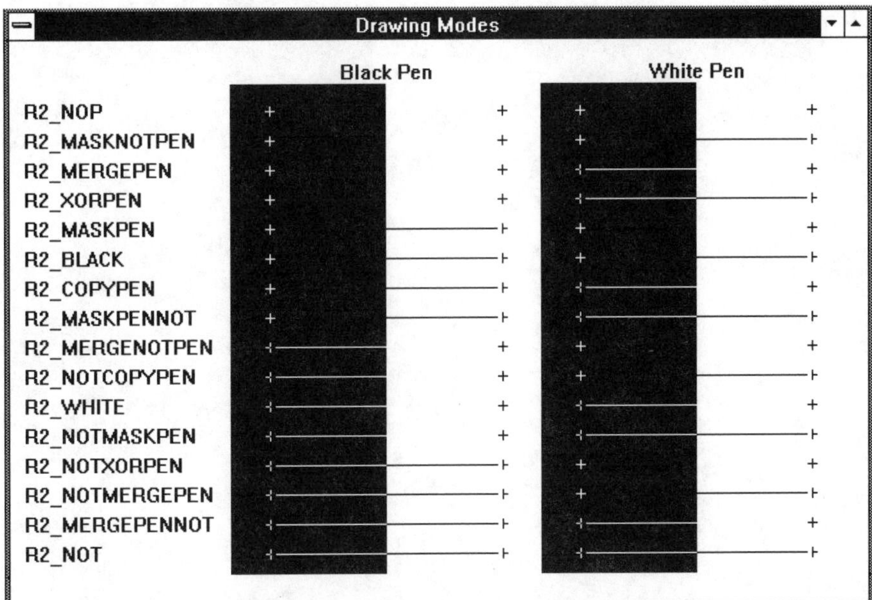

Figure 8.11 GDI's sixteen drawing modes

```
SetROP2 (hdc, R2_XORPEN);
```

In our next chapter, we're going to discuss filled figures. Every filled figure has a border, which is simply a line drawn using a GDI pen. As you will see, everything that we have discussed dealing with line drawing applies equally well to the creation of borders on GDI filled figures.

9

Drawing Filled Figures

The next set of GDI drawing routines that we're going to look at are those that create filled figures. A filled figure has two parts: an area and a border around the area. Filled figures are sometimes referred to as **closed figures** because the border closes in on itself. In line drawing terms, the starting and ending points are the same.

Figure 9.1 shows some examples of the types of filled figures that GDI can draw. Notice the variation in the thickness and style of different borders. These are the result of different pens. After all, a border is simply a line, and GDI uses pens to draw lines.

Notice also the variation in the interior area of the figures in the illustration. This is the result of another GDI drawing object: a **brush**. In the same way that different pens draw different types of lines, different brushes create different filled areas.

To understand the way that GDI draws filled figures, it is important to understand how coordinates are interpreted. Filled figure coordinates are slightly different from those used

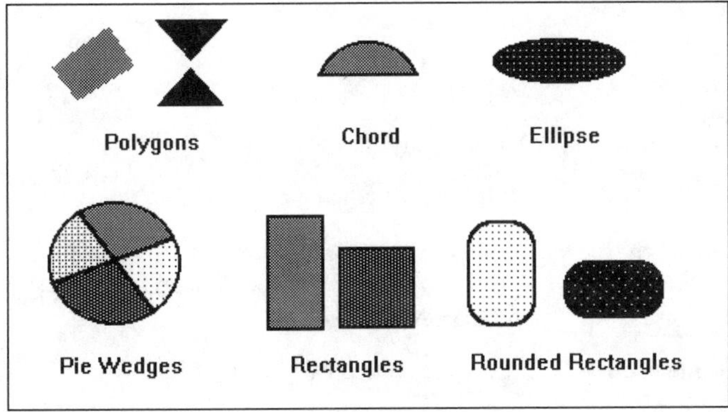

Figure 9.1 Examples of GDI filled figures

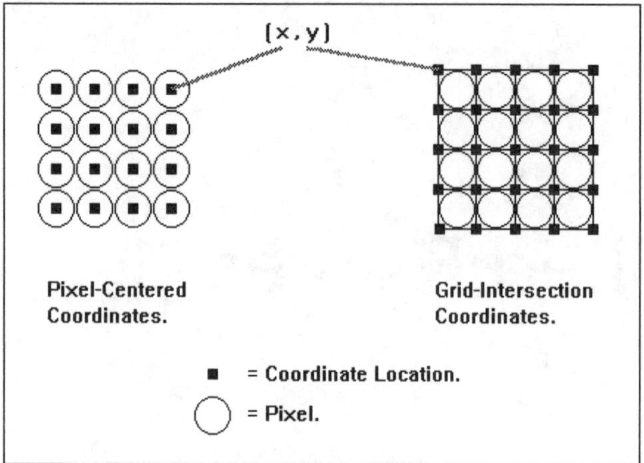

Figure 9.2 Pixel-centered and grid-intersection coordinates

in line drawing. If you draw both types of figures, you will need to make adjustments to ensure that figures are aligned in an expected manner.

In the world of graphics programming, there are two primary ways to interpret a coordinate. Put simply, the issue is: Do coordinates lie in the center of pixels or at the intersections of a grid surrounding the pixels? Figure 9.2 illustrates pixel-centered and grid-intersection coordinates.

All of GDI's line drawing primitives use **pixel-centered coordinates**. Of GDI's seven area filling primitives, two use pixel-centered coordinates and five use **grid-intersection coordinates**. While this may seem odd, each type of coordinate has its own use that makes sense in its own right. Table 9.1 shows GDI's seven area filling primitives, and the type of coordinates that each uses:

Table 9.1 GDI's Area Filling Routines

Routine	*Coordinates*	*Description*
`Polygon`	Pixel-centered	A filled polyline
`PolyPolygon`	Pixel-centered	Multiple polygons
`StrokeAndFillPath`	Pixel-centered	(Win32) Creates a filled-figure from the path defined in the DC between a `BeginPath` and `EndPath` bracket.
`Chord`	Grid-intersection	Partial arc joined by a straight line
`Ellipse`	Grid-intersection	Full arc

Table 9.1 GDI's Area Filling Routines *(Continued)*

Routine	*Coordinates*	*Description*
Pie	Grid-intersection	Pie wedge
Rectangle	Grid-intersection	Rectangle
RoundRect	Grid-intersection	Rectangle with rounded corners

Two of the Win16 filled figure routines use pixel-centered coordinates: **Polygon** and **PolyPolygon**. You can think of these routines as extensions to **Polyline**, one of GDI's line primitives. It's easy to use these routines with line drawing routines, since they use the same types of coordinates.

The other five routines use grid-intersection coordinates. These are the coordinates that GDI uses to define clipping regions. This makes it easy to use these routines with GDI's clipping routines.

GDI uses pixel-centered coordinates when the emphasis of a routine is line drawing, and grid-intersection coordinates when the emphasis is a two-dimensional area. However, if you wish to use both types of routines, it's usually a simple matter to modify the coordinates of one type of routine to fit in with the other type of routine.

When creating Win32-specific graphic output code, you can also use the **StrokeAndFillPath** routine. Like with the **StrokePath** routine discussed in the last chapter, you define a path by bracketing drawing calls between a call to **BeginPath()** and a call to **EndPath()**. After a path has been defined, the call to **StrokeAndFillPath** draws a filled figure that combines the individual component shapes.

Another Win32 enhancement is the ability to switch all filled figures to using pixel-centered coordinates. By default, Win32 drawing is compatible with Win16 drawing. But you can flip a switch by changing the "Graphics Mode" DC attribute[1]. The default value is **GM_COMPATIBLE**, but the following statement makes pixel-centered coordinates the default for filled figures:

```
dc.SetGraphicsMode (GM_ADVANCED);
```

Figure 9.3 shows the difference between pixel-centered and grid-intersection coordinates. The rectangle on the left was drawn with pixel-centered coordinates, the one on the right with grid-intersection coordinates. Square markers highlight each corner. Notice that the rectangle on the right seems to be missing a row of pixels on the bottom and left side. That's because grid-intersection coordinates only include pixels completely surrounded.

[1] The function that changes this attribute, **SetGraphicsMode**, was omitted from the OWL include files. But, like most GDI calls, it can be defined as an inline function to the native WinAPI. See Appendix H for details.

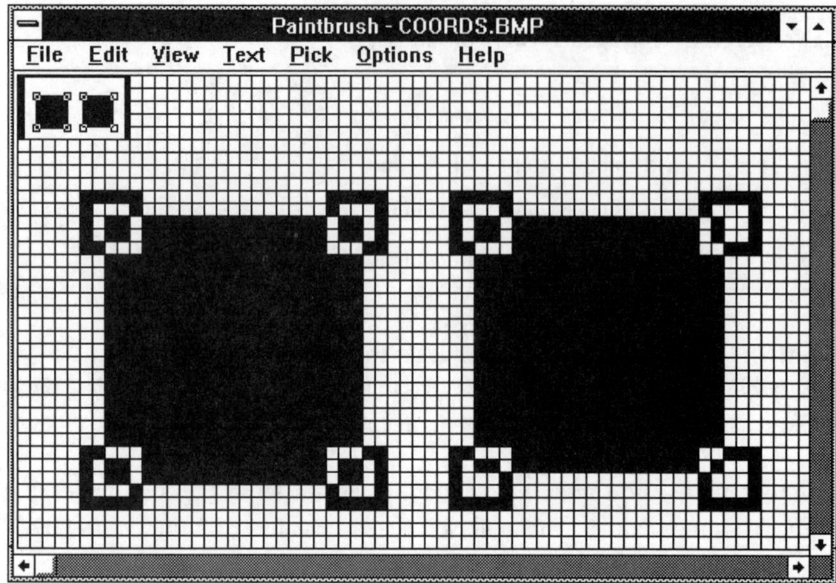

Figure 9.3 Square markers highlight the difference between pixel-centered coordinates (left) and grid-intersection coordinates (right).

This chapter's first sample program shows some simple combinations of pens and brushes—the two DC attributes which most obviously affect the appearance of filled figures. Figure 9.4 shows the various different types of rectangles that can be drawn. Here's the code to this rectangle drawing program, RECTDRAW:

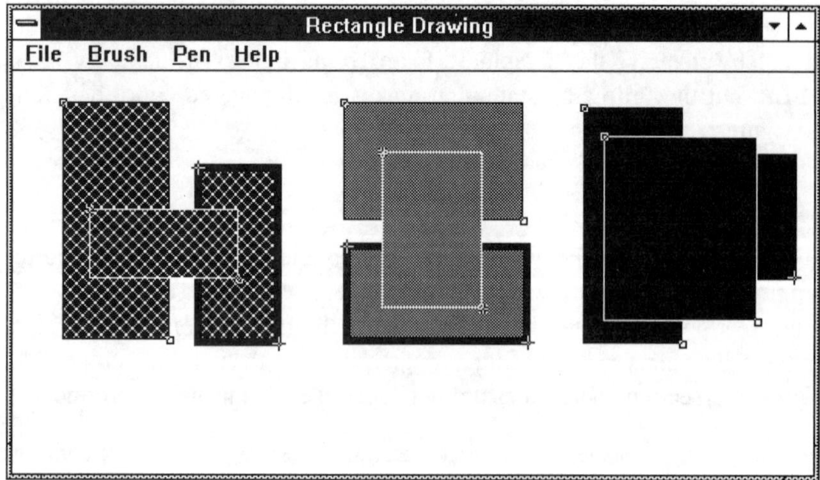

Figure 9.4 A sample of RECTDRAW's rectangle drawing

RECTDRAW.CPP

```
//
// RECTDRAW.CPP  A simple rectangle drawing program that
//               draws in response to mouse-down / mouse-up
//               input.
//

#include <owl\owlpch.h>
#include "rectdraw.h"

DEFINE_RESPONSE_TABLE1 (DFrame, TFrameWindow)
  EV_WM_INITMENU,
  EV_WM_LBUTTONDOWN,
  EV_WM_LBUTTONUP,
  EV_COMMAND(CM_FILEEXIT, CmFileExit),
  EV_COMMAND(CM_FILEERASE, CmFileErase),
  EV_COMMAND(CM_BR_HATCH, CmBrHatch),
  EV_COMMAND(CM_BR_GRAY,  CmBrGray),
  EV_COMMAND(CM_BR_BLACK, CmBrBlack),
  EV_COMMAND(CM_PN_WHITE, CmPnWhite),
  EV_COMMAND(CM_PN_BLACK1, CmPnBlack1),
  EV_COMMAND(CM_PN_BLACK2, CmPnBlack2),
  EV_COMMAND(CM_HELPABOUT, CmHelpAbout),
END_RESPONSE_TABLE;

DFrame::DFrame(char * title) : TFrameWindow(0, title)
    {
    // Mouse up/down flag.
    bMouseDown = FALSE;

    // Count of rectangles in array.
    cRects = 0;

    // Size of control-point markers.
    cxyMarkerSize = GetSystemMetrics (SM_CXICON) / 8;

    // Create brushes
    tbrHatch = new TBrush(TColor::White, HS_DIAGCROSS);
    tbrGray  = new TBrush(TColor::Gray);
    tbrBlack = new TBrush(TColor::Black);

    // Create pens
    tpnBlack = new TPen(TColor::Black);
    tpnWide  = new TPen(TColor::Black, 5);
    tpnWhite = new TPen(TColor::White);

    // Set current pen & brush.
    tbrCurrent = tbrHatch;
    tpnCurrent = tpnBlack;
    }

DFrame::~DFrame()
    {
    // Important!  Always delete any GDI object that
    // you create. Otherwise, you cause memory leaks
    // in some Win16 systems (Windows 3.1, etc.)
    delete tbrBlack;
    delete tbrGray;
    delete tbrHatch;

    delete tpnBlack;
```

```
    delete tpnWide;
    delete tpnWhite;
    }

void DFrame::CmFileExit()
    {
    CloseWindow(0); // Cause application to terminate
    }

void DFrame::CmFileErase()
    {
    // Set count of rectangles to zero...
    cRects = 0;

    // ...and force WM_PAINT message (handled by DFrame::Paint)
    Invalidate();
    }

void DFrame::CmBrHatch()  { tbrCurrent = tbrHatch; }
void DFrame::CmBrGray()   { tbrCurrent = tbrGray;  }
void DFrame::CmBrBlack()  { tbrCurrent = tbrBlack; }
void DFrame::CmPnWhite()  { tpnCurrent = tpnWhite; }
void DFrame::CmPnBlack1() { tpnCurrent = tpnBlack; }
void DFrame::CmPnBlack2() { tpnCurrent = tpnWide;  }

void DFrame::CmHelpAbout()
    {
    MessageBox("   Rectangle Drawing Program\n\n"
               "'Borland C++ 4.0 Programming\n"
               "  for Windows', by Paul Yao", Title);
    }

void DFrame::EvInitMenu(HMENU menu)
    {
    // Manage check/uncheck of brush menu items.
    MenuCheckMark(menu, CM_BR_HATCH, (tbrCurrent == tbrHatch));
    MenuCheckMark(menu, CM_BR_GRAY,  (tbrCurrent == tbrGray ));
    MenuCheckMark(menu, CM_BR_BLACK, (tbrCurrent == tbrBlack));

    // Manage check/uncheck of pen menu items.
    MenuCheckMark(menu, CM_PN_BLACK1, (tpnCurrent == tpnBlack));
    MenuCheckMark(menu, CM_PN_BLACK2, (tpnCurrent == tpnWide ));
    MenuCheckMark(menu, CM_PN_WHITE,  (tpnCurrent == tpnWhite));
    }

void DFrame::EvLButtonDown(UINT, TPoint & pt)
    {
    if (cRects == MAXRECTANGLES)
        {
        MessageBeep(MB_ICONHAND);
        MessageBox ("Cannot Create More Rectangles", Title);
        return;
        }

    // Set flag that mouse button is down.
    bMouseDown = TRUE;

    // Grab mouse for our exclusive use.
    SetCapture();

    // Record first mouse point.
    arRects[cRects].trect.left = pt.x;
```

```
    arRects[cRects].trect.top  = pt.y;

    // Place square marker at mouse location.
    TClientDC dc(HWindow);
    Marker::Square(dc, pt, cxyMarkerSize);
    }

void DFrame::EvLButtonUp(UINT, TPoint & pt)
    {
    if (!bMouseDown)
       {
       MessageBeep(MB_ICONHAND);
       return;
       }

    // Toggle that mouse is up.
    bMouseDown = FALSE;

    // Relinquish exclusive control of mouse.
    ReleaseCapture();

    // Record second mouse point.
    arRects[cRects].trect.right  = pt.x;
    arRects[cRects].trect.bottom = pt.y;

    // Record current pen & brush
    arRects[cRects].tpn = tpnCurrent;
    arRects[cRects].tbr = tbrCurrent;

    // Update rectangle count indicator.
    cRects++;

    // Force a WM_PAINT message to redraw entire window.
    Invalidate ();
    }

void DFrame::Paint (TDC& dc, BOOL, TRect&)
    {
    for (int i = 0; i < cRects ; i++ )
        {
        // Select items' pen & brush.
        dc.SelectObject (*arRects[i].tpn);
        dc.SelectObject (*arRects[i].tbr);

        // Set background BLACK so that
        // white hatch brush looks interesting.
        dc.SetBkColor (TColor::Black);

        // Draw actual rectangle
        dc.Rectangle (arRects[i].trect.left,
                      arRects[i].trect.top,
                      arRects[i].trect.right,
                      arRects[i].trect.bottom);

        // Draw markers at two control points.
        Marker::Square (dc, arRects[i].trect.left,
                            arRects[i].trect.top, cxyMarkerSize);
        Marker::Square (dc, arRects[i].trect.right,
                            arRects[i].trect.bottom, cxyMarkerSize);
        }
    }
```

```
void DFrame::MenuCheckMark(HMENU menu, int id, BOOL bCheck)
    {
    WORD wState;
    wState = (bCheck) ? MF_CHECKED : MF_UNCHECKED;
    ::CheckMenuItem (menu, id, wState);
    }

DApp::DApp() : TApplication()
    {
    }

void DApp::InitMainWindow()
    {
    SetMainWindow (new DFrame("Rectangle Drawing"));
    MainWindow->AssignMenu("MAIN");
    MainWindow->SetIcon(this, "SNAPSHOT");
    }

//
// Marker routines borrowed from CLS_MARK.CPP
// in Chapter 7's marker drawing program.
void Marker::Square (TDC& dc, int x, int y, int Size)
    {
    TPoint pt;
    pt.x = x;
    pt.y = y;
    Marker::Square(dc, pt, Size);
    }

void Marker::Square (TDC& dc, TPoint &pt, int Size)
    {
    // Request raster operation to invert pixels
    int ropOld = dc.SetROP2(R2_NOT);

    // Calculate distance from center point.
    int cxyWidth = Size / 2;

    // Draw a square marker.
    //  . . . . . . .
    //  . o o o o o .
    //  . o . . . o .
    //  . o . x . o .
    //  . o . . . o .
    //  . o o o o o .
    //  . . . . . . .
    dc.MoveTo(pt.x - cxyWidth, pt.y - cxyWidth);
    dc.LineTo(pt.x + cxyWidth, pt.y - cxyWidth);
    dc.LineTo(pt.x + cxyWidth, pt.y + cxyWidth);
    dc.LineTo(pt.x - cxyWidth, pt.y + cxyWidth);
    dc.LineTo(pt.x - cxyWidth, pt.y - cxyWidth);

    // Restore DC to the way we found it.
    dc.SetROP2 (ropOld);
    }

//
// Application main entry point.
OwlMain(int, char **)
    {
    return DApp().Run();
    }
```

RECTDRAW.H

```
#define CM_FILEEXIT  100
#define CM_FILEERASE 101
#define CM_BR_BLACK  200
#define CM_BR_GRAY   201
#define CM_BR_HATCH  202
#define CM_PN_BLACK1 300
#define CM_PN_BLACK2 301
#define CM_PN_WHITE  302
#define CM_HELPABOUT 400

const int MAXRECTANGLES = 50;
const int MARKERSIZE = 3;

//
// Marker Class
class Marker
    {
  public:
    static void Square (TDC&, TPoint&, int Size);
    static void Square (TDC&, int x, int y, int Size);
    };

//
// Rectangle Class
struct DRectangle
    {
    TBrush * tbr;
    TPen   * tpn;
    TRect    trect;
    };

//
// Main window
class DFrame : public TFrameWindow
    {
  public:
    DFrame(char * title);
    ~DFrame();
    void CmFileExit();
    void CmFileErase();
    void CmBrHatch();
    void CmBrGray();
    void CmBrBlack();
    void CmPnWhite();
    void CmPnBlack1();
    void CmPnBlack2();
    void CmHelpAbout();
    void EvInitMenu(HMENU menu);
    void EvLButtonDown(UINT, TPoint &);
    void EvLButtonUp(UINT, TPoint &);
    void Paint (TDC&, BOOL, TRect&);
    void MenuCheckMark(HMENU menu, int id, BOOL bCheck);
  private:
    BOOL       bMouseDown;
    int        cRects;
    int        cxyMarkerSize;
    DRectangle arRects [MAXRECTANGLES];
    TBrush   * tbrCurrent;
    TBrush   * tbrBlack;
    TBrush   * tbrGray;
```

```
    TBrush    * tbrHatch;
    TPen      * tpnCurrent;
    TPen      * tpnBlack;
    TPen      * tpnWide;
    TPen      * tpnWhite;

  DECLARE_RESPONSE_TABLE (DFrame);
    };

//
// Application object
class DApp : public TApplication
    {
  public:
    DApp();
    void InitMainWindow();
    };
```

RECTDRAW.RC

```
#include "rectdraw.h"

snapshot icon rectdraw.ico

main menu
    BEGIN
    POPUP "&File"
        {
        MENUITEM "&Erase", CM_FILEERASE
        MENUITEM SEPARATOR
        MENUITEM "E&xit",  CM_FILEEXIT
        }
    POPUP "&Brush"
        {
        MENUITEM "&Hatch", CM_BR_HATCH
        MENUITEM "&Gray",  CM_BR_GRAY
        MENUITEM "&Black", CM_BR_BLACK
        }
    POPUP "&Pen"
        {
        MENUITEM "&Thin Black",   CM_PN_BLACK1
        MENUITEM "&Thick Black",  CM_PN_BLACK2
        MENUITEM "&White",        CM_PN_WHITE
        }
    POPUP "&Help"
        {
        MENUITEM "&About...", CM_HELPABOUT
        }
    END
```

RECTDRAW.DEF

```
EXETYPE WINDOWS

CODE MOVEABLE DISCARDABLE
```

```
DATA MULTIPLE MOVEABLE

HEAPSIZE   512
STACKSIZE 8192
```

DYNA16.MAK

```
#  MAKE file for Win16 API using dynamic BIDS,
#  OWL and C-runtime libraries.
#
#    C> make -fstatic16.mak
#

.AUTODEPEND
CC = -c -H -H"owl\owlpch.h" -ml -R -vi -WS -X-
CD = -D_RTLDLL;_BIDSDLL;_OWLDLL;_OWLPCH;
INC = -I\BC4\INCLUDE
LIB = -L\BC4\LIB

rectdraw.exe :  rectdraw.obj rectdraw.res
  tlink -c -C -Twe $(LIB) @dyna16.lnk
  brc rectdraw.res rectdraw.exe

rectdraw.obj :  rectdraw.cpp
  bcc $(CC) $(CD) rectdraw.cpp

rectdraw.res :  rectdraw.rc rectdraw.ico rectdraw.h
  brc $(INC) -31 -R rectdraw.rc
```

DYNA16.LNK

```
\bc4\lib\c0wl.obj+
rectdraw.obj
rectdraw,rectdraw
\bc4\lib\bidsi.lib+
\bc4\lib\owlwi.lib+
\bc4\lib\import.lib+
\bc4\lib\crtldll.lib
rectdraw.def
```

DYNA32.MAK

```
#  MAKE file for Win32 API using dynamic BIDS,
#  OWL and C-runtime libraries.
#
#    C> make -fdyna32.mak
#

.AUTODEPEND
CC = -c -H -H\""owl\owlpch.h\"" -p- -R -vi -W -X-
CD = -D_RTLDLL;_BIDSDLL;_OWLDLL;_OWLPCH;
```

```
INC = -I\BC4\INCLUDE
LIB = -L\BC4\LIB

rectdraw.exe :  rectdraw.obj rectdraw.res
  tlink32 -aa -c -Tpe $(LIB) @dyna32.lnk
  brc32 rectdraw.res rectdraw.exe

rectdraw.obj :  rectdraw.cpp
  bcc32 $(CC) $(CD) rectdraw.cpp

rectdraw.res :  rectdraw.rc rectdraw.ico rectdraw.h
  brc32 $(INC) -w32 -R rectdraw.rc
```

DYNA32.LNK

```
\bc4\lib\c0w32.obj+
rectdraw.obj
rectdraw,rectdraw
\bc4\lib\bidsfi.lib+
\bc4\lib\owlwfi.lib+
\bc4\lib\import32.lib+
\bc4\lib\cw32i.lib
rectdraw.def
```

To store rectangle drawing information, RECTDRAW defines a structure **`DRectangle`**:

```
struct DRectangle
    {
    TBrush * tbr;
    TPen   * tpn;
    TRect    trect;
    };
```

Then, an array within **`DFrame`** is allocated like this:

```
DRectangle arRects[MAXRECTANGLES];
```

Each rectangle contains the following attributes: a brush for filling the interior, a pen for drawing the border, and a pair of (x,y) coordinates to hold the rectangle location. The data type used, **`TRect`**, is OWL's enhancement to the native WinAPI **`RECT`** structure. **`RECT`** is defined in Windows.H as:

```
typedef struct tagRECT
  {
    int  left;
    int  top;
    int  right;
    int  bottom;
  } RECT;
```

The elements of this array are named in a somewhat odd fashion, reflecting the use of this structure for clipping rectangles. The **`left`** and **`right`** fields contain *x* values, and the **`top`** and **`bottom`** fields contain *y* values.

The three brushes and three pens used by RECTDRAW are created in the constructor of its frame window class, **`DFrame`**. Then, to avoid problems in Win16 systems, these six objects are destroyed in **`DFrame`**'s destructor. Although you could create and destroy pens and brushes as you actually use them—which, in RECTDRAW's case, would mean in **`DFrame::Paint`**—that approach incurs additional overhead. But it's an approach that is sometimes useful when you are building your own library of graphics output routines.

RECTDRAW gets drawing location information from these two mouse messages: left-button down and left-button up (**`WM_LBUTTONDOWN`** and **`WM_LBUTTONUP`**). In OWL terms, this corresponds to the **`EvLButtonDown`** and the **`EvLButtonUp`** message response functions. Since GDI's **`Rectangle`** routine only draws rectangles that are parallel to the X and Y axes, only two points are required to uniquely define a rectangle. After the receipt of the left-button up message, a WM_PAINT message is requested by declaring the entire window damaged:

```
Invalidate();
```

which is a wrapper function for the native WinAPI function, **`InvalidateRect`**. To get a better idea of what this function does, please refer to the detailed description in the Win16/Win32 API on-line help database.

Most of the drawing action in RECTDRAW occurs in response to a **`WM_PAINT`** message. This WinAPI message gets handled by OWL's **`TWindow`** base class, which has an **`EvPaint`** message response function. It calls the WinAPI **`BeginPaint`** and **`EndPaint`** functions, and in between calls **`Paint`**. By overriding this virtual function, **`DFrame`** draws our rectangles.

Within its rectangle drawing loop, **`DFrame::Paint`** makes two calls to **`TDC::SelectObject`**—one to connect the rectangle's pen to the DC, and a second to connect the brush. So that hatch brushes are drawn against a black background, a third function is called to set the DC's background color: **`TDC::SetBkColor`**. Finally, the rectangle itself is drawn by calling **`TDC::Rectangle`**. **`TDC`** has four different versions of this routine, allowing you to pass in four integer points or two **`TPoint`** points among the various combinations. RECTDRAW uses parameters most like the WinAPI definition, which takes five parameters:

```
Rectangle (hDC, X1, Y1, X2, Y2)
```

- **`hDC`** is a handle to a device context.
- The coordinates (**`X1`**, **`Y1`**) define one rectangle corner.
- The coordinates (**`X2`**, **`Y2`**) define the opposite rectangle corner.

There are quite a few more GDI routines that draw filled figures. A discussion of the **Polygon** and **PolyPolygon** functions is next.

GDI Filled Figure Routines

This section takes a close look at each of GDI's filled figure routines. GDI has seven such routines: **Polygon**, **PolyPolygon**, **Chord**, **Ellipse**, **Pie**, **Rectangle**, and **RoundRect**.

We'll begin with the two routines that use pixel-centered coordinates.

Polygon and PolyPolygon

The **Polygon** routine is defined

```
Polygon (hDC, lpPoints, nCount)
```

- `hDC` is a handle to a device context.
- `lpPoints` is a pointer to an array of type `POINT`. It is the points to connect.
- `nCount` is the number of points to connect.

Like the **Polyline** routine that we encountered in the last chapter, this routine connects a series of points using the pen currently installed in the DC. In addition, if the first and last points are not the same, a line is drawn to close the figure, and the area inside the figure is filled using the brush currently installed in the DC.

Polygon is GDI's most flexible filled area routine, since you can use it to draw any filled figure. As a simple example, Figure 9.5 shows rectangles drawn using **Polygon**. Unlike the normal **Rectangle** routine, **Polygon** can draw *rotated* rectangles.

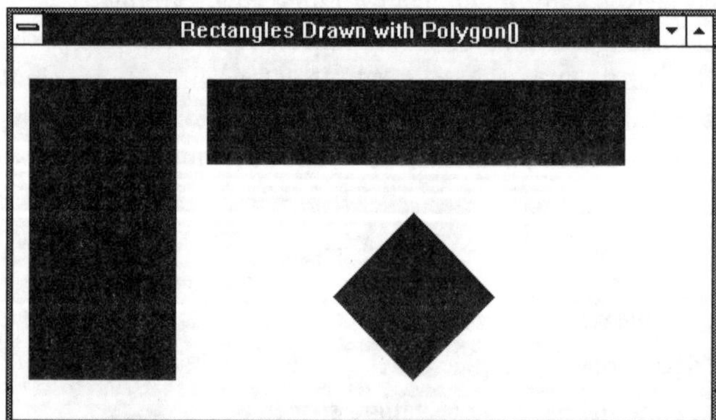

Figure 9.5 Rectangles drawn with the Polygon routine

The preceding declaration for the **Polygon** routine describes the native WinAPI function. Your clue is that the first parameter is a device context handle (**HDC**). The corresponding OWL function is a member function in OWL's **TDC** class, and is defined in DC.H as:

```
inline BOOL TDC::Polygon (const TPoint* points, int count) {
    return ::Polygon (GetHDC(), (TPoint *)points, count);
    }
```

With such functions, OWL is clearly a thin layer over the native WinAPI. For the remaining OWL GDI functions, I'll provide the WinAPI declaration and assume that the conversion to an OWL function member is straightforward enough not to require an explanation.

The **PolyPolygon** routine draws many polygons with a single call. This routine is an extension of the **Polygon** routine. Programs that draw many polygons will run faster if they call **PolyPolygon** than if they make many separate calls to **Polygon**. The speed advantage is a result of the overhead involved with making a function call.

PolyPolygon is defined as follows:

```
PolyPolygon (hDC, lpPoints, lpPolyCount, nCount);
```

- `hDC` is a handle to a device context.
- `lpPoints` is a pointer to an array of type **POINT**. It is the points to connect to create the various polygons.
- `lpPolyCount` is a pointer to an array of type **INT**. The elements of this array indicate the number of points in each polygon.
- `nCount` is an integer for the number of points in the `lpPolyCount` array. In other words, it is the number of polygons to draw.

When we talk about polygons, we normally think of figures with flat sides—like the rectangles we drew in our sample code. But we can also use the **Polygon** routines to draw curves, as long as we provide enough points. In fact, that's how GDI simulates curves—with a series of short lines. Of course, if we want to draw curves in this way, we have our work cut out for us. We'd have to calculate all of the points along the curve.

GDI has a set of routines that do this work for us and make it easy to draw filled figures with curved sides. Let's take a look at those routines.

Ellipse, Chord, and Pie

GDI has three routines that create filled figures with curved sides. As you'll see in a moment, you can think of these routines as extensions of the **Arc** routine that we covered in the last chapter. Each routine uses a bounding rectangle to draw a curve.

Here is the definition of the `Ellipse` function:

```
Ellipse (hDC, X1, Y1, X2, Y2)
```

- `hDC` is a handle to a device context.
- (`X1`, `Y1`) is a corner of the bounding rectangle.
- (`X2`, `Y2`) is the opposite corner of the bounding rectangle.

The **`Ellipse`** function creates an ellipse whose perimeter is tangent to the sides of the bounding rectangle, as illustrated in Figure 9.6.

The **`Chord`** function also makes use of a bounding rectangle to draw a partial arc connected with a line segment. This function is defined as follows:

```
Chord (hDC, X1, Y1, X2, Y2, X3, Y3, X4, Y4)
```

- `hDC` is a handle to a device context.
- (`X1`, `Y1`) and (`X2`, `Y2`) define the bounding rectangle.
- (`X3`, `Y3`) is the starting point of the line segment.
- (`X4`, `Y4`) is the ending point of the line segment.

Figure 9.7 shows a chord drawn with this function, with notation to show the bounding box and the line segment coordinates.

The **`Pie`** function takes the same parameters as the **`Chord`** function. This function draws a wedge of a pie instead of a chord. The function is defined as follows:

```
Pie (hDC, X1, Y1, X2, Y2, X3, Y3, X4, Y4)
```

- `hDC` is a handle to a device context.
- (`X1`, `Y1`) and (`X2`, `Y2`) define the bounding rectangle.
- (`X3`, `Y3`) is the starting point of the wedge.

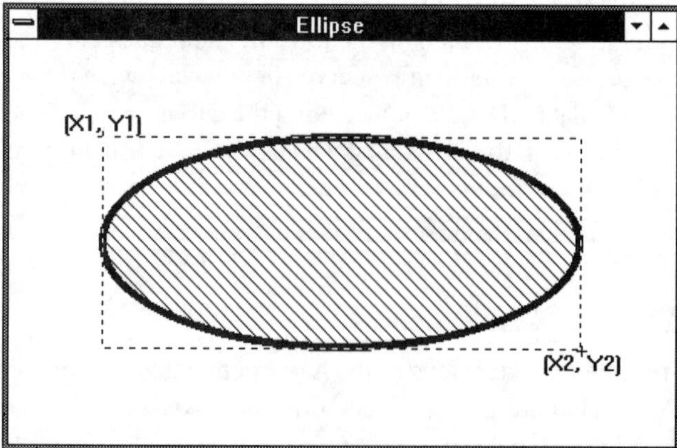

Figure 9.6 A figure drawn with the Ellipse function

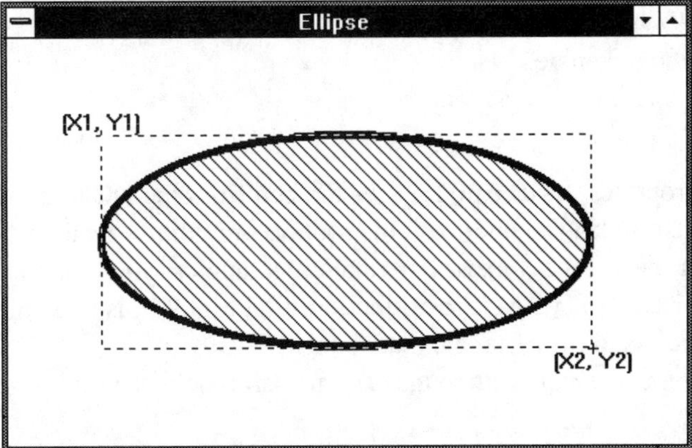

Figure 9.7 A figure drawn with the chord function

- (X4, Y4) is the ending point of the wedge.

Figure 9.8 shows a pie wedge, with the bounding box, starting point, and ending point shown.

Rectangle and RoundRect

We have seen the **`Rectangle`** function before, but for completeness sake, here is the function definition:

```
Rectangle (hDC, X1, Y1, X2, Y2)
```

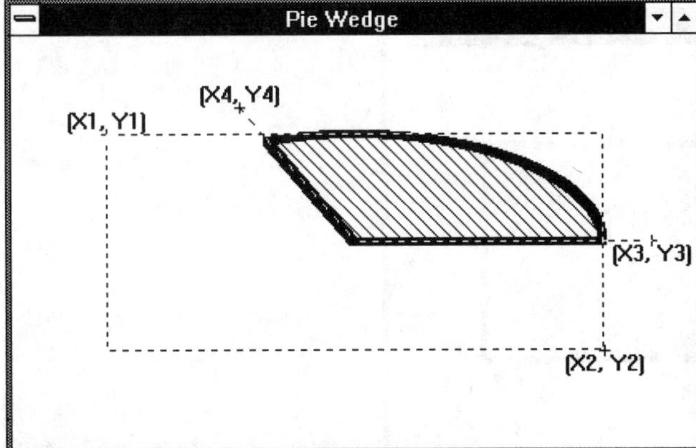

Figure 9.8 Figure drawn with the Pie function

- `hDC` is a device context handle.
- (`X1`, `Y1`) is one corner of the rectangle.
- (`X2`, `Y2`) is the opposite corner of the rectangle.

Like other GDI filled figure routines, **`Rectangle`** uses the pen from the DC to draw the rectangle border and the brush to fill the interior. This routine only draws rectangles with sides that are parallel with the *x*- and *y*-axes. For rotated rectangles, you must use either the **`Polygon`** function or the **`PolyPolygon`** function. Figure 9.9 illustrates the relationship of the two control points to the rectangle that is drawn.

The **`RoundRect`** routine draws a rectangle with rounded corners. It is defined as follows:

```
RoundRect (hDC, X1, Y1, X2, Y2, X3, Y3)
```

- `hDC` is a device context handle.
- (`X1`, `Y1`) is one corner of the rectangle.
- (`X2`, `Y2`) is the opposite corner of the rectangle.
- (`X3`, `Y3`) define a bounding box for an ellipse that is used to draw the rounded corners.

Figure 9.10 shows an example of the type of output that **`RoundRect`** can be used to create.

DC Attributes

As with other GDI drawing primitives, we must visit the device context to fully understand how much control GDI gives us over filled figures. Here is a list of the attributes that affect filled figures:

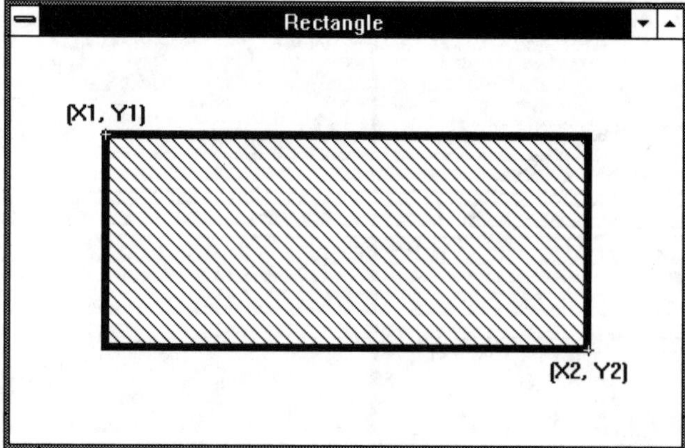

Figure 9.9 Figure drawn with the Rectangle function

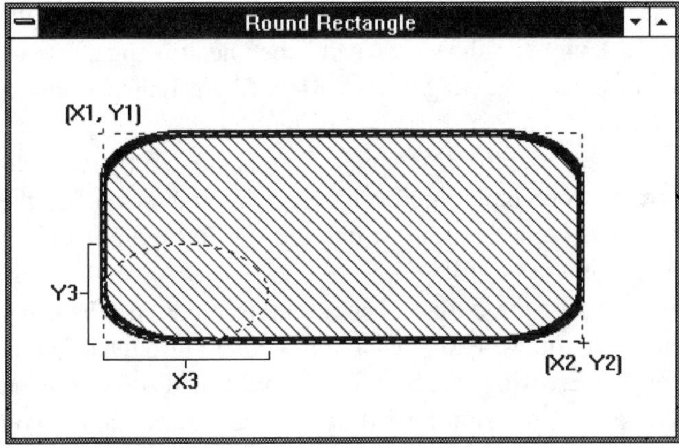

Figure 9.10 Sample of RoundRect output

Drawing Attribute	*Comments*
Background color	Second color for hatched brushes and nonsolid pens
Background mode	Turns on/off background color
Brush	Color for filling interior
Brush origin	Alignment of hatched brushes
Drawing mode	Boolean drawing operation
Graphics Mode	(Win32) When set to **GM_COMPATIBLE**, draws in a way that's compatible with Windows 3.1. When set to **GM_ADVANCED**, uses pixel-centered coordinates for all filled figure functions.
Pen	Border color, width, and style
Polygon-filling mode	For **Polygon** and **PolyPolygon** routines

Since the borders of filled figures are lines, all of the DC attributes that affect lines are also used for the borders of filled figures: background color, background mode, drawing mode, and pen. An important point to note is that, when used to draw a border, a pen is always *centered* on the border. For example, a nine-pixel-wide pen will draw a border with four pixels inside the figure, four pixels outside the figure, and one pixel on the border itself.

Pens created with a style of **PS_INSIDEFRAME**, however, never draw borders that extend beyond the border of the figure. A nine-pixel-wide **PS_INSIDEFRAME** pen, for example, will draw a border that has one pixel on the exact border and eight pixels inside the figure. This can be useful when drawing a figure which *must* occupy a specific area, and not grow beyond the rectangle which bounds the area.

Three attributes are specific to filled areas: brush, brush origin, and polygon-filling mode. Before we discuss GDI brushes, we're going to briefly discuss polygon-filling mode and drawing mode.

The names of drawing modes seem to imply that they only affect lines. For example, the default drawing mode, **R2_COPYPEN**, includes the word "pen," the line drawing attribute. In spite of this unfortunate choice of names, drawing modes affect filled figures: both the inside area and the border. Drawing modes affect pens and brushes equally.

The polygon-filling mode determines how to fill complex figures created by two routines: **Polygon** and **PolyPolygon**. For simple figures, like squares and rectangles, the polygon-filling mode has no effect. For complex figures, like the star in Figure 9.11, the polygon-filling mode determines which areas to fill.

The winding mode fills all areas inside the border. The alternate mode, on the other hand, fills only the odd areas. That is, if you were to draw a line segment through a figure, filling is turned *on* after odd boundary crossings (1, 3, 5, etc.), and turned *off* after even boundary crossings (2, 4, 6). GDI has no provision for filling the even areas, though you can achieve this effect by drawing the same figure twice.

The **SetPolyFillMode** routine, which sets this drawing attribute, is defined as follows:

```
SetPolyFillMode (hDC, nPolyFillMode)
```

- `hDC` is a handle to a device context.
- `nPolyFillMode` is either **ALTERNATE** or **WINDING**.

Now let's turn our attention to the attribute that has the most effect on the appearance of filled figures: GDI brushes.

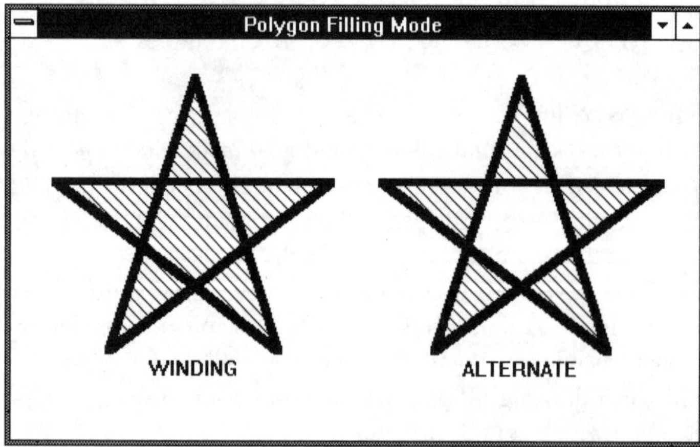

Figure 9.11 Polygon filling modes only affect complex Polygons

About Brushes

A brush is a DC drawing attribute for filling areas. Three qualities make up a brush: a style, a color, and a pattern. The size of a Win16 brush is eight pixels by eight pixels. For the sake of compatibility, Win32 brushes are also 8 x 8 pixels. But you can create a brush from a bitmap that is the size of the bitmap—so they can be as large as you'd like to make them. When we discussed GDI pens, we mentioned that attribute bundles allow a convenient way for a program to refer to several attributes at the same time. The convenience factor is certainly one of the reasons for brushes.

We mentioned earlier that pens can be shared between programs and between devices. The same is true of brushes. Just as there are stock pens, there are stock brushes. That is, GDI creates a set of brushes for use by any program. If stock brushes don't provide what you need, it is a simple matter to create your own brushes. And finally, like pens, you must be sure to clean up all of the brushes that you create. Otherwise, the memory is lost from the system. Let's look at some of the details surrounding the creation and use of brushes.

Creating and Using Brushes

At system startup time, GDI creates the following stock brushes: black, dark gray, gray, light gray, white, and null (or hollow). Like the null pen, a null brush is a placeholder. You can think of a null brush as one having a transparent color.

The **GetStockObject** routine provides a handle to stock brushes. To use a brush, install it into a DC with the **SelectObject** routine. Here is one way to draw a rectangle with a gray interior using native WinAPI routines:

```
brush = GetStockBrush (GRAY_BRUSH);// macro for GetStockObject
SelectBrush (hdc, brush);          // macro for SelectObject
Rectangle (hdc, X1, Y1, X2, Y2);
```

Here's how you get the same effect using OWL class library calls:

```
TBrush tbrGray = TBrush (TColor::Gray);
dc.SelectObject (tbrGray);
dc.Rectangle(X1, Y1, X2, Y2);
```

The OWL **TBrush** class checks for the presence of a matching stock brush *before* it creates a GDI brush, in the same way that OWL's **TPen** class checks for the presence of a stock pen. If a match is found, you use the stock brush instead of incurring the overhead of a duplicate brush.

To supplement the stock brushes, you can create custom brushes. OWL's **TBrush** class provides seven constructors to manage the brush creation process for you:

```
TBrush (HBRUSH hbr, TAutoDelete autoDelete)
TBrush (TColor color)
TBrush (TColor color, int style)
TBrush (TBitmap& pattern)
TBrush (TDib& pattern)
TBrush (LOGBRUSH far* logBrush)
```

As I cover brush creation using native WinAPI calls, I'll also mention the associated OWL constructor.

There are three types of custom brushes: solid, hatched, and pattern. Figure 9.12 shows examples of each type. GDI provides five routines to create brushes: **`CreateBrushIndirect`**, **`CreateDIBPatternBrush`**, **`CreateHatchBrush`**, **`CreatePatternBrush`**, and **`CreateSolidBrush`**.

We're going to take a close look at the last three routines in this list. Let's take a moment, though, to look at the first two. The first, **`CreateBrushIndirect`**, is able to do the job of any of the other routines. It is unique in that it takes as a parameter a pointer to a data structure that can describe any brush: a **`LOGBRUSH`** (logical brush). The OWL constructor that wraps around this routine is:

```
TBrush (LOGBRUSH far* logBrush)
```

The second routine in this list, **`CreateDIBPatternBrush`**, creates a brush from a device-independent bitmap, also known as a DIB. DIBs are bitmaps whose color information is stored in a standard format. The colors in a DIB can be correctly interpreted on any GDI device. It's OWL constructor is:

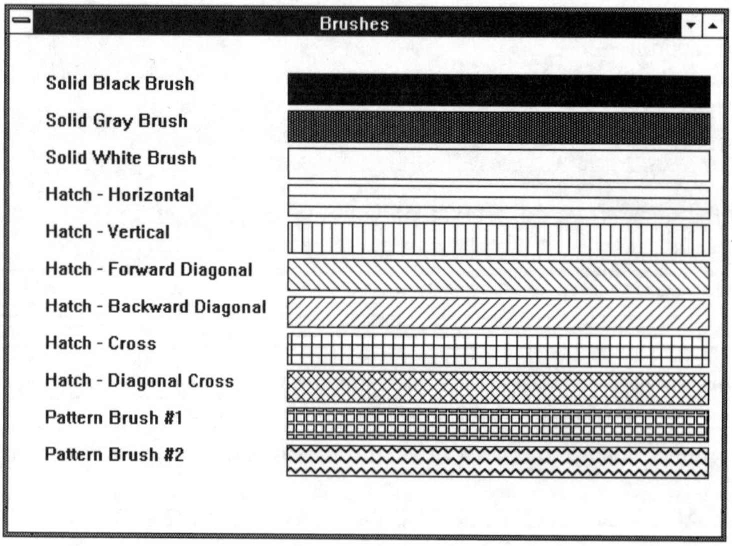

Figure 9.12 Eleven different brushes

```
TBrush (TDib& pattern)
```

Let's now turn our attention to the three types of bitmaps: solid, hatched, and pattern. As we examine each, we'll look at the three routines that we use in our sample program to create these types of brushes: **CreateSolidBrush**, **CreateHatchBrush**, and **CreatePatternBrush**.

A **solid brush** is a brush that is created from either a pure or a dithered color. We introduced dithered colors in the last chapter in our discussion of dithered pens. Dithered colors are created by mixing pure colors.

For example, the device that created Figure 9.12 has just two colors: black and white. By dithering, we can create many different shades of gray, like the one that was used to draw the rectangle labeled "Solid Gray Brush" in our figure.

The **CreateSolidBrush** routine lets you create these brushes. It is defined as

```
HBRUSH CreateSolidBrush (crColor)
```

- `crColor` is a color reference. This can be an RGB triplet, a palette index, or a palette-relative RGB value.

For example, here's how to create a white brush:

```
hbr = CreateSolidBrush (RGB (255, 255, 255));
```

The OWL constructor that calls **CreateSolidBrush** is the one defined:

```
TBrush (TColor color)
```

The OWL code for the preceding WinAPI calls to create a white brush are:

```
TBrush tbr = TBrush (TColor::White);
```

Since there is also a white stock brush, OWL accesses that one instead of creating a redundant brush.

A **hatch brush** fills areas with a pattern created with hatch marks. GDI provides six built-in hatch patterns, as shown in Figure 9.12. The **CreateHatchBrush** routine is the easiest way to create a hatch brush (although the **CreateBrushIndirect** routine can be used as well).

The syntax of **CreateHatchBrush** is as follows:

```
HBRUSH CreateSolidBrush (nIndex, crColor)
```

- `nIndex` can be any one of six values:

```
HS_BDIAGONAL
HS_CROSS
HS_DIAGCROSS
HS_FDIAGONAL
```

HS_HORIZONTAL
HS_VERTICAL

- `crColor` is a color reference. This can be an RGB triplet, a palette index, or a palette-relative RGB value.

When using the OWL **TBrush** constructors to create a hatched brush, you call the one which allows you to specify a style value. That, of course, is this one:

```
TBrush (TColor color, int style)
```

A **pattern brush** is a brush created from a bitmap pattern. If the six styles of hatch brushes aren't enough for you, a pattern brush can be created with just about any hatch pattern you'd like to use. A pattern brush can also be made to resemble a solid brush, although this is usually more work than it's worth.

To create a pattern brush, you use the **CreatePatternBrush** routine. It's syntax is as follows:

```
HBRUSH CreatePatternBrush (hBitmap)
```

- `hBitmap` is a handle to a bitmap.

To create a pattern brush, you first need a bitmap. There are many ways to create a bitmap. For now, let's look at the two methods we use in our sample program.

The first method involves using a graphic editor, such as the Resource Workshop, to draw a bitmap pattern like that shown in Figure 9.13. This pattern is saved to a file (SQUARE.BMP in our sample program). To incorporate this bitmap into our program, we make an entry in the resource script file, like the following:

```
square bitmap square.bmp
```

The following lines of code read this bitmap into memory, and use it to create a pattern brush:

```
TBitmap * ptbm;
ptbm = new TBitmap (GetApplication()->GetInstance(), "square");
tbr[9] = new TBrush (* pbtm);
delete ptbm;
```

This brush is now ready to be selected into a DC for use in filling the inside of a GDI filled figure. The corresponding **TBrush** constructor is this one:

```
TBrush (TBitmap& pattern)
```

A second method that can be used to create a bitmap is to call the **CreateBitmap** routine with a pointer to the bits to include in the bitmap. The **CreateBitmap** routine is defined as follows:

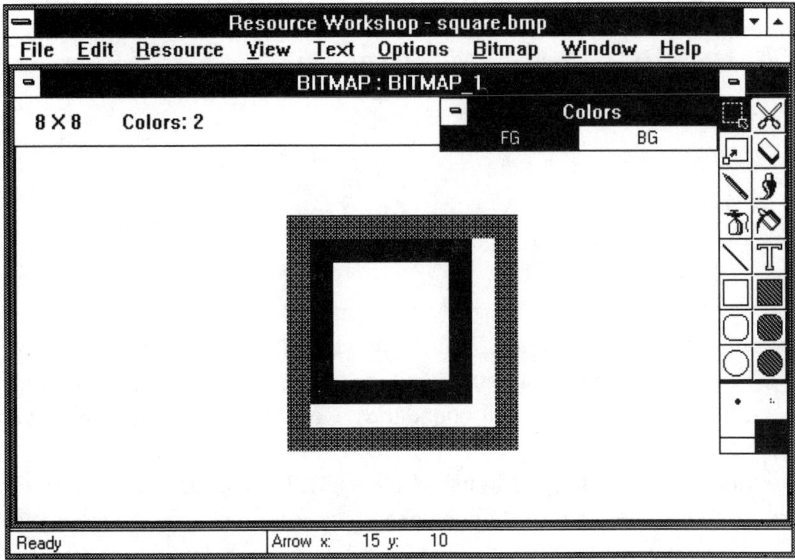

Figure 9.13 Resource Workshop used to create a bitmap.

```
HBITMAP CreateBitmap (nWidth, nHeight, nPlanes,
                       nBitCount, lpBits)
```

- `nWidth` and `nHeight` are the width and height of the bitmap in pixels. Since all GDI brushes are eight pixels wide by eight pixels high, the value of both fields must be set to `8`.
- `nPlanes` is the number of planes in the bitmap. Planes provide one means to store color information (for example, the EGA display adapter uses this method). We're going to create a monochrome bitmap, so we'll use the value `1` here.
- `nBitCount` is the number of bits per color. Packed pixels provide a second way to store color information (some modes of the CGA display adapter use this method). Since we are creating a monochrome bitmap, we set this to `1`.
- `lpBits` is a pointer to the bits to use to initialize the bitmap.

Our program creates a bitmap by calling the OWL **`TBitmap`** constructor that wraps around the **`CreateBitmap`** call. Here are the calls it makes to create the second pattern bitmap brush:

```
ptbm = new TBitmap (8, 8, 1, 1, (LPSTR)&acPattern[0]);
tbr[10] = new TBrush (*ptbm);
delete ptbm;
```

The last parameter of the **CreateBitmap** call is a pointer to an array of character values. It is defined in our program as

```
static unsigned char acPattern[] =
       {0xFF, 0,  /*  1 1 1 1 1 1 1 1  */
        0xE7, 0,  /*  1 1 1 0 0 1 1 1  */
        0xC3, 0,  /*  1 1 0 0 0 0 1 1  */
        0x99, 0,  /*  1 0 0 1 1 0 0 1  */
        0x3C, 0,  /*  0 0 1 1 1 1 0 0  */
        0x7E, 0,  /*  0 1 1 1 1 1 1 0  */
        0xFF, 0,  /*  1 1 1 1 1 1 1 1  */
        0xFF, 0}; /*  1 1 1 1 1 1 1 1  */
```

Our array is defined with hexadecimal values, but for your convenience the comment shows the values in binary. The 1's represent white pixels and the 0's represent black pixels. Since bitmap data is expected to be aligned on 16-bit boundaries, we have an additional zero byte between each of our bitmap byte values.

Each of these routines creates a **logical brush**. Like logical pens, logical brushes are requests that can be passed to any device. When asked to use a brush, the device driver *realizes* the brush—that is, it converts the logical request to a form that matches the capabilities of the specific device.

All the source files to our brush creation program, BRUSHES, are shown here:

BRUSHES.CPP

```
//
// BRUSHES.CPP  -- Shows how to create the three different
//                 types of GDI brushes.
//
//
#include <owl\owlpch.h>
#include "brushes.h"

//
// Main window
class DFrame : public TFrameWindow
    {
  public:
    DFrame(char * title);
    ~DFrame();
    void CmFileExit();
    void CmHelpAbout();
    void EvSize(UINT type, TSize &size);
    void Paint(TDC &dc, BOOL, TRect&);
  private:
    TBrush      * tbr[BRUSHCOUNT];
    char        * apszDesc[BRUSHCOUNT];
    unsigned char acPattern[PATTERNSIZE];

  DECLARE_RESPONSE_TABLE (DFrame);
    };

DEFINE_RESPONSE_TABLE1 (DFrame, TFrameWindow)
```

```
  EV_WM_SIZE,
  EV_COMMAND(CM_FILEEXIT, CmFileExit),
  EV_COMMAND(CM_HELPABOUT, CmHelpAbout),
END_RESPONSE_TABLE;


DFrame::DFrame(char * title) : TFrameWindow(0, title)
    {
    // Initialize array for dynamic bitmap creation.
    acPattern[0]  = 0xff;
    acPattern[1]  = 0;
    acPattern[2]  = 0xe7;     /*  1 1 1 1 1 1 1 1  */
    acPattern[3]  = 0;        /*  1 1 1 0 0 1 1 1  */
    acPattern[4]  = 0xc3;     /*  1 1 0 0 0 0 1 1  */
    acPattern[5]  = 0;        /*  1 0 0 1 1 0 0 1  */
    acPattern[6]  = 0x99;     /*  0 0 1 1 1 1 0 0  */
    acPattern[7]  = 0;        /*  0 1 1 1 1 1 1 0  */
    acPattern[8]  = 0x3c;     /*  1 1 1 1 1 1 1 1  */
    acPattern[9]  = 0;        /*  1 1 1 1 1 1 1 1  */
    acPattern[10] = 0x7e;
    acPattern[11] = 0;
    acPattern[12] = 0xff;
    acPattern[13] = 0;
    acPattern[14] = 0xff;
    acPattern[15] = 0;

    // Create brushes.
    apszDesc[0] = "Solid Black Brush";
    tbr[0]  = new TBrush (TColor::Black);

    apszDesc[1] = "Solid Gray Brush";
    tbr[1]  = new TBrush (TColor::Gray);

    apszDesc[2] = "Solid White Brush";
    tbr[2]  = new TBrush (TColor::White);

    apszDesc[3] = "Hatch - Horizontal";
    tbr[3]  = new TBrush (TColor::Black, HS_HORIZONTAL);

    apszDesc[4] = "Hatch - Vertical";
    tbr[4]  = new TBrush (TColor::Black, HS_VERTICAL );

    apszDesc[5] = "Hatch - Forward Diagonal";
    tbr[5]  = new TBrush (TColor::Black, HS_FDIAGONAL);

    apszDesc[6] = "Hatch - Backward Diagonal    ";
    tbr[6]  = new TBrush (TColor::Black, HS_BDIAGONAL);

    apszDesc[7] = "Hatch - Cross";
    tbr[7]  = new TBrush (TColor::Black, HS_CROSS);

    apszDesc[8] = "Hatch - Diagonal Cross";
    tbr[8]  = new TBrush (TColor::Black, HS_DIAGCROSS);

    apszDesc[9] = "Pattern Brush #1";
    TBitmap * ptbm;
    ptbm = new TBitmap (GetApplication()->GetInstance(), "square");
    tbr[9]  = new TBrush (*ptbm);
    delete ptbm;

    apszDesc[10] = "Pattern Brush #2";
    ptbm = new TBitmap (8, 8, 1, 1, (LPSTR)&acPattern[0]);
```

```
    tbr[10] = new TBrush (*ptbm);
    delete ptbm;
    }

DFrame::~DFrame()
    {
    for (int i=0;i<BRUSHCOUNT; i++)
        delete tbr[i];
    }

void DFrame::CmFileExit()
    {
    CloseWindow(0); // Cause application to terminate
    }

void DFrame::CmHelpAbout()
    {
    MessageBox("       Various GDI Brushes\n\n"
               "'Borland C++ 4.0 Programming\n"
               "  for Windows', by Paul Yao", Title);
    }

void DFrame::EvSize(UINT /* type */, TSize& /* size */)
    {
    Invalidate();
    }

void DFrame::Paint(TDC &dc, BOOL, TRect&)
    {
    /*  Divide available client area.  */
    TRect r = GetClientRect ();
    int yIncr = r.bottom/ (BRUSHCOUNT+2);
    int yText = yIncr;

    /*  Get measurements to indent text 4 spaces.  */
    TEXTMETRIC tm;
    dc.GetTextMetrics (tm);
    int xText = tm.tmAveCharWidth * 4;

    /*  Get measurements of longest text string.  */
    TSize ts = dc.GetTextExtent (apszDesc[6], lstrlen(apszDesc[6]));

    /*  Calculate width of rectangles.  */
    int xStart = xText + ts.cx;
    int xEnd   = r.right - 10;

    /*  Loop through all brushes.  */
    int yLine;
    for (int i=0;i<BRUSHCOUNT; i++, yText += yIncr)
        {
        dc.TextOut (xText, yText,apszDesc[i], lstrlen(apszDesc[i]));

        dc.SelectObject (* tbr[i]);
        yLine  = yText + yIncr - tm.tmHeight/4;
        dc.Rectangle (xStart, yText, xEnd, yLine);
        }
    }

//
// Application object
class DApp : public TApplication
    {
```

```
  public:
    DApp() : TApplication()
        {
        }
    void InitMainWindow()
        {
        SetMainWindow (new DFrame("GDI Brushes"));
        MainWindow->AssignMenu("MAIN");
        MainWindow->SetIcon(this, "SNAPSHOT");
        }
    };

//
// Application main entry point.
OwlMain(int, char **)
    {
    return DApp().Run();
    }
```

BRUSHES.H

```
#define CM_FILEEXIT 100
#define CM_HELPABOUT 200

const int BRUSHCOUNT  = 11;
const int PATTERNSIZE = 16;
```

BRUSHES.RC

```
#include "brushes.h"

snapshot icon brushes.ico

square bitmap square.bmp

main menu
    BEGIN
    POPUP "&File"
        {
        MENUITEM "E&xit", CM_FILEEXIT
        }
    POPUP "&Help"
        {
        MENUITEM "&About...", CM_HELPABOUT
        }
    END
```

BRUSHES.DEF

```
EXETYPE WINDOWS

CODE MOVEABLE DISCARDABLE
DATA MULTIPLE MOVEABLE

HEAPSIZE   512
STACKSIZE 8192
```

DYNA16.MAK

```
#  MAKE file for Win16 API using dynamic BIDS,
#  OWL and C-runtime libraries.
#
#    C> make -fstatic16.mak
#

.AUTODEPEND
CC = -c -H -H"owl\owlpch.h" -ml -R -vi -WS -X-
CD = -D_RTLDLL;_BIDSDLL;_OWLDLL;_OWLPCH;
INC = -I\BC4\INCLUDE
LIB = -L\BC4\LIB

brushes.exe :  brushes.obj brushes.res
  tlink -c -C -Twe $(LIB) @dyna16.lnk
  brc brushes.res brushes.exe

brushes.obj :  brushes.cpp
  bcc $(CC) $(CD) brushes.cpp

brushes.res :  brushes.rc brushes.ico brushes.h
  brc $(INC) -31 -R brushes.rc
```

DYNA16.LNK

```
\bc4\lib\c0wl.obj+
brushes.obj
brushes,brushes
\bc4\lib\bidsi.lib+
\bc4\lib\owlwi.lib+
\bc4\lib\import.lib+
\bc4\lib\crtldll.lib
brushes.def
```

DYNA32.MAK

```
#  MAKE file for Win32 API using dynamic BIDS,
#  OWL and C-runtime libraries.
#
#    C> make -fdyna32.mak
#
```

```
.AUTODEPEND
CC = -c -H -H\""owl\owlpch.h\"" -p- -R -vi -W -X-
CD = -D_RTLDLL;_BIDSDLL;_OWLDLL;_OWLPCH;
INC = -I\BC4\INCLUDE
LIB = -L\BC4\LIB

brushes.exe :  brushes.obj brushes.res
  tlink32 -aa -c -Tpe $(LIB) @dyna32.lnk
  brc32 brushes.res brushes.exe

brushes.obj :  brushes.cpp
  bcc32 $(CC) $(CD) brushes.cpp

brushes.res :  brushes.rc brushes.ico brushes.h
  brc32 $(INC) -w32 -R brushes.rc
```

DYNA32.LNK

```
\bc4\lib\c0w32.obj+
brushes.obj
brushes,brushes
\bc4\lib\bidsfi.lib+
\bc4\lib\owlwfi.lib+
\bc4\lib\import32.lib+
\bc4\lib\cw32i.lib
brushes.def
```

BRUSHES does its work in response to three events: window creation, window destruction, and window painting. In C++ terms, our window object class has three member functions: a constructor, a destructor, and a function to handle the **WM_PAINT** message.

At window creation time, our window creates the GDI brushes it needs. It's common for a window object to create GDI brushes in its constructor, and hold onto them for the life of the window. Although brushes take up memory, this approach allows for the fastest **WM_PAINT** processing.

Anytime you create a GDI object, you must be sure to clean it up when you're done. Since we created brushes in the constructor, it makes sense to destroy the brushes in our window object's destructor. If you overlook any GDI objects, you risk losing system memory.

In response to the **WM_PAINT** message, a default message response function calls our window object's **Paint** member function. This function divides up the available client area into 11 parts. Each part displays a rectangle that has been drawn with a different brush.

In the course of this program, we call three GDI text routines: **GetTextMetrics**, **GetTextExtent**, and **TextOut**. **GetTextMetrics** provides measurement information for the current font, or text pattern table. **GetTextExtent** is used to determine the width and height of a specific line of text. And **TextOut** displays a line of text.

In the next chapter, we're going to take a closer look at these routines and all of the other facilities that GDI provides for the creation of text output.

10

Drawing Text

In most programs, text serves as the primary output media. And yet, we have postponed a discussion of text until now because text output in GDI is quite different from text output in traditional programming environments. GDI treats text as a type of graphic object.

You may have written programs with **line-oriented output**. This method was first used on the earliest interactive computer systems, which used typewriters to display output and receive input. With today's display screens, this type of output causes lines of text to roll off the top of a screen into an imaginary "bit bucket." Interaction is simple: The computer displays a request, the user responds. Beginning C programmers always start with this type of output, because it is part of the standard C library. Here is an example:

```
printf ("Enter first number:");
scanf ("%i", &iValue);
```

The next step up is **screen-oriented output**, which treats the display screen as a grid of character cells. Programs like word processors and full screen editors in a character-oriented environment typically use this method. One popular MS-DOS database language, dBase, uses commands like these to write text and receive input on the display screen:

```
@ 10, 25 SAY "Please Enter Your Name:"
@ 10, 49 GET NAME
```

GDI's approach to text can be described as **pixel-oriented**, since GDI has no built-in idea of the size of a character cell. Instead, GDI lets you position text using the same pixel grid that you use for lines, rectangles, and other geometric shapes. This gives you a great deal of control over text placement and makes it easy to mix text with geometric figures. You can even mix different sizes and styles of text with a minimum of effort.

Unlike other graphic objects, text is not drawn using simple geometric equations. Instead, **fonts** are required to create text output. A font is a database of patterns that describe the shape and size of every letter, number, and punctuation mark. Each GDI device supports one or more fonts. Figure 10.1 shows some of the VGA display adapter's base fonts. The following box discusses GDI's base fonts.

GDI Base Fonts

Every GDI display driver is equipped with a set of base fonts, like those shown in Figure 10.1. A common set of base fonts ensures a minimum level of support will be available on all video displays.

Microsoft chose the following fonts as part of the base set:

Courier: *Provides fixed-pitch fonts for typewriter-like output.*

Tms Rmn: *A set of proportional, serif fonts available in a fairly wide range of sizes. This set can be used as a "stand-in" for other serif fonts for programs that wish to mimic a printer's output on a display screen. This font has been renamed under Windows 3.1 and later. It is now called "MS Serif."*

Helv: *A set of proportional, sans-serif Helvetica-like fonts, also available in a wide range of sizes. Like Tms Rmn, they are meant for use in programs that mimic a printer's output on a display screen. Under Windows 3.1 and later, this font is called "MS Sans Serif."*

Symbol: *An alternative character set can be used in a font; this font uses Greek letters.*

Roman, Modern, and Script: *Vector fonts, in which the letter patterns are represented as sequences of vectors, or line segments.*

Under Windows 3.1 and later, ***TrueType*** *fonts are supported. To check whether the TrueType font engine is available, call the WinAPI* **`GetRasterizerCaps`** *function. Where available, TrueType fonts provide device-independent fonts—a capability not available with the display driver base fonts described above. Here are the base TrueType fonts that ship with Windows version 3.1 and later, and with Windows NT 3.1 and later. Notice that four different styles are provided for some of these:*

Arial, Arial Bold, Arial Italic, Arial Bold Italic: *A sans-serif, Helveticalike font.*

Courier New, Courier New Bold, Courier New Italic, Courier New Bold Italic: *A fixed-pitch font for typewriterlike output.*

Symbol: *A TrueType version of the alternative character set Symbol font.*

Times New Roman, Times New Roman Bold, Times New Roman Italic, Times New Roman Bold Italic: *A proportional, serif font.*

WingDings: *A set of symbols for spicing up documents.*

To get a list of available fonts on a given system, run the Control Panel and select the "Fonts" icon. Or, run the character map program (CHARMAP.EXE) to see all the characters in the font.

The available fonts can be extended beyond this base set. An end user can purchase fonts and install them using the Windows Control Panel. Programmers can create custom fonts and incorporate them into Windows programs.

Placing text often involves determining the **font metrics**, which is a table of values that tells you height and width information for a specific font. If you wish to think in terms of a 25-line, 80-column output area, GDI gives you the tools to do so. You will find, however, that there are a few more things that you have to keep in mind—like the size of your output area (windows can shrink or grow) and the size of your text. (Every display has over 20 sizes and styles to choose from.) And you'll want to do all of this in a way that allows your program to run on any display or printer—you'll want to do this in a device-independent manner.

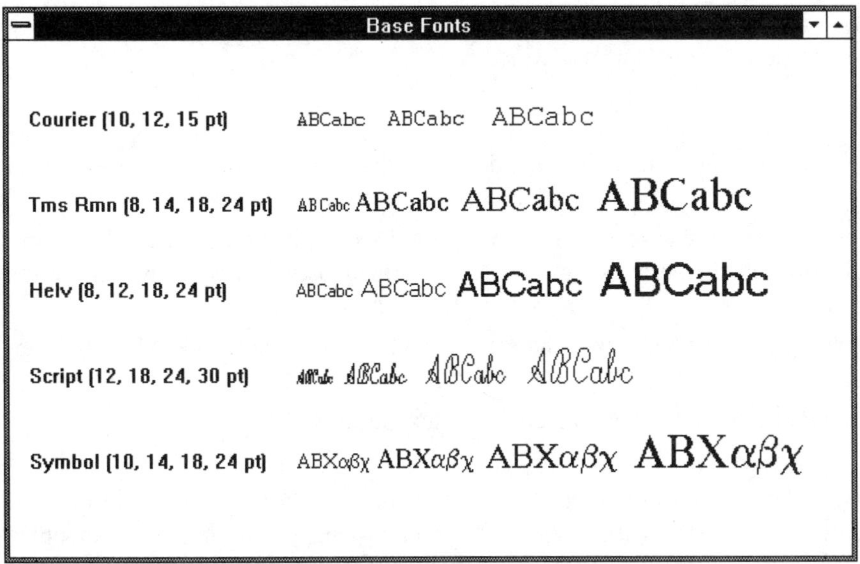

Figure 10.1 A sampling of VGA base fonts

Although it may seem strange at first to position text in a framework of pixels, this is necessary to allow you to freely mix text with other types of graphic objects. In GDI, text is positioned using the same pixel-oriented grid that we used to draw markers, lines, and rectangles.

We're going to start by reviewing the available text routines. We'll then look at the DC attributes that affect text and give special attention to the most important attribute: the font. We'll conclude this chapter with a discussion of text metrics, which is important to create device-independent text output.

Text Drawing Primitives

There are six routines for outputting text: **DrawText**, **ExtTextOut**, **GrayString**, **PolyTextOut**, **TabbedTextOut**, and **TextOut**. Strictly speaking, three of these are not part of GDI, but instead are part of the Window Manager. These routines are **DrawText**, **GrayString**, and **TabbedTextOut**. Even though these routines are not GDI routines, they provide some useful enhancements to GDI and so are worth considering in our discussion.

Let's begin by looking at **TextOut**, probably the most widely used GDI text drawing routine.

TextOut

TextOut is GDI's simplest text routine: It draws a single line of text. We used this routine to write labels in some of our earlier programs, but now it's time to give it a closer look. The WinAPI version of **TextOut** is defined as

```
TextOut (hDC, x, y, lpString, nCount)
```

- **hDC** is a DC handle. It tells GDI the device to draw on and the drawing attributes to use.
- **x** and **y** are integers that specify a **control point** used to position the text. The control point is a location in the coordinate system as defined in the DC. Since we're limiting ourselves to the MM_TEXT coordinate system, our units are pixels.
- **lpString** is a far pointer to a character string. This does not have to be a null-terminated string, since **TextOut** gets the string size from the nCount parameter.
- **nCount** is the number of characters in the text string.

By default, GDI positions a line of text with the upper-left corner at the control point. Figure 10.2 demonstrates this with a marker. Later in this chapter, when we talk about DC attributes, we'll describe other text alignment choices.

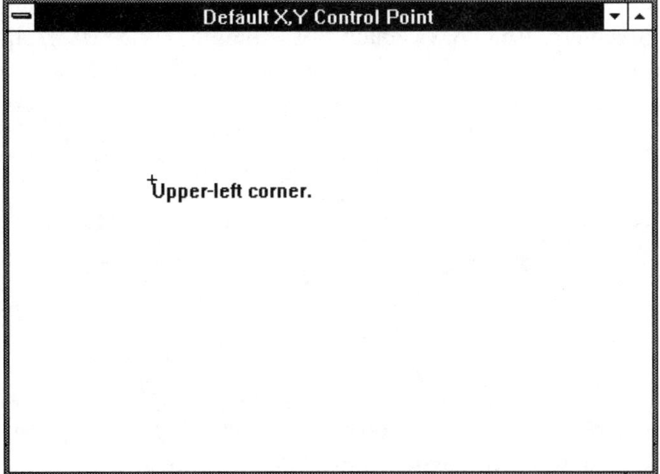

Figure 10.2 Default relationship of control point to text

It is often convenient to call **TextOut** like this:

```
static char ac[] = "Display This Text.";
BeginPaint (hwnd, &ps);
TextOut (ps.hdc, X, Y, ac, lstrlen(ac));
EndPaint (hwnd, &ps);
```

This code calculates string length "on the fly" using **lstrlen**, a Windows routine that mimics the standard **strlen** function.

Some programmers prefer to split length calculation from drawing, as in

```
static char ac[] = "Display This Text.";
static int  cb = sizeof(ac) - 1;
BeginPaint (hwnd, &ps);
TextOut (ps.hdc, X, Y, ac, cb);
EndPaint (hwnd, &ps);
```

so that text length is calculated at compile time and not at runtime. The result is faster drawing. In many cases, the time saved is hardly noticed. But when performance is critical, every little bit helps.

OWL provides some useful enhancements to this GDI function. Here are the two declarations for **TDC::TextOut** in DC.H:

```
virtual BOOL TextOut (int x, int y, const char far* str, int count=-1)
BOOL TextOut (const TPoint& p, const char far* str, int count=-1)
```

The first enhancement is that you can specify the text location using either a pair of integer (x,y) coordinates, or you can conveniently store this in a **TPoint** data object. The second enhancement has to do with the fact that the last parameters—the string length—has a default value of –1. Before calling the native GDI function, OWL calculates the string length for you. That's very convenient. An OWL version of the previous code fragment would be like this:

```
DFrame::Paint (TDC& dc, BOOL bErase, TRect trPaint)
    {
    dc.TextOut (X, Y, "Display This Text.");
    }
```

The next text routine is similar to **TextOut**, but provides some extra features.

ExtTextOut

Like **TextOut**, **ExtTextOut** draws a single line of text, but adds three options: character width control, clipping, and an opaque rectangle. You can mix and match these options as your needs require. Figure 10.3 shows text drawn with each of these options.

ExtTextOut is defined as follows:

```
ExtTextOut (hDC, X, Y, wOptions, lpRect, lpString,
            nCount, lpDx);
```

- **hDC** is a DC handle. It tells GDI the device to draw on and the drawing attributes to use.
- **x** and **y** are integers that specify a **control point** used to position the text. The control point is a location in the coordinate system as defined in the DC. Since we're limiting ourselves to the MM_TEXT coordinate system, our units are pixels.

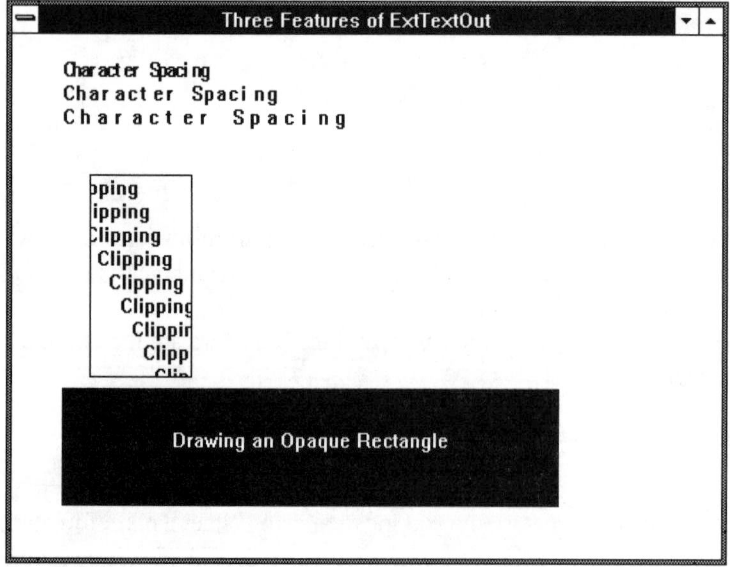

Figure 10.3 ExtTextOut

- **wOptions** is a flag for two of the three extras that this routine provides. It can be **0**, **ETO_CLIPPED**, **ETO_OPAQUE**, or a combination: **ETO_CLIPPED | ETO_OPAQUE**. We'll explain these options in a moment.
- **lpRect** is a pointer to a rectangle. Depending on the value of **wOptions**, **lpRect** may point to a clip rectangle, an opaque rectangle, or both.
- **lpString** is a far pointer to a character string. This does not have to be a null-terminated string, since **TextOut** gets the string size from the nCount parameter.
- **nCount** is the number of characters in the text string.
- **lpDx** points to an array of character width values.

The first option that we're going to discuss is character spacing, which gives you total control over the amount of space between characters. Unlike **TextOut**, which uses the default spacing defined in a font, **ExtTextOut** lets you specify your own width values for each character. You specify width values by passing an array of integers. The last parameter, **lpDx**, points to this array.

Here's the code fragment that drew the first three lines of text in the accompanying figure:

```
void DFrame::ShowSpacing (TDC& dc)
    {
    static char achString[] = "Character Spacing";
    static int  cbString   = sizeof (ac1) - 1;
    static int  ai1[] = {6, 6, 6, 6, 6, 6, 6, 6,
                         6, 6, 6, 6, 6, 6, 6, 6};
    static int  ai2[] = {9, 9, 9, 9, 9, 9, 9, 9,
                         9, 9, 9, 9, 9, 9, 9, 9};
    static int  ai3[] = {12, 12, 12, 12, 12, 12, 12, 12,
                         12, 12, 12, 12, 12, 12, 12, 12};
    TEXTMETRIC tm;

    dc.GetTextMetrics (tm);
    int yHeight = tm.tmHeight + tm.tmExternalLeading;
    int x = tm.tmAveCharWidth * 5;
    int y = yHeight;

    dc.ExtTextOut (x, y, 0, NULL, achString, cbString, ai1);
    y += yHeight;
    dc.ExtTextOut (x, y, 0, NULL, achString, cbString, ai2);
    y += yHeight;
    dc.ExtTextOut (x, y, 0, NULL, achString, cbString, ai3);
    y += yHeight;
    }
```

This hacked-together code fragment doesn't demonstrate good program design. Hopefully it *does* demonstrate how **ExtTextOut** lets you specify an array of character width values for specific character strings. In this simple example, I've hard-coded character cell width values of 6, 9 and 12. A more realistic scenario of how you get width values, however, is you'd call **GetCharWidth()**, which gives you character cell size information for a range of character cells in the font currently installed in the DC. The actual values you use would presumably be based on the default character cell width information that this function provides you.

Notice the call to **GetTextMetrics**. This provides measurement information for the current font. We use the values returned by this routine to position our first line of text one line from the top of the window, and five spaces from the left side of the window. We'll explore this routine more fully later in this chapter.

The second option available with **ExtTextOut** lets you specify a clip rectangle for text. When we introduced the DC, we said that every DC comes equipped with a clipping region. With the **ETO_CLIPPED** option, **ExtTextOut** lets you specify an additional clipping rectangle. This option provides a way to create a window of text without incurring the overhead of creating an actual window. Here is the code for the clipped text in our example:

```
void DFrame::ShowClipping (TDC& dc)
    {
    static char ach[] = "Clipping";
    static int  cch   = sizeof (ach) - 1;
    TEXTMETRIC tm;

    dc.GetTextMetrics (tm);
    int yHeight = tm.tmHeight + tm.tmExternalLeading;
    int x = tm.tmAveCharWidth * 5;
    int y = yHeight * 6;

    TRect trDraw (x + 20, y, x + 90,
                  y + tm.tmHeight * 8 + tm.tmHeight/2);
    dc.Rectangle (trDraw.left-1, trDraw.top-1,
                  trDraw.right+1, trDraw.bottom+1);

    while (y < trDraw.bottom)
        {
        dc.ExtTextOut (x, y, ETO_CLIPPED, &trDraw, ach, cch);
        y += yHeight;
        x += 8;
        }
    }
```

Once again, we rely on the **GetTextMetrics** routine to help decide where to draw lines of text. In this case, we start six lines from the top of the window and five spaces from the left side of the window.

We have arbitrarily made our clip rectangle 70 pixels wide and eight and one-half lines high. The coordinates used in a clip rectangle are **grid-intersection coordinates**, which we first encountered in the context of drawing filled areas in Chapter 9. To make the clip rectangle more readily apparent, we draw a rectangle just outside its border.

ExtTextOut's third option creates an opaque rectangle; it is like having a free call to the **Rectangle** routine. This option lets you erase a background area when drawing a line of text. As indicated in our sample code, the background color is selected by making a call to **SetBkColor**, which sets a DC attribute value that is used by all text drawing routines. We'll explore this and other DC attributes later in this chapter.

Here is the code that created the opaque rectangle:

```
void DFrame::ShowOpaquing (TDC& dc)
    {
    static char ach[] = "Drawing an Opaque Rectangle";
    static int  cch   = sizeof (ach) - 1;

    TEXTMETRIC tm;
    dc.GetTextMetrics (tm);
    int yHeight = tm.tmHeight + tm.tmExternalLeading;
    int x = tm.tmAveCharWidth * 5;
    int y = yHeight * 15;

    TRect trClient = GetClientRect ();
    trClient.top = y;
    trClient.bottom = trClient.top + (5 * tm.tmHeight);
    trClient.left = x;
    trClient.right = x + tm.tmAveCharWidth * 50;
    dc.SetBkColor (RGB (0, 0, 0));
    dc.SetTextColor (RGB (255, 255, 255));
    dc.SetTextAlign (TA_CENTER | TA_BASELINE);
    x = (trClient.left + trClient.right) / 2;
    y = (trClient.top  + trClient.bottom) / 2;
    dc.ExtTextOut (x, y, ETO_OPAQUE, &trClient, ach, cch);
    }
```

Once again, we rely on the **GetTextMetrics** routine to help us place the text and its black opaque background. In this case, the top of the rectangle is situated 15 lines from the top of the window and 5 spaces from the left side.

We set the size of our rectangle to be 5 character cells high and 50 character cells wide. To make the opaque rectangle visible, we changed two DC attributes: the text color (set to white) and the background color (set to black). We used a third DC attribute, text alignment, to center the text inside the rectangle.

TabbedTextOut

Our third text drawing primitive draws a single line of text, but expands tabs to tab stops. This provides a convenient way to align columns of data. Microsoft included this routine in the Windows library for listboxes to make it easy to create lists of column-oriented data. But it's a simple matter to use this routine in your programs to achieve the same benefit.

Figure 10.4 shows an example of text drawn with this routine. Given an array of strings like those at the bottom of the page,

```
#define COUNT 19
    static char *apch[]= {"Country \tCapital",
                          "--------------- \t------------",
                          "Afghanistan \tKabul",
                          "Albania \tTirana",
                          "Algeria \tAlgiers",
                          "Angola \tLuanda",
```

```
                                    "Antigua & Barbuda \tSt. John's",
                                    "Argentina \tBuenos Aires",
                                    "Australia \tCanberra",
                                    "Austria \tVienna",
                                    "The Bahamas \tNassau",
                                    "Bahrain \tManama",
                                    "Bangladesh \tDhaka",
                                    "Barbados \tBridgetown",
                                    "Belgium \tBrussels",
                                    "Belize \tBelmopan",
                                    "Benin \tPorto-Novo",
                                    "Bhutan \tThimphu",
                                    "Bolivia \tLa Paz"};
```

here is code that a window object's **Paint** function would use to create the output shown:

```
void DFrame::ShowTabbedText (TDC &dc)
    {
    TSize tsize;
    dc.GetTextExtent("X", 1, tsize);
    int yHeight = tsize.cy;
    int xText = 3 * tsize.cx;
    int yText = tsize.cy;
    TPoint tpDraw = TPoint (xText, yText);
    int xTab = 20 * tsize.cx;

    for (int i = 0; i < COUNT; i++, tpDraw.y += yHeight)
        {
        dc.TabbedTextOut (tpDraw, apch[i], lstrlen(apch[i]),
                          1, &xTab, xText);
        }
    }
```

A List of Countries and Capital Cities

Country	Capital
Afghanistan	Kabul
Albania	Tirana
Algeria	Algiers
Angola	Luanda
Antigua & Barbuda	St. John's
Argentina	Buenos Aires
Australia	Canberra
Austria	Vienna
The Bahamas	Nassau
Bahrain	Manama
Bangladesh	Dhaka
Barbados	Bridgetown
Belgium	Brussels
Belize	Belmopan
Benin	Porto-Novo
Bhutan	Thimphu
Bolivia	La Paz

Figure 10.4 TabbedTextOut

This code calls **GetTextExtent** to determine the width and height of the letter "X" in the current (system) font. In previous examples, we've used the **GetTextMetrics** routine to determine this information, but for the sake of variety we have chosen this alternative method.

We use the results to calculate three values: the *x* and *y* starting position of the text (one line from the top and three characters from the left) and the location of the tab-stop. In this case, we have placed the tab-stop at approximately 20 spaces from the *x* and *y* starting point. If there had been more than a single tab-stop, we would have had to allocate an array to hold them. As it is, we get by with allocating a single integer value and then passing this value to our routine.

DrawText

Like **TabbedTextOut**, **DrawText** provides some formatting capability. In our opinion, the most useful option is the ability to perform word wrapping for multiple lines of text (although this is just one of several things that **DrawText** will do for you).

Figure 10.5 shows three instances of a sample program that uses **DrawText** to display a long line of text in an area of different sizes and shapes. Given an array of characters defined like this:

```
static char *apchDesc = "The DT_WORDBREAK flag makes "
                        "DrawText split a long string "
                        "into several lines of text.  "
                        "As you can tell, the split is "
                        "only performed at normal word "
                        "breaks.";
```

window object's `Paint` member function would look like this:

```
void DFrame::Paint (TDC& dc, BOOL, TRect&)
    {
    TSize tsize;
    dc.GetTextExtent ("X", 1, tsize);
    TRect trClient = GetClientRect();
    trClient.left   += tsize.cx;
    trClient.top    += tsize.cy;
    trClient.right  -= tsize.cx;
    trClient.bottom -= tsize.cy;

    dc.DrawText (apchDesc, lstrlen(apchDesc),
                 trClient, DT_WORDBREAK);
    }
```

To insure the window gets properly updated, respond to the **WM_SIZE** message by forcing a **WM_PAINT** message—that is, by calling **TWindow::Invalidate()**.

Once more, we use **GetTextExtent** to determine the width and height of the letter "X." We use these values to offset the dimensions of our client area so that there is a margin around our text.

The **GetClientRect** routine gets the dimensions of the client area into a `TRect` variable. We then modify the values in this structure to create margins on all four sides of

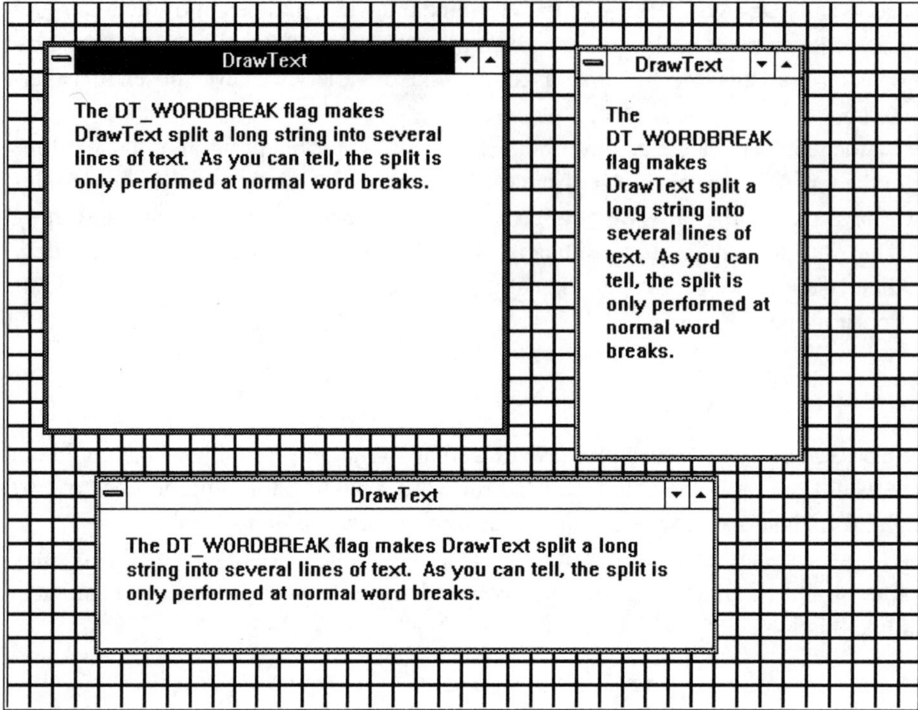

Figure 10.5 DrawText

the text. The resulting rectangle is passed to **DrawText**, which uses the values to determine where to position the text.

GrayString

The text produced by this routine is best described as checkered. But the name of the routine describes the primary reason that Microsoft created this routine: to create text with a gray appearance.

The Window Manager uses this routine for disabled menu items and disabled dialog box controls. If you write your own custom dialog box controls (discussed in Chapter 14) or create owner-drawn menu items (discussed in Chapter 12), then this routine may be quite useful to you. Figure 10.6 shows an example of a gray string.

Given the following data definitions:

```
static char acString[] = "This is a Gray String";
static int  cb = sizeof (acString) - 1;
```

this is what a window object's **Paint** member function would do to create output like that shown:

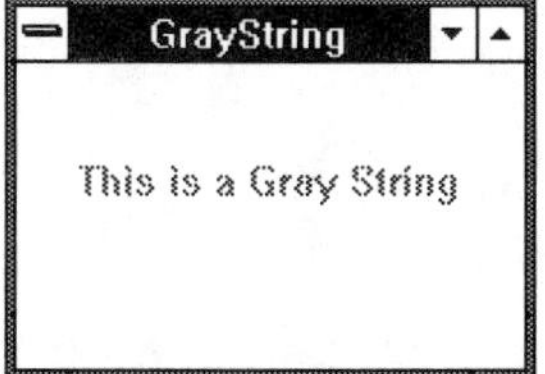

Figure 10.6 GrayString

```
void DFrame::Paint (TDC& dc, BOOL, TRect&)
    {
    static char acString[] = "This is a Gray String";
    static int cb = sizeof (acString) - 1;

    TEXTMETRIC tm;
    dc.GetTextMetrics (tm);
    int xText = tm.tmAveCharWidth * 3;
    int yText = tm.tmHeight * 2;

    TBrush tbrBlack = TBrush(TColor::Black);
    TRect  trDraw = TRect(xText, yText, xText, yText);
    dc.GrayString(tbrBlack, NULL, acString, cb, trDraw);
    }
```

As in earlier examples, we depend on the results of **GetTextMetrics** to give us some size information to help us position lines of text. Here, we place the gray string two lines from the top of the window and three character widths from the left margin.

This is the only text drawing routine that uses a brush. The color of the brush determines the foreground color of the checkered text: In this case we use a black brush, which gives the text a grayed appearance. If we had chosen a red brush, it would give the appearance of red and white checkered text.

PolyTextOut

The **PolyTextOut** routine is the only new Win32 text drawing function. The prefix "poly" means "many." In the context of text drawing, this means that a single function call can draw many lines of text. The "**TextOut**" part of the name suggests that this function is equal to many calls to **TextOut**. In fact, **PolyTextOut** can produce the same results as the **ExtTextOut** function—character spacing, text clipping, and opaque rectangle drawing. I will not argue that its name should be "**PolyExtTextOut**", though, since I'm not a fan of long function names: You get the shorter name—but keep in mind that it's more like **ExtTextOut** than **TextOut**.

To use this function, you allocate a **POLYTEXT** array. This data structure consists of little more than the **ExtTextOut** parameters layed out in a structure:

```
typedef struct _POLYTEXT {
    int     x;        // X control point.
```

```
    int      y;        // Y control point.
    UINT     n;        // Character count.
    TCHAR *  lpwstr;   // Text to be drawn.
    UINT     uiFlags;  // ETO_OPAQUE, ETO_CLIPPED, ETO_DELTAVECTOR.
    RECT     rcl;      // Opaque and/or clipping rectangle.
    int    * pdx;      // Array of character width values.
} POLYTEXT;
```

Once you've put together your array, the call to draw the lines of text is simple:

```
dc.PolyTextOut(polytext, cStrings);
```

where **`polytext`** is a pointer to an array of **`POLYTEXT`** records, and **`cStrings`** is the number of records. The key benefit to using this routine is that—for drawing many lines of text—it's much faster than making separate calls for each line. Of course, all lines of text are drawn with the same font. So if you wish to support font-aware text, this function would only help you when there are several lines of text all of the same font.

This concludes our tour of the different GDI text drawing routines. As you can see, there are quite a few different effects that you can achieve by making a single call to one of these routines. But the library routines are only half of the story. To get the complete picture of the amount of control that GDI allows you over text drawing, we need to address the issue of DC attributes that affect text appearance.

DC Attributes for Text Drawing

Six attributes affect the appearance and positioning of text:

Attribute	*Description*
Background color	Color of "empty space" in text
Background mode	Turns on/off background color
Font	Text style and size
Graphics Mode	(Win32) Allows text to be rotated along with other graphic figures when set to **`GM_ADVANCED`**. The **`GM_COMPATIBLE`** default setting forces font rotation to be handled separately from other graphic objects.
Intercharacter spacing	Extra pixels between characters for text justification
Text alignment	Relationship of text to control point
Text color	Color of letters themselves

The most important of these attributes is the font, which determines the shape and size of the individual characters. Before we delve into the way GDI handles fonts, let's explore some of the other text attributes, starting with those that control color.

Color

Three different DC attributes deal with the color of text: text color, background color, and background mode. Text can only be drawn with *pure* colors, and not dithered colors like those available for filled areas. Like pixel, pen, and brush colors, you can use any of three methods to define colors: an RGB triplet, a palette index, or an RGB palette-relative value.

The text color attribute determines the actual color of the letters. If GDI had been used to create the letters on this page, it would have been with text color set to black. To set the text color, you must call the **SetTextColor** routine. Its parameters are

```
SetTextColor (hDC, crColor);
```

- **hDC** is a DC handle. It tells GDI the device to draw on and the drawing attributes to use.
- **crColor** is the desired text color.

The **crColor** parameter is a color reference value, using one of the three methods. Here is how to set text color to blue, using an RGB triplet:

```
SetTextColor (hDC, RGB (0, 0, 0xFF));
```

The equivalent OWL statement is:

```
dc.SetTextColor (RGB(0, 0, 0xff);
```

Or, more simply:

```
dc.SetTextColor (TColor::LtBlue);
```

The background color attribute determines the color of the areas inside character cells not touched by the text color. From GDI's point of view, the text on this page has a white background, since that's the color of the space between letters and the area inside hollow letters like "O" and "Q."

As you may have noticed, the background color attribute is also used for hatched brushes and styled lines to set, respectively, the color *between* the hatches and the blank area *inside* the pattern of a style line.

To set the background color, call **SetBkColor**, which takes the same two parameters as **SetTextColor**:

```
SetBkColor (hDC, crColor);
```

- **hDC** is a DC handle. It tells GDI the device to draw on and the drawing attributes to use.
- **crColor** is the desired background color.

For example, here is how to request a green background:

```
SetBkColor (hDC, RGB (0, 0xFF, 0));
```

Request a green background using OWL class members with:

```
dc.SetBkColor (TColor::LtGreen);
```

Our third color attribute, background mode, is a toggle switch for the background color. The routine that controls this attribute, **`SetBkMode`**, takes two parameters:

```
SetBkMode (hDC, nBkMode);
```

- **`hDC`** is a DC handle. It tells GDI the device to draw on and the drawing attributes to use.
- **`nBkMode`** is the desired background mode, either **`OPAQUE`** or **`TRANSPARENT`**.

When **`nBkMode`** is **`OPAQUE`**, the background color is turned *on*. When set to **`TRANSPARENT`**, the background color is turned *off*. Call the **`TDC::SetBkMode`** function to disable the use of the background color with this line of code:

```
dc.SetBkMode (TRANSPARENT);
```

Figure 10.7 shows three lines of text, using different foreground and background colors. Notice that the second line of text is unreadable, because we set both foreground and background colors to black. Given the following data definitions:

```
char acFirst[]  = "Black on White (default)";
char acSecond[] = "Black on Black (invisible)";
char acThird[]  = "White on Black (inverted)";
```

here is **`Paint`** code that creates the output in the figure:

```
void DFrame::Paint (TDC& dc, BOOL, TRect&)
    {
    TEXTMETRIC tm;
    dc.GetTextMetrics (tm);
    int X = tm.tmAveCharWidth * 3;
    int Y = tm.tmHeight * 2;

    dc.TextOut (X, Y, acFirst, lstrlen (acFirst));
    Y += tm.tmHeight * 2;

    dc.SetBkColor(TColor::Black);
    dc.TextOut (X, Y, acSecond, lstrlen (acSecond));
    Y += tm.tmHeight * 2;

    dc.SetTextColor(TColor::White);
    dc.TextOut (X, Y, acThird, lstrlen (acThird));
    }
```

Although our example is in black and white, it is a simple matter to create red or green text on devices that support color: Supply the appropriate color reference, and GDI does the rest.

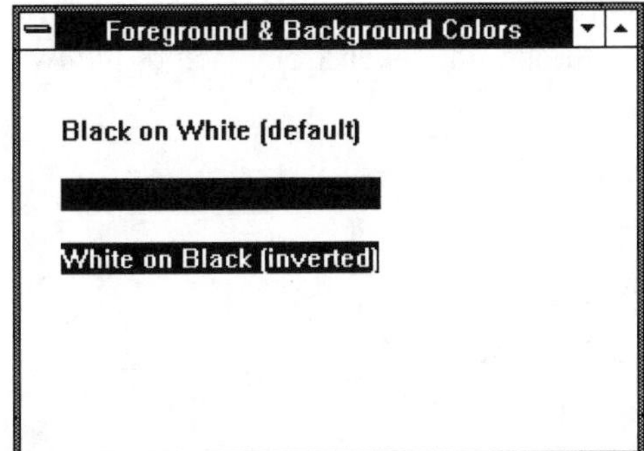

Figure 10.7 Three different foreground/ background colors

Text Alignment

The text alignment attribute lets you change the relationship between the control point, which is the (*x*,*y*) pair that is passed to each routine, and the text to be displayed. Figure 10.8 shows the nine possible ways to align text, with a marker at each control point to emphasize the alignment.

To set text alignment, you call the `SetTextAlign` routine, which has the following syntax:

```
SetTextAlign (hDC, wFlags);
```

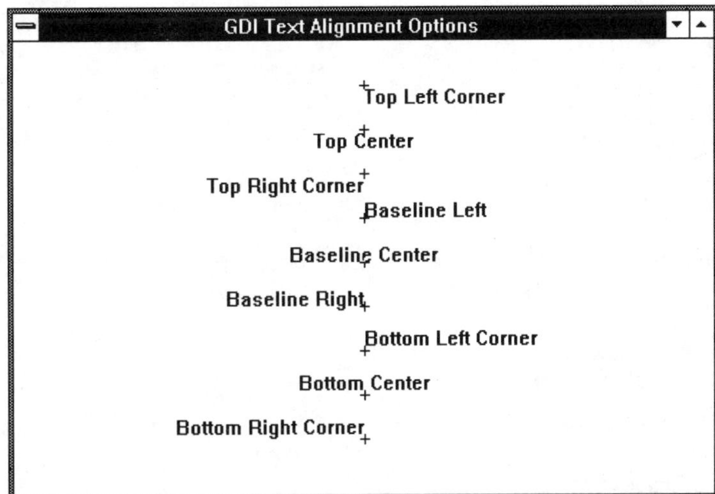

Figure 10.8 Nine different text alignments

As indicated in the example, there are nine possible alignments. Select an alignment by combining two flags from the following table, with one flag taken from each of the two categories:

Horizontal Flag	*Vertical Flag*
TA_LEFT	TA_TOP
TA_CENTER	TA_BASELINE
TA_RIGHT	TA_BOTTOM

The default alignment is **TA_LEFT | TA_TOP**. To set alignment to the bottom right, you say

```
SetTextAlign (hDC, TA_BOTTOM | TA_RIGHT);
```

Our illustration was created with the following code fragments. Given the following data definitions:

```
#define LINECOUNT 9
    static char * apchDesc[LINECOUNT] =
            { "Top Left Corner",
              "Top Center",
              "Top Right Corner",
              "Baseline Left",
              "Baseline Center",
              "Baseline Right",
              "Bottom Left Corner",
              "Bottom Center",
              "Bottom Right Corner"};
    static int  fAlign [LINECOUNT] =
            {
            TA_LEFT | TA_TOP ,
            TA_CENTER | TA_TOP ,
            TA_RIGHT | TA_TOP ,
            TA_LEFT | TA_BASELINE ,
            TA_CENTER | TA_BASELINE,
            TA_RIGHT | TA_BASELINE ,
            TA_LEFT | TA_BOTTOM ,
            TA_CENTER | TA_BOTTOM ,
            TA_RIGHT | TA_BOTTOM };
```

the drawing was done as follows:

```
void DFrame::Paint (TDC& dc, BOOL, TRect&)
    {
    TRect trClient = GetClientRect();
    int xText = trClient.right / 2;
    int yLineHeight = trClient.bottom / (LINECOUNT+1);
    TPoint tpoint = TPoint(xText, yLineHeight);

    for (int i = 0;
             i < LINECOUNT;
             i++, tpoint.y += yLineHeight)
        {
```

```
        dc.SetTextAlign (fAlign[i]);

        dc.TextOut (tpoint, apchDesc[i],
                    lstrlen(apchDesc[i]));

        Marker::Cross (dc, tpoint, Size);
        }
    }
```

In this code, we have departed from our usual practice of spacing lines. Instead of using the **GetTextMetrics** or **GetTextExtent** routines, we have split the available space in the window into 10 areas, with one line per area. Since GDI treats text as a graphic object, there is nothing to stop you from devising interesting and useful methods like this to take advantage of available screen real estate when you draw text.

Intercharacter Spacing

Intercharacter spacing allows you to insert extra pixels between characters. It provides another option (besides the **ExtTextOut** routine) to expand a line of text to fit an arbitrary margin. Figure 10.9 shows six lines of text, with extra spacing varying from zero to five pixels. It is difficult to detect the difference from one line to the next, but between the top and bottom lines the difference is quite apparent.

The code which created this drawing is as follows. First of all, we need the following data items:

```
#define COUNT 6
    static char acLine[] = "AaBbCcDdEeFfGgHhIiJjKkLlMm"
                           "NnOoPpQqRrSsTtUuVvWwXxYyZz";
    static char *apch[] = {"0", "1", "2", "3", "4", "5"};
```

Next, here is the **Paint** code to draw these lines:

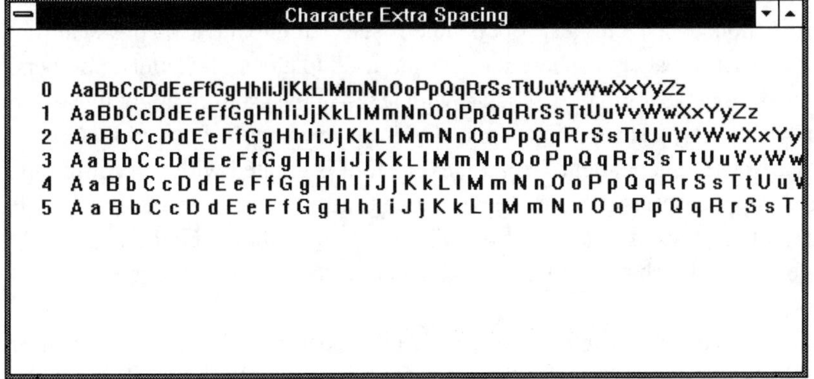

Figure 10.9 Intercharacter spacing (also known as character extra spacing)

```
void DFrame::Paint (TDC& dc, BOOL, TRect&)
    {
    TEXTMETRIC tm;
    dc.GetTextMetrics (tm);
    int X1 = tm.tmAveCharWidth * 3;
    int X2 = tm.tmHeight * 6;
    int Y  = tm.tmHeight * 2;

    for (int i=0; i < COUNT; i++, Y += tm.tmHeight)
        {
        dc.SetTextCharacterExtra (i);
        dc.TextOut (X1, Y, apch[i], -1);
        dc.TextOut (X2, Y, acLine, -1);
        }
    }
```

We have one more DC attribute to describe, which plays the most important role in determining the shape and size of letters that GDI draws: the font.

About Fonts

A font is a collection of patterns used to create text output. Fonts come in all shapes, sizes, and styles. Fonts have a lot in common with other GDI drawing objects, like pens and brushes. For one thing, fonts can be shared between programs. And like these other GDI objects, fonts are referenced using a handle. When a program is ready to use a specific font, it selects the font handle into a DC using the `SelectObject` routine:

```
SelectObject (hDC, hFont);
```

Internally, GDI recognizes two types of fonts: **logical fonts** and **physical fonts**. A logical font describes text in a standard, device-independent manner. As we'll see in a moment, a logical font consists of the set of values in the data structure **LOGFONT**. By itself, a logical font isn't enough information to draw text on a device. Instead, like other logical drawing objects, a logical font is a *request* for text with a specific appearance.

The GDI **font mapper** selects a physical font from the description contained in a logical font. The mapping is done when a logical font handle is selected into a DC. A physical font is a device-*dependent* set of patterns. These patterns are used to create the letters, numbers, and punctuation marks that we normally associate with text. A physical font might live in the device hardware, which is typical for printer fonts. Or, it may be kept in memory by GDI.

Physical fonts are device-dependent, because every font is created with a specific type of device in mind. Two measurements are used to match fonts to devices: resolution (pixels per inch) and aspect ratio (the *squareness* of the pixels). By default, the GDI mapper only selects physical fonts that match the metrics of a given device. Otherwise, the results might be very odd.

For example, a VGA display has approximately 72 pixels per inch. Today's typical laser printer has 300 pixels per inch. If you tried to mix fonts between these two devices, the results would be strange: VGA fonts on a laser printer would create text that is too small to be readable. Going the other way, if you used laser printer fonts to create text on a VGA, the resulting text would be too large.

If a program needs precise control over its text selection, it can ask for a list of available physical fonts that a device can support. This process is called **font enumeration**. When a device driver enumerates fonts, it provides a logical font description for each physical font. When a program wishes to use a specific font, it turns the process around: It gives the logical font description to GDI, which in turn makes the connection to the physical font.

Many programs don't need a lot of control over the appearance of text. Such programs can use the default fonts. Every device has a default font. And not surprisingly, the default font is the default selection in the DC.

On a video display, the default font is also called the **system font**. Windows 1.x and 2.x used a fixed-pitch system font—that is, a font in which every character is the same width. Starting with Windows 3.0, the system font is proportionally spaced: Some characters are wider than others. "W," for example, is given more room than "i." Microsoft made this change because proportionally spaced text is easier to read than fixed-pitch text and gives a better overall appearance.

Windows uses the system font for menus, titlebars, dialog box controls, and, of course, as the default font in any DC that a program gets its hands on. Microsoft has decreed that every Windows display driver must provide a system font that allows a minimum of 25 lines and 80 columns of text to be displayed. This guarantees that Windows programs will be able to display at least as much text as their MS-DOS counterparts.

To maintain compatibility with programs written for earlier versions of Windows (versions 1.x and 2.x), every display driver also maintains a fixed-pitch system font. When GDI detects that a program was written for an older version of Windows, it provides a system font that these programs expect.

Table 10.1 lists the characteristics of the default font on four popular displays and four popular printers.

Table 10.1 Default Fonts

Device	*Size of Drawing Surface*	*Default Font Height*	*Default Font Width (avg)*
CGA display	640 × 200	8	7
EGA display	640 × 350	12	7
VGA display	640 × 480	16	7
8514/a display	1024 × 768	20	9
Apple Imagewriter II printer	2550 × 3300	42	25

(continued)

Table 10.1 Default Fonts *(Continued)*

Device	*Size of Drawing Surface*	*Default Font Height*	*Default Font Width (avg)*
Epson LQ-1050 (24-pin) printer	3060 × 1980	25	36
HP LaserJet II printer	2550 × 3300	50	30
Okidata ML 320 (9-pin) printer	1020 × 792	10	12

As you can see, the size of the default font can vary quite widely from one device to another. To make sure the text created by your program looks good on every device, it's important to ask GDI about the size of a font before you start drawing. GDI provides two routines for this purpose: **`GetTextExtent`** and **`GetTextMetrics`**.

GetTextExtent

The **`GetTextExtent`** routine calculates the size of a line of text using the font currently selected in a DC. For example, here is how to calculate the width and height of the phrase "Device Independent":

```
TSize tsize;
dc.GetTextExtent("Device Independent", 18, tsize);
int yHeight = tsize.cy;
int xWidth  = tsize.cx;
```

This routine takes three parameters: a pointer to the string, the count of characters, and a reference to a **`TSize`** object. The width and height of the text that would be drawn is returned in the **`TSize`** structure, taking into account the font currently installed in the DC.

GetTextMetrics

A more complete set of font measurements is provided by the **`GetTextMetrics`** routine. Every physical font has a header record that includes font metric information. There are 20 fields, defined by the data structure **`TEXTMETRIC`**. Here is a call that retrieves the metrics of the font currently selected in a DC:

```
TEXTMETRIC tm;

dc.GetTextMetrics (tm);
```

Figure 10.10 shows five of the key fields in this data structure.

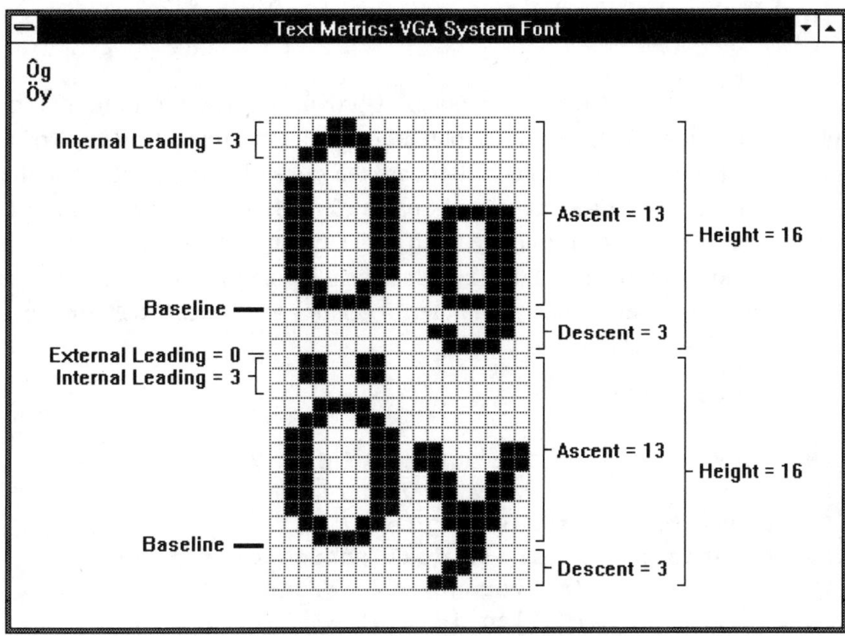

Figure 10.10 Key TextMetric fields visually defined

The **tmHeight** field defines the size of the characters in the font in pixels (since we're using the **MM_TEXT** mapping mode) or in the units of the currently selected mapping mode. Notice that this field has two components: **tmAscent**, which is the height above the baseline, and **tmDescent**, which is the height below the baseline for characters like "g" and "y."

The **tmInternalLeading** field is the difference between the "Em" height—that is, the font's true point size—and the character cell height. Some fonts fit text tightly into the text cell—with no room at the top or bottom. With other fonts, there is space left at the top and bottom to take into account the space needed between lines.

When the character call doesn't include room for interline space, a font designer can suggest the amount to use in the **tmExternalLeading** field. Notice that in our example, this field is zero. The term "leading" comes from the days when type was cast in lead and set by hand. To separate lines of text, typesetters would add a thin bar of lead between rows of type.

You may have noticed that many of our sample programs combine **tmHeight** and **tmExternalLeading** for the height of a line, as in

```
TEXTMETRIC tm;
dc.GetTextMetrics (tm);
int yLineHeight = tm.tmHeight + tm.tmExternalLeading;
```

This is a very common method for spacing lines of text.

Creating and Using Logical Fonts

As we discussed earlier, a logical font is a request. It provides a way for a program to describe the physical font it wants to use. Two routines create logical fonts: **CreateFont** and **CreateFontIndirect**. The results of both are the same: The difference is in the way parameters are passed. **CreateFont** takes 14 parameters. **CreateFontIndirect** takes a single parameter: a pointer to a structure filled with the same 14 values. We're going to limit our discussion to **CreateFontIndirect**, since it is somewhat easier to use.

CreateFontIndirect takes one parameter: a pointer to a **LOGFONT** structure. **LOGFONT** is defined in WINDOWS.H as

```
typedef struct tagLOGFONT
  {
  int   lfHeight;         /* Character Height */
  int   lfWidth;          /* Average width   */
  int   lfEscapement;     /* Text angle */
  int   lfOrientation;    /* Individual character angle
  int   lfWeight;         /* Average pixels/1000 */
  BYTE  lfItalic;         /* Flag != 0 if italic */
  BYTE  lfUnderline;      /* Flag != 0 if underlined */
  BYTE  lfStrikeOut;      /* Flag != 0 if strikeout */
  BYTE  lfCharSet;        /* Character set: ANSI, OEM */
  BYTE  lfOutPrecision;   /* Mapping precision-unused */
  BYTE  lfClipPrecision;  /* Clip precision - unused  */
  BYTE  lfQuality;        /* Draft or proof quality  */
  BYTE  lfPitchAndFamily; /* Flags for font style  */
  BYTE  lfFaceName[LF_FACESIZE]; /* Typeface name  */
  } LOGFONT;
```

There are quite a few fields in this structure, but a few fields play a decisive role in font selection: **lfFaceName**, **lfHeight**, **lfWidth**, **lfItalic**, and **lfUnderline**.

lfFaceName is a 32-character-wide field for the font name. A program can use font names to tell users about available fonts. In this way, a user can select fonts by name. Here is a list of the face names for the Windows base fonts:

Courier	Helv	Modern	Roman
Script	Symbol	System	Terminal
Tms Rmn			

Each font is available in different sizes and styles.

The **lfHeight** field is identical to the tmHeight field in the **TEXTMETRIC** data structure. Since we're dealing with the **MM_TEXT** mapping mode, the units are pixels. When another coordinate system is used, GDI converts the values to the mapping mode currently selected in the DC.

The **lfWidth** field is the average width of characters in the font. There is also a field in the **TEXTMETRIC** data structure that contains the identical information, tmAveCharWidth.

The **lfItalic** field is a flag: A nonzero value requests an italic font. The **lfUnderline** field is also a flag: A nonzero value requests an underlined font.

Every font can be described in terms of its **LOGFONT** signature. Using the Windows API, font requests are created by filling in LOGFONT data and calling **CreateFontIndirect**:

```
HFONT    hfont;
LOGFONT lf;
memset (&lf, 0, sizeof(LOGFONT));
lstrcpy (lf.lfFaceName, "Times New Roman");
lf.lfHeight = 16;
hfont = CreateFontIndirect (&lf);
```

As with other GDI objects, the font request doesn't affect any of your drawing until it's connected to a DC. In the native WinAPI, this is accomplished with a call to **SelectObject**:

```
SelectObject (hDC, hfont);
```

OWL supports GDI fonts with its **TFont** class, which has five different constructors. One of the constructors is a wrapper around the **CreateFontIndirect** call. Here's how to use the OWL libraries to get the same results as the code above:

```
TFont    * ptfont;
LOGFONT    lf;
memset (&lf, 0, sizeof(LOGFONT));
lstrcpy (lf.lfFaceName, "Times New Roman");
lf.lfHeight = 16;
ptfont = new TFont(&lf);
dc.SelectObject(*ptfont);
```

Gaining access to GDI's fonts—whether you use the native WinAPI or the OWL TFont class—involves the same thing: You provide GDI with a logical font request. In response, GDI—working with a device driver—decides which font is closest to the one you request.

The process of picking a font from your font request is called **font mapping**. There's a fairly involved process used by GDI that involves calculating a penalty for each font based on the **LOGFONT** data supplied. If you ask for a 16-pixel high Times New Roman font, you hope to get it—or something close. However, it's *possible* that you'll end up with something very different. For example, you might get 30-pixel high Courier. That would be the case if a particular device only supported one font. From GDI's perspective, this isn't a *wrong* answer—it's the best answer available.

So how do you prevent the situation in which GDI surprises you by supplying a completely different font from the one you ask for? That's easy: Before asking for a font, you ask GDI for a list of the fonts available from a particular device. The **EnumFontFamilies** function lets you create such a list. You provide a callback function, and GDI calls the function once per font family. (A font family is a font that shares the same name, "Times New Roman" for example.) GDI provides you with **LOGFONT** and **TEXTMETRIC** data for each font enumerated. Once you have a list, you can be fairly confident that any **LOGFONT** request you make for a font will get an accurate response.

An even easier way to select a font is to call the font-picker dialog box, which is one of the dialogs in Windows' common dialog box library (COMMDLG.DLL under Win16, and COMDLG32.DLL under Win32). This function displays a list of available fonts to the user, and lets the user decide which font to use. It also has a preview window, which lets users get an idea about how a font will appear before commiting to the font.

The final section of this chapter is a look at a program that—among other things—uses the common dialog box library's font-picker dialog. This program also brings together some of the other subjects covered in this chapter: creating and selecting fonts, drawing with **TextOut**, and determining font size information by calling **GetTextMetrics**. It also introduces OWL's **TScroller** class, which provides an easy way to control scrolling of data in a window.

TEXTVIEW: A Text Viewer Program

Figure 10.11 shows a text file viewing program. This program reads a text file from disk, parses the lines in the file, and displays the text. Since most text files won't fit in a single

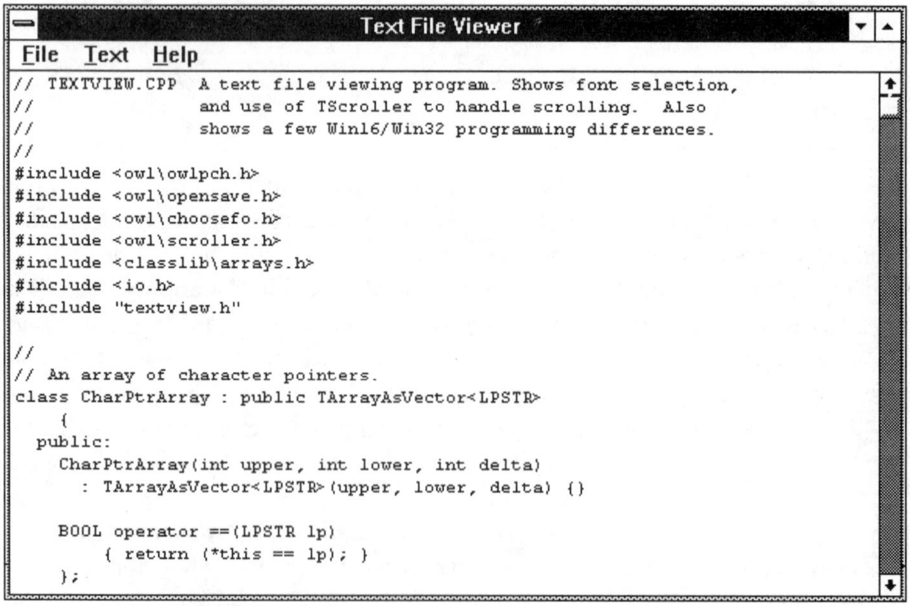

Text File Viewer

File Text Help

```
// TEXTVIEW.CPP  A text file viewing program. Shows font selection,
//               and use of TScroller to handle scrolling.  Also
//               shows a few Win16/Win32 programming differences.
//
#include <owl\owlpch.h>
#include <owl\opensave.h>
#include <owl\choosefo.h>
#include <owl\scroller.h>
#include <classlib\arrays.h>
#include <io.h>
#include "textview.h"

//
// An array of character pointers.
class CharPtrArray : public TArrayAsVector<LPSTR>
    {
  public:
    CharPtrArray(int upper, int lower, int delta)
      : TArrayAsVector<LPSTR>(upper, lower, delta) {}

    BOOL operator ==(LPSTR lp)
        { return (*this == lp); }
    };
```

Figure 10.11 TEXTVIEW displaying its own lines of code

window, it uses OWL's **`TScroller`** class to manage the scrollbars as well as the scrolling process. Here are the source files to TEXTVIEW:

TEXTVIEW.CPP

```
//
// TEXTVIEW.CPP  A text file viewing program. Shows font selection,
//               and use of TScroller to handle scrolling.  Also
//               shows a few Win16/Win32 programming differences.
//
#include <owl\owlpch.h>
#include <owl\opensave.h>
#include <owl\choosefo.h>
#include <owl\scroller.h>
#include <classlib\arrays.h>
#include <io.h>
#include "textview.h"

//
// An array of character pointers.
class CharPtrArray : public TArrayAsVector<LPSTR>
    {
  public:
    CharPtrArray(int upper, int lower, int delta)
      : TArrayAsVector<LPSTR>(upper, lower, delta) {}

    BOOL operator ==(LPSTR lp)
        { return (*this == lp); }
    };

//
// Main window
class DFrame : public TFrameWindow
    {
  public:
    DFrame(char * title);
    ~DFrame();

    void CmFileOpen();
    void CmFileExit();
    void CmTextFont();
    void CmHelpAbout();
    void EvKeyDown (UINT key, UINT repeat, UINT flags);
    void EvSize(UINT type, TSize& size);
    BOOL Create();
    void Paint (TDC& dc, BOOL bErase, TRect& trPaint);

    void GetFontMetrics(TFont& tfont);
    void BuildCharPtrArray(char * lpIn, LONG cbBuffer);
  private:
    CharPtrArray  * lpcp;          // Ptr to array of LPSTR values.
    char          * lpData;        // Ptr to data read from disk.
    int             cLines;        // Number of lines in file.
    int             ccMaxChars;    // File's largest line.
    int             cyLineHeight;  // CurFont's line height.
    int             cxAveWidth;    // CurFont's avg char width.
    TFont         * tfont;         // Ptr to current font.

    // Common dialog instance data.
```

```
    TChooseFontDialog::TData  * lpFontData;
    TOpenSaveDialog::TData    * lpFileData;

  DECLARE_RESPONSE_TABLE (DFrame);
    };

DEFINE_RESPONSE_TABLE1 (DFrame, TFrameWindow)
  EV_WM_KEYDOWN,
  EV_WM_SIZE,
  EV_COMMAND(CM_FILEEXIT, CmFileExit),
  EV_COMMAND(CM_FILEOPEN, CmFileOpen),
  EV_COMMAND(CM_TEXTFONT, CmTextFont),
  EV_COMMAND(CM_HELPABOUT, CmHelpAbout),
END_RESPONSE_TABLE;

DFrame::DFrame(char * title): TFrameWindow(0, title)
    {
    lpData       = 0;
    lpcp         = 0;
    cLines       = 0;
    ccMaxChars   = 0;
    cyLineHeight = 0;
    cxAveWidth   = 0;
    tfont        = 0;
    }

DFrame::~DFrame()
    {
    delete tfont;
    }

void DFrame::CmFileOpen()
    {
    // Create TFileOpenDialog object.
    TFileOpenDialog tfo(this, *lpFileData);

    // Display dialog box.
    int retval = tfo.Execute();

    if (retval == IDOK)
        {
#if defined (__WIN32__)
        HANDLE hf = CreateFile (lpFileData->FileName,
                                GENERIC_READ,
                                FILE_SHARE_READ,
                                NULL,
                                OPEN_EXISTING,
                                FILE_ATTRIBUTE_NORMAL,
                                0);
        // If open fails, complain.
        if (hf == INVALID_HANDLE_VALUE)
            {
            MessageBox ("Cannot Open Selected File",
                        Title, MB_ICONHAND);
            return;
            }

        // Query file size.
        DWORD cbSize = GetFileSize (hf, 0);
#else
        // Open file
        OFSTRUCT of;
```

```
        HFILE hf = OpenFile (lpFileData->FileName,
                             &of, OF_READWRITE);

        // If can't open fail, complain.
        if (hf == (HFILE)-1)
            {
            MessageBox ("Cannot Open Selected File",
                        Title, MB_ICONHAND);
            return;
            }

        // Query file size.
        UINT cbSize = (int)filelength(hf);
#endif

        // free existing file buffer.
        if (lpData)
            delete [] lpData;

        // Allocate file buffer.
        lpData = new char[cbSize + sizeof(short)];

        // Read data into buffer. Use WinAPI read because
        // Borland's RTL's "read()"  didn't work.

        // Weird cast to keep Win32 compiler happy.
        HFILE hfile = (HFILE)hf;
        LPVOID lpBuffer = (LPVOID)&lpData[sizeof(short)];
        UINT cbRead = _lread (hfile, lpBuffer, cbSize);

        // After data read, close file.
#if defined (__WIN32__)
        CloseHandle(hf);
#else
        _lclose (hf);
#endif

        // Warn if we couldn't read whole thing.
        if (cbRead != cbSize)
            MessageBox ("Unable to read entire file", Title);

        // Rebuild text array line info.
        BuildCharPtrArray (lpData, (LONG)cbRead);

        // Set scroll range info.
        TRect tr = GetClientRect();
        Scroller->SetRange (ccMaxChars - (tr.right / cxAveWidth),
                            cLines - (tr.bottom / cyLineHeight) );

        // Reposition scroll thumbs to top of window.
        Scroller->VScroll (SB_TOP, 0);

        // Force window to draw.
        Invalidate();
        }
    }

void DFrame::CmFileExit()
    {
    CloseWindow(0); // Cause application to terminate
    }
```

```
void DFrame::CmTextFont()
    {
    // Create TChooseFontDialog.
    TChooseFontDialog tcf(this, *lpFontData);

    // Display dialog box.
    int retval = tcf.Execute();

    if (retval == IDOK)
        {
        // Remove previous font.
        delete tfont;

        // Create new font.
        tfont = new TFont(&lpFontData->LogFont);

        // Init our line height.
        GetFontMetrics(*tfont);

        // Recalc scroll units & range.
        Scroller->SetUnits(cxAveWidth, cyLineHeight);
        TRect tr = GetClientRect();
        Scroller->SetRange (ccMaxChars - (tr.right / cxAveWidth),
                            cLines - (tr.bottom / cyLineHeight));

        // Force a redraw
        Invalidate();
        }
    }

void DFrame::CmHelpAbout()
    {
    MessageBox("    Text File Viewing Program\n\n"
               "'Borland C++ 4.0 Programming\n"
               "  for Windows', by Paul Yao", Title);
    }

void DFrame::EvKeyDown (UINT key, UINT /*repeat*/, UINT /*flags*/)
    {
    switch (key)
        {
        case VK_HOME:
            Scroller->VScroll(SB_TOP, 0);
            break;
        case VK_END:
            Scroller->VScroll(SB_BOTTOM, 0);
            break;
        case VK_UP:
            Scroller->VScroll(SB_LINEUP, 0);
            break;
        case VK_DOWN:
            Scroller->VScroll(SB_LINEDOWN, 0);
            break;
        case VK_PRIOR:  // Page up.
            Scroller->VScroll(SB_PAGEUP, 0);
            break;
        case VK_NEXT:   // Page down.
            Scroller->VScroll(SB_PAGEDOWN, 0);
            break;
        case VK_LEFT:
            Scroller->HScroll(SB_LINEUP, 0);
            break;
```

```
        case VK_RIGHT:
            Scroller->HScroll(SB_LINEDOWN, 0);
            break;
        }
    }

void DFrame::EvSize(UINT /*type*/, TSize& size)
    {
    Scroller->SetPageSize();
    Scroller->SetRange (ccMaxChars - (size.cx / cxAveWidth),
                        cLines - (size.cy / cyLineHeight) );
    }

// IMPORTANT!  If you override this function, always remember
//             to call TWindow::Create() to create the window.
//
BOOL DFrame::Create()
    {
    // Create File.Open instance data.
    lpFileData = new
        TOpenSaveDialog::TData(OFN_FILEMUSTEXIST,       // Flags.
                               "All Files (*.*)|*.*|"   // Filters.
                               "C++ Files (*.cpp)|*.cpp|"
                               "Include Files (*.h)|*.h|",
                               0,                // Custom Filter.
                               "",               // Initial directory.
                               "cpp");           // Default Extension.

    // Error checking.
    if (! lpFileData)
        return FALSE;

    // Create Text.Font instance data.
    lpFontData = new TChooseFontDialog::TData();

    // Select initial font.
    tfont = new TFont("Courier New");

    // Error checking.
    if (!lpFontData  || !tfont)
        return FALSE;

    // Init structure.
    lpFontData->Flags = CF_INITTOLOGFONTSTRUCT |
                        CF_FORCEFONTEXIST      |
                        CF_SCREENFONTS;
    lpFontData->Error = 0;
    lpFontData->DC = 0;
    tfont->GetObject (lpFontData->LogFont);
    lpFontData->PointSize = 0;
    lpFontData->Color = 0;
    lpFontData->Style = "";
    lpFontData->FontType = SCREEN_FONTTYPE;
    lpFontData->SizeMin = 0;
    lpFontData->SizeMax = 0;

    // Get line height for default font.
    GetFontMetrics(*tfont);

    // Request scroll bars from TWindow base class.
    Attr.Style |= WS_VSCROLL | WS_HSCROLL;
```

```
        // IMPORTANT! Call original virtual function.
        TWindow::Create();

        // Connect a TScroller object.
        Scroller = new TScroller (this, cxAveWidth, cyLineHeight,
                                  ccMaxChars, cLines);

        // Disable scroller origin setting (since it
        // has a range limitation of +-32767).
        Scroller->AutoOrg = FALSE;

        return TRUE;
        }

void DFrame::Paint (TDC& dc, BOOL, TRect&)
        {
        // Set viewport origin for DC.
        TRect rClient = GetClientRect();
        Scroller->BeginView (dc, rClient);

        // Y-Axis: (1) Calculate starting & ending lines.
        int ipszStart = Scroller->YPos;
        int ipszEnd   = ipszStart + rClient.bottom / cyLineHeight + 1;
        if (ipszEnd > cLines)
            ipszEnd = cLines;

        // Y-Axis: (2) Start drawing at top of window.
        int   yLine = 0;

        // X-Axis: Calculate X-offset based on scroller data.
        int   xLine = cxAveWidth / 2 - (Scroller->XPos * Scroller->XUnit);

        // Select current font.
        dc.SelectObject(*tfont);

        // Draw lines of text.
        for (int i=ipszStart; i < ipszEnd; i++)
            {
            LPSTR lpText = (*lpcp)[i];
            short   ccLine = (*(short *)(lpText-sizeof(short)));
            dc.TextOut (xLine, yLine, lpText, ccLine);
            yLine += cyLineHeight;
            }

        // Update scroll bar position.
        Scroller->EndView ();
        }

//
// This function takes a char [] array as input
// and builds a LPSTR[] array to point to the
// beginning of each line. It also modifies the
// original char[] array to store line-length
// information at the start of each string.
// For example, with an input array like this:
//
// char [0] =       <sizeof(short) left empty>
//      [2] = "Language shapes the way we think,<CR><LF>"
//            "And determines what we can think about.<CR><LF>"
//            "- B.L.Whorf<CR><LF>"
//
// This array is created:
```

```
//
//     LPSTR [0] = &char[2]
//           [1] = &char[37]
//           [2] = &char[78]
//
// And these elements are filled with line-length information:
//
//     char [ 0] = (int)33
//     char [35] = (int)39
//     char [76] = (int)11
//
void DFrame::BuildCharPtrArray(char * lpIn, LONG cbBuffer)
    {
    // Delete existing char ptr array.
    if (lpcp)
       delete lpcp;

    // Allocate char ptr array.
    lpcp = new CharPtrArray(250, 0, 250);

    // Insert start of buffer as first array element.
    lpcp->Add((char *)(lpIn+sizeof(short)));

    // Use sizeof(short) bytes at start for line length info.
    short * lpiLength = (short *)lpIn;

    // Initialize buffer pointer to AFTER length info.
    lpIn += (sizeof(short));

    // Init file info values: line count & max line width.
    cLines = 0;
    ccMaxChars = 0;

    // Loop until end-of-buffer.
    while (cbBuffer > 0)
        {
        int cbLine = 0;

        // Loop until end-of-line.
        while (*lpIn != CR && *lpIn != LF)
            {
            lpIn++;
            cbLine++;
            cbBuffer--;
            }

        // Increment line count.
        cLines++;

        // Update max line width value.
        if (cbLine > ccMaxChars)
            ccMaxChars = cbLine;

        // Update previous line length info.
        *lpiLength = cbLine;

        // Set pointer to current buffer location.
        lpiLength = (short *)lpIn;

        // Update pointer to start of next line.
        lpIn += sizeof(short);
```

```
            // Decrement buffer character count.
            cbBuffer-=sizeof(short);

            // If we're not at the end, add line to list.
            if (cbBuffer > 0)
                lpcp->Add(lpIn);
            }
        }

void DFrame::GetFontMetrics(TFont& tfont)
    {
    TClientDC  dc(0);
    TEXTMETRIC tm;

    // Check for failure in getting DC.
    if (!dc)
        return;

    dc.SelectObject (tfont);
    dc.GetTextMetrics(tm);
    cyLineHeight = tm.tmHeight + tm.tmExternalLeading;
    cxAveWidth   = tm.tmAveCharWidth;
    }

//
// Application object
class DApp : public TApplication
    {
  public:
    DApp() : TApplication()
        {
        }
    void InitMainWindow()
        {
        SetMainWindow (new DFrame("Text File Viewer"));
        MainWindow->AssignMenu("MAIN");
        MainWindow->SetIcon(this, "SNAPSHOT");
        }
    };

//
// Application main entry point.
OwlMain(int, char **)
    {
    return DApp().Run();
    }
```

TEXTVIEW.H

```
#define CM_FILEEXIT  100
#define CM_FILEOPEN  101
#define CM_TEXTFONT  200
#define CM_HELPABOUT 300

const char LF = 0x0a;
const char CR = 0x0d;
```

TEXTVIEW.RC

```
#include "textview.h"

snapshot icon textview.ico

main menu
    BEGIN
    POPUP "&File"
        {
        MENUITEM "Open...", CM_FILEOPEN
        MENUITEM SEPARATOR
        MENUITEM "E&xit",   CM_FILEEXIT
        }
    POPUP "&Text"
        {
        MENUITEM "&Font...", CM_TEXTFONT
        }
    POPUP "&Help"
        {
        MENUITEM "&About...", CM_HELPABOUT
        }
    END
```

TEXTVIEW.DEF

```
EXETYPE WINDOWS

CODE MOVEABLE DISCARDABLE
DATA MULTIPLE MOVEABLE

HEAPSIZE   512
STACKSIZE 8192
```

DYNA16.MAK

```
#  MAKE file for Win16 API using dynamic BIDS,
#  OWL and C-runtime libraries.
#
#     C> make -fstatic16.mak
#

.AUTODEPEND
CC = -c -H -H"owl\owlpch.h" -ml -R -vi -WS -X-
CD = -D_RTLDLL;_BIDSDLL;_OWLDLL;_OWLPCH;
INC = -I\BC4\INCLUDE
LIB = -L\BC4\LIB

textview.exe :  textview.obj textview.res
  tlink -c -C -Twe $(LIB) @dyna16.lnk
  brc textview.res textview.exe

textview.obj :  textview.cpp
  bcc $(CC) $(CD) textview.cpp

textview.res :  textview.rc textview.ico textview.h
  brc $(INC) -31 -R textview.rc
```

DYNA16.LNK

```
\bc4\lib\c0wl.obj+
textview.obj
textview,textview
\bc4\lib\bidsi.lib+
\bc4\lib\owlwi.lib+
\bc4\lib\import.lib+
\bc4\lib\crtldll.lib
textview.def
```

DYNA32.MAK

```
#  MAKE file for Win32 API using dynamic BIDS,
#  OWL and C-runtime libraries.
#
#    C> make -fdyna32.mak
#

.AUTODEPEND
CC = -c -H -H\""owl\owlpch.h\"" -p- -R -vi -W -X-
CD = -D_RTLDLL;_BIDSDLL;_OWLDLL;_OWLPCH;
INC = -I\BC4\INCLUDE
LIB = -L\BC4\LIB

textview.exe :  textview.obj textview.res
  tlink32 -aa -c -Tpe $(LIB) @dyna32.lnk
  brc32 textview.res textview.exe

textview.obj :  textview.cpp
  bcc32 $(CC) $(CD) textview.cpp

textview.res :  textview.rc textview.ico textview.h
  brc32 $(INC) -w32 -R textview.rc
```

DYNA32.LNK

```
\bc4\lib\c0w32.obj+
textview.obj
textview,textview
\bc4\lib\bidsfi.lib+
\bc4\lib\owlwfi.lib+
\bc4\lib\import32.lib+
\bc4\lib\cw32i.lib
textview.def
```

From the point of view of graphic output, the handling of the **`WM_PAINT`** message is usually the most interesting part of a Windows program. With TEXTVIEW, however, you need to look at where it gets its data to understand how this program works. That means you need to look at the place where a file gets opened and data read in—the **`CmFileOpen`** message response function. This function gets called when the user selects the **File.Open...** command.

The File.Open dialog box itself is handled by the common dialog box library, so the amount of code needed for that is just a few lines. You'll notice that file opening is handled a little differently for Win16 programs than for Win32 programs. For some reason, the Win16 **`OpenFile`** routine failed to work under Win32, so I resorted to the native Win32 **`CreateFile`** function.

Once the file is open, a buffer gets allocated and the data is read in. I didn't get fancy with allocating a buffer, which means that—when running in Win16—only files that are 64K or smaller can be read in. That, of course, is the maximum size of a memory segment under the Intel-86 family's memory management scheme.

After the data's been read in, the **`BuildCharPtrArray`** function parses the entire file to determine the length of each line. Line length information is stored within the text buffer itself, overwriting the carriage-return and line-feed characters that ordinarily sit between lines of text. At the same time, a pointer is added to a list of **`char *`** pointers. The list itself is built using one of OWL's container template classes, the **`TArrayAsVector`** template class. This proved to be a useful way to dynamically build a list that could still be referenced using the convenient square bracket array notation.

Whenever the font changed, a private function—**`GetFontMetrics`**—initialized line height information and character width information by calling **`GetTextMetrics`**. This information, stored in **`cyLineHeight`** and **`cxAveCharWidth`**, served to help paint the lines of text.

Support for the **`TScroller`** class starts in the **`TWindow`** base window class, which provides a data member—**`Scroller`**—for a pointer to a **`TScroller`** object. Once the scroller object has been created and provided with the appropriate scroll units and the scroll range, it tracks the numbers for you. All that's required is using the values it stores when painting the window.

As you can see, GDI treats text as a graphic object. This means that you get a great deal of control over the placement, sizing, and color of text. You can freely mix text and geometric shapes, and combine text of different sizes and styles on the same page. We think you'll find that the extra effort required is well worth the device-independent punch that GDI packs in text creation.

For programmers who don't need a lot of variety in text, GDI guarantees that you will find a default font for every GDI device. This will provide reasonable-looking text output with a minimum of effort on your part.

PART FOUR

USER INTERFACE OBJECTS

11

Commands: Menu and Accelerator Basics

Windows has built-in support for two user-interface objects that retrieve command input from users: menus and accelerators. Menus allow a program to show users available actions and options, and encourage users to explore the capabilities of a program. Menus help beginners by eliminating the need to memorize commands. More advanced users can take advantage of accelerators, which translate keystrokes into program commands. To bridge the gap between menus and accelerators, programs often list accelerator keys inside menus.

Programs that adhere to the Windows standards for accelerators and menus are easier for users to learn than programs that do not. Therefore, it's important for programmers who plan to design menus to first learn these standards. There are two things you can do that will help you become familiar with these standards: You can use Windows, and you can read the style guidelines that Microsoft includes with the software development kit. Learning the standards is time well spent, since it will minimize the time required for a user to become comfortable with your program. Users who are familiar with the "look and feel" that pervades Windows programs will be put off by programs that ignore widely accepted standards.

Let's start with a quick look at some of the things that users expect to find in menus.

User-Interface Standards

Users expect to find two types of items in a menu: **actions** and **options**. A menu action is usually expressed as a verb, or as a noun-verb combination. For example, many programs have an *Open* menu item inside a "File" menu. Menu actions usually act on a specific object that the user has selected. But menu actions can also cause a change that will affect an entire program. The *Close* item in a system menu, for example, can cause a program to terminate when the window being closed is the program's main, top-level window.

Options are toggle switches. Unlike menu actions, which create a short-lived response, options have a more long-lasting effect that is usually reversible. Programs often display check marks in menus to indicate whether an option is active or not. For example, the Program Manager has an Options menu that lets the user enable and disable two features: "Auto Arrange" and "Minimize on Use." While certain important options are set inside menus, most large programs make use of dialog boxes to allow the user to control a program's settable options. In other words, you don't need to put every available option inside menus. The less frequently required options can be placed into dialog boxes, which we'll discuss in more detail in Chapter 14.

Users expect to see **visual clues** in menus. Visual clues can be subtle, like the ellipses (...) that appear when the selection of a menu item causes a dialog box to appear. Or, can be as obvious as the way menu items are grouped. Here is a list of some of the different visual clues that can be incorporated into menus to indicate special handling of menu items:

- **Accelerator keystrokes** tell the user the accelerator key that matches the menu selection.
- An **arrow** indicates that a menu item is a doorway to a nested menu. The nested menu appears when the user touches the menu item, either by dragging the mouse or moving to the menu selection using keyboard cursor keys.
- A **separator** divides longer menus into smaller groups of menu items.
- A **check mark** next to a menu item indicates that the option has been turned on.
- An **ellipsis** (...) after a menu item tells the user to expect a dialog box when the menu item is selected.
- An **exclamation point** at the end of a menu item in a top-level menu indicates that the menu item causes an action and will not cause a popup menu to appear.
- A **grayed** menu item is unavailable. In the system menu, for example, several menu items are grayed when a window is maximized.
- An **underlined** *letter* in the menu item text indicates the letter can be used to select the menu item. Such a letter is called a **mnemonic**. To make a popup menu appear, the [Alt] key is pressed with the mnemonic of the popup menu. Once a popup has appeared, menu items can be selected by pressing the mnemonic corresponding to the desired menu item.

Figure 11.1 shows a menu with an example of each of these different visual clues.

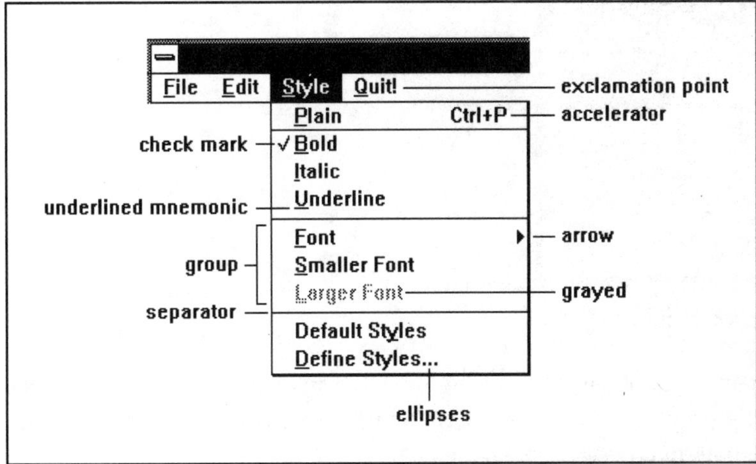

Figure 11.1 Menu showing various visual clues

Users expect every program to have a **system menu**. From a programming point of view, this is easily accomplished, since Windows creates and maintains the system menu for you. In general, programs should not alter the contents of the system menu without a very good reason. A program may *add* certain items to the system menu. In particular, programs which only run in a minimized (or iconic) state can add private menu items to the system menu. The system menu, after all, is the only menu to appear when a program is iconic. Tiny utility and toy applications can add items to the system menu as well, to avoid the fuss of creating private menus. It's not something you'll do often, but under certain conditions it makes sense to. Figure 11.2 shows a standard system menu.

In programs that work with data files, users expect to find a **File** popup menu. This menu provides access to the commands involved with opening, closing, and printing files. Notice, as shown in Figure 11.3, the *Exit* menu item is a standard part of the File menu. When selected, this item causes the program to terminate. While this duplicates the *Close*

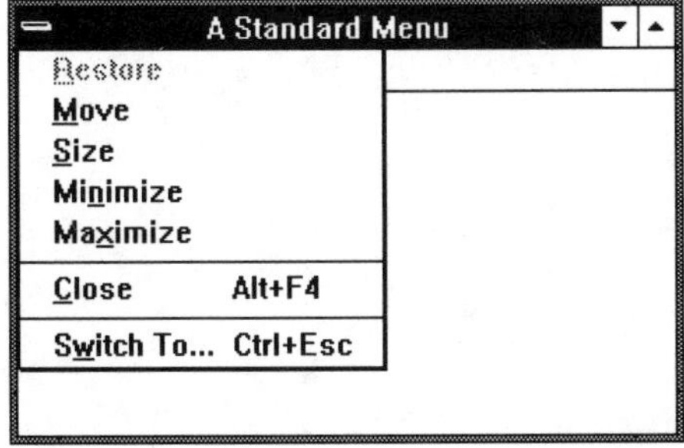

Figure 11.2 The standard system menu

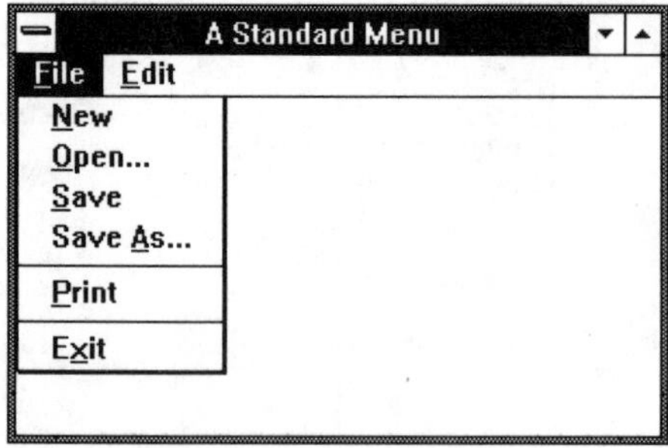

Figure 11.3 A typical file menu

menu item in the system menu of a top-level window, it is a standard that users have come to expect. If you write a program that does *not* have a File menu, you'll still want to put an *Exit* menu item at the bottom of your first popup menu.

Another standard menu that users expect is the **Edit** popup menu. This menu lists general-purpose editing actions, including clipboard control, search and replace, undo previous actions, and repeat previous actions. A program can add other items to the standard Edit menu to allow an application-specific object to be manipulated. For example, a word processing program might list an action in its Edit menu to allow a user to edit the header or footer of a document. Figure 11.4 shows a typical Edit menu, which is part of the first program we're going to write.

Menus can be accessed using any combination of mouse and keyboard input. For example, after a mouse click makes a popup menu appear, users can browse through menu items by pressing arrow keys and can select a menu item by pressing the return key. As an alternative, users can activate a popup menu from the keyboard by pressing the [Alt] or the [F10] key. Menu browsing and selection can then be done with the mouse.

This ability to choose between the mouse and the keyboard for menu operations is part of a larger plan to allow these devices to be used interchangeably in other actions as well. Of course, there are limits—entering characters with the mouse is difficult. But aside from these extremes, this ability to choose is important for program designers to keep in mind. Some users will rely solely on the keyboard—either because they don't have a mouse or

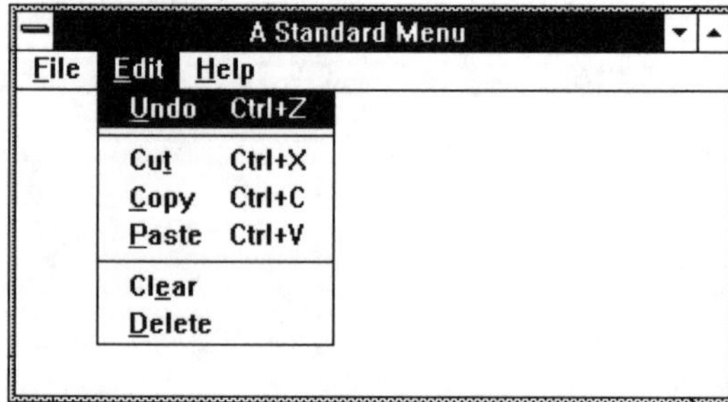

Figure 11.4 A typical edit menu

because they prefer the keyboard. Others may switch between the two input methods, depending on the operation and their personal preference. In Chapters 15 and 16, when we discuss mouse and keyboard input in more detail, we'll reiterate this choice as an important part of the overall design for Windows programs. For now, let's get into the programming details of creating menus.

Menu Programming Issues

Windows has a very robust, flexible menuing system that is, at the same time, quite easy to work with. While menus are easy to create for Windows programmers, the creation of the menuing system proved one of the most challenging tasks in the creation of Windows. The code that supports menuing has been reworked, tuned, and rewritten more than any other part of the system. One of the reasons has to do with performance: From the beginning, menus had to be snappy. Otherwise, the system itself would risk appearing sluggish. To help menus disappear quickly with minimum performance impact, a bitmap "snapshot" is taken of the screen where a menu is going to be drawn. When a user has finished using a menu, the snapshot is used to restore the area where the menu had been.

After all of Microsoft's efforts to make menus work quickly and efficiently, you'll be happy to know that menu creation is easy. As we'll see shortly, the quickest way to create a menu involves writing a short menu description in a program's resource file. You activate a menu by connecting it to a window, which makes it available to a user.

Since we're working with a message-driven system, it probably won't surprise you to learn that menus created in Windows use messages to communicate with your program. Or, more precisely, messages are used to communicate with your *window object*. The most important menu message is the **WM_COMMAND** message, which is sent to notify you that a menu item has been selected.

Table 11.1 shows the different steps in the operation of a menu, the mouse and keyboard actions that lead to each step, and the associated messages. Notice that identical message traffic occurs whether the mouse or the keyboard is used. The details of the interaction between the user and your menus are hidden in the menu system, so that your program can simply respond to the messages with complete trust that the menuing system is taking care of the rest.

Table 11.1 Menu Operation and Menu Messages

Menu Operation	*Mouse Action*	*Keyboard Action*	*Message*
Initiate menu use	n/a	F10 or Alt key	WM_INITMENU
Display a popup	n/a	arrow or mnemonic keys	WM_INITMENUPOPUP

(continued)

Table 11.1 Menu Operation and Menu Messages *(Continued)*

Menu Operation	*Mouse Action*	*Keyboard Action*	*Message*
Initiate and display popup	<Click>	Alt + mnemonic key	WM_INITMENU and WM_INITMENUPOPUP
Browse a menu item	<Drag>	arrow keys	WM_MENUSELECT
Select a menu item	<Release>	Enter key or mnemonic key	WM_COMMAND

While the **WM_COMMAND** message is the most useful, you'll want to understand the role of the other messages since there are times that they can be useful as well. For example, if a program wishes to initialize a top-level menu before the user makes a selection, it would respond to the **WM_INITMENU** message. To initialize a popup menu before it appears, a program would respond to **WM_INITMENUPOPUP**. Programs that use the clipboard often respond to one of these initialization messages to let the user know, for example, whether or not there is data on the clipboard that can be pasted. If there is, the *Paste* item in the Edit menu is enabled. Otherwise, it is grayed.

As the user browses through the items in a menu, the **WM_MENUSELECT** message tells a program the specific menu item that the user is highlighting at every moment in time. This information can be used to support an "information area" to display hints about the meaning of each menu item. This might be another window on the screen where information is displayed for the user to see. Quite a few commercial Windows programs provide this feature to assist in the selection of menu items. In Chapter 13, where we discuss issues relating to windowing, we'll show you a program that creates an OWL gadget window and processes **WM_MENUSELECT** messages in this way.

Menu Template

The simplest menus start with a menu template. A menu template defines the popup menus and menu items that make up a menu. A menu template is a hierarchical data structure, like the DOS file system with its root directory and subdirectories. At the top of the hierarchy—the root directory—are the items for the menu bar, also known as the **action bar**. At this top level, items can be either menu items, which send command messages when selected, or the tops of popup menus. As a side note, it's something of a curiosity that another term used to refer to a popup menu is **pull-down menu**.

Popup menus are like subdirectories that are one level below the root directory in the DOS file hierarchy. And in the same way that subdirectories can themselves contain *other* subdirectories, a popup menu can contain other popup menus. There isn't any limit to the number of nested menu levels that the menu subsystem will provide. But common sense would indicate that three levels of menus—the main menu bar and two levels of popup menus—is the deepest you will most likely want to go. Otherwise, you risk losing your user in a sea of menus.

The quickest and easiest way to create a menu template is from within the Resource Workshop. As shown in Figure 11.5, this editor makes it easy to change a menu, since it lets you instantly see the results of a change. You can also create a menu template using a text editor. Whichever method you choose, our discussion will give you all the details of menu template creation:

```
menuID MENU [load option] [memory option]
BEGIN
    MENUITEM or POPUP statement
    MENUITEM or POPUP statement
    .
    .
    .
END
```

The **`[load option]`** can be either **`PRELOAD`** or **`LOADONCALL`**, and the **`[memory option]`** can be **`FIXED`**, **`MOVEABLE`**, or **`DISCARDABLE`**. These describe how the menu data itself is handled as a memory object. **`PRELOAD`** causes a menu resource to be loaded into memory before a program starts running. **`LOADONCALL`** causes the menu item to be loaded only when it is needed. The other three options, **`FIXED`**, **`MOVEABLE`**, and **`DISCARDABLE`**, describe how the memory object should behave once it has been loaded into memory. In

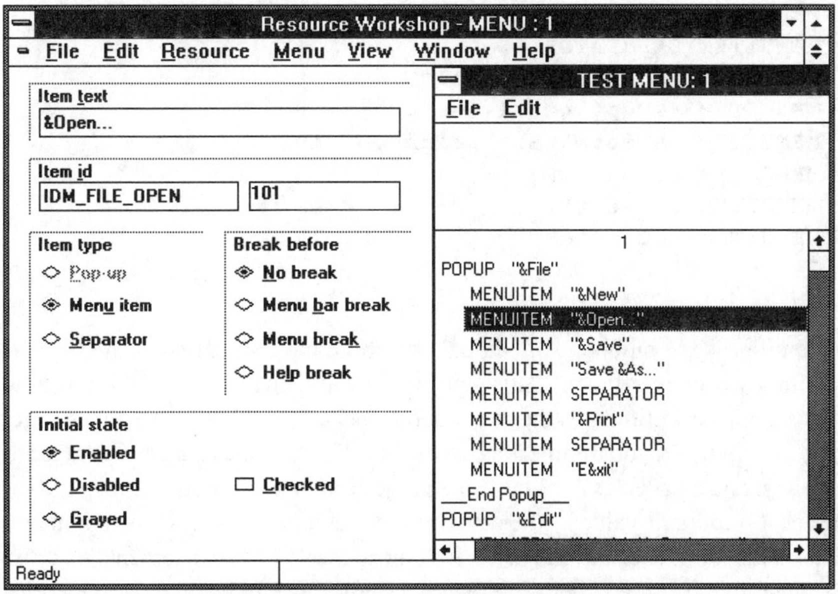

Figure 11.5 Defining a menu with Resource Workshop

Chapter 17, we'll describe in detail the meaning of these three options. Since the default behavior of **LOADONCALL** and the memory option of **DISCARDABLE** are good enough for now, we won't bother specifying these options in our menu examples.

Each **MENUITEM** statement defines a menu item that, when selected, causes a **WM_COMMAND** message to be sent. Each **POPUP** statement starts the definition of a popup menu, with a **BEGIN** and an **END** statement to bracket other **MENUITEM** or **POPUP** statements. Incidentally, if you want to save yourself some typing, you can use the C language squiggly brackets "{" and "}" in place of the **BEGIN** and **END** statements. Here is the menu definition for the File and Edit menus that we discussed earlier in this chapter:

```
7 MENU
    {
    POPUP "&File"
        {
        MENUITEM "&New",                           1
        MENUITEM "&Open...",                       2
        MENUITEM "&Save",                          3
        MENUITEM "Save &As...",                    4
        MENUITEM SEPARATOR
        MENUITEM "&Print",                         5
        MENUITEM SEPARATOR
        MENUITEM "E&xit",                          6
        }
    POPUP "&Edit"
        {
        MENUITEM "&Undo\tAlt+Backspace", 7
        MENUITEM SEPARATOR
        MENUITEM "Cu&t\tShift+Del",        8
        MENUITEM "&Copy\tCtrl+Ins",        9
        MENUITEM "&Paste\tShift+Ins",     10
        MENUITEM SEPARATOR
        MENUITEM "Cl&ear",                        11
        MENUITEM "&Delete",                       12
        }
    }
```

The menu identifier is the number 7. Although we could have specified an ASCII text string, using a number is more efficient. This identifier is our name for the menu; it is how we'll identify this menu definition to Windows. Each ampersand (&) defines a mnemonic, which is a letter used in the keyboard interface to menus. The **\t** causes a tab character to be generated, to separate an accelerator keystroke name from a menu item name.

Perhaps the most important value in the definition of each menu item is the command result code. This is the number at the end of each of these **MENUITEM** statements that distinguishes one menu item from another. The menu system uses the result code to identify menu items for the **WM_COMMAND** and **WM_MENUSELECT** messages.

The general syntax of the **POPUP** statement is

```
POPUP text [,optionlist]
```

and the **MENUITEM** statement has the following syntax:

```
MENUITEM text, result-code [,optionlist]
```

The big difference between the two statements is that a **MENUITEM** statement has a result code and the **POPUP** statement does not. As far as `[optionlist]` goes, there are five options that can be selected. The first three select the initial state of the menu item:

- **CHECKED**. Places a check mark next to the popup or menu item name. This only affects items inside a popup menu, and not items in the top-level menu.
- **GRAYED**. Item is initially grayed and inactive.
- **INACTIVE**. Item appears normally, but cannot be selected. The **GRAYED** option is better, since it provides the user with visual feedback that a menu item isn't available.

The other two options change the physical layout of the menu itself:

- **MENUBREAK**. Causes a menu break. For horizontal (top-level) menus, this means a break in the vertical direction. For vertical (popup) menus, this means a break in the horizontal direction. If used with wild abandon, you could have vertical top-level and horizontal popup menus.
- **MENUBARBREAK**. Causes a menu break. In popup menus, the break is accompanied by a vertical bar.

In a top-level menu, these last two options have the same effect, which is to cause a menu item to start on a new line. For example, consider the following menu definition:

```
7 MENU
    {
    MENUITEM "Item-1", 1
    MENUITEM "Item-2", 2, MENUBREAK
    MENUITEM "Item-3", 3
    MENUITEM "Item-4", 4
    MENUITEM "Item-5", 5, MENUBARBREAK
    MENUITEM "Item-6", 6
    }
```

As depicted in Figure 11.6, the two break statements, **MENUBREAK** and **MENUBARBREAK**, cause the menu to wrap on the second and the fifth menu items. Windows itself will break top-level menus when the window is too narrow. But if you want to control when and how this occurs, these options are what you'll need.

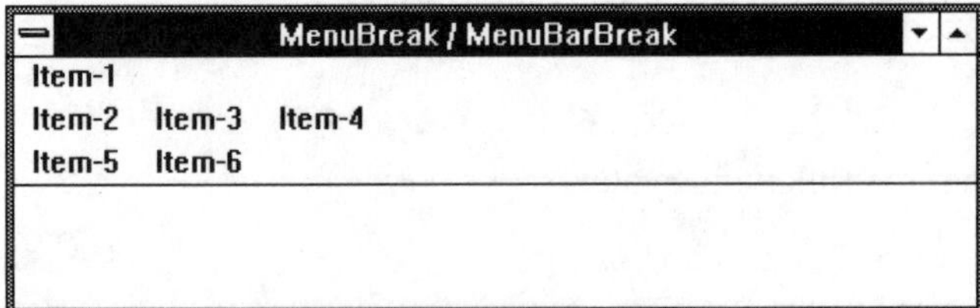

Figure 11.6 Results of a MENUBREAK and MENUBARBREAK option on a top-level menu

To see the effect of these two options in a popup menu, consider the following menu template:

```
7 MENU
    {
    POPUP "Popup"
        {
        MENUITEM "Item-1", 1
        MENUITEM "Item-2", 2, MENUBREAK
        MENUITEM "Item-3", 3
        MENUITEM "Item-4", 4
        MENUITEM "Item-5", 5, MENUBARBREAK
        MENUITEM "Item-6", 6
        }
    }
```

Figure 11.7 shows the resulting popup menu. Notice that both options cause the menus to begin a new column, but that the **MENUBARBREAK** option adds a vertical bar to separate the different columns of menu items that are created.

An additional option is listed in the documentation—**HELP**—but it no longer applies to the current standard for menus and so it has no effect. The old standard put the Help menu on the far right side of the top-level menu, with a vertical bar separating it from the other menu items. The current standard simply calls for making the Help menu the last item on the top-level menu. If you experiment with this option, you'll see that the menu system

Figure 11.7 Results of a MENUBREAK and a MENUBARBREAKoption in a popup menu

simply ignores it. On the other hand, if you want popup menus to appear on the right side of the menu bar, you'll need to create the menu dynamically and use the `MF_HELP` flag.

Let's take a look at a full-blown program that incorporates a menu. The menus we'll use are the standard File and Edit menus that we looked at earlier.

A Sample Program: STANMENU

This program shows all of the pieces that must be put together to get a working menu. The menu itself is defined in the resource file, STANMENU.RC. But a resource by itself is just a data definition. To bring it into a program and make it work requires some code.

One way to connect a menu to a window is to associate the menu with a WinAPI window class. This involves overriding **TWindow::GetClassName** and **TWindow::GetWindowClass** to define your own, custom WinAPI window class. If you developed Windows applications in C, this technique would be familiar to you.

Since the OWL C++ classes provide richer capabilities than native WinAPI window classes, they are all but disabled by the OWL class library[1]. When using OWL, then, it makes more sense to connect a menu to an individual window than to a window class. That's the role of **TWindow::AssignMenu**, which has been called by every program in this book in **DApp::InitMainWindow**:

```
MainWindow->AssignMenu ("MAIN");
```

The string "MAIN" is the name of the menu resource in the resource script (.RC) file.

Here is the code to our sample menu program, STANMENU:

STANMENU.CPP

```
//
// STANMENU.CPP  Shows a standard File & Edit menu.
//
//
#include <owl\owlpch.h>
#include "stanmenu.h"

//
// Main window
class DFrame : public TFrameWindow
    {
  public:
    DFrame(char * title);
    void CmFileNew();
    void CmFileOpen();
    void CmFileSave();
```

[1] Actually, the OWL library registers a single WinAPI window class—**OwlWindow**—for all **TWindow**-derived classes.

```
    void CmFileSaveAs();
    void CmFilePrint();
    void CmFileExit();
    void CmEditUndo();
    void CmEditCut();
    void CmEditCopy();
    void CmEditPaste();
    void CmEditClear();
    void CmEditDelete();
    void CmHelpAbout();

  DECLARE_RESPONSE_TABLE (DFrame);
    };

DEFINE_RESPONSE_TABLE1 (DFrame, TFrameWindow)
  EV_COMMAND(CM_FILE_NEW,  CmFileNew),
  EV_COMMAND(CM_FILE_OPEN, CmFileOpen),
  EV_COMMAND(CM_FILE_SAVE, CmFileSave),
  EV_COMMAND(CM_FILE_SAVEAS, CmFileSaveAs),
  EV_COMMAND(CM_FILE_PRINT, CmFilePrint),
  EV_COMMAND(CM_FILE_EXIT, CmFileExit),
  EV_COMMAND(CM_EDIT_UNDO, CmEditUndo),
  EV_COMMAND(CM_EDIT_CUT,  CmEditCut),
  EV_COMMAND(CM_EDIT_COPY, CmEditCopy),
  EV_COMMAND(CM_EDIT_PASTE, CmEditPaste),
  EV_COMMAND(CM_EDIT_CLEAR, CmEditClear),
  EV_COMMAND(CM_EDIT_DELETE, CmEditDelete),
  EV_COMMAND(CM_HELP_ABOUT, CmHelpAbout),
END_RESPONSE_TABLE;

DFrame::DFrame(char * title) : TFrameWindow(0, title)
    {
    }

void DFrame::CmFileNew()
    {
    MessageBox ("File.New Selected", Title);
    }
void DFrame::CmFileOpen()
    {
    MessageBox ("File.Open... Selected", Title);
    }
void DFrame::CmFileSave()
    {
    MessageBox ("File.Save Selected", Title);
    }
void DFrame::CmFileSaveAs()
    {
    MessageBox ("File.Save As... Selected", Title);
    }
void DFrame::CmFilePrint()
    {
    MessageBox ("File.Print Selected", Title);
    }
void DFrame::CmFileExit()
    {
    MessageBox ("File.Exit Selected", Title);
    CloseWindow(0); // Cause application to terminate
    }
void DFrame::CmEditUndo()
    {
    MessageBox ("Edit.Undo Selected", Title);
```

```
    }
void DFrame::CmEditCut()
    {
    MessageBox ("Edit.Cut Selected", Title);
    }
void DFrame::CmEditCopy()
    {
    MessageBox ("Edit.Copy Selected", Title);
    }
void DFrame::CmEditPaste()
    {
    MessageBox ("Edit.Paste Selected", Title);
    }
void DFrame::CmEditClear()
    {
    MessageBox ("Edit.Clear Selected", Title);
    }
void DFrame::CmEditDelete()
    {
    MessageBox ("Edit.Delete Selected", Title);
    }

void DFrame::CmHelpAbout()
    {
    MessageBox("  Standard File & Edit Menus\n\n"
               "'Borland C++ 4.0 Programming\n"
               "  for Windows', by Paul Yao", Title);
    }

//
// Application object
class DApp : public TApplication
    {
  public:
    DApp() : TApplication()
        {
        }
    void InitMainWindow()
        {
        SetMainWindow (new DFrame("A Standard Menu"));
        MainWindow->AssignMenu("MAIN");
        MainWindow->SetIcon(this, "SNAPSHOT");
        }
    };

//
// Application main entry point.
OwlMain(int, char **)
    {
    return DApp().Run();
    }
```

STANMENU.H

```
#define CM_FILE_NEW    100
#define CM_FILE_OPEN   101
#define CM_FILE_SAVE   102
#define CM_FILE_SAVEAS 103
#define CM_FILE_PRINT  104
```

```
#define CM_FILE_EXIT   105

#define CM_EDIT_UNDO   200
#define CM_EDIT_CUT    201
#define CM_EDIT_COPY   202
#define CM_EDIT_PASTE  203
#define CM_EDIT_CLEAR  204
#define CM_EDIT_DELETE 205

#define CM_HELP_ABOUT   300
```

STANMENU.RC

```
#include "stanmenu.h"

snapshot icon stanmenu.ico

main menu
    BEGIN
    POPUP "&File"
        {
        MENUITEM "&New",        CM_FILE_NEW
        MENUITEM "&Open...",    CM_FILE_OPEN
        MENUITEM "&Save",       CM_FILE_SAVE
        MENUITEM "Save &As...", CM_FILE_SAVEAS
        MENUITEM SEPARATOR
        MENUITEM "&Print",      CM_FILE_PRINT
        MENUITEM SEPARATOR
        MENUITEM "E&xit",       CM_FILE_EXIT
        }
    POPUP "&Edit"
        {
        MENUITEM "&Undo\tCtrl+Z",  CM_EDIT_UNDO
        MENUITEM SEPARATOR
        MENUITEM "Cu&t\tCtrl+X",   CM_EDIT_CUT
        MENUITEM "&Copy\tCtrl+C",  CM_EDIT_COPY
        MENUITEM "&Paste\tCtrl+V", CM_EDIT_PASTE
        MENUITEM SEPARATOR
        MENUITEM "Cl&ear",         CM_EDIT_CLEAR
        MENUITEM "&Delete",        CM_EDIT_DELETE
        }
    POPUP "&Help"
        {
        MENUITEM "&About...", CM_HELP_ABOUT
        }
    END
```

STANMENU.DEF

```
EXETYPE WINDOWS

CODE MOVEABLE DISCARDABLE
DATA MULTIPLE MOVEABLE

HEAPSIZE   512
STACKSIZE 8192
```

DYNA16.MAK

```
#  MAKE file for Win16 API using dynamic BIDS,
#  OWL and C-runtime libraries.
#
#    C> make -fstatic16.mak
#

.AUTODEPEND
CC = -c -H -H"owl\owlpch.h" -ml -R -vi -WS -X-
CD = -D_RTLDLL;_BIDSDLL;_OWLDLL;_OWLPCH;
INC = -I\BC4\INCLUDE
LIB = -L\BC4\LIB

stanmenu.exe :  stanmenu.obj stanmenu.res
  tlink -c -C -Twe $(LIB) @dyna16.lnk
  brc stanmenu.res stanmenu.exe

stanmenu.obj :  stanmenu.cpp
  bcc $(CC) $(CD) stanmenu.cpp

stanmenu.res :  stanmenu.rc stanmenu.ico stanmenu.h
  brc $(INC) -31 -R stanmenu.rc
```

DYNA16.LNK

```
\bc4\lib\c0wl.obj+
stanmenu.obj
stanmenu,stanmenu
\bc4\lib\bidsi.lib+
\bc4\lib\owlwi.lib+
\bc4\lib\import.lib+
\bc4\lib\crtldll.lib
stanmenu.def
```

DYNA32.MAK

```
#  MAKE file for Win32 API using dynamic BIDS,
#  OWL and C-runtime libraries.
#
#    C> make -fdyna32.mak
#

.AUTODEPEND
CC = -c -H -H\""owl\owlpch.h\"" -p- -R -vi -W -X-
CD = -D_RTLDLL;_BIDSDLL;_OWLDLL;_OWLPCH;
INC = -I\BC4\INCLUDE
LIB = -L\BC4\LIB

stanmenu.exe :  stanmenu.obj stanmenu.res
  tlink32 -aa -c -Tpe $(LIB) @dyna32.lnk
  brc32 stanmenu.res stanmenu.exe

stanmenu.obj :  stanmenu.cpp
  bcc32 $(CC) $(CD) stanmenu.cpp

stanmenu.res :  stanmenu.rc stanmenu.ico stanmenu.h
  brc32 $(INC) -w32 -R stanmenu.rc
```

DYNA32.LNK

```
\bc4\lib\c0w32.obj+
stanmenu.obj
stanmenu,stanmenu
\bc4\lib\bidsfi.lib+
\bc4\lib\owlwfi.lib+
\bc4\lib\import32.lib+
\bc4\lib\cw32i.lib
stanmenu.def
```

When a user selects a menu item, a command message—**WM_COMMAND**—gets sent to the menu's window object with the menu item ID encoded in message parameters. To handle a typical WinAPI message, you create a message response function and reference it in the window's response table. While you could create an **EvCommand** function, it's simpler to allow **TWindow::EvCommand** to receive **WM_COMMAND** messages and parse them for you.

To take advantage of this facility, you define one function per menu item. Here, for example, is the function for handling the **File.New** menu item in STANMENU:

```
void DFrame::CmFileNew()
    {
    MessageBox ("File.New Selected", Title);
    }
```

As a member of **DFrame**, **CmFileNew** is declared in the **DFrame** class declaration. Connecting it to the message response function involves the following line in the message response table:

```
EV_COMMAND(CM_FILE_NEW, CmFileNew),
```

The simple menu in STANMENU has enough sophistication for most Windows programs. However, you may decide you need to get more involved with the handling of a menu. This would be the case if you wanted to change your menu at runtime: to add a menu item, or to make a menu item grayed or checked. For programs (and programmers) that demand more, Windows has 26 menu support routines that you can use. To help you get a grasp of them, we've divided these routines into six main types. We're going to discuss each type in turn.

Menu Support Routines

Windows has 26 menu support routines, which can be divided into six categories. Each category describes a different type of activity that can be performed on a menu. The categories are creation, connect to a window, destruction, modification, query, and tracking. When you need more than just the simplest menu operations, you'll find that you can go to each group of routines and find one or more that will help you with whatever problem you have. Table 11.2 summarizes the various categories of menu functions.

Table 11.2 A Summary of Menu Functions

Category	*Routine*	*Description*
Creation (4)	CreateMenu	Creates an empty menu in memory.
	CreatePopupMenu	Creates an empty popup menu in memory.
	LoadMenu	Creates a menu from a disk-based (.EXE or .DLL file) menu resource.
	LoadMenuIndirect	Creates a menu from a memory-based menu resource.
Connect to a Window (1)	SetMenu	Attaches a top-level menu to a window.
Destruction (2)	DeleteMenu	Removes a menu item from a top-level or popup menu, and destroys any associated popup menus.
	DestroyMenu	Destroys a specific top-level or popup menu and all the menus below it.
Modification (10)	AppendMenu	Adds items to the end of a top-level or popup menu.
	ChangeMenu	Old Windows 1.x and 2.x menu modification function.
	CheckMenuItem	Toggles a checkmark inside a popup menu.
	DrawMenuBar	Forces the top-level menu to be redrawn after it has been changed.
	EnableMenuItem	Enables, disables, and grays menu items.
	HiliteMenuItem	Toggles highlighting of an item in a top-level menu.
	InsertMenu	Puts a new item into a menu.
	ModifyMenu	Changes an item in a menu.
	RemoveMenu	Removes a menu item or a popup menu. After a popup menu is removed, it is not destroyed, which means it can be reused.

(continued)

Table 11.2 A Summary of Menu Functions *(Continued)*

Category	*Routine*	*Description*
	SetMenuItemBitmaps	Defines two bitmaps to be used in place of the default checked and unchecked display.
Query (8)	GetMenu	Retrieves the menu handle for a window's top-level menu.
	GetMenuCheckMark Dimensions	Gets the size of the default menu check mark, as set by the display driver.
	GetMenuItemCount	Returns the number of items in a top-level or popup menu.
	GetMenuItemID	Finds the menu ID for a given menu item.
	GetMenuState	Returns the flags that are set for a given menu item.
	GetMenuString	Returns the label of a menu item.
	GetSubMenu	Retrieves the menu handle of a popup menu.
	GetSystemMenu	Retrieves a handle to a system menu.
Tracking (1)	TrackPopupMenu	Creates a floating popup menu to appear anywhere on the display screen.

Although OWL provides `TMenu` and `TMenuPopup` classes, these are such a thin layer over the native Windows API that I don't bother using them. OWL's own `TWindow` class, in fact, does not use either class for menu operations. From the following discussion, which focuses entirely on the WinAPI, you will have enough details to figure out how to make the OWL classes work for you.

Let's look at each type of menu routine, starting with the menu creation routines.

Menu Creation

To the user, menus are user-interface objects that sit inside windows. All of the work that Windows does to support a menu remains hidden behind the scenes. It's the programmer's job, however, to understand what goes on behind the scenes, to make sure that things operate smoothly and efficiently. From a programmer's point of view, menu support requires that certain data structures be created that define the shape and behavior of a menu. Most programs take the easy route to menu creation by attaching a menu resource to a window class. As the window is created, the menu is automatically created as well.

But a program can become more intimately involved in a menu's internal data structures. We have already seen that a program can call **LoadMenu** to request that a menu resource be loaded. Let's see what other possibilities are available.

Using the **CreateMenu** and **CreatePopup** routines, a program can build empty menus, which can then be filled with menu command items and connected to other popup menus. Adding a menu item can involve any of several of the menu modification routines. In the following example, we've decided to use **AppendMenu**. This code fragment creates from scratch a menu like the one that STANMENU built using a menu resource:

```
{
HMENU hSub;
HMENU hTop;
hTop = CreateMenu ();
hSub = CreatePopupMenu ();
AppendMenu (hSub, MF_STRING, 1,  "&New");
AppendMenu (hSub, MF_STRING, 2,  "&Open...");
AppendMenu (hSub, MF_STRING, 3,  "&Save");
AppendMenu (hSub, MF_STRING, 4,  "Save &As...");
AppendMenu (hSub, MF_SEPARATOR, 0, 0);
AppendMenu (hSub, MF_STRING, 5,  "&Print");
AppendMenu (hSub, MF_SEPARATOR, 0, 0);
AppendMenu (hSub, MF_STRING, 6,  "E&xit");
AppendMenu (hTop, MF_POPUP, hSub, "&File");
hSub = CreatePopupMenu ();
AppendMenu (hSub, MF_STRING, 7,  "&Undo\tAlt+Backspace");
AppendMenu (hSub, MF_SEPARATOR, 0, 0);
AppendMenu (hSub, MF_STRING, 8,  "Cu&t\tShift+Del");
AppendMenu (hSub, MF_STRING, 9,  "&Copy\tCtrl+Ins");
AppendMenu (hSub, MF_STRING,10,  "&Paste\tShift+Ins");
AppendMenu (hSub, MF_SEPARATOR, 0, 0);
AppendMenu (hSub, MF_STRING,11,  "Cl&ear");
AppendMenu (hSub, MF_STRING,12,  "&Delete");
AppendMenu (hTop, MF_POPUP, hSub, "&Edit");
SetMenu (hTop);
}
```

The **AppendMenu** routine provides the glue to put the different menu pieces together. It attaches menu items to menus and connects popup menus to top-level menus. **AppendMenu** is defined as

```
BOOL AppendMenu (hMenu, wFlags, wIDNewItem, lpNewItem)
```

- **hMenu** is a handle to a menu, either a popup or a top-level menu.
- **wFlags** is a combination of one or more of the `MF_` flags, as described below.

- **wIDNewItem** is the result code delivered with the **WM_COMMAND** message, or a handle to a popup menu when a popup menu is being appended.
- **lpNewItem** is a long value that can contain three different types of values. When inserting a string, it is a long pointer to a text string. When inserting a bitmap, it is a bitmap handle. Otherwise, if you are creating an **owner-draw** menu item, it identifies the specific item that you wish to draw.

AppendMenu has several different uses, depending on whether you are attaching a regular menu item or a popup menu, and whether the new item will display a string, a bitmap, or an owner-draw menu item. To put a new string item in a menu for a regular command item, you can call **AppendMenu** like this:

```
AppendMenu (hMenu, MF_STRING, wID, "Open...");
```

The value of wID is the command result code that will be sent with the **WM_COMMAND** message when the user selects the menu item, which will be identified by the label "Open..."

Alternatively, **AppendMenu** can be used to attach a popup menu to a top-level menu (or a popup menu to another popup menu). In such cases, it could be called like this:

```
AppendMenu (hMenuTop, MF_POPUP, hMenuPopup,"File");
```

In this case, the value of the third parameter, **hMenuPopup**, is not a command result code, but it is a handle to a popup menu that is to be appended to the end of the menu identified by the hMenuTop menu handle. When the popup is added, it will be identified with the string "File."

AppendMenu can also be used to install a bitmap in place of a string as the label that is displayed for a menu item. When a bitmap is used, the last parameter is used to hold the bitmap handle, instead of a long pointer to a string. In the following example, the variable **hbm** is a bitmap handle, and it is packed into the last parameter using the **MAKELONG** macro:

```
AppendMenu (hMenu, MF_BITMAP, wID, MAKELONG(hbm, 0));
```

Of the 12 flags for the **wFlags** field, 10 duplicate features that can be requested from a resource file entry. The other two are only available for dynamically generated menus: **MF_BITMAP** and **MF_OWNERDRAW**. In Chapter 12, you'll find sample programs that show how to use these two types of menu items. Table 11.3 lists and describes each menu flag. To put these flags into a slightly different perspective, there are four general categories of flags: type of object, checked or not, enabled or not, and menu break or not. Table 11.4 lists each of the categories and the flags that are in each. The top item in each list is the default value.

The only menu creation routine we have not investigated is **LoadMenuIndirect**. This routine builds a menu from a memory-resident menu template. This routine is just like **LoadMenu**, except that **LoadMenu** creates a menu from a disk-based menu template.

LoadMenuIndirect creates a menu using data that is memory-resident. Thus, you can create a menu template "on the fly" and give it to the menu system for use in creating a menu. Doing this requires that you duplicate what the resource compiler does in creating

Table 11.3 The MF–Menu Creation Flags

Menu Flag	*Available in a Resource*	*Description*
MF_BITMAP	No	Displays a GDI bitmap instead a text string for a menu item. It provides one way that graphic images can be displayed in a menu. The other way involves an MF_OWNERDRAW menu item.
MF_CHECKED	Yes	Puts a checkmark next to a menu item.
MF_DISABLED	Yes	Disables a menu item. Use the MF_GRAYED flag instead, since it provides the user with visual feedback.
MF_ENABLED	Yes	Enables a menu item.
MF_GRAYED	Yes	Disables and grays a menu item.
MF_MENUBARBREAK	Yes	Creates a menu break, and a vertical bar for items inside a popup menu.
MF_MENUBREAK	Yes	Creates a menu break.
MF_OWNERDRAW	No	The creator of the menu is sent a message, WM_DRAWITEM, which includes a handle to a device context to be used for drawing custom menu labels using GDI drawing calls. Cannot be used for top-level menu items.
MF_POPUP	Yes	A popup menu is being attached to a top-level menu, or to another popup.
MF_SEPARATOR	Yes	A horizontal separator should be created in a menu item.
MF_STRING	Yes	A text string is being supplied for a menu item label.
MF_UNCHECKED	Yes	Menu item should be drawn without a check mark.

Table 11.4 Four Categories of Menu Flags

Type of Object	*Checked*	*Enabled*	*Menu Break*
MF_STRING	MF_UNCHECKED	MF_ENABLED	<none>

(continued)

Table 11.4 Four Categories of Menu Flags *(Continued)*

Type of Object	*Checked*	*Enabled*	*Menu Break*
MF_POPUP	MF_CHECKED	MF_GRAYED	MF_MENUBARBREAK
MF_BITMAP		MF_DISABLED	MF_MENUBREAK
MF_SEPARATOR			
MF_OWNERDRAW			

a memory object that describes a menu. The data structures in WINDOWS.H that have been defined for this purpose include the **MENUITEMTEMPLATEHEADER** and **MENU-ITEMTEMPLATE**.

The next routine that we're going to cover is **SetMenu**. This routine provides the one and only way to attach a menu to a window.

Connect to a Window

A single Windows function supports the placement of a menu in a window: **SetMenu**. This single function gets its own category because it provides the only way to replace a top-level menu. In addition, there are some system memory cleanup issues that this routine raises, which we'll describe in a moment. The syntax of this routine is

```
BOOL SetMenu (hWnd, hMenu)
```

- **hWnd** is a window handle to a **WS_OVERLAPPED** or **WS_POPUP** window. A menu cannot be attached to a **WS_CHILD** window.
- **hMenu** is the handle of a top-level menu to be attached to a window.

A program can create several menus and make a different menu available to the user at different times during the operation of a program. There are several reasons why a program might want to do this. One has to do with supporting different levels of users. A beginner might only want to see short menus, with a program's most basic commands. More advanced users can set a program option to allow them to view a program's longer, more complete menus.

Another reason for a program to have multiple menus involves program security. Different menus can be used to enforce privilege levels in a program. For example, a program might ask for a password at program startup time. The menu that is installed will depend on which password is used. A regular user might get an abbreviated set of menus, while more privileged users get a more complete set of menus giving them the ability to do more privileged operations.

Yet another reason for a program to have different menus is to support the Multiple Document Interface (MDI) standard. This user-interface standard opens a new document window for each new document that a user asks to work with. Different types of documents may need different menus. For example, Microsoft's Excel spreadsheet has two types of documents: worksheets and charts. There are two menus, one for each type of document. Excel switches between the two menus, depending on the type of document with which the user is working.

Whatever your reason for having different menus, **SetMenu** lets you quickly switch from one menu to another. If you do this, however, a word of caution is in order. When you remove a menu from a window, Windows forgets about the menu. If your program terminates without explicitly destroying this menu, the memory taken up by the menu is lost forever (or until the user exits Windows). Therefore, be sure to destroy menus that have been detached from a window. Otherwise, your program will inadvertently waste system memory (in the USER module's data segment) every time it runs. The next section discusses how to destroy menus.

Hint If you replace a menu by calling **SetMenu**, be sure to hold onto the handle of the old menu. Then, when your program exits, destroy the menu since menus that aren't attached to windows are not cleaned up automatically.

Menu Destruction

Windows has two routines that destroy menus and free the memory associated with them: **DestroyMenu** and **DeleteMenu**.

The **DestroyMenu** routine destroys menus that are *not* connected to any window. If you pass it the menu handle for a menu connected to a window, your program will crash. **DestroyMenu** is defined as follows:

```
BOOL DestroyMenu (hmenu)
```

- **hmenu** is the handle of a top-level or popup menu that is to be destroyed. The menu specified and all associated popup menus are destroyed.

Here is code that will determine the currently installed menu, remove it from the window, and destroy it:

```
HMENU hmenu;

hmenu = GetMenu(hwnd);   /* Find out menu handle. */
SetMenu (hwnd, NULL);    /* Remove menu.          */
DestroyMenu (hmenu);     /* Destroy the menu.     */
```

You don't have to do this for every menu you create, though, because a menu that is attached to a window is automatically destroyed when the window is destroyed.

The second menu destruction routine, **DeleteMenu**, actually does two things: It removes a menu item from a menu and destroys whatever popup menus are associated with the menu item. This routine frees the memory used by the menu in the same way that **DestroyMenu** does.

DeleteMenu is defined as

```
BOOL DeleteMenu (hMenu, nPosition, wFlags)
```

- **hMenu** is a handle to either a top-level or a popup menu.
- **nPosition** identifies the menu item of interest. The meaning of this field depends on the value of the last parameter, **wFlags**.
- **wFlags** is either **MF_BYPOSITION** or **MF_BYCOMMAND**.

If **wFlags** is **MF_BYPOSITION**, then the menu item is selected by its relative position in the menu: The first item in a menu has an offset of zero, the next has an offset of one, and so forth. This is necessary to reference popup menus, which don't have an associated result code. Here is one way to remove the Edit popup menu from the top-level menu in the STANMENU program:

```
HMENU hmenu;
...
hmenu = GetMenu (hwnd);
DeleteMenu (hmenu, 1, MF_BYPOSITION);
DrawMenuBar (hwnd);
```

As we'll discuss in the next section, the call to **DrawMenuBar** is necessary whenever the top-level menu changes, to request that it be completely redrawn.

The **MF_BYPOSITION** flag also can be used to remove an item in a popup menu. But you must first get a handle to the popup menu that contains the item by calling **GetSubMenu**. For example, here is how to delete the *Copy* command, which is the fourth item in our standard menu:

```
HMENU hmenu;
HMENU hmenuEdit;
hmenu = GetMenu (hwnd);
hmenuEdit = GetSubMenu (hMenu, 1);
DeleteMenu (hmenuEdit, 3, MF_BYPOSITION);
```

Menu items can also be deleted by using the command result code, by using the **MF_BYCOMMAND** flag in **DeleteMenu**'s last parameter. For deleting items in popup menus, using the command result code is faster than using the relative position, since the command result code lets you reference any item in the menu hierarchy by referencing the handle to the top-level menu. For example, here is another way to remove the *Copy* command from the Edit menu in STANMENU:

```
HMENU hmenu;
...
hmenu = GetMenu (hwnd);
DeleteMenu (hmenu, 9, MF_BYCOMMAND);
```

Our discussion of **DeleteMenu** has introduced two more menu flags: **MF_BYCOMMAND** and **MF_BYPOSITION**. These two, plus the 12 flags that were introduced in the discussion of the **AppendMenu** routine, bring to 14 the total number of menu flags that we have encountered. These 14 form the core set that you will use in just about all of the work you do with menus.

The next set of routines that we're going to look at are used to modify a menu once it has been created.

Menu Modification

Once a program has created a menu and attached it to a window, there is no reason for the menu to remain unchanged. In fact, Windows provides 10 routines that let you fiddle with menus as much as you need to. We've looked at one of them already, **AppendMenu**. Four other routines change the structure of an existing menu: **ChangeMenu**, **InsertMenu**, **ModifyMenu**, and **RemoveMenu**. In general, the **ChangeMenu** routine should be avoided since it was created for an earlier version of Windows and is somewhat clumsy and complicated to use. More to the point, its capabilities are replaced by the other three menu modification routines.

InsertMenu installs a new menu item or popup menu into an existing menu. Unlike **AppendMenu**, which can only create new items at the *end* of a menu, **InsertMenu** creates new items anywhere. The **ModifyMenu** routine *changes* an existing menu item. For example, it can be used to change the menu string, change the command result code, enable a grayed menu item, or gray and disable a menu item. The **RemoveMenu** routine detaches a popup menu from a top-level menu or other popup menus. This routine leaves the internal menu structure intact, so that a menu can be reused later. Of course, if you remove a menu item from a menu, you must remember to destroy the menu item before your program exits, since otherwise the memory will be lost to the system.

Our first routine, **InsertMenu**, is defined as follows:

```
BOOL InsertMenu( hMenu, nPosition, wFlags, wID, lpNew)
```

- **hMenu** is a handle to a popup or top-level menu.
- **nPosition** indicates the menu item before which the new item is to be created. This value can be either the relative position of a menu item or the result code of a menu item, depending on whether the **MF_BYPOSITION** or **MF_BYCOMMAND** flag is selected.

- **wFlags** is a combination of the 12 menu flags that were described earlier with the AppendMenu routine. Two other flags indicate how the new item location is selected: **MF_BYPOSITION** and **MF_BYCOMMAND**.
- **wID** is the result code for a new menu item and is the value delivered with the **WM_COMMAND** message. Or, when a popup menu is being inserted, it is a popup menu handle.
- **lpNew** is a long value that can contain three different types of values. When inserting a string, it is a long pointer to a text string. When inserting a bitmap, it is a bitmap handle. Otherwise, if you are creating an owner-draw menu item, it identifies the specific item that you wish to draw.

Here is one way to add a *Close* command to the File menu, underneath the *Open* ... menu item:

```
HMENU hmenu;
HMENU hmenuFile;
...
hmenu = GetMenu (hwnd);
hmenuFile = GetSubMenu (hmenu, 0);
InsertMenu (hmenuFile, 2, MF_BYPOSITION, 13, "&Close");
```

This code fragment uses the **MF_BYPOSITION** method to specify the location of the new menu item. Since we're inserting a menu item in a popup menu, this approach requires us to get a handle to the popup menu. The **GetMenu** routine gets a handle to the top-level menu. The **GetSubMenu** routine gets a handle to the File menu, since it's the first (zeroth) item in the top-level menu. Once we have a handle to the correct popup menu, the **InsertMenu** routine inserts a new menu command that will produce a result code of 13. The second parameter, 2, specifies that the menu item is to be inserted *before* menu item 2. In zero-based counting, that means before the *third* item. Figure 11.8 shows the File menu with the newly added *Close* menu item.

Another slightly simpler way to add this menu item involves using the **MF_BYCOMMAND** option to specify the position for the new menu item. This approach is simpler, since it can

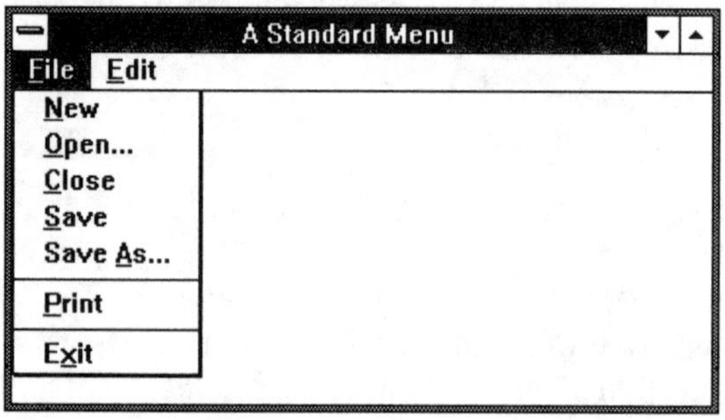

Figure 11.8 File menu with newly added Close menu item

be done using a handle to the top-level menu instead of requiring a handle to the specific popup where we're going to insert our new item:

```
HMENU hmenu;
...
hmenu = GetMenu (hwnd);
InsertMenu (hmenu, 3, MF_BYCOMMAND, 13, "&Close");
```

This code fragment also creates a Close menu item in the File menu. This time, however, the **MF_BYCOMMAND** parameter lets us specify the location using a command result code. In this case, the value of 3 is chosen since this is the result code for the *Save* menu item, before which we wish to have a menu item inserted.

The **ModifyMenu** routine, which can change any aspect of a menu item, takes the same parameters and flags as **InsertMenu**. This routine uses the same two methods for specifying a specific menu item: **MF_BYPOSITION** and **MF_BYCOMMAND**. Of course, since this routine modifies existing menu items instead of inserting new menu items, the way an item is specified is a little different. With **InsertMenu**, we point to the item that will follow the new menu item. **ModifyMenu**, on the other hand, requires us to point to the item itself.

ModifyMenu can put a new label on a menu item, gray a regular menu item, or enable a grayed menu item. It can be used to change a regular menu item into a bitmap or into an owner-draw menu item. In brief, anything that can be added to a menu with **InsertMenu** or **AppendMenu** can be changed using **ModifyMenu**. For example, here is how **ModifyMenu** can be used to change the labels on a menu item. We're going to change the Edit menu's *Cut*, *Copy*, and *Paste* menu items so that each menu item displays the equivalent French phrase instead. Using the **MF_BYPOSITION** option, we would say

```
HMENU hmenu;
HMENU hmenuEdit;
...
hmenu = GetMenu (hwnd);
hmenuEdit = GetSubMenu (hmenu, 1);
ModifyMenu (hmenuEdit, 2, MF_BYPOSITION, 8,  "Couper");
ModifyMenu (hmenuEdit, 3, MF_BYPOSITION, 9,  "Copier");
ModifyMenu (hmenuEdit, 4, MF_BYPOSITION, 10, "Coller");
```

As we saw in earlier examples, the **MF_BYPOSITION** option requires us to get the handle of the specific menu or submenu that contains the item of interest. A simpler approach involves using the **MF_BYCOMMAND** option. Here is how to use the **MF_BYCOMMAND** option to achieve the same results as in our previous example, except it requires no call to **GetSubMenu**:

```
HMENU hmenu;
...
hmenu = GetMenu (hwnd);
ModifyMenu (hmenu,  8, MF_BYCOMMAND,  8, "Couper");
ModifyMenu (hmenu,  9, MF_BYCOMMAND,  9, "Copier");
ModifyMenu (hmenu, 10, MF_BYCOMMAND, 10, "Coller");
```

Our next menu modification function, **RemoveMenu**, removes items from a menu. If an item is a command, it is removed and the memory associated with it is freed. However, if an item is a popup menu, it is not destroyed so that it can be used again. **RemoveMenu** is defined as

```
BOOL RemoveMenu (hMenu, nPosition, wFlags)
```

- **hMenu** is a handle to a popup or top-level menu.
- **nPosition** indicates the menu item to be removed. This value is either the relative position of a menu item or the result code of a menu item, depending on whether the **MF_BYPOSITION** or **MF_BYCOMMAND** flag is selected.
- **wFlags** is either **MF_BYPOSITION** or **MF_BYCOMMAND**.

Using the **MF_BYCOMMAND** flag, we could delete the *Clear* menu item with

```
HMENU hmenu;
...
hmenu = GetMenu (hwnd);
RemoveMenu (hmenu, 11, MF_BYCOMMAND);
```

If we wanted to remove the entire Edit menu, we would have to use the **MF_BYPOSITION** flag as shown here:

```
HMENU hmenu;
...
hmenu = GetMenu (hwnd);
hmenuEdit = GetSubMenu (hmenu, 1);
RemoveMenu (hmenu, 1, MF_BYPOSITION);
DrawMenuBar (hwnd);
```

Since we are removing a popup menu from the menu hierarchy, unless we attach it later on we're going to have to be sure to destroy the menu before our program terminates:

```
DestroyMenu (hmenuEdit);
```

so that the memory associated with the Edit menu is freed.

You may have noticed the call to **DrawMenuBar** after the popup menu is removed. Whenever a change is made to a top-level menu, **DrawMenuBar** should be called. The reason is that the menu modification routines *only* change the internal data structures that support a menu. For the user to see the change, **DrawMenuBar** must be called to redraw the newly modified menu. Otherwise, the change does not appear to the user, which is sure to result in some confusion.

All of the remaining routines in this group are used to change the state of existing menu items. **CheckMenuItem**, for example, is used to place a check mark next to a menu item, or to remove a check mark. Incidentally, if you don't like the shape of the default check mark, you can create a bitmap that has an image that you do like and associate it with a menu item by calling **SetMenuItemBitmaps**. This routine also lets you select the bitmap to be displayed when a menu item is not checked. In Chapter 12, when we discuss how to enhance menu items using graphics, we'll show you exactly how this is done.

The **EnableMenuItem** routine lets you pick one of three enable states for a menu item: enabled, disabled, and grayed. As we mentioned earlier, because the disabled state provides no visual feedback to the user, it is probably best to avoid using it. For the other two, *enabled* is the default state of a menu in which it can be selected and manipulated in a normal manner. A *grayed* menu item, on the other hand, is displayed in a grayed text and cannot be selected by the user.

A final routine, **HiliteMenuItem**, lights up items in the top-level menu. This routine is used by the keyboard accelerator support code when a keyboard accelerator is pressed. The top-level menu item that is associated with the selected menu item is highlighted for a moment. Unless you plan to simulate this functionality yourself, you'll probably not find occasion to use this routine.

Our next set of routines perform a query—that is, they ask the menu system for some information.

Query

The Query routines let you ask for information about menus. There are two types of routines: one set returns a handle to a menu, the other provides menu attribute information. In general, if you can set a value or a flag, there is a query routine to let you know the currently selected value or flag associated with a menu item.

Three query routines give you menu handle information: **GetMenu**, **GetSubMenu**, and **GetSystemMenu**. Figure 11.9 gives a graphic depiction of the menu handles

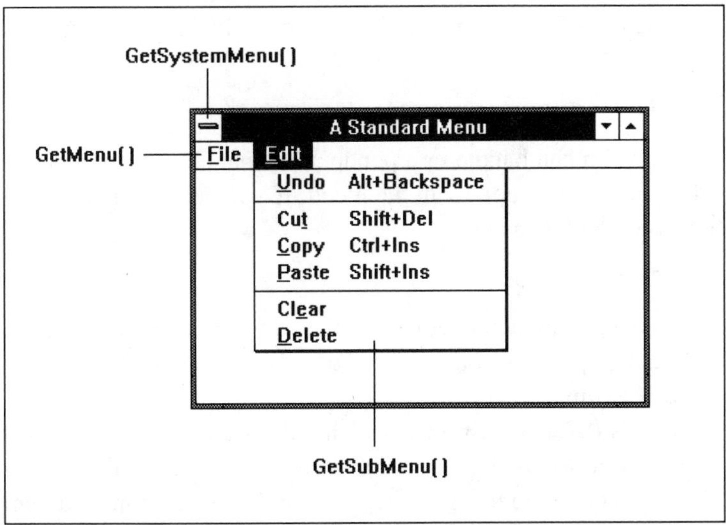

Figure 11.9 Three query routines return menu handles

returned by these three routines. **GetMenu** gives you a handle to the top-level menu that is attached to a window. Here is how it is called:

```
hmenuTop = GetMenu (hwnd);
```

Once you have the handle to a top-level menu, you get a handle to one of its popups by calling

```
hmenu = GetSubMenu (hmenuTop, nPosition);
```

where `nPosition` is the zero-based index of the popup in the top-level menu, or the index of a popup within another popup menu. Once you have a popup menu handle, it can be used with any of the menu modification routines to add, remove, or modify any item in the menu.

The **GetSystemMenu** routine has two uses to handle the special nature of the system menu. Most programs will use the default system menu, and so Windows only maintains a single copy. However, a copy is automatically created for a window if it calls **GetSystemMenu** like this:

```
hmenuSys = GetSystemMenu (hwnd, 0);
```

The zero in the second parameter tells the menu system to give you a handle to a private system menu that you can modify. If, after changing the system menu, you decide that you want to return to the original system menu, you make a call like this:

```
hmenuSys = GetSystemMenu (hwnd, 1);
```

A nonzero value in the second parameter attaches the default system menu to your window, which cannot be modified by you.

The other five query routines return menu attribute information. Figure 11.10 shows the specific attribute for four of the routines. To find out the number of items in a menu, you call

```
w = GetMenuItemCount (hMenu);
```

where `hMenu` is either a top-level menu handle or a popup menu handle. The number of items includes the vertical separators that appear in the menu. If you need to find out the result code for a menu item command, you can call

```
w = GetMenuItemID (hMenu, nPosition);
```

This routine can't tell you about a popup menu item, since they don't have result codes. If you ask for the result code for a popup menu, you get a `-1`. To find out the handle of a popup menu, you need to call **GetSubMenu**.

Another menu query routine is **GetMenuState**, which tells you the current settings for various menu flags. If you want to test for a specific menu flag, you use the logical AND function. For example, this code fragment gets the flags for the menu command item that has a result code of `38`, then checks to see if the menu item is grayed or not:

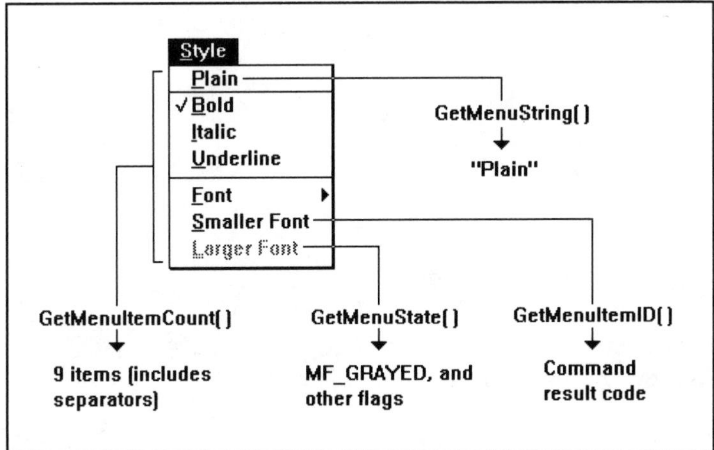

Figure 11.10 Menu attributes that a program can query

```
WORD wFlags;
...
wFlags = GetMenuState (hmenu, 38, MF_BYCOMMAND);
if (wFlags & MF_GRAYED)
    {
    .
    .
    .
```

Be careful when using this routine, however. All of the default flags (**MF_STRING**, **MF_UNHILITE**, **MF_ENABLED**, and **MF_UNCHECKED**) have a value of zero. You really can't test for them with the logical AND, since ANDing with zero always gives a result of zero. Instead, to test for any of the default flags, you need to check whether the flags that represent the opposite are present. For example, here is how to check whether or not a menu is enabled:

```
WORD wFlags
...
wFlags = GetMenuState (hmenu, 38, MF_BYCOMMAND);
if (!(wFlags & (MF_DISABLED | MF_GRAYED))
    {
    .
    .
    .
```

If the disabled and grayed flags are not set, this conditional statement returns a value of true. While it may seem like an odd way to test for the presence of a flag, it is necessary because of the way that the default flag information is stored. Notice that the **GetMenuState** routine lets you choose between the **MF_BYCOMMAND** and **MF_BYPOSITION** flags for picking a specific menu item.

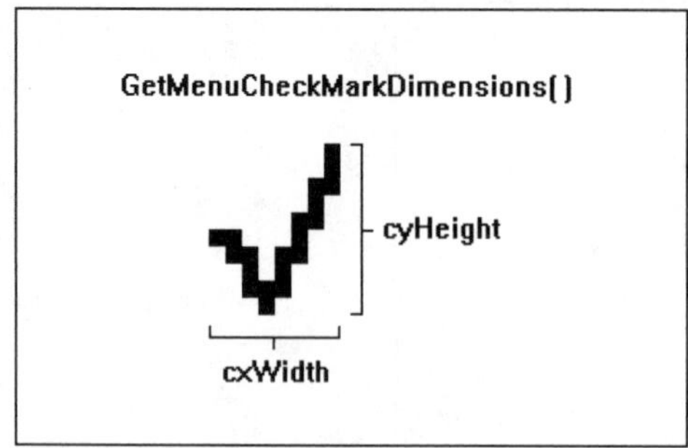

Figure 11.11 Check-mark dimensions returned by GetMenuCheckMarkDimensions

If you have a menu item that displays a string (as opposed to a separator, a bitmap, or an owner-draw item), you can retrieve a copy of the string by calling

```
cbSize = GetMenuString (hmenu, wID, lpBuff, bufsize, wFlag);
```

where `hmenu` is a menu handle, `wID` is either a command result code or the relative position of an item, `lpBuff` is a long pointer to a character buffer, `bufsize` is the buffer size, and `wFlag` is either **`MF_BYCOMMAND`** or **`MF_BYPOSITION`**. The return value, `cbSize`, is the number of bytes that were copied.

Our last menu query routine has perhaps the longest routine name in Windows: **`GetMenuCheckMarkDimensions`**. As indicated in Figure 11.11, this routine returns the width and height of a default menu check mark. This is useful for programs that wish to install custom check marks to replace the default check mark. In addition, a program can install a mark that is displayed when the menu item is *not* checked. This routine returns a four-byte value that must be split apart to yield the two size values:

```
DWORD dwCheck;
int cxWidth;
int cyHeight;
dwCheck  = GetMenuCheckMarkDimensions();
cxWidth  = LOWORD (dwCheck);
cyHeight = HIWORD (dwCheck);
```

As indicated in the code example, this routine takes no parameters.

There is one more category to look at that deals with tracking, which is the support of a popup menu outside a window's regular menu.

Tracking

Our final category of menu routines is made up of a single routine that is used for menu tracking. This routine, **`TrackPopupMenu`**, allows a program to create a popup menu anywhere on the display screen. Menus that are not attached to a top-level menu are sometimes referred to as **tear-off** menus, since they look like regular popup menus, except that they can appear anywhere. **TrackPopupMenu** is defined as

```
BOOL TrackPopupMenu (hMenu, 0, x, y, 0, hWnd, 0L)
```

- **hMenu** is a handle to a popup menu.
- **x** is the *x* value of the upper-left corner of the menu, in screen coordinates.
- **y** is the *y* value of the upper-left corner of the menu, in screen coordinates.
- **hWnd** is a handle of the window to which the **WM_COMMAND** and other menu messages are sent.
- The second, fifth, and seventh parameters are reserved values and must be zero, as shown here.

An important point to keep in mind with this routine is that the popup menu is *not* positioned in client area coordinates but in **screen coordinates**. Like client area coordinates, screen coordinates are a pixel-based coordinate system. However, the origin (0,0) in screen coordinates is always the upper-left corner of the display screen. If you wish to put a popup menu in your client area, you must convert client area coordinates to screen coordinates. The **ClientToScreen** routine does this for you quite nicely.

When the **TrackPopupMenu** function first appeared in the Windows API, it seemed an interesting but odd addition to the system's menuing capabilities. Since then, there has been a growing trend to make use of these floating menus. An emerging standard is to display an object-specific menu when the user clicks the *right mouse button* on an object. Figure 11.12 shows a sample program that does this.

This program, RECTMENU, is an enhancement to the RECTDRAW program from Chapter 8. The original program drew rectangles in response to left mouse clicks. This enhancement allows a new pen or brush to be used for specific rectangles. The source files to RECTMENU appear here:

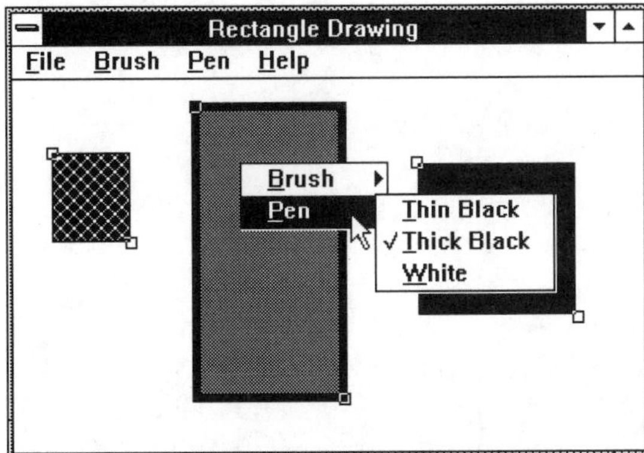

Figure 11.12 A right mouse click summons RECTMENU's rectangle property menu.

RECTMENU.CPP

```
//
// RECTMENU.CPP  Enhancement of RECTDRAW.EXE program (in Chapter 9)
//               to use Right mouse button clicks to get object-
//               specific menus.
//

#include <owl\owlpch.h>
#include "rectmenu.h"

//
// Main window
class DFrame : public TFrameWindow
    {
  public:
    DFrame(char * title);
    ~DFrame();
    void CmFileExit();
    void CmFileErase();
    void CmBrHatch();
    void CmBrGray();
    void CmBrBlack();
    void CmPnWhite();
    void CmPnBlack1();
    void CmPnBlack2();
    void CmHelpAbout();
    void CmBrPopupHatch();
    void CmBrPopupGray();
    void CmBrPopupBlack();
    void CmPnPopupWhite();
    void CmPnPopupBlack1();
    void CmPnPopupBlack2();
    void EvInitMenu(HMENU menu);
    void EvLButtonDown(UINT, TPoint &);
    void EvLButtonUp(UINT, TPoint &);
    void EvRButtonDown(UINT, TPoint &);
    BOOL Create();
    void Paint (TDC&, BOOL, TRect&);
    void MenuCheckMark(HMENU menu, int id, BOOL bCheck);
  private:
    BOOL        bCtorSuccess;
    BOOL        bMouseDown;
    int         cRects;
    int         cxyMarkerSize;
    DRectangle arRects [MAXRECTANGLES];
    TBrush    * tbrCurrent;
    TBrush    * tbrBlack;
    TBrush    * tbrGray;
    TBrush    * tbrHatch;
    TMenu     * tmenuRect;
    TPen      * tpnCurrent;
    TPen      * tpnBlack;
    TPen      * tpnWide;
    TPen      * tpnWhite;

    int         irChange;      // Popup menu support.
    TPen      * tpnChange;     // Popup menu support.
    TBrush    * tbrChange;     // Popup menu support.

  DECLARE_RESPONSE_TABLE (DFrame);
    };
```

```
DEFINE_RESPONSE_TABLE1 (DFrame, TFrameWindow)
  EV_WM_INITMENU,
  EV_WM_LBUTTONDOWN,
  EV_WM_LBUTTONUP,
  EV_WM_RBUTTONDOWN,
  EV_COMMAND(CM_FILEEXIT, CmFileExit),
  EV_COMMAND(CM_FILEERASE, CmFileErase),
  EV_COMMAND(CM_BR_HATCH, CmBrHatch),
  EV_COMMAND(CM_BR_GRAY,  CmBrGray),
  EV_COMMAND(CM_BR_BLACK, CmBrBlack),
  EV_COMMAND(CM_PN_WHITE, CmPnWhite),
  EV_COMMAND(CM_PN_BLACK1, CmPnBlack1),
  EV_COMMAND(CM_PN_BLACK2, CmPnBlack2),
  EV_COMMAND(CM_HELPABOUT, CmHelpAbout),
  EV_COMMAND(CM_BR_PU_HATCH, CmBrPopupHatch),
  EV_COMMAND(CM_BR_PU_GRAY,  CmBrPopupGray),
  EV_COMMAND(CM_BR_PU_BLACK, CmBrPopupBlack),
  EV_COMMAND(CM_PN_PU_BLACK1, CmPnPopupBlack1),
  EV_COMMAND(CM_PN_PU_BLACK2, CmPnPopupBlack2),
  EV_COMMAND(CM_PN_PU_WHITE,  CmPnPopupWhite),
END_RESPONSE_TABLE;



DFrame::DFrame(char * title) : TFrameWindow(0, title)
    {
    // Mouse up/down flag.
    bMouseDown = FALSE;

    // Count of rectangles in array.
    cRects = 0;

    // Size of control-point markers.
    cxyMarkerSize = GetSystemMetrics (SM_CXICON) / 5;

    // Create brushes
    tbrHatch = new TBrush(TColor::White, HS_DIAGCROSS);
    tbrGray  = new TBrush(TColor::Gray);
    tbrBlack = new TBrush(TColor::Black);

    // Create pens
    tpnBlack = new TPen(TColor::Black);
    tpnWide  = new TPen(TColor::Black, 5);
    tpnWhite = new TPen(TColor::White);

    // Set current pen & brush.
    tbrCurrent = tbrHatch;
    tpnCurrent = tpnBlack;

    // Create popup menu for R-button mouse clicks.
    tmenuRect = new TMenu (GetApplication()->GetInstance(), "RectMenu");

    // Notify DFrame::Create of success or failure in creation.
    bCtorSuccess = (tbrHatch && tbrGray && tbrBlack &&
                    tpnBlack && tpnWide && tpnWhite &&
                    tmenuRect);
    }

DFrame::~DFrame()
    {
    // Important!  Always delete any GDI object that
    // you create. Otherwise, you cause memory leaks
    // in some Win16 systems (Windows 3.1, etc.)
    delete tbrBlack;
    delete tbrGray;
    delete tbrHatch;
```

```
    delete tpnBlack;
    delete tpnWide;
    delete tpnWhite;

    delete tmenuRect;
    }

void DFrame::CmFileExit()
    {
    CloseWindow(0); // Cause application to terminate
    }

void DFrame::CmFileErase()
    {
    // Set count of rectangles to zero...
    cRects = 0;

    // ...and force WM_PAINT message (handled by DFrame::Paint)
    Invalidate();
    }

void DFrame::CmBrHatch()  { tbrCurrent = tbrHatch; }
void DFrame::CmBrGray()   { tbrCurrent = tbrGray;  }
void DFrame::CmBrBlack()  { tbrCurrent = tbrBlack; }
void DFrame::CmPnWhite()  { tpnCurrent = tpnWhite; }
void DFrame::CmPnBlack1() { tpnCurrent = tpnBlack; }
void DFrame::CmPnBlack2() { tpnCurrent = tpnWide;  }

void DFrame::CmHelpAbout()
    {
    MessageBox("   Rectangle Drawing Program\n"
               "Showing Right Mouse Button Menu\n\n"
               " 'Borland C++ 4.0 Programming\n"
               "    for Windows', by Paul Yao", Title);
    }

void DFrame::CmBrPopupHatch()
    {
    arRects[irChange].tbr = tbrHatch;
    }
void DFrame::CmBrPopupGray()
    {
    arRects[irChange].tbr = tbrGray;
    }
void DFrame::CmBrPopupBlack()
    {
    arRects[irChange].tbr = tbrBlack;
    }
void DFrame::CmPnPopupWhite()
    {
    arRects[irChange].tpn = tpnWhite;
    }
void DFrame::CmPnPopupBlack1()
    {
    arRects[irChange].tpn = tpnBlack;
    }
void DFrame::CmPnPopupBlack2()
    {
    arRects[irChange].tpn = tpnWide;
    }

void DFrame::EvInitMenu(HMENU menu)
    {
    // Manage check/uncheck of brush menu items.
    MenuCheckMark(menu, CM_BR_HATCH, (tbrCurrent == tbrHatch));
```

```
    MenuCheckMark(menu, CM_BR_GRAY,  (tbrCurrent == tbrGray ));
    MenuCheckMark(menu, CM_BR_BLACK, (tbrCurrent == tbrBlack));

    // Manage check/uncheck of pen menu items.
    MenuCheckMark(menu, CM_PN_BLACK1, (tpnCurrent == tpnBlack));
    MenuCheckMark(menu, CM_PN_BLACK2, (tpnCurrent == tpnWide ));
    MenuCheckMark(menu, CM_PN_WHITE,  (tpnCurrent == tpnWhite));

    // Manage check/uncheck of brush items for popup menu.
    MenuCheckMark(menu, CM_BR_PU_HATCH, (tbrChange == tbrHatch));
    MenuCheckMark(menu, CM_BR_PU_GRAY,  (tbrChange == tbrGray ));
    MenuCheckMark(menu, CM_BR_PU_BLACK, (tbrChange == tbrBlack));

    // Manage check/uncheck of pen items for popup menu.
    MenuCheckMark(menu, CM_PN_PU_BLACK1, (tpnChange == tpnBlack));
    MenuCheckMark(menu, CM_PN_PU_BLACK2, (tpnChange == tpnWide ));
    MenuCheckMark(menu, CM_PN_PU_WHITE,  (tpnChange == tpnWhite));
    }

void DFrame::EvLButtonDown(UINT, TPoint & pt)
    {
    if (cRects == MAXRECTANGLES)
        {
        MessageBeep(MB_ICONHAND);
        MessageBox ("Cannot Create More Rectangles", Title);
        return;
        }

    // Set flag that mouse button is down.
    bMouseDown = TRUE;

    // Grab mouse for our exclusive use.
    SetCapture();

    // Record first mouse point.
    arRects[cRects].trect.left = pt.x;
    arRects[cRects].trect.top  = pt.y;

    // Place square marker at mouse location.
    TClientDC dc(HWindow);
    Marker::Square(dc, pt, cxyMarkerSize);
    }

void DFrame::EvLButtonUp(UINT, TPoint & pt)
    {
    if (!bMouseDown)
       {
       MessageBeep(MB_ICONHAND);
       return;
       }

    // Toggle that mouse is up.
    bMouseDown = FALSE;

    // Relinquish exclusive control of mouse.
    ReleaseCapture();

    // Record second mouse point.
    arRects[cRects].trect.right  = pt.x;
    arRects[cRects].trect.bottom = pt.y;

    // Record current pen & brush
    arRects[cRects].tpn = tpnCurrent;
    arRects[cRects].tbr = tbrCurrent;

    // Update rectangle count indicator.
```

```
    cRects++;

    // Force a WM_PAINT message to redraw entire window.
    Invalidate ();
    }

void DFrame::EvRButtonDown(UINT, TPoint &pt)
    {
    // Init "found" index.
    irChange = (-1);

    // Walk rectangle list to find clicked one.
    // Start at end of list - since they are 'topmost'.
    for (int i = cRects-1; i >= 0; i--)
        {
        if (PtInRect (&arRects[i].trect, pt))
            {
            irChange = i;
            break;
            }
        }

    // If missed, complain to user.
    if (irChange == (-1))
        {
        MessageBeep(MB_ICONHAND);
        return;
        }

    // Save away current pen & brush to help init menu.
    tbrChange = arRects[irChange].tbr;
    tpnChange = arRects[irChange].tpn;

    // Convert mouse coordinate for popup menu positioning.
    ClientToScreen (pt);

    // Use a popup menu to get pen / brush info.
    ::TrackPopupMenu (::GetSubMenu(HMENU(*tmenuRect), 0),
                      TPM_LEFTALIGN | TPM_RIGHTBUTTON,
                      pt.x, pt.y, 0, HWindow, 0);

    // Redraw.
    Invalidate();
    }

BOOL DFrame::Create()
    {
    // If constructor object creation failed...
    if (!bCtorSuccess)
        {
        // .. notify user...
        MessageBox (" Low Memory -- Close Other\n"
                    "Applications and Try Again.",
                    Title, MB_ICONHAND);

        // ...notify TModule's WinAPI message loop...
        #if defined(__WIN32__)
          ::PostThreadMessage(GetCurrentThreadId(), WM_QUIT, 0, 0);
        #else
          ::PostAppMessage(GetCurrentTask(), WM_QUIT, 0, 0);
        #endif

        // ...and notify TWindowFrame & TWindow.
        return FALSE;
        }
```

```
    // Important!  Always call base class
    // version of Create.
    return TFrameWindow::Create();
    }

void DFrame::Paint (TDC& dc, BOOL, TRect&)
    {
    for (int i = 0; i < cRects ; i++ )
        {
        // Select items' pen & brush.
        dc.SelectObject (*arRects[i].tpn);
        dc.SelectObject (*arRects[i].tbr);

        // Set background BLACK so that
        // white hatch brush looks interesting.
        dc.SetBkColor (TColor::Black);

        // Draw actual rectangle
        dc.Rectangle (arRects[i].trect.left,
                      arRects[i].trect.top,
                      arRects[i].trect.right,
                      arRects[i].trect.bottom);

        // Draw markers at two control points.
        Marker::Square (dc, arRects[i].trect.left,
                            arRects[i].trect.top, cxyMarkerSize);
        Marker::Square (dc, arRects[i].trect.right,
                            arRects[i].trect.bottom, cxyMarkerSize);
        }
    }

void DFrame::MenuCheckMark(HMENU menu, int id, BOOL bCheck)
    {
    WORD wState;
    wState = (bCheck) ? MF_CHECKED : MF_UNCHECKED;
    ::CheckMenuItem (menu, id, wState);
    }

//
// Application object
class DApp : public TApplication
    {
  public:
    DApp() : TApplication()
        {
        }
    void InitMainWindow()
        {
        SetMainWindow (new DFrame("Rectangle Drawing"));
        MainWindow->AssignMenu("MAIN");
        MainWindow->SetIcon(this, "SNAPSHOT");
        }
    };

//
// Marker routines borrowed from CLS_MARK.CPP
// in Chapter 7's marker drawing program.
void Marker::Square (TDC& dc, int x, int y, int Size)
    {
    TPoint pt;
    pt.x = x;
    pt.y = y;
```

```
     Marker::Square(dc, pt, Size);
     }

void Marker::Square (TDC& dc, TPoint &pt, int Size)
     {
     // Request raster operation to invert pixels
     int ROP2 = dc.SetROP2(R2_NOT);

     // Temporarily need a thin black pen --
     // "normal" way to do it is too costly.
     HANDLE h = ::SelectObject (HDC(dc), ::GetStockObject(BLACK_PEN));

     // Calculate distance from center point.
     int cxyWidth = Size / 2;

     // Draw a square marker.
     //  . . . . . . .
     //  . o o o o o .
     //  . o . . . o .
     //  . o . x . o .
     //  . o . . . o .
     //  . o o o o o .
     //  . . . . . . .
     dc.MoveTo(pt.x - cxyWidth, pt.y - cxyWidth);
     dc.LineTo(pt.x + cxyWidth, pt.y - cxyWidth);
     dc.LineTo(pt.x + cxyWidth, pt.y + cxyWidth);
     dc.LineTo(pt.x - cxyWidth, pt.y + cxyWidth);
     dc.LineTo(pt.x - cxyWidth, pt.y - cxyWidth);

     // Restore DC to the way we found it.
     dc.SetROP2(ROP2);
     ::SelectObject (HDC(dc), h);
     }

//
// Application main entry point.
OwlMain(int, char **)
     {
     return DApp().Run();
     }
```

RECTMENU.H

```
#define CM_FILEEXIT  100
#define CM_FILEERASE 101
#define CM_BR_BLACK  200
#define CM_BR_GRAY   201
#define CM_BR_HATCH  202
#define CM_PN_BLACK1 300
#define CM_PN_BLACK2 301
#define CM_PN_WHITE  302
#define CM_HELPABOUT 400

// Popup menu IDs.
#define CM_BR_PU_HATCH  500
#define CM_BR_PU_GRAY   501
#define CM_BR_PU_BLACK  502
#define CM_PN_PU_BLACK1 600
#define CM_PN_PU_BLACK2 601
#define CM_PN_PU_WHITE  602
```

```
const int MAXRECTANGLES = 50;
const int MARKERSIZE = 3;

//
// Marker Class
class Marker
    {
  public:
    static void Square (TDC&, TPoint&, int Size);
    static void Square (TDC&, int x, int y, int Size);
    };

//
// Rectangle Class
struct DRectangle
    {
  public:
    TBrush * tbr;
    TPen   * tpn;
    TRect    trect;
    };
```

RECTMENU.RC

```
#include "rectmenu.h"

snapshot icon rectmenu.ico

main menu
    BEGIN
    POPUP "&File"
        {
        MENUITEM "&Erase", CM_FILEERASE
        MENUITEM SEPARATOR
        MENUITEM "E&xit",  CM_FILEEXIT
        }
    POPUP "&Brush"
        {
        MENUITEM "&Hatch", CM_BR_HATCH
        MENUITEM "&Gray",  CM_BR_GRAY
        MENUITEM "&Black", CM_BR_BLACK
        }
    POPUP "&Pen"
        {
        MENUITEM "&Thin Black",   CM_PN_BLACK1
        MENUITEM "&Thick Black",  CM_PN_BLACK2
        MENUITEM "&White",        CM_PN_WHITE
        }
    POPUP "&Help"
        {
        MENUITEM "&About...", CM_HELPABOUT
        }
    END

RectMenu menu
    BEGIN
    POPUP "RandomMenuName"
        {
        POPUP "&Brush"
```

```
            {
            MENUITEM "&Hatch", CM_BR_PU_HATCH
            MENUITEM "&Gray",  CM_BR_PU_GRAY
            MENUITEM "&Black", CM_BR_PU_BLACK
            }
        POPUP "&Pen"
            {
            MENUITEM "&Thin Black",   CM_PN_PU_BLACK1
            MENUITEM "&Thick Black",  CM_PN_PU_BLACK2
            MENUITEM "&White",        CM_PN_PU_WHITE
            }
        }
    END
```

RECTMENU.DEF

```
EXETYPE WINDOWS

CODE MOVEABLE DISCARDABLE
DATA MULTIPLE MOVEABLE

HEAPSIZE   512
STACKSIZE 8192
```

DYNA16.MAK

```
#  MAKE file for Win16 API using dynamic BIDS,
#  OWL and C-runtime libraries.
#
#    C> make -fstatic16.mak
#

.AUTODEPEND
CC = -c -H -H"owl\owlpch.h" -ml -R -vi -WS -X-
CD = -D_RTLDLL;_BIDSDLL;_OWLDLL;_OWLPCH;
INC = -I\BC4\INCLUDE
LIB = -L\BC4\LIB

rectmenu.exe :  rectmenu.obj rectmenu.res
  tlink -c -C -Twe $(LIB) @dyna16.lnk
  brc rectmenu.res rectmenu.exe

rectmenu.obj :  rectmenu.cpp
  bcc $(CC) $(CD) rectmenu.cpp

rectmenu.res :  rectmenu.rc rectmenu.ico rectmenu.h
  brc $(INC) -31 -R rectmenu.rc
```

DYNA16.LNK

```
\bc4\lib\c0wl.obj+
rectmenu.obj
rectmenu,rectmenu
```

```
\bc4\lib\bidsi.lib+
\bc4\lib\owlwi.lib+
\bc4\lib\import.lib+
\bc4\lib\crtldll.lib
rectmenu.def
```

DYNA32.MAK

```
#  MAKE file for Win32 API using dynamic BIDS,
#  OWL and C-runtime libraries.
#
#    C> make -fdyna32.mak
#

.AUTODEPEND
CC = -c -H -H\""owl\owlpch.h\"" -p- -R -vi -W -X-
CD = -D_RTLDLL;_BIDSDLL;_OWLDLL;_OWLPCH;
INC = -I\BC4\INCLUDE
LIB = -L\BC4\LIB

rectmenu.exe :  rectmenu.obj rectmenu.res
  tlink32 -aa -c -Tpe $(LIB) @dyna32.lnk
  brc32 rectmenu.res rectmenu.exe

rectmenu.obj :  rectmenu.cpp
  bcc32 $(CC) $(CD) rectmenu.cpp

rectmenu.res :  rectmenu.rc rectmenu.ico rectmenu.h
  brc32 $(INC) -w32 -R rectmenu.rc
```

DYNA32.LNK

```
\bc4\lib\c0w32.obj+
rectmenu.obj
rectmenu,rectmenu
\bc4\lib\bidsfi.lib+
\bc4\lib\owlwfi.lib+
\bc4\lib\import32.lib+
\bc4\lib\cw32i.lib
rectmenu.def
```

The relevant part of this program is the **EvRButtonDown** response function, which gets called when the user clicks the right-mouse button. This function compares the location of a mouse click with each of the rectangles in the **arRects** rectangle array by calling the **PtInRect** routine. If no rectangle is hit, the program complains to the user by beeping, but takes no further action. If a rectangle is hit, a popup menu is displayed to let the user change the rectangle's pen or brush.

If you look in the resource file, RECTMENU.RC, you'll notice that this program has *two* menus—one is the program's main menu and the second is our tear-off menu. You might notice that the tear-off menu consists of two **POPUP** statements embedded in another

POPUP statement. This odd arrangement reflects how the **TrackPopupMenu** function expects to find a popup menu structured.

A simpler way to get a tear-off menu is to use a popup menu already connected to your window. You get a handle to your application's menu handle by calling **TWindow::GetMenu**. Getting a handle to a specific popup menu involves calling **GetSubMenu**. Here is how to get a menu handle to a window's first popup menu:

```
HMENU hmenu = GetSubMenu(GetMenu(), 0);
```

In addition to having a separate menu resource, the tear-off menu also has separate message response functions for each menu item. These are needed so that the state of an individual rectangle can be changed without changing all the rectangles in the program.

Although menus allow a program to show the user the commands that are available, some users prefer to enter keyboard commands. To help you give these users what they want, Windows supports the creation of keyboard accelerators. Keyboard accelerators provide a seamless connection between keyboard input and menu commands. The connection is so good that accelerator commands even cause a menu item to be briefly illuminated to let the user know that a command has been selected. Let's take a look at the capabilities that are available with keyboard accelerators and see how they can be incorporated into a Windows program.

Keyboard Accelerators

Keyboard accelerator support was one of the last pieces to be put in place when Microsoft was getting ready to ship the first version of Windows in 1985. Windows' original design called for a user interface that relied primarily on the mouse for command input. But after taking a second look at the existing base of computers—most of which didn't have a mouse—Microsoft had second thoughts. Another factor that strongly influenced their decision to put accelerator support into Windows was feedback from software developers who were considering the use of Windows for their applications. Some of the software developers had successful DOS programs that relied heavily on a keyboard interface, and they were concerned about the suitability of Windows for their products. Microsoft's response was to provide keyboard accelerators.

Keyboard accelerators tie together keyboard input and menu command selection. For users who don't have a mouse, or who prefer to use the keyboard to enter commands, accelerators link keystrokes with the creation of messages that match the menu messages we described earlier in this chapter. For programmers, this means that a minimum amount of effort is required to incorporate accelerator support in a Windows program.

Microsoft did such a good job of creating accelerator support that programmers usually think of accelerators as little more than an extension to the menu system. In fact, it is a separate part of Windows that can support commands that have no menu equivalent. Carried to an extreme, you could even write programs that rely *solely* on accelerator keystrokes for command input, and which make no use of menus. Of course, you probably won't want to do this since the presence of *both* menus and accelerators makes for a very flexible user interface.

In Chapter 15, when we discuss keyboard input, you'll see that keyboard input goes through a *two-step* translation process. Keyboard hardware generates **scan codes** to report keyboard activity. In fact, every key on the keyboard has *two* scan codes: one that says the key is being pressed and another that says the key is being released. A scan code lets the keyboard hardware report that a change has taken place. In general, scan codes are not interesting to most programs since they are too low-level to work with, and because Windows' keyboard driver translates scan codes into more useful information.

The first translation process converts scan codes into **virtual key codes**. Virtual key codes get us one step closer to character information, but they don't distinguish, for example, between a capital "A" and a lowercase "a." This is because virtual key codes don't represent characters, but keyboard keys. From the point of view of accelerators, virtual key codes are the most useful way to think about keyboard input. After all, when a user enters a keyboard command such as [Ctrl]+[A], it should have the same effect whether or not the [Caps Lock] key is active. In other words, there shouldn't be a difference between [Ctrl]+[A] (capital "A") and [Ctrl]+[a] (lowercase"a").

The second translation process converts virtual key codes into the extended ASCII character set that Windows supports. Programs that wish to receive character input—such as a word processor—are most interested in ASCII characters and ignore scan codes and virtual key codes. From the point of view of accelerators, a program *can* incorporate ASCII characters as accelerators. But this could be very limiting, for example, to a word processing program if certain letters were command keys and not interpreted as data. Of course, if you're writing a program that uses keyboard input *only* for command input, there is no reason not to use ASCII characters.

Windows lets you define accelerator keys using either virtual key code information or ASCII characters. Virtual keys are the more common type of accelerator, because they do not rely on the state of shift keys, such as the [Caps Lock] key. But if you wish to create a case-sensitive command key, then ASCII character accelerators are what you need.

For a program to get access to accelerators, an accelerator table must be created. Programs can have more than one accelerator table, but only one can be active at any moment. Acclerator tables are created by making an entry in a program's resource file using the **ACCELERATORS** keyword. As shown in Figure 11.13, the Resource Workshop has a built-in accelerator editor which makes it easy to create an accelerator table. Or, you can use a text editor to create your accelerator definitions.

Here's a template showing the two basic types of accelerator table entries. Each line in the table represents a different keyboard accelerator:

```
table-name ACCELERATORS
    {
    <key>,<cmd>,VIRTKEY,  [,NOINVERT][,ALT][,SHIFT][,CONTROL]
```

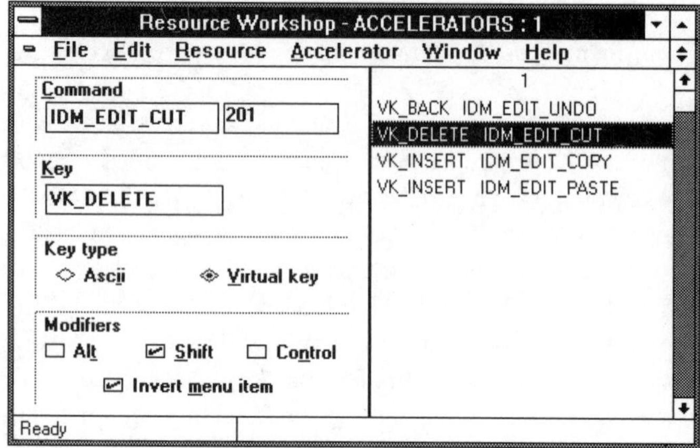

Figure 11.13 The Resource Workshop's Accelerator Editor

```
<key>,<cmd>,ASCII     [,NOINVERT][,ALT][,SHIFT][,CONTROL]
}
```

- <key> is the key, either text in quotes, "A," or a virtual key constant from WINDOWS.H, like `VK_F1`. It can also be a numeric value, like `58` or `0x6C`.
- <cmd> is the command result code to be included with the `WM_COMMAND` message to notify a program that an accelerator key combination has been pressed.
- **VIRTKEY** specifies that the value of <key> represents a virtual key code.
- **ASCII** specifies that <key> is an ASCII key code.
- **NOINVERT** inhibits the automatic highlighting of the related menu command.
- **ALT** indicates that an accelerator uses the [Alt] key.
- **SHIFT** indicates that an accelerator uses the [Shift] key.
- **CONTROL** indicates that an accelerator uses the [Ctrl] key.

Here is an example of an accelerator table containing only ASCII values:

```
AscKeys ACCELERATORS
    {
    "A", 25, ASCII
    "a", 26, ASCII
    "1", 27, ASCII
    }
```

This approach means using regular character values as commands. Notice, though, that the use of ASCII makes your commands case sensitive. The capital A command is created when either the [Shift] key is pressed *or* [Caps Lock] is on. As you're probably aware, when both keys are active, they cancel each other out, to create lowercase letters.

Instead of using ASCII accelerators, most programs use virtual key code accelerators. Virtual key codes let you define accelerators in a case-insensitive fashion. They also allow you to combine keys with any combination of the [Alt], [Shift], and [Ctrl] keys. Here is another accelerator table showing how virtual key accelerators can be defined:

```
VirtKeys ACCELERATORS
    {
    "A",   35, VIRTKEY, CONTROL
    VK_F1, 36, VIRTKEY
    VK_F8, 37, VIRTKEY, ALT, CONTROL, SHIFT
    }
```

This table defines three virtual key accelerators: [Ctrl]+[A], [F1], and [Alt]+[Ctrl]+[Shift]+[F8]. Because virtual key codes are tied to keyboard *keys* and not ASCII code values, the [Ctrl]+[A] accelerator ignores the state of the [Caps Lock] key. For this reason, virtual key accelerators are less confusing to the user. The second accelerator in this table causes the [F1] function key to send a **WM_COMMAND** message with a value of `36` in the **wParam** parameter. The last accelerator in this table shows that an accelerator can be defined using all three shift keys: [Alt], [Ctrl], and [Shift]. Of course, it's probably *not* a good idea to use all three shift keys in a single accelerator, since you'd be asking your user to press four keys simultaneously just to make a command selection. Of course, if you *do* need this capability, you will sleep better at night knowing that it's available.

Certain key combinations should not be used as accelerator keys. Some of them are shown in this accelerator table:

```
AvoidThese ACCELERATORS
  {
  VK_TAB,      99, VIRTKEY, ALT     ; switch programs
  VK_SPACE,   100, VIRTKEY, ALT     ; system menu
  VK_F10,     101, VIRTKEY          ; menu hot key
  VK_F4,      102, VIRTKEY, ALT     ; close window
  VK_ESCAPE,  103, VIRTKEY, CONTROL ; get task list
  VK_ESCAPE,  104, VIRTKEY, ALT     ; switch programs

  VK_MENU,    105, VIRTKEY          ; Alt key
  VK_SHIFT,   106, VIRTKEY          ; Shift key
  VK_CONTROL,107, VIRTKEY           ; Control key

  VK_DELETE, 108, VIRTKEY, CONTROL, ALT  ; Reboot!
  }
```

The first set of accelerator definitions are key combinations that are reserved for Windows' use. If you create an accelerator key for one of them, you will prevent that key combination from playing its standard role in the user interface. The second set of accelerator keys involves the use of the [Alt], [Shift], and [Ctrl] keys alone. The keyboard accelerator system ignores these keys when used alone, since they are reserved for use with other keys. The very last accelerator key in this table needs no further explanation other than to say that you will never use it as an accelerator key command.

You'll want to avoid another set of accelerator key combinations, except when you need them for the actions for which they are reserved. [Shift]+[Del], for example, is reserved for the *Edit/Cut* menu item, a standard menu item for programs that use the clipboard. Table 11.5 summarizes these reserved accelerator keys and describes the use of each. From this set, you can see that the number of reserved accelerator keys is small and that you are left with a very wide range of keyboard combinations to choose from.

Table 11.5 Reserved Accelerator Key Combinations

Key Combination	*Description*
Alt + Backspace	Edit / Undo menu item.
Shift + Del	Edit / Cut menu item to remove an item to the clipboard.
Ctrl + Ins	Edit / Copy to place a copy of an item on the clipboard.
Shift + Ins	Edit / Paste to copy the contents of the clipboard into a document.
Del	Edit / Clear or Edit / Delete to remove data without affecting the contents of the clipboard.
F1	Help.
F6	Switch to a different panel in a split window.
Ctrl + F6	Switch to a different window under the multiple document interface.

If you are creating a Windows program that may someday be translated for use in a different language, you will probably want to avoid creating any accelerators that combine [Alt] with a letter key, for example, [Alt] + [A.] Such accelerators create the possibility of a conflict with mnemonic keystrokes. As we discussed earlier, a mnemonic keystroke lets the user strike [Alt] + a letter key to call up a popup menu. If an accelerator is defined for such a keystroke, like [Alt] + [A], and a popup menu uses the letter as a mnemonic, the mnemonic is disabled because accelerator key combinations have a higher priority.

At first glance, you might think that the solution would be simply to avoid creating accelerators that conflict with mnemonic letters. Consider a program with two popups: File and Edit. If [Alt]+[F] and [Alt]+[E] are the only two mnemonic keystrokes that the program uses, you might think that you can use [Alt]+[T] without any problem. But when the time comes for you to convert your product to be used in Finland, where the word for file is "Tiedosto," you will find that your accelerator, [Alt]+[T], has collided with the most obvious mnemonic for this menu. See Figure 11.14 for an example of how a Finnish program might appear.

As you can see from looking at this program, either an [Alt]+[T] or [Alt]+[M] accelerator would collide with the mnemonics in the Finnish version of our program for the File (Tie-

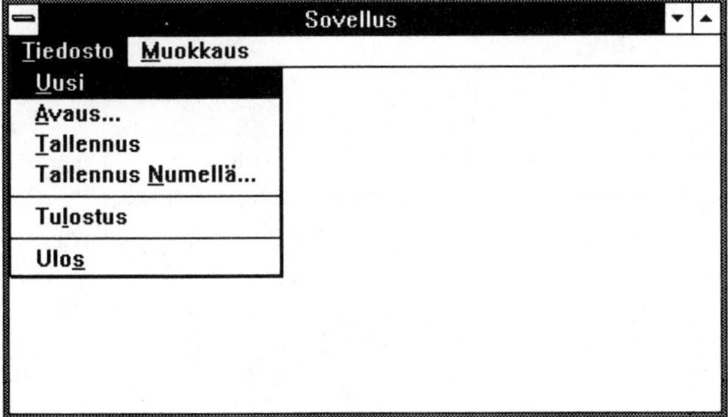

Figure 11.14 A sample Finnish program

dosto) or Edit (Muokkaus) menus. The easiest way to avoid this problem is simply to avoid creating accelerator keys that consist of [Alt] and a letter key alone.

Once an accelerator table has been defined in the resource file, bringing it into a program requires a call to the **LoadAccelerators** routine. This is defined as

```
HANDLE LoadAccelerators (hInstance, lpTableName)
```

- **hInstance** is an instance handle passed to a program as a parameter to **WinMain**.
- **lpTableName** is a long pointer to a character string containing the name of an accelerator table in the program's resource file.

The return value is a handle to an accelerator table, which identifies the specific set of accelerator keystrokes to be used. You would load an accelerator table named VIRTKEYS as shown here:

```
HANDLE hAccel;
hAccel = LoadAccelerators (hInstance, "VIRTKEYS");
```

Just like other resources (such as the menus described earlier), a numeric value can be used to identify an accelerator table, as in

```
23 ACCELERATORS
    {
    "A",  35, VIRTKEY, CONTROL
    .
    .
    }
```

To load this accelerator table into memory, you would make a call like this:

```
hAccel = LoadAccelerators (hInstance, "#23");
```

Or, the **MAKEINTRESOURCE** macro can be used to package the value in another way so that it is recognized as a numeric identifier:

```
hAccel=LoadAccelerators(hInstance,MAKEINTRESOURCE(23));
```

OWL's **TWindow** class automatically loads an accelerator table for you, as long as you provide the accelerator's resource ID in the window's **Attr.AccelTable** field. KEYCMD, our sample program, assigns a value to this field in its frame window constructor like this:

```
Attr.AccelTable = TResID("main");
```

Once the accelerator resource ID has been assigned, TWindow can load the accelerator table at the right time.

Once an accelerator table has been loaded, using it requires calling **TranslateAccelerator** in a message loop. Since the OWL application object already calls this routine for us, you don't need to know too much about it. If you're curious about the details, though, you can learn about **TranslateAccelerator** in the accompanying boxed discussion.

Accelerator keys generate the same messages as a corresponding menu selection. In particular, the **WM_COMMAND** message brings the command to a window object. As with menu commands, you can create a single message response function to handle all **WM_COMMAND** messages. Or, you can create a different message response function for each command.

Acclerator Translation

Acclerator keystrokes are automatically translated into their menu equivalents by the **TranslateAccelerator** routine, when it is embedded in a program's message loop. The OWL application object already calls this routine for us, in its message loop. **TranslateAccelerator** is defined as

```
int TranslateAccelerator (hWnd, haccTable, lpMsg)
```

- **hWnd** is a handle of the window that is to receive the command and menu control messages created by keyboard accelerators. This window will normally have a menu attached, so that menu and accelerator support can be seamlessly integrated.
- **haccTable** is a handle to an accelerator table loaded with the **LoadAccelerators** routine.
- **lpMsg** is a long pointer to an **MSG** data structure.

The most common way to use accelerators is to modify the standard **GetMessage** loop in your **WinMain** function. Here is the standard **GetMessage** loop:

```
while (GetMessage(&msg, 0, 0, 0))
    {
    TranslateMessage(&msg);  /*  Keyboard input. */
```

```
        DispatchMessage(&msg);
        }
```

TranslateAccelerator can check the message traffic received by **GetMessage** and convert it to the appropriate menu messages. If it performs a translation, it provides a return code of TRUE. Otherwise, the return code is FALSE. Here is the most common way to incorporate this routine into a standard message loop:

```
    while (GetMessage(&msg, 0, 0, 0))
        {
        if (!TranslateAccelerator(hwnd, hAccel, &msg))
            {
            TranslateMessage(&msg);  /*  Kbd input. */
            DispatchMessage(&msg);
            }
        }
```

If **TranslateAccelerator** does not find an accelerator, it returns a value of FALSE. This causes the message to be handled normally by **TranslateMessage** and **DispatchMessage**. Otherwise, if an accelerator was found, then no other steps are required by the **GetMessage** loop, since it is handled entirely by **TranslateAccelerator**.

Here is a complete program that shows how an accelerator table can be implemented. This program is built on the standard menu program we introduced at the beginning of this chapter, STANMENU. We have added the four standard accelerators that support the standard clipboard operations: *undo*, *cut*, *copy*, and *paste*.

KEYCMD.CPP

```
//
// KEYCMD.CPP   Shows the creation of keyboard command accelerators.
//
//
#include <owl\owlpch.h>
#include "keycmd.h"

//
// Main window
class DFrame : public TFrameWindow
    {
  public:
    DFrame(char * title);
    void CmFileNew();
    void CmFileOpen();
    void CmFileSave();
    void CmFileSaveAs();
    void CmFilePrint();
    void CmFileExit();
    void CmEditUndo();
    void CmEditCut();
    void CmEditCopy();
    void CmEditPaste();
    void CmEditClear();
```

```
      void CmEditDelete();
      void CmHelpAbout();

    DECLARE_RESPONSE_TABLE (DFrame);
      };

  DEFINE_RESPONSE_TABLE1 (DFrame, TFrameWindow)
    EV_COMMAND(CM_FILE_NEW,  CmFileNew),
    EV_COMMAND(CM_FILE_OPEN, CmFileOpen),
    EV_COMMAND(CM_FILE_SAVE, CmFileSave),
    EV_COMMAND(CM_FILE_SAVEAS, CmFileSaveAs),
    EV_COMMAND(CM_FILE_PRINT, CmFilePrint),
    EV_COMMAND(CM_FILE_EXIT, CmFileExit),
    EV_COMMAND(CM_EDIT_UNDO, CmEditUndo),
    EV_COMMAND(CM_EDIT_CUT,  CmEditCut),
    EV_COMMAND(CM_EDIT_COPY, CmEditCopy),
    EV_COMMAND(CM_EDIT_PASTE, CmEditPaste),
    EV_COMMAND(CM_EDIT_CLEAR, CmEditClear),
    EV_COMMAND(CM_EDIT_DELETE, CmEditDelete),
    EV_COMMAND(CM_HELP_ABOUT, CmHelpAbout),
  END_RESPONSE_TABLE;

  DFrame::DFrame(char * title) : TFrameWindow(0, title)
      {
      Attr.AccelTable = TResId("main");
      }

  void DFrame::CmFileNew()
      {
      MessageBox ("File.New Selected", Title);
      }
  void DFrame::CmFileOpen()
      {
      MessageBox ("File.Open... Selected", Title);
      }
  void DFrame::CmFileSave()
      {
      MessageBox ("File.Save Selected", Title);
      }
  void DFrame::CmFileSaveAs()
      {
      MessageBox ("File.Save As... Selected", Title);
      }
  void DFrame::CmFilePrint()
      {
      MessageBox ("File.Print Selected", Title);
      }
  void DFrame::CmFileExit()
      {
      MessageBox ("File.Exit Selected", Title);
      CloseWindow(0); // Cause application to terminate
      }
  void DFrame::CmEditUndo()
      {
      MessageBox ("Edit.Undo Selected", Title);
      }
  void DFrame::CmEditCut()
      {
      MessageBox ("Edit.Cut Selected", Title);
      }
  void DFrame::CmEditCopy()
      {
      MessageBox ("Edit.Copy Selected", Title);
      }
  void DFrame::CmEditPaste()
      {
```

```
        MessageBox ("Edit.Paste Selected", Title);
        }
    void DFrame::CmEditClear()
        {
        MessageBox ("Edit.Clear Selected", Title);
        }
    void DFrame::CmEditDelete()
        {
        MessageBox ("Edit.Delete Selected", Title);
        }

    void DFrame::CmHelpAbout()
        {
        MessageBox(" Standard File & Edit Menus\n"
                   "  with Standard Accelerators\n\n"
                   "'Borland C++ 4.0 Programming\n"
                   "  for Windows', by Paul Yao", Title);
        }

    //
    // Application object
    class DApp : public TApplication
        {
      public:
        DApp() : TApplication()
            {
            }
        void InitMainWindow()
            {
            SetMainWindow (new DFrame("Standard Accelerators"));
            MainWindow->AssignMenu("MAIN");
            MainWindow->SetIcon(this, "SNAPSHOT");
            }
        };

    //
    // Application main entry point.
    OwlMain(int, char **)
        {
        return DApp().Run();
        }
```

KEYCMD.H

```
#define CM_FILE_NEW     100
#define CM_FILE_OPEN    101
#define CM_FILE_SAVE    102
#define CM_FILE_SAVEAS  103
#define CM_FILE_PRINT   104
#define CM_FILE_EXIT    105

#define CM_EDIT_UNDO    200
#define CM_EDIT_CUT     201
#define CM_EDIT_COPY    202
#define CM_EDIT_PASTE   203
#define CM_EDIT_CLEAR   204
#define CM_EDIT_DELETE  205

#define CM_HELP_ABOUT    300
```

KEYCMD.RC

```
#include "keycmd.h"

snapshot icon keycmd.ico

main menu
    BEGIN
    POPUP "&File"
        {
        MENUITEM "&New",        CM_FILE_NEW
        MENUITEM "&Open...",    CM_FILE_OPEN
        MENUITEM "&Save",       CM_FILE_SAVE
        MENUITEM "Save &As...", CM_FILE_SAVEAS
        MENUITEM SEPARATOR
        MENUITEM "&Print",      CM_FILE_PRINT
        MENUITEM SEPARATOR
        MENUITEM "E&xit",       CM_FILE_EXIT
        }
    POPUP "&Edit"
        {
        MENUITEM "&Undo\tCtrl+Z",  CM_EDIT_UNDO
        MENUITEM SEPARATOR
        MENUITEM "Cu&t\tCtrl+X",   CM_EDIT_CUT
        MENUITEM "&Copy\tCtrl+C",  CM_EDIT_COPY
        MENUITEM "&Paste\tCtrl+V", CM_EDIT_PASTE
        MENUITEM SEPARATOR
        MENUITEM "Cl&ear",         CM_EDIT_CLEAR
        MENUITEM "&Delete",        CM_EDIT_DELETE
        }
    POPUP "&Help"
        {
        MENUITEM "&About...", CM_HELP_ABOUT
        }
    END

main ACCELERATORS
    {
    ; Windows 3.1 Edit menu accelerators.
    "Z",      CM_EDIT_UNDO,   VIRTKEY, CONTROL
    "X",      CM_EDIT_CUT,    VIRTKEY, CONTROL
    "C",      CM_EDIT_COPY,   VIRTKEY, CONTROL
    "V",      CM_EDIT_PASTE,  VIRTKEY, CONTROL

    ; Old-style Edit menu accelerators.
    VK_BACK,   CM_EDIT_UNDO,  VIRTKEY, ALT
    VK_DELETE, CM_EDIT_CUT,   VIRTKEY, SHIFT
    VK_INSERT, CM_EDIT_COPY,  VIRTKEY, CONTROL
    VK_INSERT, CM_EDIT_PASTE, VIRTKEY, SHIFT
    }
```

KEYCMD.DEF

```
EXETYPE WINDOWS

CODE MOVEABLE DISCARDABLE
DATA MULTIPLE MOVEABLE

HEAPSIZE   512
STACKSIZE 8192
```

DYNA16.MAK

```
#  MAKE file for Win16 API using dynamic BIDS,
#  OWL and C-runtime libraries.
#
#    C> make -fstatic16.mak
#

.AUTODEPEND
CC = -c -H -H"owl\owlpch.h" -ml -R -vi -WS -X-
CD = -D_RTLDLL;_BIDSDLL;_OWLDLL;_OWLPCH;
INC = -I\BC4\INCLUDE
LIB = -L\BC4\LIB

keycmd.exe :  keycmd.obj keycmd.res
  tlink -c -C -Twe $(LIB) @dyna16.lnk
  brc keycmd.res keycmd.exe

keycmd.obj :  keycmd.cpp
  bcc $(CC) $(CD) keycmd.cpp

keycmd.res :  keycmd.rc keycmd.ico keycmd.h
  brc $(INC) -31 -R keycmd.rc
```

DYNA16.LNK

```
\bc4\lib\c0wl.obj+
keycmd.obj
keycmd,keycmd
\bc4\lib\bidsi.lib+
\bc4\lib\owlwi.lib+
\bc4\lib\import.lib+
\bc4\lib\crtldll.lib
keycmd.def
```

DYNA32.MAK

```
#  MAKE file for Win32 API using dynamic BIDS,
#  OWL and C-runtime libraries.
#
#    C> make -fdyna32.mak
#

.AUTODEPEND
CC = -c -H -H\""owl\owlpch.h\"" -p- -R -vi -W -X-
CD = -D_RTLDLL;_BIDSDLL;_OWLDLL;_OWLPCH;
INC = -I\BC4\INCLUDE
LIB = -L\BC4\LIB

keycmd.exe :  keycmd.obj keycmd.res
  tlink32 -aa -c -Tpe $(LIB) @dyna32.lnk
  brc32 keycmd.res keycmd.exe

keycmd.obj :  keycmd.cpp
  bcc32 $(CC) $(CD) keycmd.cpp

keycmd.res :  keycmd.rc keycmd.ico keycmd.h
  brc32 $(INC) -w32 -R keycmd.rc
```

DYNA32.LNK

```
\bc4\lib\c0w32.obj+
keycmd.obj
keycmd,keycmd
\bc4\lib\bidsfi.lib+
\bc4\lib\owlwfi.lib+
\bc4\lib\import32.lib+
\bc4\lib\cw32i.lib
keycmd.def
```

Adding accelerator support to this program involved the addition of a single line of code to the C++ source file:

```
Attr.AccelTable = TResID("main");
```

`Attr` is a structure of type **`TWindowAttr`** inherited from **`TWindow`**, the OWL class that provides primary support for a WinAPI window. The **`Attr`** structure contains some basic window attribute information that's used to create the WinAPI window, such as initial size and location, menu resource id, style bits and accelerator table resource id.

A quick look in KEYCMD.RC shows what this refers to—the keyboard commands that make up KEYCMD's accelerators. The first line of this accelerator table contains the name of the accelerator table as follows:

```
main ACCELERATORS
```

This explains why **`AccelTable`** was set equal to "main," above.

Windows gives you a comprehensive set of menu creation and management routines and lets you create accelerator keystrokes to define keyboard commands. It communicates via messages each action taken by the user with menus. The menu system is robust, fast, and flexible. You can create static menu templates, build menus on the fly, or change any part of an existing menu.

In the next chapter, you're going to see how to get a little more sparkle out of menus by adding graphics. We're going to explore two techniques to allow us to use GDI drawing routines to change the appearance of menu items: owner-draw menu items and custom check marks. I'll also show a technique for using **Windows hooks** to make keyboard accelerators a little more versatile.

12

Enhancing Menus with Graphics and Hooks

Windows uses the system font, a bold, Helveticalike, proportionally spaced font, to draw the text inside menus. This default font was chosen because it is easy to read and has a slick, modern look. However, there may be times when you want to use another font inside a menu. Or, you might want to create a menu that contains geometric figures or graphic images. When you want to do this, Windows lets you hook into its menu creation mechanism so that you can enhance the look of your menus with graphical objects. In this chapter, you're going to look at two methods that are available to you: owner-draw menu items and custom checkmarks. I'll also show how to use Window hooks to make accelerator key commands available when a menu is visible—something that Windows does not normally allow to happen.

Owner-Draw Menu Items

All of the menus that we've created up to now have used a text label drawn with the system font. For most applications, this is a reasonable approach to take. But there may be times when you wish to replace the text with a graphic object. Or, you may wish to change the font that is used. Owner-draw menu items give you the ability to create graphical menu images using GDI drawing calls. Thus, instead of just *telling* users what a menu item will produce, you can *show* them. A drawing program might use this capability to show the user the different lines, shapes, and fonts that are available. A flowchart program might put different flowchart elements into menus to provide instant feedback on which flowchart elements are available.

Because the resource compiler does not provide any support for owner-draw menu items, you have to dynamically create the menu items by calling one of the menu modification routines we discussed in the last chapter. If you want an owner-draw menu item to appear in your menu the first time your window appears, you'll probably want to add the menu item in response to the **WM_CREATE** message. You won't be able to add owner-draw menu items at window object creation time (i.e., in your window object constructor) since the MS-Windows window hasn't been created yet. Instead, override **TFrameWindow::SetupWindow** and add your owner draw menu items from that function.

After an owner-draw menu item has been inserted into a menu, two messages will be sent to the window procedure to measure and draw the menu item: **WM_MEASUREITEM** and **WM_DRAWITEM**. The **WM_MEASUREITEM** message arrives before the menu item is ever drawn. Your program must respond to this message by filling in a data structure that describes the width and height of your menu item in pixels. The second message, **WM_DRAWITEM**, is sent whenever drawing is needed for the menu item. Drawing is needed when a menu is displayed and when the menu item is highlighted to provide the user with visual feedback while menu items are browsed.

Before we look at the handling of these two messages in detail, it's worth mentioning that these two messages are also sent for the other types of owner-draw objects: buttons, comboboxes, and listboxes. As you'll see, there are elements of the owner-draw mechanism, intended for use with the other owner-draw objects, that can be safely ignored when dealing with owner-draw menu items. As we look at each part of this mechanism, we'll be sure to identify these elements for you.

The WM_MEASUREITEM Message

An owner-draw item can be as small or as large as you would like to make it. The **WM_MEASUREITEM** message provides a way for you to let the menu system know the exact size that you need to draw the menu item. The units are in pixels, but since you're going to use GDI routines to draw, you can use GDI's coordinate mapping system.

When calculating the size of the area that you'll need in an owner-draw menu item, you need to take into account space for a margin around the menu item. For one thing, you'll want to allow enough space between your menu item and other menu items. It's also a good idea to reserve space for a checkmark on the left side of your menu. You can call the **GetMenuCheckMarkDimensions** routine for information about the default width and height of a checkmark. Even if you don't use a checkmark for your owner-draw menu item, you'll still want to do this. The width of a checkmark is the standard left margin of a menu item; using this value will help give your owner-draw menu items a consistent look with normal menu items.

To accommodate the higher resolution of devices that we may see some day, it's a good idea to avoid hard-coding any specific sizes for owner-draw menu items. Instead, you should make your drawing relative to the size of system objects, because they are automatically scaled for different device resolutions. Icons are a type of system object that can serve as a good reference point for owner-draw menu items. Icon dimensions are determined by the system display device driver. To determine the dimensions of an icon, you call **GetSystemMetrics**. If you wanted to make your menu items the same size as an icon, here's how you could do it:

```
DWORD dwCheckMark;
int cxWidth, cyHeight;

cxWidth  = GetSystemMetrics (SM_CXICON); /* Width.  */
cyHeight = GetSystemMetrics (SM_CYICON); /* Height. */

/* Adjust for check mark.  */
dwCheckMark = GetMenuCheckMarkDimensions();
cxWidth +=      LOWORD(dwCheckMark);
cyHeight = max (HIWORD(dwCheckMark), cyHeight);
```

We add a value for the width of the checkmark, and we also update `cyHeight` to make sure that it can accommodate the height of a checkmark.

As an alternative, you can base the size of your owner-draw items on the metrics of the system font. When we discuss dialog boxes in Chapter 14, you'll see that the dialog box manager uses this approach to provide device-independent **dialog box coordinates**. To calculate the dimensions of an owner-draw menu item that is twice as tall as the system font, and which has a width equal to that of 15 characters, you can say

```
DWORD dwCheckMark;
HDC hdc
int cxWidth, cyHeight;
TEXTMETRIC tm;

hdc = GetDC (HWindow);
GetTextMetrics (hdc, &tm);
ReleaseDC (HWindow, hdc);

cxWidth  = tm.tmMaxCharWidth * 15;
cyHeight = tm.tmHeight * 2;

/*  Adjust for check mark. */
dwCheckMark = GetMenuCheckMarkDimensions();
cxWidth +=      LOWORD(dwCheckMark);
cyHeight = max (HIWORD(dwCheckMark), cyHeight);
```

The **GetTextMetrics** routine, which we first discussed in Chapter 10, gets the metrics of the font that is currently installed in a DC. In the absence of special window class styles (discussed in Chapter 13), **GetDC** returns a DC with the system font installed. As in the earlier example, this code includes the dimensions of a menu checkmark in the overall dimensions of the owner-draw item.

Whichever method you choose, one **WM_MEASUREITEM** message is sent for each owner-draw menu item. When it arrives, it includes a pointer to a structure of type **MEASUREITEMSTRUCT**. This structure is defined in WINDOWS.H as

```
typedef struct tagMEASUREITEMSTRUCT
  {
```

```
    WORD   CtlType;     /*  ODT_MENU           */
    WORD   CtlID;       /*  Ignore for menus.  */
    WORD   itemID;
    WORD   itemWidth;   /*  Return width.      */
    WORD   itemHeight;  /*  Return height.     */
    DWORD  itemData;
  } MEASUREITEMSTRUCT;
```

When you get a **WM_MEASUREITEM** message, the two fields that you use to return the width and height of your owner-draw item are **itemWidth** and **itemHeight**. The other fields in this data structure help you identify a specific owner-draw item, since you will have one **WM_MEASUREITEM** message for each owner-draw menu item that you have. When working with owner-draw menu items, one of these fields can be ignored since it's only used for owner-draw dialog box controls: **CtlID**.

The **CtlType** field describes the type of owner-draw item. It is set to **ODT_MENU** for menus. The presence of this field means a single body of code can support owner-draw objects in menus, listboxes, or comboboxes.

itemID is the command result code for a menu item. It is the value that gets sent in the wParam parameter of a **WM_COMMAND** message. As we'll see in a moment, this value is set when a menu item is created.

The **itemData** field provides another way to identify an owner-draw menu item. It is a 32-bit field that you create and provide when you create an owner-draw menu item. When you create an owner-draw popup menu (as opposed to a regular command menu item), this field provides the only way to distinguish one owner-draw popup menu from another, since popup menu items do not have a command result code.

If you create an owner-draw menu item by calling **AppendMenu** like this:

```
AppendMenu (hmenu, MF_OWNERDRAW, 38, (LPSTR)200);
```

it creates a menu item with an **itemID** of 38 and an **itemData** value of 200. The last parameter is cast as an **LPSTR** because that is how this routine is prototyped. Otherwise, the compiler issues an unnecessary warning message. If the variables **cxWidth** and **cyHeight** contained the desired dimensions of this menu item, we could respond to the **WM_MEASUREITEM** message like this:

```
void DFrame::EvMeasureItem(UINT /* ctrlId */,
                           MEASUREITEMSTRUCT far& msrInfo)
    {
    if (msrInfo.itemID == 38)
        {
        msrInfo.itemWidth = cxWidth;
        msrInfo.itemHeight = cyHeight;
        }
    }
```

Another approach involves checking **itemData** for the specific owner-draw menu item:

```
void DFrame::EvMeasureItem(UINT /* ctrlId */,
                           MEASUREITEMSTRUCT far& msrInfo)
    {
    if (msrInfo.itemData == 200)
        {
        msrInfo.itemWidth = cxWidth;
        msrInfo.itemHeight = cyHeight;
        }
    }
```

A program only receives a single **WM_MEASUREITEM** message for each owner-draw item. After that, the menu system remembers the dimensions of the menu item and sends a **WM_DRAWITEM** message whenever it needs a menu item to be drawn.

The WM_DRAWITEM Message

A **WM_DRAWITEM** message is sent to your window procedure when a popup menu is opened that contains an owner-draw menu item. Then, as the user browses through a menu, this message is sent to toggle menu highlighting. As you'll see in a moment, the **WM_DRAWITEM** message provides flags that let you know the effect that the menu system requires.

When the **WM_DRAWITEM** message is sent, it contains a pointer to a structure of type **DRAWITEMSTRUCT**, defined in WINDOWS.H as follows:

```
typedef struct tagDRAWITEMSTRUCT
    {
    WORD   CtlType;     /* ODT_MENU.                     */
    WORD   CtlID;       /* Ignore for menus.             */
    WORD   itemID;
    WORD   itemAction;  /* Ignore for menus.             */
    WORD   itemState;   /* Selected,grayed,checked.      */
    HWND   hwndItem;    /* Handle to popup menu.         */
    HDC    hDC;
    RECT   rcItem;      /* Bounding rectangle.           */
    DWORD  itemData;
    } DRAWITEMSTRUCT;
```

Four of the items in this data structure are identical to items in the data structure that is sent with the **WM_MEASUREITEM** message: `CtlType`, `CtlID`, `itemID`, and `itemData`.

The `CtlType` field describes the type of owner-draw item. It is set to **ODT_MENU** for menus.

The `CtlID` field can be ignored for owner-draw menu items, since it is only used for owner-draw dialog box controls.

`itemID` is the command result code for a menu item, which is the value sent to a window procedure in the `wParam` parameter of a **WM_COMMAND** message.

The **itemData** field provides another way to identify an owner-draw menu item and is the only way to distinguish one owner-draw popup menu from another.

The **itemAction** field describes the action the menu system wants you to perform. However, since menu items are drawn to reflect the menu item state, you can usually ignore this field and determine the menu state from the next field.

The **itemState** field defines the current state of the menu item, as shown here:

Value	*Menu Item State*
ODS_CHECKED	Checkmark is to appear in the menu.
ODS_DISABLED	Menu to be drawn disabled.
ODS_FOCUS	Ignore—not used for menus.
ODS_GRAYED	Menu to be drawn grayed.
ODS_SELECTED	Menu to be drawn selected.

The most important flag is **ODS_SELECTED**. When this bit is set, it indicates that the menu item needs to be highlighted. A highlighted menu item is drawn in a different color from a regular menu item to provide visual feedback while the user is browsing a menu. You should draw highlighted menu items using two system colors that are defined for this purpose. To obtain the RGB values of the required system colors, call the **GetSysColor** routine. Here are the color indices that you should use for menu highlights:

Value	*Description*
COLOR_HIGHLIGHT	Background color of a selected object.
COLOR_HIGHLIGHTTEXT	Foreground color of a selected object.
COLOR_MENU	Background color of a normal object.
COLOR_MENUTEXT	Foreground color of a normal object.

If you plan to set the state of an owner-draw menu item to checked, or if you plan to gray the menu item, your response to the **WM_DRAWITEM** message must provide for this. You will need to test the value in the **itemState** field and change the way you draw your menu item according to the desired effect. For example, you might use a shade of gray in your drawing to indicate a grayed menu item. You can draw a checkmark using a bitmap that is built into the display driver. Here is the WinAPI way to obtain a handle to that bitmap, and draw with it:

```
hbm = LoadBitmap (NULL,MAKEINTRESOURCE(OBM_CHECK));
hdcBitmap = CreateCompatibleDC (hDC);
hbmOld = SelectBitmap (hdcBitmap, hbm);

dwDimensions = GetMenuCheckMarkDimensions();
cxWidth  = LOWORD(dwDimensions);
cyHeight = HIWORD(dwDimensions);
```

```
    BitBlt (ps.hdc, 0, 0, cxWidth, cyHeight,
            hdcBitmap, 0, 0, SRCCOPY);

    SelectBitmap (hdcBitmap, hbmOld);
    DeleteDC (hdcBitmap);
```

In spite of its name, the **hwndItem** field is not a window handle but instead is a popup menu handle for the menu that contains the owner-draw item. Its name comes from its use with owner-draw dialog box controls, when it does contain a window handle. When a program receives a **WM_DRAWITEM** message, it might wish to use the popup menu handle to call a menu query routine to find out, for example, the number of items that are in the current menu, or the state of other menu items.

The **hDC** field is a handle to a device context for drawing in the menu. Be sure to restore the DC to its initial state when you are done, otherwise you risk causing problems for the menu system when it draws other parts of your menu.

The **rcItem** field defines a rectangle within which you can draw your menu item. You should not go beyond this rectangle, since doing so risks overwriting other menu items.

The owner-draw items supported by these messages and data structures give a program a remarkable amount of flexibility in deciding how a menu item should appear. Let's look at a sample program that shows how to put these messages and data structures to work for you.

A Sample Program: GRAFMENU

Figure 12.1 shows GRAFMENU, a program that uses owner-draw menu items to let a user select a marker. Without the ability to create owner-draw items, text descriptions would be used for the three markers. Instead, this menu shows users the shape of available markers. In the figure, the cross marker is displayed in a selected state—with white foreground pixels and black background pixels. The other markers are displayed in a nonselected state. The appearance of each menu item is no accident—if you scan through the

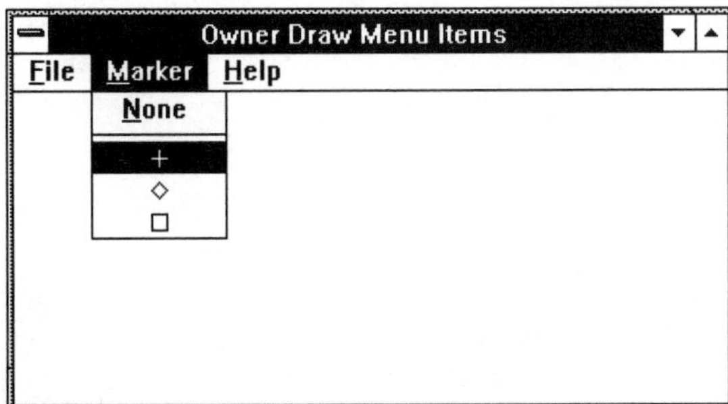

Figure 12.1 GRAFMENU's owner draw menu items

following source code files to GRAFMENU, you can figure out how it draws selected and unselected menu items.

GRAFMENU.CPP

```
//
// GRAFMENU.CPP  Shows the creation & maintenance of
//               owner-draw menu items.
//
#include <owl\owlpch.h>
#include "grafmenu.h"
#include "cls_mark.h"

DEFINE_RESPONSE_TABLE1 (DFrame, TFrameWindow)
  EV_WM_DRAWITEM,
  EV_WM_MEASUREITEM,
  EV_COMMAND(CM_FILEEXIT, CmFileExit),
  EV_COMMAND(CM_MARK_NONE,     CmNone),
  EV_COMMAND(CM_MARK_CROSS,    CmCross),
  EV_COMMAND(CM_MARK_DIAMOND, CmDiamond),
  EV_COMMAND(CM_MARK_SQUARE,   CmSquare),
  EV_COMMAND(CM_HELPABOUT, CmHelpAbout),
END_RESPONSE_TABLE;

DFrame::DFrame(char * title) : TFrameWindow(0, title)
    {
    // Init marker size.
    cxyMarkerSize = GetSystemMetrics (SM_CYICON) / 4;
    cmMarker = CM_MARK_CROSS;

    // Init menu colors.
    tcrMenuSelectText = GetSysColor(COLOR_HIGHLIGHTTEXT);
    tcrMenuSelectBack = GetSysColor(COLOR_HIGHLIGHT);
    tcrMenuNormalText = GetSysColor(COLOR_MENUTEXT);
    tcrMenuNormalBack = GetSysColor(COLOR_MENU);

    // Create foreground & background pens & brushes.
    tpnSelect = new TPen(tcrMenuSelectText);
    tpnNormal = new TPen(tcrMenuNormalText);
    tbrSelect = new TBrush(tcrMenuSelectBack);
    tbrNormal = new TBrush(tcrMenuNormalBack);
    }

DFrame::~DFrame()
    {
    // As usual, any NEW'ed objects get DEL'ed.
    delete tpnSelect;
    delete tpnNormal;
    delete tbrSelect;
    delete tbrNormal;
    }

void DFrame::CmFileExit()
    {
    CloseWindow(0); // Cause application to terminate
    }

void DFrame::CmNone()    { cmMarker=CM_MARK_NONE;    Invalidate(); }
void DFrame::CmCross()   { cmMarker=CM_MARK_CROSS;   Invalidate(); }
void DFrame::CmDiamond() { cmMarker=CM_MARK_DIAMOND; Invalidate(); }
```

```
void DFrame::CmSquare()  { cmMarker=CM_MARK_SQUARE;  Invalidate(); }

void DFrame::CmHelpAbout()
    {
    MessageBox("    Owner Draw Menu Items\n\n"
               "'Borland C++ 4.0 Programming\n"
               "  for Windows', by Paul Yao", Title);
    }

void DFrame::EvDrawItem (UINT /* ctrlID */, DRAWITEMSTRUCT far& dis)
    {
    // Temp's to save DC state.
    COLORREF crBackground;

    // Calculate marker location.
    TPoint ptCenter;
    ptCenter.x = (dis.rcItem.left + dis.rcItem.right) / 2;
    ptCenter.y = (dis.rcItem.bottom + dis.rcItem.top) / 2;

    // Set colors.
    HPEN hpen;
    if (dis.itemState & ODS_SELECTED)
        {
        hpen = HPEN(*tpnSelect);
        crBackground = SetBkColor(dis.hDC, tcrMenuSelectBack);
        }
    else
        {
        hpen = HPEN(*tpnNormal);
        crBackground = SetBkColor(dis.hDC, tcrMenuNormalBack);
        }

    // Draw background. Used this way, this function doesn't
    // draw text -- instead it fills the specified rectangle
    // using the background color attribute in the DC (which
    // was set a few lines earlier in the call to SetBkColor).
    ExtTextOut(dis.hDC, 0, 0, ETO_OPAQUE, &dis.rcItem, 0, 0, 0);

    switch (dis.itemID)
        {
        case CM_MARK_CROSS:
            Marker::Cross (dis.hDC, ptCenter, cxyMarkerSize,
                           hpen, R2_COPYPEN);
            break;
        case CM_MARK_DIAMOND:
            Marker::Diamond (dis.hDC, ptCenter, cxyMarkerSize,
                             hpen, R2_COPYPEN);
            break;
        case CM_MARK_SQUARE:
            Marker::Square (dis.hDC, ptCenter, cxyMarkerSize,
                            hpen, R2_COPYPEN);
            break;
        }

    // Restore DC before returning.
    SetBkColor(dis.hDC, crBackground);
    }

void DFrame::EvMeasureItem (UINT /* ctrlID */,
                            MEASUREITEMSTRUCT far& mis)
    {
    // Calculate the pixel width & height of 3 X's.
```

```
    TClientDC dc(HWindow);
    TSize size;
    dc.GetTextExtent ("XXX", 3, size);

    // Get menu checkmark width for left & right margins.
    TSize tsCheckMark = GetMenuCheckMarkDimensions();

    // Menu height = text line height
    mis.itemHeight = size.cy;

    // Menu width = Width of X's + 2 * margin values.
    mis.itemWidth  = size.cx + (2 * tsCheckMark.cx);
    }

typedef void (* DRAWFUNC)(HDC, TPoint&, int, HPEN, int);

void DFrame::Paint (TDC& dc, BOOL, TRect&)
    {
    // Don't draw if "None" selected.
    if (cmMarker == CM_MARK_NONE)
        return;

    // For speed, this switch statement was moved from
    // inner loop. Crazy C-language tricks still doable.
    DRAWFUNC df;
    switch (cmMarker)
        {
        case CM_MARK_CROSS:
            df = Marker::Cross;
            break;
        case CM_MARK_DIAMOND:
            df = Marker::Diamond;
            break;
        case CM_MARK_SQUARE:
            df = Marker::Square;
            break;
        }

    // Get area to fill with markers.
    TRect trClient = GetClientRect();

    // Loop through client area & fill with selected marker.
    TPoint ptDraw;
    for (int y = cxyMarkerSize;
             y < trClient.bottom; y+= cxyMarkerSize)
        {
        for (int x = cxyMarkerSize;
                 x < trClient.right; x += cxyMarkerSize)
            {
            ptDraw.x = x;
            ptDraw.y = y;

            df (HDC(dc), ptDraw, cxyMarkerSize, 0, R2_COPYPEN);
            }
        }
    }

void DFrame::SetupWindow()
    {
    // Call base class to get things set up.
    TFrameWindow::SetupWindow();
```

```
    // Fetch window handle submenus.
    HMENU hmenu = GetMenu();
    HMENU hsubmenu = GetSubMenu (hmenu, MARKER_MENU_POS);

    // Add owner-drawn items to Marker submenu.
    tmenuMarker = new TMenu(hsubmenu);
    tmenuMarker->AppendMenu(MF_OWNERDRAW, CM_MARK_CROSS, 0);
    tmenuMarker->AppendMenu(MF_OWNERDRAW, CM_MARK_DIAMOND, 0);
    tmenuMarker->AppendMenu(MF_OWNERDRAW, CM_MARK_SQUARE,  0);
    }

void DFrame::CleanupWindow()
    {
    delete tmenuMarker;
    }

DApp::DApp() : TApplication()
    {
    }

void DApp::InitMainWindow()
    {
    SetMainWindow (new DFrame("Owner Draw Menu Items"));
    MainWindow->AssignMenu("MAIN");
    MainWindow->SetIcon(this, "SNAPSHOT");
    }

//
// Application main entry point.
OwlMain(int, char **)
    {
    return DApp().Run();
    }
```

GRAFMENU.H

```
#define CM_FILEEXIT     100

#define CM_MARK_NONE    200
#define CM_MARK_CROSS   201
#define CM_MARK_DIAMOND 202
#define CM_MARK_SQUARE  203

#define CM_HELPABOUT    300

// Sub-menu ordinal values.
const int MARKER_MENU_POS =  1;

// Main window
class DFrame : public TFrameWindow
    {
  public:
    DFrame(char * title);
    ~DFrame();
    void CmFileExit();
    void CmNone();
    void CmCross();
    void CmDiamond();
    void CmSquare();
```

```
    void CmHelpAbout();
    void EvDrawItem (UINT ctrlID, DRAWITEMSTRUCT far& dis);
    void EvMeasureItem (UINT ctrlID, MEASUREITEMSTRUCT far& mis);
    void Paint (TDC&, BOOL, TRect&);
    void SetupWindow();
    void CleanupWindow();
  private:
    int      cxyMarkerSize;
    int      cmMarker;
    TColor   tcrMenuSelectText;
    TColor   tcrMenuSelectBack;
    TColor   tcrMenuNormalText;
    TColor   tcrMenuNormalBack;
    TMenu  * tmenuMarker;
    TPen   * tpnSelect;
    TPen   * tpnNormal;
    TBrush * tbrSelect;
    TBrush * tbrNormal;

  DECLARE_RESPONSE_TABLE (DFrame);
    };

// Application object
class DApp : public TApplication
    {
  public:
    DApp();
    void InitMainWindow();
    };
```

GRAFMENU.RC

```
#include "grafmenu.h"

snapshot icon grafmenu.ico

main menu
    BEGIN
    POPUP "&File"
        {
        MENUITEM "E&xit", CM_FILEEXIT
        }
    POPUP "&Marker"
        {
        MENUITEM "&None", CM_MARK_NONE
        MENUITEM SEPARATOR
        }
    POPUP "&Help"
        {
        MENUITEM "&About...", CM_HELPABOUT
        }
    END
```

GRAFMENU.DEF

```
EXETYPE WINDOWS

CODE MOVEABLE DISCARDABLE
DATA MULTIPLE MOVEABLE

HEAPSIZE   512
STACKSIZE 8192
```

DYNA16.MAK

```
#  MAKE file for Win16 API using dynamic BIDS,
#  OWL and C-runtime libraries.
#
#    C> make -fstatic16.mak
#

.AUTODEPEND
CC = -c -H -H"owl\owlpch.h" -ml -R -vi -WS -X-
CD = -D_RTLDLL;_BIDSDLL;_OWLDLL;_OWLPCH;
INC = -I\BC4\INCLUDE
LIB = -L\BC4\LIB

grafmenu.exe :  grafmenu.obj cls_mark.obj grafmenu.res
  tlink -c -C -Twe $(LIB) @dyna16.lnk
  brc grafmenu.res grafmenu.exe

grafmenu.obj :  grafmenu.cpp
  bcc $(CC) $(CD) grafmenu.cpp

cls_mark.obj :  cls_mark.cpp
  bcc $(CC) $(CD) cls_mark.cpp

grafmenu.res :  grafmenu.rc grafmenu.ico grafmenu.h
  brc $(INC) -31 -R grafmenu.rc
```

DYNA16.LNK

```
\bc4\lib\c0wl.obj+
grafmenu.obj+cls_mark.obj
grafmenu,grafmenu
\bc4\lib\bidsi.lib+
\bc4\lib\owlwi.lib+
\bc4\lib\import.lib+
\bc4\lib\crtldll.lib
grafmenu.def
```

DYNA32.MAK

```
#  MAKE file for Win32 API using dynamic BIDS,
#  OWL and C-runtime libraries.
#
#    C> make -fdyna32.mak
```

```
#

.AUTODEPEND
CC = -c -H -H\""owl\owlpch.h\"" -p- -R -vi -W -X-
CD = -D_RTLDLL;_BIDSDLL;_OWLDLL;_OWLPCH;
INC = -I\BC4\INCLUDE
LIB = -L\BC4\LIB

grafmenu.exe :  grafmenu.obj cls_mark.obj grafmenu.res
  tlink32 -aa -c -Tpe $(LIB) @dyna32.lnk
  brc32 grafmenu.res grafmenu.exe

grafmenu.obj :  grafmenu.cpp
  bcc32 $(CC) $(CD) grafmenu.cpp

cls_mark.obj :  cls_mark.cpp
  bcc32 $(CC) $(CD) cls_mark.cpp

grafmenu.res :  grafmenu.rc grafmenu.ico grafmenu.h
  brc32 $(INC) -w32 -R grafmenu.rc
```

DYNA32.LNK

```
\bc4\lib\c0w32.obj+
grafmenu.obj+cls_mark.obj
grafmenu,grafmenu
\bc4\lib\bidsfi.lib+
\bc4\lib\owlwfi.lib+
\bc4\lib\import32.lib+
\bc4\lib\cw32i.lib
grafmenu.def
```

As with the other programs you've encountered up to now, this program has two objects: an application object and a window object. We pretty much use the OWL application object as is. It performs all the required initialization, and manages our message loop.

As expected, the window object's constructor initializes the window object's various data members. First of all, the marker size—**`cxyMarkerSize`**—is set to 1/4 the size of an icon. The **`GetSysColor`** routine is called to ask for the current default colors, then the pens and brushes that will be needed for the menu are created. As always, these GDI objects get cleaned up in the destructor.

In response to the **`WM_CREATE`** message—that is, in **`DFrame::SetupWindow`**—GRAFMENU creates an OWL **`TMenu`** wrapper around the submenu that will contain the three owner-draw items. You won't be able to attach a menu to a window in the window object's constructor, since the MS-Windows window doesn't exist yet. Instead, like GRAFMENU, you'll need to rely on the `WM_CREATE` message to initialize an owner-draw menu item. In fact, the same holds true for any object that you wish to attach to a window.

Once the measurement information has been provided, our window procedure starts to receive **`WM_DRAWITEM`** messages. Since we're not interested in grayed or disabled items, GRAFMENU doesn't check for these flags. We also don't check whether or not the item should display a checkmark. If we wanted a checkmark, we would have to draw it ourselves in response to the **WM_DRAWITEM** message. That is to say, if we are going to draw *part* of a menu item, we must draw the *entire* menu item.

Keyboard mnemonics are not supported in owner-draw menu items. In general, this makes sense, since a graphic image can hardly be expected to have an associated keyboard keystroke. However, if you *did* have text within your graphic image, there is a way for you to make this available to users as a mnemonic. You start by underlining the specific mnemonic letter. Then, in response to the **WM_MENUCHAR** message, you check for the mnemonic letters and indicate either an error or a menu selection in the return value. The **WM_MENUCHAR** message is sent when the user strikes a keystroke that doesn't correspond to any mnemonic or accelerator key. When the default window procedure receives this message, it provides a return value that tells the menu system to beep at the user. But processing this message yourself would allow you to provide the necessary return value so that the menu system would handle the keystroke as a regular mnemonic.

The use of owner-draw items gives a program the greatest control and flexibility in the appearance of menu items. From one moment to the next, a menu item may change in response to some outside event. It requires a bit of work, but the results are well worth it. You should be aware that Windows supports another method for putting graphics into a menu: using GDI bitmaps. This is an older method that doesn't produce very attractive results. In particular, when an item is selected, the correct colors are not selected. I suggest you stick with owner-draw menu items for placing any graphic object within a menu.

The one possible exception involves checkmarks. Every display driver comes with its own built-in checkmark bitmaps. As you'll see in the next section, it's quite easy to replace the default checkmarks with your own checkmark bitmaps. This solution still suffers from the problem that the checkmark doesn't change to the right color when an item is selected, but it's a relatively minor problem. If you're really interested in pixel-perfect custom checkmarks, consider drawing them within the context of an owner draw menu item.

Creating Custom Menu Checkmarks

In the last chapter, we mentioned that checkmarks provide one type of visual clue in menus. Although the standard checkmark is useful in many situations, you may want to use a different symbol in your menus. You can call GDI routines to create your own custom checkmarks and install them into menus. When you do this, the menu system lets you attach *two* different bitmaps to every menu item. One bitmap is displayed when the menu item is in a *checked* state; the other is for the *unchecked* state.

Creating a checkmark bitmap starts with the creation of a regular GDI bitmap. In OWL terms, you create a **TBitmap**, and a **TMemoryDC**. By itself, the bitmap is a drawing surface disconnected from GDI. As with any drawing surface—the display screen or a printer, for example—it must be connected to a DC to be useful. A call to **TDC::SelectObject** creates the required connection. From there, you use GDI routines to draw whatever figure you wish to use to reflect the checked and unchecked states. You have to be careful, though, because your drawing has to be small enough to fit in the space that the menu system has set aside for checkmarks.

To determine the proper size to use, you call **GetMenuCheckMarkDimensions**. This routine takes no parameters, but returns a **DWORD** (unsigned long) value into which is packed the required dimensions of a checkmark bitmap. Here is how to extract the dimension information from the return value:

```
DWORD dwCheck;
int cxWidth, cyHeight;

dwCheck  = GetMenuCheckMarkDimension();
cxWidth  = LOWORD (dwCheck);
cyHeight = HIWORD (dwCheck);
```

Using the size information provided by this routine, you can create a pair of bitmaps, draw checked and unchecked images that you wish to use, and attach the bitmaps to specific menu items. Since bitmaps are shared GDI objects, you can create a single pair of checkmark bitmaps and use them in many different menu items. To attach a bitmap to a menu item, you call the **SetMenuItemBitmaps** routine, which is defined:

```
BOOL SetMenuItemBitmaps (hMenu, nPosition, wFlags,
                         hbmUnchecked, hbmChecked)
```

- **hMenu** is a menu handle.
- **nPosition** identifies the menu item to which the pair of bitmaps are to be attached. If the next parameter, wFlags, is **MF_BYCOMMAND**, then **nPosition** is a command result code. If it is **MF_BYPOSITION**, **nPosition** is the relative position of the menu item in the menu identified by **hMenu**.
- **wFlags** is either **MF_BYCOMMAND** or **MF_BYPOSITION**.
- **hbmUnchecked** is a handle of a GDI bitmap to be displayed when the menu is not checked.
- **hbmChecked** is a handle of a GDI bitmap to be displayed when the menu item is checked.

Once the checkmark bitmaps are attached to a menu item, they are used automatically without requiring any additional effort from your program. All you need to do at this point is call **CheckMenuItem** to set the checked state to either **MF_CHECKED** or **MF_UNCHECKED**.

If, at any time, you wish to remove a custom checkmark, you call **SetMenuItemBitmaps** with a NULL value in the bitmap handle parameter corresponding to the bitmap that you wish to have removed. Figure 12.2 shows the menu with the custom checkmark.

Although the menu system lets you connect *two* different checkmark bitmaps to a menu, CHEKMENU only creates one for checked menu items. For the unchecked state, the default bitmap is used. This particular set of menu items was inspired by Microsoft's Word

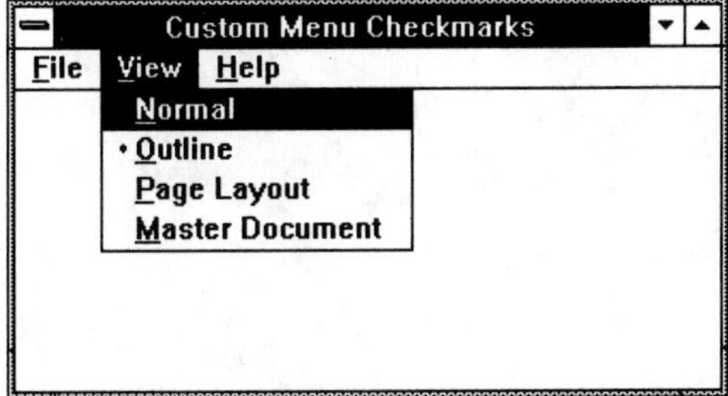

Figure 12.2 Custom menu checkmark created by CHECKMENU

for Windows (version 6.0). The tiny round checkmark suggests that these menu items are treated more like radio buttons than like check boxes: Only one document view state is ever selected at any time. Here are the source files to CHEKMENU:

CHEKMENU.CPP

```
//
// CHEKMENU.CPP  Shows the creation of custom menu checkmarks.
//
//
#include <owl\owlpch.h>
#include "chekmenu.h"

DEFINE_RESPONSE_TABLE1 (DFrame, TFrameWindow)
  EV_WM_INITMENU,
  EV_COMMAND(CM_FILE_EXIT, CmFileExit),
  EV_COMMAND(CM_VW_NORMAL,  CmViewNormal),
  EV_COMMAND(CM_VW_OUTLINE, CmViewOutline),
  EV_COMMAND(CM_VW_LAYOUT,  CmViewLayout),
  EV_COMMAND(CM_VW_MASTER,  CmViewMaster),
  EV_COMMAND(CM_HELP_ABOUT, CmHelpAbout),
END_RESPONSE_TABLE;

DFrame::DFrame(char * title) : TFrameWindow(0, title)
    {
    // Set initial "current view."
    CurView = CM_VW_NORMAL;

    // Fetch checkmark info.
    TSize sizCheck;
    TMenu::GetMenuCheckMarkDimensions (sizCheck);

    // Borrow display DC.
    TScreenDC dcScr;

    // Create a bitmap of correct size.
    tbmCheck = new TBitmap (dcScr, sizCheck.cx, sizCheck.cy, FALSE);

    // Create DC and connect to bitmap.
    TMemoryDC dc(dcScr);
    dc.SelectObject (*tbmCheck);
```

```
    // Get desired colors.
    TColor tcrBackground = GetSysColor(COLOR_MENU);
    TColor tcrForeground = GetSysColor(COLOR_MENUTEXT);

    // Erase bitmap background.
    dc.TextRect(0, 0, sizCheck.cx, sizCheck.cy, tcrBackground);

    // Calculate location of checkmark.
    TPoint pt;
    pt.x = (6 * sizCheck.cx) / 10;
    pt.y = (3 * sizCheck.cy) / 10;

    // Calculate checkmark size.
    TEXTMETRIC tm;
    dc.GetTextMetrics(tm);
    int cyHeight = tm.tmDescent;
    int cxWidth  = tm.tmDescent - 1;

    // Draw "selected" radio button.
    for (int y = pt.y; y <= pt.y + cyHeight; y++)
        {
        for (int x = pt.x; x <= pt.x + cxWidth; x++)
            dc.SetPixel(x, y, tcrForeground);
        }

    // Finish bitmap by zapping four corners to round them off.
    dc.SetPixel(pt.x,         pt.y,          tcrBackground);
    dc.SetPixel(pt.x,         pt.y+cyHeight, tcrBackground);
    dc.SetPixel(pt.x+cxWidth, pt.y,          tcrBackground);
    dc.SetPixel(pt.x+cxWidth, pt.y+cyHeight, tcrBackground);

    }

DFrame::~DFrame()
    {
    // Important!  Always destroy your GDI objects.
    delete tbmCheck;
    }

void DFrame::CmFileExit()
    {
    MessageBox ("File.Exit Selected", Title);
    CloseWindow(0); // Cause application to terminate
    }
void DFrame::CmViewNormal()
    {
    MessageBox ("View.Normal Selected", Title);
    CurView = CM_VW_NORMAL;
    }
void DFrame::CmViewOutline()
    {
    MessageBox ("View.Outline Selected", Title);
    CurView = CM_VW_OUTLINE;
    }
void DFrame::CmViewLayout()
    {
    MessageBox ("View.Page Layout Selected", Title);
    CurView = CM_VW_LAYOUT;
    }
void DFrame::CmViewMaster()
    {
```

```
        MessageBox ("View.Master Document Selected", Title);
        CurView = CM_VW_MASTER;
        }

    void DFrame::CmHelpAbout()
        {
        MessageBox("   Custom Menu Checkmarks\n\n"
                   "'Borland C++ 4.0 Programming\n"
                   "  for Windows', by Paul Yao", Title);
        }

    void DFrame::EvInitMenu(HMENU hmenu)
        {
        MenuCheckMark (hmenu, CM_VW_NORMAL , (CurView==CM_VW_NORMAL ));
        MenuCheckMark (hmenu, CM_VW_OUTLINE, (CurView==CM_VW_OUTLINE));
        MenuCheckMark (hmenu, CM_VW_LAYOUT , (CurView==CM_VW_LAYOUT ));
        MenuCheckMark (hmenu, CM_VW_MASTER , (CurView==CM_VW_MASTER ));
        }

    void DFrame::SetupWindow()
        {
        TFrameWindow::SetupWindow();

        HMENU hmenu = GetMenu();
        if (!hmenu)
            ::MessageBox (HWindow, "Aaarrrgghhh -- No Menu", "Test", MB_OK);

        ::SetMenuItemBitmaps(hmenu, CM_VW_NORMAL , MF_BYCOMMAND, NULL,
HBITMAP(*tbmCheck));
        ::SetMenuItemBitmaps(hmenu, CM_VW_OUTLINE, MF_BYCOMMAND, NULL,
HBITMAP(*tbmCheck));
        ::SetMenuItemBitmaps(hmenu, CM_VW_LAYOUT , MF_BYCOMMAND, NULL,
HBITMAP(*tbmCheck));
        ::SetMenuItemBitmaps(hmenu, CM_VW_MASTER , MF_BYCOMMAND, NULL,
HBITMAP(*tbmCheck));
        }

    void DFrame::MenuCheckMark(HMENU menu, int id, BOOL bCheck)
        {
        WORD wState;
        wState = (bCheck) ? MF_CHECKED : MF_UNCHECKED;
        ::CheckMenuItem (menu, id, wState);
        }

    DApp::DApp() : TApplication()
        {
        }

    void DApp::InitMainWindow()
        {
        SetMainWindow (new DFrame("Custom Menu Checkmarks"));
        MainWindow->AssignMenu("MAIN");
        MainWindow->SetIcon(this, "SNAPSHOT");
        }

    //
    // Application main entry point.
    OwlMain(int, char **)
        {
        return DApp().Run();
        }
```

CHEKMENU.H

```
#define CM_FILE_EXIT      100

#define CM_VW_NORMAL    200
#define CM_VW_OUTLINE   201
#define CM_VW_LAYOUT    202
#define CM_VW_MASTER    203

#define CM_HELP_ABOUT     300

// Main window
class DFrame : public TFrameWindow
    {
  public:
    DFrame(char * title);
    ~DFrame();
    void CmFileExit();
    void CmViewNormal();
    void CmViewOutline();
    void CmViewLayout();
    void CmViewMaster();
    void CmHelpAbout();
    void EvInitMenu(HMENU hmenu);
    void SetupWindow();
    void MenuCheckMark(HMENU menu, int id, BOOL bCheck);
  private:
    TBitmap  * tbmCheck;
    UINT       CurView;

  DECLARE_RESPONSE_TABLE (DFrame);
    };

// Application object
class DApp : public TApplication
    {
  public:
    DApp();
    void InitMainWindow();
    };
```

CHEKMENU.RC

```
#include "chekmenu.h"

snapshot icon chekmenu.ico

main menu
    BEGIN
    POPUP "&File"
        {
        MENUITEM "E&xit",        CM_FILE_EXIT
        }
    POPUP "&View"
        {
        MENUITEM "&Normal",           CM_VW_NORMAL
        MENUITEM "&Outline",          CM_VW_OUTLINE
        MENUITEM "&Page Layout",      CM_VW_LAYOUT
        MENUITEM "&Master Document",  CM_VW_MASTER
```

```
        }
    POPUP "&Help"
        {
        MENUITEM "&About...", CM_HELP_ABOUT
        }
    END
```

CHEKMENU.DEF

```
EXETYPE WINDOWS

CODE MOVEABLE DISCARDABLE
DATA MULTIPLE MOVEABLE

HEAPSIZE   512
STACKSIZE 8192
```

DYNA16.MAK

```
#  MAKE file for Win16 API using dynamic BIDS,
#  OWL and C-runtime libraries.
#
#    C> make -fstatic16.mak
#

.AUTODEPEND
CC = -c -H -H"owl\owlpch.h" -ml -R -vi -WS -X-
CD = -D_RTLDLL;_BIDSDLL;_OWLDLL;_OWLPCH;
INC = -I\BC4\INCLUDE
LIB = -L\BC4\LIB

chekmenu.exe :  chekmenu.obj chekmenu.res
  tlink -c -C -Twe $(LIB) @dyna16.lnk
  brc chekmenu.res chekmenu.exe

chekmenu.obj :  chekmenu.cpp
  bcc $(CC) $(CD) chekmenu.cpp

chekmenu.res :  chekmenu.rc chekmenu.ico chekmenu.h
  brc $(INC) -31 -R chekmenu.rc
```

DYNA16.LNK

```
\bc4\lib\c0wl.obj+
chekmenu.obj
chekmenu,chekmenu
\bc4\lib\bidsi.lib+
\bc4\lib\owlwi.lib+
\bc4\lib\import.lib+
\bc4\lib\crtldll.lib
chekmenu.def
```

DYNA32.MAK

```
#  MAKE file for Win32 API using dynamic BIDS,
#  OWL and C-runtime libraries.
#
#     C> make -fdyna32.mak
#

.AUTODEPEND
CC = -c -H -H\""owl\owlpch.h\"" -p- -R -vi -W -X-
CD = -D_RTLDLL;_BIDSDLL;_OWLDLL;_OWLPCH;
INC = -I\BC4\INCLUDE
LIB = -L\BC4\LIB

chekmenu.exe :  chekmenu.obj chekmenu.res
  tlink32 -aa -c -Tpe $(LIB) @dyna32.lnk
  brc32 chekmenu.res chekmenu.exe

chekmenu.obj :  chekmenu.cpp
  bcc32 $(CC) $(CD) chekmenu.cpp

chekmenu.res :  chekmenu.rc chekmenu.ico chekmenu.h
  brc32 $(INC) -w32 -R chekmenu.rc
```

DYNA32.LNK

```
\bc4\lib\c0w32.obj+
chekmenu.obj
chekmenu,chekmenu
\bc4\lib\bidsfi.lib+
\bc4\lib\owlwfi.lib+
\bc4\lib\import32.lib+
\bc4\lib\cw32i.lib
chekmenu.def
```

CHEKMENU combines menu functionality into the window object. As with the other programs in this chapter, this was done to focus on the Windows API considerations rather than to demonstrate object-oriented design principles.

The initialization and creation of checkmarks in the menu was divided into two parts: in the window object constructor, the checked bitmap was created. In response to **`WM_CREATE`**—that is, during **`DFrame::SetupWindow`**—the bitmap was attached to each of the four menu items. Once connected to the menu system, our custom checkmark gets displayed when a menu item is "checked." Checking and unchecking menu items is performed by the **`CheckMenuItem`** WinAPI function, which in this program is wrapped within the **`DFrame::MenuCheckMark`** function.

The use of graphic menus can make your program easier to use by providing clearly defined visual clues to your users. There are some other refinements that you can make to the menu system, however. One of them is the subject of the next section.

Enabling Accelerators in the Menu System

From a user's perspective, a program's menus and its accelerators seem tightly integrated: Accelerator keystroke equivalents often appear within the text of a menu, and both represent ways for commands to get entered. From the perspective of the Windows API—and of a Windows program—the two are quite distinct. This is mostly an accident of history, since accelerators were added fairly late in the development cycle to support MS-DOS program developers that relied heavily on keyboard input.

Whatever the reason, the two are separate. Although it's not very difficult, it does take some effort to make sure that menus and accelerators are in synch with each other. For example, you must make sure that menu identifiers match the accelerator command IDs—the Edit.Cut menu item should have the same ID as its keyboard equivalent, [Ctrl]+X, or you've got a bug.

In one subtle way, however, the Windows system puts them at odds with each other. From a user's perspective, an accelerator key isn't enabled when a menu is visible. For example, when a user summons the Edit menu, the accelerator key equivalents are clearly printed on the menu: to cut, type [Ctrl]+X, to copy type [Ctrl]+C, etc. *But if the user decides to strike these keys while the menu is visible, the keys don't work—the system beeps at the user!*

The following program shows one way to remove this rough edge from your Windows application[1]. This program, which is based on the KEYCMD program in the last chapter, is named KEYCMD2. Here are the source files to KEYCMD2:

KEYCMD2.CPP

```
//
// KEYCMD2.CPP    Enhancement to KEYCMD from Chapter 11. Uses
//                a hook to make accelerators operational when
//                menu is visible. Subtle but useful improvement
//                to Windows User Interface.
//
#include <owl\owlpch.h>
#include "keycmd2.h"

DApp * DApplication;

DEFINE_RESPONSE_TABLE1 (DFrame, TFrameWindow)
  EV_COMMAND(CM_FILE_NEW,   CmFileNew),
  EV_COMMAND(CM_FILE_OPEN, CmFileOpen),
  EV_COMMAND(CM_FILE_SAVE, CmFileSave),
  EV_COMMAND(CM_FILE_SAVEAS, CmFileSaveAs),
  EV_COMMAND(CM_FILE_PRINT, CmFilePrint),
```

[1] In an environment as rich and complex as Windows, there are usually several ways to accomplish any given task. An alternative to the method shown here, for example, involves responding to the **WM_MENUCHAR** message.

```
  EV_COMMAND(CM_FILE_EXIT, CmFileExit),
  EV_COMMAND(CM_EDIT_UNDO, CmEditUndo),
  EV_COMMAND(CM_EDIT_CUT,  CmEditCut),
  EV_COMMAND(CM_EDIT_COPY, CmEditCopy),
  EV_COMMAND(CM_EDIT_PASTE, CmEditPaste),
  EV_COMMAND(CM_EDIT_CLEAR, CmEditClear),
  EV_COMMAND(CM_EDIT_DELETE, CmEditDelete),
  EV_COMMAND(CM_HELP_ABOUT, CmHelpAbout),
END_RESPONSE_TABLE;

DFrame::DFrame(char * title) : TFrameWindow(0, title)
    {
    Attr.AccelTable = TResId("main");
    }

void DFrame::CmFileNew()
    {
    MessageBox ("File.New Selected", Title);
    }
void DFrame::CmFileOpen()
    {
    MessageBox ("File.Open... Selected", Title);
    }
void DFrame::CmFileSave()
    {
    MessageBox ("File.Save Selected", Title);
    }
void DFrame::CmFileSaveAs()
    {
    MessageBox ("File.Save As... Selected", Title);
    }
void DFrame::CmFilePrint()
    {
    MessageBox ("File.Print Selected", Title);
    }
void DFrame::CmFileExit()
    {
    MessageBox ("File.Exit Selected", Title);
    CloseWindow(0); // Cause application to terminate
    }
void DFrame::CmEditUndo()
    {
    MessageBox ("Edit.Undo Selected", Title);
    }
void DFrame::CmEditCut()
    {
    MessageBox ("Edit.Cut Selected", Title);
    }
void DFrame::CmEditCopy()
    {
    MessageBox ("Edit.Copy Selected", Title);
    }
void DFrame::CmEditPaste()
    {
    MessageBox ("Edit.Paste Selected", Title);
    }
void DFrame::CmEditClear()
    {
    MessageBox ("Edit.Clear Selected", Title);
    }
void DFrame::CmEditDelete()
    {
```

```
    MessageBox ("Edit.Delete Selected", Title);
    }

void DFrame::CmHelpAbout()
    {
    MessageBox("        Global Accelerators\n\n"
               "'Borland C++ 4.0 Programming\n"
               "  for Windows', by Paul Yao", Title);
    }

HACCEL DFrame::GetAccel()
    {
    return hAccel;
    }

DApp::DApp() : TApplication()
    {
    // Save for use by hook function.
    DApplication = this;

    // Install hook.
    hhMsgFilter =
        SetWindowsHookEx (WH_MSGFILTER,  // Menu hook.
                          MsgHook,       // Hook function.
                          GetInstance(), // Who owns.
    #if defined (__WIN32__)
                          GetCurrentThreadId()); // Our Win32 thread.
    #else
                          GetCurrentTask());     // Our Win16 task.
    #endif
    }

DApp::~DApp()
    {
    // Remove hook.
    UnhookWindowsHookEx (hhMsgFilter);
    }

void DApp::InitMainWindow()
    {
    SetMainWindow (new DFrame("Global Accelerators"));
    MainWindow->AssignMenu("MAIN");
    MainWindow->SetIcon(this, "SNAPSHOT");
    }

void DApp::InitInstance()
    {
    TApplication::InitInstance();
    hwndMain  = HWND(*MainWindow);
    hAppAccel = ((DFrame *)MainWindow)->GetAccel();
    }


//
// Application main entry point.
OwlMain(int, char **)
    {
    return DApp().Run();
    }
```

KEYCMD2.H

```
#define CM_FILE_NEW    100
#define CM_FILE_OPEN   101
#define CM_FILE_SAVE   102
#define CM_FILE_SAVEAS 103
#define CM_FILE_PRINT  104
#define CM_FILE_EXIT   105

#define CM_EDIT_UNDO   200
#define CM_EDIT_CUT    201
#define CM_EDIT_COPY   202
#define CM_EDIT_PASTE  203
#define CM_EDIT_CLEAR  204
#define CM_EDIT_DELETE 205

#define CM_HELP_ABOUT   300

// Prototype for hook function.
LRESULT CALLBACK MsgHook(int nCode, WPARAM wParam, LPARAM lParam);

//
// Main window
class DFrame : public TFrameWindow
    {
  public:
    DFrame(char * title);
    void   CmFileNew();
    void   CmFileOpen();
    void   CmFileSave();
    void   CmFileSaveAs();
    void   CmFilePrint();
    void   CmFileExit();
    void   CmEditUndo();
    void   CmEditCut();
    void   CmEditCopy();
    void   CmEditPaste();
    void   CmEditClear();
    void   CmEditDelete();
    void   CmHelpAbout();
    HACCEL GetAccel();

  DECLARE_RESPONSE_TABLE (DFrame);
    };

//
// Application object
class DApp : public TApplication
    {
  public:
    DApp();
    ~DApp();
    void InitMainWindow();
    void InitInstance();

    HACCEL hAppAccel;
    HHOOK hhMsgFilter;
    HWND  hwndMain;
    };

typedef DApp FAR * LPDAPP;
```

MSGHOOK.CPP

```
#include <owl\owlpch.h>
//#include <owl\module.h>
#include "keycmd2.h"

extern DApp * DApplication;

LRESULT CALLBACK MsgHook(int nCode, WPARAM wParam, LPARAM lParam)
    {
    HACCEL haccel;
    HWND   hwnd;
    LPMSG lpmsg = (LPMSG)lParam;

    // Check for accelerator.
    haccel = DApplication->hAppAccel;
    hwnd   = DApplication->hwndMain;

    if (nCode == MSGF_MENU &&
        TranslateAccelerator (hwnd, haccel, lpmsg) )
        {
        // Since it's one of our accelerator keys, dismiss
        // menus by pumping <Esc> keys into msg queue.
        PostMessage (lpmsg->hwnd, WM_KEYDOWN, VK_ESCAPE, 0L);
        PostMessage (lpmsg->hwnd, WM_KEYDOWN, VK_ESCAPE, 0L);

        // Put key back into queue.
        PostMessage (lpmsg->hwnd,   lpmsg->message,
                     lpmsg->wParam, lpmsg->lParam);

        return (LRESULT)TRUE;   // Say "we stole message".
        }

    // Say "we ignore message".
    return CallNextHookEx (DApplication->hhMsgFilter, nCode,
                           wParam, lParam);
    }
```

KEYCMD2.RC

```
#include "keycmd2.h"

snapshot icon keycmd2.ico

main menu
    BEGIN
    POPUP "&File"
        {
        MENUITEM "&New",        CM_FILE_NEW
        MENUITEM "&Open...",    CM_FILE_OPEN
        MENUITEM "&Save",       CM_FILE_SAVE
        MENUITEM "Save &As...", CM_FILE_SAVEAS
        MENUITEM SEPARATOR
        MENUITEM "&Print",      CM_FILE_PRINT
        MENUITEM SEPARATOR
        MENUITEM "E&xit",       CM_FILE_EXIT
        }
    POPUP "&Edit"
        {
```

```
        MENUITEM "&Undo\tCtrl+Z",  CM_EDIT_UNDO
        MENUITEM SEPARATOR
        MENUITEM "Cu&t\tCtrl+X",   CM_EDIT_CUT
        MENUITEM "&Copy\tCtrl+C",  CM_EDIT_COPY
        MENUITEM "&Paste\tCtrl+V", CM_EDIT_PASTE
        MENUITEM SEPARATOR
        MENUITEM "Cl&ear",         CM_EDIT_CLEAR
        MENUITEM "&Delete",        CM_EDIT_DELETE
        }
    POPUP "&Help"
        {
        MENUITEM "&About...", CM_HELP_ABOUT
        }
    END

main ACCELERATORS
    {
    ; Windows 3.1 Edit menu accelerators.
    "Z",      CM_EDIT_UNDO,   VIRTKEY, CONTROL
    "X",      CM_EDIT_CUT,    VIRTKEY, CONTROL
    "C",      CM_EDIT_COPY,   VIRTKEY, CONTROL
    "V",      CM_EDIT_PASTE,  VIRTKEY, CONTROL

    ; Old-style Edit menu accelerators.
    VK_BACK,   CM_EDIT_UNDO,  VIRTKEY, ALT
    VK_DELETE, CM_EDIT_CUT,   VIRTKEY, SHIFT
    VK_INSERT, CM_EDIT_COPY,  VIRTKEY, CONTROL
    VK_INSERT, CM_EDIT_PASTE, VIRTKEY, SHIFT
    }
```

KEYCMD2.DEF

```
EXETYPE WINDOWS

CODE MOVEABLE DISCARDABLE
DATA MULTIPLE MOVEABLE

HEAPSIZE   512
STACKSIZE 8192
```

DYNA16.MAK

```
#  MAKE file for Win16 API using dynamic BIDS,
#  OWL and C-runtime libraries.
#
#    C> make -fstatic16.mak
#

.AUTODEPEND
CC = -c -H -H"owl\owlpch.h" -ml -R -vi -WS -X-
CD = -D_RTLDLL;_BIDSDLL;_OWLDLL;_OWLPCH;
INC = -I\BC4\INCLUDE
LIB = -L\BC4\LIB

keycmd2.exe :  keycmd2.obj msghook.obj keycmd2.res
  tlink -c -C -Twe $(LIB) @dyna16.lnk
```

```
  brc keycmd2.res keycmd2.exe

keycmd2.obj :  keycmd2.cpp
  bcc $(CC) $(CD) keycmd2.cpp

msghook.obj :  msghook.cpp
  bcc $(CC) $(CD) msghook.cpp

keycmd2.res :  keycmd2.rc keycmd2.ico keycmd2.h
  brc $(INC) -31 -R keycmd2.rc
```

DYNA16.LNK

```
\bc4\lib\c0wl.obj+
keycmd2.obj+msghook.obj
keycmd2,keycmd2
\bc4\lib\bidsi.lib+
\bc4\lib\owlwi.lib+
\bc4\lib\import.lib+
\bc4\lib\crtldll.lib
keycmd2.def
```

DYNA32.MAK

```
#  MAKE file for Win32 API using dynamic BIDS,
#  OWL and C-runtime libraries.
#
#    C> make -fdyna32.mak
#

.AUTODEPEND
CC = -c -H -H\""owl\owlpch.h\"" -p- -R -vi -W -X-
CD = -D_RTLDLL;_BIDSDLL;_OWLDLL;_OWLPCH;
INC = -I\BC4\INCLUDE
LIB = -L\BC4\LIB

keycmd2.exe :  keycmd2.obj msghook.obj keycmd2.res
  tlink32 -aa -c -Tpe $(LIB) @dyna32.lnk
  brc32 keycmd2.res keycmd2.exe

keycmd2.obj :  keycmd2.cpp
  bcc32 $(CC) $(CD) keycmd2.cpp

msghook.obj :  msghook.cpp
  bcc32 $(CC) $(CD) msghook.cpp

keycmd2.res :  keycmd2.rc keycmd2.ico keycmd2.h
  brc32 $(INC) -w32 -R keycmd2.rc
```

DYNA32.LNK

```
\bc4\lib\c0w32.obj+
keycmd2.obj+msghook.obj
keycmd2,keycmd2
\bc4\lib\bidsfi.lib+
\bc4\lib\owlwfi.lib+
\bc4\lib\import32.lib+
\bc4\lib\cw32i.lib
keycmd2.def
```

KEYCMD2 accepts an accelerator key even when a menu is visible thanks to a Windows hook that gets called when a menu is visible. Before getting into the specific operation of KEYCMD2's message hook, I'm going to start by describing the role of **Windows hooks** in general.

As discussed in Chapter 4, a Windows program calls **GetMessage**[2] to receive input and to receive queued messages. In addition, many user-interface messages are not queued but delivered directly to a window procedure. In both cases, if you write the code for the message handling, you can do what you want with a message.

Sometimes, however, you need to intercept a message intended for someone else and that's where hooks are useful. A hook is a callback function that receives a message before the intended recipient. In some cases, hooks can swallow a message so the original recipient never sees it. In other cases, the hook can learn about a message but not do anything to change it.

There are 12 different kinds of hooks defined in the WinAPI, as listed in this table:

Hook Type	*Description*
WH_CALLWNDPROC	Called when a window procedure is about to be delivered a nonqueued message.
WH_CBT	The Computer Based Training (CBT) hook gets notification when a window is activated, created, destroyed, minimized, maximized, gets the focus, or gets a system command message.
WH_DEBUG	Called before all other hooks in the system, this hook will help debug hook code.
WH_GETMESSAGE	Called right before a queued message is retrieved by **GetMessage** / **PeekMessage**.
WH_HARDWARE	A hook for nonstandard hardware devices.
WH_JOURNALPLAYBACK	Plays prerecorded mouse and keyboard events.

[2] OWL programs call **PeekMessage**, a close cousin of **GetMessage**. For our purposes, the two functions behave identically.

Hook Type	*Description*
WH_JOURNALRECORD	Records mouse and keyboard events for later playback.
WH_KEYBOARD	For notification about keyboard input.
WH_MOUSE	For notification about mouse input.
WH_MSGFILTER	For notification from the message loop of menus and dialogs.
WH_SHELL	Notification about creation and destruction of top-level application windows.
WH_SYSMSGFILTER	For systemwide notifications from the message loop of menus and dialogs.

The **WH_CALLWNDPROC** and **WH_GETMESSAGE** hooks used together allow you to intercept any message in the system. This is how Borland's WinSight utility is able to eavesdrop on messages intended for any window in the system. Other hooks provide a subset of this information: **WH_MOUSE** and **WM_KEYBOARD**, for example, are the subset of queued messages that pertain to mouse and keyboard input. A good use for a keyboard hook is to detect the [F1] key in support of context-sensitive help. For details on individual hooks, refer to the **SetWindowsHookEx** function in the Win16/Win32 help database.

KEYCMD2 uses a **WH_MSGFILTER** hook. Even though a Windows program has its own message loop, when the system displays a menu or a modal dialog box, it provides its own message loop. In most cases, you'll never notice the difference. But since accelerator support requires that a message loop call WinAPI's **TranslateAccelerator** function, accelerators are disabled. Deep within the menu system—and in the dialog manager as well—there lurks a message loop like the following:

```
while (bContinue)
    {
    GetMessage (&msg, 0, 0, 0);
    if (! CallMsgFilter (&msg, nCode)
        {
        TranslateMessage(&msg);
        DispatchMessage(&msg);
    }
```

The WinAPI **CallMsgFilter** function calls the **WH_MSGFILTER** hook function and only processes the message if the hook function returns FALSE. Otherwise, the message gets swallowed up by the hook function.

The critical component of KEYCMD2 is **MsgHook()**, the **WH_MSGFILTER** Windows-hook function. This function gets called from the message loops in the menu system and in the dialog manager. The first parameter to this function, **nCode**, will be set to **MSGF_MENU** when the menu message loop is calling. When this is the case, the hook function calls the **TranslateAccelerator** function to see if the incoming message is an accelerator in our accelerator table. If not, the next hook in the hook chain gets called. If it *is* an accelerator, then three messages get put into our message queue: two that correspond to the [Esc] key being pushed, then the original accelerator keystroke. The first two messages cause the menu system to dismiss the current menu. The third message is required because accelerators are disabled when the menu system is active. Only by putting a message back into the message queue can we hope to see the result of the accelerator keystroke.

The other important part of this program is the installation and removal of the hook. Not surprisingly, these are done in the the application class constructor (**DApp**) and destructor (**~DApp**). Installation involves a call to **SetWindowsHookEx**, and removal involves the call to **UnhookWindowsHookEx**. This program also shows some of the differences between Win16 hooks and Win32 hooks—Win16 hooks accept a task handle where Win32 hooks expect a thread ID.

While the code in KEYCMD2 is simple, it's important to look for ways to refine your applications to make them easier to use. The current versions of Windows represent a good step forward in improved usability, but—as this program shows—there are still many tiny ways that a Windows program can improve on what the system provides.

Our next chapter returns to a subject first touched on in Chapter 2 when you first saw the minimum Windows program. The issue is windowing—the creation of WinAPI windows that make up an application's user-interface. While a program doesn't need to have more than one window, you'll find there are times when having more windows is indispensable for providing a good user interface. And even if you never create more than one window in your application, some of the Window Manager's special capabilities are hidden in the window creation process. Also, OWL provides some very useful capabilities in the form of new window classes. Let's roll up our sleeves and see what the Windows API and OWL have to offer in terms of windowing capabilities.

13

Windowing

The fundamental user-interface object—under Windows 3.1, Windows NT, and anticipated future versions of Windows—is the window. Since a major part of what these operating systems add is a standard user-interface, in some sense every chapter in this book relates to some aspect or other of windowing. This chapter addresses basic issues of windowing—what is a window, and when should a window be used?

After an overview of the Windows and OWL support for windowing, I'll delve into the WinAPI **`RegisterClass`** and **`CreateWindow`** routines. There are some interesting capabilities hidden by these two routines—particularly in each routine's **style field**. I'll review all of the parameters and the choices involved in using these routines, and show how to access these capabilities under OWL.

This chapter has two sample programs: OWNSIZE and GADGETS. OWNSIZE shows how to create a top-level window that sets the size of its main window instead of relying on the Window Manager to handle this chore. The second sample, GADGETS, shows how OWL's **`TGadgetWindow`** and related classes let you create control bars, status windows, etc.

Fundamentals

A window is like every other system object in Windows—the native WinAPI is wrapped in one or more OWL classes. One difference, however, is that half the OWL classes wrap around one type of window or another. Just as the window is the primary object under the native Windows API, then, it also holds the position of the primary object under OWL.

What Is a Window?

A window is a **virtual console** for communicating between a user and an application program. In this context, the term "virtual" means it's a technique for multiplexing some resource, just like virtual memory allows an operating system to multiplex physical RAM. Where a computer might have one *physical* console, windowing allows for the creation of ***multiple virtual consoles***. Just like a physical console—like the old style TTYs—there is an input side and an output side.

A window is an input port for mouse and keyboard operations. As you'll see in Chapters 15 and 16, mouse and keyboard input arrives in the form of messages. When working with multiple windows, only one is the **active window**—which means, only one will receive mouse and keyboard input. If other windows want input, they must wait for the user to activate them—perhaps with a mouse click or through the task list.

A window is also an output device, and it displays command choices, status information, and user data. By "command choices," I mean control bar buttons, scroll bars, and menus. Even though a menu is a separate user-interface object, once connected to a window it loses its identity and becomes part of the window. By "status information," I mean the caption, scroll bar positions, and other feedback provided by an application to a user. While not every application provides editing capability, by "user data" I mean user-supplied values that can be entered, changed, or saved.

From a user's perspective, a window normally has a caption bar and system menu. This includes dialog boxes as well as an application's "main" window. Thick (sizable) borders and scroll bars are common, as are the minimize and maximize buttons, but the savvy user knows these other elements are not part of every window.

To a programmer, the user's view is only partially correct. As actually implemented by Windows applications, main windows and dialog box windows are often used as containers for one or more *other* windows. For example, a dialog box window holds a set of smaller windows called **dialog box controls** (or just "controls"). And a main window might contain a control bar window or a status bar window. There are perhaps smaller windows hiding within larger, captioned windows.

The situation is not as clear-cut as it might seem, however. For example, in many Microsoft applications, push buttons are not WinAPI windows but bitmaps. And some of the gizmos drawn in a toolbar are not windows, but one of several items within a container window. You'll see how the OWL `TGadgetWindow` is a window, but the `TGadget` objects contained within are not windows. An important decision that Windows programmers must make, then, is when to use a WinAPI window and when not to.

When to Use a Window?

The question of what should be a window has no simple answer. Should every graphic unit be in its own window—for example, should every letter and every punctuation mark in a word processing program be a window? Or, should multiple objects be implemented together? There is no one right answer for everyone. Here are some things to consider to help you decide.

The overhead associated with a window is in the range of 50 to 100 bytes[1]. In memory use terms, it doesn't make sense to spend 100 bytes to store 1 character. If you look at a commercial application like a word processor or a spreadsheet, for example, you'll find that individual words and cells are *not* put in their own windows—instead whole documents and spreadsheets are the unit of windowing. You can prove this to yourself by running WinSight—included with Borland C++ 3.0 and later—which helps you detect what windows an application has created.

Another overhead issue involves the messaging associated with a window. Although faster processors and displays may someday make this a nonissue, the current crop of x386-based systems can get bogged down by the message traffic required to maintain a window. The classic example is the Program Manager in Windows version 3.0. In case that application isn't around on the version of Windows that's available when you read this, the Program Manager was the Windows 3.x program launcher.

In the Windows 3.x Program Manager, programs were organized into program groups. Under Windows 3.0, two windows were used for each program: one to display the program icon and one to display the program title. Ten groups with ten programs each required 200 windows. Not only did it consume a large part of the system's resources, but it ran slow because each window got a torrent of messages every time the user worked with the Program Manager. This was fixed in Windows version 3.1, where all the programs in a program group shared one window. In the newer version, only ten windows were needed to hold the 100 programs described above.

Another issue is a limit to the *total number of windows* that can be created in the system. Running on Windows 3.x, the 100 bytes per window cost is charged against a 64K data area[2]. This means that—if only windows are counted, and not other user-interface objects that use this same data area—there is a systemwide limit of only 640 windows. Based on this limit, my rules for the number of windows to create are:

Number of Windows	*Impact on System*
1 to 9	Great—plenty of room to run other applications.
10 to 49	Ok—doable, but still running heavy.
50 to 100	Huh?—You're chewing up more than 10% of this system's resources. Do you *really* need this many?

(continued)

---

[1] It's not my goal to explore the contents of a window, but to point out the scale of the overhead involved. It's not 1 byte per window, and it's not 1000 bytes per window—something between 50 and 100 bytes is about right, depending on the length of the title, window property information, extra bytes, etc.

[2] Since 12K is used for static data, the actual space left for window data is closer to 52K. For the sake of simplicity, however, I use 64K.

Number of Windows	*Impact on System*
100 +	Stop!—Your application might not even run in a low-memory situation.

What should you make a window within your application? Don't use a window to contain objects that are very tiny—words or spreadsheet cells, for example—because the overhead will be too high. On the other extreme, don't try putting all your application's graphical objects into a single window—that one window will be too complicated. Instead, balance the overhead of a window against the volume of data and the complexity with which users require for working with the data.

This discussion of when to use a window has focused on **data windows**—the places where data gets displayed and perhaps edited. In most cases, your data windows will reside in an application's main window or in a dialog box—what I call a **caption windows**, out of respect for the user's view that these have a caption bar. Let's take a look at what the Windows API provides for each type, and the enhancements provided by OWL.

Caption Windows

The term "caption window" means a window—either an application's main window or a dialog box—that has a caption bar. These are standalone windows that can be dismissed from a system menu, or perhaps with an Ok or Cancel button. They are sometimes sizable, but don't have to be. When a user summons the Task List by striking [Ctrl] + [Esc], a list of main windows shows up. When the user clicks on a menu item with an ellipsis (...), a dialog shows up.

For an application's main window, the Windows API provides **overlapped windows**. You create an overlapped window when the **`WS_OVERLAPPED`** bit gets set in the call to **`CreateWindow`** (something that will be covered in more detail shortly). An overlapped window always has a caption bar and a system menu. For dialog boxes, **popup windows** are provided. These can have caption bars and system menus—by convention, they always do—but the WinAPI doesn't require this. User-interface standards, however, make this a strongly suggested component. Incidentally, you can take a dialog box and make it an application's main window—something described in Chapter 14.

The OWL libraries take these two types of windows and rewrap them to provide the following six types of top-level, captioned windows:

OWL Class	*Description*
`TFrameWindow`	Basic container for holding an application—described in detail in Chapter 4.
`TDecoratedFrame`	A **`TFrameWindow`** with one or more embedded **`TGadgetWindow`** windows. This class provides control bars, status bars, and other **`TGadget`** gadget-filled windows. See the GADGETS example later in this chapter.

OWL Class	*Description*
TDecoratedMDIFrame	A **TMDIFrame** window that supports gadget windows.
TDialog	A dialog box window, covered in detail in Chapter 14.
TFloatingFrame	The same as a frame window, except it has a tiny caption bar (thanks to the **TTinyCaption** class). Some applications use this window type for tool collections.
TMDIFrame	A **TFrameWindow** derived class for use as a multiple document interface (MDI) frame window. This book doesn't have an example of this, but several are provided in the OWL compiler samples.

With the exception of **TDialog**, each of these classes are derived from **TFrameWindow**. All trace their class ancestry to **TWindow**, the base class that wraps the Windows API windows.

Data Windows

You can put user data into any type of WinAPI window. More complex applications, however, tend to focus overlapped and popup windows on tasks related to application management. The WinAPI window type for creating data windows is a **child window**, or more precisely a window created with the **WS_CHILD** style bit set in the call to **CreateWindow**. WinAPI child windows differ from popup and overlapped windows in that a child window *must* have a parent window—and the child window's pixels are always borrowed from its parents. This means, for example, that when a user tries to move a child window beyond the border of its parent window, the child window gets clipped—it's invisible—outside the boundary of its parent.

The OWL libraries provide the following wrapper classes built on WinAPI child windows:

OWL Class	*Description*
TControl	The base class for all the control classes that wrap around the **WS_CHILD** windows that make up dialog box controls. Described in more detail in Chapter 14.
TGadgetWindow	A **WS_CHILD** window for holding gadgets. There are several kinds of gadgets—bitmaps, buttons, text, separators, and controls. With the exception of control gadgets, these are not WinAPI windows.
TMDIChild	A document editing window in an MDI application.

Like the caption windows, all the data windows are derived from **TWindow**, and therefore you can use any of the many WinAPI windowing functions to manipulate them—

move them, show them, hide them, etc. You can also use a raw **TWindow** as the client window in a **TFrameWindow**, for situations when you don't need the extras provided by the other OWL classes.

These are the fundamentals of windowing with the Windows API and OWL. In the next two sections, I'm going to cover the two step process involved in creating a WinAPI window. While OWL handles much of this for you, nonetheless you'll want to know how it works so you can understand how to fine tune it for your own needs.

The Window Creation Process

In Chapter 2, we introduced the minimum Windows program. At the time, we said that window creation was a two-step process. We introduced you to the two routines that control the operation of each of those steps, **RegisterClass** and **CreateWindow**; but we refrained from going into more detail until now. As you'll see, the window creation process is quite involved and gives you quite a few choices over the shape, size, style, and behavior of a window. When I first described the window creation process, you probably suspected that I was holding out on you. OK. It's time to come clean with you. Let's start by looking at the first part of the window creation process, which revolves around a single data structure: the window class.

Window Classes

In the same way that a C++ class is a template to create instances of different objects, a window class is a template for creating windows. While a C++ class can have multiple member functions, a window class has only *one* function, called a window procedure. The structure of the OWL application framework lets you define a set of message response functions, to redirect the flow of window messages. Nonetheless, it's important for you to understand the way Windows itself is working for you.

Let's take a closer look at the window class registration process to understand what data members are associated with a window class. Here is how a non-OWL program would handle registering a window class:

```
WNDCLASS wc;

wc.lpszClassName = "MIN:MAIN";
wc.hInstance     = hInstance;
wc.lpfnWndProc   = MinWndProc;
wc.hCursor       = LoadCursor(hInstance, "hand");
wc.hIcon         = LoadIcon(hInstance,"snapshot");
wc.lpszMenuName  = NULL;
wc.hbrBackground = COLOR_WINDOW+1;
wc.style         = NULL;
wc.cbClsExtra    = 0;
wc.cbWndExtra    = 0;

RegisterClass( &wndclass);
```

The **lpszClassName** field defines an ASCII text string for the class name. Although in earlier versions of Windows there was a problem creating names that were identical with existing class names, in Windows 3.0 and later all window classes are **private classes** by default. A private window class is only accessible from a single program. This means that you can use any name you'd like and know that it won't interfere with the class names of other programs. Avoid the predefined dialog box classes to avoid interfering with dialog boxes: **button**, **combobox**, **edit**, **listbox**, **scroll bar**, and **static**. In addition, to avoid getting in the way of Windows' MDI support, don't create a class with the name **mdiclient**.

The **hInstance** field tells Windows which program created the window class. The primary reason has to do with internal housekeeping. After every instance of a program has terminated, Windows de-registers the classes that the program created.

The **lpfnWndProc** field identifies the function that will process messages for the windows in the class. A window procedure can support multiple windows because each window has a unique window handle. When a message is delivered to a window procedure, the window handle tells the window procedure exactly *which* window is sending the message. If you want to treat different windows in a different manner, you can look at the window handle to know who is calling.

The **hCursor** field is a handle to a cursor shared by all members of a window class. The default window procedure uses this to install the correct cursor whenever it receives a **WM_SETCURSOR** message. If you want a window to have a *private* cursor, different from the class cursor, you need to process this message. If you need further information, skip ahead to Chapter 16, which covers issues relating to the mouse, mouse message traffic, and custom cursors.

The **hIcon** field is a handle to an icon that is displayed when a window in the class is minimized. Not every kind of window will use its icon. Icons are only displayed for top-level windows (windows that have no parents) and document windows in programs that use MDI. The typical way for a program to define an icon handle is to load the icon, as shown here:

```
wc.hIcon  =  LoadIcon(hInstance,"snapshot");
```

A program can also draw an icon on the fly by defining a null icon:

```
wc.hIcon = NULL;
```

When the window is iconized, it appears as a tiny, empty window. Creating a drawing for the icon is surprisingly simple: You handle the **WM_PAINT** message just as you would when the window is *not* iconized. The only difference is that you need to be prepared to draw into a very tiny area.

A window created from a window class with a null icon has one issue to deal with. That issue involves the choice of icons to display when the user drags the iconic program. When the user drags a program that does have an icon, the mouse cursor changes to the shape of that icon. But when a program's window doesn't have an icon, it has two choices: It can let the system display a default icon, or it can provide one in response to the **WM_QUERYDRAGICON** message. Here, for example, is what a program without an icon might do when sent this message:

```
HANDLE DFrame::EvQueryDragIcon ()
    {
    return GetApplication()->LoadIcon("DRAGICON");
    }
```

A top-level window without an icon will see other message traffic that is different from that which is sent to windows that *do* have an icon. A top-level window without an icon will receive a **WM_PAINT** message when it's time to draw its iconized image. Top-level windows *with* icons receive a **WM_PAINTICON** message instead. The default window procedure responds to this message by displaying the icon for the window class. A program that had a class icon that wanted to draw a custom icon could respond to the **WM_PAINTICON** message and create an on-the-fly icon if it wanted to.

The **lpszMenuName** field identifies the class menu by name. This value can take one of three forms. For a menu resource defined like this:

```
15 MENU
    {
    POPUP "File"
        {
        MENUITEM "New", IDM_NEW
        ...
```

the menu name can be a character string preceded by a # sign:

```
wc.lpszMenuName   = "#15";
```

Alternatively, the **MAKEINTRESOURCE** macro can be used to sneak in an integer value in place of a long pointer to a string. Here is an example showing how the **MAKEINTRESOURCE** macro can be used:

```
wc.lpszMenuName   = MAKEINTRESOURCE(15);
```

A third choice, but a less attractive one because it consumes more memory and is slower, involves using a regular character string:

```
MyMenu MENU
    {
    POPUP "File"
        {
        MENUITEM "New", IDM_NEW
        .
        .
        .
```

To load this menu into memory, you provide the name of the menu in the **WNDCLASS** data structure, as shown here:

```
wc.lpszMenuName   = "MyMenu";
```

The disadvantage to this approach is that a string takes up more space than an integer. Also, an integer identifier allows faster loading than a string identifier since an integer compare is faster than a string compare. From the point of view of performance and memory use, integer values are better.

The **hbrBackground** field is a handle to a brush used to fill the background before any drawing is done. The default window procedure fills in the background in response to the **WM_ERASEBACKGROUND** message. This seems like a funny name for the message, since in fact the background is really *painted* and not erased. However, it *does* suggest the idea that whatever was in the window before is removed to provide a clean surface on which to draw. There are two types of values that can be placed in this field: a brush handle and an index to a system color. Here is how to use a stock black brush for the background:

```
wc.hbrBackground = GetStockObject (BLACK_BRUSH);
```

A better alternative, however, involves using a "magic number" for the background color, like this:

```
wc.hbrBackground = COLOR_WINDOW+1;
```

When the default window procedure sees this value, it uses the default window background color that the user has defined from the Control Panel.

The **cbClsExtra** field defines the number of bytes that are added at the end of the class definition as a reserved data area. These bytes are known as **class extra bytes**. This data area can be used by a program for any purpose, but Windows does not provide a pointer to the data area itself. Instead, you must set these values using the **SetClassWord** and **SetClassLong** routines, and retrieve them using the **GetClassWord** and **GetClassLong** routines. If you don't plan to use class extra bytes, be sure to initialize **cbClsExtra** to zero. If you don't explicitly initialize this field to zero, it is possible that some random, large value will be passed as the number of bytes to be allocated. Initializing to zero avoids an accidental waste of memory.

The **cbWndExtra** field, like the **cbClsExtra** field, defines a reserved data area for the private use of your application. These bytes are referred to as **window extra bytes**. Unlike class extra bytes, which are shared by every window in a class, window extra bytes are reserved for the private use of each individual window. They provide a way for a window to have its own "bank account" for bytes that it wishes to use—like having a Swiss bank account. To read the value of the window extra bytes, a program calls either **GetWindowWord** or **GetWindowLong**. These routines take a window handle as a parameter to identify exactly whose bytes are to be accessed. To write values into the window extra bytes, a program must call the **SetWindowWord** or **SetWindowLong** routines. These routines also take a window handle, which lets the Window Manager know into whose bank account you wish to make a deposit.

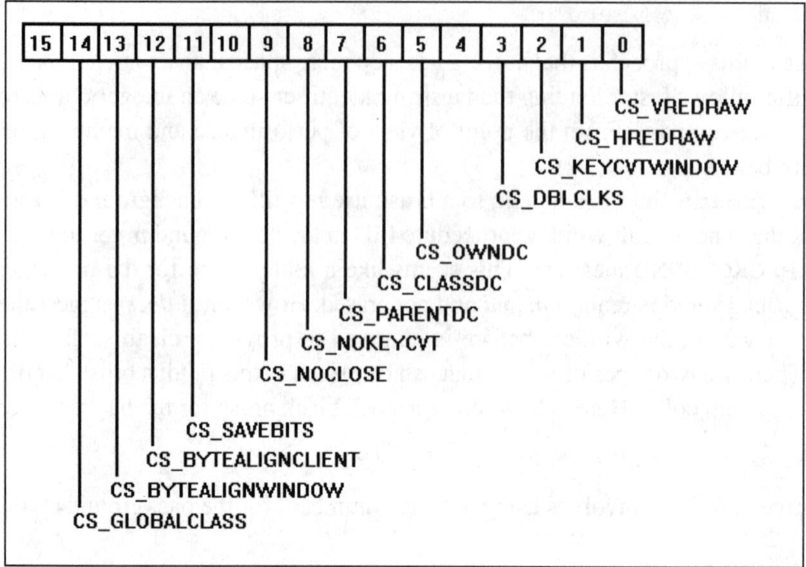

Figure 13.1 The thirteen WNDCLASS style bits

The **style** field is a 16-bit field that contains a set of flags that describe various features of the window class. There are 13 style flags, as shown in Figure 13.1. Let's look at each of the window class style bits in detail.

Window Class Style Bits

A lot of the subtlety in creating windows actually comes from certain class style bits that you can select. Let's take a look at all of them, to try to understand where they can be useful in a Windows program.

The **CS_VREDRAW** and **CS_HREDRAW** styles determine whether the window should be completely redrawn when the user changes the window size in either the vertical (**CS_VREDRAW**) or horizontal (**CS_HREDRAW**) direction. In other words, they determine whether a WinAPI call like the following is made when a window's size changes:

```
InvalidateRect (hwnd, NULL, TRUE);
```

As you probably remember, the `InvalidateRect` routine is used to mark a portion of a window as damaged, which means that a **WM_PAINT** message will eventually be generated to repair the window. A `NULL` value in the second parameter declares the *entire* window to be damaged. The TRUE value in the last parameter requests that the damaged area (in this case, the entire window) be erased before being redrawn.

Two style bits are referenced in WINDOWS.H but not mentioned in the documentation: **CS_KEYCVTWINDOW** and **CS_NOKEYCVT**. They seem to be remnants of support for a Kanji conversion window for Japanese Windows. However, Microsoft has created a separate version of Windows for the Japanese market, which also requires its own special version of the Windows Software Development Kit. Therefore, even though these style bits promise built-in Kanji support, you must obtain the special Software Development Kit to develop Windows programs for the Japanese-speaking market.

If you want a window to receive double-click mouse messages (**WM_LBUTTONDBLCLK, WM_MBUTTONDBLCLK,** or **WM_RBUTTONDBLCLK**), then you must use the **CS_DBLCLKS** style bit. As you'll see in Chapter 16, if you don't set this style bit, every mouse click message gets treated as single mouse click messages. From the point of view of the Windows API, a window only gets double-click messages when it wants one. The OWL library, by contrast, sets this bit by default for every OWL window.

Two style bits allow a window to have a private device context (DC): **CS_OWNDC** and **CS_CLASSDC**. When we introduced the device context in Chapter 6, we mentioned that most programs borrow a DC from the system DC cache. But because of the overhead associated with checking out and returning a DC, some programs prefer to have their own. In the same way that library books require more effort than books that you own, borrowed DCs require more effort. Of course, like private book collections, private DCs cost more in terms of memory required.

How much *does* a private DC cost? Although there has been talk among Windows programmers for some years that a DC is 800 bytes, in fact the actual size is about 200 bytes, all of which are allocated from GDI's local heap. While this doesn't seem like a lot, the allocation of a private DC has to be weighed against the fact that, as we'll discuss in Chapter 18, GDI's local heap space is a shared resource that all programs compete for. Therefore, avoid allocating a private DC unless you really need it.

So when is the cost of a private DC justified? In general, programs that do a lot of drawing, and programs that interact with the user *while* drawing, may run faster with a private DC. A word processor program, for example, that displays text as the user types may get a performance boost by getting its own, private DC. Or a drawing package that interacts with the user to interactively draw pictures may get a slight performance benefit from a private DC. In general, in a program that uses keystrokes or mouse clicks to draw, you might find that a private DC is faster to work with than a shared, system DC.

The **CS_OWNDC** style bit gives a private DC to *every window* in a class. This type of DC is the most expensive, in terms of memory used, but gives the fastest response. It is the most expensive because one DC is allocated for each window in a class. It is fastest because you don't incur the overhead of borrowing and returning the DC every time you draw. As illustrated in the following code fragment, a window created from a class with the **CS_OWNDC** style bit can get a DC handle during the **WM_CREATE** message and use it when it needs to draw for any other message:

```
class DFrame : public TFrameWindow
    {
    TClientDC * tdc;
    }

void DFrame::SetupWindow()
```

```
    {
    TFrameWindow::SetupWindow();
    tdc = new TClientDC(HWindow);
    }

void DFrame::EvLButtonDown(UINT modkeys, TPoint& pt)
    {
    tdc->TextOut(pt, "Draw anytime");
    }

void DFrame::CleanupWindow()
    {
    delete tdc;
    TFrameWindow::CleanupWindow();
    }
```

Besides the **WM_CREATE** message, the only other time this window procedure asks for a DC is in response to a **WM_PAINT** message, when a regular **BeginPaint/EndPaint** sandwich is used. This contrasts sharply with the approach that programs must take when they use a system DC. As shown in this code fragment, such programs must borrow and return a DC for each message:

```
void DFrame::EvLButtonDown(UINT modkeys, TPoint& pt)
    {
    // TDC created as local variable.
    TClientDC dc = TClientDC(HWindow);
    dc.TextOut(pt, "Draw anytime");
    }
```

From this, you can see that one advantage of a private DC is that programs don't have to borrow a DC every time they wish to draw. A second advantage is that a program can set up the DC's drawing attributes and then not have to worry about them again. In contrast with this is the way programs must work with system DCs. Every time a system DC is borrowed, its drawing attributes are reset to their initial, default state. Programs that use a system DC have to set up the DC drawing attributes every time they wish to draw.

Programs with a private DC must still use a **BeginPaint/EndPaint** sandwich in response to a **WM_PAINT** message. This is because the **WM_PAINT** message can only be turned off by the use of these two routines. **BeginPaint** is smart enough to recognize when a window has a private DC, and it returns the correct DC handle inside the **PAINTSTRUCT** structure. The only difference is that the DC will have a clipping region installed to limit drawing to the damaged part of the window.

The **CS_CLASSDC** style provides a DC that is similar to a private DC except that it is shared by an entire class of Windows and not owned by a single window. Like a private DC, the drawing attributes in a class DC are not reset every time the DC is returned. This gives us a slight performance improvement over a regular system DC, in which drawing attributes *are* reset. Therefore, a class DC has some of the benefits of a private DC except that it is shared between several windows of the same class. Because it is shared between windows, a class DC must be handled like a system DC. In other words, it must be borrowed when needed—using either **`GetDC`** or **`BeginPaint`**—and returned when it is not needed—using either **`ReleaseDC`** or **`EndPaint`**.

The **`CS_PARENTDC`** style can also help improve performance when drawing in a window. Unlike the private DC and the class DC, however, a parent DC does not cause a new DC to be allocated in the system. Instead, a window with this style bit will receive a regular DC from the system's DC cache.

The difference lies in the way that clipping is set in the DC. Unlike a regular DC, in which clipping is set either to the visible part of the client area (by **`GetDC`**) or to the damaged part of a window (by **`BeginPaint`**), clipping in a parent DC is set to the boundaries of the parent window. Figure 13.2 compares the clipping that is set up in a regular system DC and in a parent DC. With the parent DC, the child window can draw anywhere in the client area of its parent's window. If you have children, this may sound like a familiar state of affairs. Even if your children have their own rooms, they certainly are not shy about wandering into other rooms in your home.

You might be wondering why on earth anyone would give a child window the ability to draw into its parent's client area. This is a performance optimization to help in situations when the child is drawing in a very small space and may accidentally draw outside its own border (kids will be kids).

The parent DC style bit is set for the predefined classes that create Windows' dialog box controls. As you will see when we discuss dialog boxes in Chapter 14, dialog box controls are given a size and a position using a special set of coordinates called **dialog box coordinates**. Since there can be some degree of imprecision with these coordinates, the parent DC style bit gives the dialog box controls room to maneuver. If you create your own custom dialog box controls, you may wish to use the **`CS_PARENTDC`** style bit for them as well.

The **`CS_PARENTDC`** style bit is not compatible with the **`WS_CLIPCHILDREN`** style that we'll discuss when we look at **`CreateWindow`** style bits. If the parent window has

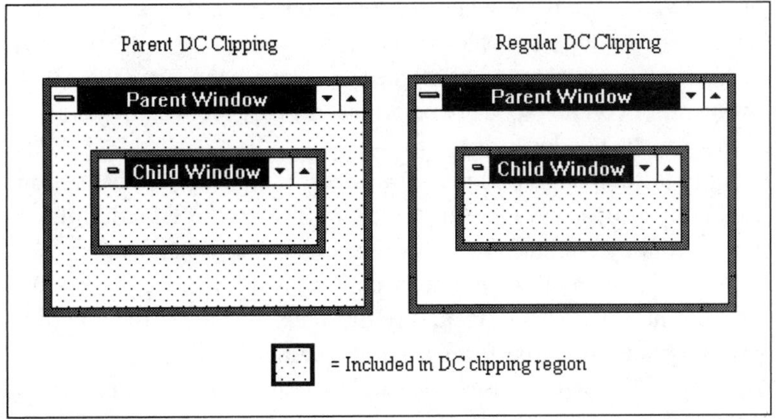

Figure 13.2 Comparison of clipping in a system cache DC and in a parent DC

this window style bit set, then its child windows cannot draw in the parent's window. You might call this the "Aunt Edna" style bit, since the kids don't run around as much (or at all) when your Aunt Edna comes over (she has a way with kids).

The **CS_NOCLOSE** class style removes the *Close* item from the system menu. You use this with windows that have a system menu, which shouldn't be closed by the user. Of course, as we discussed in Chapter 11, another way to achieve the same result involves modifying the system menu using the various menu modification routines. This style bit provides a simpler way to achieve the same end, providing that you need this behavior for every window in the window class.

The **CS_SAVEBITS** class style is a performance bit that you set for windows that visit the display screen for very short periods of time. The save-bits style asks the Window Manager to take a snapshot of the bits that the window overwrites when it appears. You may recall that this is how menus are able to make a graceful exit when they leave. After a menu disappears, a window never gets a **WM_PAINT** message to redraw the area that the menu had occupied. Menus are very polite: They don't damage any window on the display screen.

The save-bits style asks every window in a class to provide the same courtesy. The class of windows that are used to create dialog boxes are set up this way. For the most part, when a dialog box visits your window, it can disappear quickly and easily without requiring your window to be sent a **WM_PAINT** message to redraw. But sometimes things happen that thwart the save-bits style. For example, if the dialog box moves, the bitmap snapshot of the area behind the dialog box can no longer be used to restore the area after the dialog box is removed. Or, if any drawing is done underneath the dialog box, then the bitmap snapshot will also be unusable to restore the area covered by the dialog box. In both cases, a **WM_PAINT** message is generated to repair the damage caused by the exit of the dialog box (or the other window).

Two class style bits are used to specify how a window should be positioned on the display screen: **CS_BYTEALIGNWINDOW** and **CS_BYTEALIGNCLIENT**. These style bits never affect the height of a window or its placement on the *y*-axis. However, they *do* affect the width of a window and its placement on the *x*-axis. As the names suggest, these style bits force either a window or its client area to be aligned on a byte boundary. This allows a performance improvement for certain types of operations: moving the window, drawing menu items, and drawing into the window.

Byte-aligned drawing is faster on certain types of devices: monochrome displays and color displays that use multiple planes to represent color. In fact, the only kind of device that doesn't really benefit from byte-aligned drawing is a color display that uses a packed pixel approach to storing data. Since all of the most popular display devices are either monochrome or color with multiple planes (including EGA, VGA, and 8514), the byte-aligned style can give a program a slight performance improvement.

The **CS_GLOBALCLASS** class style is used for window classes that are going to be shared among different programs. For example, if you are going to create a custom dialog box control, you'll want to register the window class of your dialog box control as a global class. This allows a single window class to be shared among several programs. For example, you could use your custom dialog box control to create your spreadsheet program, your word processing program, and even for your database program.

Once a window class has been registered, you can create as many copies of the window as you like. There are two Windows library routines that do this for you, which is what we're going to look at next.

Creating a Window

In general, an OWL program creates a window by creating a window object. In every program in this book, an application object member function—**InitMainWindow**—creates a window object (and an MS-Windows window). To get the most from an MS-Windows window, though, you need to understand all the capabilities which are embodied in the window creation routines.

First, let's take a brief look at the **TWindowAttr** structure. Every descendent of **TWindow** has a data member of this type called **Attr**. You control the MS-Windows window creation process by changing values in this data structure. For the changes to affect the window creation process, the changes must be made in a window object's constructor. Here is **TWindowAttr**, as defined in WINDOW.H:

```
struct TWindowAttr {
    DWORD       Style;
    DWORD       ExStyle;
    int         X, Y, W, H;
    TResId      Menu;          // Menu resource id
    int         Id;            // Child ID
    char far*   Param;
    TResId      AccelTable;    // Accelerator table resource id
    };
```

These parameters are passed to one of the MS-Windows window creation routines, **CreateWindowEx**. Let's examine both window creation routines.

Two Windows library routines create a window: **CreateWindow** and **CreateWindowEx**. The "Ex" at the end of the second routine's name stands for "extended." The extended routine does all of the things that the first routine can do, plus a little more. The **CreateWindowEx** routine was created because Windows ran out of style bits in the **CreateWindow** routine. This being the case, we're going to start by looking at the parameters to these routines and then consider all of the available style bits—both regular and extended.

CreateWindow is defined as follows:

```
CreateWindow (lpClassName, lpWindowName,
              dwStyle, X, Y, nWidth, nHeight,
              hWndParent, hMenu, hInstance, lpParaml)
```

The extended style bits parameter is the first one in **CreateWindowEx**, which is defined as

```
CreateWindowEx (dwExStyle, lpClassName, lpWindowName,
                dwStyle, X, Y, nWidth, nHeight,
                hWndParent, hMenu, hInstance, lpParaml)
```

The value of **dwExStyle** is an unsigned long (**DWORD**) value of the extended style bits for use with the **CreateWindowEx** routine. We'll discuss the regular and extended style bits in a moment.

The **lpClassName** parameter is a long pointer to a character string for the class name. This is the class name that you defined using the **RegisterClass** routine, or it can be the name of a public window class that was created by someone else. For example, Windows makes available the following public window classes: **button**, **combobox**, **edit**, **listbox**, **scroll bar**, and **static**. We'll take a closer look at each of these classes when we discuss dialog boxes in Chapter 14. There isn't a **TWindowAttr** data member for the window class. The reason is that the window class name is provided by the **GetClassName** member function, which you'll need to override to define the window class for your window object.

The **lpWindowName** parameter is a long pointer to a character string for the window text. The window text is displayed in the titlebar (also known as a caption bar) for windows that have a titlebar. When a window is minimized—is put into an iconic state—the window text is displayed as a label for the icon. Certain types of windows that don't have a titlebar, like pushbuttons, use the window text as a window label.

The **dwStyle** parameter is an unsigned long (**DWORD**) value that contains a set of flags to define the shape, size, and behavior of the window you wish to create. We'll discuss style bits, along with the extended style bits, in a moment.

The **X** and **Y** parameters identify the *x* and *y* coordinates of the upper-left corner of the window. For top-level windows—that is, windows that don't have parents—this location is relative to the upper-left corner of the display screen, also known as **screen coordinates**. For child windows, this is relative to the upper-left corner of the parent window's client area, also known as client area coordinates.

The Window Manager calculates the location of a top-level window when the value of the *x* coordinate is set to **CW_USEDEFAULT**. When this option is used, each subsequent top-level window is given an initial position that cascades from the previous window. This option arranges top-level windows in an orderly fashion, like soldiers in a row. Figure 13.3 shows the cascading effect created by this flag.

The **nWidth** and **nHeight** fields allow you to define the width and height of a window. For top-level windows, you can set nWidth to **CW_USEDEFAULT**. This tells the Window Manager to set the size of your window for you. But this feature is not available for child windows, so you will have to calculate their size yourself.

When you calculate the size of a window—whether it is a child window or a top-level window—you'll need to keep in mind that **CreateWindow** and **CreateWindowEx** expect the size of the *entire* window and not just the client area. Many programmers make the mistake of calculating the size of the client area and using those dimensions. But an additional

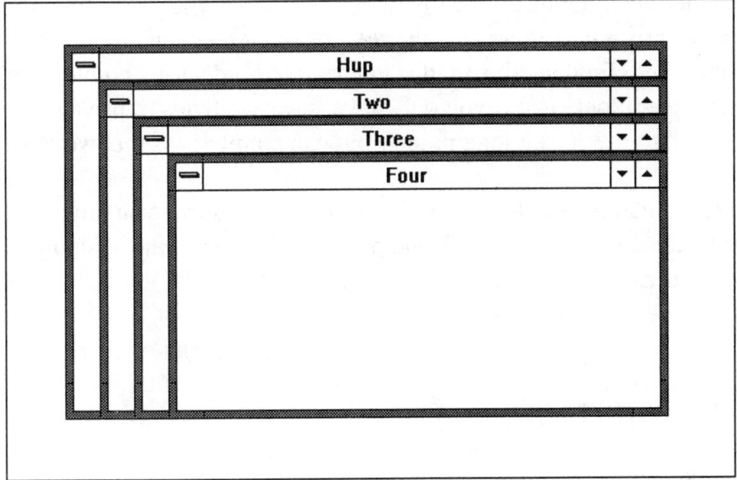

Figure 13.3 Cascading effect of the CW_USEDEFAULT FLAG

step is required: You must add in the size of the various nonclient area objects. When we discuss the issue of window metrics later in this chapter, we'll describe two different ways to calculate the size of the actual window to get a client area of the desired size.

The **hwndParent** parameter identifies the window that is to be the parent of the newborn window. Windows that don't have a parent can pass a NULL value in this field, which effectively makes the window a child of the desktop window. Children of the desktop are considered top-level windows and are shown in the Task List window that appears with the [Ctrl] + [Esc] key combination.

When we discuss window style bits, you'll see that there are three different kinds of windows: overlapped, popup, and child. When you create a child window, it *must* have a parent window. This agrees with the way we think of human parents and children: Children depend on their parents for their well-being. The other two types of windows do not require a parent.

The **hMenu** parameter identifies the menu that is to be associated with a window. We have already seen that a menu name can be supplied in the **lpszMenuName** field when we register a window class. But, to use a menu that is different from the default class menu, we can specify a menu handle in this field. As we discussed in Chapter 11 when we introduced menus, the **LoadMenu** routine provides one way to obtain a menu handle when a menu has been defined in a program's resource file:

```
HMENU hmenu = GetApplication()->LoadMenu("MENUNAME");
```

The OWL libraries call LoadMenu for you, which is why you provide a menu name (and not a handle) *both* when you register a window class *and* when in the **Attr** window creation structure.

The **lpParam** parameter is an optional, four-byte-long value that you can use to pass private data to your window procedure along with the **WM_CREATE** message. If you translate this Hungarian notation into English, this field is intended to hold a long pointer, presumably to a private parameter block. But if you only have, say, two bytes of private data to pass, then you don't need to use it as a long pointer but can simply pass the two bytes inside the pointer field.

If you *do* wish it to pass a parameter block, here is an example to show you how to go about doing it. We start by allocating a data block and passing a pointer to the block in the last parameter of **CreateWindow**:

```
LPSTR lp;
RECT  rPrivate;

rPrivate.left = 10;    rPrivate.top    = 20;
rPrivate.right = 200; rPrivate.bottom = 100;

lp = (LPSTR)&rPrivate;

hwnd = CreateWindow("MIN:MAIN",     /* Class name.   */
            "Minimum",              /* Title.        */
            WS_OVERLAPPEDWINDOW,    /* Style bits.   */
            CW_USEDEFAULT,          /* x - default.  */
            0,                      /* y - default.  */
            CW_USEDEFAULT,          /* cx - default. */
            0,                      /* cy - default. */
            NULL,                   /* No parent.    */
            NULL,                   /* Class menu.   */
            hInstance,              /* Creator.      */
            lp);                    /* Params.       */
```

In this example, our data block is simply a **RECT** structure containing two (*x*,*y*) pairs that presumably are of interest to our window procedure. A pointer to this structure is placed in the `lpParam` parameter, which is the last parameter of **CreateWindow**.

Within the OWL framework, you'll pass the data block by defining it in the **Param** member of the **TWindowAttr** data structure, like this:

```
Attr.Param = lp
```

The time to get a pointer to our data block is during the processing for the **WM_CREATE** message. The **lParam** parameter of our window procedure will contain a pointer to a data structure defined in WINDOWS.H as **CREATESTRUCT**. It is defined in WINDOWS.H as:

```
typedef struct tagCREATESTRUCT
    {
    LPSTR lpCreateParams;
    HANDLE hInstance;
    HANDLE hMenu;
    HWND hwndParent;
    int cy;
    int cx;
```

```
int y;
int x;
LONG  style;
LPSTR lpszName;
LPSTR lpszClass;
DWORD dwExStyle;
} CREATESTRUCT;
```

The first item in this structure, **`lpCreateParams`**, is the value that we passed as our last parameter to **`CreateWindow`**. Here is one way to create a pointer to our rectangle data:

```
void DFrame::EvCreate(CREATESTRUCT far& cs)
    {
    LPRECT lpr = (LPRECT)cs.lpCreateParams;
    int xTop = lpr->top // == 20;

    TFrameWindow::EvCreate(cs);
    }
    {
    int xTop;
    LPCREATESTRUCT lpcs;
    LPRECT lpr;

    lpcs = (LPCREATESTRUCT)Msg.LParam;
    lpr  = (LPRECT)lpcs->lpCreateParams;

    xTop = lpr -> top; /* =20   */
    ...
```

If you pass a pointer to a data block, you'll want to make a local copy of the data block for your window procedure, since the pointer may not be valid after the conclusion of the **`WM_CREATE`** message. The pointer may become invalid, for example, if the caller decides to free the memory that had been allocated to hold the data object.

At this point, we have discussed all of the parameters to **`CreateWindow`** and **`CreateWindowEx`**. To get a complete picture of what these routines have to offer, we need to dig a little deeper and investigate the different style bits that can be passed in the `dwExStyle` and `dwStyle` parameters.

Window Creation Style Bits

There are five categories of style bits to control window creation for **`CreateWindow`** and **`CreateWindowEx`**: type of window, window border, nonclient area components, the window's initial state, and performance bits. These are summarized in Table 13.1.

Type of Window

The best way to explain the three types of windows is to describe the intended use of each. The **`WS_OVERLAPPED`** window, for example, is meant to serve as a program's main, top-level window. A window created with the **`WS_POPUP`** style has some things in common with overlapped

Table 13.1 Summary of CreateWindow and CreateWindowEx Style Bits

Category	*Style Bit*	*Description*
Type of Window (3)	`WS_OVERLAPPED`	Create an overlapped window, suitable for use as a top-level window. Overlapped windows always have a caption whether or not you specify the WS_CAPTION style. And they always have a border. A border of type WS_BORDER is used if no other type has been requested.
	`WS_POPUP`	Create a popup window, suitable for use as a dialog box or secondary window.
	`WS_CHILD`	Create a child window, suitable for dividing up the area of overlapped, popup, and other child windows into smaller functional areas.
Window Border (4)	`WS_BORDER`	Window is to have a thin border. This is the default when a caption bar has been requested (with the WS_CAPTION style).
	`WS_DLGFRAME`	Window is to have a thick, solid border. In previous versions of Windows, this was the standard for dialog boxes. The WS_EX_DLGMODALFRAME style bit is used in Windows 3.0 instead.
	`WS_THICKFRAME`	Window is to have a thick frame. The presence of this border indicates that a window can be resized. The WS_CAPTION style must accompany this selection.
	`WS_EX_DLGMODALFRAME`	Window is to have an extended dialog frame, to include a system menu and caption bar, if requested. This is the standard style for dialog boxes.
Non-Client Components (6)	`WS_CAPTION`	Window has a caption, also known as a titlebar. A caption is always accompanied by a border, with the WS_BORDER selected by default.

(continued)

Table 13.1 Summary of CreateWindow and CreateWindowEx Style Bits *(Continued)*

Category	*Style Bit*	*Description*
	`WS_HSCROLL`	Specifies to create the window with a horizontal scroll bar. Scroll bars created using this style bit are always on the bottom edge of the window. To place a scroll bar in another part of a window, you must create a scroll bar control.
	`WS_MAXIMIZEBOX`	Window is to have a maximize box. The WS_CAPTION style must accompany this selection.
	`WS_MINIMIZEBOX`	Window is to have a minimize box. The WS_CAPTION style must accompany this selection.
	`WS_SYSMENU`	Window is to have a system menu. The WS_CAPTION style must accompany this selection.
	`WS_VSCROLL`	Window is to have a vertical scroll bar. Scroll bars created using this style bit are always placed on the right edge of the window. To locate a scroll bar at another location, you must create a scroll bar control.
Initial State (5)	`WS_DISABLED`	Window is initially disabled, which means that mouse and keyboard input is not delivered to the window. If the user tries to click on a disabled window, a warning beep is generated.
	`WS_ICONIC`	Window is initially iconic or minimized, which means that window is closed, and only its icon is displayed.
	`WS_MAXIMIZE`	Window is initially maximized. For top-level windows, this means it occupies the complete display screen. For child windows, it means it occupies its parent's entire client area.
	`WS_MINIMIZE`	Window is initially iconic. This style bit is the same as the WS_ICONIC style bit.

(continued)

Table 13.1 Summary of CreateWindow and CreateWindowEx Style Bits *(Continued)*

Category	*Style Bit*	*Description*
	`WS_VISIBLE`	Window is initially visible. This is a very important style bit, since without it a window will not appear.
Performance Bits (3)	`WS_CLIPCHILDREN`	Clipping in software is expensive; therefore, a parent window usually does not clip, to avoid drawing in its children. However, if you wish a parent window to avoid overwriting its children, the parent must have this style set.
	`WS_CLIPSIBLINGS`	Clipping in software is expensive; therefore, sibling windows≈that is, windows that have the same parent≈do not make any extra effort to avoid drawing over each other. This style bit ensures that siblings do not overwrite each other. It prevents what some Windows programmers refer to as "sibling rivalry."
	`WS_EX_NOPARENTNOTIFY`	By default, a child window sends quite a few notification messages to its parent, in the form of the WM_PARENTNOTIFY message. Notification messages are sent when the child is created, when it receives mouse click messages, and when it is destroyed. This style bit prevents a child from writing so many letters home. This decreased message traffic helps improve performance. Dialog box controls, for example, are always created with this style.

windows, and this style is intended for dialog boxes and other secondary "free-floating" windows outside a program's main window. **`WS_CHILD`** windows are used to organize the use of overlapped, popup, and other child windows into functional areas. An example of child window use is as a dialog box control (pushbutton, listbox, etc.) in a dialog box.

When you create a window with the **`WS_OVERLAPPED`** style, the Window Manager gives you some help in making sure that the window meets the minimum standards required of a top-level window. For one thing, it makes sure that your window has a caption bar and a border. (But you'll still need to specify the **WS_CAPTION** style if you wish to create a system menu or other caption bar elements.) Since overlapped windows are expected to serve as the top-level windows, the Window Manager will automatically size and position an overlapped window using the **CW_USEDEFAULT** flag. And finally, an overlapped window is always positioned in screen coordinates. This means that, even if an overlapped window has a parent, it is positioned independent of its parent.

A window created with the **WS_POPUP** style is a popup window. In many respects, a popup window behaves like an overlapped window: It can reside anywhere on the display screen and is positioned in screen coordinates. So why have two different styles? It's mostly an accident of history.

Version 1.x of Windows used *tiled windows* as main program windows. Popup windows were the only kind of overlapping window that could be created, and these were used for dialog boxes. Starting with version 2.x of Windows, overlapping windows replaced tiled windows as the style used for main program windows. Since then, the differences between overlapped and popup windows have been mostly cosmetic, since they behave in exactly the same way.

With Windows 3.x, the differences between the two types have been reduced even further. For one thing, starting with Windows 3.x, dialog boxes have titlebars. So then, what's the difference between the two? It is mostly an issue of conventional usage. As we said earlier, overlapped windows are intended for a program's main window. Popup windows are intended for dialog boxes. Presumably, if a difference should appear between these two uses in a future version of Windows, programs that follow this convention will have no problem running with whatever convention is adopted.

A window created with the **WS_CHILD** style is a child window. Child windows are used to divide other windows—overlapped, popup, and other child windows—into smaller functional areas. Since this is the case, a child window *must* have a parent. At window creation time, the parent is the window whose handle is passed as the **hwndParent** parameter of the **CreateWindow** and **CreateWindowEx** routines. Like human children, child windows require a parent because the parent provides a place to live. A child window is only visible when positioned inside the client area of its parent. If it is moved outside the client area by either a program or by a user action, any portion that lies outside of the parent's client area will not be visible.

Window Border

Figure 13.4 shows the four types of borders that are available. Notice that, among the different window border styles, only the **WS_DLGFRAME** cannot be used with a caption. This is an older style that has been replaced by the **WS_EX_DLGMODALFRAME** border for dialog boxes but is still present to maintain compatibility with programs created for older versions of Windows.

As we mentioned earlier, a **WS_OVERLAPPED** window must have a border. If a border is not specified, the thin **WS_BORDER** is automatically created for the window. The other

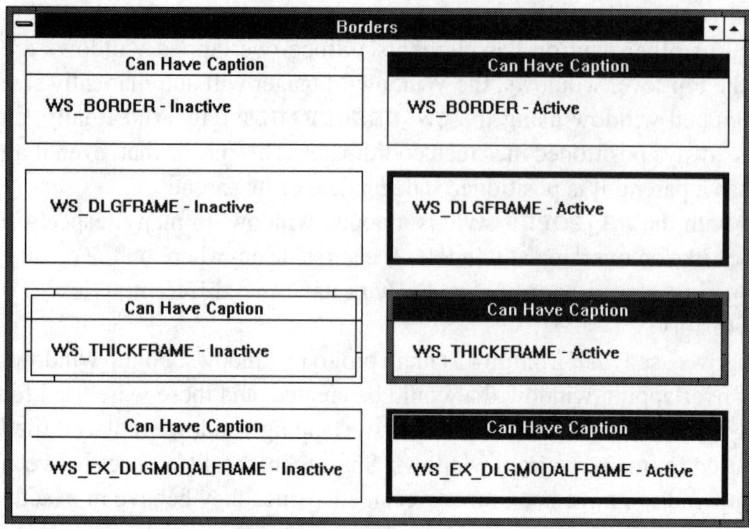

Figure 13.4 The four types of borders, shown in both inactive and active states

types of windows do not require a border, which is convenient when you wish to use a child window to invisibly divide up a larger window. However, it doesn't make sense to create a popup window without a border. Without a border, a popup can easily be lost as windows are shuffled around the screen.

The border of a window and the caption bar change colors to let the user see a difference between active windows and inactive windows, as shown in Figure 13.4. The borders of top-level windows are changed automatically by the system, which sends a **WM_NCACTIVATE** message to inform a window to redraw its nonclient area to reflect either an active or an inactive state. However, this message is not sent for child windows. If you wish to change a child window's border and caption to reflect an active state, you can use the following line of code to transmit your message:

```
SendMessage (hwndChild, WM_NCACTIVATE, TRUE, 0L);
```

Changing the border and caption to reflect an inactive state involves the same message, with a zero or **FALSE** value for the **wParam**:

```
SendMessage (hwndChild, WM_NCACTIVATE, FALSE, 0L);
```

Nonclient Area Components

Figure 13.5 shows a window with all of the nonclient area components with a style flag labeling the corresponding part. With the exception of the two scroll bars, each nonclient area component is managed by the default window procedure. This means, of course, that

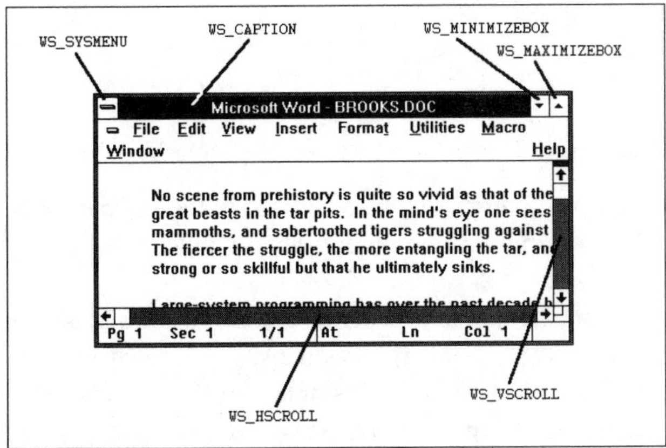

Figure 13.5 The nonclient area components of a window

a window procedure must forward the various nonclient area messages on to the window procedure for these components to work properly. But this is hardly a new requirement, since you are used to the idea that the messages you don't process yourself are always sent on to the default window procedure.

The one exception involves scroll bars. Scroll bars send messages that let a window know how the user is interacting with the scroll bar. There are two messages that scroll bars send: A **WM_HSCROLL** message is sent by horizontal scroll bars, and **WM_VSCROLL** is sent by vertical scroll bars.

Initial State

Of the four style bits that set a window's initial state, perhaps the most important is the **WS_VISIBLE**. Without this style bit, a window does not appear at creation time. Of course, a window can be created invisible and later made visible by calling routines like **ShowWindow**, but it is often easier for you to simply make a window visible at window creation time. One exception to this, of course, is the way that top-level windows are ordinarily handled in a program's **WinMain** function. Every OWL program, in fact, creates an invisible top-level window and then calls **ShowWindow** to make it appear, by calling these two routines:

```
hwnd = CreateWindow("MIN:MAIN",    /* Class name.    */
             "Minimum",/* Title.*/
             WS_OVERLAPPEDWINDOW,/* Style bits.*/
             CW_USEDEFAULT,/* x - default.*/
             0,/* y - default.*/
             CW_USEDEFAULT,/* cx - default.*/
             0,/* cy - default.*/
             NULL,/* No parent.*/
             NULL,/* Class menu.*/
```

```
                hInstance,/* Creator.*/
                NULL/* Params.*/
                ) ;

    ShowWindow (hwnd, cmdShow);
```

As we discussed earlier, the **cmdShow** parameter is the value passed as the last parameter in the **WinMain** function, which tells a program how its top-level window should first appear.

The **WS_MINIMIZE** and **WS_MAXIMIZE** style bits describe whether a window should be initially minimized (iconic) or maximized (zoomed). This is usually limited to a program's top-level window, since users have come to expect a single top-level window in an application. Of course, the Multiple Document Interface changes this a bit, since a document window can be minimized and rest inside the client area of its parent window. The Program Manager provides a good example of how windows other than a program's top-level window can be managed when either minimized or maximized. In older Windows programs, you may see the **WS_ICONIC** style used instead of **WS_MINIMIZE**. If you check WINDOWS.H, you'll notice that these two flags have identical values, and therefore can be used interchangeably.

The **WS_DISABLED** style bit lets you create a window that may be visible but is not available for user interaction. This is like having a door that is locked and that displays a "Closed" sign. All of the predefined dialog box controls take on a grayed appearance when they are disabled. In this way, not only is the user locked out from using the window, but the window provides visual feedback to make this aspect clear. You may wish to use this same approach if you plan to have windows that are visible, but not accessible. The two pushbuttons in Figure 13.6 show one way to let the user know that a window is not available.

Performance Bits

When we discussed the various style bits that are available for window classes, we looked at several style flags that we referred to as performance bits. In those cases, each of those

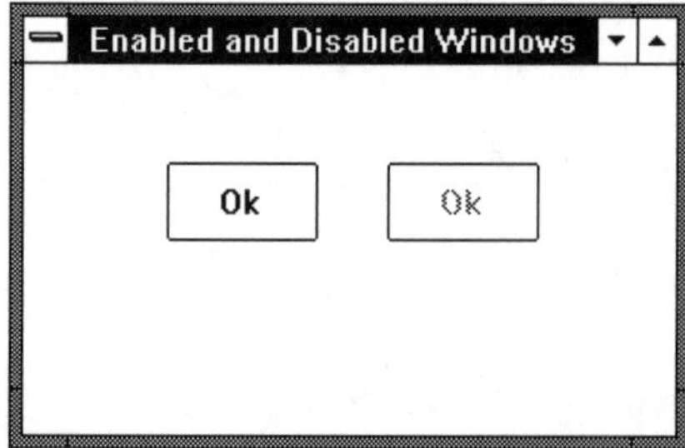

Figure 13.6 A disabled pushbutton displays its label in grayed text

performance bits provided a way to give a bit of a boost in speed for certain types of operations.

Of the three flags that we call performance bits, only one of them actually improves the performance of the system. The other two actually cause things to slow down a bit, although from your viewpoint they mean that less effort is required by your program to make things work right. For this reason, we feel justified in calling them performance bits, although perhaps a better term would be "performance-*relate*d" style bits.

The first two styles, **WS_CLIPCHILDREN** and **WS_CLIPSIBLINGS**, control the amount of clipping that is set up in the DC when drawing in a window. In Chapter 6, when we first discussed the role of clipping, we mentioned that clipping allows windowing. Without clipping, one program might accidentally overwrite another program's window. Between two windows that don't belong to the same program, clipping is automatically provided.

But between windows that belong to the same program, clipping is not so strictly enforced. In particular, there is no automatic mechanism to prevent a parent window from overwriting a child (**WS_CHILD**) window. And between child windows, there is no automatic clipping to prevent one child window from overwriting another. The primary reason that clipping is turned *off* in these situations is performance. If a program has put a window in a particular spot, the Window Manager assumes that the program will not allow other windows to interfere with the operation of that window. This works well and eliminates the overhead that would otherwise occur when a window has more than a few child windows.

However, things begin to break down when the user is able to move windows. In this case, a program has less control over the placement of child windows. When there is the risk that the user will cause two windows to interfere with each other, the **WS_CLIPSIBLINGS** style bit should be used to avoid "sibling rivalry," which is a tongue-in-cheek term for what happens when two child windows don't respect each other's boundaries.

The other clipping style bit, **WS_CLIPCHILDREN**, is used to prevent a parent window from overwriting its children. This is required when (a) a user can pick up a child window and move it around and (b) the window's parent draws in its own client area. The fix involves using this style bit to force the Window Manager to do a little more work in setting up the clipping that will cause the parent window to respect the boundaries of its children.

The last performance bit is **WS_EX_NOPARENTNOTIFY**. This performance bit reduces the number of messages that a child window sends to its parent. By default, a child window sends its parent a message when it is created, when it receives mouse click messages, and when it is destroyed. This message prevents the **WM_PARENTNOTIFY** message from being sent when child windows are created and destroyed (but still sends notify messages for mouse clicks). While it seems like a lot of effort to eliminate two messages, when there are a lot of windows being created or destroyed at one time, it slows things down a bit. This is why, for example, dialog box controls use this style.

Compound Window Styles

The last three styles that we're going to look at are values that have been defined in WINDOWS.H for the sake of convenience: **WS_OVERLAPPEDWINDOW**, **WS_POPUPWINDOW**, and **WS_CHILDWINDOW**. These compound styles are defined as follows:

```
#define WS_OVERLAPPEDWINDOW
                    (WS_OVERLAPPED | WS_CAPTION |
                     WS_SYSMENU | WS_THICKFRAME |
                     WS_MINIMIZEBOX | WS_MAXIMIZEBOX)
#define WS_POPUPWINDOW
                    (WS_POPUP | WS_BORDER | WS_SYSMENU)
#define WS_CHILDWINDOW
                    (WS_CHILD)
```

These values are available for the sake of convenience, to make it easier to select the most commonly selected style bits.

Top-Level Window Considerations

A program's top-level window is the main doorway through which users access your program. When it first opens, it creates an initial impression of what a user can expect from your program. For this reason, it would seem that programmers would wish to make that initial impression a favorable one. And yet, that doesn't seem to be the case in many of today's programs. We're not interested in flashy graphics, spiffy logos, or sexy animation. What we're concerned with is much simpler than any special effects: A program will give a distinct impression based on the initial position and size of its main window.

On the one hand, quite a few programs use the **CW_USEDEFAULT** flag and let the Window Manager control the size and positioning of a program's main window. But, if you spend very much time using Windows, you soon find that this behavior can be annoying. Even though Windows creates this effect by keeping careful track of the location of each new top-level window that it positions, to the user the effect is one of chaos. The process of starting a program can seem to a user to be out of control, since programs seem to start up at seemingly random positions. The cascading effect creates more work for the user, since the first thing a user does is reposition the window of a newly started program to a convenient location.

If you agree that this is a problem, there are several possible solutions. One involves always creating your program's top-level window at a fixed location and with a fixed size. For example, a program might create its top-level window with a location of (10, 10) and make its window 320 pixels wide and 240 pixels high. The problem with hard-coding values like this is that the effect you produce is dependent on the type of display the user happens to be using. For example, a window of this size would occupy about one half of a CGA screen, which is 640 × 200 pixels. But on an 8514, which has a resolution of 1024 × 768, this window would only occupy one twelfth of the screen.

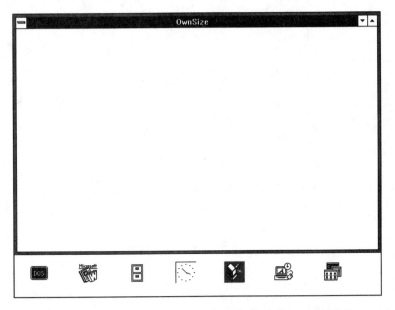

Figure 13.7 A top-level window that defines its own size

As an alternative, a program can call **GetSystemMetrics** to determine the size of the display screen and then set the size of the top-level window accordingly. Our next sample program, OWNSIZE, does just that. It creates a top-level window that is equal to the width of the display screen. It makes the window almost as tall as the display screen but leaves enough room at the bottom of the display screen so that program icons that are resting there are visible. Figure 13.7 shows our program's top-level window when it is first created.

Here is the source code to OWNSIZE:

OWNSIZE.CPP

```
//
// OWNSIZE.CPP -- Demonstrates window creation using system
//                metric values and the use of a profile file.
//
#include <owl\owlpch.h>
#include "ownsize.h"

enum WindowSize { REOPEN_NORMAL,
                  REOPEN_ZOOM,
                  REOPEN_DEFAULT };

// Profile file values.
char achPr[]   = "OWNSIZE";     /*  Profile file key name. */
char achFile[] = "OWNSIZE.INI"; /*  Profile file name.     */

//
```

```
// Main window
class DFrame : public TFrameWindow
    {
  public:
    DFrame(char * title);
    void CmFileExit();
    void CmHelpAbout();
    void EvDestroy();
    LPSTR GetClassName ();
    void  GetWindowClass (WNDCLASS&);

  DECLARE_RESPONSE_TABLE (DFrame);
    };

DEFINE_RESPONSE_TABLE1 (DFrame, TFrameWindow)
  EV_WM_DESTROY,
  EV_COMMAND(CM_FILEEXIT, CmFileExit),
  EV_COMMAND(CM_HELPABOUT, CmHelpAbout),
END_RESPONSE_TABLE;

DFrame::DFrame(char * title) : TFrameWindow(0, title)
    {
    int iReopen;
    int x, y, cx, cy;

    if (!GetApplication()->hPrevInstance)
        {
        /*
         *  For first instance, set position & size to that
         *  of window when we last ran.
         */

        x  = GetPrivateProfileInt (achPr, "x", 0, achFile);
        y  = GetPrivateProfileInt (achPr, "y", 0, achFile);

        cx = GetSystemMetrics (SM_CXSCREEN);
        cx = GetPrivateProfileInt (achPr, "cx", cx, achFile);
        cy = GetSystemMetrics (SM_CYSCREEN) -
             GetSystemMetrics (SM_CYICON)   -
            (GetSystemMetrics (SM_CYCAPTION) * 2);
        cy = GetPrivateProfileInt (achPr, "cy", cy, achFile);

        iReopen = GetPrivateProfileInt (achPr, "Reopen", 0,
                                        achFile);

        if (iReopen == REOPEN_ZOOM)
            GetApplication()->nCmdShow = SW_SHOWMAXIMIZED;
        if (iReopen == REOPEN_DEFAULT)
            {
            x  = CW_USEDEFAULT;
            cx = CW_USEDEFAULT;
            }
        }
    else
        {
        /*  Other instances, use default position & size.      */
        x = cx = CW_USEDEFAULT;
        y = cy = 0;
        }

    Attr.X = x;
    Attr.Y = y;
```

```
    Attr.W = cx;
    Attr.H = cy;
    }

void DFrame::CmFileExit()
    {
    CloseWindow(0); // Cause application to terminate
    }

void DFrame::CmHelpAbout()
    {
    MessageBox("   A Window with a Memory\n\n"
               "'Borland C++ 4.0 Programming\n"
               "  for Windows', by Paul Yao", Title);
    }

void DFrame::EvDestroy()
    {
    char ach[80];
    int  iReopen;

    //  Update window position information.

    wsprintf (ach, "%d",Attr.X);
    WritePrivateProfileString (achPr, "x", ach, achFile);

    wsprintf (ach, "%d",Attr.Y);
    WritePrivateProfileString (achPr, "y", ach, achFile);

    wsprintf (ach, "%u",Attr.W);
    WritePrivateProfileString (achPr, "cx", ach, achFile);

    wsprintf (ach, "%d",Attr.H);
    WritePrivateProfileString (achPr, "cy", ach, achFile);

    /*
     *  Write reopen flags for iconic/zoomed windows.
     */
    iReopen = REOPEN_NORMAL;
    if (IsZoomed ())  iReopen = REOPEN_ZOOM;
    if (IsIconic ())  iReopen = REOPEN_DEFAULT;

    wsprintf (ach, "%d", iReopen);
    WritePrivateProfileString (achPr, "Reopen", ach, achFile);

    TWindow::EvDestroy();
    }

LPSTR DFrame::GetClassName ()
    {
    return "OwnSize:MAIN";
    }

void DFrame::GetWindowClass (WNDCLASS& wc)
    {
    TFrameWindow::GetWindowClass (wc);
    wc.hIcon=LoadIcon (wc.hInstance, "snapshot");
    wc.lpszMenuName = "MAIN";
    wc.style != CS_HREDRAW | CS_VREDRAW;
    }

//
```

```
// Application object
class DApp : public TApplication
    {
  public:
    DApp();
    void InitMainWindow();
    };

DApp::DApp() : TApplication()
    {
    }

void DApp::InitMainWindow()
    {
    SetMainWindow (new DFrame("OwnSize"));
    }

//
// Application main entry point.
OwlMain(int, char **)
    {
    return DApp().Run();
    }
```

OWNSIZE.H

```
#define CM_FILEEXIT 100
#define CM_HELPABOUT 200
```

OWNSIZE. RC

```
#include "ownsize.h"

snapshot icon ownsize.ico

main menu
    BEGIN
    POPUP "&File"
        {
        MENUITEM "E&xit", CM_FILEEXIT
        }
    POPUP "&Help"
        {
        MENUITEM "&About...", CM_HELPABOUT
        }
    END
```

OWNSIZE.DEF

```
EXETYPE WINDOWS

CODE MOVEABLE DISCARDABLE
DATA MULTIPLE MOVEABLE
```

```
HEAPSIZE   512
STACKSIZE 8192
```

DYNA16.MAK

```
#  MAKE file for Win16 API using dynamic BIDS,
#  OWL and C-runtime libraries.
#
#    C> make -fstatic16.mak
#

.AUTODEPEND
CC = -c -H -H"owl\owlpch.h" -ml -R -vi -WS -X-
CD = -D_RTLDLL;_BIDSDLL;_OWLDLL;_OWLPCH;
INC = -I\BC4\INCLUDE
LIB = -L\BC4\LIB

ownsize.exe :  ownsize.obj ownsize.res
  tlink -c -C -Twe $(LIB) @dyna16.lnk
  brc ownsize.res ownsize.exe

ownsize.obj :  ownsize.cpp
  bcc $(CC) $(CD) ownsize.cpp

ownsize.res :  ownsize.rc ownsize.ico ownsize.h
  brc $(INC) -31 -R ownsize.rc
```

DYNA16.LNK

```
\bc4\lib\c0wl.obj+
ownsize.obj
ownsize,ownsize
\bc4\lib\bidsi.lib+
\bc4\lib\owlwi.lib+
\bc4\lib\import.lib+
\bc4\lib\crtldll.lib
ownsize.def
```

DYNA32.MAK

```
#  MAKE file for Win32 API using dynamic BIDS,
#  OWL and C-runtime libraries.
#
#    C> make -fdyna32.mak
#

.AUTODEPEND
CC = -c -H -H\""owl\owlpch.h\"" -p- -R -vi -W -X-
CD = -D_RTLDLL;_BIDSDLL;_OWLDLL;_OWLPCH;
INC = -I\BC4\INCLUDE
```

```
LIB = -L\BC4\LIB

ownsize.exe :  ownsize.obj ownsize.res
  tlink32 -aa -c -Tpe $(LIB) @dyna32.lnk
  brc32 ownsize.res ownsize.exe

ownsize.obj :  ownsize.cpp
  bcc32 $(CC) $(CD) ownsize.cpp

ownsize.res :  ownsize.rc ownsize.ico ownsize.h
  brc32 $(INC) -w32 -R ownsize.rc
```

DYNA32.LNK

```
\bc4\lib\c0w32.obj+
ownsize.obj
ownsize,ownsize
\bc4\lib\bidsfi.lib+
\bc4\lib\owlwfi.lib+
\bc4\lib\import32.lib+
\bc4\lib\cw32i.lib
ownsize.def
```

OWNSIZE demonstrates two programming techniques that may be interesting to you. First, it uses the **GetSystemMetrics** routine to determine the size of its top-level window when it is first run. When OWNSIZE is about to exit, it writes the size of its window to a private **profile file**. A profile file is an ASCII text file that a program can use to store values that it wants to remember. OWNSIZE uses a profile file to save the location and dimensions of its window, so the next time it is run it can start up with the same size. Also, the profile sets a flag if the window was zoomed, so that the next time the program is started it can make its window zoomed as well. The profile file provides a sense of continuity for a program.

The initial width of the window in OWNSIZE is set to the width of the display screen. To determine the width of the display screen, the window object's constructor calls **GetSystemMetrics** with the SM_CXSCREEN parameter, as shown here:

```
cx = GetSystemMetrics (SM_CXSCREEN);
```

The initial height of the window in OWNSIZE is set so that when the window is open, the row of icons at the bottom of the display screen is visible. To calculate the required value, we make three calls to **GetSystemMetrics**. The first determines the screen height; the second determines the height of an icon; and the third call determines the height of a caption, since each icon is accompanied by a caption. Here is the line of code that does this calculation:

```
cy = GetSystemMetrics (SM_CYSCREEN) -
     GetSystemMetrics (SM_CYICON)   -
```

```
(GetSystemMetrics (SM_CYCAPTION) * 2);
```

The caption height is multiplied by two just to make sure there is enough room.

GetSystemMetrics provides measurement information for quite a few objects that make up the Windows user interface. Included are the sizes of cursors, icons, menus, and captions, as well as the widths of the different types of borders. Let's take a moment to look at some of the different measurement values that this routine can provide.

System Metrics

Table 13.2 lists all of the system metrics that are defined for Windows, along with the symbolic value for the index. To give a better idea of what each value represents, Figures 13.8 through 13.10 provide the same information in a visual form.

Table 13.2 Windows System Metrics

Type	*Index*	*Description*
Screen Metrics (4)	SM_CXSCREEN	Screen width in pixels.
	SM_CYSCREEN	Screen height in pixels.
	SM_CXFULLSCREEN	Screen width in pixels.
	SM_CYFULLSCREEN	Screen height in pixels minus the height of a window caption.
Border Sizes (6)	SM_CXBORDER	Width of a border created with the WS_BORDER style.
	SM_CYBORDER	Height of a border created with the WS_BORDER style.
	SM_CXFRAME	Width of a border on a window created with the WS_THICKFRAME style bit.
	SM_CYFRAME	Height of a border on a window created with the WS_THICKFRAME style bit.
	SM_CXDLGFRAME	Width of a border on a window with either a WS_EX_DLGMODALFRAME or WS_DLGFRAME style border.
	SM_CYDLGFRAME	Height of a border on a window with either a WS_EX_DLGMODALFRAME or WS_DLGFRAME style border.

(continued)

Table 13.2 Windows System Metrics *(Continued)*

Type	*Index*	*Description*
Scroll Bar Metrics (6)	SM_CXVSCROLL	Width of the arrow bitmap in a vertical scroll bar.
	SM_CYHSCROLL	Height of the arrow bitmap in a horizontal scroll bar.
	SM_CYVSCROLL	Height of the arrow bitmap in a vertical scroll bar.
	SM_CXHSCROLL	Width of the arrow bitmap in a horizontal scroll bar.
	SM_CYVTHUMB	Height of the thumb in a vertical scroll bar.
	SM_CXHTHUMB	Width of the thumb in a horizontal scroll bar.
Window Components (8)	SM_CYCAPTION	Height of a caption bar.
	SM_CYMENU	Height of a single-line menu item.
	SM_CXICON	Width of an icon.
	SM_CYICON	Height of an icon.
	SM_CXCURSOR	Width of a cursor.
	SM_CYCURSOR	Height of a cursor.
	SM_CXSIZE	Width of the system menu, minimize and maximize icons.
	SM_CYSIZE	Height of the system menu, minimize and maximize icons.
Window Tracking (4)	SM_CXMIN	Minimum width of a window.
	SM_CYMIN	Minimum height of a window.
	SM_CXMINTRACK	Minimum tracking width of a window.
	SM_CYMINTRACK	Minimum tracking height of a window.
Miscellaneous Flags (4)	SM_DEBUG	Nonzero if the debug version of Windows is installed.
	SM_SWAPBUTTON	Nonzero if the left and right mouse buttons are swapped.

(continued)

Table 13.2 Windows System Metrics *(Continued)*

Type	*Index*	*Description*
	SM_MOUSEPRESENT	Nonzero if a mouse is present.
	SM_CMETRICS	Count of the number of system metric values.

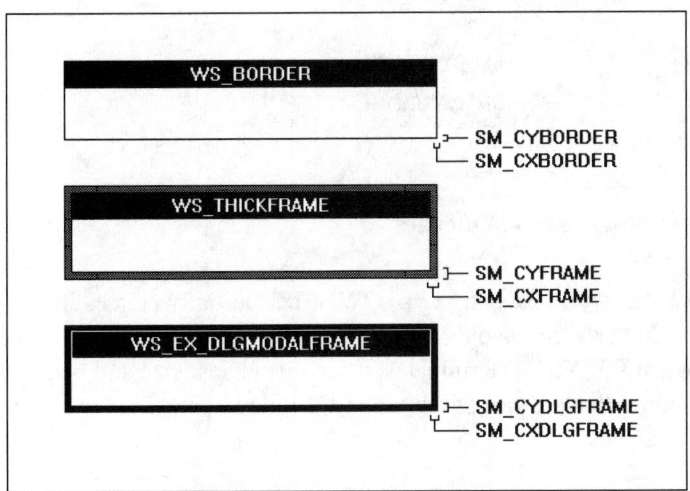

Figure 13.8 Border size system metrics

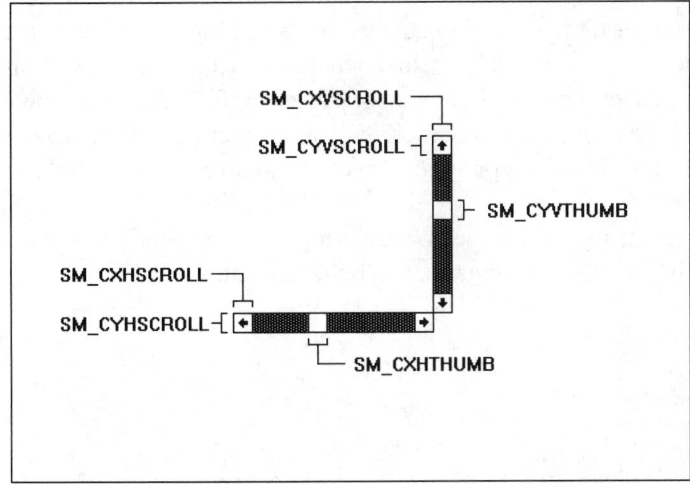

Figure 13.9 Scroll bar system metrics

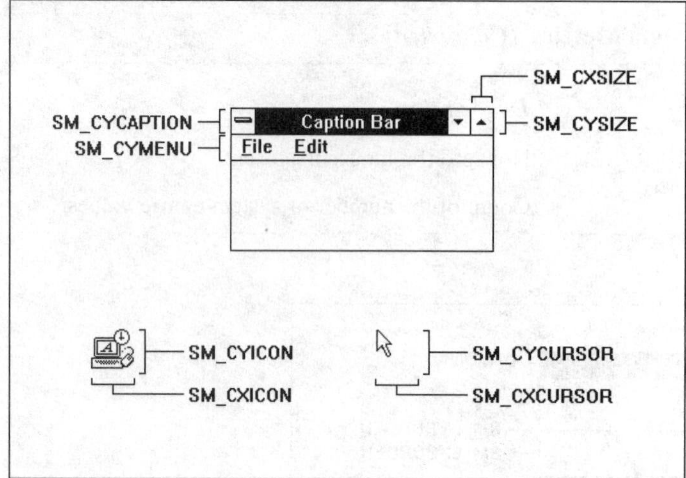

Figure 13.10 Window component system metrics

By using the values from **`GetSystemMetrics`**, OWNSIZE initially creates its top-level window with a reasonable size and avoids the cascading effect that seems to serve only to confuse the user. When OWNSIZE terminates, it records its last size and position onto disk. It uses a set of routines that are part of the support Windows provides for private profile files.

Private Profile Files

One way that a program can improve its rapport with a user is to remember the preferences that the user has expressed. This might mean remembering the menu options that were selected, the preferred color to use for negative numbers, or something as simple as the position of the program's top-level window. To help make this easy for you to do, Windows includes a set of routines that support the creation of private profile files, also known as private initialization files. Of course, you might prefer to keep user preference data in your own format, but the profile file support provides an easy way to read and write user preference information.

A profile file is an ASCII text file, which means that users can modify the file using a text editor. Here is the profile file that our program, OWNSIZE, created:

```
[OWNSIZE]
x=0
y=0
cx=640
cy=408
Reopen=0
```

As you can tell from this example, profile files have the following format:

```
 [application name]
keyname1 = value1
keyname2 = value2
keyname3 = value3
```

OWNSIZE keeps four numeric values that correspond to the location and the dimensions of the window when OWNSIZE was last run. These are associated with the keynames `x`, `y`, `cx`, and `cy`. A fifth numeric value, associated with the keyname `Reopen`, is used when the window has been either zoomed or iconized (maximized or minimized), in which case the program provides special handling.

Windows provides six routines that can be used to read and write profile files. Three of them are for reading and writing WIN.INI, which is the profile file used by Windows and older Windows programs: **`GetProfileInt`**, **`GetProfileString`**, and **`WriteProfileString`**. The other three provide support for private initialization files: **`GetPrivateProfileInt`**, **`GetPrivateProfileString`**, and **`WritePrivateProfileString`**.

OWNDRAW writes into its private profile file, OWNDRAW.INI, by calling **`WritePrivateProfileString`**, which is defined

```
WritePrivateProfileString (lpApplication, lpKey,
                           lpString, lpFile)
```

- **`lpApplication`** is a long pointer to the application name. This is the name placed in square brackets in the profile file to identify a group of keyname/value pairs.
- **`lpKey`** is the long pointer to the name of the data identifier. That is, it is the string on the left of the equal sign in a keyname/value pair.
- **`lpString`** is a long pointer to the string to be placed on the right side of the equal sign in a keyname/value pair.
- **`lpFile`** is a long pointer to a character string for the file name to be used as a profile file. If no directory is given, the profile file is written into Windows' directory.

Here, for example, is how OWNSIZE writes the *x* location of the window:

```
wsprintf (ach, "%d",Attr.X);
WritePrivateProfileString (achPr, "x", ach, achFile);
```

When OWNDRAW starts up, it calls **`GetPrivateProfileInt`** to retrieve the various numeric values that it uses for the initial size and position of its window. This routine allows a program to establish a default value in case the requested integer value is not available. **`GetPrivateProfileInt`** is defined as follows:

```
WORD GetPrivateProfileInt (lpApp, lpKey, nDefault,
                           lpFile)
```

- **`lpApplication`** is a long pointer to the application name. This is the name placed in square brackets in the profile file to identify a group of keyname/value pairs.
- **`lpKey`** is the long pointer to the name of the data identifier. That is, it is the string on the left of the equal sign in a keyname/value pair.
- **`nDefault`** is the value to be used if the keyname is not available in the initialization file, or if the initialization file does not exist.
- **`lpFile`** is a long pointer to a character string for the file name to be used as a profile file. If no directory is given, the profile file is written into Windows' directory.

The return value is an unsigned integer value that is the value in the private profile file, or the default value if the profile entry could not be found. Here is how OWNDRAW retrieves the (*x*,*y*) location from the private profile file:

```
x   = GetPrivateProfileInt (achPr, "x", 0, achFile);
y   = GetPrivateProfileInt (achPr, "y", 0, achFile);
```

The next topic we're going to discuss is the use of child windows in a program's top-level window. And in particular, the use of the OWL gadget windows for creating a control bar window and a message bar window.

Creating a TGadgetWindow

If you glance at the OWL class hierarchy[3], you'll notice a group of classes called "Gadget Classes." Within this group there are two distinct class hierarchies: the **`TGadgetWindow`** classes and the **`TGadget`** classes. The **`TGadgetWindow`** classes are derived from **`TWindow`**, and therefore wrap around a WinAPI window. You'll create gadget windows within a decorated frame[4] and place within the gadget window one or more gadgets—that is, an object created from the classes derived from **`TGadget`**.

In general, **`TGadget`** objects are not themselves windows. This doesn't mean that they aren't useful, just that there isn't any **`HWindow`** member of **`TGadget`** and the window manipulation API—which can be so helpful in moving, sizing, and modifying windows—cannot be used with **`TGadget`** objects. The one exception is **`TControlGadget`** objects. These gadgets are dialog box controls and, as you'll see in Chapter 14, that means that they are windows and *can* be manipulated with the various windowing API.

Figure 13.11 shows GADGETS, a program that uses two gadget windows and each available gadget type. One gadget window sits below the menu, the other at the bottom of the frame window (with the text, "A sample push button gadget"). The upper gadget win-

---

[3] A copy of the OWL class hierarchy appears at the very end of this book, on the 2 next-to-last pages.

[4] In OWL terms, a **`TDecoratedFrame`** or a **`TDecoratedMDIFrame`** window.

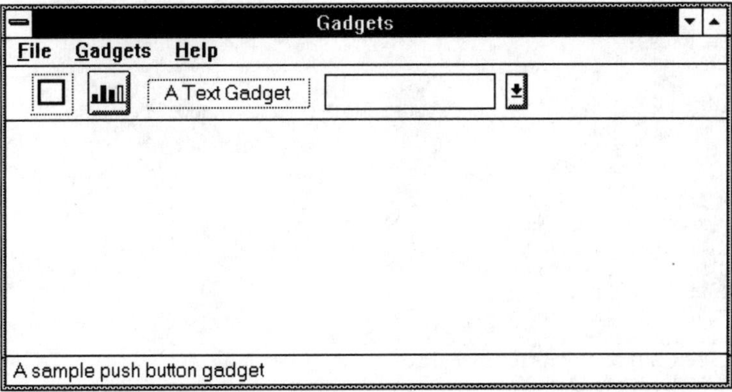

Figure 13.11 GADGETS creates every type of TGadget object.

dow is a **control bar**—in OWL terms a **`TControlBar`** window—used to hold program status indicators and program command gadgets. The lower gadget window is a message bar—a **`TMessageBar`**—used to display helpful messages to the user. Some messages appear when the user browses a menu to help the user decide which menu item to pick. Other messages—like the one shown here—appear when the user browses (moves the mouse cursor over) button gadgets. (The button gadget is the graph in the control bar.)

There are a few quirks to gadgets, but in general they are very helpful and visually attractive. Just from looking at this simple example, it should be clear that they provide two items—a control bar and a message window—that many application developers will want to use. Here are the source files to GADGETS:

GADGETS.CPP

```
//
// GADGETS.CPP  Shows the creation of a toolbar and a status line
//              using OWL's TGadgetWindow and the various TGadget
//              descendents.
//
#include <owl\owlpch.h>
#include <owl\decframe.h>
#include <owl\statusba.h>
#include <owl\controlba.h>
#include <owl\gadget.h>
#include <owl\textgadg.h>
#include <owl\buttonga.h>
#include <owl\bitmapga.h>
#include <owl\controlg.h>
#include <owl\combobox.h>
#include "gadgets.h"

DDecFrame::DDecFrame(TWindow * twParent, const char * Title,
                     TWindow * twClient) :
    TDecoratedFrame (twParent, Title, twClient, TRUE)
    {
    pdApp = (DApp *) GetApplication();
```

```
    bButtonEnable = FALSE;
    }

DEFINE_RESPONSE_TABLE3 (DDecFrame, TDecoratedFrame, TFrameWindow, TWindow)
  EV_WM_INITMENU,
  EV_WM_MOVE,
  EV_WM_SIZE,
  EV_COMMAND(CM_BM_SQUARE, CmBmSquare),
  EV_COMMAND(CM_BM_ROUND,  CmBmRound),
  EV_COMMAND(CM_BU_ENABLE, CmBuEnable),
  EV_COMMAND(CM_BU_DISABLE,CmBuDisable),
  EV_COMMAND(CM_FILEEXIT, CmFileExit),
  EV_COMMAND(CM_HELPABOUT, CmHelpAbout),
  EV_COMMAND(CM_BUTTON, CmButton),
  EV_COMMAND_ENABLE(CM_BUTTON, CmButtonEnable),
  EV_COMMAND(CM_CONTROL, CmControl),
END_RESPONSE_TABLE;

DClient::DClient(char * Title) : TWindow(0, Title, 0)
    {
    }

DClient::~DClient()
    {
    }
void DDecFrame::EvInitMenu(HMENU /*hmenu*/)
    {
    // Tell combobox listbox to disappear.
    pdApp->pcwComboBox->HideList();
    }

void DDecFrame::EvMove(TPoint& ptOrigin)
    {
    TDecoratedFrame::EvMove(ptOrigin);

    // Tell combobox listbox to disappear.
    pdApp->pcwComboBox->HideList();
    }

void DDecFrame::EvSize(UINT sizeType, TSize& size)
    {
    TDecoratedFrame::EvSize(sizeType, size);

    // Tell combobox listbox to disappear.
    pdApp->pcwComboBox->HideList();
    }

void DDecFrame::CmFileExit()
    {
    CloseWindow(0); // Cause application to terminate
    }

void DDecFrame::CmBmSquare()
    {
    pdApp->pgBitmap->SelectImage(BM_SQUARE, FALSE);
    }

void DDecFrame::CmButtonEnable(TCommandEnabler& handler)
    {
    handler.Enable(bButtonEnable);
    }
```

```
void DDecFrame::CmBmRound()
    {
    pdApp->pgBitmap->SelectImage(BM_ROUND, FALSE);
    }

void DDecFrame::CmBuEnable()
    {
    bButtonEnable = TRUE;
    }

void DDecFrame::CmBuDisable()
    {
    bButtonEnable = FALSE;
    }

void DDecFrame::CmHelpAbout()
    {
    MessageBox(" Creating and Using Gadgets\n\n"
               "'Borland C++ 4.0 Programming\n"
               "  for Windows', by Paul Yao", Title);
    }

void DDecFrame::CmButton()
    {
    MessageBox ("Button Clicked", Title);
    }

void DDecFrame::CmControl()
    {
    MessageBeep(0);
    }

DApp::DApp() : TApplication()
    {
    }

void DApp::InitInstance()
    {
    // Create application's windows.
    TApplication::InitInstance();

    // Time to init WinAPI combobox window.
    // First, add strings, then...
    pcwComboBox->AddString("Borland");
    pcwComboBox->AddString("C++ 4.0");
    pcwComboBox->AddString("Programming for");
    pcwComboBox->AddString("Windows");

    // ...Resize.  Query current size...
    TRect trWindow;
    pcwComboBox->GetWindowRect(trWindow);

    // ...calculate new size...
    TEXTMETRIC tm;
    TClientDC dc(0);
    dc.GetTextMetrics(tm);
    int cy = tm.tmHeight * 6;
    int cx = trWindow.Width();

    // ...Call WinAPI to resize.
    pcwComboBox->SetWindowPos(HWND_TOP, 0, 0, cx, cy, SWP_NOMOVE);
    }
```

```
   void DApp::InitMainWindow()
       {
       // Create client & frame windows.
       pdcWindow = new DClient("Gadgets");
       pdfWindow = new DDecFrame(0, "Gadgets", pdcWindow);

       // Create control bar and connect to decorated frame.
       pgwControlBar = new TControlBar (pdfWindow);
       pdfWindow->Insert (*pgwControlBar, TDecoratedFrame::Top);

       // Ask for hints -- text in TMessageBar window --
       // for TButtonGadget gadgets.
       pgwControlBar->SetHintMode (TGadgetWindow::EnterHints);

       // A Separator makes control bar visually pleasing.
       pgSeparator1 = new TSeparatorGadget (10);
       pgwControlBar->Insert(*pgSeparator1);

       // Create & insert bitmap display gadget.
       pgBitmap    = new TBitmapGadget ("shapes", CM_BITMAP, TGadget::Embossed ,
 2, 0);
       pgwControlBar->Insert(*pgBitmap);

       pgSeparator2 = new TSeparatorGadget (10);
       pgwControlBar->Insert(*pgSeparator2);

       // Create & insert pushbutton gadget.
       pgButton    = new TButtonGadget ("graph", CM_BUTTON);
       pgwControlBar->Insert(*pgButton);

       pgSeparator3 = new TSeparatorGadget (10);
       pgwControlBar->Insert(*pgSeparator3);

       // Create & insert text display gadget.
       pgText = new TTextGadget (CM_TEXT,              // Gadget id.
                                 TGadget::Embossed,    // Border.
                                 TTextGadget::Center, // Alignment.
                                 10,                   // Max string.
                                 "A Text Gadget");     // Init string.
       pgwControlBar->Insert(*pgText);

       pgSeparator4 = new TSeparatorGadget (10);
       pgwControlBar->Insert(*pgSeparator4);

       // Calculate size for combobox control...
       TEXTMETRIC tm;
       TClientDC dc(0);
       dc.GetTextMetrics(tm);
       int cxControl = tm.tmMaxCharWidth * 10;
       int cyControl = tm.tmHeight * 2;

       // Create combobox...
       pcwComboBox = new TComboBox (pgwControlBar, CM_CONTROL,
                                    0, 0, cxControl, cyControl,
                                    CBS_DROPDOWN, 20);

       // ...and connect combobox to control bar.
       pgControl   = new TControlGadget (*pcwComboBox);
       pgwControlBar->Insert(*pgControl);

       // Create message window and connect to decorated frame.
```

```
    pgwMessage = new TMessageBar (pdfWindow);
    pdfWindow->Insert (*pgwMessage, TDecoratedFrame::Bottom);

    // Perform normal application start-up work.
    SetMainWindow (pdfWindow);
    MainWindow->AssignMenu("MAIN");
    MainWindow->SetIcon(this, "SNAPSHOT");
    }

//
// Application main entry point.
OwlMain(int, char **)
    {
    return DApp().Run();
    }
```

GADGETS.H

```
// Command identifiers are sequential to make
// resource string table compact. Reason is
// that these ID's are used as string ID's.
#define CM_FILEEXIT   100

#define CM_BM_SQUARE  101
#define CM_BM_ROUND   102
#define CM_BU_ENABLE  103
#define CM_BU_DISABLE 104
#define CM_TX_COUNT   105

#define CM_HELPABOUT  106

#define CM_BITMAP     107
#define CM_BUTTON     108
#define CM_TEXT       109
#define CM_CONTROL    110

// Gadget defines.
#define BM_SQUARE     0
#define BM_ROUND      1

class DClient;
class DApp;

//
// Main Window
class DDecFrame : public TDecoratedFrame
    {
  public:
    DDecFrame(TWindow *, const char *, TWindow *);

    void CmFileExit();
    void CmBmSquare();
    void CmBmRound();
    void CmBuEnable();
    void CmBuDisable();
    void CmHelpAbout();
    void CmButton();
    void CmButtonEnable(TCommandEnabler& handler);
    void CmControl();
```

```
    void EvInitMenu(HMENU hmenu);
    void EvMove(TPoint& ptOrigin);
    void EvSize(UINT sizeType, TSize& size);
  private:
    BOOL      bButtonEnable;
    DApp    * pdApp;

  DECLARE_RESPONSE_TABLE (DDecFrame);
    };

//
// Client window
class DClient : public TWindow
    {
  public:
    DClient(char * Title);
    ~DClient();
    };

//
// Application object
class DApp : public TApplication
    {
  public:
    DApp();
    void InitInstance();
    void InitMainWindow();

    TBitmapGadget    * pgBitmap;
    TButtonGadget    * pgButton;

    DClient          * pdcWindow;
    TDecoratedFrame  * pdfWindow;

    TMessageBar      * pgwMessage;
    TTextGadget      * pgText;

    TControlBar      * pgwControlBar;
    TTextGadget      * ptText;
    TSeparatorGadget * pgSeparator1;
    TSeparatorGadget * pgSeparator2;
    TSeparatorGadget * pgSeparator3;
    TSeparatorGadget * pgSeparator4;
    TControlGadget   * pgControl;
    TComboBox        * pcwComboBox;
    };
```

GADGETS. RC

```
#include "gadgets.h"

snapshot icon gadgets.ico

main menu
    BEGIN
    POPUP "&File"
        {
        MENUITEM "E&xit", CM_FILEEXIT
        }
```

```
    POPUP "&Gadgets"
        {
        MENUITEM "Square Bitmap",   CM_BM_SQUARE
        MENUITEM "Round Bitmap",    CM_BM_ROUND
        MENUITEM SEPARATOR
        MENUITEM "Enable Button",   CM_BU_ENABLE
        MENUITEM "Disable Button",  CM_BU_DISABLE
        }
    POPUP "&Help"
        {
        MENUITEM "&About...", CM_HELPABOUT
        }
    END

shapes bitmap shapes.bmp

graph bitmap graph.bmp

;
; String ID's correspond to menu IDs since
; the TMessageBar will automatically display
; strings with the same string ID -- IFF the
; TDecoratedFrame window was created with
; trackMenuSelection = TRUE.
;
; The one gadget ID, CM_BUTTON, is because the
; TButtonGadget will display helpful info. You
; need to tell the TControlBar how much help to
; give, which you do by call its SetHintMode
; function (actually TGadgetWindow has this).
;
STRINGTABLE
    {
    CM_FILEEXIT, "Exit application"

    CM_BM_SQUARE, "Display square bitmap in bitmap gadget"
    CM_BM_ROUND,  "Display round bitmap in bitmap gadget"
    CM_BU_ENABLE, "Disable pushbutton gadget"
    CM_BU_DISABLE, "Enable pushbutton gadget"

    CM_HELPABOUT,  "About this application..."

    CM_BUTTON, "A sample push button gadget"
    }
```

GADGETS.DEF

```
EXETYPE WINDOWS

CODE MOVEABLE DISCARDABLE
DATA MULTIPLE MOVEABLE

HEAPSIZE   512
STACKSIZE 8192
```

DYNA16.MAK

```
#  MAKE file for Win16 API using dynamic BIDS,
#  OWL and C-runtime libraries.
#
#    C> make -fstatic16.mak
#

.AUTODEPEND
CC = -c -H -H"owl\owlpch.h" -ml -R -vi -WS -X-
CD = -D_RTLDLL;_BIDSDLL;_OWLDLL;_OWLPCH;
INC = -I\BC4\INCLUDE
LIB = -L\BC4\LIB

gadgets.exe :  gadgets.obj gadgets.res
  tlink -c -C -Twe $(LIB) @dyna16.lnk
  brc gadgets.res gadgets.exe

gadgets.obj :  gadgets.cpp
  bcc $(CC) $(CD) gadgets.cpp

gadgets.res :  gadgets.rc gadgets.ico gadgets.h
  brc $(INC) -31 -R gadgets.rc
```

DYNA16.LNK

```
\bc4\lib\c0wl.obj+
gadgets.obj
gadgets,gadgets
\bc4\lib\bidsi.lib+
\bc4\lib\owlwi.lib+
\bc4\lib\import.lib+
\bc4\lib\crtldll.lib
gadgets.def
```

DYNA32.MAK

```
#  MAKE file for Win32 API using dynamic BIDS,
#  OWL and C-runtime libraries.
#
#    C> make -fdyna32.mak
#

.AUTODEPEND
CC = -c -H -H\""owl\owlpch.h\"" -p- -R -vi -W -X-
CD = -D_RTLDLL;_BIDSDLL;_OWLDLL;_OWLPCH;
INC = -I\BC4\INCLUDE
LIB = -L\BC4\LIB

gadgets.exe :  gadgets.obj gadgets.res
  tlink32 -aa -c -Tpe $(LIB) @dyna32.lnk
  brc32 gadgets.res gadgets.exe

gadgets.obj :  gadgets.cpp
  bcc32 $(CC) $(CD) gadgets.cpp

gadgets.res :  gadgets.rc gadgets.ico gadgets.h
  brc32 $(INC) -w32 -R gadgets.rc
```

DYNA32.LNK

```
\bc4\lib\c0w32.obj+
gadgets.obj
gadgets,gadgets
\bc4\lib\bidsfi.lib+
\bc4\lib\owlwfi.lib+
\bc4\lib\import32.lib+
\bc4\lib\cw32i.lib
gadgets.def
```

Although it may not be immediately evident, GADGETS has five separate WinAPI windows. The outermost window is a frame window—**TDecoratedFrame**, to be exact. There are two **TGadgetWindow** windows—one for the control bar and one for the message bar. One of the gadgets is a WinAPI combo box control, which is a WinAPI window. And finally, GADGETS creates an empty **TWindow** derived class, **DClient**, as a place holder for your client windows.

Although most programs in this book have a single frame window *without* a client window, the OWL frame window classes provide a place holder for a client window. The idea apparently is to allow the frame window to handle application-level operations—the application menu, accelerator keys, and application shutdown. The client window can then focus on handling the display and editing of user data.

Within GADGETS, gadget setup is a two step operation. The first step involves creating two gadget window objects and filling them with gadgets—tasks accomplished in **DApp::SetupMainWindow**. The second step is to initialize the combo box control within the **TGadgetControl** window—this is done in **DApp::InitInstance**. The second step is necessary because the combo box—itself a WinAPI window—cannot be initialized until it has been created. That is, even though an OWL **TControlBox** object has been created, the associated WinAPI window doesn't get created until later[5].

The four different OWL **TGadgetWindow** classes are:

OWL Class	*Description*
TToolBox	Arranges gadgets into a grid. You specify the number of rows and columns you need for your particular set of gadgets. It also sizes itself to accommodate the number of rows it contains.
TMessageBar	Has a single text gadget for displaying application messages.

(continued)

[5] The creation of WinAPI windows is performed by **TApplication::InitInstance**, which creates the application's main window object, then calls **TWindow::Create** (which calls **TWindow::PerformCreate**) to create the WinAPI window. When the WinAPI **WM_CREATE** message arrives at the main window (the **EvCreate** message response function), the **SetupWindow** function gets called which in turn calls **TWindow::CreateChildren** to create the WinAPI child windows.

OWL Class	*Description*
TStatusBar	Derived from **TMessageBar**, this gadget window allows for additional text gadgets and "mode indicators." A mode indicator is a text gadget that displays the status of—for example—the Caps Lock key, the Num Lock key, etc. There are six different mode indicators defined for the status bar.
TControlBar	A gadget window that resides by default under the application menu for application command buttons. It sets its height based on the tallest gadget. Gadgets themselves are arranged in a single row, and gadgets that extend outside the window are not wrapped or accommodated in any way.

From this set of gadget windows, you'll probably use **TMessageBar** or **TStatusBar**, but probably not both at the same time. The same holds true for the other two: You'll probably use either **TToolBox** or **TControlBar**, but not both within your application's main window. If you have several different tool sets, you might put each in its own **TFloatingFrame** window.

The **TMessageBar** in GADGETS echoes helpful information about menu items as the user browses through them. It works this way because a string table in GADGETS.RC provides a string for each menu item. If you study this string table, you'll notice that the string IDs match the command IDs for the menu items, which is how the message bar connects a menu to its description. The message bar can also display descriptive information for button gadgets (but only button gadgets—not for any other types) if a string entry is provided for it as well. This capability, which is turned off by default, can be enabled by calling **TControlBar::SetHintMode**.

Gadget windows are useful because of the gadgets they contain. As mentioned earlier, gadgets are not WinAPI windows but instead are graphic objects drawn within a **TGadgetWindow** window[6]. Here are the available **TGadget**-derived classes:

OWL Class	*Description*
TBitmapGadget	Output-only. This gadget accepts a GDI bitmap containing multiple images, and lets you select which image to display.
TButtonGadget	Input/Output. This gadget accepts a GDI bitmap for use as a pushbutton style gadget. OWL defines a new message, **WM_COMMAND_ENABLE**, that gets sent to determine if a particular menu item or button gadget is enabled. As shown in the GADGETS sample, respond to this message for each button gadget to enable and disable. The class handles proper drawing of a disabled button for you.

[6] The exceptions, as mentioned earlier, are the dialog box control windows that are wrapped within **TControlGadget** objects.

OWL Class	*Description*
`TTextGadget`	Output-only. Draws a line of text.
`TSeparatorGadget`	Output-only. Used to create empty space between gadgets. The units used are "gadget-units," set equal to the width of a nonsizable border (see the **`GetSystemMetrics`** function, the **`SM_CXBORDER`** and **`SM_CYBORDER`** values).
`TControlGadget`	Input/Output. Wrapper for holding WinAPI dialog box control as a gadget. In the GADGETS example, a combo box is shown being used as a gadget.

Once you create a gadget, it only becomes useful when installed in a gadget window. For most gadgets, it's fairly straightforward. With control gadgets, however, you can run into minor snags. As mentioned earlier, you must, for the WinAPI window is created before attempting to initialize a control gadget. With a combo box control gadget, create the gadget the size of the closed combo box. Then, after the WinAPI combo box window is created, resize it to its open size.

This futzing is necessary because a combo box uses its size information to decide how large to make its listbox, but when closed the combo box is typically quite a bit smaller. But since a gadget window uses the combo box size to adjust the gadget window size and/or spacing, you can end up with lots of useless blank screen space. The solution, as shown in GADGETS, is to create the TControlGadget object at its closed size and insert it into the gadget window. Then, after the listbox window has been created, resize the window with WinAPI function calls to its open size. Everyone is then happy.

A quirk of the button gadget is that when a **`WM_COMMAND_ENABLE`** message arrives, you need to explicitly enable the button. Otherwise, the button stays in a permanently disabled state. As shown in GADGETS, when this message arrives it provides a pointer to a command enabler object. Just call the handler's **`Enable`** member, passing **`TRUE`** to enable and **`FALSE`** to disable your button.

The two sample programs in this chapter, OWNSIZE and GADGETS, provide a template that you can use to fine-tune the handling of windows in your own programming projects. But this is only the beginning of how to take advantage of Windows' windows. In the next chapter, I'm going to cover an important user interface object built on top of windowing. I'm referring, of course, to Windows' support for dialog boxes.

14

Dialog Boxes

Dialog boxes are windows that provide a standard way for a program to ask users for additional information that may be required to complete a command. For example, a user may select the **Open...** menu item from a program's File popup menu. The ellipsis (...) at the end of the menu text indicates that a dialog box will appear. For the program to determine *which* file to open, it displays a dialog box. The user can either type the name of the file to be opened or select a file from a list. Figure 14.1 shows a standard file-open dialog box.

A dialog box itself is a window that contains child windows. In the context of dialog boxes, these child windows are called **dialog box controls**. Windows provides six window classes to support a wide range of dialog box controls. Dialog box controls can be created using the button, combobox, edit, listbox, scroll bar, and static window classes. And, if these predefined window classes don't provide the exact type of control that is needed, creating a custom dialog box control is as easy as creating a new window class.

Dialog boxes come in two flavors: modal and modeless. A **modal dialog box** prevents the user from interacting with other windows in a program. **System modal dialog boxes** are a

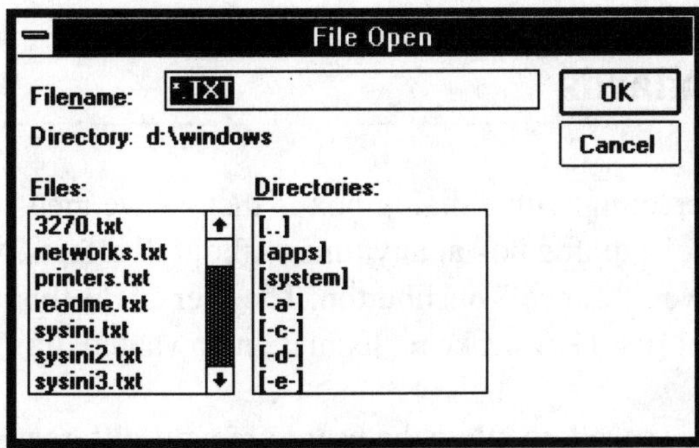

Figure 14.1 A standard file-open dialog box

special type of modal dialog box that prevents the user from interacting with any window in the *system*. A **modeless dialog box**, on the other hand, doesn't interfere with a user's interaction with other windows, but instead lets the user choose the window to work with.

Internally, the difference between the two has to do with the way the flow of messages is controlled. A modal dialog box cuts off the flow of mouse and keyboard messages to its parent and sibling windows by making its parent window **disabled**. If the user tries to interact with the disabled parent window by clicking the mouse in its client area, in its menu, or in any other part of its nonclient area, the system responds with a warning beep. A second way that modal dialog boxes control message flow is that each has its own message processing loop. Instead of using OWL's standard **`PeekMessage`** loop, a modal dialog box establishes its own. This means that keyboard accelerators, which depend on the call to **`TranslateAccelerator`** in the message loop, will be disabled when a modal dialog box is present.

A modeless dialog box, on the other hand, does not alter the flow of messages to any part of your program. Once a modeless dialog box has been opened, the user is free to work with other windows in your program or to access keyboard accelerators. Modeless dialog boxes act like the windows that a program can create by calling **`CreateWindow`**. In fact, this is how both modeless *and* modal dialog boxes are created. As we'll discuss, dialog box creation routines simply make a sequence of calls to **`CreateWindow`** on your behalf.

At first glance, modeless dialog boxes may seem more attractive than modal dialog boxes, since they give the user more choices over the structure of an interaction. In spite of this initial impression, most dialog boxes are modal. A modal dialog box provides an ideal way to focus the user's attention on the command he has selected. Once you have his attention, he must decide whether to complete the command or to cancel it. The ability to cancel a modal dialog box is one reason that modal dialogs can be so strict in their interactions with users.

Dialog boxes are an important part of the Windows user interface, and there is a standard set of dialog box controls that users quickly learn how to manipulate. The success of your dialog box programming depends to a large degree on how well you understand these conventions. We're going to start by looking at some of the conventions that have been developed for dialog boxes and dialog box controls.

Dialog Box User-Interface Standards

Perhaps the first thing to be said about interacting with a dialog box is that, as we mentioned earlier, a user should be able to cancel a dialog box at any time without ill effects. For this reason, every dialog box should have a "Cancel" pushbutton. The user clicks this button with the mouse or uses the equivalent [Esc] keystroke to dismiss an unwanted dialog box.

A dialog box will have other pushbuttons as well, to allow the user to request different types of actions. A pushbutton marked "Ok" provides a standard way for the user to indicate that all data has been entered into the dialog box, and that the program should perform whatever action had been requested that first caused the dialog to be created. In the same way that a dialog box can be canceled by either mouse or keyboard action, the user can click with the mouse on the Ok button, or use the [Tab] key to position the keyboard focus indicator and strike [Enter] to push the Ok button. At a minimum, users expect to see two pushbuttons: one to accept the changes and one to reject them.

There are other types of pushbuttons that a programmer can create, including a pushbutton that displays a text label followed by an ellipsis (...). Like its counterpart in menus, this pushbutton causes a dialog box to be displayed. A variation on this theme is a pushbutton with a chevron (> >) after the button label. When such a button is pushed, it causes the dialog box to grow and reveal hidden dialog box controls. Figure 14.2 shows four types of pushbuttons: Ok, Cancel, ellipsis (...), and chevron (> >).

Pushbuttons indicate the set of actions that users can request from a dialog box. When a dialog box opens, one pushbutton will be the default, which means it is selected when the user strikes the [Enter] key. The default pushbutton has a thicker border than normal, so that the user knows it at a glance. When the user strikes the [Tab] key to move between dialog box controls, the pushbutton that has the keyboard focus will always be the default pushbutton.

Two other types of buttons are **radio buttons** and **check boxes**. Radio buttons always come in groups. A group of radio buttons is like a question in a multiple-choice test: At least one of the answers must be correct. A check box is like an on/off switch: When it is checked, it is turned on and when it is not checked, it is turned off. Figure 14.3 shows a dialog box containing radio buttons and check boxes.

An **edit control** lets the user enter and edit text. There are several different styles of edit controls, including single line and multiline, automatic conversion to either uppercase or lowercase, and character masking to hide text when entering passwords. Like most of the other standard parts of the Windows user interface, edit controls can be manipulated with

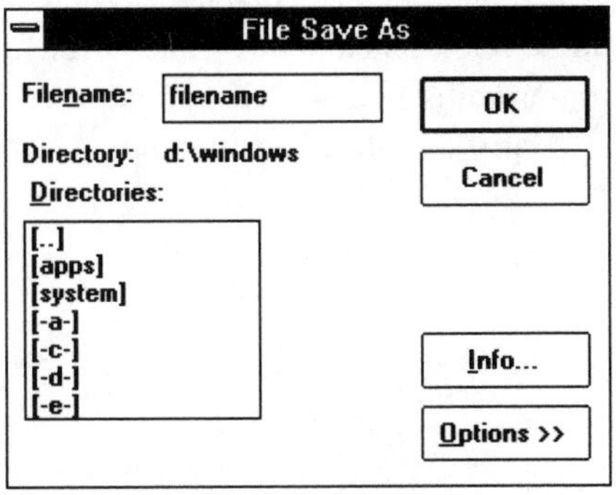

Figure 14.2 Four pushbutton types, from the Paintbrush program's Save As dialog box

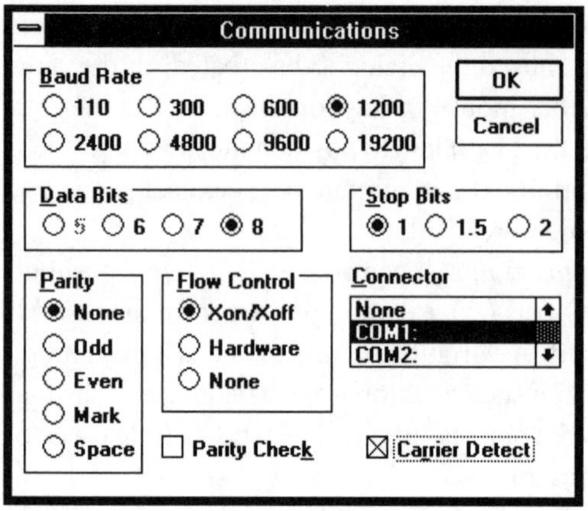

Figure 14.3 Radio buttons and check boxes

the mouse or the keyboard. Either device can be used to select a character or a range of characters, or move the insertion point. A multiline edit control can be equipped with a scroll bar for when the text might not be able to fit into the area available in an edit control. Figure 14.4 shows a typical edit control.

The **static** window class creates controls that are used to display icons, text labels, and empty and filled rectangles. Figure 14.5 shows a group of static controls in a dialog box.

A **listbox** shows the user a set of choices that are available. The most common type of listbox contains text, but graphic images can also be drawn into a listbox when the set of choices is best represented by pictures instead of by words. Listboxes can have scroll bars, which are necessary when the items in a list cannot all be displayed simultaneously. Figure 14.6 shows a listbox.

A **combobox** combines a listbox with an edit control or a listbox with a static text control. A combobox can hide its listbox until the user clicks on an arrow icon to call up the listbox. Like regular listboxes, a combobox can have a scroll bar and can display either text or graphic images. From a user's point of view, a combobox looks and acts exactly like a listbox paired with a static or edit control. From a programming point of view, however, a combobox is much easier to support. Figure 14.7 shows an example of a combobox.

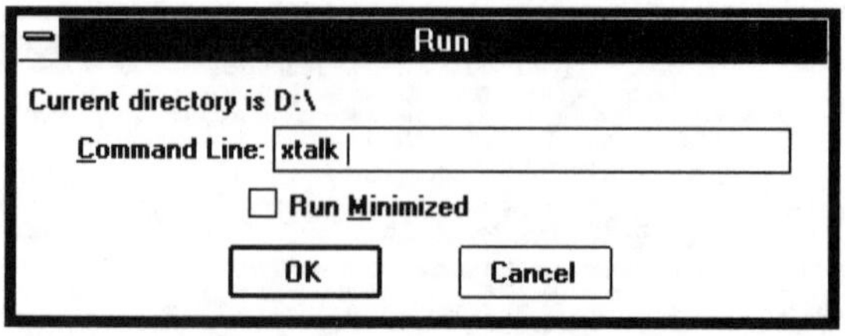

Figure 14.4 An edit control from the File Manager

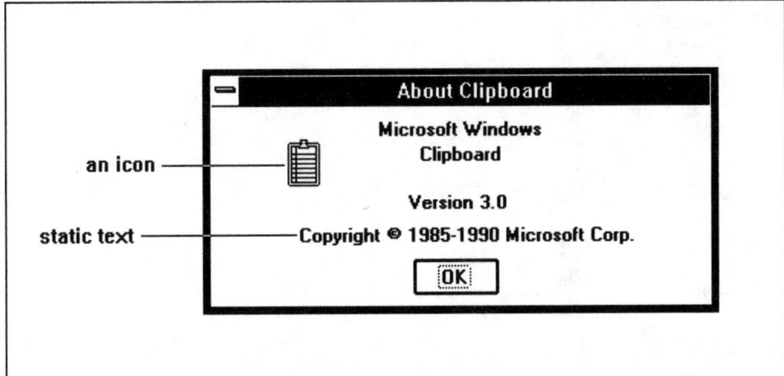

Figure 14.5 A group of static controls in a dialog box

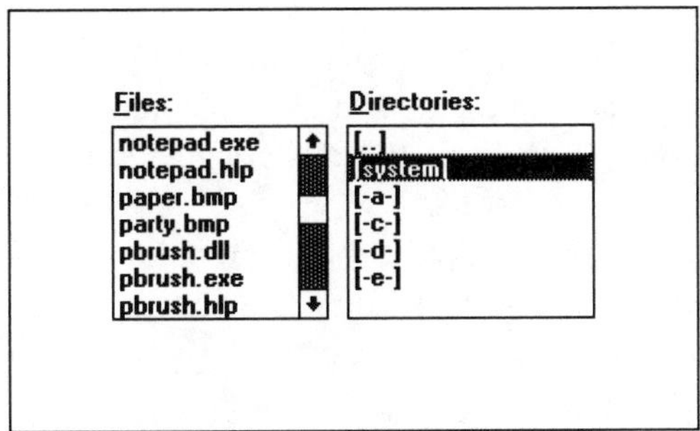

Figure 14.6 A pair of listboxes: one with and one without a scroll bar

A **scroll bar** is a graphical representation of three related numbers: a minimum, a maximum, and a current value that lies between the two. You may recall that a scroll bar is installed in a regular window that was created with either the **WS_HSCROLL** or

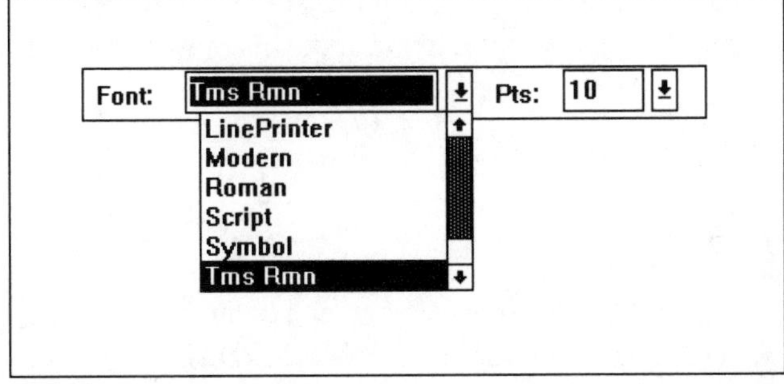

Figure 14.7 A pair of comboboxes: one showing and one hiding a listbox

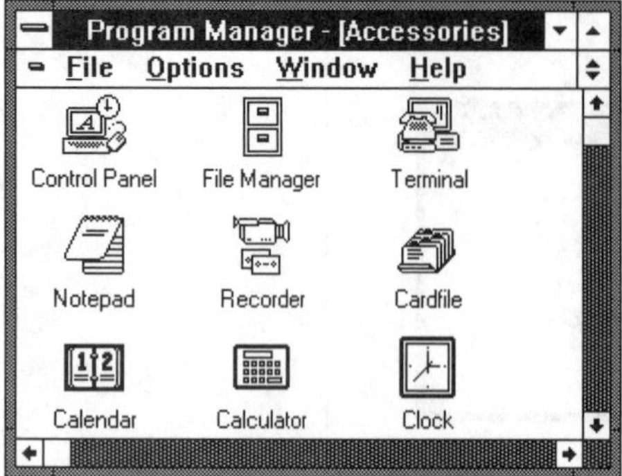

Figure 14.8 Vertical and horizontal scroll bars

WS_VSCROLL style bits. Also, as we mentioned earlier, listboxes and edit controls can be created with a built-in scroll bar. However, you can request a stand-alone scroll bar as a dialog box control. Figure 14.8 shows a vertical and a horizontal scroll bar in the Program Manager application.

Programs that have special input requirements that cannot be met by Windows' predefined dialog box controls can provide their own. Custom dialog box controls can be incorporated into a dialog box alongside Windows' own dialog box controls.

Now that you've seen Windows' predefined dialog box controls, it's time to look at what's involved writing code to support a dialog box. In general, you create a dialog, initialize its controls, and let the controls handle the low-level nitty-gritty work for you. As the user interacts with each control, you receive notification messages to help you keep track of the user's progress. When the user dismisses a dialog—with a click on an Ok or Cancel button, for example—you collect the contents of each control and apply them as necessary.

Before showing you the ins and outs of a modal and a modeless dialog box, I'm going to touch briefly on Windows' **common dialog boxes**. These are eight dialog boxes that Microsoft provides as part of Windows. In addition to helping standardize the user-interface between applications, the common dialog boxes help cut down the work required to build Windows applications.

Common Dialog Boxes

Before you build your own dialog box, you'll want to check whether a common dialog box can do the job for you. Windows 3.1 comes equipped with COMMDLG.DLL, which contains everything needed to support Windows' eight common dialog boxes. While this DLL does not come standard with Windows 3.0, it's easy to get a royalty-free license from

Microsoft to ship this DLL to customers using this older version of Windows. Under Windows NT, the common dialogs are provided by COMDLG32.DLL. These libraries contain hundreds of lines of code that you get to access for free.

Under OWL, the common dialogs are derived from **`TCommonDialog`**, which itself is derived from **`TDialog`**, OWL's base dialog box class. Summoning one of these dialogs is as simple as initializing a data structure, creating an OWL common dialog box object, then creating the WinAPI dialog box objects. The total amount of code involved is between 10 and 20 lines—a far cry from the hundreds of lines that would be required for all the work these dialogs do for you.

There are two dialogs in each of these four categories: file selection, printing, searching and graphic selection. The file selection dialogs support the **File.Open...** and **File.Save As...** menu items. The user gets shown lists of files, directories, and disk drives. A user can even access network drives by clicking on a Network... push button.

The two printing dialog boxes accept user input for selecting a range of pages to print, and for selecting a particular printer to use. The printing dialogs can even create a printer DC for you, taking into account the user's desired printer configuration.

One of the search dialog boxes lets the user specify a string to search for. The second dialog lets the user specify both a search string and a replace string. Both are created as modeless dialog boxes, which means the user can continue editing while the dialog boxes are present.

The two graphic selection common dialogs provide color picker and font selection support. The color picker dialog resembles the dialog used by the Windows' Control Panel for setting desktop colors. In fact, the same developer at Microsoft—Clark Cyr—built the Windows Control Panel and the common dialog box library. The font picker dialog box lets a user pick from available system and device fonts. The text viewer program in Chapter 10, TEXTVIEW, uses this dialog to let you select a font to use for text display. It provides the **`LOGFONT`** data needed to create a GDI logical font, and so provides a convenient way to do font selection.

The following sample program demonstrates the use of one of the common dialog boxes, the file open dialog. As you get started using these dialog boxes, you'll see that this dialog has elements used by the other seven: you start by filling in a data structure. Next, you create an OWL dialog object. Finally, you create the WinAPI object by calling **`TDialog`**'s **`Execute`** member for a modal dialog, or **`Create`** for a modeless dialog.

OPENFILE.CPP

```
//
// OPENFILE.CPP  Demonstrate call to Windows File.Open...
//               common dialog box.
//
#include <owl\owlpch.h>
#include <owl\opensave.h>
#include "openfile.h"
```

```
DEFINE_RESPONSE_TABLE1 (DFrame, TFrameWindow)
  EV_COMMAND(CM_FILEOPEN, CmFileOpen),
  EV_COMMAND(CM_FILEEXIT, CmFileExit),
  EV_COMMAND(CM_HELPABOUT, CmHelpAbout),
END_RESPONSE_TABLE;

DFrame::DFrame(char * title) : TFrameWindow(0, title)
    {
    }

void DFrame::CmFileOpen()
    {
    // Create TFileOpenDialog object.
    TFileOpenDialog tfo(this, *lpFileData);

    // Display dialog box.
    int retval = tfo.Execute();

    // Did user hit <Ok> or <Cancel>?
    if (retval == IDOK)
        {
        // Query filename & extension
        tfo.GetFileTitle(lpFileData->FileName, lpszFileTitle, 16);

        // Set main window caption w/file title.
        ((DApp *)GetApplication())->SetFileCaption(lpszFileTitle);

        // Force a repaint.
        Invalidate();
        }
    else
        {
        MessageBox ("File Open Cancelled", Title);
        }
    }

void DFrame::CmFileExit()
    {
    CloseWindow(0); // Cause application to terminate
    }

void DFrame::CmHelpAbout()
    {
    MessageBox("       Open File Dialog Box\n\n"
               "'Borland C++ 4.0 Programming\n"
               "  for Windows', by Paul Yao", Title);
    }

BOOL DFrame::Create()
    {
    // Create File.Open instance data.
    lpFileData = new TOpenSaveDialog::TData(
                         OFN_FILEMUSTEXIST,       // Flags.
                         "All Files (*.*)|*.*|"  // Filters.
                         "Text Files (*.txt)|*.txt|"
                         "Help Databases (*.hlp)|*.hlp|"
                         "Programs (*.exe)|*.exe|"
                         "Libraries (*.dll)|*.dll|",
                         0,               // Custom Filter.
                         "",              // Initial directory.
                         "txt");          // Default Extension.
```

```
    // Error checking.
    if (! lpFileData)
        return FALSE;

    // IMPORTANT! Call original base class function.
    return TFrameWindow::Create();
    }

void DFrame::Paint (TDC& dc, BOOL, TRect&)
    {
    char ach[256];
    wsprintf (ach, "Full Path: %s", lpFileData->FileName);

    dc.TextOut(10, 10, ach);
    }

DApp::DApp() : TApplication()
    {
    achBaseTitle = "Open File";
    }

void DApp::InitMainWindow()
    {
    SetMainWindow (new DFrame(achBaseTitle));

    MainWindow->AssignMenu("MAIN");
    MainWindow->SetIcon(this, "SNAPSHOT");
    }

void DApp::SetFileCaption(LPSTR lpFileName)
    {
    char ach[120];
    lstrcpy (ach, achBaseTitle);
    lstrcat (ach, " - ");
    lstrcat (ach, lpFileName);

    MainWindow->SetCaption(ach);
    }

// Application main entry point.
OwlMain(int, char **)
    {
    return DApp().Run();
    }
```

OPENFILE.H

```
#define CM_FILEOPEN  100
#define CM_FILEEXIT  101
#define CM_HELPABOUT 200

// Main window
class DFrame : public TFrameWindow
    {
  public:
    DFrame(char * title);
    void CmFileOpen();
    void CmFileExit();
    void CmHelpAbout();
```

```
    BOOL Create();
    void Paint (TDC& dc, BOOL, TRect&);

    TOpenSaveDialog::TData    * lpFileData;
    char lpszFileTitle[16];

  DECLARE_RESPONSE_TABLE (DFrame);
    };

// Application object
class DApp : public TApplication
    {
  public:
    DApp();
    void InitMainWindow();
    void SetFileCaption(LPSTR lpFileName);
  private:
    LPSTR achBaseTitle;
    };
```

OPENFILE.RC

```
#include "openfile.h"

snapshot icon openfile.ico

main menu
    BEGIN
    POPUP "&File"
        {
        MENUITEM "&Open...", CM_FILEOPEN
        MENUITEM SEPARATOR
        MENUITEM "E&xit",   CM_FILEEXIT
        }
    POPUP "&Help"
        {
        MENUITEM "&About...", CM_HELPABOUT
        }
    END
```

OPENFILE.DEF

```
EXETYPE WINDOWS

CODE MOVEABLE DISCARDABLE
DATA MULTIPLE MOVEABLE

HEAPSIZE   512
STACKSIZE 8192
```

DYNA16.MAK

```
#  MAKE file for Win16 API using dynamic BIDS,
#  OWL and C-runtime libraries.
#
#    C> make -fstatic16.mak
#

.AUTODEPEND
CC = -c -H -H"owl\owlpch.h" -ml -R -vi -WS -X-
CD = -D_RTLDLL;_BIDSDLL;_OWLDLL;_OWLPCH;
INC = -I\BC4\INCLUDE
LIB = -L\BC4\LIB

openfile.exe :  openfile.obj openfile.res
  tlink -c -C -Twe $(LIB) @dyna16.lnk
  brc openfile.res openfile.exe

openfile.obj :  openfile.cpp
  bcc $(CC) $(CD) openfile.cpp

openfile.res :  openfile.rc openfile.ico openfile.h
  brc $(INC) -31 -R openfile.rc
```

DYNA16.LNK

```
\bc4\lib\c0wl.obj+
openfile.obj
openfile,openfile
\bc4\lib\bidsi.lib+
\bc4\lib\owlwi.lib+
\bc4\lib\import.lib+
\bc4\lib\crtldll.lib
openfile.def
```

DYNA32.MAK

```
#  MAKE file for Win32 API using dynamic BIDS,
#  OWL and C-runtime libraries.
#
#    C> make -fdyna32.mak
#

.AUTODEPEND
CC = -c -H -H\""owl\owlpch.h\"" -p- -R -vi -W -X-
CD = -D_RTLDLL;_BIDSDLL;_OWLDLL;_OWLPCH;
INC = -I\BC4\INCLUDE
LIB = -L\BC4\LIB

openfile.exe :  openfile.obj openfile.res
  tlink32 -aa -c -Tpe $(LIB) @dyna32.lnk
  brc32 openfile.res openfile.exe
```

```
openfile.obj :  openfile.cpp
  bcc32 $(CC) $(CD) openfile.cpp

openfile.res :  openfile.rc openfile.ico openfile.h
  brc32 $(INC) -w32 -R openfile.rc
```

DYNA32.LNK

```
\bc4\lib\c0w32.obj+
openfile.obj
openfile,openfile
\bc4\lib\bidsfi.lib+
\bc4\lib\owlwfi.lib+
\bc4\lib\import32.lib+
\bc4\lib\cw32i.lib
openfile.def
```

Unlike many other programs, OPENFILE does its main window initialization by overriding **TFrameWindow::Create** instead of **TFrameWindow::SetupWindow**. While this may seem like an arbitrary choice, in fact **Create** can fail, while **SetupWindow** can't. In a low memory situation, for example, an application can be notified when a failure occurs during initialization.

At initialization, a **TOpenSaveDialog::TData** block gets created. This is all the state information required for a file open dialog. But by itself, it doesn't represent a file open dialog box. The creation of the OWL file open dialog occurs in **DFrame::CmFileOpen**, when the OWL **TFileOpenDialog** object is created. It might strike you as odd that this object gets created as a local variable on the stack. This is a feature of a modal dialog box, which forces the caller to wait until the dialog box has been dismissed before returning. In the context of OPENFILE, the call to **Execute** creates the associated WinAPI objects and doesn't return until the user has struck **Ok** or **Cancel**.

Once the dialog has been dismissed, it's a simple matter to query the **TFileOpenDialog** object for bits of information that might be needed. In the sample program, the file name—name and extension minus path information—gets incorporated into the main window's caption. Notice, however, that the fully qualified path gets retained in the initialization data block, and gets displayed in response to a **WM_PAINT** message.

Of course, there will be times when the common dialog boxes don't meet your specific requirements. At those times, you'll build your own dialog from the ground up. Let's take a look at what's involved in building a dialog box yourself.

Creating Dialog Boxes

Creating a dialog box—whether modal or modeless—requires a combination of three ingredients: a dialog box template, code to create the dialog box, and code to maintain the dialog box. Each of these elements puts a different twist on the dialog box creation process, so we're going to look at them one at a time.

Dialog Box Template

A dialog box template is a data object that defines the size of the dialog box, the type of controls in the dialog box, as well as the size and positioning of each dialog box control. The most common type of dialog box template is one built with a graphic editor like the one built into the Resource Workshop. The dialog box editor creates a template like this:

```
FIND DIALOG LOADONCALL MOVEABLE DISCARDABLE
            9, 27, 216, 47
CAPTION "Find"
STYLE WS_BORDER | WS_CAPTION | WS_DLGFRAME | WS_SYSMENU |
      WS_VISIBLE | WS_POPUP
BEGIN
    CONTROL "&Find What:", -1, "static",
            SS_LEFT | WS_CHILD, 9, 7, 39, 10
    CONTROL "", IDD_EDIT, "edit",
            ES_LEFT | WS_BORDER | WS_TABSTOP | WS_CHILD,
            52, 6, 146, 12
    CONTROL "Find &Next", IDD_FIND, "button",
            BS_DEFPUSHBUTTON | WS_TABSTOP | WS_CHILD,
            83, 26, 61, 14
END
```

The **`DIALOG`** statement is a lot like the **`MENU`** statement, which is the resource keyword for defining a menu. The syntax of the **`DIALOG`** statement is

```
dialogID DIALOG [load option] [memory option] x, y, cx, cy
```

- **`dialogID`** identifies the dialog box resource.
- **`[load option]`** is either **`PRELOAD`** or **`LOADONCALL`**. **`PRELOAD`** causes a dialog to be loaded into memory before a program starts running. **`LOADONCALL`** causes the dialog to be loaded only when it is needed.
- **`[memory option]`** is **`FIXED`**, **`MOVEABLE`**, or **`DISCARDABLE`**, and describes the behavior of the object once it has been loaded. For more details on these options, refer to the discussion in Chapter 18.
- **`x`** and **`y`** is the position of the dialog box window, in dialog box coordinates, relative to the client area of the dialog box's parent window.
- **`cx`** and **`cy`** are the width and height of the control, in dialog box coordinates.

Each **CONTROL** statement in the dialog box definition defines a different dialog box control. The general syntax of the **CONTROL** statement is

```
CONTROL <text>, nID, <class>, <styles>, x, y, cx, cy
```

- **<text>** is a character string in double quotes that later becomes the window text of the window that is created.
- **nID** is an integer value that uniquely identifies the dialog control window.
- **<class>** is the character string name of the window class from which a dialog control is to be created.
- **<styles>** are a set of generic window class styles and control-specific styles that are ORed together.
- **x** and **y** is the position of the control in the dialog box window, in dialog box coordinates.
- **cx** and **cy** are the width and height of the control, in dialog box coordinates.

You may have noticed that the position and size of the dialog box itself, and of each control in the dialog box, are specified in a coordinate system called **dialog box coordinates**. This coordinate system helps a dialog box definition be somewhat device-independent, since the units are defined relative to the size of the system font. In dialog box coordinates, units in the *x* direction are approximately 1/4 of the average width of the system font. In the *y* direction, they are 1/8 of the height of the system font. **GetDialogBoxUnits** provides the necessary base units, which can be used to convert between dialog box units and pixels using code like the following:

```
int  xBase,  yBase;
int  xDlg,   yDlg;
int  xPixel, yPixel;
LONG lBase;

lBase = GetDialogBoxUnits();
xBase = LOWORD (lBase);
yBase = HIWORD (lBase);
xPixel = (xDlg * xBase)/4;
yPixel = (yDlg * yBase)/8;
```

The **STYLE** statement in the **DIALOG** statement lists the window styles that are part of the dialog box window when it is created. From this, you may have already guessed that the dialog box template is little more than a convenient way to list the parameters of the **CreateWindow** routine. Your guess would be correct. One of the tasks performed by the dialog box routines is to parse the dialog box template, making appropriate calls to **CreateWindow**.

If you find that you're a bit overwhelmed by all the details that are involved in the definition of the dialog box template, you'll be glad to know there is an easier way. Rather than messing with the creation of a dialog box template by hand, there is a tool that is part of the Borland Resource Workshop: the dialog box editor.

The Resource Workshop Dialog Box Editor

The very first Windows programmers, back at the beginning of (Windows) time, had to create dialog box templates from scratch. This involved taking pencil to graph paper to create dialogs that looked somewhat reasonable. Getting a dialog box to look good required many hours of work. Fortunately, those days are long gone, and Windows programmers can take advantage of a graphic tool that allows them to draw dialog boxes and create dialog templates from these images.

Figure 14.9 shows the Resource Workshop's dialog box editor displaying the image of the dialog box definition that we saw earlier. The editor lets you adjust a dialog until it looks right. It supports all of the predefined types of dialog box controls, as well as custom controls which reside in a dynamic link library. The editor has quite a few convenient features.

To fine-tune a specific dialog box control, you select the Control.Style... menu or double-click on the control. This causes a customizing dialog box to appear, which allows you to change a control's text, its ID value, and the specific style bits that will control the appearance and behavior of the control. There is a different customizing dialog box for each class of dialog box control, since each class has its own, private style bits. Figure 14.10 shows the customizing dialog box that allows you to select the different styles available for static class dialog box controls.

The dialog box editor also lets you edit include (.H) files. Select the Resource.Identifiers... menu to view and change the symbolic constants you have created for control

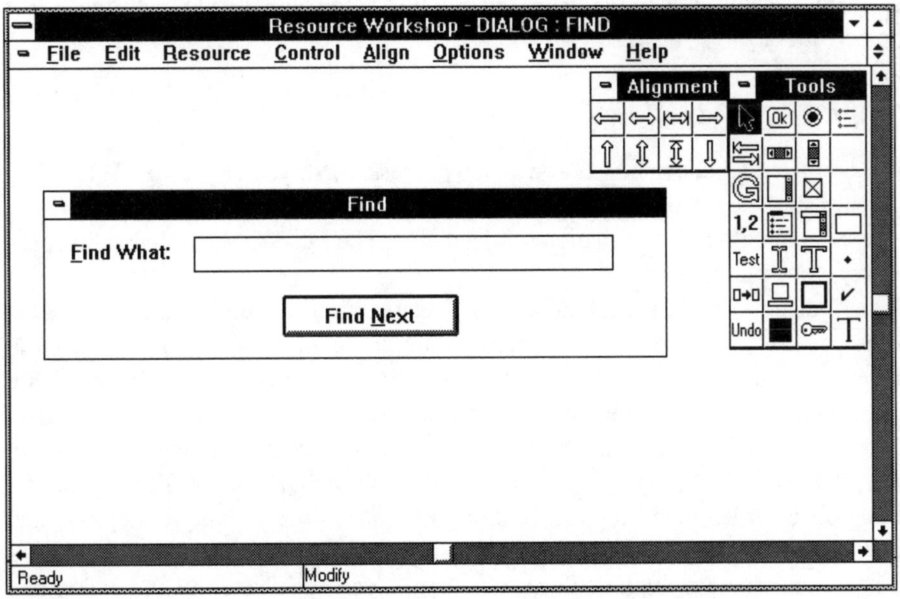

Figure 14.9 The Dialog Box editor

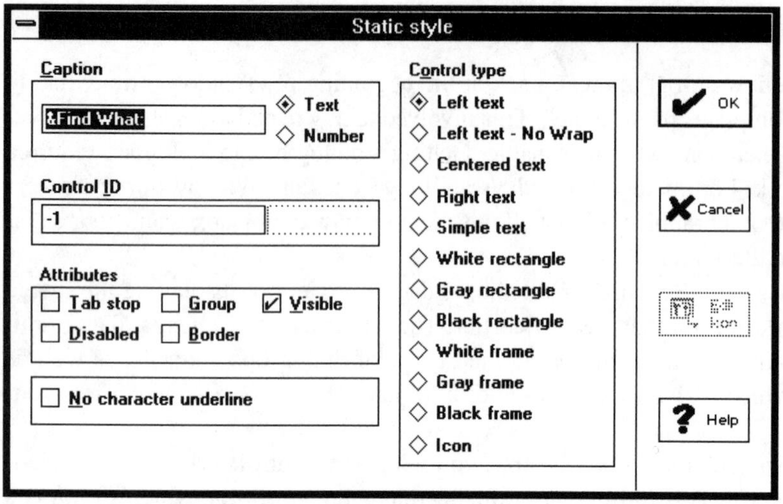

Figure 14.10 Selecting static control styles

command IDs. I usually create a separate include file for each dialog box, to simplify the process of reusing templates for different projects.

Creating the dialog box template involves creating a resource object that describes the shape, size, and position of the dialog box itself and those of each control in a dialog box. This object is placed into your program's resource file, along with the icon, resource, and menu definitions that are part of your application program. With the resource defined, the next ingredient that you'll need to create a dialog box is the actual code that triggers the dialog box creation.

Creating a Modal Dialog Box

The creation of a modal dialog box is a two-step process. First, you create an OWL dialog object. Then, using the dialog object, you create an MS-Windows dialog box. The OWL dialog object maintains state information for the dialog. The MS-Windows dialog box handles the interaction with the user.

OWL has a dialog box class, **`TDialog`**, which can serve as a foundation for the dialog box classes you create in your applications. For simple dialog boxes, you don't need to define a new class. Simply let **`TDialog`** handle everything. For more involved dialog boxes, of course, you'll want to derive classes from **`TDialog`**.

`TDialog` itself is derived from **`TWindow`**. As you may recall from the discussion in Chapter 5, **`TWindow`** is the primary wrapper around WinAPI windows. To truly understand dialog boxes, it helps to keep this in mind. Put more simply: every dialog box and every dialog box control *is* a WinAPI window. Anything you can do to a WinAPI window—create them, move them, hide them, size them—you can also do to any dialog box window *using the same window-manipulation API.*

TDialog has only a few data members:

Type	*Name*	*Description*
PUBLIC:		
TDialogAttr	**Attr**	Structure for dialog box attributes.
BOOL	**IsModal**	Flag set if dialog box is modal.

And, of course, it also has the member it inherits from **TWindows**. The **TDialogAttr** structure is defined in DIALOG.H, an OWL include file, as follows:

```
struct TDialogAttr {
    char far* Name;
    DWORD Param;
};
```

Name refers to the resource ID for the dialog box template. This value is provided as a parameter to the constructor. **Param** provides a way to pass initialization data to a dialog box. You can assign a value to this field in the constructor of classes derived from **TDialog**.

TDialog contains 28 member functions: 23 are public, 3 are protected, and 2 are private. Here is a list of the more commonly called and more commonly overridden member functions:

Commonly Called Member Functions:

Function Name	*Description*
TDialog()	Constructor.
~TDialog()	Destructor.
Execute()	Creates an MS-Windows modal dialog box from a resource template.
Create()	Creates an MS-Windows *modeless* dialog box from a resource template.
CloseWindow()	Closes a dialog box.
SendDlgItemMsg()	Sends a message to an MS-Windows dialog box control.

Commonly Overridden Member Functions:

Function Name	*Description*
EvInitDialog()	Respond to the **WM_INITDIALOG** message. Call the overridden function, since it performs some initialization processing as well.
Ok()	Override to process **WM_COMMAND** notification codes from an Ok pushbutton.

Function Name	*Description*
`Cancel()`	Override to process **`WM_COMMAND`** notification from a Cancel pushbutton.

To create an OWL dialog box, start by creating an OWL **`TDialog`** object (or an object from a class derived from **`TDialog`**). You can instantiate the OWL dialog object as a local variable to create a modal dialog box:

```
TFindDialog tdFind(this, "FIND", achFind, BUFSIZE);
tdFind.Execute();
```

When creating a modeless dialog boxes, however, you'll probably call the C++ **`new`** operator to dynamically allocate the OWL dialog object:

```
ptdFind = new TFindDialog(this, "FIND", achFind, BUFSIZE);
ptdFind->Create();
```

`TDialog::Create()` returns immediately after creating the WinAPI modeless dialog box, so a local variable can't be used. **`TDialog::Execute()`**, on the other hand, doesn't return until the modal dialog is dismissed, which is why a local variable can be used. Since dynamic allocation (**`new`**) method works for both modal and modeless dialog boxes, it's safest to use all the time.

When creating a modal dialog box, you call **`TDialog::Execute()`**. This function, in turn, calls a WinAPI function—**`DialogBoxParam`**—to create the Windows dialog box object. For details on this routine, see the accompanying boxed discussion.

The `DialogBoxParam` Routine

Four MS-Windows routines create a modal dialog box: **`DialogBox`**, **`DialogBoxIndirect`**, **`DialogBoxIndirectParam`**, and **`DialogBoxParam`**. The OWL dialog box object, **`TDialog`**, calls the last of these routines to create an MS-Windows dialog box: **`DialogBoxParam`**. This routine is defined

```
int DialogBoxParam (hInstance, lpszTemplate,
                    hwndParent,lpDialogProc, dwParam);
```

- **`hInstance`** is the instance handle of the program or dynamic link library that owns the dialog box definition. The application object holds a copy of this for you.
- **lpszTemplate** is a far pointer to a character string for the name of the dialog box definition, as defined in the dialog box template. Alternatively, it can be an integer value wrapped inside the

MAKEINTRESOURCE macro, when an integer is used in place of a character string to identify the dialog box template. **TDialog** gets the resource ID from your dialog box constructor.

- **hwndParent** is a handle to the parent window of the dialog box. The parent window of a modal dialog box is disabled when the dialog box is displayed. You identify the parent of a dialog box to **TDialog**'s constructor.
- **lpDialogProc** is a far pointer to a piece of code that maintains the dialog box while it being displayed. This is a function that is referred to as a dialog box procedure. The address passed in this parameter is not the actual address of the routine itself, but the instance thunk created by the **MakeProcInstance** routine for the dialog box procedure. This mechanism is covered in detail in Chapter 19.
- **dwParam** is a DWORD (unsigned long) value for an (optional) parameter to be passed to the dialog box at creation time. This value is copied from the **Attr** data member of the **TDialog** class.

The first and third parameters are relatively straightforward, since we have encountered instance handles and window handles before. Let's take a closer look at the second and fourth parameters.

The second parameter to **DialogBox** is defined as an **LPSTR** value, which means it can hold a far pointer to a character string. The second parameter identifies the dialog box template from the resource file definition. This can be a regular character string for dialog box templates that are defined that way:

```
DialogBoxParam (hInst, "MYDIALOG", hwndParent,
                lpproc, 0L);
```

As an alternative, an integer value can be used to define a dialog box template. When this is the case, a program can use the **MAKEINTRESOURCE** macro to disguise an integer value in a character string position:

```
DialogBoxParam (hInst, MAKEINTRESOURCE(15),
                hwndParent, lpproc, 0L);
```

Or, instead of the **MAKEINTRESOURCE** macro, a pound sign can be placed in a character string to identify a dialog box template with a numeric identifier:

```
DialogBoxParam (hInst, "#15", hwndParent,
                lpproc, 0L);
```

The fourth parameter to **DialogBoxParam** identifies a function which maintains the dialog box while it is opened. This procedure, known as a **dialog box procedure**, processes messages for a dialog box in the same way that a window procedure processes messages for an MS-Windows window. OWL provides a dialog box procedure, and dispatches messages to an OWL program's **message response functions**.

A non-OWL dialog box requires the creation of a **dialog box procedure**. This is a function defined to handle the MS-Windows messages sent to the dialog box. OWL programs, on the other hand, process MS-Windows dialog box messages by creating message response functions. As you may recall from our discussion of the window object classes in Chapter 5, these class member functions each process one MS-Windows message *or* one specific type of WM_COMMAND message.

Let's take a closer look at these member functions, since they play a key role in the maintenance of a dialog box.

Maintaining the Dialog Box

Although a dialog box is a regular MS-Windows window, you'll deal with a different set of messages from those in a normal window. In particular, there are two messages which are interesting in a dialog box: **WM_INITDIALOG** and **WM_COMMAND**. To handle these messages, you'll create two member functions in a dialog box class: **EvInitDialog** and **EvCommand**. As with menu commands, you may decide to create a different message response function for each type of **WM_COMMAND** message you receive.

The **WM_INITDIALOG** message is sent to the dialog box procedure after all of the dialog box control windows have been created, but before they have been made visible. In response to this message, a dialog box procedure initializes each of the dialog box controls to the correct initial state. For example, it might fill a listbox with the items to be viewed by the user. Or, it might set the state of radio buttons or check box buttons to a state that reflects the current settings. If there is an edit control in the dialog box, the dialog box procedure might insert a string at initialization time.

Once the dialog box controls have been given their initial settings, they work on their own to accept user input, modify the current settings, and keep out of each other's way. As they work, they send **WM_COMMAND** messages to the dialog box procedure to notify it of just about every action that the user takes. In some respects, dialog box controls are like children away at summer camp, who write home to tell their parents about the day's activities:

Dear Mom and Dad Window,

Camp is fun. Today we went hiking, played volleyball, received the input focus from the user, and a mouse click or two.

Your child window control,
Check-Box

The **WM_COMMAND** notification messages allow the dialog box procedure to respond to the changes that take place in a dialog box control. In some respects, the **WM_COMMAND** message sent from a dialog box control is just like the **WM_COMMAND** message sent from a menu item when the user has made a menu selection. The **wParam** contains the value of the identifier assigned to the control in its resource file definition. The **lParam** parameter contains other information: The high-order word contains a **notification code**, and the low-order word contains the control's window handle. Figure 14.11 graphically depicts the contents of the parameters to the **WM_COMMAND** message.

Symbolic constants have been assigned for each control's notification codes. With some controls, only a few notification codes have been assigned. This is the case with pushbuttons, which only have two notification codes: **BN_CLICKED** and **BN_DOUBLECLICKED**. These notification codes communicate, respectively, that a button has been clicked and double-clicked with the mouse. Notifications for comboboxes start with CBN_, as in **CBN_DBLCLK**, **CBN_DROPDOWN**, **CBN_EDITCHANGE**, etc. Edit control notifications start with EN_ (**EN_CHANGE**, **EN_HSCROLL**, etc.). Listbox notifications start with LBN_ (**LBN_DBLCLK**, **LBN_KILLFOCUS**, etc.). For more details, refer to the Windows API documentation.

In addition to the messages that a dialog box procedure receives, you'll send quite a few messages *from* your dialog box objects *to* the dependent controls. Sending messages provides the primary mechanism by which your dialog box objects communicate with their controls. At initialization (WM_INITDIALOG) time, a dialog box object sets the initial state of controls by sending messages. As the dialog box object receives notification messages, it may send more messages to fine-tune the controls based on the content of the notifications.

A final issue that needs addressing is the termination of a dialog box. For both modal and modeless dialog boxes, **TDialog**'s **CloseWindow** member function does the work

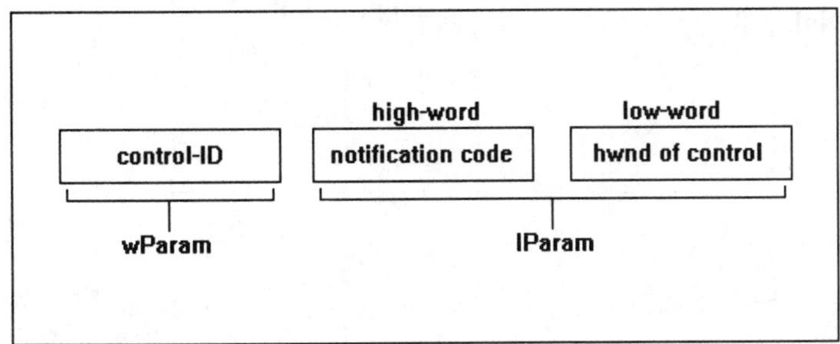

Figure 14.11 The parameters in a Win16 WM_COMMAND notification message

for you. If you've ever written dialog box support code in C, you might recall modal and modeless dialog boxes each require special handling. One of the niceties of the OWL libraries is that they hide these types of differences from you, allowing a single function to do all the dirty work for you.

Now that you've seen the basics of dialog box creation, here's a program that shows the creation of both modal and modeless dialog boxes. The same dialog box template is used, so that you can see the specific differences between the two types of dialog boxes.

Modal and Modeless Dialog Boxes: FIND

The dialog boxes in this sample program is basically a single dialog box that will be created as both a modal and a modeless dialog box. This dialog box is modeled after a dialog box displayed by Write (the word processor that's bundled with Windows) when the user selects the **Edit.Find...** menu item. This program uses this dialog as a modeless dialog box, which means a user can continue editing even when the dialog box is visible. The dialog would be left open to support ongoing string searches, while also allowing a user to continue editing once a desired text block is found. Figure 14.12 shows the dialog box created by our program. Here are the source files to this program:

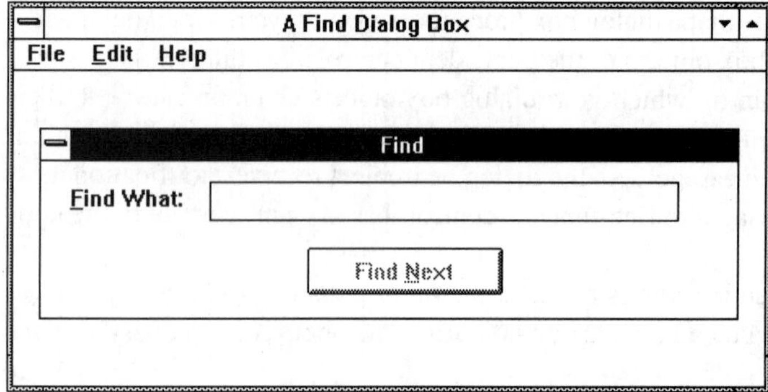

Figure 14.12 The Find Dialog Box

FIND.CPP

```
//
// FIND.CPP   Modal and modeless dialog boxes
//
#include <owl\owlpch.h>
#include "find.h"

DEFINE_RESPONSE_TABLE1 (TFindDialog, TDialog)
  EV_CHILD_NOTIFY_ALL_CODES(IDD_FIND, CmFind),
  EV_CHILD_NOTIFY_ALL_CODES(IDD_EDIT, CmEdit),
```

```
END_RESPONSE_TABLE;

TFindDialog::TFindDialog(DFrame * twParent, LPSTR lpszName,
                         LPSTR lpFindData, WORD cbBufSize)
            : TDialog (twParent, lpszName)
    {
    lpBuffer = lpFindData;
    cbBuffer = cbBufSize;
    }

void TFindDialog::SetupWindow()
    {
    TDialog::SetupWindow();

    // Disable button when text buffer is empty.
    HWND hCtl = GetItemHandle (IDD_FIND);
    ::EnableWindow(hCtl, FALSE);
    }

void TFindDialog::CmFind(UINT /* notify */ )

    {
    // Copy data to parent's find buffer.
    GetDlgItemText (IDD_EDIT, lpBuffer, cbBuffer);

    // Notify parent that find request has been made.
    Parent->HandleMessage(PM_FIND, 0, 0L);
    }

void TFindDialog::CmEdit(UINT notify)
    {
    if (notify == EN_CHANGE)
        {
        HWND hwndEdit = GetDlgItem (IDD_EDIT);
        HWND hwndFind = GetDlgItem (IDD_FIND);
        int cc = Edit_GetTextLength (hwndEdit);
        Button_Enable (hwndFind, cc);
        }
    }

DEFINE_RESPONSE_TABLE1 (DFrame, TFrameWindow)
  EV_MESSAGE(PM_FIND, CmFindData),
  EV_COMMAND(CM_FILEEXIT, CmFileExit),
  EV_COMMAND(CM_EDITFIND, CmEditFind),
  EV_COMMAND(CM_EDITFINDMODAL, CmEditFindModal),
  EV_COMMAND(CM_HELPABOUT, CmHelpAbout),
END_RESPONSE_TABLE;

DFrame::DFrame(char * title) : TFrameWindow(0, title)
    {
    ptdFind = 0;
    }

void DFrame::CmFileExit()
    {
    CloseWindow(0); // Cause application to terminate
    }

// Create a modeless dialog.
void DFrame::CmEditFind()
    {
    // If Find dialog already exists, make it active.
    if (ptdFind && ptdFind->IsWindow())
        {
        ptdFind->SetActiveWindow();
```

```
        return;
        }

    // Create OWL dialog box object.
    ptdFind = new TFindDialog (this, "FIND", achFind, BUFSIZE);

    // Create WinAPI dialog box.
    ptdFind->Create();
    }

// Create a modal dialog.
void DFrame::CmEditFindModal()
    {
    // A local variable works for a modal dialog box,
    // but not for modeless dialogs.
    TFindDialog tdFind(this, "FIND", achFind, BUFSIZE);
    tdFind.Execute();
    }

void DFrame::CmHelpAbout()
    {
    MessageBox("Modal and Modeless Dialog Boxes\n\n"
               "   'Borland C++ 4.0 Programming\n"
               "    for Windows', by Paul Yao", Title);
    }

LRESULT DFrame::CmFindData (WPARAM, LPARAM)
    {
    MessageBox (achFind, "Find Request Received", MB_OK);

    return 0L;
    }

DApp::DApp() : TApplication()
    {
    }

void DApp::InitMainWindow()
    {
    SetMainWindow (new DFrame("A Find Dialog Box"));

    MainWindow->AssignMenu("MAIN");
    MainWindow->SetIcon(this, "SNAPSHOT");
    }

//
// Application main entry point.
OwlMain(int, char **)
    {
    return DApp().Run();
    }
```

FIND.H

```
// Menu IDs.
#define CM_FILEEXIT      100
#define CM_EDITFIND      200
#define CM_EDITFINDMODAL 201
#define CM_HELPABOUT     300

// Dialog IDs.
#define IDD_EDIT     101
```

```
#define IDD_FIND     102

#define BUFSIZE       (80)

#define PM_FIND      (WM_USER+1)

class TFindDialog;
class DFrame;
class DApp;

// Find dialog.
class TFindDialog : public TDialog
  {
  public:

    TFindDialog(DFrame * pwParent, LPSTR lpszName,
                LPSTR lpFindData, WORD cbBufSize);

    void SetupWindow();
    void CmFind(UINT notify);
    void CmEdit(UINT notify);

  private:
    LPSTR lpBuffer;
    WORD  cbBuffer;
  DECLARE_RESPONSE_TABLE(TFindDialog);
  };

// Main window
class DFrame : public TFrameWindow
    {
  public:
    DFrame(char * title);
    void CmFileExit();
    void CmEditFind();
    void CmEditFindModal();
    void CmHelpAbout();
    LRESULT CmFindData (WPARAM wParam, LPARAM lParam);

  private:
    TFindDialog * ptdFind;
    char  achFind[BUFSIZE];
  DECLARE_RESPONSE_TABLE (DFrame);
    };

// Application object
class DApp : public TApplication
    {
  public:
    DApp();
    void InitMainWindow();
    };


// WindowsX.H macro borrowed & given global scope.
#define Edit_GetTextLength(hwndCtl) \
        ::GetWindowTextLength(hwndCtl)
#define Button_Enable(hwndCtl, fEnable) \
        ::EnableWindow((hwndCtl), (fEnable))
```

FIND.RC

```
#include "find.h"

snapshot icon find.ico

main menu
    BEGIN
    POPUP "&File"
        {
        MENUITEM "E&xit", CM_FILEEXIT
        }
    POPUP "&Edit"
        {
        MENUITEM "&Find...",       CM_EDITFIND
        MENUITEM "&Modal Find...", CM_EDITFINDMODAL
        }
    POPUP "&Help"
        {
        MENUITEM "&About...", CM_HELPABOUT
        }
    END

FIND DIALOG LOADONCALL MOVEABLE DISCARDABLE
            9, 27, 216, 47
CAPTION "Find"
STYLE WS_BORDER | WS_CAPTION | WS_DLGFRAME | WS_SYSMENU |
      WS_VISIBLE | WS_POPUP
BEGIN
    CONTROL "&Find What:", -1, "static",
            SS_LEFT | WS_CHILD, 9, 7, 39, 10
    CONTROL "", IDD_EDIT, "edit",
            ES_LEFT | WS_BORDER | WS_TABSTOP | WS_CHILD,
            52, 6, 146, 12
    CONTROL "Find &Next", IDD_FIND, "button",
            BS_DEFPUSHBUTTON | WS_TABSTOP | WS_CHILD,
            83, 26, 61, 14
END
```

FIND.DEF

```
EXETYPE WINDOWS

CODE MOVEABLE DISCARDABLE
DATA MULTIPLE MOVEABLE

HEAPSIZE   512
STACKSIZE 8192
```

DYNA16.MAK

```
#  MAKE file for Win16 API using dynamic BIDS,
#  OWL and C-runtime libraries.
#
#    C> make -fstatic16.mak
#
```

```
.AUTODEPEND
CC = -c -H -H"owl\owlpch.h" -ml -R -vi -WS -X-
CD = -D_RTLDLL;_BIDSDLL;_OWLDLL;_OWLPCH;
INC = -I\BC4\INCLUDE
LIB = -L\BC4\LIB

find.exe :  find.obj find.res
  tlink -c -C -Twe $(LIB) @dyna16.lnk
  brc find.res find.exe

find.obj :  find.cpp
  bcc $(CC) $(CD) find.cpp

find.res :  find.rc find.ico find.h
  brc $(INC) -31 -R find.rc
```

DYNA16.LNK

```
\bc4\lib\c0wl.obj+
find.obj
find,find
\bc4\lib\bidsi.lib+
\bc4\lib\owlwi.lib+
\bc4\lib\import.lib+
\bc4\lib\crtldll.lib
find.def
```

DYNA32.MAK

```
#  MAKE file for Win32 API using dynamic BIDS,
#  OWL and C-runtime libraries.
#
#     C> make -fdyna32.mak
#

.AUTODEPEND
CC = -c -H -H\""owl\owlpch.h\"" -p- -R -vi -W -X-
CD = -D_RTLDLL;_BIDSDLL;_OWLDLL;_OWLPCH;
INC = -I\BC4\INCLUDE
LIB = -L\BC4\LIB

find.exe :  find.obj find.res
  tlink32 -aa -c -Tpe $(LIB) @dyna32.lnk
  brc32 find.res find.exe

find.obj :  find.cpp
  bcc32 $(CC) $(CD) find.cpp

find.res :  find.rc find.ico find.h
  brc32 $(INC) -w32 -R find.rc
```

DYNA32.LNK

```
\bc4\lib\c0w32.obj+
find.obj
find,find
\bc4\lib\bidsfi.lib+
\bc4\lib\owlwfi.lib+
\bc4\lib\import32.lib+
\bc4\lib\cw32i.lib
find.def
```

Two menu commands will summon dialog boxes: **Edit.Find...** and **Edit.Modal Find...** As suggested by the menu names, the second command creates a modal dialog box. When creating a modal dialog box, the application's main window is disabled—and along with it, the application's menu. A modeless dialog box, on the other hand, allows access to the main window and its menu. Unfortunately, this means that a user could bring up multiple modeless dialog boxes unless we do something to stop them.

Our sample program only allows one copy of the modeless dialog box. When the user tries to create a second one, the response is to activate the first one—that's what the call to **`SetActiveWindow`** is all about within **`DFrame::CmEditFind`**. Otherwise, the user could create a huge pile of modeless dialog boxes that could create some confusion.

With a modal dialog box, on the other hand, no such care is necessary. It disables its parent window—that is, the application's main window—and the application's menu along with it. A modal dialog box, then, doesn't have the same dialog-box-pile-up problem that modeless dialog boxes do. What *does* occur, however, is that a modal dialog box *doesn't* disable the modeless dialog boxes that were present before the modal dialog box appeared. In our sample program, this creates the interesting problem that it's possible to have *two* Find dialogs present at the same time: the modal version and the modeless version.

Within the dialog box itself, the *Find* pushbutton is initially grayed, to notify the user that it can't be selected. Our dialog box doesn't gray the control itself, but rather disables it with a call to **`EnableWindow`**. When disabled, the control grays its text to tell the user that it's "out to lunch." **`EnableWindow`** is defined:

```
BOOL EnableWindow (HWND hwnd, BOOL bEnabled)
```

- **hwnd** is a handle to a window to be enabled or disabled.
- **bEnabled** is TRUE (nonzero) to enable and FALSE (zero) to disable.

The dialog box object only enables the push-button when there are characters in the edit control.

The easiest way to detect characters in an edit control is to wait for the edit control's **`EN_CHANGE`** notification. As mentioned earlier, notifications arrive as part of a **`WM_COMMAND`** message. This particular notification gets sent whenever characters are added or removed from the edit control.

The **TFindDialog::CmEdit** function handles all edit control notifications. It makes two calls to **TWindow::GetDlgItem**, which returns the WinAPI window handle for the edit control and the button control. The call to **Edit_GetTextLength** is actually a macro defined in WindowsX.h. This file contains lots of very useful, but poorly documented, macros. A quick peek in this file will show you that this macro is defined as follows:

```
#define Edit_GetTextLength(hwndCtl) GetWindowTextLength(hwndCtl)
```

I prefer to use this macros over making native WinAPI calls because the macros make code easier to read. The **Button_Enable** macro is another WindowsX.h macro that takes the place of a call to **EnableWindow**. Both macros have been copied from WindowsX.h to FIND.H, and modified with the **::** operator to give them global scope.

Since **TFindDialog** is a descendent of OWL's **TWindow** class, it can get messages. If you look at the way the message response table is defined, you'll notice the **EV_CHILD_NOTIFY_ALL_CODES** macro. This sets up a single message response function to handle all the different types of notifications that all get sent as part of a **WM_COMMAND** message. The meaning of each message gets passed to the individual response functions as the **notify** parameter.

Let's take a closer look at some of the things that make a modeless dialog box different from a modal dialog box.

Modeless Dialog Boxes

The three elements needed to create a modeless dialog box are the same as those needed for a modal dialog box: a dialog template, code to create the dialog, and code to maintain the dialog once it has been created. From an MS-Windows point of view, modal and modeless dialog boxes are similar but different. The OWL libraries hide these differences from you, to simplify your programming tasks.

Dialog Box Template

The dialog box template for a modeless dialog box is almost identical to the template you'd use for a modal dialog box. However, there are a few subtle things you'll want to change. For example, you'll want to set the dialog's window styles in a particular way. You do this from the Resource Workshop's Window Style dialog box, shown in Figure 14.14. You access this dialog by selecting the dialog box frame. Then, either select the *Control.Style...* menu item or double-click on the dialog box frame.

For a modeless dialog box, be sure to click the check box marked *Initially Visible*. This adds the **WS_VISIBLE** style to the dialog box templates. You don't need this style for a modal dialog box, since modal dialogs are automatically made visible. It makes sense: Otherwise, a modal dialog would disable its parent, then remain hidden. A modeless dialog without this style, on the other hand, simply would not appear—leaving you wondering what went wrong!

Another useful style is **WS_CAPTION**, which is controlled by the radio button marked *Caption* in the "Frame style" group. This gives users something to grab when they need to move a modeless dialog box out of the way, using the mouse. The *System Menu* check box requests the **WS_SYSMENU** style. A system menu lets a user control a dialog using keyboard commands.

Although it's not used in our programming example, notice that the "Window style" dialog box in Figure 14.13 lets you change the font used in a dialog box. This adds a FONT statement to a dialog template, causing the selected font to be used in all of the dialog's controls. The dialog and each of its controls change size to match the selected font's proportions.

For the dialog box template, the only difference between a modal and a modeless dialog box is the style bits. Let's look at how a modeless dialog differs from a modal dialog in its creation.

Creating a Modeless Dialog Box

Creating a modeless dialog box is similar to creating a modal dialog box: First create a dialog box object, and then use this object to create an MS-Windows dialog box.

Like a modal dialog box, you can derive classes from the OWL **TDialog**. For example, this class would process the standard **WM_INITDIALOG** and **WM_COMMAND** messages:

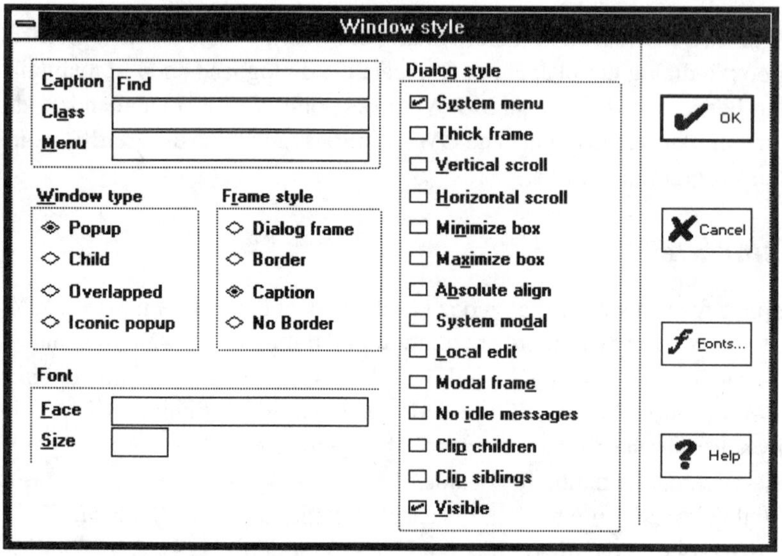

Figure 14.13 Resource Workshop's "Window style" dialog box

```
class TSampleDialog : public TDialog
    {
  public:
    TSampleDialog (TWindow* parent, TResID id);
    LRESULT EvCommand(UINT id, HWND hwndCtl, UINT notify);
    BOOL EvInitDialog(HWND hwndFocus);
    };
```

As discussed already, a modeless **`TDialog`** object can't be allocated as a local variable, so a pointer like the following has to be allocated—perhaps in its parent window's instance data:

```
TSampleDialog * ptModeless;
```

At the appropriate time, we'd create an instance of this object as follows:

```
ptModeless = new TSampleDialog (ptParent, "DLGTEMP");
```

To instantiate the actual WinAPI dialog box, we call **`TDialog::Create()`**, like this:

```
ptModeless->Create();
```

This routine, in turn, calls **`CreateDialogParam`**, a WinAPI routine for creating modeless dialog boxes. For details on this routine, see the accompanying boxed discussion.

The `CreateDialogParam` Routine

Four MS-Windows routines create a modeless dialog box: **`CreateDialog`**, **`CreateDialogIndirect`**, **`CreateDialogIndirectParam`**, and **`CreateDialogParam`**. OWL uses the last one to create a modeless dialog box. This routine is defined

```
int CreateDialogParam (hInstance, lpszTemplate,
                       hwndParent,lpDialogProc,
                       dwParam);
```

- **`hInstance`** is the instance handle of the program or dynamic link library that owns the dialog box definition.
- **`lpszTemplate`** is a far pointer to a character string for the name of the dialog box definition, as defined in the dialog box template. Alternatively, it can be an integer value wrapped inside the **`MAKEINTRESOURCE`** macro, when an integer is used in place of a character string to identify the dialog box template.
- **`hwndParent`** is a handle to the parent window of the dialog box.

- **lpDialogProc** is a far pointer to a piece of code that maintains the dialog box while it is being displayed. This is a function that is referred to as a dialog box procedure. The address passed in this parameter is not the actual address of the routine itself, but the instance thunk created by the **MakeProcInstance** routine for the dialog box procedure. For details on thunks, see Chapter 19.
- **dwParam** is a DWORD (unsigned long) value for an (optional) parameter to be passed to the dialog box at creation time. This value is copied from the **Attr** data member of the **TDialog** class.

The parameters to **CreateDialogParam** are identical with those of **DialogBoxParam** (discussed earlier). Even though you probably will never create a dialog box that is both modal and modeless, the similarity between these two routines makes it possible. One of the reasons for the similarity is that **DialogBox** itself calls **CreateDialog** to build the actual dialog box. The difference between the two, of course, is that **DialogBox** disables its parent and has its own message loop, while **CreateDialog** simply returns when the dialog box has been built.

As you can see, the creation of a modeless dialog box is quite similar to a modal dialog box. Where a modeless dialog box differs is in the fact that its parent window will be enabled. In other words, it can receive mouse and keyboard input. One issue this raises for modeless dialog is that you'll need to prevent *two* (or more) copies of a modeless dialog from being created. After all, with the parent enabled, the user can access the commands which will request a second dialog box. (This isn't a problem with *modal* dialogs, since the parent window—and its menu—is disabled.) To prevent this from happening, as you saw in the FIND sample program, you simply need a flag. To round out this discussion, let's look at some of the message processing concerns of modeless dialog boxes.

Maintaining a Modeless Dialog Box

One issue specific to modeless dialog boxes involves keyboard input. In particular, the [Tab], [Enter], and arrow keys have certain expected behavior in a dialog box. A *modal* dialog box, with its private message loop, already handles this. With a *modeless* dialog box, on the other hand, special handling is required. In particular, the message loop must be modified to make a call to the **IsDialogMessage** routine. Fortunately, as you may recall from our discussion of the message loop in Chapter 4, the OWL application object handles this for us. While you don't need to understand the particulars, if you're curious, you can read the accompanying boxed discussion.

The keyboard interface to a *modal* dialog box consists of support for several keys: [Tab], [Enter], [Esc], and the arrow keys. These keys allow the user to move between controls and dismiss the dialog box. They are automatically available for modal dialog boxes because, as you may recall, a modal dialog box has its own message loop. To get these keys to work in a *modeless* dialog box, you must modify your program's message loop to include a call to **IsDialogMessage**. This routine is defined as

```
BOOL IsDialogMessage (hDlg, lpMsg)
```

- **hDlg** is a handle to a modeless dialog box.
- **lpMsg** is a far pointer to a structure of type MSG.

IsDialogMessage returns TRUE when the message was for a dialog box or a dialog box control. In this case, **IsDialogMessage** makes the necessary calls to **TranslateMessage** and **DispatchMessage**. **IsDialogMessage** returns FALSE when the message was not for the dialog box or any control in the dialog box. In that case, the message loop can handle the message in the usual way.

Here is an example of a message loop that has been modified to correctly call **IsDialogMessage** to handle the keyboard interface for a modeless dialog box:

```
while (GetMessage(&msg, 0, 0, 0))
    {
    if (hwndFindDialog)
        if (IsDialogMessage(hwndFindDialog,&msg))
            continue;
      TranslateMessage(&msg);
      DispatchMessage(&msg);
    }
```

Notice that **IsDialogMessage** is only called if the value of **hwndFindDialog** is nonzero. This is the variable in which is stored either the window handle of a modeless dialog box or a zero when the modeless dialog box is not open.

To terminate a modeless dialog, call **TDialog**'s **CloseWindow** member function. This same routine closes modal dialogs. Under the hood, MS-Windows requires a different routine to be called to close each type of dialog. Once again, OWL simplifies the Windows programming interface for you.

At this point, you've seen several working examples of dialog boxes, which should give you a starting point when creating your own dialog boxes. Also, refer to the various OWL sample dialog box programs for more examples of working with dialog boxes using OWL.

A nice feature of dialog box controls is that they handle all low-level (mouse and keyboard) input for you. A user can type into an edit control, for example, and the text entry is handled for you. A user can click on a button and that gets translated into a higher-level notification message to your code. There are times, however, when your application wants to more closely tap into the system's mouse and keyboard input. This is the subject of the next two chapters.

PART FIVE

Message Driven Input

15

Keyboard Input

In earlier chapters, we looked at the way a Windows program creates graphics output. The facilities available for graphics output can be considered quite high-level: Sophisticated drawing can be accomplished with a minimum of effort. In particular, this is the case if you consider how much code would be required to accomplish the same results without the help of GDI.

In this chapter and the one that follows, we're going to look at the way that Windows handles *input*. In contrast to GDI's high-level output, the form in which input arrives can be regarded as very low-level. That is, keyboard input arrives in the form of individual keystroke messages, with two or three messages generated per key typed. And the actions of the mouse are reported as a stream of messages that give a blow-by-blow account of the actions of this pointing device.

This chapter discusses keyboard input, leaving the next chapter to describe mouse input.

How a Windows Program Receives Keyboard Input

Figure 15.1 shows all the pieces that play a role in handling keyboard input. The black lines represent data flow.

We'll start our study of keyboard input by tracing the flow of data from the keyboard, through the various software layers into a typical Windows program. Every Windows program has a **`GetMessage`** (or **`PeekMessage`**) loop which is responsible for pulling all keyboard messages into a program. But as you'll see, that's only half the story; once raw keyboard data arrives in a Windows program, a special Windows library routine must be called to cook the data to create truly useful character input. We introduced this routine in Chapter 4, in the context of an OWL program's application object: **`TranslateMessage`**. This routine is a standard part of every Windows program's message loop. While

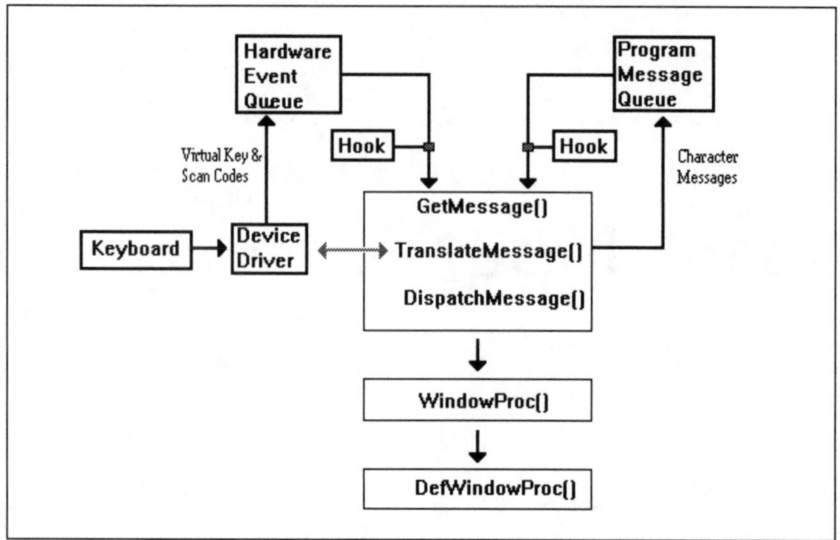

Figure 15.1 The flow of keyboard data

Windows provides an abundant set of messages to describe keyboard activity, you will find that you can concentrate your efforts on a subset of these messages, which we'll describe as we follow the path of the wily keyboard messages. Keyboard input starts in the hardware of the keyboard, so that's where we'll begin.

The Keyboard

Windows runs on IBM-compatible personal computers, and so the range of keyboards you're likely to encounter is small. Nonetheless, since IBM introduced its first PC in 1981, the keyboard has changed. The first IBM PC had an 83-key keyboard. IBM introduced a new keyboard with its PC/AT, which moved a few keys around and added the [SysReq] key, for a total of 84 keys. With its current line of PS/2 computers, IBM has adopted yet another keyboard, the Enhanced 101/102-key keyboard. This keyboard added two function keys, but most of the new keys were simply duplicates of keys already on the keyboard. With some minor variations, makers of IBM-compatible computers have adopted the same keyboard layout as IBM machines.

Although successive keyboards have moved a key here and added a key there, the basic operation of all keyboards has stayed the same. Every time you press or release a key, the keyboard hardware generates a one- or two-byte **scan code** that uniquely identifies the key. Every key produces two different scan codes, depending on whether the key is pressed or released. When you press a key, the value of the scan code is between 01H and 58H (for IBM-compatible keyboards). When you release the key, the value of the scan code is 80H higher. For example, when you press the letter "Z," the keyboard generates a scan code of 2CH. When it is released, the keyboard generates a scan code of ACH (2CH + 80H).

From the keyboard's point of view, the two scan codes are the only meaningful information associated with a given key. The meaning of the scan code is interpreted by the software that receives the keyboard input. In our case, that means the Windows keyboard device driver. Consider the two scan codes from the previous example: 2CH and ACH. When the keyboard driver is told that a US English keyboard is present, these codes are interpreted as the letter "Z." But the same scan codes will be interpreted as the letter "W" if the keyboard driver is told that a French keyboard is present. From this example, you can see how international support is provided: The keyboard driver simply needs the correct scan code to virtual key code and virtual key code to ASCII translation tables.

As keys are pressed and released, scan codes are sent via the keyboard cable to control circuitry on the system board of the computer. When the control circuitry senses that keyboard input is available, it generates a hardware interrupt 09H. When DOS is present, this interrupt results in a call to the ROM BIOS keyboard handler. But when Windows is present, another mechanism is put into place which meets the special requirements that Windows has for handling keyboard input. That mechanism is part of the Windows keyboard device driver, which we'll look at next.

The Windows Keyboard Device Driver

During Windows startup, the Windows keyboard driver installs an interrupt handler to receive keyboard scan codes. The interrupt handler is called any time a key is pressed or released. It reads scan values from the keyboard port and maps these onto a set of **virtual key** values that make up the **Windows virtual keyboard**.

The virtual keyboard defines a standard set of keys for all keyboards currently on the market. It also defines keys that don't correspond to any current keyboard, to allow room for growth. Table 15.1 lists all of the keys in the virtual keyboard, along with the symbolic names as defined in WINDOWS.H.

Table 15.1 The Windows Virtual Keys

(hex)	*(dec)*	*Symbolic Name*	*Key Pressed (US English 101/102 Keyboard)*
1	1	VK_LBUTTON	
2	2	VK_RBUTTON	
3	3	VK_CANCEL	Ctrl+Break
4	4	VK_MBUTTON	
8	8	VK_BACK	Backspace

(continued)

Table 15.1 The Windows Virtual Keys *(Continued)*

(hex)	*(dec)*	*Symbolic Name*	*Key Pressed (US English 101/102 Keyboard)*
9	9	VK_TAB	Tab
C	12	VK_CLEAR	5 on numeric keypad with Num Lock off
D	13	VK_RETURN	Enter
10	16	VK_SHIFT	Shift
11	17	VK_CONTROL	Ctrl
12	18	VK_MENU	Alt
13	19	VK_PAUSE	Pause (or Ctrl+Num Lock)
14	20	VK_CAPITAL	Caps Lock
1B	27	VK_ESCAPE	Esc
20	32	VK_SPACE	Spacebar
21	33	VK_PRIOR	Page Up
22	34	VK_NEXT	Page Down
23	35	VK_END	End
24	36	VK_HOME	Home
25	37	VK_LEFT	Left Arrow
26	38	VK_UP	Up Arrow
27	39	VK_RIGHT	Right Arrow
28	40	VK_DOWN	Down Arrow
29	41	VK_SELECT	<unused>
2A	42	VK_PRINT	<unused>
2B	43	VK_EXECUTE	<unused>
2C	44	VK_SNAPSHOT	Print Screen
2D	45	VK_INSERT	Ins
2E	46	VK_DELETE	Del
2F	47	VK_HELP	<unused>
30–39	48–57	VK_0 to VK_9	0 through 9 above letter keys
41–5A	65–90	VK_A to VK_Z	A through Z
60	96	VK_NUMPAD0	0 on numeric keypad with Num Lock on

Table 15.1 The Windows Virtual Keys *(Continued)*

(hex)	*(dec)*	*Symbolic Name*	*Key Pressed (US English 101/102 Keyboard)*
61	97	VK_NUMPAD1	1 on numeric keypad with Num Lock on
62	98	VK_NUMPAD2	2 on numeric keypad with Num Lock on
63	99	VK_NUMPAD3	3 on numeric keypad with Num Lock on
64	100	VK_NUMPAD4	4 on numeric keypad with Num Lock on
65	101	VK_NUMPAD5	5 on numeric keypad with Num Lock on
66	102	VK_NUMPAD6	6 on numeric keypad with Num Lock on
67	103	VK_NUMPAD7	7 on numeric keypad with Num Lock on
68	104	VK_NUMPAD8	8 on numeric keypad with Num Lock on
69	105	VK_NUMPAD9	9 on numeric keypad with Num Lock on
6A	106	VK_MULTIPLY	* on numeric keypad
6B	107	VK_ADD	+ on numeric keypad
6C	108	VK_SEPARATOR	<unused>
6D	109	VK_SUBTRACT	- on numeric keypad
6E	110	VK_DECIMAL	. on numeric keypad with Num Lock on
6F	111	VK_DIVIDE	/ on numeric keypad
70	112	VK_F1	F1 function key
71	113	VK_F2	F2 function key
72	114	VK_F1	F3 function key
73	115	VK_F4	F4 function key
74	116	VK_F5	F5 function key
75	117	VK_F6	F6 function key
76	118	VK_F7	F7 function key
77	119	VK_F8	F8 function key
78	120	VK_F9	F9 function key
79	121	VK_F10	F10 function key
7A	122	VK_F11	F11 function key
7B	123	VK_F12	F12 function key
7C	124	VK_F13	

(continued)

Table 15.1 The Windows Virtual Keys *(Continued)*

(hex)	*(dec)*	*Symbolic Name*	*Key Pressed (US English 101/102 Keyboard)*
7D	125	VK_F14	
7E	126	VK_F15	
7F	127	VK_F16	
90	144	VK_NUMLOCK	Num Lock
91	145		Scroll Lock
		The following codes apply to US keyboards only	
BA	186		colon/semicolon
BB	187		plus/equal
BC	188		less than/comma
BD	189		underscore/hyphen
BE	190		greater than/period
BF	191		question/slash
C0	192		tilde/back accent
DB	219		left squiggle brace/left square brace
DC	220		horizontal bar/backslash
DD	221		right squiggle brace/right square brace
DE	222		double quote/single quote

Once the keyboard driver has translated the scan code information into a virtual key code, it calls Windows. Windows puts both scan code and virtual key data into a special buffer called the **hardware event queue**. We briefly discussed the role of this buffer in Chapter 4, when we talked about the message loop. Let's return to this topic to see how it affects keyboard input.

The Hardware Event Queue

From the point of view of keyboard input, the hardware event queue is simply a type-ahead buffer. It can hold up to 120 hardware events, which means 60 characters worth of data since two events are generated when a keyboard key is pressed and released. Even for the fastest typists, this should be enough to prevent data loss.

A type-ahead buffer is necessary because of the way that a Windows program retrieves keyboard input. As you may recall from an earlier discussion, Windows' multitasking is nonpreemptive. That is, the operating system does not interrupt one program to allow another to run. Instead, programs interrupt themselves. This polite form of multitasking works because it is built into Windows' message delivery mechanism. All input to a program, including keyboard input, is delivered in the form of messages. Since Windows does not interrupt programs to deliver keyboard information, the data has to be stored someplace: That place is the hardware event queue. Otherwise, a fast typist might outpace a program's ability to retrieve keyboard input.

The contents of the hardware event queue are eventually delivered to a Windows program in the form of two messages: **`WM_KEYDOWN`** and **`WM_KEYUP`**. These correspond to the two types of scan codes: key press and key release. As indicated by the diagram in Figure 15.1, a program gets these two messages from the hardware event queue by calling **`GetMessage`**.

But the real meaning of keyboard messages comes from the values stored in one 2-byte integer value and one 4-byte integer value which make up the **`wParam`** and **`lParam`** parameters of a window procedure. The format of these two fields is the same for both messages.

`wParam` contains the virtual key code of the key that was pressed or released. The keyboard driver generates this value from the scan code that it received from the keyboard hardware. By far and away, this is the most important field that Windows provides with these two messages. After all, the virtual key code represents how the keyboard driver views a keyboard event in the context of Windows taking into account the type of keyboard that is currently attached to the system.

The **`lParam`** parameter is divided into six fields, as shown in Figure 15.2. Let's review these one at a time:

- **Repeat Count**. Built into the hardware of the keyboard is the ability to automatically repeat a single character if a key is held down: a feature that IBM calls **typematic**. To prevent such keys from overflowing the hardware event queue, Windows increments the repeat count when it finds that a new keyboard event is identical with the previous keyboard event that is still in the queue. In doing so, Windows combines several `WM_KEYDOWN` messages into a single message. A repeat count greater than 1 means that keyboard events are occurring faster than your program is able to pro-

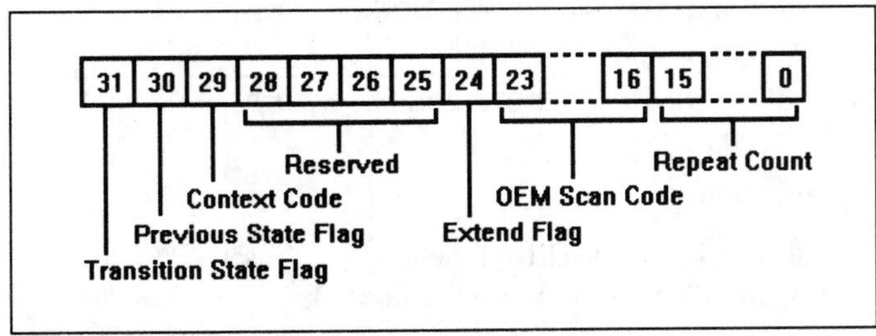

Figure 15.2 Six Fields of IPARAM for keystroke messages

cess them. In such cases, a program can interpret each `WM_KEYDOWN` message as multiple messages, depending on the repeat value.

- **OEM Scan Code**. This field contains the scan code value as it was sent from the keyboard. For most programs, the virtual key code is more useful, since it represents a device-independent code for a keystroke. Because the scan code represents a hardware-dependent value, in most cases you'll want to avoid using this field. But sometimes it is necessary to use the scan code information to tell the difference, for example, between the left shift key and the right shift key. For certain keys, the keyboard driver uses the hardware scan code to translate the `WM_KEYDOWN` message into a `WM_CHAR` message. This is the case, for example, with keys in the numeric keypad.
- **Extend Flag**. This field is actually an extension of the OEM Scan Code. In effect, it tells a program that the key that was pressed was one of the duplicate keys on IBM's extended keyboard. Like the scan code, the value of this field is device-dependent, and so great care should be taken when using it.
- **Context Code**. This flag is `1` if the [Alt] key is down; otherwise it has a value of `0`.
- **Previous State Flag**. This flag helps to identify messages generated by typematic action. It has a value of `1` if the previous state of the key was down, and a value of `0` if the previous state of the key was up.
- **Transition State Flag**. This flag is `1` if the key is being released and `0` if the key is being pressed. It will always be `1` for **`WM_KEYUP`** and `0` for the **`WM_KEYDOWN`** message.

From these messages, a program receives both the raw keyboard scan codes and the half-cooked virtual key codes. As you'll see shortly, the most useful keyboard data arrive as fully cooked character messages. But there are some keystrokes that are not available as character messages, since they do not represent characters but rather keyboard commands.

Table 15.2 shows a list of the keystrokes that can only be detected with the **`WM_KEYDOWN`** and **`WM_KEYUP`** messages. In a moment, we'll discuss the **`WM_CHAR`** message, which provides ASCII character information. The keys in this table do not produce ASCII characters, and so they do not generate **`WM_CHAR`** messages. Therefore, if you are interested in detecting keystrokes generated by these keys, you'll watch for the **`WM_KEYDOWN`** message.

Table 15.2 Keystrokes available only with `WM_KEYDOWN` and `WM_KEYUP`

Keystroke	*Description*
F1–F9, F11–F16	Function keys. The [F10] function key is reserved for Windows' use as the Menu Select hot-key.

Table 15.2 Keystrokes available only with `WM_KEYDOWN` and `WM_KEYUP` *(Continued)*

Keystroke	*Description*
Shift, Ctrl, Alt	Shift keys. The [Alt] key is a reserved system key and does not generate WM_KEYDOWN or WM_KEYUP unless the [Ctrl] key is down. Normally, it only generates WM_SYSKEYDOWN and WM_SYSKEYUP messages.
Caps Lock, Num Lock, Scroll Lock.	Toggle keys
Print Screen	Reserved key for copying screen to clipboard ([PrtSc] alone), or for copying the active window to the clipboard ([Alt] + [PrtSc]). Windows eats the WM_KEYDOWN message, leaving WM_KEYUP.
Pause	Pause key
Insert, Delete, Home, End, Page Up, Page Down	Text editing keys. Although there are two of each of these keys on the 101/102 keyboard, each pair has only one virtual key code. However, they can be distinguished with the Extend flag.
Up, Left, Down, Right	Direction keys. Although there are eight keys in this set, like the text editing keys the duplicate keys do not have a separate virtual key code. However, they can be distinguished with the Extend flag.

To detect one of these keys in a Windows program, you'll test the value of `wParam` against the virtual key values listed in Table 15.1. For example, here is code that checks for a key-down transition of the [F1] function key:

```
void DFrame::EvKeyDown(UINT key, UINT repeat,  UINT flags)
    {
    if (key == VK_F1)
        {
        // user pressed [F1] key...
        }
    }
```

For programming the function keys, it is often easier to define an Accelerator.

While it would involve a lot of work, it would be possible to receive all the keyboard input that you might require using **WM_KEYDOWN** and **WM_KEYUP** messages. Notice, however, that to tell the difference between a capital letter and a lowercase letter would require you to know the state of the shift key in addition to detecting the keystroke message. There's no reason to go to all that work, since Windows has a built-in facility that will do the work for you. The routine that provides this service is a standard part of every message loop: **TranslateMessage**.

The GetMessage Loop

The minimum standard message loop is as follows:

```
while (GetMessage (&msg, 0, 0, 0))
    {
    TranslateMessage (&msg);
    DispatchMessage (&msg);
    }
```

GetMessage reads messages from two places: the hardware event queue and a program's private message queue. For every message it retrieves, a call is made to **TranslateMessage**, which ignores every message except two: **WM_KEYDOWN** and **WM_SYSKEYDOWN**.

WM_SYSKEYDOWN is one of three **system keyboard messages**. The other two are **WM_SYSKEYUP** and **WM_SYSCHAR**. The behavior of these messages parallels the behavior of the three regular keyboard messages, but system keyboard messages are used primarily as part of the keyboard interface to menus. We'll look at another use of these messages when we discuss the window procedure in a short while.

The role of **TranslateMessage** is simple. It takes the virtual key data from the **WM_KEYDOWN** (or **WM_SYSKEYDOWN**) message and calls the keyboard device driver to convert the virtual key code into an ASCII code. For keys with no ASCII equivalent, no translation is done. For the rest, a **WM_CHAR** (or **WM_SYSCHAR**) message is generated and placed in the private message queue.

The sequence of messages created in response to hitting the "w" key, for example, is as follows:

Key	*wParam Contains*
WM_KEYDOWN	Virtual key W
WM_CHAR	ASCII code w
WM_KEYUP	Virtual key W

And when a capital letter is struck, the sequence of messages is even more involved. Here is the message traffic when the user types "W":

Key	*wParam Contains*
WM_KEYDOWN	Virtual key VK_SHIFT
WM_KEYDOWN	Virtual key W
WM_CHAR	ASCII code W
WM_KEYUP	Virtual key W
WM_KEYUP	Virtual key VK_SHIFT

On some non-English keyboards (French and German, to name two), special key combinations are used to create diacritic marks over vowels. For example, to type the words château (the French word for "castle") and München (the German name for the city of Munich) on a French keyboard, you need to use special key combinations because there are no dedicated "â" and "ü" keys.

These special keys are called **dead-keys**, since they are not expected to produce characters, but modify the keystroke that follows. In response to a **WM_KEYDOWN** (or **WM_SYSKEYDOWN**) for such keys, **TranslateMessage** generates a **WM_DEADCHAR** (or **WM_SYSDEADCHAR**) message. You can safely ignore these messages, since Windows will create the correct character message from the keystrokes that follow.

If you'd like to experiment with dead-key processing, you can install a different keyboard translation table using the Control Panel. Bring up the International Settings dialog box and select the country whose keyboard layout you want to work with. If you bring up the French keyboard, you'll discover that the "A" and "Q" keys have been switched, as have the "W" and "Z" keys. The dead-key for the circumflex is located at the key marked "[," and the dead-key for the umlaut is [Shift]+"[."

The message sequence that is generated on a French keyboard to produce the letter "â" is as follows:

Key	*wParam Contains*
WM_KEYDOWN	Scan code for pressing circumflex key
WM_DEADCHAR	Dead character message for circumflex key
WM_KEYUP	Scan code for releasing circumflex key
WM_KEYDOWN	Scan code for pressing "a"
WM_CHAR	Character message for "â"
WM_KEYUP	Scan code for releasing "a"

With the exception of the keys listed in Table 15.2, keyboard input will normally come from the **WM_CHAR** messages that are created by **TranslateMessage**. The translation that takes place takes into account the state of the various shift keys, to provide uppercase and lowercase letters, numbers, and punctuation marks. Since the ASCII character set includes a complete range of accented vowels, this mechanism also supports international keyboards.

After **TranslateMessage** generates the **WM_CHAR** (or **WM_SYSCHAR**) message, it returns control to the message loop. The **DispatchMessage** routine then pushes the **WM_KEYDOWN** or **WM_SYSKEYDOWN** message to the window procedure for processing.

Since the character message is placed on the program's message queue, it does not become available to the program until **GetMessage** is called to read a new message. At that time, the **WM_CHAR** (or **WM_SYSCHAR**) message is read in, passed to **Translate-Message** (which ignores it), and finally sent on to the window procedure by **Dispatch-Message**. Although the key-down message causes the character message to be generated, by the time the window procedure sees the character message, the key-down message has already been processed.

The window procedure parameters for the **WM_CHAR** message are similar to those for the other keyboard messages we discussed earlier. That is, the **lParam** field in a character message contains the same six fields as the **WM_KEYDOWN** and **WM_KEYUP** messages.

The **WM_CHAR** message is different, however, in that the **wParam** parameter contains the ASCII code of the character whose key was pressed. It's the job of the window procedure to trap this message and read whatever character input is required.

To build bullet-proof processing for character input, you'll probably want to filter out some of the **WM_CHAR** messages which are created for keystrokes that aren't ordinarily printed. These include the tab, backspace, and return keys. These, along with the others in the list in Table 15.2, will require special processing apart from the regular character messages:

	ASCII Value		
Keystroke	*(hex)*	*(dec)*	*Description*
Ctrl+A to Ctrl+G	1–7	1–7	Nonprintable characters.
Backspace	8	8	Backspace key (VK_BACK).
Ctrl+H	8	8	Surrogate backspace key (VK_BACK).
Tab	9	9	Tab key (VK_TAB).
Ctrl+I	9	9	Surrogate tab key (VK_TAB).
Ctrl+J	A	10	Linefeed.
Ctrl+K to Ctrl+L	B–C	11–12	Nonprintable characters.
Return	D	13	Return key (VK_RETURN).
Ctrl+M	D	13	Surrogate return key (VK_RETURN).
Ctrl+N to Ctrl+Z	E–1A	15–26	Nonprintable characters.
Esc	1B	27	Escape key (VK_ESCAPE).

When an accelerator has been defined with a [Ctrl] + letter key combination, then no **WM_CHAR** is generated for that keystroke. We explored accelerators in Chapter 11.

The Window Object

We've traced the path that keyboard data takes on its way from the hardware to our program. Although some handling of keyboard input is done in the message loop, the bulk of processing is handled in the OWL window object message response functions.

Table 15.3 summarizes all of the keyboard messages that we have encountered so far. You can safely ignore most of them, however, and concentrate your efforts on two messages: **WM_CHAR** for all character input, and **WM_KEYDOWN** for all noncharacter function key input. In the example program, KEYINPUT, these are the only messages we rely on to create a text-entry and editing window.

Table 15.3 A Summary of Keyboard Messages

WM_KEYDOWN	Key pressed
WM_CHAR	Character input
WM_DEADCHAR	Dead-character
WM_KEYUP	Key released
WM_SYSKEYDOWN	System key pressed
WM_SYSCHAR	System character input
WM_SYSDEADCHAR	System dead-character
WM_SYSKEYUP	System key released

In certain situations, you may wish to process system keyboard messages as well. In particular, when the active window in the system is iconic, Windows substitutes the system keyboard messages (**WM_SYSKEYDOWN**, **WM_SYSKEYUP**, **WM_SYSCHAR**) in place of the regular keyboard messages. Since most programs are not interested in keyboard input when they are iconic, this convention helps avoid spurious input. If you *do* want to receive keyboard input in this situation, however, you'll need to pay attention to the system keyboard messages.

In general, however, you'll ignore system keyboard messages, which are primarily used by Windows for its own internal housekeeping purposes. Since some of this housekeeping is done in the default window procedure, you'll want to be sure that—like other unused messages—these messages get passed on.

The Default Window Procedure

All of the messages that a window procedure does not use should be passed on to the default window procedure. The default window procedure ignores all regular keyboard messages, so window procedures that don't use keyboard messages can safely pass them on.

But the default window procedure plays an important role in handling the system keyboard messages. System keyboard messages are usually generated in place of regular keyboard messages when the [Alt] key is down. In this way, system keyboard messages are used by the default window procedure to provide keyboard access to menus.

For example, when a window has a system menu icon, the system menu will appear when you strike the [Alt] + [Spacebar] keys. When we discuss menus in Chapters 11 and 12, you saw that you can define your own menu hot-key that will cause a pull-down menu to appear when the hot-key is hit with the [Alt] key. A menu hot-key is also called a **mnemonic**, since it is always a letter in the name of the menu. These keystrokes are handled as system keyboard messages.

The default window procedure also plays a role in making certain keyboard combinations operate correctly. For example, you can quit an application by typing [Alt] + [F4], go to the Task List by pressing [Ctrl] + [Esc], and switch the active program with [Alt] + [Tab]. For these system hot-keys to work properly, the default window procedure must get all system keyboard messages.

In our look at the path taken by keyboard events, there is one item that we have overlooked: hooks. The subject of hooks is outside the scope of this book, but it is important for you to be aware of them because they can affect the path of keyboard input.

Hooks

A hook is a subroutine that is installed into Windows' message handling mechanism. Hooks allow you to monitor and trap certain types of messages. Figure 15.1 shows the relationship of hooks to the flow of keyboard data.

Windows has a total of seven different hooks, although we're going to limit our discussion to two of them: keyboard hooks and "getmessage" hooks. All hooks are installed on a systemwide basis. That is, if a program installs a hook, it affects every program running in the system.

The keyboard hook taps into the flow of keyboard messages coming out of the hardware event queue and provides a means of listening to all keyboard input in the system. Creating a keyboard hook in Windows is comparable to stealing the keyboard interrupt under DOS; it gives you complete control over the flow of keystroke messages (**WM_KEYDOWN** and **WM_KEYUP**) in the system.

One use of a keyboard hook is to watch for special hot-keys. For example, you might want to give a user the ability to call up your program at any time by simply typing the [Alt] + [F12] key combination. You accomplish this by installing a keyboard hook when your program starts running. The hook lets all keyboard input pass, until it encounters the desired keystroke. At that time, it lets Windows know that it wants the key for itself, which causes the key to be ignored by the rest of the system. The hook then notifies the program (perhaps via a message) that the hot-key has been struck. At that time, it is up to the program to respond in a way that makes sense. Perhaps that means opening a window to offer some service to the user.

The second type of hook that affects keyboard input is the getmessage hook. This hook is actually called by the **GetMessage** routine for every message that it receives before it gives the message to a program. This hook can do anything it wants to the message, including change any of the parameters, or even the value of the message!

Since a getmessage hook has access to every message that is received by the **GetMessage** routine, it can be used for many different types of applications. A hot-key could be implemented using a getmessage hook, for example. Or, it could be used to detect mouse button messages on a given window—perhaps to prevent a user from accessing any other window until a password has been typed correctly. The getmessage hook can be used for any messages that **GetMessage** retrieves, which means all keyboard and mouse messages as well as the **WM_PAINT** and **WM_TIMER** messages.

A Sample Program

To demonstrate the way a program can receive keyboard input, we have written KEYINPUT. This program creates a simple single-line text entry window. Figure 15.3 shows a sample of the output created by this program.

KEYINPUT shows how the **WM_CHAR** and **WM_KEYDOWN** messages can be used to receive character input and perform some simple editing. The following cursor movement keys are recognized: Home, End, Left Arrow, and Right Arrow. In addition, the backspace and delete keys can be used to erase characters.

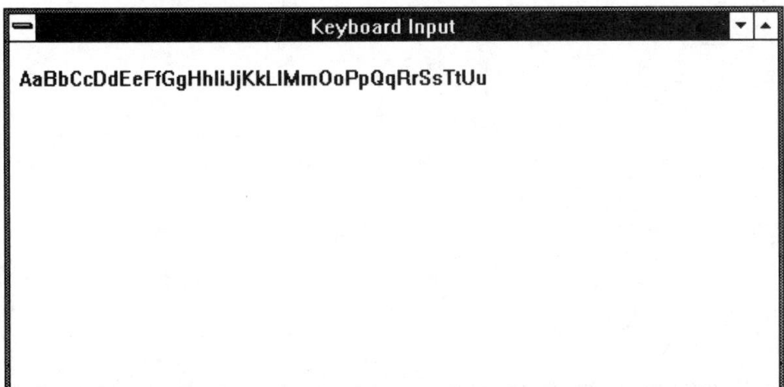

Figure 15.3 Output from KEYINPUT program

KEYINPUT.CPP

```
//
// KEYINPUT.CPP  Shows receiving raw keyboard input.
//
//
#include <owl\owlpch.h>
#include "keyinput.h"

DEFINE_RESPONSE_TABLE1 (DFrame, TFrameWindow)
  EV_WM_CHAR,
  EV_WM_KEYDOWN,
  EV_COMMAND(CM_FILEEXIT, CmFileExit),
  EV_COMMAND(CM_HELPABOUT, CmHelpAbout),
END_RESPONSE_TABLE;

DFrame::DFrame(char * title) : TFrameWindow(0, title)
    {
    TScreenDC dc;

    TEXTMETRIC tm;
    dc.GetTextMetrics (tm);

    yLineHeight = tm.tmHeight + tm.tmExternalLeading;
    xLeftMargin = tm.tmAveCharWidth;

    achInput[0] = '\0';
    cchInput = 0;
    ichNext = 0;
    }

void DFrame::CmFileExit()
    {
    CloseWindow(0); // Cause application to terminate
    }

void DFrame::CmHelpAbout()
    {
    MessageBox(" Receiving Raw Keyboard Input\n\n"
               "'Borland C++ 4.0 Programming\n"
               "  for Windows', by Paul Yao", Title);
    }

void DFrame::EvChar (UINT key, UINT, UINT)
    {
    if (key == VK_BACK)    //  Backspace.
        {
        if (ichNext == 0)
            MessageBeep(0);
        else                            //  Remove a character.
            {
            ichNext--;
            for (int i=ichNext;i<cchInput;i++)
                achInput[i]=achInput[i+1];
            cchInput--;
            Invalidate ();
            }
        return;
        }

    // Complain if character out of range or if buffer is full.
    if ((key <= VK_ESCAPE) || (cchInput >= BUFSIZE))
```

```
        {
        MessageBeep(0);
        return;
        }

    // Make room for next char.
    for (int i=cchInput;i>ichNext;i--)
        achInput[i]=achInput[i-1];

    /*  Put new char in buffer.  */
    achInput[ichNext] = (unsigned char)key;

    // Increment count of characters.
    cchInput++;

    // Update display.
    TClientDC dc(HWindow);
    TSize size;
    dc.GetTextExtent ((LPSTR)&achInput[0], ichNext, size);
    dc.TextOut (xLeftMargin+size.cx,
                yLineHeight,
                (LPSTR)&achInput[ichNext],
                cchInput - ichNext);

    // Increment index to next character.
    ichNext++;
    }

void DFrame::EvKeyDown (UINT key, UINT, UINT)
    {
    switch (key)
        {
        case VK_DELETE:
            /*  If end of buffer, complain.  */
            if (ichNext == cchInput)
                MessageBeep(0);
            else  /*  Remove a character.  */
                {
                int i;
                for (i=ichNext;i<cchInput;i++)
                    achInput[i]=achInput[i+1];
                cchInput--;
                Invalidate();
                }
            break;
        case VK_END:
            ichNext = cchInput;
            break;
        case VK_HOME:
            ichNext = 0;
            break;
        case VK_LEFT:
            if (ichNext > 0) ichNext--;
            else MessageBeep(0);
            break;
        case VK_RIGHT:
            if (ichNext < cchInput) ichNext++;
            else MessageBeep(0);
            break;
        }
    }
```

```
void DFrame::Paint (TDC& dc, BOOL, TRect&)
    {
    dc.TextOut (xLeftMargin, yLineHeight,
                (LPSTR)achInput, cchInput);
    }

DApp::DApp() : TApplication()
    {
    }

void DApp::InitMainWindow()
    {
    SetMainWindow (new DFrame("Keyboard Input"));

    MainWindow->AssignMenu("MAIN");
    MainWindow->SetIcon(this, "SNAPSHOT");
    }

//
// Application main entry point.
OwlMain(int, char **)
    {
    return DApp().Run();
    }
```

KEYINPUT.H

```
#define CM_FILEEXIT 100
#define CM_HELPABOUT 200

const int BUFSIZE = 120;

// Main window
class DFrame : public TFrameWindow
    {
  public:
    DFrame(char * title);
    void CmFileExit();
    void CmHelpAbout();
    void EvChar (UINT key, UINT repeat, UINT flags);
    void EvKeyDown (UINT key, UINT repeat, UINT flags);
    void Paint (TDC&, BOOL, TRect&);

  private:
    unsigned char achInput[BUFSIZE];
    int  cchInput;
    int  ichNext;
    int  yLineHeight;
    int  xLeftMargin;

  DECLARE_RESPONSE_TABLE (DFrame);
    };

// Application object
class DApp : public TApplication
    {
  public:
    DApp();
    void InitMainWindow();
    };
```

KEYINPUT.RC

```
#include "keyinput.h"

snapshot icon keyinput.ico

main menu
    BEGIN
    POPUP "&File"
        {
        MENUITEM "E&xit", CM_FILEEXIT
        }
    POPUP "&Help"
        {
        MENUITEM "&About...", CM_HELPABOUT
        }
    END
```

KEYINPUT.DEF

```
EXETYPE WINDOWS

CODE MOVEABLE DISCARDABLE
DATA MULTIPLE MOVEABLE

HEAPSIZE   512
STACKSIZE 8192
```

DYNA16.MAK

```
#  MAKE file for Win16 API using dynamic BIDS,
#  OWL and C-runtime libraries.
#
#    C> make -fstatic16.mak
#

.AUTODEPEND
CC = -c -H -H"owl\owlpch.h" -ml -R -vi -WS -X-
CD = -D_RTLDLL;_BIDSDLL;_OWLDLL;_OWLPCH;
INC = -I\BC4\INCLUDE
LIB = -L\BC4\LIB

keyinput.exe :  keyinput.obj keyinput.res
  tlink -c -C -Twe $(LIB) @dyna16.lnk
  brc keyinput.res keyinput.exe

keyinput.obj :  keyinput.cpp
  bcc $(CC) $(CD) keyinput.cpp

keyinput.res :  keyinput.rc keyinput.ico keyinput.h
  brc $(INC) -31 -R keyinput.rc
```

DYNA16.LNK

```
\bc4\lib\c0wl.obj+
keyinput.obj
keyinput,keyinput
\bc4\lib\bidsi.lib+
\bc4\lib\owlwi.lib+
\bc4\lib\import.lib+
\bc4\lib\crtldll.lib
keyinput.def
```

DYNA32.MAK

```
#  MAKE file for Win32 API using dynamic BIDS,
#  OWL and C-runtime libraries.
#
#    C> make -fdyna32.mak
#

.AUTODEPEND
CC = -c -H -H\""owl\owlpch.h\"" -p- -R -vi -W -X-
CD = -D_RTLDLL;_BIDSDLL;_OWLDLL;_OWLPCH;
INC = -I\BC4\INCLUDE
LIB = -L\BC4\LIB

keyinput.exe :  keyinput.obj keyinput.res
  tlink32 -aa -c -Tpe $(LIB) @dyna32.lnk
  brc32 keyinput.res keyinput.exe

keyinput.obj :  keyinput.cpp
  bcc32 $(CC) $(CD) keyinput.cpp

keyinput.res :  keyinput.rc keyinput.ico keyinput.h
  brc32 $(INC) -w32 -R keyinput.rc
```

DYNA32.LNK

```
\bc4\lib\c0w32.obj+
keyinput.obj
keyinput,keyinput
\bc4\lib\bidsfi.lib+
\bc4\lib\owlwfi.lib+
\bc4\lib\import32.lib+
\bc4\lib\cw32i.lib
keyinput.def
```

Like the other sample programs in this book, KEYINPUT was built on top of the minimum Windows program that we introduced in Chapter 2. This program handles three different messages: **`WM_CHAR`**, **`WM_KEYDOWN`**, and **`WM_PAINT`**. As you may have noticed, we've organized the functions in our source code by class, then in alphabetical order by member function name. If you find this helps, you might wish to adopt this convention in your own programs.

As the **WM_CHAR** keyboard character messages occur, KEYINPUT accumulates the characters in a character array defined as

```
unsigned char achInput[BUFSIZE];
```

The use of the *unsigned* character type is a good practice that will help when working with the extended ASCII character set that Windows supports. It helps avoid the confusion that otherwise can occur with normal signed characters, which use the high-order bit as a sign bit. Since Windows' extended ASCII uses this high-order bit for the characters between 128 and 255 (80H to ffh), this can cause unexpected results. Consider the following lines of code:

```
unsigned char chUnsigned;
char chSigned;

chUnsigned = 'â';   /*  In Windows' extended ASCII,   */
chSigned   = 'â';   /*      <131> = e2h.                  */

if (chSigned == 'â')
    {
    /*  This will never be true.   */
    }

if (chUnsigned == 'â')
    {
    /*  This will always be true.   */
    }
```

The problem occurs because of the way compilers interpret the numeric value of characters. Character values are converted into two-byte word values before a comparison is done. When this happens, the sign bit is extended to provide the correct word value. If you use unsigned `char` arrays, you will avoid this problem.

Getting back to our sample program, KEYINPUT has two variables that keep track of the contents of **achInput**: **cchInput** and **ichNext**. **cchInput** is the count of characters in the array. **ichNext** is an index into the array, and serves as the insertion point when new characters are typed. KEYINPUT increments and decrements these two fields as characters are entered and deleted.

Every time characters are entered, KEYINPUT draws the newly entered letters. On the other hand, when characters are erased, KEYINPUT generates a **WM_PAINT** message by calling **Invalidate**:

```
Invalidate();
```

which tells Windows, in effect, that the entire window is damaged and that it should be completely erased and redrawn. This is a pretty radical step to take. To erase characters, the entire line must be redrawn. It guarantees that the contents of the window is always correct, since the **WM_PAINT** message reads the character array with the changes in place.

One way to improve this program involves eliminating this excessive drawing, which means replacing the calls to **Invalidate** with actions that erase a single character in response to a backspace. This requires a little more work, but avoids the annoying blinking that occurs when characters are erased.

Quite a few other improvements could be made to this program, but it is enough to give you the basic idea about how keyboard input can be collected and displayed. We'll come back to this program in a minute, to see how a **caret** can be used to highlight the current insertion point. Before that, we need to discuss some issues that are critical in correctly handling character data: character sets and other internationalization issues.

Character Sets and International Support

As keyboard data travels from the keyboard to your program, it undergoes a number of conversions: Keyboard data starts out as scan codes, which are converted by the device driver into virtual key information. And finally, virtual key codes are converted into ASCII character values to provide upper- and lowercase letters, numbers, and punctuation marks. Figure 15.4 shows Windows' ANSI character set.

What is a character set? It is a convention or a standard that helps avoid confusion. For example, according to the ANSI character set, the value 41H (65 decimal) stands for a capital "A." Microsoft adopted the ANSI character set to allow the data created by a Windows program to be readable by other Windows programs, and interpreted correctly on different

ANSI Character Set - Code Page 1004

	0-	1-	2-	3-	4-	5-	6-	7-	8-	9-	A-	B-	C-	D-	E-	F-
-0	I	I		0	@	P	`	p	I	I		°	À	Ð	à	ð
-1	I	I	!	1	A	Q	a	q	I	‘	¡	±	Á	Ñ	á	ñ
-2	I	I	"	2	B	R	b	r	I	’	¢	²	Â	Ò	â	ò
-3	I	I	#	3	C	S	c	s	I	I	£	³	Ã	Ó	ã	ó
-4	I	I	$	4	D	T	d	t	I	I	¤	´	Ä	Ô	ä	ô
-5	I	I	%	5	E	U	e	u	I	I	¥	µ	Å	Õ	å	õ
-6	I	I	&	6	F	V	f	v	I	I	¦	¶	Æ	Ö	æ	ö
-7	I	I	'	7	G	W	g	w	I	I	§	·	Ç	×	ç	÷
-8	I	I	(	8	H	X	h	x	I	I	¨	¸	È	Ø	è	ø
-9	I	I	)	9	I	Y	i	y	I	I	©	¹	É	Ù	é	ù
-A	I	I	*	:	J	Z	j	z	I	I	ª	º	Ê	Ú	ê	ú
-B	I	I	+	;	K	[	k	{	I	I	«	»	Ë	Û	ë	û
-C	I	I	,	<	L	\	l	|	I	I	¬	¼	Ì	Ü	ì	ü
-D	I	I	-	=	M	]	m	}	I	I	-	½	Í	Ý	í	ý
-E	I	I	.	>	N	^	n	~	I	I	®	¾	Î	Þ	î	þ
-F	I	I	/	?	O	_	o	I	I	I	¯	¿	Ï	ß	ï	ÿ

Figure 15.4 ANSI Character Set

brands of computers and different brands of printers, as well as computers and peripherals in different countries.

Windows uses the ANSI character set to interpret how a text character should be displayed, and to provide a standard that allows file sharing between different Windows computers. But this isn't the only character set that you'll want to know how to work with. In addition to the ANSI character set, every Windows computer has a second character set that DOS uses. For example, IBM-compatible computers that are manufactured for use in the United States have a character set that IBM calls code page 437. Figure 15.5 shows the characters in code page 437. This is the character set that DOS programs use when they create data files, and is the character set used by DOS for file names.

For upper- and lowercase letters, numbers, and punctuation marks, this character set is identical to the Windows' ANSI character set. Thus, if you are writing a Windows program for use only in the United States, you can mix and match data files between DOS and Windows programs with little chance for confusion. This will be true as long as your Windows and DOS programs use printable characters in the range 20h to 7eh (32 to 126 decimal).

For Windows programs to work on computers outside the United States, some effort is required on your part. In the first place, other code pages besides 437 are used on computers manufactured for different languages. For example, code page 860 substitutes 16

OEM Character Set - Code Page 437

	0-	1-	2-	3-	4-	5-	6-	7-	8-	9-	A-	B-	C-	D-	E-	F-
-0		►		0	@	P	`	p	Ç	É	á	░	└	╨	α	≡
-1	☺	◄	!	1	A	Q	a	q	ü	æ	í	▒	┴	╤	ß	±
-2	☻	↕	"	2	B	R	b	r	é	Æ	ó	▓	┬	╥	Γ	≥
-3	♥	‼	#	3	C	S	c	s	â	ô	ú	│	├	╙	π	≤
-4	♦	¶	$	4	D	T	d	t	ä	ö	ñ	┤	─	╘	Σ	⌠
-5	♣	§	%	5	E	U	e	u	à	ò	Ñ	╡	┼	╒	σ	⌡
-6	♠	▬	&	6	F	V	f	v	å	û	ª	╢	╞	╓	µ	÷
-7	•	↨	'	7	G	W	g	w	ç	ù	º	╖	╟	╫	τ	≈
-8	◘	↑	(	8	H	X	h	x	ê	ÿ	¿	╕	╚	╪	Φ	°
-9	○	↓	)	9	I	Y	i	y	ë	Ö	⌐	╣	╔	┘	Θ	∙
-A	◙	→	*	:	J	Z	j	z	è	Ü	¬	║	╩	┌	Ω	·
-B	♂	←	+	;	K	[	k	{	ï	¢	½	╗	╦	█	δ	√
-C	♀	∟	,	<	L	\	l	¦	î	£	¼	╝	╠	▄	∞	ⁿ
-D	♪	↔	-	=	M	]	m	}	ì	¥	¡	╜	═	▌	φ	²
-E	♫	▲	.	>	N	^	n	~	Ä	₧	«	╛	╬	▐	ε	■
-F	☼	▼	/	?	O	_	o	⌂	Å	ƒ	»	┐	╧	▀	∩	

Figure 15.5 DOS Character Set in the United States: Code Page 437

accented characters that are not available in code page 437 that are required for computers sold in Portugal. Code page 863 has 22 new accented and other special characters to meet the requirements of French Canada. And code page 865 has four characters that change the US code page for use in creating Norwegian data files.

Therefore, every machine that runs Windows will have at least two character sets: Windows' ANSI character set (sometimes known as code page 1004), which has the most complete support for accented characters, and what Microsoft calls an OEM character set, which is the character set that DOS uses to meet the language needs of different countries (code page 437).

When a DOS program is running in a window, Windows uses a font that contains characters that match the OEM character set. In this way, the character set provides backward compatibility between Windows and DOS. If you are writing a program to display a text file created by a DOS program, there is a stock font available that uses the OEM character set. You can access this font by saying

```
hfontOEM = GetStockObject (OEM_FIXED_FONT);
SelectObject (hdc, hfontOEM);
```

Converting between Character Sets

If a Windows program reads files that are written by DOS programs, for the program to work properly on all non-US machines, the files must be converted from the OEM character set to Windows' ANSI character set. Conversely, if a Windows program writes to a file that a DOS program may read, the Windows program should convert from the ANSI character set to the native OEM character set that DOS programs expect in order to work outside the United States. Fortunately, some Windows library routines are available to do the conversion for you:

Routine	*Description*
AnsiToOem	Convert null-terminated ANSI string to DOS characters
AnsiToOemBuff	Convert *n* ANSI characters to DOS characters
OemToAnsi	Convert null-terminated DOS characters to ANSI
OemToAnsiBuff	Convert *n* DOS characters to ANSI

In addition to DOS data files, the DOS file system itself uses the OEM character set for file names. However, if you use the **OpenFile** Windows library routine, your file names are automatically converted to the OEM character set before DOS is called.

Upper- and Lowercase Conversion

Programmers in the United States who work with characters exclusively in the range 20Hto 7ef (32 to 126 decimal) often play tricks to convert text to upper- or lowercase. In this range, the upper- and lowercase letters are 20H (32) apart, like those shown here:

	ASCII				
Uppercase	*(hex)*	*(dec)*	*Lowercase*	*(hex)*	*(dec)*
A	41H	65	a	61H	97
B	42H	66	b	62H	98
C	43H	67	c	63H	99
.					
.					
Z	5aH	90	z	7aH	122

In this range, uppercase conversion is easy; here is code that does this for us:

```
for (i=0;i<cc;i++)
    {
    if (ach[i] >= 'a' && ach[i] <= 'z')
        ach[i] -= 32;
    }
```

But consider the following pairs of upper- and lowercase accented letters:

	ASCII				
Uppercase	*(hex)*	*(dec)*	*Lowercase*	*(hex)*	*(dec)*
Á	c0h	192	á	e0h	224
Ç	c7h	199	ç	e7h	231
È	c8h	200	è	e8h	232
Ï	cfh	207	ï	efh	239
Õ	d5h	213	õ	f5h	245
Û	dbh	219	û	fbh	251

If the array in our earlier example included any of the lowercase letters in this table, the case conversion would not have worked correctly. If you are writing a program that will be sold outside the United States, you should use the following Windows library routines for upper- and lowercase conversion instead of writing your own.

Routine	*Description*
`AnsiLower`	Converts null-terminated string to lowercase
`AnsiLowerBuff`	Converts *n* characters to lowercase
`AnsiUpper`	Converts null-terminated string to uppercase
`AnsiUpperBuff`	Converts *n* characters to uppercase

To convert a null-terminated character string to all uppercase, you could pass a long pointer to **AnsiUpper**, as in

```
AnsiUpper (lpszConvert);
```

or, using **AnsiUpperBuff**, you could say:

```
i = lstrlen (lpszConvert);
AnsiUpperBuff (lpszConvert, i);
```

Another set of routines tests whether character information is upper- or lowercase, whether it is an alphabetic character, or whether it is alphanumeric:

Routine	*Description*
`IsCharAlpha`	Returns TRUE if character is alphabetic character.
`IsCharAlphaNumeric`	Returns TRUE if character is either alphabetic or numeric character.
`IsCharLower`	Returns TRUE if character is lowercase.
`IsCharUpper`	Returns TRUE if character is uppercase.

Sorting Character Strings

Accented characters require special handling when converting text strings to uppercase or to lowercase. The same is true when sorting character strings. Programs that perform a simple numeric sort of character strings will put words with accents out of order. For example, the following sort order results from a simple numeric sort:

cheese
chocolate
church
château

Of course, the problem is that the numeric value of the character “â” is e2h (226 decimal), which comes after “e” (65h or 101 decimal), “o” (6fh or 111 decimal), and “u” (75h or 117 decimal). Since this is the way that the C-runtime library routine, **strcmp**, works, this routine should be avoided if you want your product to work correctly outside the United States.

Putting “château” at the top of the list, where it belongs, requires that we call a Windows library routine to perform string comparison for us during our sort. Actually, there are two such routines: one that compares in a case-insensitive fashion, **lstrcmpi**, and one that compares in a case-sensitive fashion, **lstrcmp**.

String Tables

Windows has a facility that will help in the effort to prepare a product for translation to another language—a process that Microsoft calls **localization**. The facility is the **string table**. A string table allows you to put all the strings from a program in a central place: the resource file. When your program needs to access a string, it makes a call to Windows using a numeric index. In this way, all messages for the user are centralized in one place. The job of a translator is simplified, since there is only one file that must be converted to localize an entire application.

To create a string table, entries are made in the .RC resource file, like the following:

```
#include "myinclude"

STRINGTABLE
    {
    FILENOTFOUND, "File Not Found."
    HELPPROMPT, "For Help, Type F1."
    RECALCMESSAGE, "Recalculating."
    }
```

The file MYINCLUDE would contain definitions like the following:

```
#define FILENOTFOUND  101
#define HELPPROMPT    102
#define RECALCMESSAGE 103
```

These provide a unique, numeric ID for each string. When the time comes to use a string, a Windows library routine, **`LoadString`**, is called:

```
char acMessage[BUFSIZE];

LoadString (hInstance,     // instance handle
            FILENOTFOUND,  // string id value
            acMessage,     // character buffer
            BUFSIZE);      // buffer size
```

Then the string can be displayed, perhaps using the **`TextOut`** routine.

There are other benefits to using string tables besides the international support issue. Objects in a string table are read-only data, and as such Windows loads them when needed and purges them from memory when not needed. In other words, the benefit of string tables is that they are very efficient in terms of the memory that is used.

Entering Characters from the Numeric Keypad

You may be aware that, when running DOS, you can enter ASCII codes directly from the numeric keypad. Windows provides the same mechanism, which is supported by the Windows keyboard driver. You can actually enter characters from either the ANSI or OEM character sets.

To enter characters from the ANSI character set, with [Num Lock] toggled on, hold down the [Alt] key and enter a zero followed by the decimal ASCII character code. To enter the letter “A,” for example, you hold down [Alt] and type 0192.

You can enter characters from the OEM character set as well, although they will be mapped to the corresponding ANSI character set value. With the [Num Lock] toggled on, hold down the [Alt] key and enter the decimal OEM character code. For example, to enter the letter “à,” you hold down [Alt] and type 160.

Multitasking Issues

Now that we've covered the basics of handling keyboard input and dealing with different character sets, there are a few more issues that you must be aware of in order to make effective use of the keyboard.

Windows is multitasking, which means there has to be a mechanism for sharing devices like the keyboard. There are two concepts that Windows uses to direct where keyboard input is sent: the **active window** and the **focus**.

When a program creates a window, the program decides whether the window is a **top-level window** or a child of another top-level window. Most programs create a single top-level window. This window serves as the primary means by which the user interacts with the program. One characteristic of top-level windows is that they appear on the Task List that is displayed in response to the [Ctrl] + [Esc] key combination. The Task List, shown in Figure 15.6, lets the user select the top-level window that he wishes to make active.

The active window, then, is simply the top-level window that the user has decided to work with. Of course, there are other ways to make a window active besides selecting from the Task List. For example, a user could click with the mouse to make a window active, or hit the [Alt] + [Tab] key combination continuously to circulate among the top-level windows. The active window is always on top of every other top-level window in the system.

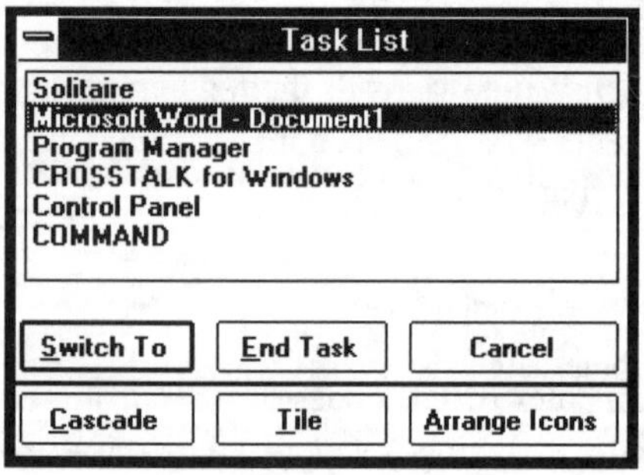

Figure 15.6 The Windows Task List

This makes sense, for if the user has decided to work with a particular window, it should be completely visible.

When a top-level window becomes active, Windows sends it a **WM_ACTIVATE** message with a nonzero value in `wParam`. This tells the window, in effect, that "the boss wants to see you. Now." Windows also sends a **WM_NCACTIVATE** message, which causes the window's caption bar to change colors so that the user has a visual clue to the active window. Like other nonclient area messages, this one is handled by the default window procedure.

In response to a **WM_ACTIVATE** message, the default window procedure gives the active window the focus. Here is the actual code from **DefWindowProc**:

```
case WM_ACTIVATE:
    if (wParam)
        SetFocus (hWnd);
```

The focus is simply an indicator within Windows that identifies which window should get keyboard input. In effect, when a window has the focus, it has the keyboard. It alone will receive keyboard messages.

When a window receives the focus, Windows lets it know by sending it a message: **WM_SETFOCUS**. But before it does that, it sends a **WM_KILLFOCUS** message to the window that is losing the keyboard. By watching these two messages, a window procedure can keep track of whether it has control of the keyboard or not.

But why should a window care whether it has the keyboard or not? Won't it still get the proper keyboard messages? The answer is, Yes. But sometimes a window procedure will want to know when it has the focus, and will want to take special steps. One such case occurs when we wish to have a keyboard pointer, or **caret**, in a window. That is the next topic that we plan to discuss.

Creating a Keyboard Pointer: Carets

As a program receives keyboard input, it's quite common to display a keyboard pointer to let the user know where the next character will be entered. In most environments, this is called a **cursor**. But Windows uses the term cursor to refer to the mouse pointer, and instead uses the term caret to refer to a keyboard pointer.

A caret is a rectangular blinking bitmap that lets the user know several things. First of all, it lets the user know which window has the keyboard—that is, which window has the focus. Second, as we mentioned a moment ago, it lets the user know the current position—the location where text (or some other object) will appear next.

While the most obvious use of a caret is to highlight a text entry point, that is certainly not the only use. For example, a caret can be used to indicate the "current object" in a drawing program, and is used in listboxes to show the user which item would be affected by keyboard input.

Windows has four routines for creating and maintaining the keyboard caret:

Routine Name	*Description*
`CreateCaret`	Creates a caret
`SetCaretPos`	Positions the caret
`ShowCaret`	Makes a caret visible
`DestroyCaret`	Destroys a caret

You might be tempted to create a caret at the beginning of your program and hold onto it until your program exits, but this wouldn't give you the results you expect. The reason is that internally, Windows is only able to recognize one caret for the entire system. Thus, you cannot keep a caret for the life of your program. You can only keep it for as long as you have the focus. For this reason, do not create a caret like this:

```
// Do Not Create Carets Like This!
void DFrame::SetupWindow()
    {
    CreateCaret(HWindow, 0, xWidth, yHeight);
    }

void DFrame::CleanupWindow()
    {
    DestroyCaret();
    }
```

Instead, the proper way to create and destroy a caret is in response to the **`WM_SETFOCUS`** and **`WM_KILLFOCUS`** messages. Every time your window gains the keyboard focus, it will create a caret, and every time it loses the keyboard focus, it destroys its caret. It might seem that this is a lot of trouble for a tiny, blinking bitmap, but this approach is necessary to properly maintain a caret in a Windows program:

```
// Correct way to create & destroy carets.
void DFrame::EvSetFocus (HWND /*hwndLostFocus*/)
    {
    CreateCaret (hwnd, 0, xWidth, yHeight);
    }

void DFrame::EvKillFocus (HWND /*hwndGetFocus*/)
    {
    DestroyCaret();
    }
```

The **`CreateCaret`** routine is defined as follows:

```
void CreateCaret (hWnd, hBitmap, nWidth, nHeight)
```

- **`hWnd`** is a handle to the window where the caret is to be located.
- **`hBitmap`** is a handle to a bitmap. It can be `0`, `1`, or a real bitmap handle.
- **`nWidth`** is the caret width.

- **nHeight** is the caret height.

The second field, **hBitmap**, is the key field that determines the shape and color of the caret. If it is set to zero, then the bitmap will be a black square `nWidth` by `nHeight`. If set to one, the bitmap is a gray square `nWidth` by `nHeight`. Otherwise, if it is a GDI bitmap, the caret takes on the shape of the bitmap.

When we create a caret, we'll want to make sure it is large enough to be visible. Since we're going to use the caret to highlight a text entry point, it makes sense to make the caret the same height as the text. Here is how to create a black caret that fits the bill:

```
class DFrame : TFrameWindow
    {
    int cyCaretHeight;
    ...
    };
...
void DFrame::SetupWindow()
    {
    TClientDC hdc(HWindow);
    TEXTMETRICS tm;
    dc.GetTextMetrics(tm);
    cyCaretHeight = tm.tmHeight;
    }

void DFrame::EvSetFocus (HWND /*hwndLostFocus*/)
    {
    CreateCaret (hwnd,
                 0,     // default black caret.
                 0,     // default width.
                 cyCaretHeight);
    }
```

Here is how to create a gray caret that is the same size:

```
CreateCaret (hwnd,
             1,     // default gray caret
             0,     // default width
             cyCaretHeight);
```

By selecting a width of zero, we let Windows use the default size. This will be the width of a window border, to make sure that the caret is visible.

We could also create a bitmap, draw onto it using GDI drawing routines, and use it as a caret. We're going to create a monochrome bitmap. The portion of the bitmap that is black will be ignored while the portion that is white will blink. Here is how to make a caret in the shape of an I-beam. Notice that most of the work involves creating the bitmap and drawing onto it:

```
void TSampleWindow::SetupWindow()
    {
    HBITMAP hbmOld;
    HDC hdc;
    HDC hdcBitmap;
```

```
    TEXTMETRIC tm;

    hdc = GetDC (hwnd);
    GetTextMetrics (hdc, &tm);
    yLineHeight = tm.tmHeight + tm.tmExternalLeading;
    ReleaseDC (hwnd, hdc);

    hdcBitmap = CreateCompatibleDC (hdc);
    hbm = CreateBitmap (xLeftMargin,
                        yLineHeight,
                        1, 1, NULL);
    hbmOld = SelectBitmap (hdcBitmap, hbm);

    /*  Blank out bitmap.  */
    SelectBrush (hdcBitmap,
                 GetStockBrush (BLACK_BRUSH));
    Rectangle (hdcBitmap, 0, 0,
               xLeftMargin, yLineHeight);

    /*  Do actual drawing in white.  */
    SelectPen (hdcBitmap,
               GetStockPen (WHITE_PEN));
    MoveTo (hdcBitmap, 0, 0);
    LineTo (hdcBitmap, xLeftMargin+1, 0);
    MoveTo (hdcBitmap, xLeftMargin/2, 0);
    LineTo (hdcBitmap, xLeftMargin/2, yLineHeight-1);
    MoveTo (hdcBitmap, 0, yLineHeight-1);
    LineTo (hdcBitmap, xLeftMargin+1, yLineHeight-1);
    SelectBitmap (hdcBitmap, hbmOld);
    DeleteDC (hdcBitmap);
    ...
    }

void TSampleWindow::CleanupWindow()
    {
    DeleteBitmap (hbm);
    }

void TSampleWindow::EvKillFocus(HWND)
    {
    DestroyCaret();
    }

void TSampleWindow::EvSetFocus(HWND)
    {
    CreateCaret(HWindow,
                hbm,    // hBitmap
                0,      // xWidth
                0);     // yWidth
    SetCaretPos (x, y);
    ShowCaret(HWindow);
    }
```

And, of course, this code fragment assumes that a bitmap handle has been allocated as a static object:

```
static HBITMAP hbm;
```

Let's look at an actual program that uses a caret. We've modified the KEYINPUT program so that it uses a caret. In addition to creating and deleting the caret properly, it also moves the caret in response to the cursor movement keys on the keyboard. Here is our caret-handling program: CARET.

CARET.CPP

```
//
// CARET.CPP  Demonstrate the creation & use of a keyboard
//            pointer (a.k.a. 'caret').
//
#include <owl\owlpch.h>
#include "cl_caret.h"
#include "caret.h"

DEFINE_RESPONSE_TABLE1 (DFrame, TFrameWindow)
  EV_WM_CHAR,
  EV_WM_KEYDOWN,
  EV_WM_SETFOCUS,
  EV_WM_KILLFOCUS,
  EV_COMMAND(CM_FILEEXIT, CmFileExit),
  EV_COMMAND(CM_HELPABOUT, CmHelpAbout),
END_RESPONSE_TABLE;

DFrame::DFrame(char * title) : TFrameWindow(0, title)
    {
    TScreenDC dc;

    TEXTMETRIC tm;
    dc.GetTextMetrics (tm);

    yLineHeight = tm.tmHeight + tm.tmExternalLeading;
    xLeftMargin = tm.tmAveCharWidth;

    achInput[0] = '\0';
    cchInput = 0;
    ichNext = 0;
    }

void DFrame::CmFileExit()
    {
    CloseWindow(0); // Cause application to terminate
    }

void DFrame::CmHelpAbout()
    {
    MessageBox(" Creating & Managing a Caret\n\n"
               "'Borland C++ 4.0 Programming\n"
               "  for Windows', by Paul Yao", Title);
    }

void DFrame::EvChar (UINT key, UINT, UINT)
    {
    if (key == VK_BACK)    //  Backspace.
        {
        if (ichNext == 0)
            MessageBeep(0);
        else               //  Remove a character.
            {
            ichNext--;
            pcCaret->SetCharPosition(ichNext);
```

```
            for (int i=ichNext;i<cchInput;i++)
                achInput[i]=achInput[i+1];
            cchInput--;
            Invalidate ();
            }
        return;
        }

    // Complain if character out of range or if buffer is full.
    if ((key <= VK_ESCAPE) || (cchInput >= BUFSIZE))
        {
        MessageBeep(0);
        return;
        }

    // Make room for next char.
    for (int i=cchInput;i>ichNext;i--)
        achInput[i]=achInput[i-1];

    /*  Put new char in buffer.  */
    achInput[ichNext] = (unsigned char)key;

    // Increment count of characters.
    cchInput++;

    pcCaret->Hide();

    // Update display.
    TClientDC dc(HWindow);
    TSize size;
    dc.GetTextExtent ((LPSTR)&achInput[0], ichNext, size);
    dc.TextOut (xLeftMargin+size.cx,
                yLineHeight,
                (LPSTR)&achInput[ichNext],
                cchInput - ichNext);

    pcCaret->Show();

    // Increment index to next character.
    ichNext++;
    pcCaret->SetCharPosition(ichNext);
    }

void DFrame::EvSetFocus(HWND /* hwndLostFocus */)
    {
    pcCaret->SetCharPosition(ichNext);
    pcCaret->SetState(CARET_ACTIVE);
    }

void DFrame::EvKillFocus(HWND /* hwndGetFocus */)
    {
    pcCaret->SetState(CARET_INACTIVE);
    }

void DFrame::EvKeyDown (UINT key, UINT, UINT)
    {
    BOOL fCaretMoved = FALSE;

    switch (key)
        {
        case VK_DELETE:
            /*  If end of buffer, complain.  */
```

```
            if (ichNext == cchInput)
                MessageBeep(0);
            else  /*  Remove a character.  */
                {
                int i;
                for (i=ichNext;i<cchInput;i++)
                    achInput[i]=achInput[i+1];
                cchInput--;
                Invalidate();
                }
            break;
        case VK_END:
            ichNext = cchInput;
            fCaretMoved = TRUE;
            break;
        case VK_HOME:
            ichNext = 0;
            fCaretMoved = TRUE;
            break;
        case VK_LEFT:
            if (ichNext > 0)
                {
                ichNext--;
                fCaretMoved = TRUE;
                }
            else
                MessageBeep(0);
            break;
        case VK_RIGHT:
            if (ichNext < cchInput)
                {
                ichNext++;
                fCaretMoved = TRUE;
                }
            else
                MessageBeep(0);
            break;
        }

    if (fCaretMoved)
        pcCaret->SetCharPosition(ichNext);
    }
void DFrame::Paint (TDC& dc, BOOL, TRect&)
    {
    dc.TextOut (xLeftMargin, yLineHeight, achInput, cchInput);
    }

void DFrame::SetupWindow()
    {
    TFrameWindow::SetupWindow();

    HFONT hFont = (HFONT)::GetStockObject (SYSTEM_FONT);
    pcCaret = new Caret (HWindow, hFont);

    pcCaret->SetAnchor (xLeftMargin, yLineHeight);
    pcCaret->SetStringPtr ((LPSTR)&achInput[0]);
    }

void DFrame::CleanupWindow()
    {
    delete pcCaret;
```

```
    TFrameWindow::CleanupWindow();
    }

DApp::DApp() : TApplication()
    {
    }

void DApp::InitMainWindow()
    {
    SetMainWindow (new DFrame("Caret"));

    MainWindow->AssignMenu("MAIN");
    MainWindow->SetIcon(this, "SNAPSHOT");
    }

// Application main entry point.
OwlMain(int, char **)
    {
    return DApp().Run();
    }
```

CARET.H

```
#define CM_FILEEXIT 100
#define CM_HELPABOUT 200

const int BUFSIZE = 120;

// Main window
class DFrame : public TFrameWindow
    {
  public:
    DFrame(char * title);
    void CmFileExit();
    void CmHelpAbout();
    void EvChar (UINT key, UINT repeat, UINT flags);
    void EvKeyDown (UINT key, UINT repeat, UINT flags);
    void Paint (TDC&, BOOL, TRect&);
    void SetupWindow();
    void CleanupWindow();
    void EvSetFocus(HWND hwndLostFocus);
    void EvKillFocus(HWND hwndGetFocus);
  private:
    Caret * pcCaret;
    char achInput[BUFSIZE];
    int  cchInput;
    int  ichNext;
    int  yLineHeight;
    int  xLeftMargin;

  DECLARE_RESPONSE_TABLE (DFrame);
    };

// Application object
class DApp : public TApplication
    {
  public:
    DApp();
    void InitMainWindow();
    };
```

CL_CARET.CPP

```
//
// CL_CARET.CPP  Caret class definition.
//

#include <owl\owlpch.h>
#include "cl_caret.h"

 // Caret class constructor.
Caret::Caret(HWND hwndIn, HFONT hFontIn)
    {
    HFONT      hfontOld;
    TEXTMETRIC tm;

    hdcInfo = CreateIC ("DISPLAY", 0, 0, 0);
    hfontOld = (HFONT)::SelectObject (hdcInfo, hFontIn);
    GetTextMetrics (hdcInfo, &tm);
    SelectObject (hdcInfo, hfontOld);

    hwnd          = hwndIn;
    hFont         = hFontIn;
    iCharPos      = 0;
    iFlag         = CARET_INACTIVE;
    cxCaretWidth  = GetSystemMetrics (SM_CXBORDER);
    cyCaretHeight = tm.tmHeight;
    ptPixelPos.x  = 0;
    ptPixelPos.y  = 0;
    ptAnchor.x    = 0;
    ptAnchor.y    = 0;
    lpString      = (LPSTR)0L;
    }

// Caret class destructor.
Caret::~Caret()
    {
    if (iFlag & CARET_ACTIVE)
        {
        HideCaret(hwnd);
        DestroyCaret();
        }

    DeleteDC (hdcInfo);
    }

void Caret::Hide()
    {
    HideCaret(hwnd);
    }

void Caret::Show()
    {
    ShowCaret(hwnd);
    }

int     Caret::GetAnchorX()
    {
    return ptAnchor.x;
    }

int     Caret::GetAnchorY()
    {
    return ptAnchor.y;
```

```
    }

int     Caret::GetCharPosition ()
    {
    return iCharPos;
    }

HFONT Caret::GetFontHandle()
    {
    return hFont;
    }

int     Caret::GetState ()
    {
    return iFlag;
    }

LPSTR  Caret::GetStringPtr()
    {
    return lpString;
    }

void   Caret::SetAnchor (int X, int Y)
    {
    ptAnchor.x = X;
    ptAnchor.y = Y;
    }

void   Caret::SetCharPosition (int iChar)
    {
    DWORD  dwSize;
    HFONT  hFontOld;
    int    xWidth;

    iCharPos = iChar;

    // Calculate width of character string.
    hFontOld = (HFONT)::SelectObject (hdcInfo, hFont);
    dwSize = GetTextExtent (hdcInfo, lpString, iCharPos);
    xWidth = LOWORD(dwSize);
    SelectObject (hdcInfo, hFontOld);

    // Update caret position information.
    ptPixelPos.x = ptAnchor.x + xWidth;
    ptPixelPos.y = ptAnchor.y;

    // If caret is active, update location.
    if (iFlag & CARET_ACTIVE)
        {
        SetCaretPos (ptPixelPos.x, ptPixelPos.y);
        }
    }

void   Caret::SetFontHandle(HFONT hFontIn)
    {
    HFONT      hfontOld;
    TEXTMETRIC tm;

    hfontOld = (HFONT)::SelectObject (hdcInfo, hFontIn);
    GetTextMetrics (hdcInfo, &tm);
    SelectObject (hdcInfo, hfontOld);

    hFont         = hFontIn;
```

```
    cyCaretHeight = tm.tmHeight;
    }

void   Caret::SetState (int AFlag)
    {
    if (iFlag == AFlag)
        return;

    if (AFlag & CARET_ACTIVE)
        {
        CreateCaret (hwnd, 0, cxCaretWidth, cyCaretHeight);
        SetCaretPos (ptPixelPos.x, ptPixelPos.y);
        ShowCaret (hwnd);
        }

    if (AFlag & CARET_INACTIVE)
        {
        DestroyCaret ();
        }

    iFlag = AFlag;
    }

void Caret::SetStringPtr(LPSTR lpstrIn)
    {
    lpString = lpstrIn;
    }
```

CL_CARET.H

```
const int CARET_ACTIVE   = 0x01;
const int CARET_INACTIVE = 0x02;

// The Caret class.
class Caret
  {
  public:
    Caret(HWND hwndIn, HFONT hFontIn);
    ~Caret();

    virtual void   Hide();
    virtual void   Show();

    virtual int    GetAnchorX();
    virtual int    GetAnchorY();
    virtual int    GetCharPosition ();
    virtual HFONT  GetFontHandle();
    virtual int    GetState ();
    virtual LPSTR  GetStringPtr();

    virtual void   SetAnchor (int X, int Y);
    virtual void   SetCharPosition (int iChar);
    virtual void   SetFontHandle(HFONT hFontIn);
    virtual void   SetState (int AFlag);
    virtual void   SetStringPtr(LPSTR lpstrIn);
  private:
    HFONT   hFont;
    HDC     hdcInfo;
    HWND    hwnd;
```

```
    int      iCharPos;
    int      iFlag;
    int      cxCaretWidth;
    int      cyCaretHeight;
    POINT    ptPixelPos;
    POINT    ptAnchor;
    LPSTR    lpString;
};
```

CARET.RC

```
#include "caret.h"

snapshot icon caret.ico

main menu
    BEGIN
    POPUP "&File"
        {
        MENUITEM "E&xit", CM_FILEEXIT
        }
    POPUP "&Help"
        {
        MENUITEM "&About...", CM_HELPABOUT
        }
    END
```

CARET.DEF

```
EXETYPE WINDOWS

CODE MOVEABLE DISCARDABLE
DATA MULTIPLE MOVEABLE

HEAPSIZE   512
STACKSIZE 8192
```

DYNA16.MAK

```
#  MAKE file for Win16 API using dynamic BIDS,
#  OWL and C-runtime libraries.
#
#    C> make -fstatic16.mak
#

.AUTODEPEND
CC = -c -H -H"owl\owlpch.h" -ml -R -vi -WS -X-
CD = -D_RTLDLL;_BIDSDLL;_OWLDLL;_OWLPCH;
INC = -I\BC4\INCLUDE
LIB = -L\BC4\LIB

caret.exe :  caret.obj cl_caret.obj caret.res
```

```
  tlink -c -C -Twe $(LIB) @dyna16.lnk
  brc caret.res caret.exe

cl_caret.obj :  cl_caret.cpp
  bcc $(CC) $(CD) cl_caret.cpp

caret.obj :  caret.cpp
  bcc $(CC) $(CD) caret.cpp

caret.res :  caret.rc caret.ico caret.h
  brc $(INC) -31 -R caret.rc
```

DYNA16.LNK

```
\bc4\lib\c0wl.obj+
caret.obj+cl_caret.obj
caret,caret
\bc4\lib\bidsi.lib+
\bc4\lib\owlwi.lib+
\bc4\lib\import.lib+
\bc4\lib\crtldll.lib
caret.def
```

DYNA32.MAK

```
#  MAKE file for Win32 API using dynamic BIDS,
#  OWL and C-runtime libraries.
#
#    C> make -fdyna32.mak
#

.AUTODEPEND
CC = -c -H -H\""owl\owlpch.h\"" -p- -R -vi -W -X-
CD = -D_RTLDLL;_BIDSDLL;_OWLDLL;_OWLPCH;
INC = -I\BC4\INCLUDE
LIB = -L\BC4\LIB

caret.exe :  caret.obj cl_caret.obj caret.res
  tlink32 -aa -c -Tpe $(LIB) @dyna32.lnk
  brc32 caret.res caret.exe

cl_caret.obj :  cl_caret.cpp
  bcc32 $(CC) $(CD) cl_caret.cpp

caret.obj :  caret.cpp
  bcc32 $(CC) $(CD) caret.cpp

caret.res :  caret.rc caret.ico caret.h
  brc32 $(INC) -w32 -R caret.rc
```

DYNA32.LNK

```
\bc4\lib\c0w32.obj+
caret.obj+cl_caret.obj
caret,caret
\bc4\lib\bidsfi.lib+
\bc4\lib\owlwfi.lib+
\bc4\lib\import32.lib+
\bc4\lib\cw32i.lib
caret.def
```

In this program, we've created a caret class, **`TCaret`**, which manages an MS-Windows caret. There is certainly room for improvement of this class, but it does provide a sufficient base on which to build a real-world application's caret class. Let's examine the data members and member functions which make up **`TCaret`**, starting with the data members:

Type	*Name*	*Description*
`HFONT`	`hFont`	Font used for display of string, used to calculate string width information.
`HDC`	`hdcInfo`	Permanent Information Context (IC) used to derive character/font width information.
`HWND`	`hwnd`	Window in which font resides.
`int`	`iCharPos`	Position of caret, in character cells.
`int`	`iFlag`	Active/inactive flag.
`int`	`cxCaretWidth`	Width of caret, in pixels. Width is equal to the border width of a window.
`int`	`cyCaretHeight`	Height of caret, in pixels. Height is equal to height of currently selected font.
`POINT`	`ptPixelPos`	Position (*x,y*) of caret, in pixels.
`POINT`	`ptAnchor`	Anchor point (*x,y*) of string, from which caret location is calculated.
`LPSTR`	`lpString`	Points to the character string relative to which the caret is to be placed.

The **`TCaret`** class handles managing the movement of a caret through a character string. It does so by keeping track of every piece of information relative to the caret: an MS-Windows handle to the text window, a pointer to the character string, the font used, and the relative location of the string in the text window. Once these values have been set up, the only thing which must be supplied is the character position of the caret, **`iCharPos`**. This is accomplished by calling the **`SetCharPosition`** member function. Let's look at the other member functions:

Function Name	*Description*
`TCaret`	Constructor.
`~TCaret`	Destructor.
`Hide`	Hides a caret. To avoid a conflict with output in a window, you'll need to hide the caret when drawing in a window.
`Show`	Shows a caret.
`GetAnchorX`	Retrieves the *x* value of the string anchor position.
`GetAnchorY`	Retrieves the *y* value of the string anchor position.
`GetCharPosition`	Retrieves the character position.
`GetFontHandle`	Retrieves the font handle.
`GetState`	Retrieves the active/inactive state.
`GetStringPtr`	Retrieves a pointer to the current character string.
`SetAnchor`	Sets the string anchor position.
`SetCharPosition`	Set the character position of the caret.
`SetFontHandle`	Sets the font handle.
`SetState`	Sets the active/inactive state.
`SetStringPtr`	Sets the current string pointer.

One important aspect of carets is that they must be hidden when you draw in a window. In particular, if you draw during any message besides the **WM_PAINT** message, you'll need to hide the caret while you are drawing. This is necessary because the drawing of a caret occurs asynchronously with system messages. Before calling **GetDC**, you must hide the caret by calling **HideCaret**. After you've gotten rid of the DC by calling **ReleaseDC**, it's safe to restore the caret by calling `ShowCaret`. That's exactly what **TCaret**'s **Hide** and **Show** member functions do in this fragment taken from our sample program (from **DFrame:EvChar**, to be exact):

```
pcCaret->Hide();

// Update display.
TClientDC dc(HWindow);
TSize size;
dc.GetTextExtent ((LPSTR)&achInput[0], ichNext, size);
dc.TextOut (xLeftMargin+size.cx,
            yLineHeight,
            (LPSTR)&achInput[ichNext],
            cchInput - ichNext);

pcCaret->Show();
```

Perhaps the single most important thing that should be said about carets is that they must be created in response to the **WM_SETFOCUS** message and destroyed in response to

WM_KILLFOCUS. With **TCaret**, both actions are performed by the **SetState** member function. When called with the **CARET_ACTIVE** flag, the caret is created and displayed. When called with the **CARET_INACTIVE** flag, the caret is destroyed. If a program fails to destroy a caret in response to the **WM_KILLFOCUS** message, the Window Manager will get confused. It seems that the Window Manager assumes there will be only one caret in the system at any time. If your program fails to follow these rules, you will get an orphaned caret in a window. Avoiding this is easy: Create and destroy carets in response to the proper messages.

This concludes our look at keyboard input, and at carets. You see now that keyboard input goes through a two-step conversion process: from scan code to virtual key and from virtual key to ASCII character code. This two-step process helps Windows be an international operating system, and allows Windows programs to run unchanged around the world.

In the next chapter, we're going to look at the other type of input device available to Windows programs: the mouse. Ideally, a Windows program will allow a user to switch between the mouse and the keyboard for all of its operations. Let's see what this involves.

16

Mouse Input

A mouse is a pointing device about the size of a deck of playing cards connected via cable to a computer. The first mouse was developed in the mid-1960s at the Stanford Research Institute (SRI). During the 1970s, the mouse played a key role in the computer research done at Xerox's Palo Alto Research Center (PARC). But the mouse didn't come into widespread use until the 1980s, with the advent and immense popularity of personal computers.

The mouse allows a user to quickly point to different objects and locations on the display screen. Objects can be picked up, moved, and directly manipulated with a versatility that is not possible with the keyboard alone. The advantage of the mouse over the keyboard is that pointing is a very natural, human action that we are capable of from a very young age. Pressing letter combinations on a keyboard is arguably a less natural way to communicate.

The mouse is a very important input device in Windows. Used alone, quite a bit of interaction is possible: Programs can be started, windows moved, menu items selected, and, in programs that allow it, data objects can be directly manipulated. As you begin to create Windows programs, you'll want to keep in mind the tremendous possibilities that are possible through the simple act of pointing.

Even though Windows and Windows applications make significant use of the mouse, not every Windows computer will have a mouse. And even on computers that are equipped with a mouse, there may be times when a particular user prefers to avoid the mouse. Early in the development of Windows, this issue was raised by the developers of some popular software packages. In particular, the developers of DOS-based programs that relied primarily on keyboard input were concerned with the suitability of Windows for their programs. In response, Windows was changed so that all available mouse functions would be available from the keyboard as well. Ideally, programs should allow users to switch from one to the other at any time.

This approach is built into the way that Windows handles menus. Consider the system menu. When you want to see the system menu, you can click the mouse on the system menu icon or strike the [Alt] + [Spacebar] keys. Once the system menu has made its appearance, you can select system menu commands using either the mouse or the keyboard. Using the mouse, you click on the desired menu item. Using the keyboard, there are two choices: You can use the arrow keys followed by the return key, or simply strike a letter key that matches an underlined letter in a menu item name. On the other hand, having seen the system menu, you might decide that you don't want to select any of its commands after all. Again, there is a keyboard approach and a mouse approach to dismissing the system menu. From the keyboard, you hit the [Esc] key. Using the mouse, simply click anywhere outside the system menu.

This flexibility allows the user to alternate between the two devices based on personal preference. We suggest that you take a similar approach while designing the user interface to your Windows programs. It will require some thought on your part to create a robust, flexible interface—but the increased *usability* of your program will most likely cause an increase in the *use* of your program.

If you have never used a mouse before, you might be skeptical about its usefulness as an input device. There's a story about a researcher at Xerox PARC, Larry Tesler, who used to think that way. He set up an experiment to prove that the mouse wasn't a very useful input device. He took people off the streets, and taught them to use a full-screen editor with cursor keys. After an hour or so, he would introduce the mouse as an alternative to the cursor keys. After playing with the mouse a little, most people ended up ignoring the cursor keys in favor of the mouse. The experiment backfired: Although he was trying to demonstrate that the mouse was an unsuitable input device, Tesler found that most users were more comfortable using the mouse instead of the keyboard to select input locations on a display screen.

Perhaps, like many programmers, you are primarily oriented toward keyboard input. If so, it might be worth your time to practice using the mouse. This will help you become a better Windows programmer, since it will help you to better understand the benefits that the mouse can provide to your users. To get you started, the next section discusses some of the common uses of the mouse in Windows.

The Uses of a Mouse

We're going to start our discussion of the mouse from the point of view of the user. That is, we're going to answer the question: What is a mouse used for? If you're an experienced mouse user, you might wish to skip ahead a few pages to where our discussion of programming issues begins.

In use, the mouse rests on a flat surface like a desktop. It controls the movement of a tiny symbol on the display screen called a **cursor**. The cursor sometimes changes shape to let you know that a particular location on the screen has significance. For example, some windows have a thick border for use in resizing the window. When positioned on top of such a border, the cursor changes into a two-headed arrow to let you know that resizing can take place.

A mouse may have one or more buttons. While the cursor location is important, it's actually the use of the buttons that triggers an action. There are several different uses of the mouse buttons that are common in the world of Windows, including clicking, double-clicking, clicking with a shift key, and dragging. We're going to discuss each of these briefly, to introduce the basic mouse actions, and to discuss some of the techniques that you'll see mentioned in this chapter. A more complete discussion of mouse interaction techniques can be found in the IBM publication *Systems Application Architecture, Common User Access: Advanced Interface Design Guide* (SC26-4582-0). This document describes a set of user-interface standards that have been adopted for Windows programs. You should consider getting a copy of this important guide.

The first mouse action that we're going to describe is **clicking**. Clicking involves pressing and releasing a mouse button without moving the mouse. A click is used to select objects and actions. For example, clicking causes menus to appear and is used to make scroll bars operate.

Double-clicking involves two clicking operations at the same location in a very short time interval. The default time interval is one-half second, but this can be changed using the Control Panel. While a single click makes a selection, a double-click means "do the default action." For example, a double-click on the system menu icon means "close this window." A double-click on a program icon in the Program Manager means "start this program." In general, a double-click should extend the action that was started by a single click.

Clicking with a shift key involves holding down one of the shift keys ([Shift] or [Ctrl]) while clicking a mouse button. The shift key modifies the mouse click, in the same way that a shift key modifies a keyboard key. [Shift] + [A], for example, gives us a capital "A." The meaning of [Shift] + click or [Ctrl] + click will depend on the program. In general, though, [Shift] + click is a request to extend a selection that was started with a single click.

Dragging is a two-part mouse action, which starts with clicking to select an object, and then—with the mouse button still pressed—involves moving the mouse to cause the selected object to move. When the object has arrived at the desired location, the mouse button is released. Dragging is perhaps the hardest operation for new Windows users to master, since it combines mouse button action and mouse movement. But it is also a widely used action. For example, in graphics programs, dragging allows a user to directly manipulate objects on the display screen. In the Windows interface itself, dragging is an important mouse action: Dragging is used to move windows, select menu items, and operate scroll bars.

This brief introduction to mouse actions is not a substitute for your working with the Windows user interface and becoming comfortable with each of these techniques. If you are a regular Windows user, it will help make you a better Windows programmer. But now, let's roll up our sleeves and start to investigate some of the issues that will help you program for the mouse. In the same way that we traced the path of keyboard data from the hardware into our program, we're going to follow the path that mouse data takes in hopes of understanding how a Windows program can best make use of this device.

How a Windows Program Receives Mouse Input

The path that mouse data takes is illustrated in Figure 16.1. In many respects, mouse data is much simpler than keyboard data, and so this figure is correspondingly simpler than the diagram that we saw in the last chapter. Nevertheless, mouse input has some unique qualities, and understanding these qualities will help you use mouse input.

The Mouse

Although there are other pointing devices besides the mouse—including track balls, joy sticks, touch screens, and cat's paws—none has experienced the same popularity as the mouse. At present, a relatively small number of companies ship mice, including Hewlett-Packard, Logitech, Microsoft, and Mouse Systems. Among these companies, there aren't many differences between the mouse each provides. Some have two buttons and others have three. Some detect movement by the motion of a rubber-coated steel ball, while others use optical detection methods. There is also little variety in the way different mice connect to the computer system. Some mice use a communication port, while others connect to a special bus adapter card, and still others connect to the system through the keyboard.

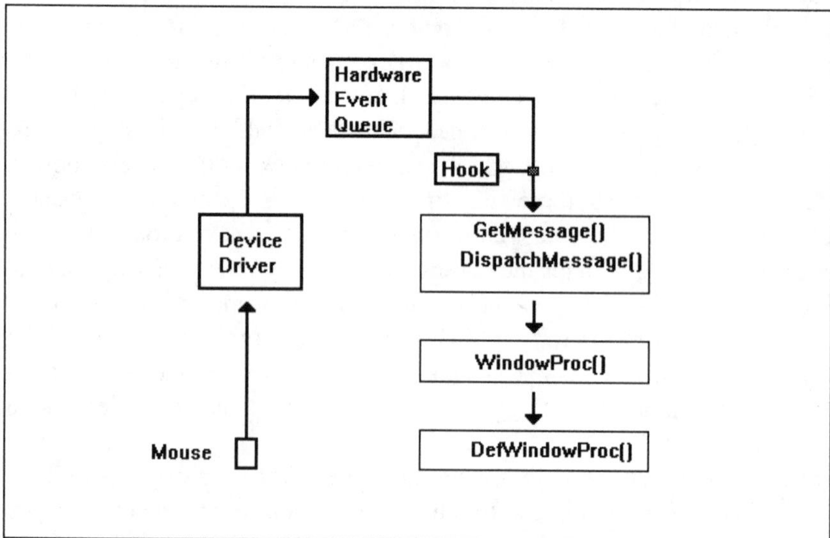

Figure 16.1 The flow of mouse data

When a mouse reports its location, it does so in terms of movement along the *x*- and *y*-axes. And, like keyboard activity, mouse button actions are reported as button down and button up actions. When one of these events occurs, a signal is sent which results in a hardware interrupt being generated. The handling of the interrupt is the job of the next component we're going to look at: the device driver.

The Mouse Device Driver

When Windows starts up, the mouse driver loads itself and goes off in search of a mouse. When Windows asks, the device driver lets Windows know whether a mouse is present in the system. If so, Windows calls the driver to provide an address of a procedure to be called to report mouse events. From that point on, the job of the device driver is simple: Whenever a mouse event occurs, the driver calls Windows to report mouse actions.

When Windows is notified of a mouse event, one of the first things it does is to check whether the mouse has moved. If so, it calls the display driver to move the mouse cursor. In this way, the movement of the mouse cursor always occurs at interrupt time, and will preempt almost all other activities. But this happens in the background, so you never need to worry that it might disrupt the proper operation of your programs.

Like keyboard events, mouse events are not delivered to programs at interrupt time. The disruption that this would cause to Windows' nonpreemptive scheduling system would make writing Windows programs very difficult. Instead, mouse events are handled like keyboard events and placed into Windows' hardware event queue.

The Hardware Event Queue

Mouse events are written into the hardware event queue, where they wait for delivery to the message loop of a program. When we introduced the hardware event queue in our discussion of keyboard input, we mentioned that it had room for 120 events. While this is easily enough to keep ahead of most typists, you might be concerned that the queue can overflow if the mouse were to be quickly moved across the screen.

In anticipation of this problem, Windows regards mouse movement in a very special way. Before a new mouse move event is written to the hardware event queue, a check is made to see if the previous hardware event was also reporting mouse movement. If so, the previous event is overwritten with the latest mouse move information. After all, when the user is moving the mouse, the destination is more important than every point traversed by the mouse.

The events in the hardware event queue don't yet belong to any particular program, until they are claimed by the **`GetMessage`** routine. This is necessary for the proper operation of the system. After all, one mouse message might cause a window to move or to close. This would change the way that subsequent mouse messages are handled, since mouse input is based on mouse cursor location. That decision is made by the next link in the mouse handling chain: the **`GetMessage`** loop.

The GetMessage Loop

Every program has a **GetMessage** loop, which serves as one of the gateways for messages to enter a program for processing. As discussed earlier, this message passing mechanism also serves to keep Windows' multitasking system working properly.

When a program calls **GetMessage**, it opens the possibility that Windows may decide to put the program to sleep and wake up another program. This is precisely what happens when **GetMessage** finds that the hardware event queue contains a mouse event for another program. It puts the first program to sleep, and wakes up the second program. The second program can then return from its own call to **GetMessage**, where it has been sleeping, with a mouse message to process.

GetMessage decides which program should receive a mouse message by finding out which program owns the window where the mouse cursor resides. For now, though, let's set aside these multitasking issues and concentrate on the way **GetMessage** operates once it has decided that a specific program should receive a mouse message.

Even after **GetMessage** has found a mouse event for one of our windows, it still isn't ready to bring a message back to our program. The problem is simple: There are two types of mouse messages, depending on where the cursor is resting. Table 16.1 provides a list of the two types: client area and nonclient area messages. The distinction is important, since Windows itself takes care of mouse messages in the nonclient area of the window, and lets our program handle client area mouse messages.

Table 16.1 Client Area and Nonclient Area Mouse Messages

Client Area Messages	*Nonclient Area Message*
WM_LBUTTONDOWN	WM_NCLBUTTONDOWN
WM_LBUTTONUP	WM_NCLBUTTONUP
WM_LBUTTONDBLCLK	WM_NCLBUTTONDBLCLK
WM_MBUTTONDOWN	WM_NCMBUTTONDOWN
WM_MBUTTONUP	WM_NCMBUTTONUP
WM_MBUTTONDBLCLK	WM_NCMBUTTONDBLCLK
WM_RBUTTONDOWN	WM_NCRBUTTONDOWN
WM_RBUTTONUP	WM_NCRBUTTONUP
WM_RBUTTONDBLCLK	WM_NCRBUTTONDBLCLK
WM_MOUSEMOVE	WM_NCMOUSEMOVE

As you can tell by looking at the messages in Table 16.1, Windows has messages for up to three mouse buttons, which are called the left, middle, and right buttons. Since some mice have only two buttons, few programs rely on the middle button for mouse input. In addition, Windows itself relies exclusively on the left button, and many programs follow this practice.

In case you are worried that this is unfair to users who prefer the right mouse button, Windows has a built-in solution. The Control Panel lets a user swap the left and right mouse buttons. When this is done, Windows automatically converts all right button messages into left button messages. Therefore, if a program uses only one mouse button, it can safely rely on left button messages and still satisfy users who prefer to use the right button.

To determine where the mouse cursor is resting in a window, and therefore what type of message is needed, the **GetMessage** routine sends a message to the window procedure: **WM_NCHITTEST**. To understand how this works, we need to review Windows' message passing mechanisms.

In Chapter 4, we introduced two types of message processing: push-model and pull-model processing. At the time, we said that the **GetMessage** routine takes care of pull-model processing to read hardware event information. And yet, to determine the location of the mouse cursor, **GetMessage** relies on push-model processing. In more familiar terms, the **GetMessage** routine calls your window procedure as if it were a subroutine.

It does so using a Windows library routine that we have not yet encountered: **SendMessage**. This routine bypasses the message queues to deliver messages directly to a window object. In a sense, it behaves as if it were directly calling a window object's window procedure. This routine incorporates the push-model processing that we first discussed in Chapter 4. A window procedure cannot be called directly. Instead, the **SendMessage** routine performs immediate message delivery for us. You call **SendMessage** like this:

```
lRetVal = SendMessage (hwnd, msg, wValue, lValue);
```

Since this is like a function call, we get back whatever return value the window procedure has decided to give us.

The return value is very important in the context of the **WM_NCHITTEST** message that **GetMessage** sends to our window procedure. This message asks the window procedure to identify where the mouse cursor is resting. Most programs pass this message on to the default window procedure, which studies the location of the mouse cursor, and provides a **hit-test code** as a return value. The hit-test codes are shown in Figure 16.2.

Most of the hit-test codes describe a location on the window border, like **HTTOP** and **HTTOPLEFT**. Others identify different nonclient area objects like scroll bars and menus. One of the hit-test codes, **HTCLIENT**, refers to the window's client area. **GetMessage** uses the hit-test code to decide the type of mouse message to generate. When the hit-test code is equal to **HTCLIENT**, a client area message is generated; all other hit-test codes cause nonclient area mouse messages to be generated.

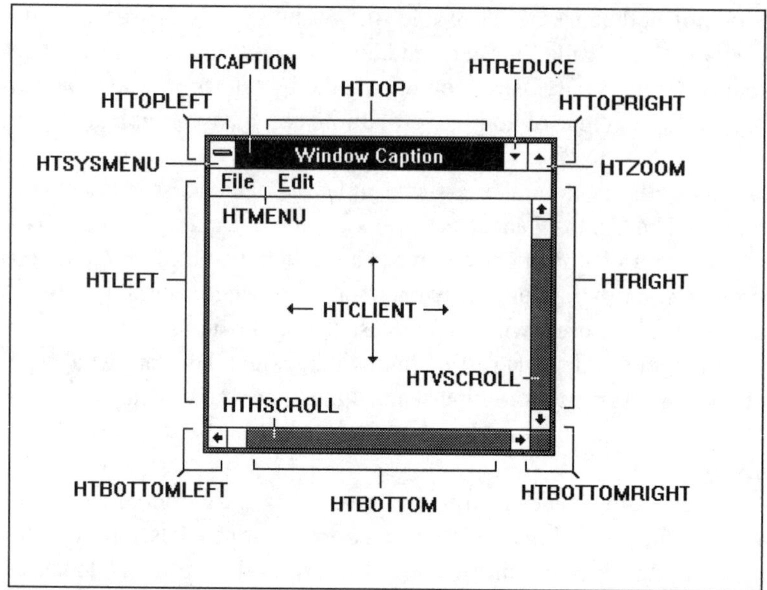

Figure 16.2 Windows hit-test codes

Before **GetMessage** returns a mouse message to our program, there is still one more thing it does: It makes sure the shape of the mouse cursor is correct for the location of the mouse. To do this, it sends yet another message to our window procedure: **WM_SETCURSOR**. Like the **WM_NCHITTEST** message, most programs ignore this message and allow the default window procedure to do the right thing. The hit-test code is included with the message as the low word of the `lParam` parameter, so that the default window procedure knows how to correctly set the cursor shape. For example, the **HTTOP** hit-test code indicates that a two-headed arrow cursor is needed to show the user that window resizing is available, while the **HTMENU** code summons the normal arrow cursor.

Figure 16.3 shows an example of WinSight listening to mouse messages. This is typical mouse message traffic. With one exception, which we'll cover when we discuss *mouse capture*, the **WM_NCHITTEST** and **WM_SETCURSOR** messages always precede a mouse message. The reason now should be evident: Windows must first find the location of the mouse cursor to know whether to generate a client area or a nonclient area message. Once the location is known, Windows makes sure that the user knows by setting the mouse cursor to the correct shape.

When we discussed keyboard input, we mentioned that Windows allows for the installation of message hooks, which can be used to alter the flow of messages. While we aren't going to take the time now to describe how to install a hook, you should be aware that a **WH_GETMESSAGE** hook can alter the flow of any client area or nonclient area mouse message. Once **GetMessage** is ready to bring a message into our program, it makes a call to the hook to see if any changes need to be made before the message itself is delivered to a program.

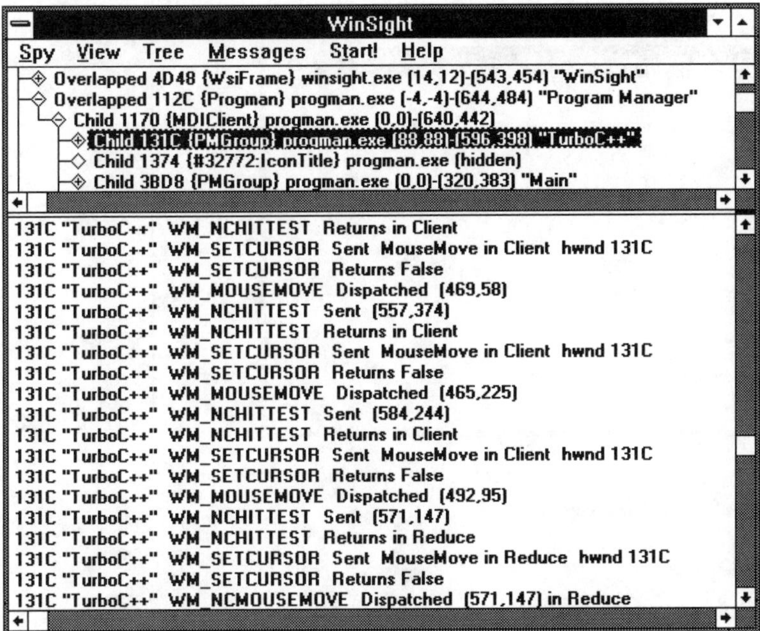

Figure 16.3 WinSight listening to mouse messages

Once **`GetMessage`** has brought a mouse message into our program, the message is sent on to the correct window procedure by the **`DispatchMessage`** routine. From the point of view of our program, the window procedure is where all the action is. So, let's take a look at how a window object can handle mouse traffic.

The Mouse and the Window Object

Of the 20 mouse messages that exist in Windows, 10 are nonclient area messages and can be safely ignored by a window object. After all, the nonclient area of a window is maintained by Windows. Among the 10 client area messages, one lets our program know the location of the mouse in our client area: **`WM_MOUSEMOVE`**. We'll take a detailed look at this message shortly. Of the other nine messages, three are for the left button, three for the middle button, and three for the right button. Since the processing for each set of messages is the same, and because most programs ignore the middle and right buttons, we're going to focus our attention on the left mouse button and its three messages: **`WM_LBUTTONDOWN`**, **`WM_LBUTTONUP`**, and **`WM_LBUTTONDBLCLK`**.

The WM_LBUTTONDOWN Message

When the user pushes the left mouse button with the cursor in our client area, our window object receives a **`WM_LBUTTONDOWN`** message. Besides telling us that a click has occurred

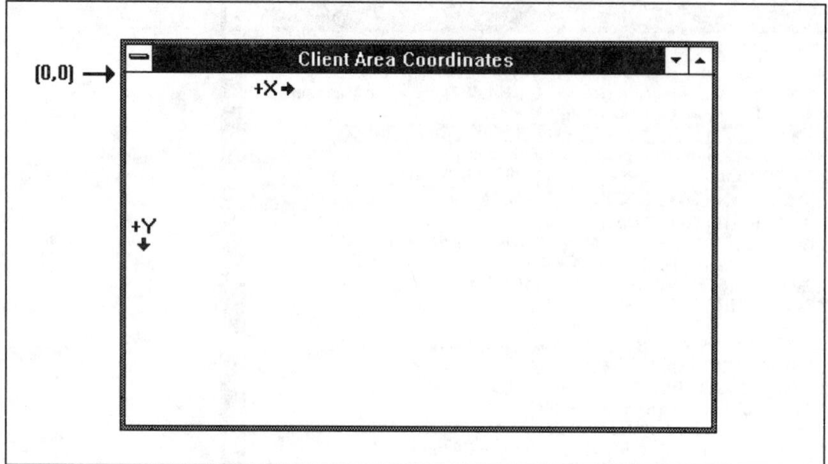

Figure 16.4 Client area coordinates

in our client area, the message parameters, **wParam** and **lParam**, tell us quite a bit more about the message. Incidentally, the **wParam** and **lParam** values are the same for all client area mouse messages.

The **lParam** value in a mouse message contains the location of the mouse cursor, in client area coordinates. We introduced client area coordinates in Chapter 6. This coordinate system places the origin in the upper-left corner of the client area, with one unit equal to one pixel. Figure 16.4 shows how client area coordinates flip the normal Cartesian coordinate system upside down, with the *y*-axis positive going downward.

Fortunately, the OWL message response function hides these ugly parameter values from us. Every mouse message response function takes the same two parameters. Here is the message response function for the **WM_LBUTTONDOWN** message:

```
void EvLButtonDown (UINT modkeys, TPoint& point)
    {
    xValue = point.x;
    yValue = point.y;
    }
```

A mouse message's **WParam** parameter contains flags that describe the state of the mouse buttons and the state of the [Shift] and [Ctrl] keys. Figure 16.5 shows the layout of these flags.

The value of a field is `1` if the corresponding mouse button or keyboard key is down; otherwise the value is `0`. To test whether a specific field is down, you can use the C language bitwise-AND operator, `&`. Here is how to see if the shift key is down in response to a left button down message:

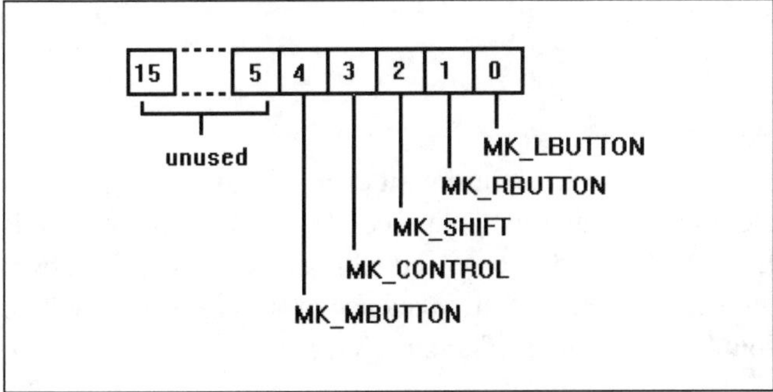

Figure 16.5 Five fields of wParam for client area mouse messages

```
void EvLButtonDown (UINT modkeys, TPoint& point)
    {
    if (modkeys & MK_SHIFT)
        {
        // Shift key is down.
        }
    }
```

The WM_LBUTTONUP Message

This message signals that the left mouse button has been released. In many ways, this message is analogous to the **WM_KEYUP** keyboard message. And yet, Windows programs rarely pay attention to the **WM_KEYUP** message when handling keyboard input. The **WM_LBUTTONUP** message, on the other hand, is quite important. If you are writing a program that uses the mouse to draw, for example, this message will tell you when to stop drawing. In the enhanced rectangle drawing program that you'll find later in this chapter, this message is used both to finish drawing rectangles and to finish the job when we drag a rectangle across the window.

The WM_LBUTTONDBLCLK Message

At the beginning of this chapter, we introduced double-clicking as a common user action. To be effective, a program that responds to a double-click should be careful that the double-click is an extension of a single click. The reason is that a single click message will always be received before a double-click message.

For a window to receive double-click messages, it must have been defined with a special class style: **CS_DBLCLKS**. To add this style, you'd add the following line to the **GetWindowClass** member function of a window class:

```
...
wc.style = CS_DBLCLKS;
...
```

When a window has this bit set in its class style definition, it changes the way that mouse button down messages are handled. In particular, when a second button down message is received within a short (one-half second) period of time, a double-click message is substituted for the second button down message. Here is the sequence of messages that will be sent when the user performs a double-click on the left mouse button:

Message	*Comment*
WM_LBUTTONDOWN	First button down message
WM_LBUTTONUP	
WM_LBUTTONDBLCLK	Replaces second button down message
WM_LBUTTONUP	

All of the programs in this book let the OWL libraries register a window class named "OwlWindow" that has this bit set. This means that double-clicking is *enabled* by default. If double-click messages really aren't interesting to you, then call **EvLButtonDown** from **EvLButtonDblClk**—which lets you ignore the double-click messages entirely.

The WM_MOUSEMOVE Message

The fourth and final message that we're going to look at is the mouse movement message. As we mentioned earlier, Windows has a built-in mechanism to prevent mouse move messages from overflowing the hardware event queue. Thus, the mouse movement messages that a program receives might only provide a sampling of all of the places that the mouse visited. But this sampling is sufficient for most programs to track the movement of this pointing device.

In a moment, we'll look at some sample programs that show the use of each of these mouse messages. But first, let's look at the last component that plays an important role in handling mouse messages, the default window procedure.

The Default Window Procedure

When we first introduced the default window procedure, we described it as the central reason that Windows programs behave in such a uniform manner. It provides all the basic, minimum processing that allows a common set of user actions to produce the same results from different Windows programs. Menus, scroll bars, and windows can all be accessed using the same set of user actions. This uniformity assumes, of course, that Windows programmers pass along all their "extra" messages. In the case of mouse messages, the default window procedure ignores the client area messages and instead relies on nonclient area messages.

The default window procedure is also responsible for providing a common mouse and keyboard interface. It does this by translating input into a set of system commands, which show up as **WM_SYSCOMMAND** messages. And finally, the default window procedure handles the **WM_NCHITTEST** and **WM_SETCURSOR** messages which pave the way for almost all mouse messages.

When a mouse message gets to the default window procedure, it has arrived at its final destination. Starting at the mouse itself, mouse input follows a pretty direct route into a program. But, as we've seen, that route may cause Windows' multitasking switcher to stop feeding messages to one program and start feeding them to another. And finally, we've seen that half of the mouse messages that occur can be safely ignored—that is, assuming we pass our ignored messages on to the default window procedure.

For all this mouse theory to be helpful to you in building Windows programs, it would help to see some practical examples. In this chapter, we're going to show you three such examples. The first program, CARET2, will show how a mouse click can be used in a text input window to move a caret. Our second program, DRAGRECT, is a revision of the rectangle drawing program first encountered in Chapter 9. We'll explore the application of GDI raster operations to create stretchable rectangles and dragable objects. Our final program, DYNACURS, creates a mouse cursor "on the fly." It echoes the mouse location, using a dynamic cursor.

A Mouse Input Sample: CARET2

In the last chapter, we introduced a program that receives keyboard input. We then enhanced this program with a caret so that the user could always see the current text entry position. Using the keyboard cursor keys, the user moves the caret to different positions in the text. Now that we've been discussing the use of the mouse, the time has come to enhance our program one more time so that the mouse can be used to move the caret.

CARET2.CPP

```
//
// CARET2.CPP  Demonstrates moving the caret with the mouse.
//
#include <owl\owlpch.h>
#include "cl_caret.h"
#include "caret2.h"

DEFINE_RESPONSE_TABLE1 (DFrame, TFrameWindow)
  EV_WM_CHAR,
  EV_WM_KEYDOWN,
  EV_WM_SETFOCUS,
  EV_WM_KILLFOCUS,
```

```
    EV_WM_LBUTTONDOWN,
    EV_COMMAND(CM_FILEEXIT, CmFileExit),
    EV_COMMAND(CM_HELPABOUT, CmHelpAbout),
END_RESPONSE_TABLE;

DFrame::DFrame(char * title) : TFrameWindow(0, title)
    {
    TScreenDC dc;

    TEXTMETRIC tm;
    dc.GetTextMetrics (tm);

    yLineHeight = tm.tmHeight + tm.tmExternalLeading;
    xLeftMargin = tm.tmAveCharWidth;

    achInput[0] = '\0';
    cchInput = 0;
    ichNext = 0;
    }

void DFrame::CmFileExit()
    {
    CloseWindow(0); // Cause application to terminate
    }

void DFrame::CmHelpAbout()
    {
    MessageBox(" Caret and Mouse Interaction\n\n"
               "'Borland C++ 4.0 Programming\n"
               "  for Windows', by Paul Yao", Title);
    }

void DFrame::EvChar (UINT key, UINT, UINT)
    {
    if (key == VK_BACK)    //  Backspace.
        {
        if (ichNext == 0)
            MessageBeep(0);
        else                              //  Remove a character.
            {
            ichNext--;
            pcCaret->SetCharPosition(ichNext);

            for (int i=ichNext;i<cchInput;i++)
                achInput[i]=achInput[i+1];
            cchInput--;
            Invalidate ();
            }
        return;
        }

    // Complain if character out of range or if buffer is full.
    if ((key <= VK_ESCAPE) || (cchInput >= BUFSIZE))
        {
        MessageBeep(0);
        return;
        }

    // Make room for next char.
    for (int i=cchInput;i>ichNext;i--)
        achInput[i]=achInput[i-1];
```

```
    //  Put new char in buffer.
    achInput[ichNext] = (unsigned char)key;

    // Increment count of characters.
    cchInput++;

    pcCaret->Hide();

    // Update display.
    TClientDC dc(HWindow);
    TSize size;
    dc.GetTextExtent ((LPSTR)&achInput[0], ichNext, size);
    dc.TextOut (xLeftMargin+size.cx,
                yLineHeight,
                (LPSTR)&achInput[ichNext],
                cchInput - ichNext);

    pcCaret->Show();

    // Increment index to next character.
    ichNext++;
    pcCaret->SetCharPosition(ichNext);
    }

void DFrame::EvSetFocus(HWND /* hwndLostFocus */)
    {
    pcCaret->SetCharPosition(ichNext);
    pcCaret->SetState(CARET_ACTIVE);
    }

void DFrame::EvKillFocus(HWND /* hwndGetFocus */)
    {
    pcCaret->SetState(CARET_INACTIVE);
    }

void DFrame::EvKeyDown (UINT key, UINT, UINT)
    {
    BOOL fCaretMoved = FALSE;

    switch (key)
        {
        case VK_DELETE:
            //  If end of buffer, complain.
            if (ichNext == cchInput)
                MessageBeep(0);
            else  //  Remove a character.
                {
                int i;
                for (i=ichNext;i<cchInput;i++)
                    achInput[i]=achInput[i+1];
                cchInput--;
                Invalidate();
                }
            break;
        case VK_END:
            ichNext = cchInput;
            fCaretMoved = TRUE;
            break;
        case VK_HOME:
            ichNext = 0;
            fCaretMoved = TRUE;
            break;
```

```
        case VK_LEFT:
            if (ichNext > 0)
                {
                ichNext--;
                fCaretMoved = TRUE;
                }
            else
                MessageBeep(0);
            break;
        case VK_RIGHT:
            if (ichNext < cchInput)
                {
                ichNext++;
                fCaretMoved = TRUE;
                }
            else
                MessageBeep(0);
            break;
        }

    if (fCaretMoved)
        pcCaret->SetCharPosition(ichNext);
    }

void DFrame::EvLButtonDown(UINT, TPoint& pt)
    {
    //  First check:  is it in our hit area?
    if (PtInRect(&rHitArea, pt))
        {
        TClientDC dc(HWindow);
        int xTotWidth = xLeftMargin;
        int xPrevHalfWidth = xLeftMargin;

        ichNext = cchInput;    // Default = end of string.

        //  Next: loop through characters.
        int xNextHalfWidth;
        for (int i=0;i<cchInput;i++)
            {
            TSize size;
            dc.GetTextExtent ((LPSTR)&achInput[i], 1, size);
            xNextHalfWidth = size.cx/2;
            if ((xTotWidth - xPrevHalfWidth) <= pt.x &&
                (xTotWidth + xNextHalfWidth) >  pt.x)
                {
                //  A hit!  Set caret position.
                ichNext = i;
                break;
                }
            xPrevHalfWidth = xNextHalfWidth;
            xTotWidth += size.cx;
            }

        //  Mousing around in the hit rectangle makes caret move
        pcCaret->SetCharPosition(ichNext);
        }
    }

void DFrame::Paint (TDC& dc, BOOL, TRect&)
    {
    dc.TextOut (xLeftMargin, yLineHeight, achInput, cchInput);
    }
```

```
void DFrame::SetupWindow()
    {
    TFrameWindow::SetupWindow();

    HFONT hFont = (HFONT)::GetStockObject (SYSTEM_FONT);
    pcCaret = new Caret (HWindow, hFont);

    pcCaret->SetAnchor (xLeftMargin, yLineHeight);
    pcCaret->SetStringPtr ((LPSTR)&achInput[0]);

    // Init mouse hit rectangle.
    rHitArea.left   = 0;
    rHitArea.right  = 9999;
    rHitArea.top    = yLineHeight;
    rHitArea.bottom = yLineHeight + yLineHeight;
    }

void DFrame::CleanupWindow()
    {
    delete pcCaret;

    TFrameWindow::CleanupWindow();
    }

DApp::DApp() : TApplication()
    {
    }

void DApp::InitMainWindow()
    {
    SetMainWindow (new DFrame("Caret with Mouse"));

    MainWindow->AssignMenu("MAIN");
    MainWindow->SetIcon(this, "SNAPSHOT");
    MainWindow->SetCursor(NULL, IDC_IBEAM);
    }

// Application main entry point.
OwlMain(int, char **)
    {
    return DApp().Run();
    }
```

CARET2.H

```
#define CM_FILEEXIT 100
#define CM_HELPABOUT 200

const int BUFSIZE = 120;

// Main window
class DFrame : public TFrameWindow
    {
  public:
    DFrame(char * title);
    void CmFileExit();
    void CmHelpAbout();
    void EvChar (UINT key, UINT repeat, UINT flags);
    void EvKeyDown (UINT key, UINT repeat, UINT flags);
```

```
    void EvLButtonDown(UINT, TPoint&);
    void Paint (TDC&, BOOL, TRect&);
    void SetupWindow();
    void CleanupWindow();
    void EvSetFocus(HWND hwndLostFocus);
    void EvKillFocus(HWND hwndGetFocus);
  private:
    Caret * pcCaret;
    char  achInput[BUFSIZE];
    int   cchInput;
    int   ichNext;
    int   yLineHeight;
    int   xLeftMargin;
    TRect rHitArea;

  DECLARE_RESPONSE_TABLE (DFrame);
    };

// Application object
class DApp : public TApplication
    {
  public:
    DApp();
    void InitMainWindow();
    };
```

CL_CARET.CPP

```
//
// CL_CARET.CPP  Caret class definition.
//

#include <owl\owlpch.h>
#include "cl_caret.h"

 // Caret class constructor.
Caret::Caret(HWND hwndIn, HFONT hFontIn)
    {
    HFONT      hfontOld;
    TEXTMETRIC tm;

    hdcInfo = CreateIC ("DISPLAY", 0, 0, 0);
    hfontOld = (HFONT)::SelectObject (hdcInfo, hFontIn);
    GetTextMetrics (hdcInfo, &tm);
    SelectObject (hdcInfo, hfontOld);

    hwnd           = hwndIn;
    hFont          = hFontIn;
    iCharPos       = 0;
    iFlag          = CARET_INACTIVE;
    cxCaretWidth   = GetSystemMetrics (SM_CXBORDER);
    cyCaretHeight  = tm.tmHeight;
    ptPixelPos.x   = 0;
    ptPixelPos.y   = 0;
    ptAnchor.x     = 0;
    ptAnchor.y     = 0;
    lpString       = (LPSTR)0L;
    }

// Caret class destructor.
```

```
Caret::~Caret()
    {
    if (iFlag & CARET_ACTIVE)
        {
        HideCaret(hwnd);
        DestroyCaret();
        }

    DeleteDC (hdcInfo);
    }

void Caret::Hide()
    {
    HideCaret(hwnd);
    }

void Caret::Show()
    {
    ShowCaret(hwnd);
    }

int    Caret::GetAnchorX()
    {
    return ptAnchor.x;
    }

int    Caret::GetAnchorY()
    {
    return ptAnchor.y;
    }

int    Caret::GetCharPosition ()
    {
    return iCharPos;
    }

HFONT Caret::GetFontHandle()
    {
    return hFont;
    }

int    Caret::GetState ()
    {
    return iFlag;
    }

LPSTR  Caret::GetStringPtr()
    {
    return lpString;
    }

void   Caret::SetAnchor (int X, int Y)
    {
    ptAnchor.x = X;
    ptAnchor.y = Y;
    }

void   Caret::SetCharPosition (int iChar)
    {
    DWORD  dwSize;
    HFONT  hFontOld;
    int    xWidth;
```

```
    iCharPos = iChar;

    // Calculate width of character string.
    hFontOld = (HFONT)::SelectObject (hdcInfo, hFont);
    dwSize = GetTextExtent (hdcInfo, lpString, iCharPos);
    xWidth = LOWORD(dwSize);
    SelectObject (hdcInfo, hFontOld);

    // Update caret position information.
    ptPixelPos.x = ptAnchor.x + xWidth;
    ptPixelPos.y = ptAnchor.y;

    // If caret is active, update location.
    if (iFlag & CARET_ACTIVE)
        {
        SetCaretPos (ptPixelPos.x, ptPixelPos.y);
        }
    }

void   Caret::SetFontHandle(HFONT hFontIn)
    {
    HFONT      hfontOld;
    TEXTMETRIC tm;

    hfontOld = (HFONT)::SelectObject (hdcInfo, hFontIn);
    GetTextMetrics (hdcInfo, &tm);
    SelectObject (hdcInfo, hfontOld);

    hFont         = hFontIn;
    cyCaretHeight = tm.tmHeight;
    }

void   Caret::SetState (int AFlag)
    {
    if (iFlag == AFlag)
        return;

    if (AFlag & CARET_ACTIVE)
        {
        CreateCaret (hwnd, 0, cxCaretWidth, cyCaretHeight);
        SetCaretPos (ptPixelPos.x, ptPixelPos.y);
        ShowCaret (hwnd);
        }

    if (AFlag & CARET_INACTIVE)
        {
        DestroyCaret ();
        }

    iFlag = AFlag;
    }

void Caret::SetStringPtr(LPSTR lpstrIn)
    {
    lpString = lpstrIn;
    }
```

CL_CARET.H

```
const int CARET_ACTIVE   = 0x01;
const int CARET_INACTIVE = 0x02;

// The Caret class.
class Caret
  {
  public:
    Caret(HWND hwndIn, HFONT hFontIn);
    ~Caret();

    virtual void   Hide();
    virtual void   Show();

    virtual int    GetAnchorX();
    virtual int    GetAnchorY();
    virtual int    GetCharPosition ();
    virtual HFONT  GetFontHandle();
    virtual int    GetState ();
    virtual LPSTR  GetStringPtr();

    virtual void   SetAnchor (int X, int Y);
    virtual void   SetCharPosition (int iChar);
    virtual void   SetFontHandle(HFONT hFontIn);
    virtual void   SetState (int AFlag);
    virtual void   SetStringPtr(LPSTR lpstrIn);
  private:
    HFONT   hFont;
    HDC     hdcInfo;
    HWND    hwnd;
    int     iCharPos;
    int     iFlag;
    int     cxCaretWidth;
    int     cyCaretHeight;
    POINT   ptPixelPos;
    POINT   ptAnchor;
    LPSTR   lpString;
  };
```

CARET2.RC

```
#include "caret2.h"

snapshot icon caret2.ico

main menu
    BEGIN
    POPUP "&File"
        {
        MENUITEM "E&xit", CM_FILEEXIT
        }
    POPUP "&Help"
        {
        MENUITEM "&About...", CM_HELPABOUT
        }
    END
```

CARET2.DEF

```
EXETYPE WINDOWS

CODE MOVEABLE DISCARDABLE
DATA MULTIPLE MOVEABLE

HEAPSIZE   512
STACKSIZE 8192
```

DYNA16.MAK

```
#  MAKE file for Win16 API using dynamic BIDS,
#  OWL and C-runtime libraries.
#
#    C> make -fstatic16.mak
#

.AUTODEPEND
CC = -c -H -H"owl\owlpch.h" -ml -R -vi -WS -X-
CD = -D_RTLDLL;_BIDSDLL;_OWLDLL;_OWLPCH;
INC = -I\BC4\INCLUDE
LIB = -L\BC4\LIB

caret2.exe :  caret2.obj cl_caret.obj caret2.res
  tlink -c -C -Twe $(LIB) @dyna16.lnk
  brc caret2.res caret2.exe

cl_caret.obj :  cl_caret.cpp
  bcc $(CC) $(CD) cl_caret.cpp

caret2.obj :  caret2.cpp
  bcc $(CC) $(CD) caret2.cpp

caret2.res :  caret2.rc caret2.ico caret2.h
  brc $(INC) -31 -R caret2.rc
```

DYNA16.LNK

```
\bc4\lib\c0wl.obj+
caret2.obj+cl_caret.obj
caret2,caret2
\bc4\lib\bidsi.lib+
\bc4\lib\owlwi.lib+
\bc4\lib\import.lib+
\bc4\lib\crtldll.lib
caret2.def
```

DYNA32.MAK

```
#  MAKE file for Win32 API using dynamic BIDS,
#  OWL and C-runtime libraries.
#
#    C> make -fdyna32.mak
```

```
#

.AUTODEPEND
CC = -c -H -H\""owl\owlpch.h\"" -p- -R -vi -W -X-
CD = -D_RTLDLL;_BIDSDLL;_OWLDLL;_OWLPCH;
INC = -I\BC4\INCLUDE
LIB = -L\BC4\LIB

caret2.exe :  caret2.obj cl_caret.obj caret2.res
  tlink32 -aa -c -Tpe $(LIB) @dyna32.lnk
  brc32 caret2.res caret2.exe

cl_caret.obj :  cl_caret.cpp
  bcc32 $(CC) $(CD) cl_caret.cpp

caret2.obj :  caret2.cpp
  bcc32 $(CC) $(CD) caret2.cpp

caret2.res :  caret2.rc caret2.ico caret2.h
  brc32 $(INC) -w32 -R caret2.rc
```

DYNA32.LNK

```
\bc4\lib\c0w32.obj+
caret2.obj+cl_caret.obj
caret2,caret2
\bc4\lib\bidsfi.lib+
\bc4\lib\owlwfi.lib+
\bc4\lib\import32.lib+
\bc4\lib\cw32i.lib
caret2.def
```

Cursors

All of the programs in prior chapters use the arrow cursor, a built in system cursor. Nothing in any program specifically asked for this cursor, but instead OWL provides it as a default cursor for the **OwlWindow** class it registers for us. CARET2 doesn't use the arrow cursor, but instead uses a system cursor more suitable for working with text: the I-beam cursor. This tall, skinny cursor helps work in the narrow spaces between text characters.

There are three basic ways to use cursors: as the default window class cursor, as an on-the-fly cursor, or as a subwindow area indicator. The first way is to connect a cursor to a window at window creation time by calling **TWindow::SetCursor**. The second way is to call the WinAPI **::SetCursor** function. The third way is to process the **WM_SETCURSOR** message, then call either cursor setting function.

To connect a cursor to a window at window creation time, you call **TWindow::SetCursor**. This function is like its cousin, **TWindow::SetIcon**, which every program in this book uses to access an icon. This function is defined:

```
BOOL TWindow::SetCursor (TModule* module, TResID resID)
```

- **module** describes which executable file has the desired cursor. In particular, this parameter identifies the module object which owns the cursor. In **DApp::InitMainWindow**, the **this** pointer refers to our application's executable file. To load a cursor from a random DLL, specify the DLL's module object. To get a system cursor, specify **NULL**, which asks the system to search for a display driver cursor.
- **resID** identifies a specific cursor resource.

Figure 16.6 shows all of Windows' predefined system cursors, which reside in the system's display driver. Here, then, is how caret gets its I-beam cursor:

```
MainWindow->SetCursor(NULL, IDC_IBEAM);
```

A second way to use a cursor is to bypass OWL and call the WinAPI `::SetCursor` function. You'd do this either when you don't have a window, or when you want to change the cursor for just a moment. This function is defined:

```
HCURSOR SetCursor (HCURSOR hcr)
```

- **hcr** identifies a cursor that has already been loaded into the system.

As a native WinAPI function, you need to get access to a native WinAPI cursor handle. The simplest way to do this involves calling the WinAPI `LoadCursor` function, defined as:

```
HCURSOR LoadCursor (HMODULE hInstance, LPSTR lpResID)
```

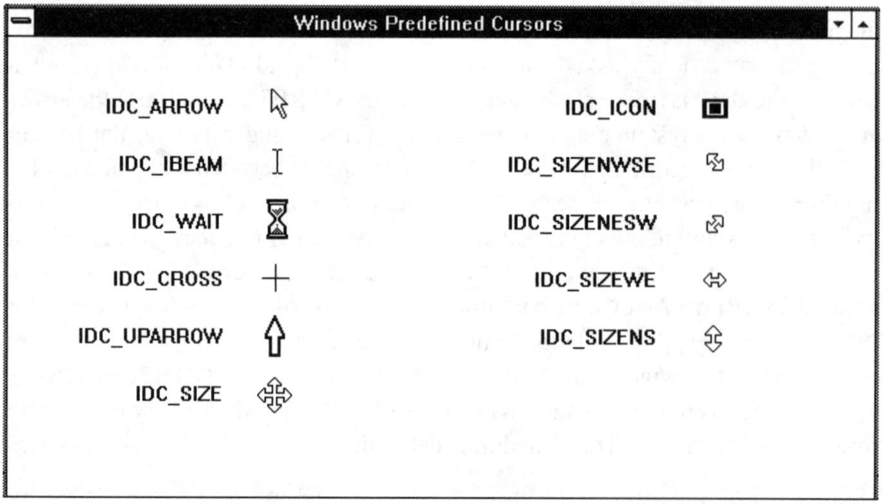

Figure 16.6 Windows' predefined system cursors

- **hInstance** is the instance handle of an application, a module handle of a DLL, or NULL for a system cursor.
- **lpResID** identifies the specific cursor resource.

For example, if it takes a few moments for your application to perform its initialization, you might decide to display the hourglass cursor before your application's main window is visible. Here's how you might do it:

```
HCURSOR hcrWait = LoadCursor (NULL, IDC_WAIT);
SetCursor(hcrWait);
```

Or, if we performed a lengthy operation in some utility function, to change the cursor to an hourglass and then change it back, we could do something like this:

```
HCURSOR hcrWait = LoadCursor (NULL, IDC_WAIT);
HCURSOR hcrOld = SetCursor(hcrWait);
// ...Lengthy operation here...
SetCursor (hcrOld);
```

The third way to use a cursor is to respond to the **WM_SETCURSOR** message. This gives you the most control, and is in fact how both OWL and the Windows API change cursors. OWL's **TWindow** class responds to this message for client area mouse messages and displays the appropriate cursor. For nonclient area messages, **TWindow** passes the messages on to the WinAPI **DefWindowProc** function, which displays the proper cursor for nonclient area messages. If you process this message, you'll want to follow this approach as well.

You might use this approach to show a program's current operating mode (text editing mode versus line drawing mode). Or, it could be used to give feedback about different areas in a window. One word processing program, for example, uses the left margin for selecting multiple lines of text instead of individual words or characters. When the cursor goes into the left margin, it changes to reflect this fact.

As an example, assume two variables have been defined for two cursor handles:

```
HCURSOR hcrIBeam;
HCURSOR hcrCross;
```

You have to initialize these, perhaps in response to the **WM_CREATE** message, which really means in a function that overrides **TWindow::SetupWindow**:

```
void DFrame::SetupWindow()
    {
    TFrameWindow::SetupWindow();
    hcrIBeam = ::LoadCursor (NULL, IDC_IBEAM);
    hcrCross = ::LoadCursor (NULL, IDC_CROSS);
    }
```

In response to the **WM_SETCURSOR** message, set the cursor like this:

```
BOOL DFrame::EvSetCursor (HWND, UINT hitTest, UINT)
    {
    if (hitTest == HTCLIENT)
        {
        if (Area == TEXT) ::SetCursor(hcrIBeam);
        if (Area == GRAPHICS) ::SetCursor(hcrCross);
        return TRUE; // we set the cursor
        }
    else
        return (BOOL)DefaultProcessing();
    }
```

When processing the **WM_SETCURSOR** message, check the hit test code to insure that your cursor only appears in your program's client area. The nonclient area cursors, after all, are handled for you by Windows' default message processor.

Later in this chapter, I'll point out other alternatives for changing a cursor, including the dynamic creation of cursors on-the-fly.

Hit-Testing

Besides using the I-beam system cursor, the primary difference between CARET2 and CARET has to do with the way that the **WM_LBUTTONDOWN** message is handled. CARET ignores this message, and CARET2 uses it to detect where to place the mouse cursor.

Connecting mouse input to objects that are drawn on the display is called **hit-testing**. There are two Windows library routines for hit-testing: **PtInRegion** and **PtInRect**. Both routines tell you if a point lies inside a specified area. The **PtInRect** routine lets you define the area in terms of a simple rectangle, while **PtInRegion** lets the area be defined in terms of a region. As you may recall from our discussion of clipping in Chapter 10, a region is defined by a set of rectangles. Let's take a closer look at **PtInRect**, which is the routine that CARET2 used.

The **PtInRect** routine is defined as follows:

```
BOOL PtInRect (lpRect, Point)
```

- **lpRect** is a long pointer to a **TRect** data structure that contains the rectangle against which the hit-testing is performed.
- **Point** is a variable of type **TPoint**. That is, it is an *x* and a *y* value.

The return value is `TRUE` if the point is inside the rectangle; otherwise it returns `FALSE`. CARET2 uses the **PtInRect** routine to determine if the cursor is located within a hit rectangle.

The **PtInRect** routine is only used for preliminary hit-testing to see if the cursor is located anywhere inside an imaginary rectangle that bounds the text and extends to the left and right borders of the window. But we need to do some more work to determine exactly where the cursor is resting to properly place the caret.

Actually, since a caret should always be placed between two characters, the real issue involves figuring out the letter break that lies closest to the cursor. CARET2 has it easy, since the caret position is defined in terms of character cells by the variable **ichNext**. CARET2 calculates the hit area by looping through the array of characters, **achInput**.

The key to understanding the character hit-test loop lies with three variables: **xTotWidth**, **xPrevHalfWidth**, and **xNextHalfWidth**, visually depicted in Figure 16.7. Notice first of all that we're only interested in *x* values. The reason is simple: The **PtInRect** test has already determined that we're in the proper *y* range. The value of **xTotWidth** is the total width of the text, including the margin. This means that **xTotWidth** is the distance from the left border measured in client area coordinates. The **xPrevHalfWidth** variable holds a value equal to one half the width of the previous character. **xNextHalfWidth** holds a value of one half the width of the next character. As we loop through the array of characters, hit-testing becomes simple: We test whether the point is between the beginning of the previous character and the end of the next character, as shown here:

```
if ((xTotWidth - xPrevHalfWidth) <= pt.x &&
    (xTotWidth + xNextHalfWidth) >  pt.x)
    {
    /*  A hit!  Set caret position.  */
    ichNext = i;
    break;
    }
```

Once a hit is made, it's a simple matter to set the current character position variable, **ichNext**, break out of the loop, and call the TCaret class caret moving routine, **SetCharPosition**. Naturally, this routine calls the Windows routine, **SetCaretPos**, to do the actual work.

CARET2 has shown a number of things: the use of predefined system cursors, and one approach to take in combining mouse input with text. Of course, part of the challenge in working with the system font is the fact that it is nonproportional. Hit-testing a fixed pitch

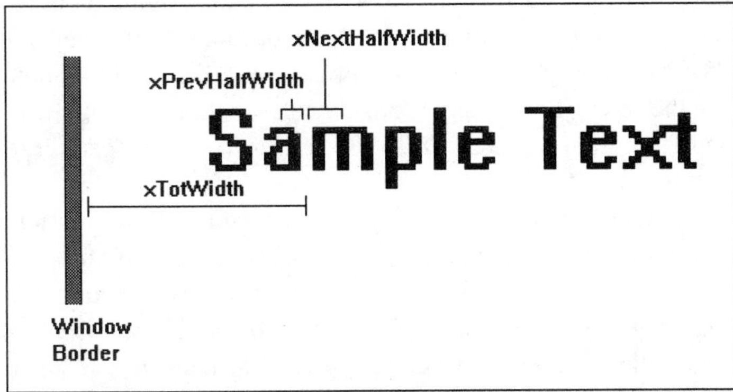

Figure 16.7 Hit testing characters in CARET2

font, after all, would be quite a bit easier. But Windows gives you all the tools you need to make the hit-testing work.

There is certainly room for improvement in this program. For example, it would probably be more efficient to calculate the width of each character cell ahead of time. Once stored away, much of the hit-testing and caret movement becomes simpler. Of course, this improvement has its trade-off in memory used.

Now let's look at our second sample program. This time, we've improved on the rectangle drawing program from Chapter 14.

Dragable Objects and Stretchable Rectangles

As the mouse cursor travels across the system display, it seems to perform a little magic. It can go anywhere on the display screen, and yet it never causes any damage to any of the objects it walks over. In most cases, this magic is the result of software. A well-written device driver gives the illusion that the mouse cursor isn't part of the rest of the display. In other cases, the magic is part of the hardware. Some display adapters have a built-in ability to support cursors. Whichever approach is taken, the result is the same: The cursor never causes any damage to any objects on the display screen.

A similar effect is seen when a window is moved. If the user clicks on the caption bar of a window (or selects the *Move* item on the system menu), a dotted outline of the window lets the user see the proposed location for the window as it is moved. Thus, the user can preview the results of the move before actually committing to the move.

The same type of "floating images" can be very useful in a Windows program. Such images can be used to help the user reposition objects in a window. Since they don't damage other objects in the window, the user can arrange objects in different ways before committing to one arrangement or another.

These effects can be achieved using GDI **raster operation (ROP) codes**. We first discussed the topic of ROP codes in Chapter 13. We did not provide a programming example then, however, since ROP codes are most easily understood in the context of the mouse.

As you may recall, a raster operation is a combination of one or more Boolean operations applied between a source, which might be a pen or a brush, and a destination. Some of the raster operations ignore the source and simply change the destination. In a moment, we're going to look at a sample program, DRAGRECT, which uses the NOT operator to produce the effect of dragable and stretchable rectangles.

A dragable rectangle can be grabbed (using the mouse) and placed in a new position. Although our demonstration program uses rectangles, the principle is the same if you wish to drag any object that is drawn using GDI's pixel, line, or filled area routines. Figure 16.8 shows an example of a rectangle being dragged in our sample program. Notice how the outline of the rectangle is always visible, no matter what color is part of the background. Also, as it is moved, it doesn't damage the other rectangles. Both of these qualities are achieved using raster operations.

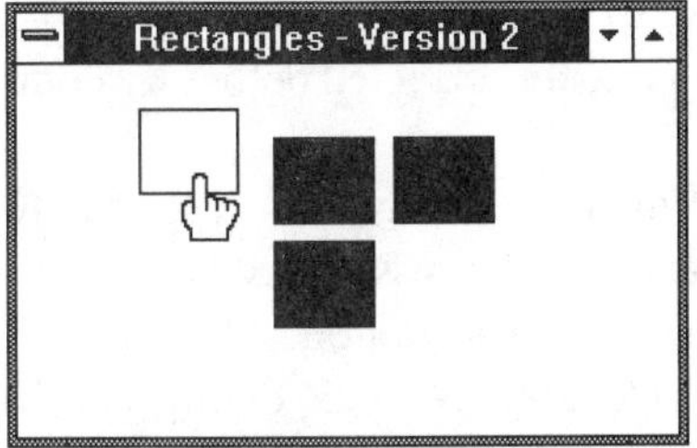

(a) Click to start dragging.

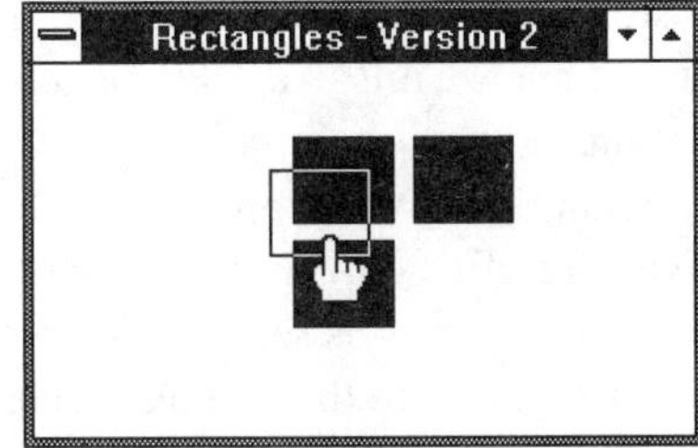

(b) Dragging over other rectangles.

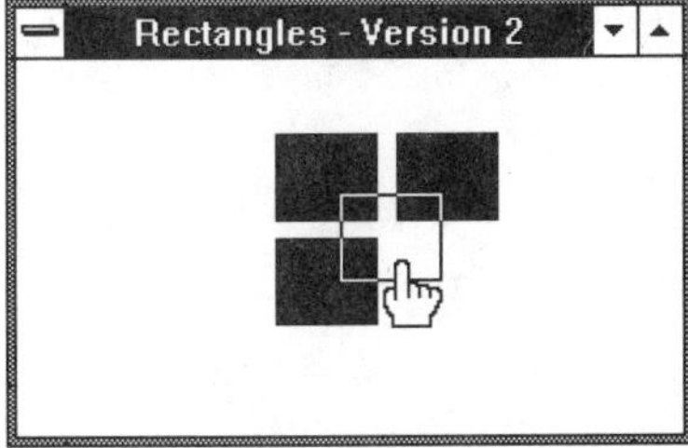

(c) Still dragging.

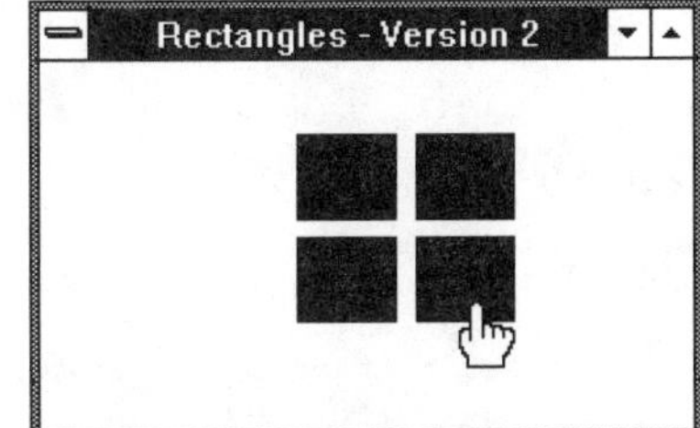

(d) Release to place rectangle.

Figure 16.8 A dragable rectangle

A stretchable rectangle is also drawn using raster operations. A stretchable rectangle lets you preview the rectangle as it is drawn. By providing this feedback, the rectangle drawing program makes it easy to avoid unwanted effects. Figure 16.9 shows how a stretchable

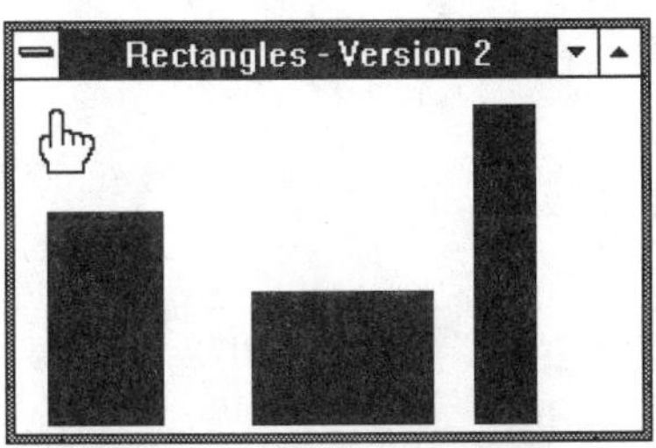

(a) Click to start.

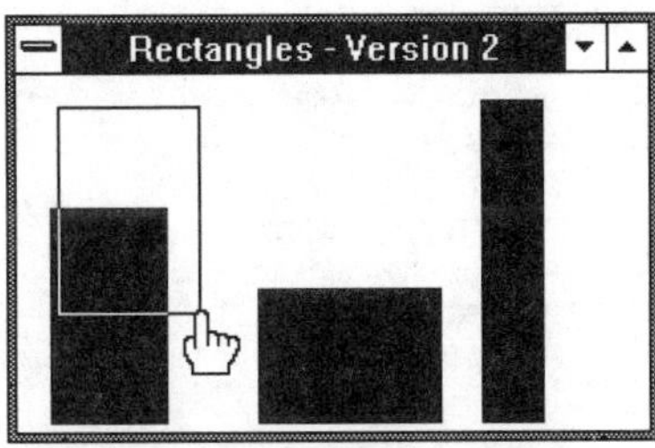

(b) Oops. Too far down.

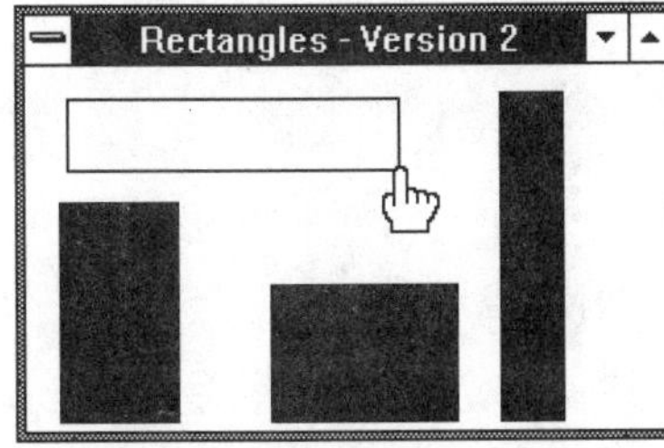

(c) That's where it should be.

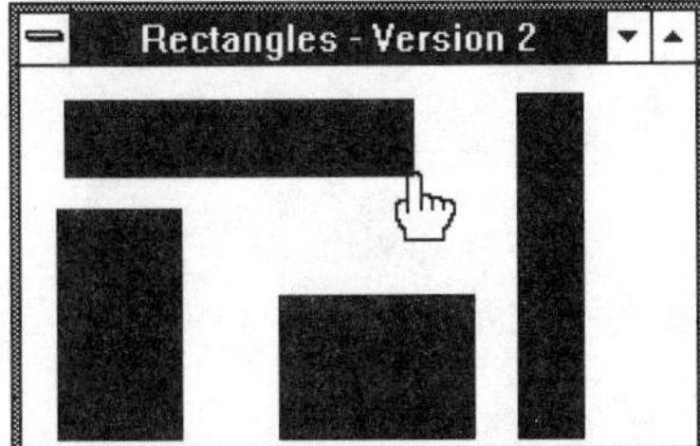

(d) Release to finish.

Figure 16.9 A stretchable rectangle

rectangle helps position a rectangle as it is drawn. In the (b) panel, this preview capability helps us see that we've made a mistake. But this mistake is easily corrected before we commit to our final rectangle.

Like our first rectangle drawing program, RECT2 draws rectangles in response to mouse button activity. The first corner of a rectangle is selected by pressing the mouse button. The second, opposing corner is selected by releasing the mouse button. As the mouse is dragged from the first corner to the second corner, a stretchable rectangle outline is echoed to the user to let him know where the final rectangle is to be placed. RECT2 has also been enhanced to allow the user to drag rectangles. The drag action is differentiated from a drawing operation by the use of the [Shift] key to accompany a button click.

DRAGRECT.CPP

```
// DRAGRECT.CPP  Rectangle dragging program -- when drawing
//               rectangles, this program echoes a stretchable
//               rubber rectangle. Click on existing rectangles
//               using [Shift] key enables rectangle dragging.
//

#include <owl\owlpch.h>
#include "dragrect.h"

DEFINE_RESPONSE_TABLE1 (DFrame, TFrameWindow)
  EV_WM_INITMENU,
  EV_WM_LBUTTONDOWN,
  EV_WM_LBUTTONUP,
  EV_WM_MOUSEMOVE,
  EV_COMMAND(CM_FILEEXIT, CmFileExit),
  EV_COMMAND(CM_FILEERASE, CmFileErase),
  EV_COMMAND(CM_BR_HATCH, CmBrHatch),
  EV_COMMAND(CM_BR_GRAY,  CmBrGray),
  EV_COMMAND(CM_BR_BLACK, CmBrBlack),
  EV_COMMAND(CM_PN_WHITE, CmPnWhite),
  EV_COMMAND(CM_PN_BLACK1, CmPnBlack1),
  EV_COMMAND(CM_PN_BLACK2, CmPnBlack2),
  EV_COMMAND(CM_HELPABOUT, CmHelpAbout),
END_RESPONSE_TABLE;

DFrame::DFrame(char * title) : TFrameWindow(0, title)
    {
    // Mouse up/down flag.
    bMouseDown = FALSE;

    // Count of rectangles in array.
    cRects = 0;

    // Size of control-point markers.
    cxyMarkerSize = GetSystemMetrics (SM_CXICON) / 8;

    // Create brushes
    tbrHatch = new TBrush(TColor::White, HS_DIAGCROSS);
    tbrGray  = new TBrush(TColor::Gray);
    tbrBlack = new TBrush(TColor::Black);
```

```
    // Create pens
    tpnBlack = new TPen(TColor::Black);
    tpnWide  = new TPen(TColor::Black, 5);
    tpnWhite = new TPen(TColor::White);

    // Set current pen & brush.
    tbrCurrent = tbrHatch;
    tpnCurrent = tpnBlack;

    // Rectangle drag & capture flags.
    fDrag = FALSE;
    bCapture = FALSE;
    }

DFrame::~DFrame()
    {
    // Important!  Always delete any GDI object that
    // you create. Otherwise, you cause memory leaks
    // in some Win16 systems (Windows 3.1, etc.)
    delete tbrBlack;
    delete tbrGray;
    delete tbrHatch;

    delete tpnBlack;
    delete tpnWide;
    delete tpnWhite;
    }

void DFrame::CmFileExit()
    {
    CloseWindow(0); // Cause application to terminate
    }

void DFrame::CmFileErase()
    {
    // Set count of rectangles to zero...
    cRects = 0;

    // ...and force WM_PAINT message (handled by DFrame::Paint)
    Invalidate();
    }

void DFrame::CmBrHatch()  { tbrCurrent = tbrHatch; }
void DFrame::CmBrGray()   { tbrCurrent = tbrGray;  }
void DFrame::CmBrBlack()  { tbrCurrent = tbrBlack; }
void DFrame::CmPnWhite()  { tpnCurrent = tpnWhite; }
void DFrame::CmPnBlack1() { tpnCurrent = tpnBlack; }
void DFrame::CmPnBlack2() { tpnCurrent = tpnWide;  }

void DFrame::CmHelpAbout()
    {
    MessageBox("Rectangle Drawing & Dragging Program\n\n"
               "     'Borland C++ 4.0 Programming\n"
               "        for Windows', by Paul Yao", Title);
    }

void DFrame::EvInitMenu(HMENU menu)
    {
    // Manage check/uncheck of brush menu items.
    MenuCheckMark(menu, CM_BR_HATCH, (tbrCurrent == tbrHatch));
    MenuCheckMark(menu, CM_BR_GRAY,  (tbrCurrent == tbrGray ));
```

```
    MenuCheckMark(menu, CM_BR_BLACK, (tbrCurrent == tbrBlack));

    // Manage check/uncheck of pen menu items.
    MenuCheckMark(menu, CM_PN_BLACK1, (tpnCurrent == tpnBlack));
    MenuCheckMark(menu, CM_PN_BLACK2, (tpnCurrent == tpnWide ));
    MenuCheckMark(menu, CM_PN_WHITE,  (tpnCurrent == tpnWhite));
    }

void DFrame::EvLButtonDown(UINT keycode, TPoint & pt)
    {
    if (cRects == MAXRECTANGLES)
        {
        MessageBeep(MB_ICONHAND);
        MessageBox ("Cannot Create More Rectangles", Title);
        return;
        }

    // If shift key is down, we're dragging...
    if (MK_SHIFT & keycode)
        {
        iDrag = -1;
        for (int i = cRects-1; i >= 0; i--)
            {
            if (arRects[i].trect.Contains(pt))
                {
                iDrag = i;
                break;
                }
            }

        if (iDrag == -1)
            return;

        rScratch = arRects[i].trect;

        InvalidateRect (rScratch);
        UpdateWindow ();

        ptDrag.x = pt.x;
        ptDrag.y = pt.y;
        fDrag = TRUE;
        }
    else
        {
        // Record first mouse point.
        arRects[cRects].trect.left = pt.x;
        arRects[cRects].trect.top  = pt.y;

        // Place marker at mouse location.
        TClientDC dc(HWindow);
        Marker::Square(dc, pt, cxyMarkerSize);

        rScratch.left   = rScratch.right  = pt.x;
        rScratch.top    = rScratch.bottom = pt.y;
        }

    pdrStretch = new DragRect(rScratch.left,
                              rScratch.top,
                              rScratch.right,
                              rScratch.bottom);

    if (fDrag)
```

```
        {
        TClientDC dc(HWindow);
        pdrStretch->Invert(HDC(dc));
        }

    // Set flag that mouse button is down.
    bMouseDown = TRUE;

    // Grab mouse for our exclusive use.
    SetCapture();
    }

void DFrame::EvMouseMove(UINT, TPoint & pt)
    {
    if (!bMouseDown)
        return;

    if (fDrag)
        {
        ptDrag.x -= pt.x;    // Calculate relative movement.
        ptDrag.y -= pt.y;

        rScratch.left   -= ptDrag.x;
        rScratch.top    -= ptDrag.y;
        rScratch.right  -= ptDrag.x;
        rScratch.bottom -= ptDrag.y;

        ptDrag.x = pt.x;     // Save draw rectangle for next time.
        ptDrag.y = pt.y;

        }
    else
        {
        rScratch.right  = pt.x;
        rScratch.bottom = pt.y;
        }

    // Move rubber rectangle.
    TClientDC dc(HWindow);
    pdrStretch->Move (HDC(dc), rScratch.left, rScratch.top,
                               rScratch.right, rScratch.bottom);
    }

void DFrame::EvLButtonUp(UINT, TPoint & pt)
    {
    int index;

    if (!bMouseDown)
       {
       MessageBeep(MB_ICONHAND);
       return;
       }

    // Erase rubber rectangle
    TClientDC dc(HWindow);
    pdrStretch->Invert(HDC(dc));

    // Delete rectangle inverter
    delete pdrStretch;

    if (fDrag)
        {
```

```
            // Update rectangle location.
            arRects[iDrag].trect = rScratch;
            }
        else
            {
            // Set coordinates in min/max order to
            // help TRect::Contains, which requires it.
            int x1 = pt.x;
            int y1 = pt.y;
            int x2 = rScratch.left;
            int y2 = rScratch.top;
            rScratch.left   = min (x1, x2);
            rScratch.top    = min (y1, y2);
            rScratch.right  = max (x1, x2);
            rScratch.bottom = max (y1, y2);

            // Save mouse coordinates.
            arRects[cRects].trect  = rScratch;

            // Record current pen & brush
            arRects[cRects].tpn = tpnCurrent;
            arRects[cRects].tbr = tbrCurrent;

            // Update rectangle count indicator.
            cRects++;
            }

        // Force a WM_PAINT message to redraw entire window.
        Invalidate ();

        // Relinquish exclusive control of mouse.
        ReleaseCapture();

        // Reset dragging & drawing flags.
        bCapture = FALSE;
        fDrag = FALSE;
        iDrag = -1;

        // Toggle that mouse is up.
        bMouseDown = FALSE;
        }

    void DFrame::Paint (TDC& dc, BOOL, TRect&)
        {
        for (int i = 0; i < cRects ; i++ )
            {
            // Select items' pen & brush.
            dc.SelectObject (*arRects[i].tpn);
            dc.SelectObject (*arRects[i].tbr);

            // Set background BLACK so that
            // white hatch brush looks interesting.
            dc.SetBkColor (TColor::Black);

            // Draw actual rectangle
            dc.Rectangle (arRects[i].trect.left,
                          arRects[i].trect.top,
                          arRects[i].trect.right,
                          arRects[i].trect.bottom);

            // Draw markers at two control points.
            Marker::Square (dc, arRects[i].trect.left,
```

```
                            arRects[i].trect.top, cxyMarkerSize);
        Marker::Square (dc, arRects[i].trect.right,
                            arRects[i].trect.bottom, cxyMarkerSize);
        }
    }

void DFrame::MenuCheckMark(HMENU menu, int id, BOOL bCheck)
    {
    WORD wState;
    wState = (bCheck) ? MF_CHECKED : MF_UNCHECKED;
    ::CheckMenuItem (menu, id, wState);
    }

DApp::DApp() : TApplication()
    {
    }

void DApp::InitMainWindow()
    {
    SetMainWindow (new DFrame("Rectangle Drawing & Dragging"));
    MainWindow->AssignMenu("MAIN");
    MainWindow->SetIcon(this, "SNAPSHOT");
    }

//
// Marker routines borrowed from CLS_MARK.CPP
// in Chapter 7's marker drawing program.
void Marker::Square (TDC& dc, int x, int y, int Size)
    {
    TPoint pt;
    pt.x = x;
    pt.y = y;
    Marker::Square(dc, pt, Size);
    }

void Marker::Square (TDC& dc, TPoint &pt, int Size)
    {
    // Request raster operation to invert pixels
    int ropOld = dc.SetROP2(R2_NOT);

    // Calculate distance from center point.
    int cxyWidth = Size / 2;

    // Draw a square marker.
    //  . . . . . . .
    //  . o o o o o .
    //  . o . . . o .
    //  . o . x . o .
    //  . o . . . o .
    //  . o o o o o .
    //  . . . . . . .
    dc.MoveTo(pt.x - cxyWidth, pt.y - cxyWidth);
    dc.LineTo(pt.x + cxyWidth, pt.y - cxyWidth);
    dc.LineTo(pt.x + cxyWidth, pt.y + cxyWidth);
    dc.LineTo(pt.x - cxyWidth, pt.y + cxyWidth);
    dc.LineTo(pt.x - cxyWidth, pt.y - cxyWidth);

    // Restore DC to the way we found it.
    dc.SetROP2 (ropOld);
    }

DragRect::DragRect(int x1, int y1, int x2, int y2)
```

```
        {
        hbrNull = (HBRUSH)::GetStockObject (NULL_BRUSH);

        rLocation.left   = x1;
        rLocation.top    = y1;
        rLocation.right  = x2;
        rLocation.bottom = y2;
        }

    void DragRect::Move(HDC hdc, int x1, int y1, int x2, int y2)
        {
        Invert (hdc);

        rLocation.left   = x1;
        rLocation.top    = y1;
        rLocation.right  = x2;
        rLocation.bottom = y2;

        Invert (hdc);
        }

    void DragRect::Invert (HDC hdc)
        {
        HBRUSH hbrOld;
        int    ropOld;

        hbrOld = (HBRUSH)::SelectObject (hdc, hbrNull);
        ropOld = SetROP2 (hdc, R2_NOT);

        Rectangle (hdc, rLocation.left,  rLocation.top,
                        rLocation.right, rLocation.bottom);

        SelectObject (hdc, hbrOld);
        SetROP2 (hdc, ropOld);
        }

    //
    // Application main entry point.
    OwlMain(int, char **)
        {
        return DApp().Run();
        }
```

DRAGRECT.H

```
    #define CM_FILEEXIT  100
    #define CM_FILEERASE 101
    #define CM_BR_BLACK  200
    #define CM_BR_GRAY   201
    #define CM_BR_HATCH  202
    #define CM_PN_BLACK1 300
    #define CM_PN_BLACK2 301
    #define CM_PN_WHITE  302
    #define CM_HELPABOUT 400

    const int MAXRECTANGLES = 50;
    const int MARKERSIZE = 3;

    // Rubber rectangle class.
    class DragRect
```

```
  {
  public:
    DragRect (int x1, int y1, int x2, int y2);
    virtual void Move(HDC hdc, int x1, int y1, int x2, int y2);
    virtual void Invert (HDC hdc);

  private:
    HBRUSH hbrNull;
    RECT   rLocation;
  };

// Marker Class
class Marker
    {
  public:
    static void Square (TDC&, TPoint&, int Size);
    static void Square (TDC&, int x, int y, int Size);
    };

// Rectangle Class
struct DRectangle
    {
    TBrush * tbr;
    TPen   * tpn;
    TRect    trect;
    };

// Main window
class DFrame : public TFrameWindow
    {
  public:
    DFrame(char * title);
    ~DFrame();
    void CmFileExit();
    void CmFileErase();
    void CmBrHatch();
    void CmBrGray();
    void CmBrBlack();
    void CmPnWhite();
    void CmPnBlack1();
    void CmPnBlack2();
    void CmHelpAbout();
    void EvInitMenu(HMENU menu);
    void EvLButtonDown(UINT, TPoint &);
    void EvLButtonUp(UINT, TPoint &);
    void EvMouseMove(UINT, TPoint & pt);
    void Paint (TDC&, BOOL, TRect&);
    void MenuCheckMark(HMENU menu, int id, BOOL bCheck);
  private:
    BOOL       bMouseDown;
    int        cRects;
    int        cxyMarkerSize;
    DRectangle arRects [MAXRECTANGLES];
    TBrush   * tbrCurrent;
    TBrush   * tbrBlack;
    TBrush   * tbrGray;
    TBrush   * tbrHatch;
    TPen     * tpnCurrent;
    TPen     * tpnBlack;
    TPen     * tpnWide;
    TPen     * tpnWhite;
    BOOL       fDrag;
```

```
    BOOL        bCapture;
    TRect       rScratch;
    int         iDrag;
    TPoint      ptDrag;
    DragRect * pdrStretch;

  DECLARE_RESPONSE_TABLE (DFrame);
    };

// Application object
class DApp : public TApplication
    {
  public:
    DApp();
    void InitMainWindow();
    };
```

DRAGRECT.RC

```
#include "dragrect.h"

snapshot icon dragrect.ico

main menu
    BEGIN
    POPUP "&File"
        {
        MENUITEM "&Erase", CM_FILEERASE
        MENUITEM SEPARATOR
        MENUITEM "E&xit",  CM_FILEEXIT
        }
    POPUP "&Brush"
        {
        MENUITEM "&Hatch", CM_BR_HATCH
        MENUITEM "&Gray",  CM_BR_GRAY
        MENUITEM "&Black", CM_BR_BLACK
        }
    POPUP "&Pen"
        {
        MENUITEM "&Thin Black",   CM_PN_BLACK1
        MENUITEM "&Thick Black",  CM_PN_BLACK2
        MENUITEM "&White",        CM_PN_WHITE
        }
    POPUP "&Help"
        {
        MENUITEM "&About...", CM_HELPABOUT
        }
    END
```

DRAGRECT.DEF

```
EXETYPE WINDOWS

CODE MOVEABLE DISCARDABLE
DATA MULTIPLE MOVEABLE

HEAPSIZE   512
STACKSIZE 8192
```

DYNA16.MAK

```
#  MAKE file for Win16 API using dynamic BIDS,
#  OWL and C-runtime libraries.
#
#     C> make -fstatic16.mak
#

.AUTODEPEND
CC = -c -H -H"owl\owlpch.h" -ml -R -vi -WS -X-
CD = -D_RTLDLL;_BIDSDLL;_OWLDLL;_OWLPCH;
INC = -I\BC4\INCLUDE
LIB = -L\BC4\LIB

dragrect.exe :  dragrect.obj dragrect.res
  tlink -c -C -Twe $(LIB) @dyna16.lnk
  brc dragrect.res dragrect.exe

dragrect.obj :  dragrect.cpp
  bcc $(CC) $(CD) dragrect.cpp

dragrect.res :  dragrect.rc dragrect.ico dragrect.h
  brc $(INC) -31 -R dragrect.rc
```

DYNA16.LNK

```
\bc4\lib\c0wl.obj+
dragrect.obj
dragrect,dragrect
\bc4\lib\bidsi.lib+
\bc4\lib\owlwi.lib+
\bc4\lib\import.lib+
\bc4\lib\crtldll.lib
dragrect.def
```

DYNA32.MAK

```
#  MAKE file for Win32 API using dynamic BIDS,
#  OWL and C-runtime libraries.
#
#     C> make -fdyna32.mak
#

.AUTODEPEND
CC = -c -H -H\""owl\owlpch.h\"" -p- -R -vi -W -X-
CD = -D_RTLDLL;_BIDSDLL;_OWLDLL;_OWLPCH;
INC = -I\BC4\INCLUDE
LIB = -L\BC4\LIB

dragrect.exe :  dragrect.obj dragrect.res
  tlink32 -aa -c -Tpe $(LIB) @dyna32.lnk
  brc32 dragrect.res dragrect.exe

dragrect.obj :  dragrect.cpp
  bcc32 $(CC) $(CD) dragrect.cpp

dragrect.res :  dragrect.rc dragrect.ico dragrect.h
  brc32 $(INC) -w32 -R dragrect.rc
```

DYNA32.LNK

```
\bc4\lib\c0w32.obj+
dragrect.obj
dragrect,dragrect
\bc4\lib\bidsfi.lib+
\bc4\lib\owlwfi.lib+
\bc4\lib\import32.lib+
\bc4\lib\cw32i.lib
dragrect.def
```

Dragging and Stretching

Any program that does any dragging or stretching will be interested in three mouse messages: button down, mouse move, and button up. In response to the button down message, the window procedure does whatever initialization it needs to do to make the dragging or stretching work. The mouse move message means the mouse cursor has moved, and that the dragged or stretched object needs to be modified to reflect that movement. The simplest way to handle this is to erase the image of the object at the old location and create a copy of the object at the new location. The button up message means that no more movement is required, so dragging or stretching can be turned off and the object made permanent.

While movement is going on, the raster operations provide a convenient manner to quickly draw and erase the moveable/stretchable rectangles. The particular raster operation that we use is the one associated with the NOT operation, **R2_NOT**. A nice feature of this raster operation is that it virtually guarantees that the object you draw will appear. Every white pixel encountered will turn black, and every black pixel encountered will turn white. Pixels that have colors other than black and white will be changed to the logical inverse color. You'll find that this produces some slightly unexpected results—like the fact that **R2_NOT** of blue on a 16-color VGA adapter gives yellow (instead of orange). This is a limitation of the hardware, and a compromise to allow a reasonable set of colors to be available on this device.

In spite of this odd behavior with color, the second—and most important—advantage of the **R2_NOT** raster operation is that everything is easily reversible. Let's look at the two-color monochrome case to convince ourselves that this is true. The *first* time a figure (say a rectangle) is drawn, every white pixel turns black and every black pixel turns white. The *second* time the same figure is drawn, every white pixel turns black and every black pixel turns white. But after the figure is drawn the second time, the figure itself disappears. Put together, the two advantages of the **R2_NOT** raster operation are ideal for drawing dragable and stretchable rectangles.

In DRAGRECT, the work of creating and maintaining the **R2_NOT** rectangles is done by the **DragRect** class object. In particular, the **Invert** member function selects the stock null brush into the DC, so it only draws the rectangle outline. It sets the raster operation to **R2_NOT** by calling the **SetROP2** routine, then draws a rectangle. The routine itself doesn't know (or care) whether it is drawing the first rectangle—to make one appear—or the second rectangle—to make it disappear.

A second issue that is raised by the DRAGRECT program is that of the mouse capture, which we're going to discuss next.

The Mouse Capture

Mouse messages are always sent to the window lying under the mouse cursor. In this way, the user is free to move the cursor to the desired program and start it running with a mouse click. But there are times when it makes sense to restrict all mouse messages to one window. In particular, it is useful when some operation has started that must be completed in order to leave the program in a stable, known state. Rectangle dragging and stretching are two such times.

In DRAGRECT, when the **WM_LBUTTONDOWN** message is received, the program gets set up to draw a new rectangle or to move an existing rectangle. The program expects to receive another message—a **WM_LBUTTONUP**—before things are returned to "normal." If a second **WM_LBUTTONDOWN** message is received before a **WM_LBUTTONUP** message, it will cause some confusion in the program and a mess in the window.

To make sure that our window gets the expected sequence of messages, the window procedure **captures** the mouse. This is done by calling **SetCapture**, which takes a single parameter: a window handle. **SetCapture** is called in response to **WM_LBUTTONDOWN**, to reserve all mouse messages for our window until the capture is released.

Releasing the capture is done by making a call to **ReleaseCapture**. DRAGRECT calls **ReleaseCapture** in response to a **WM_LBUTTONUP**, to allow other programs to receive mouse messages.

The final point to be made about the mouse capture is that the hit-testing and cursor setting messages are disabled when the mouse is captured. That is, you will not encounter the **WM_NCHITTEST** or **WM_SETCURSOR** messages when the mouse is captured. The hit-testing message, **WM_NCHITTEST**, after all, tests whether a client area or nonclient area message should be sent, and only client area messages are sent when the mouse is captured. And the **WM_SETCURSOR** is not sent since Windows doesn't expect the cursor to change when one window has reserved all mouse input for itself.

At this point, we're going to turn our attention to the third sample program of this chapter, which creates a mouse cursor on the fly.

Creating Dynamic Cursors

MIN, which was first introduced in Chapter 2, uses the system's default arrow cursor, thanks to work done by OWL's **TWindow** class. A program in this chapter, CARET2, used the system's I-beam cursor. If the built-in cursors don't meet your needs, you can always use the Resource Workshop utility to draw your own cursor, in the same way that we drew a custom icon for MIN. All these cursors are static.

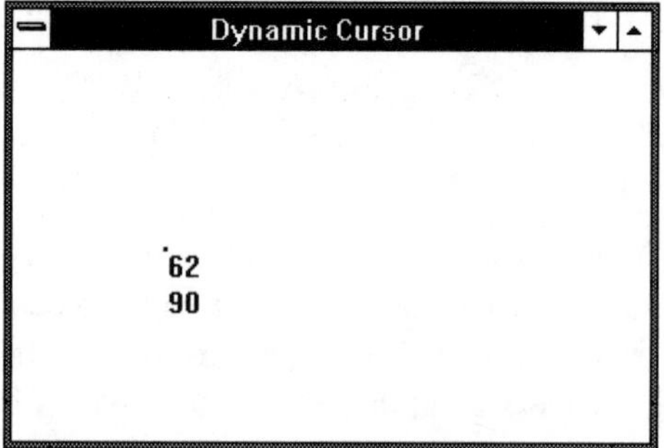

Figure 16.10 The cursor in DYNACURS echoes the mouse location

While a static custom cursor will serve most of your needs, there may be times when you need to create a dynamic cursor. A dynamic cursor is one that is created by a Windows program at execution time, instead of during program development time. One way to create a dynamic cursor is to create a GDI bitmap and then use GDI routines to draw the desired shape. This is the approach we will take. This simple description hides the fact that quite a bit of shuffling is required to create a custom cursor.

The DYNACURS Program

Our dynamic cursor program echoes the current mouse location. Figure 16.10 shows a sample of its output. The "hot-spot" of the cursor is in the cursor's upper-left corner, marked by a dot. The top number is the *x* location of the cursor, and the bottom number is the *y* location.

One of the first things you notice when you run this program is the way the cursor seems to blink a lot. That is, as the mouse moves and the cursor changes, the dynamic cursor doesn't have the smooth quality that we associate with a normal cursor. The reason has to do with the fact that the background—the area "behind" the cursor—must be restored every time the cursor changes.

DYNACURS.CPP

```
// DYNACURS.CPP  Creates a dynamic cursor on the fly.
//
#include <owl\owlpch.h>
#include "dynacurs.h"

DEFINE_RESPONSE_TABLE1 (DFrame, TFrameWindow)
  EV_WM_SETCURSOR,
  EV_COMMAND(CM_FILEEXIT, CmFileExit),
  EV_COMMAND(CM_HELPABOUT, CmHelpAbout),
END_RESPONSE_TABLE;
```

```
DFrame::DFrame(char * title) : TFrameWindow(0, title)
    {
    }

void DFrame::CmFileExit()
    {
    CloseWindow(0); // Cause application to terminate
    }

void DFrame::CmHelpAbout()
    {
    MessageBox("     Dynamic Mouse Cursor\n\n"
               "'Borland C++ 4.0 Programming\n"
               "  for Windows', by Paul Yao", Title);
    }

void DFrame::SetupWindow()
    {
    // Call base class member first.
    TFrameWindow::SetupWindow();

    //  Find out expected size of cursor.
    cxCursor = GetSystemMetrics (SM_CXCURSOR);
    cyCursor = GetSystemMetrics (SM_CYCURSOR);

    //  Create scratch objects...

    //  ...a bitmap....
    hbm = CreateBitmap (cxCursor,  // width
                        cyCursor,  // height
                        1,         // planes
                        1,         // bits per pixel
                        NULL);     // initial data

    //  ...A DC for the bitmap...
    HDC hdc = GetDC (HWindow);
    hdcBitmap = CreateCompatibleDC (hdc);
    ReleaseDC (HWindow, hdc);

    //  Connect the bitmap to the DC.
    hbmOld = (HBITMAP)SelectObject (hdcBitmap, hbm);

    //  Some memory scratch space.
    cbSize = (cxCursor/8) * cyCursor;
    hmemAND = GlobalAlloc (GMEM_MOVEABLE,    // flags
                           (DWORD)cbSize);   // size

    lpAND = (LPSTR)GlobalLock (hmemAND);
    if (lpAND == NULL)
        goto ErrorExit;

    hmemXOR = GlobalAlloc (GMEM_MOVEABLE,    // flags
                           (DWORD)cbSize);   // size

    lpXOR = (LPSTR)GlobalLock (hmemXOR);
    if (lpXOR == NULL)
        goto ErrorExit;

    //  Get GDI objects to use.
    hbrWhite = new TBrush(TColor::White);
    hbrBlack = new TBrush(TColor::Black);
```

```
    // Error checking.
    if (hbm == NULL      || hdcBitmap == NULL ||
        hmemAND == NULL || hmemXOR == NULL    ||
        cxCursor%8 != NULL)
        {
ErrorExit:
        MessageBox ("Unable to Initialize", Title);
        }

    return;
    }

void DFrame::CleanupWindow()
    {
    SelectObject (hdcBitmap, hbmOld);
    DeleteDC (hdcBitmap);
    DeleteObject (hbm);
    DestroyCursor(hcrPrev);

    delete hbrWhite;
    delete hbrBlack;

    GlobalUnlock (hmemAND);
    GlobalUnlock (hmemXOR);
    GlobalFree (hmemAND);
    GlobalFree (hmemXOR);
    }

BOOL DFrame::EvSetCursor(HWND hwnd,
                         UINT hitTest,
                         UINT mouseMsg)
    {
    // Ignore non-client area messages.
    if (hitTest != HTCLIENT)
        return TFrameWindow::EvSetCursor(hwnd,
                                         hitTest,
                                         mouseMsg);

    //  Set up AND Mask.
    SelectObject (hdcBitmap, HBRUSH(*hbrWhite));
    PatBlt (hdcBitmap, 0, 0, cxCursor, cyCursor,
            PATCOPY);

    // Light up the hot-spot.
    SetPixel (hdcBitmap, 1, 0, 0L);
    SetPixel (hdcBitmap, 1, 1, 0L);
    SetPixel (hdcBitmap, 1, 2, 0L);
    SetPixel (hdcBitmap, 0, 1, 0L);
    SetPixel (hdcBitmap, 2, 1, 0L);

    //  Where is the mouse cursor?
    TPoint pt;
    GetCursorPos (pt);

    ScreenToClient (pt);

    char    acLine1[8];
    char    acLine2[8];
    int cc1 = wsprintf (acLine1,"%d", pt.x);
    int cc2 = wsprintf (acLine2,"%d", pt.y);

    //  Write coordinates to bitmap.
```

```
    TextOut (hdcBitmap, 3, 0, acLine1, cc1);
    TextOut (hdcBitmap, 3, cyCursor/2, acLine2, cc2);

    GetBitmapBits (hbm, (DWORD)cbSize, lpAND);

    //  Set up XOR Mask.
    SelectObject (hdcBitmap, HBRUSH(*hbrBlack));
    PatBlt (hdcBitmap, 0, 0, cxCursor, cyCursor,
            PATCOPY);

    GetBitmapBits (hbm, (DWORD)cbSize, lpXOR);

    //  Spin a cursor on the fly.
    HCURSOR hcrTemp = CreateCursor (
         GetApplication()->GetInstance(),
         1,          // X-hotspot
         1,          // Y-hotspot
         cxCursor,   // width
         cyCursor,   // height
         lpAND,      // AND bitmask
         lpXOR);     // XOR bitmask

    ::SetCursor (hcrTemp);  // Select new cursor.

    //  Remove old cursor.
    if (hcrPrev != NULL) DestroyCursor(hcrPrev);

    hcrPrev = hcrTemp;

    return TRUE;
    }

DApp::DApp() : TApplication()
    {
    }

void DApp::InitMainWindow()
    {
    SetMainWindow (new DFrame("Dynamic Cursor"));

    MainWindow->AssignMenu("MAIN");
    MainWindow->SetIcon(this, "SNAPSHOT");
    }

//
// Application main entry point.
OwlMain(int, char **)
    {
    return DApp().Run();
    }
```

DYNACURS.H

```
#define CM_FILEEXIT 100
#define CM_HELPABOUT 200

// Main window
class DFrame : public TFrameWindow
    {
  public:
    DFrame(char * title);
    void CmFileExit();
```

```
      void CmHelpAbout();
      void SetupWindow();
      void CleanupWindow();
      BOOL EvSetCursor(HWND hwnd, UINT hitTest, UINT mouseMsg);
    private:
      HCURSOR   hcrPrev;
      HBITMAP   hbm;
      HBITMAP   hbmOld;
      TBrush  * hbrWhite;
      TBrush  * hbrBlack;
      HDC       hdcBitmap;
      HGLOBAL   hmemAND;
      HGLOBAL   hmemXOR;
      LPSTR     lpAND;
      LPSTR     lpXOR;
      int       cbSize;
      int       cxCursor;
      int       cyCursor;

    DECLARE_RESPONSE_TABLE (DFrame);
      };

  // Application object
  class DApp : public TApplication
      {
    public:
      DApp();
      void InitMainWindow();
      };
```

DYNACURS.RC

```
#include "dynacurs.h"

snapshot icon dynacurs.ico

main menu
    BEGIN
    POPUP "&File"
        {
        MENUITEM "E&xit", CM_FILEEXIT
        }
    POPUP "&Help"
        {
        MENUITEM "&About...", CM_HELPABOUT
        }
    END
```

DYNACURS.DEF

```
EXETYPE WINDOWS

CODE MOVEABLE DISCARDABLE
DATA MULTIPLE MOVEABLE

HEAPSIZE   512
STACKSIZE 8192
```

DYNA16.MAK

```
#  MAKE file for Win16 API using dynamic BIDS,
#  OWL and C-runtime libraries.
#
#     C> make -fstatic16.mak
#

.AUTODEPEND
CC = -c -H -H"owl\owlpch.h" -ml -R -vi -WS -X-
CD = -D_RTLDLL;_BIDSDLL;_OWLDLL;_OWLPCH;
INC = -I\BC4\INCLUDE
LIB = -L\BC4\LIB

dynacurs.exe :  dynacurs.obj dynacurs.res
  tlink -c -C -Twe $(LIB) @dyna16.lnk
  brc dynacurs.res dynacurs.exe

dynacurs.obj :  dynacurs.cpp
  bcc $(CC) $(CD) dynacurs.cpp

dynacurs.res :  dynacurs.rc dynacurs.ico dynacurs.h
  brc $(INC) -31 -R dynacurs.rc
```

DYNA16.LNK

```
\bc4\lib\c0wl.obj+
dynacurs.obj
dynacurs,dynacurs
\bc4\lib\bidsi.lib+
\bc4\lib\owlwi.lib+
\bc4\lib\import.lib+
\bc4\lib\crtldll.lib
dynacurs.def
```

DYNA32.MAK

```
#  MAKE file for Win32 API using dynamic BIDS,
#  OWL and C-runtime libraries.
#
#     C> make -fdyna32.mak
#

.AUTODEPEND
CC = -c -H -H\""owl\owlpch.h\"" -p- -R -vi -W -X-
CD = -D_RTLDLL;_BIDSDLL;_OWLDLL;_OWLPCH;
INC = -I\BC4\INCLUDE
LIB = -L\BC4\LIB

dynacurs.exe :  dynacurs.obj dynacurs.res
  tlink32 -aa -c -Tpe $(LIB) @dyna32.lnk
  brc32 dynacurs.res dynacurs.exe

dynacurs.obj :  dynacurs.cpp
  bcc32 $(CC) $(CD) dynacurs.cpp

dynacurs.res :  dynacurs.rc dynacurs.ico dynacurs.h
  brc32 $(INC) -w32 -R dynacurs.rc
```

DYNA32.LNK

```
\bc4\lib\c0w32.obj+
dynacurs.obj
dynacurs,dynacurs
\bc4\lib\bidsfi.lib+
\bc4\lib\owlwfi.lib+
\bc4\lib\import32.lib+
\bc4\lib\cw32i.lib
dynacurs.def
```

DYNACURS is interested in three messages: **WM_CREATE**, **WM_DESTROY**, and **WM_SETCURSOR**. In response to the **WM_CREATE** message, that is, in **DFrame::Set-upWindow,** several objects are created and initialized that will be needed to support the cursor creation. This includes a monochrome memory bitmap, a device context to connect to the bitmap, and some dynamically allocated memory. The **WM_SETCURSOR** message triggers the dynamic cursor creation, which involves determining the mouse cursor location, calling GDI routines to write this location to the memory bitmaps, and then calling the **CreateCursor** routine to convert this data into a full-fledged cursor. In response to the third message, **WM_DESTROY**, that is, in **DFrame::CleanupWindow,** DYNACURS cleans up and deallocates the objects that were created in response to the **WM_CREATE** message. To understand why these objects are needed, it will help to explore the insides of a cursor, so that you'll know what makes it tick.

How Cursors Work

A cursor is a data object that consists of two parts. Each part is a monochrome bitmap that is combined with the pixels of the display surface to create the cursor image. The first part is called the AND mask, to reflect the fact that the pixels of this bitmap are combined with the surface using the logical AND operation. The second part of the cursor is called the XOR mask, which again reflects the fact that a logical operation, XOR, is used to combine this bitmap with the display surface.

When the display driver draws a cursor, it starts by making a copy of the pixels that are already on the display surface. This ensures that the old image can be restored, and is key in maintaining the integrity of the image on the display surface. Once the copy has been made, the AND mask is applied to the surface, followed by the XOR mask. Through the magic of Boolean operations, this two-step process allows four different effects: black, white, display, and not-display. By "display," we mean that the cursor is transparent and allows the background to show through. By "not-display," we mean the pixels on the background are inverted. This is a rarely used combination, but it can provide some interesting effects. For example, the not-display effect might be used on a cursor in the shape of a magnifying glass to help suggest the fuzzy distortion of the lens surface. Table 16.2 has a truth table that shows how pixels of the AND mask and XOR mask combine to create the four effects.

Table 16.2 The AND Mask and XOR Mask

AND Mask	*XOR Mask*	*Cursor*
0 (Black)	0 (Black)	Black
0 (Black)	1 (White)	White
1 (White)	0 (Black)	Display
1 (White)	1 (White)	Not-display

To create an all-black cursor, you need to set both masks to black. An all-white cursor would result from an all-black AND mask and an all-white XOR mask. DYNACURS creates black text on a transparent (display colored) background by combining an AND mask of black text on a white background with an all-black XOR mask.

The routine that creates a dynamic cursor is **`CreateCursor`**, defined as

```
CreateCursor (hInstance, xHotSpot, yHotSpot, nWidth,
              hHeight, lpANDbitPlane, lpXORbitPlane);
```

- **`hInstance`** is the instance handle that was passed to our program as a parameter to **`WinMain`**. We retrieve the application object's copy of this value by saying

  ```
  GetApplication()->GetInstance()
  ```

- **`xHotSpot`** is the *x* coordinate for the cursor hot-spot.
- **`yHotSpot`** is the *y* coordinate for the cursor hot-spot.
- **`nWidth`** is the width in pixels of the cursor. If the size we provide doesn't match the size desired by the display driver, our cursor will be stretched (or shrunk). To make sure we have a match, we ask Windows to provide the size that the display driver expects. The following call provides the correct width value:

  ```
  GetSystemMetrics (SM_CXCURSOR);
  ```

- **`nHeight`** is the height in pixels of the cursor. We set this value to match the size desired by the display driver by calling the following routine:

  ```
  GetSystemMetrics (SM_CYCURSOR);
  ```

- **`lpANDbitPlane`** is an `LPSTR (char far *)` pointer to the bits that make up the AND mask.
- **`lpXORbitPlane`** is an `LPSTR (char far *)` pointer to the bits that make up the XOR mask.

Most of the work that we need to do to create a custom cursor involves creating the two bit masks. Understanding what DYNACURS does to get these two bit masks requires an understanding of two topics, GDI bitmaps and dynamic memory allocation. Since these two topics will be the subject of later chapters, we're going to limit our discussion to a brief introduction.

Creating a GDI Bitmap

In our introduction to GDI in Chapter 6, we described a bitmap as a type of pseudodevice that is used primarily to store pictures. If you think of a bitmap as nothing more than a type of device, you will be half way to understanding how to use them. The other half involves understanding how to get a handle to a DC that will allow you to write on a bitmap. The following calls accomplish that:

```
//  Create scratch objects...

//  ...a bitmap....
hbm = CreateBitmap (cxCursor,   // width
                    cyCursor,   // height
                    1,          // planes
                    1,          // bits per pixel
                    NULL);      // initial data

//  ...A DC for the bitmap...
HDC hdc = GetDC (HWindow);
hdcBitmap = CreateCompatibleDC (hdc);
ReleaseDC (HWindow, hdc);

//  Connect the bitmap to the DC.
hbmOld = (HBITMAP)SelectObject (hdcBitmap, hbm);
```

The first routine, **CreateBitmap**, asks GDI to allocate the memory that will be used to store the bits of our bitmap. The width and height values, `cxCursor` and `cyCursor`, come from Windows itself, which tells us, via the **GetSystemMetrics** routine, the size of the cursor that the current display driver expects to use:

```
/*  Find out expected size of cursor.  */
cxCursor = GetSystemMetrics (SM_CXCURSOR);
cyCursor = GetSystemMetrics (SM_CYCURSOR);
```

To build a cursor, we need a monochrome bitmap, which is the reason we set the number of planes to `1` and the bits per pixel to `1`. The **CreateBitmap** routine returns a handle to a bitmap, of the type **HBITMAP**, which we store in the variable **hbm**.

By itself, a bitmap is just a block of memory. We need to create a connection to the memory, and also a set of drawing tools that will allow us to send output to the bitmap just like we send output to the display device. We need a device context. The simplest way to create a DC is to ask GDI to make a copy of an existing DC for us. This is accomplished with the following calls:

```
//  ...A DC for the bitmap...
HDC hdc = GetDC (HWindow);
hdcBitmap = CreateCompatibleDC (hdc);
ReleaseDC (HWindow, hdc);
```

We borrow and return a DC with a **GetDC/ReleaseDC** pair, and create a new DC with the call to **CreateCompatibleDC**. The value returned by **CreateCompatibleDC** is a handle to a DC. But by itself, it has no connection to our bitmap (or any device, for that matter), so we need to create a connection. We do this by calling the SelectObject function.

As you may recall, we use the **SelectObject** routine to install pens, brushes, and other drawing objects into a DC. But the bitmap is more than just a drawing object—it is a full-fledged drawing surface. Or, as we have said earlier, a *pseudodevice*. Once the bitmap and DC are connected, we draw to the bitmap by calling any GDI drawing routine and providing the DC handle as a parameter. When the bitmap is connected to the DC that **SelectObject** provides, we save the value returned by **SelectObject** so that we can later disconnect the bitmap from the DC. At cleanup time, this will make it easy to destroy both objects.

At this point, we've seen how to create a bitmap. Let's look at how DYNACURS uses the bitmap.

Using the GDI Bitmap

When DYNACURS receives a **WM_SETCURSOR** message, it draws into our bitmap to create the desired pixel patterns for the AND and XOR bit masks. The bits are then copied from the bitmap into two dynamically allocated pieces of memory, since **CreateCursor** does not read a bitmap directly but instead reads the bit masks as blocks of memory. These bit masks are passed to **CreateCursor** via the two pointers that make up **CreateCursor**'s last two parameters.

The first bit mask that gets set up is the AND mask. First, we set all the bits to white, using a routine called **PatBlt**. This GDI routine fills a rectangular area on a drawing surface using the currently selected brush. Here is the code that does this for us:

```
//  Set up AND Mask.
SelectObject (hdcBitmap, HBRUSH(*hbrWhite));
PatBlt (hdcBitmap, 0, 0, cxCursor, cyCursor,  PATCOPY);
```

Drawing the four-pixel-square hot-spot involves four calls to **SetPixel**:

```
// Light up the hot-spot.
SetPixel (hdcBitmap, 1, 0, 0L);
SetPixel (hdcBitmap, 1, 1, 0L);
SetPixel (hdcBitmap, 1, 2, 0L);
SetPixel (hdcBitmap, 0, 1, 0L);
SetPixel (hdcBitmap, 2, 1, 0L);
```

DYNACURS then makes a call to **GetCursorPos**, which finds out the location of the mouse cursor in **screen coordinates**. Like client area coordinates, screen coordinates are pixel units. But they differ from client area coordinates in that the origin (0,0) is at the upper-left corner of the entire screen instead of the upper-left corner of the client area. To convert from one to the other, a call is made to **ScreenToClient**. Then, the coordinates are converted from integer values to a character string, and the two lines are written onto the bitmap:

```
// Where is the mouse cursor?
TPoint pt;
GetCursorPos (pt);

ScreenToClient (pt);

char    acLine1[8];
char    acLine2[8];
int cc1 = wsprintf (acLine1,"%d", pt.x);
int cc2 = wsprintf (acLine2,"%d", pt.y);

// Write coordinates to bitmap.
TextOut (hdcBitmap, 3, 0, acLine1, cc1);
TextOut (hdcBitmap, 3, cyCursor/2, acLine2, cc2);
```

At this point, the bitmap contains the image that we want to use for the AND mask on the cursor. But we have to ask GDI to make a copy of the bits in a form that **CreateCursor** will accept. This is the job of the **GetBitmapBits** routine. **GetBitmapBits** is defined as follows:

```
DWORD GetBitmapBits (hBitmap, dwCount, lpBits)
```

- **hBitmap** is a handle to a bitmap.
- **dwCount** is a `DWORD` value for the size of the storage area.
- **lpBits** is a `char far * (LPSTR)` that points to the data area to hold the bits.

The following line of code from DYNACURS copies the bits from the bitmap into a block of dynamically allocated memory, suitable for passing to **CreateCursor**:

```
GetBitmapBits (hbm, (DWORD)cbSize, lpAND);
```

The creation of the XOR bit mask is similar, but much simpler. The **PatBlt** routine is called to set every pixel in the bitmap to black. Once this is done, a call is made to **GetBitmapBits** to copy the bits from the bitmap to a piece of dynamically allocated memory. To fully understand how DYNACURS works, we need to explore further the allocation and use of dynamically allocated memory.

Dynamically Allocating Memory

The reason that dynamically allocated memory is necessary is that there is no way to anticipate the amount of memory that may be required to hold the bits of a cursor. For example, here are the cursor sizes and memory requirement for some of today's popular display adapters:

Display Adapter	*Cursor Size*	*Memory Required*
CGA	32 × 16	64 bytes
EGA/VGA	32 × 32	128 bytes
8514/a	32 × 32	128 bytes

New display adapters may come along tomorrow that require larger blocks of memory to store the AND and XOR bit masks, so, to be safe, we depend upon dynamic memory allocation to provide the memory we need.

If you've done a lot of C language programming, you're probably familiar with **malloc**, the C-runtime library routine which dynamically allocates memory. For reasons that we'll describe in Chapter 18, Windows programmers don't use this routine, but instead rely on two sets of memory allocating routines that are built into Windows. Here are the routines that DYNACURS uses:

Routine Name	*Description*
GlobalAlloc	Allocates a block (segment) of memory.
GlobalLock	Locks the memory in place and provides a far pointer.
GlobalUnlock	Unlocks the memory to allow it to move.
GlobalFree	Deallocates a block of memory.

To determine the amount of memory that is required, we start by asking Windows for the cursor size that the display adapter requires:

```
cxCursor = GetSystemMetrics (SM_CXCURSOR);
cyCursor = GetSystemMetrics (SM_CYCURSOR);
```

Since **cxCursor** is the width in pixels and **cyCursor** is the height in pixels, we can get the total size in bytes necessary to store this object by dividing **cxCursor** by eight and then multiplying by `cyCursor`, like this:

```
cbSize = (cxCursor/8) * cyCursor;
```

We allocate two blocks of memory: one for the AND mask and one for the XOR mask using the **GlobalAlloc** routine, as shown here:

```
hmemAND = GlobalAlloc (GMEM_MOVEABLE,     // flags
                       (DWORD)cbSize); // size

hmemXOR = GlobalAlloc (GMEM_MOVEABLE,     // flags
                       (DWORD)cbSize); // size
```

The **GMEM_MOVEABLE** flag tells Windows that it can move the object when we aren't using it. This is necessary because Windows runs in the real mode of the Intel-86 family of CPUs. This particular mode doesn't provide any hardware assistance to manage memory. And so Windows programs must manage memory in a way that cooperates with Windows and with other Windows programs. The **GMEM_MOVEABLE** flag offers a reasonable compromise between usefulness and cooperativeness. We'll explore the use of this and other flags more fully in Chapter 18.

GlobalAlloc returns a handle to the memory block, which serves to identify a block of memory, although it does not tell us where moveable memory is located. To find that out, we must lock the memory down using the **GlobalLock** routine. This routine returns a far pointer to the memory block, which is how we can access it. **GlobalLock** is defined as follows:

```
LPSTR GlobalLock (hMem)
```

- **hMem** is a handle to a global memory object, allocated with the **GlobalAlloc** routine.

Here are the lines of code from DYNACURS that lock the memory so it can be accessed. Notice that we check the return value to make sure that we have retrieved a valid pointer. This is a good habit to get into, since a NULL pointer can cause problems depending on Windows' operating mode. In real mode, it allows you to trash the interrupt vectors located at the very low end of memory. In protect mode, it causes a protection violation which results in the termination of your program. Neither alternative is attractive, and it is quick and easy to avoid these problems.

```
lpAND = (LPSTR) GlobalLock (hmemAND);
if (lpAND == NULL) goto ErrorExit;

lpXOR = (LPSTR) GlobalLock (hmemXOR);
if (lpXOR == NULL) goto ErrorExit;
```

After we are done using a block of dynamically allocated memory, we unlock the memory objects by calling **GlobalUnlock**. The primary reason we do this is to allow our programs to behave nicely when Windows is running in real mode:

```
GlobalUnlock (hmemAND);
GlobalUnlock (hmemXOR);
```

The final issue that we need to address is the freeing of our memory objects when DYNACURS gets a **WM_DESTROY** message. That is the job of the **GlobalFree** routine. Windows is smart enough to reclaim unused memory when a program exits, but we think it's a good programming practice to clean up after yourself. After all, someone may later use your code as part of a larger programming project and may not check to make sure that you have cleaned up properly. And since GDI objects do not automatically get cleaned up, you must make sure to destroy the GDI objects that you have created. Here is how DYNACURS cleans up the memory, the leftover cursor, and the GDI objects that it created:

```
void DFrame::CleanupWindow()
    {
    SelectObject (hdcBitmap, hbmOld);
    DeleteDC (hdcBitmap);
    DeleteObject (hbm);
    DestroyCursor(hcrPrev);

    delete hbrWhite;
    delete hbrBlack;

    GlobalUnlock (hmemAND);
    GlobalUnlock (hmemXOR);
    GlobalFree (hmemAND);
    GlobalFree (hmemXOR);
    }
```

While creating a dynamic cursor takes a lot of work, it provides a way to create custom cursors at runtime. You might create a cursor in the shape of a clock face or a timer to count down a lengthy operation. You can even let users define their own private, custom cursors. And any cursor you create can be used as an icon as well, since the two user-interface objects share the exact same format.

As a pointing device, the mouse is a fairly simple device. But its operation and use can prove quite involved, depending on how much control you give the user—in terms of picking up and dragging objects, for example. There are also very rich methods for providing feedback to the user, as shown by both static and dynamic mouse cursors.

This concludes my look into the use of the keyboard and mouse input. In the next section, I'll address operating systems considerations by addressing memory management issues and dynamic linking.

PART SIX

Operating System Considerations

17

Memory, Part I: System Memory Management

With the introduction of Windows NT in July of 1993, understanding how Windows manages memory started getting at the same time simpler, yet also more complex. Things are getting simpler because the Win32 API supports a flat, 32-bit address space. Issues related to the ugly, segmented addressing of the Win16 API will be going away. For example, the distinction between `near` and `far` pointers are a nonissue in Win32. Having to deal with a 64K limit of data per segment isn't a problem for a programmer writing to a Win32 application.

Things are more complex because the Win16 API is still with us, and until it goes away—which it someday must—programmers writing code for both environments will occasionally get bitten by incompatibilities. Issues like memory sharing, calling a Win16 library from a Win32 program (or vice-versa), and the different ways DLLs get handled will get in the way of moving code easily between Win16 and Win32. It's also more complex because you'll want to test your code on multiple operating systems, and perhaps on multiple hardware platforms.

Greater complexity isn't all bad, however, since the new Win32-aware systems add features and capabilities that help more than they get in the way. Features like memory mapped file i/o, thread local storage, and structured exception handling help simplify the software development process. New capabilities, like better system swap tuning and larger GDI and USER heap areas, are largely invisible yet represent greater system capabilities, and therefore lower the risk of running out of critical system resources.

From the start, Windows was built with the more advanced chips in mind. The architect of memory management in Windows 1.x was Steve Wood, a former Yale graduate student who started working for Microsoft in June 1983. He laid the foundation for Windows' memory management, which he modeled after the protected mode of the Intel 80286 processor. In those days, Microsoft was contemplating a successor to DOS, and planned for Windows to run with the new operating system. Of course, today we know that Windows NT is that operating system. It gives Windows programmers a choice of creating 16-bit or 32-bit Windows application programs. As of this writing, a successor to Windows 3.1—code named CHICAGO—is scheduled for delivery by the end of 1994. While still under development, this system promises mass-market support for the Win32 API while still supporting the currently popular base of Win16 applications.

Each subsequent version of Windows built on the original design to improve memory use. The architect of Windows' memory management for Windows 2.x and 3.x, David Weise, was also one of the designers of the EMS 4.0 Memory Specification. This allowed him to build EMS support into Windows 2.x and to continue that support in Real-Mode Windows 3.0. This latest version of Windows has a flexible approach to memory use that allows it to push the limits of whatever processor it finds itself running with.

In this chapter, I'm going to discuss how the various Windows systems manage memory—that is, I'm going to provide an *operating system* perspective on memory management. If you're in a hurry to see how *applications* manage memory, I suggest you skip this chapter and go directly to Chapter 18, which describes the memory choices available in both Win16 and Win32 environments. What follows, then, is background material for fully understanding how the various Windows systems manage memory.

Since Windows 3.x today still represents the current mainstream system, I'm going to start with a look at the segmented memory support provided by Win16 systems. As you probably know, the Windows 3.x systems support three memory modes: Real, Standard, and 386-Enhanced Mode. These represent roughly the native capabilities of the 8088, 80286 and 80386 processors. Even though support for Real Mode went away with Windows 3.1, Windows itself was born in Real Mode so I'll cover it to give you an historical perspective on where Windows has been.

The flat address space of Win32 relieves programmers of the worry of segmented addressing. In my discussion of this system, then, I'll focus on issues that might get in the way of porting Win16 code to the Win32 API, and describe new features and capabilities provided by these new systems. Let's start, then, with a look at system memory management under the Win16 API.

Win16 System Memory Management

To truly understand Win16 memory management, you need to understand the operation of the Intel-86 family of processors. While Win16 applications run on non-Intel processors, thanks to emulation layers provided by companies like Insignia Systems, this API was built for this processor. In fact, when you look at the emulation software source code, you find that—register for register, feature for feature, quirk for quirk—the essence of the Intel processors has

been captured. This, then, is a description of how the native hardware works. I'll focus on the 8088, 80286, and 80386 processors, since these represent both significant milestones for this processor family, and Windows' own Real, Standard, and 386-Enhanced Modes.

The Physical Address Space

One important aspect worth considering with any microprocessor is the maximum amount of memory that it can access—that is, the size of its address space. One way to determine this is to count the number of memory addressing lines that connect the processor to system memory. That number raised to a power of 2 is the size of the address space. For example, the 8088 has 20 address lines, which translates into a 2^{20} or 1-megabyte (1,048,576 bytes) address space. With 24 address lines, the 80286 can address 2^{24} or 16 megabytes (16,777,216 bytes) of physical RAM. And finally the 80386, with its 32 address lines, can use up to 2^{32} or 4 gigabytes (4,294,967,296 bytes) of system memory.

Every byte of memory in the system has its own unique physical address, starting at zero on up to n–1 for a system with n bytes of memory. For example, the 8088 has a memory address range from 0 to 1,048,575. In this regard, the Intel-86 family of processors is like any other processor. The physical address allows the CPU to communicate with the memory addressing hardware. But this is not how software communicates an address to the CPU. Instead, to application software, the address space is only available through a segmented memory addressing scheme.

Segmented Memory

All members of the Intel-86 family use segmented memory addressing. It may help to understand this if you think about building addresses in the physical world. The Prime Minister of Great Britain, for example, lives at Number 10 Downing Street; the President of the United States lives at 1600 Pennsylvania Avenue. A two-part logical address gives each program the freedom to divide its address space into many small "streets" or **segments**, each of which can hold from one to 65,535 "houses" or *bytes*. And, if we may push the analogy further, this approach permits operating-system software to give each program its own "city"—that is, its own private address space.

To programmers unaccustomed to the Intel-86 family of processors, segmented addressing can be both confusing and frustrating. But it provides some benefits worth considering. For experienced DOS and OS/2 1.x programmers, segmented addressing will be very familiar, although you should pay attention to the particular way that Windows operates in this environment.

A key benefit of segmented addressing is software migration. This architecture was first selected by Intel to allow software to migrate from the older 8-bit 8080 processor to the first member of this family, the 8088. The continued adoption of this addressing scheme has allowed DOS to run on all members of the Intel-86 family when they run in real mode. It is also one of the reasons that DOS programs can run under the various Intel-86-based operating systems, like Windows, OS/2, and Unix. And finally, it gives properly written Windows programs a migration path from the earlier versions of Windows to the protected mode operation of Windows 3.x, and on into future versions.

From the point of view of software development, segmented addressing is helpful in program debugging. A program can be divided into multiple code and data segments to create "fire walls" between different parts of an application. Fire walls prevent bad memory references in one part of an application from contaminating the data in another part of the application, and therefore make programs easier to debug. In protected mode, the processor complains loudly when an invalid segment reference is made, or when a program tries to read or write beyond the end of a memory segment.

And finally, a benefit of segmented programs is that they provide the operating system with hints about the **working sets** of a program. These hints can result in improved performance and lower memory requirements. A working set is a division of a program that performs a task or a set of tasks for the user. Since Windows incorporates an overlay facility called **dynamic linking**, at any given moment only *part* of a program has to be loaded into memory (see Chapter 19 for details on dynamic linking). If each working set in a program is a cleanly defined set of code segments, memory use is optimized. In a low-memory situation, Windows discards code segments from the current working set *last*. In this way, a program with well-defined working sets—what Windows programmers call "well-tuned"—will have lower memory requirements than the same program that hasn't been tuned. The latter program will slow down in a low-memory situation, since Windows will have to continually reread previously discarded code segments from disk: a situation commonly called **disk-thrashing**.

The Logical Address

While a CPU uses a physical address to read and write in physical memory, programmers use a higher level abstraction called a **logical address**. It's the job of the CPU to translate logical addresses into physical addresses to access memory locations in the physical address space. This is illustrated in Figure 17.1.

The translation process that takes place in the CPU might be very simple or very involved, depending on the current operating mode of the CPU. In **real mode**, for example, simple bit shifting and addition are involved. In the various **protected modes**, however, the CPU uses a lookup table to determine how to map a logical address into a physical address. This lookup table allows the operating system to move memory objects so that it can minimize fragmentation of physical memory. The operating system can even play tricks like writing memory to disk to implement virtual memory. If you are familiar with the operation of OS/2 version 1.x, you know that its virtual memory manager writes segments to disk. And finally, the higher-end 80386 and 80486 chips have special hardware that, when enabled, provides an additional level of indirection that divides memory into 4K pages. This paging mechanism is particularly useful in creating a very efficient virtual memory system, which is how the Windows memory manager implements virtual memory in 386 Enhanced Mode.

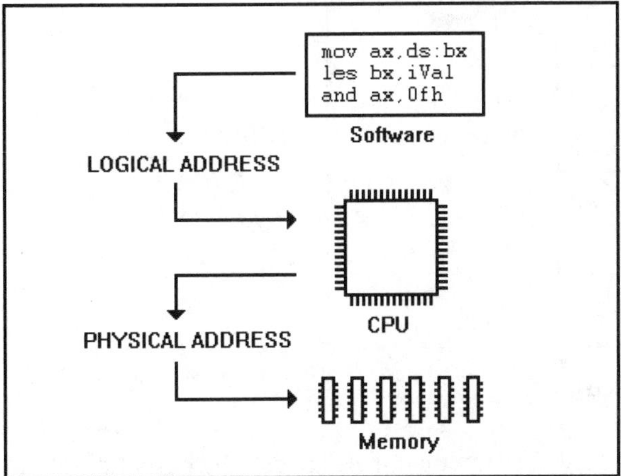

Figure 17.1 The Translation of a logical address to a physical address

In a moment, we're going to take a close look at each of the operating modes that Windows uses. But first, let's look at the pieces that make up a logical address. Every processor in the Intel-86 family uses a two-part logical address, made up of a **segment identifier** and an **offset**.

The segment identifier specifies the segment of memory that we are interested in. The segment identifier is a 16-bit value that is the "street name" that we're working on. In the logical-to-physical address translation process, it answers the question "where in the world is the segment." The answer might be within the physical address space of the CPU, or, in a virtual memory system, temporarily moved out to disk.

The second part of a logical address, the offset, indicates the distance within a particular segment. If the segment identifier is the street name, then the offset is the house number. Or, you can think of a segment as an array and the offset as an array index. In any event, both segment identifier and offset are used together to address specific bytes in system memory.

With this introduction to the basics of memory addressing for the Intel-86 family, let's take a look at how the Intel-86 family supports Windows' operating modes: real mode, standard mode, and 386-Enhanced Mode. To check the current mode, a user can look at the About box in the Program Manager. From a program, you can find this out by calling the `GetWinFlags` routine. (This call has been replaced in Win32 by `GetSystemInfo`.)

Real Mode Operation

While all members of the Intel-86 family can operate efficiently in real mode, it is usually associated with the oldest members of this family, the 8086 and 8088. With 20 address lines, these chips have a one-megabyte address space. To maintain complete compatibility,

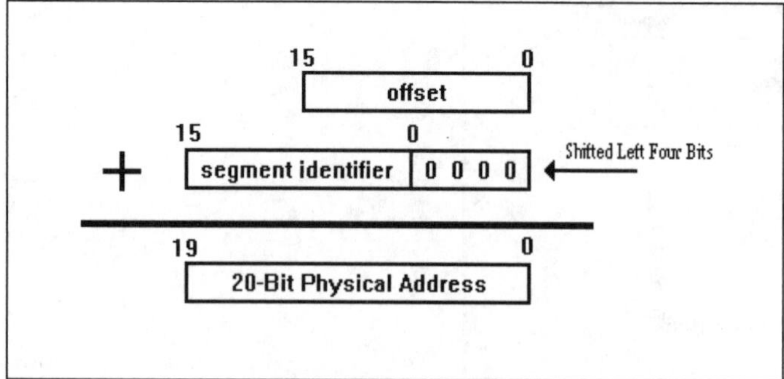

Figure 17.2 Real mode address calculation

the other processors in this family share this same address space when emulating real mode.

Real mode gets its name from the fact that a logical address is equivalent to the *real* physical address. To convert a logical address to the physical address, the CPU starts by shifting the 16-bit segment value left by four bits to create a 20-bit value. To this, it adds the 16-bit offset. Figure 17.2 illustrates this process.

Because the segment value is shifted left by four bits, which effectively multiplies it by 16, the smallest segment in real mode is 16 bytes long. Intel calls this a **paragraph**. Because of the way Windows operates in real mode, the granularity of segments is actually two paragraphs, or 32 bytes. Another way to visualize the logical-to-physical address conversion is shown in Figure 17.3.

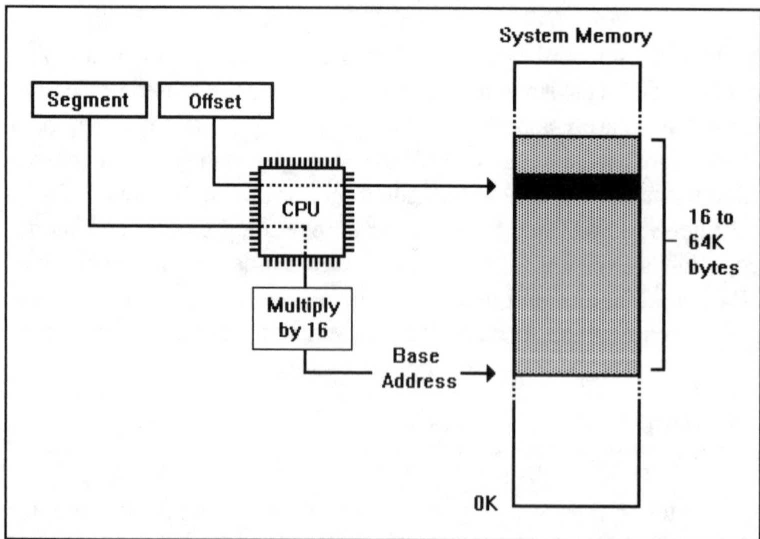

Figure 17.3 Another view of Real Mode address calculation

The Real Mode Address Space

Since Windows runs as an extension to DOS, it inherits the DOS environment. In memory terms, this means the one-megabyte address space of real mode, divided into several parts, as depicted in Figure 17.4.

In this figure, dotted lines are meant to suggest that the size of each piece can vary. DOS, its device drivers, and terminate-and-stay-resident (TSR) programs get first crack at the lowest end of memory. When Windows starts up, it requires a minimum of 200K or so for its device drivers, resident fonts, and the fixed code and data used by the Windows' core components: Kernel, User, and GDI. The space marked as "application area" is used for both Windows programs and for the discardable parts of Windows over and above the minimum set needed.

The well-publicized "640K limit" on DOS applications results from the design of the DOS address space, which reserves the area between 640K and 1024K for system uses: video adapter cards, ROM, and other uses. Since this memory area is occupied by hardware, Windows can't do anything to make it available for its own use, except in real mode, when it is used for EMS support.

However, on 80286 and 80386 CPUs, Windows gets an extra 64K of memory from the **High Memory Area** (HMA), located just above the one-megabyte address line, when an XMS (eXtended Memory Specification) driver is installed, such as HIMEM.SYS. This is the beginning of the extended memory area, which is usually only available in protected mode. But this memory is available in real mode through tricks that an XMS driver plays.

Above and beyond the HMA, real mode Windows is able to make other uses of extended memory. The SMARTDRV disk-caching device driver, for example, can be set up to optimize disk transfer operations. And the RAMDRIVE driver emulates a disk drive in RAM, to create fast temporary files. In addition, if the Windows Memory Manager finds

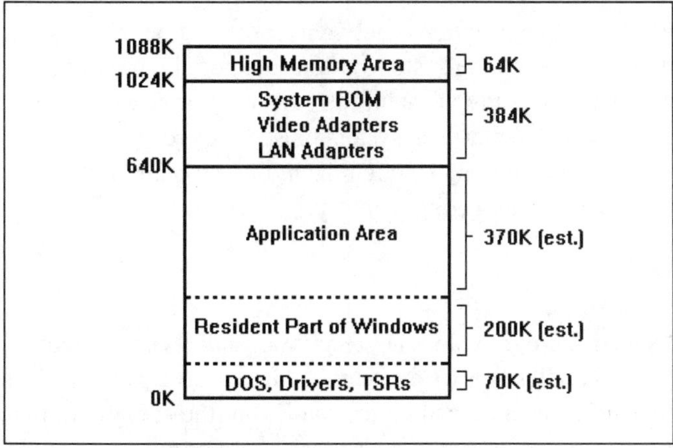

Figure 17.4 The real mode address space

extra, unused extended memory, it uses it to store code segments that it would otherwise discard. For this reason, if you are running in real mode, it's a good idea to leave about 256K or so of extended RAM unallocated. Windows will put this memory to good use, to provide better performance.

In real mode, the amount of memory available to a Windows program varies from 300K to 450K, depending on the amount of space taken up by DOS device drivers, and the availability of the high memory area. While this may seem a very small amount of memory, Windows' dynamic linking facility allows a program 10 times this size (or *larger*) to run. In such situations, the performance might be sluggish, which would encourage a hardware upgrade to accommodate one of Windows' more advanced operating modes. But, such a program *can* run.

Real Mode and Windows

Prior to Windows 3.0, all versions of Windows ran exclusively in real mode. Windows was limited to real mode for practical reasons: The installed base of microcomputers consisted of machines that could only be run in real mode—computers based on the Intel 8088 and 8086 CPUs. The memory manager was first built for real mode, but it was designed with the protected modes of the higher-end chips in mind, which is one of the reasons that Windows 3.0 is able to operate in all of its different modes.

Real mode addressing is fast and efficient, since there is very little overhead involved in translating logical addresses to physical addresses. To seasoned DOS programmers, it may seem like the most open, accessible way to work. And it is, until you try to create a multitasking operating system.

The job of an operating system is to manage and distribute resources. This is true whether the resource is processor time, disk space, or memory. The problem with real mode addressing is that it makes it very difficult for an operating system to manage memory. It's easy enough to allocate memory to a program—the operating system carves off a piece of system memory and assigns it to a program—but great care must be taken in the *way* memory is assigned. If a real mode operating system assigns memory by providing an address, it is almost impossible for the operating system to move that block of memory. But memory movement is precisely what an operating system must do in order to avoid the problems associated with memory fragmentation. To circumvent this problem, real mode Windows uses a handle-based approach to allocating memory.

Moveable Memory

When a block of memory is allocated, a program does not receive an addresss, but a handle that identifies the memory. Like the handles that we encountered in our discussion of GDI drawing objects, the value of a handle has no meaning to anyone but the subsystem that issued the handle. Like a claim check at a restaurant coat room, a program can trade the memory handle for a memory address whenever it needs to access the memory. At that time, Windows provides a pointer to the memory and locks the segment in place. All other times, the Windows Memory Manager is free to move and compact system memory to reduce fragmentation. Or, in coat room terms, your hat and coat can be moved to another room or even to another floor when the main coat room gets too crowded.

A handle-based, moveable memory system helps the Windows' memory manager to avoid memory loss due to fragmentation. But another mechanism is needed to deal with the problem of running out of physical memory: a situation sometimes referred to as "memory overcommit." In the world of mainframe computers, virtual memory systems solve this problem by copying portions of memory to disk. But this requires fast disks and, in the best of cases, hardware support for memory management. When the first version of Windows was being created, neither was available on the computers for which Windows was being written.

The first version of Windows was targeted to run on a 4.77-MHz 8088-based system with 256K of memory and two floppy diskette drives. When Microsoft started building Windows in 1983, hard disks were not widely used, and the 80286-based PC/AT had not yet been introduced. Given the low power of this target machine, even if the 8088 had any sophisticated memory management capabilities (which it doesn't), the two floppy drives of a minimally configured system did not provide fast enough response or a large enough capacity for implementing a virtual memory system. Instead, Microsoft implemented what some might call a "poor-man's" virtual memory system: dynamic linking. This facility depends on the second type of memory that we're going to discuss: discardable memory.

Discardable Memory

To help ease the memory crunch, the Windows memory manager can do more than just move memory around. If it needs to, it can **discard** objects from memory. A discarded object is purged from memory and is overwritten by whatever objects are allocated in its place. The most obvious type of discardable memory object is code. In most cases, code is not modified. So code that is not needed can be discarded, and reread when it is needed again.

Discardable, read-on-demand code is the basis of Windows' dynamic link mechanism. This is a very flexible mechanism that allows code to be removed from system memory when it is not used. In some ways, this mechanism has a lot in common with memory overlay facilities that are used by some DOS programs, and even in some very old mainframe systems. But the difference between Windows' dynamic linking mechanism and overlays is that dynamic linking is transparent to the application programmer. Overlays, on the other hand, typically must be designed with great care to avoid a deadlock—a situation in which the system must halt because it cannot read in the next overlay that it needs to continue operating properly. Windows' dynamic link mechanism does the work to ensure that deadlocks do not occur.

Besides code, another type of object is commonly placed into discardable memory objects: **resources**. To the Windows Memory Manager, a resource is a block of read-only data. When a resource is needed, it is read from disk into a discardable memory block. Later, when system memory gets crowded, the Memory Manager can discard resources to allow other objects to take their place.

There are quite a few kinds of resources in Windows. Some are used to support the user interface, like menu and dialog box templates, icons, and cursors. Others are used to store GDI objects like fonts and bitmaps. Beyond these, programmers can create custom resources for private read-only data if they wish. Like discardable code, discardable resources give the Windows Memory Manager the freedom to purge objects that might otherwise clog system memory.

We've looked at two types of memory objects that can be allocated in Windows: moveable and discardable. Both types allow a flexible, dynamic memory management system to be implemented on top of the relatively inflexible addressing of real mode. Windows supports a third type of memory, which application programmers should avoid, but which is important for the well-being and overall efficient operation of certain parts of the system: fixed memory.

Fixed Memory

While moveable and discardable memory objects are necessary for the Memory Manager to meet the demands of Windows' multitasking, there are situations that require memory that won't be moved or discarded. For example, an interrupt handler will require a fixed location in memory since it must always be ready to process an interrupt. For such uses, the Windows Memory Manager allows the allocation of segments that reside at a fixed location.

Of course, the use of fixed memory should be limited to special cases like device drivers. If a Windows program allocated fixed memory for regular uses, it would quickly use up this scarce resource and cause the system to slow down. When we talk about dynamic memory allocation in the next chapter, you'll see that a program *can* allocate as many fixed memory objects as it requires. But, before you do this, be sure that the other types of memory truly cannot satisfy your requirements.

EMS and Real Mode Windows

The second major revision of Windows, version 2.x, introduced support for EMS memory, which is memory that is made available according to the **expanded memory specification**. EMS describes a software interface for bank switching memory to increase the total amount of memory that DOS programs can access. Since real mode Windows ran on top of DOS, it took advantage of EMS. In fact, Windows programs can directly communicate with the expanded memory manager to allocate pages just like their DOS counterparts. But Windows programs don't have to do anything special to benefit from the presence of EMS memory. Instead, the Windows Memory Manager does all the work behind the scenes to increase total available system memory.

EMS does not increase the size of the hardware address space. Instead, it switches extra memory into unused parts of the DOS address space. In this way, EMS allows up to 32 additional megabytes of memory to be accessible in the DOS address space. At first glance, this seems to be enough memory to satisfy the needs of *any* DOS or Windows program. However, because its gobs of memory are not *simultaneously* accessible, EMS is only a limited solution to the memory crunch.

For example, in one configuration, a 64K memory window serves as the only access point for all of the memory on an EMS card. This memory window, which is also called the **EMS page frame**, is typically divided into pages that are 16K bytes. Thus, our 64K memory window consists of four 16K memory pages. If a program wanted to access more than 64K of EMS memory at a time, it would have to decide which EMS pages to use and which pages to ignore. With its tiny memory window, EMS cannot be a general-purpose memory management solution. But there is no denying that it has helped ease the memory shortage of real mode systems. Figure 17.5 illustrates the relationship of the real mode address space to EMS memory pages.

Windows' use of EMS is transparent to Windows programs. When a Windows program starts running, the program receives a private EMS bank. The program is guaranteed to have private use of this memory, free from competition with other programs. As Windows' multitasking switcher lets other programs run, it communicates with the EMS memory manager to map the correct EMS bank into the EMS page frame. The net result is reduced competition for memory between different programs, more total available memory, and better overall performance. The improved performance comes from postponing low-memory situations, when code must be discarded and reread from disk.

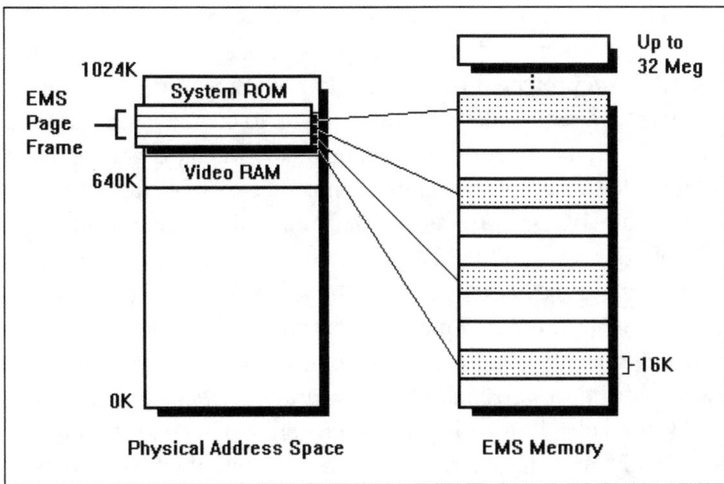

Figure 17.5 EMS lets real-mode programs peek at a larger address space

When running in real mode, Windows 3.0 allocates EMS memory for programs in the same way that Windows 2.x did. But in its other operating modes, Windows ignores EMS memory. That is, Windows does not use EMS memory for Windows programs in either standard mode or 386-Enhanced Mode. These other modes have access to extended memory, which doesn't suffer the same shortcomings of EMS memory. Extended memory, after all, is accessible without bank switching and has the added advantage of virtual memory support in 386-Enhanced Mode.

EMS is important in another way. It represents the first time that Windows' memory management supported the concept of a **private address space** for application programs. A private address space helps protect applications from the misbehavior of other applications, since a private address space can only be accessed by its owner. In Windows 3.0 protected mode, which we're going to discuss in a moment, the idea of a private address space is also starting to be implemented with the memory protection that is provided. A private, per address space became available starting with Windows NT. Before discussing this new operating system—and the other new Win32 features—let's look at the two other Win16 operating modes: Standard Mode and 386-Enhanced Mode.

Standard and Enhanced Mode

As we mentioned earlier, when Windows' memory management system was first being designed, it was with an eye toward someday moving Windows to the protected modes of the Intel-86 family. With Windows 3.0, this vision is realized in not one but *two* operating modes: Windows standard mode and 386-Enhanced Mode.

Standard mode gives Windows the benefits of protected mode on the 80286 and 80386 processors. In this mode, Windows programs get a physical address space that breaks the one-megabyte boundary of real mode and can be as large as 16 megabytes. Unlike the bank-switched memory of EMS, in protected mode the additional memory is **extended memory**—that is, the memory is a directly addressable extension to the real mode address space. Protected mode provides special memory management support that is not available in real mode. This support includes the enforcement of memory access rules that help preserve the integrity of each program, of each program's data, and of the system itself.

In 386-Enhanced Mode, Windows gets all the benefits of standard mode, plus an even larger address space. When running in this mode, don't be alarmed when the Program Manager tells you that the system has more *free* memory than you have RAM installed in your system. During the development of Windows, someone complained about this problem in a bug report, and was told simply: *"Welcome to the world of virtual memory!"*

The virtual memory of 386-Enhanced Mode is provided by an 80386 control program, WIN386.EXE, that works with the memory paging hardware built into the 80386 processor. In this mode, the address space can grow to a size that is up to four times the available physical memory[1]. For example, five megabytes of physical memory can support a virtual address space of 20 megabytes. And 16 megabytes of RAM can support a 64-megabyte virtual memory address space. These examples assume, of course, enough disk space to hold the memory pages that have been written to the page file.

Protected Mode

The term **protected mode** refers to a state of the processor in which certain rules are enforced when memory is addressed. These rules minimize the risk that a program will overwrite—either accidentally or intentionally—memory that doesn't belong to it. A program that violates these rules is subject to a serious penalty: It is terminated.

This harsh treatment contrasts sharply with the way a similar action is treated in real mode. For example, it's quite common for a DOS program to busy itself poking around the DOS data areas, installing private interrupt handlers, and in general making itself at home. Since DOS is a single-tasking system, such liberties are allowable since they don't interfere with the operation of other programs.

But Windows is a multitasking system, and even though programs can fiddle with any part of system memory in real mode Windows, this should be avoided. Programs should refrain from actions that might have adverse side effects for other programs. Such actions may cause a program to be incompatible with protected mode Windows.

And yet, an otherwise "well-behaved" program might mistakenly overwrite memory belonging to another program—or even memory that belongs to Windows itself. Without the memory protection of protected mode, such actions can lead to data corruption and even a system crash. Protected mode provides increased system integrity because of its memory protection features.

Memory Addressing in Protected Mode

When a program addresses memory in protected mode, it uses a two-part segment address just like a program in real mode, with a segment identifier and an offset. But in protected mode, the logical-to-physical addresss conversion is a simple operation. Instead, the processor relies on special tables called **descriptor tables** that are created and maintained by the operating system. There are two types of descriptor tables: **Global Descriptor Tables** (GDT) and **Local Descriptor Tables** (LDT). (A third type of descriptor table, the Interrupt Descriptor Table or IDT, is used to hold interrupt vectors. Its use is beyond this discussion.)

Intel designed its protected mode with a lot of flexibility in the way that descriptor tables can be used by different operating systems. In general, a descriptor table contains an array of segment information records, known as **segment descriptors**. In protected mode, the part of a memory address that we have been calling a "segment identifier" is referred to as

---

[1] Under Windows 3.1, the `[386Enh].PageOverCommit` SYSTEM.INI switch changes this multiplier from its default value of 4.

a **segment selector**. A segment selector contains an index into the array of descriptors that make up a descriptor table. It identifies the segment descriptor that provides the detail needed to access the segment data. Here is what a segment descriptor contains:

Segment Descriptor Field	*80286 Size*	*80386 Size*
Segment location (aka base address)	3 bytes	4 bytes
Segment size (aka segment limit)	2 bytes	2 1/2 bytes
Flags	1 byte	1 1/2 bytes
Unused	2 bytes	0 bytes
	8 bytes	8 bytes

When a program references a memory location, the CPU loads the segment descriptor into special registers for use in determining the physical address of the segment. The offset is added to the base address, to access the desired bytes of memory. This process is illustrated in Figure 17.6.

Actually, only 13 of the 16 bits in a segment value are used as a descriptor table index. As shown in Figure 17.7, the other three bits are two additional fields that play an important part in the addressing scheme and protection mechanism of protected mode. Bit 2 is a flag that indicates which descriptor table to use. This field allows an operating system to set up an address space of a program using two descriptor tables: one GDT and one LDT. The idea is that the GDT contains all the memory that is shared system wide. The LDT, on the other hand, represents a program's private address space.

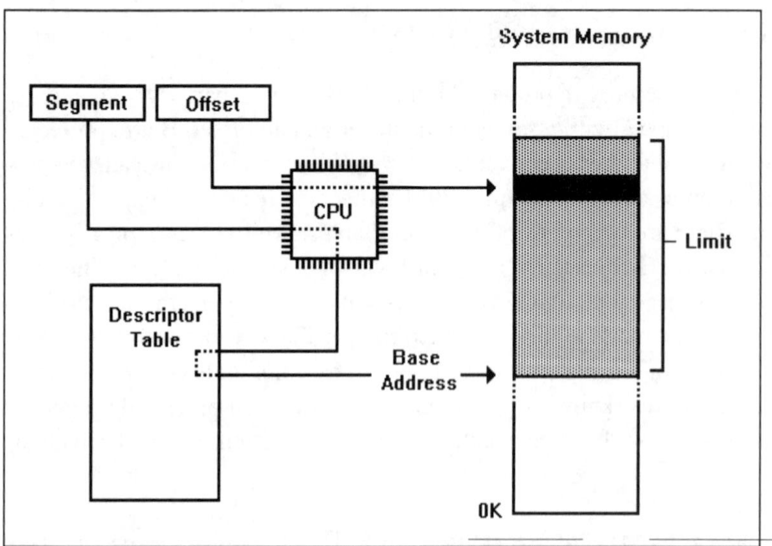

Figure 17.6 The segment value is an index into a descriptor table

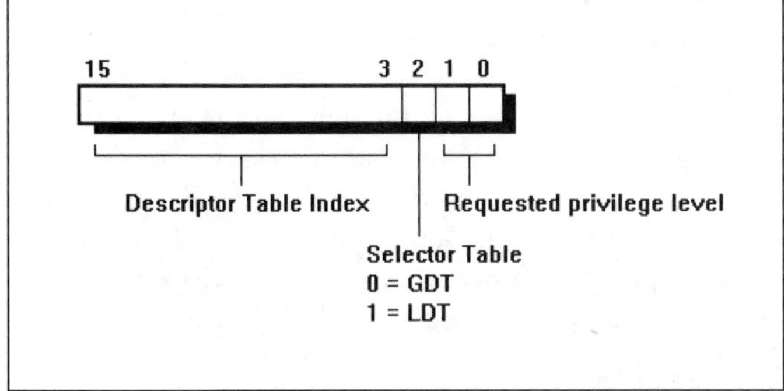

Figure 17.7 Structure of a protected mode selector

Bits 0 and 1 describe the segment's **requested privilege level** (**RPL**). These bits are set by operating-system software to create and enforce a memory protection scheme with four privilege levels, 0 to 3. Zero is the highest privilege level, and is reserved for the most trusted operating-system software. In Windows standard mode, the DOS Protected Mode Interface (DPMI) code has the highest privilege level, also known as ring 0.

The DPMI support code resides in DOSX.EXE (in standard mode) and in WIN386.EXE (in 386-Enhanced Mode). DPMI provides access to memory above the 640K line. Memory in the range 640K to 1024K is known as **upper memory blocks** (**UMB**s). The 64K from 1024K to 1088K is called the **high memory area** (**HMA**). And finally, memory allocated above the 1088K line is called **extended memory blocks** (**EMB**s). In 386-Enhanced Mode, the 80386 control program has ring 0 privileges.

In this architecture, memory protection is enforced in the following way. A memory error causes an exception to occur—that is, a CPU interrupt. In Windows, this results in the offending program being terminated with an error message like that shown in Figure 17.8. If you ran some of the earliest, prerelease versions of Windows 3.0, you'd see the word "Trayf"—Yiddish for "not kosher"—in this message. An apt description for an invalid memory reference.

Several types of errors cause this message to appear. For example, if a program tries to address memory using an invalid segment selector, the CPU catches the error and reports it to the operating system. Or, if a program tries to access memory beyond the end of a seg-

Figure 17.8 Windows' fatal error message

ment—that is, if the offset value is greater than the segment limit—the memory management hardware prevents the program from accessing memory that does not belong to it. It notifies the operating system that a program has violated the rules for the proper use of memory.

When such an error occurs and a debugger like Turbo Debugger is present, Windows refrains from displaying the error message. Instead, it passes control to the debugger. At that time, Turbo Debugger shows you where the error occurred. If it is within your program, you'll see which line of your source code caused the error. But if it was not in your code—for example, if the error occurred in a device driver or in one of Windows' libraries—the debugger shows you the machine instruction responsible for the error.

Windows and Protected Mode

When we described real mode memory management, we talked about the three types of memory objects: moveable, discardable, and fixed. An operating system needs all three types of objects to be able to do an effective job of managing system memory. For this reason, real mode Windows implements these types of memory objects in software, since there wasn't any hardware support for them.

When running in protected mode, things operate a little more efficiently because Windows has help from the processor's memory management hardware. Since programs don't have access to physical addresses as they do in real mode, the Windows Memory Manager can reorganize memory whenever it needs to. The only thing it has to worry about is updating the descriptor table to reflect the new location of a memory object. From a program's point of view, even if an object is moved in physical memory, it still appears at the same logical address, since the address references a descriptor table entry and not a physical address. In protected mode Windows, discardable objects behave in the same way that they do under real mode Windows. After all, discarding is a very efficient way to make more memory available when more memory is needed.

Fixed memory objects, which are the third type of memory object that Windows supports, are treated much the same as they are under real mode. But, just like moveable objects, a fixed object can move. The reason is that, even though the fixed object will maintain its logical address, Windows can move the object in the physical address space. Of course, certain operations require that fixed objects do not move in physical memory, such as an interrupt handler in a device driver DLL. For such uses, Windows allows segments to have a fixed logical address as well as a fixed physical address.

Windows Virtual Memory Support

All that we have said about protected mode operation applies equally to standard mode and to 386-Enhanced Mode. But there is an important capability that is only available in 386-Enhanced Mode: support for virtual memory.

Virtual memory support works alongside the protected mode addressing mechanism that we have been discussing. In other words, the segment value in an address is still used as an index into a descriptor table to determine the base address of a segment. And the offset is added to this base address to determine the exact bytes to be worked on.

The difference between regular protected mode and the virtual memory protected mode on the 80386 has to do with how this base + offset address is interpreted. In regular protected mode, it is interpreted as a physical memory address. But in 386-Enhanced Mode, the paging hardware built into the Intel 80386 processor is enabled, allowing addresses to be treated as virtual memory addresses. Figure 17.9 illustrates how this translation is done.

This figure shows how the segment and offset values are decoded into an address in the virtual address space. This address space is divided into 4K pages, each of which resides in either physical memory or in a page file on disk. When a reference is made to a location that resides on disk, a page fault is triggered, which is simply an internal CPU interrupt. At such times, the virtual memory manager reads the desired page from disk to provide access to the required code or data. The instruction that triggered the page fault is then restarted so that paging is entirely transparent to software.

The virtual memory manager packs segments into the virtual address space as tightly as it can. In other words, as suggested in Figure 17.9, the beginning and end of a segment do not have to coincide with a page boundary. The net result is that the virtual memory manager avoids wasting even a single byte. The paging hardware behaves in a traditional manner, so that part of a segment can be on disk while another part is in physical memory. As

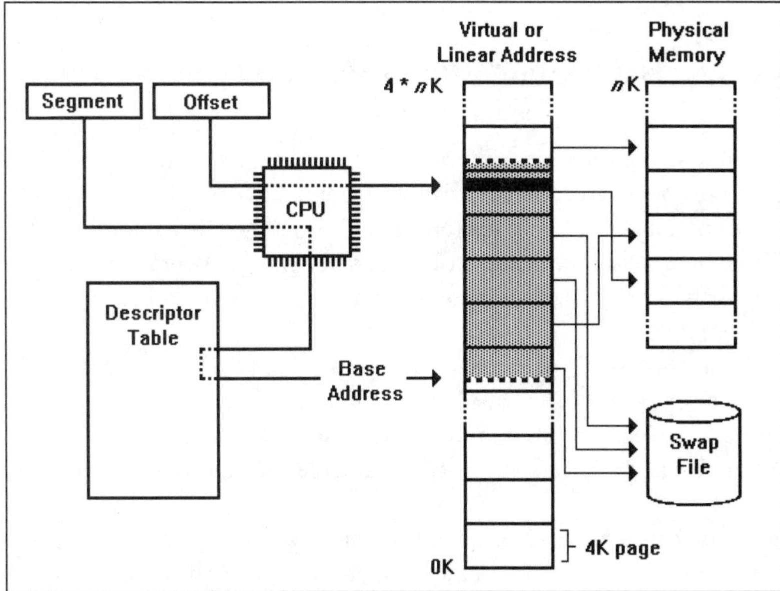

Figure 17.9 Virtual memory addressing

you might expect, the portions that are in physical memory do not have any special relationship with each other. Instead, the virtual memory manager can relocate a page of memory anywhere that is convenient.

Even when virtual memory is available, Windows can still discard segments when it starts running out of memory. However, in Windows 3.x, discarding only occurs when the Windows Memory Manager has used up the virtual address space. For this reason, the current implementation of 386-Enhanced Mode has a slight inefficiency built in: It *swaps* discardable code and resources instead of *discarding* them.

The reason this happens is that 386-Enhanced Mode uses two different memory managers: Windows' protected mode global heap manager and the 80386 control program's virtual memory manager. Windows' global heap manager allocates segments in Windows' address space. The 80386 control program provides virtual memory support, EMS emulation, and management of the 8086 virtual machines in which DOS programs run.

Since the lower-level 80386 control program provides paging support, it creates the net effect that *Enhanced Mode Windows prefers paging over discarding*. A mistake programmers sometimes make is to allocate pages based on the assumption that discarding occurs before paging, but the reverse is true. There are two reasons this approach was taken: First, Microsoft assumed (correctly) that it would be improving the bandwidth to the paging file—something that has been accomplished with 32-bit protected mode file access. Second, it costs more to reread and reproduce certain key discardable objects—like TrueType fonts—than to page them out to disk and back again. Given these tradeoffs, the only issue is that you be aware that the system works this way. Let's take a quick look at how the Windows' segment discarding mechanism works.

How Windows Selects a Segment for Discarding

In all of its operating modes, Windows can purge code and data segments that are marked as *discardable* when it runs out of free memory. Understanding how Windows chooses to discard one segment over another will help you understand Windows' behavior in a low-memory situation. This, in turn, will help you write programs that can operate effectively even when memory is scarce, either because many programs are running or because Windows is operating in real mode.

Windows discards segments on a *least recently used* basis. That is, when it needs to discard a segment, it picks a segment that has resided in system memory the longest without being used. To determine the least recently used segment, Windows maintains a table of discardable segments known as the **LRU list**. Every discardable code and data segment has an entry on the LRU list.

Every one-quarter second, on a hardware timer tick, Windows scans an access flag associated with each discardable code segment in the system. If the segment has been accessed since the last time the flag was checked, the segment gets moved to the bottom of the LRU list. That is, it gets promoted to the most recently used position in the table. Once a segment has been promoted, the access flag gets cleared so that it is ready to be tripped again if the segment is used again.

A drawback to this approach is that it isn't exact. In other words, it doesn't distinguish between a segment that was accessed 30 times and one that was accessed just once. But this approach was chosen because it is fast.

The access flags for discardable code segments reside in different places depending on whether the system is running in real or protected mode. In real mode, the Windows Memory Manager supports a data structure called a **module database** for every program and dynamic link library (we'll take a closer look at this data structure later in this chapter). The access flags are stored as an array of bytes in the module database, with one byte per discardable code segment.

In protected mode, the Intel-86 family provides support for an access flag in hardware. To be more precise, the access flag is a one-bit field of the segment descriptor in the descriptor tables (in the LDT). The memory management hardware automatically sets this bit when a segment has been accessed. Windows checks this bit when it scans all discardable segments to update the LRU list.

Data segments are treated a little differently, but the idea is the same. Windows doesn't keep an access flag for data segments. Instead, the LRU list is automatically updated by the locking and unlocking mechanism that is used to access discardable data objects. After all, a segment must be locked to access it. Then, when it is unlocked, the segment gets automatically promoted to the bottom of the LRU list, to make it the most recently used segment.

You might find yourself working on an application that doesn't work well with the "least recently used" discarding algorithm. Consider, for example, a database program that walks a circular linked list of data segments. As it makes the round of these segments, the very next segment that the program wants to use will also be the least recently used and therefore the one most likely to be discarded. In such cases, there are Windows library routines that can be used to directly modify the LRU tables: **`GlobalLRUNewest`**, which makes a segment the least likely to be discarded, and **`GlobalLRUOldest`**, which makes a segment the most likely to be discarded.

The LRU mechanism is largely transparent to Windows programs running in protected mode. In real mode, if you run the SYMDEB debugger, you might run across a single machine instruction that is added to help update the LRU list. This instruction is embedded in a piece of dynamic link code called a **thunk**, which we discuss in more detail in Chapter 19:

```
SAR  CS:[xxxx], 1
```

This *shift arithmetic right* instruction trips the access byte of a discardable code segment. Segments that are fixed or that are not present have a value of `FFh`. Segments that haven't been accessed since the last LRU timer tick have a value of `01h`. This instruction leaves the `FFh` value unchanged, while it changes the value of `01h` to `00h`. The bytes that are modified by this instruction are scanned by Windows as it updates the LRU list.

Now that we've looked at the way that Windows manages memory, let's take a look at the data objects that Windows itself allocates. In this chapter, we're going to focus on the data objects that the Windows KERNEL allocates. In the next chapter, when we discuss application memory use, we'll look at the memory used by Windows' other two core components: USER.EXE and GDI.EXE.

The Win16 KERNEL's Private Memory Use

When Windows' three main components are doing work for Windows programs, they consume memory. For the most part, a Windows programmer doesn't have to know how this memory is consumed. But it can help if you're interested in knowing what makes Windows tick. Also, there are certain system limits that you will understand only when you know how Windows uses memory.

KERNEL Data Objects

The KERNEL is responsible for dynamic linking, memory management, and interacting with DOS when Windows programs require DOS system services. Although there are many tiny data structures tucked away throughout the system that the KERNEL uses, we're going to limit our discussion to three of the most important: the Burgermaster, the task database, and the module databases. In protected mode, the Burgermaster goes away because its job is taken over by the protected mode descriptor tables and other internal data structures.

The Burgermaster

The Burgermaster gets its name from a fast-food restaurant that is next door to the building where Windows was first developed. In those days, two numbers were programmed into the telephone auto-dialer at Microsoft; one was the number of the take-out service at Burgermaster. (The other was the number of the athletic club to which Microsoft employees were given memberships.) This object was named in honor of this restaurant, because the members of the development team that worked on the KERNEL ate lunch at Burgermaster almost every day.

The Burgermaster is the master memory handle table for moveable and discardable objects in Windows. In other words, like the descriptor tables in protected mode, the Burgermaster maintains the physical addresses of moveable memory objects. When a program needs to get the address of such a segment, it makes a call to one of several Windows library routines, which look it up in the Burgermaster.

The Task Database

A Task Database (or TDB) is created for every instance of every program that runs in Windows. For example, when a single copy of CLOCK is running, there is a single TDB. A TDB always sits in a fixed segment and contains pointers to all of the things that make an instance of a program unique. Here is a partial list of some of the things that are stored in the TDB:

TDB Field	*Comment*
Array of `MakeProcInstance` thunks	Created by `MakeProcInstance` routine for use by dialog box procedures, and other "call-back" procedures, but *not* for window procedures.
Current MS-DOS disk directory	On a task switch, Windows sets up the current disk and directory for the active program.
EMS allocation data	Real mode only.
Application message queue	Keeps private messages that have been posted to a program (using the `PostMessage` routine).
Module database handle	Memory object that contains directory of objects in the module's .EXE or .DLL file.
Private interrupt vector table	Contains the private interrupts that a program has installed. Only a small set can be installed, including interrupts 0, 2, 4, 6, 7. These deal with errors in arithmetic functions. Can be changed by calling interrupt `21h` (DOS services), function number `25h`.
Pointer to DOS program database	Also known as the DOS Program Segment Prefix or PSP. Windows provides a copy of this data structure for each Windows program that runs. A program can get the address of this by calling `GetCurrentPDB`.
Task switch save area	Saves CPU registers between task switches.

This list is not complete, nor is this the order of the actual TDB. The contents of the TDB are not publicly documented, which means it can change in a future version. But it's included here to give you an idea of the type of data that Windows saves for every instance of every program. For example, from the list you can see that Windows keeps track of the current disk and directory for each program. A program can freely change these and not be worried about any adverse effects on other programs. Also, in case you wondered where the application's private message queue lives, it lives in the TDB. Notice that the TDB has a private interrupt vector table. If you want to trap the interrupts that are generated when certain arithmetic errors occur, you can install your own interrupt handler. For example, interrupt vector 0 is issued when a divided-by-zero error occurs. Programs that don't handle those interrupts themselves are terminated when such errors occur.

Windows always creates one TDB per instance of every program that runs. When an instance of a program terminates, the TDB is removed from memory. Knowing this, you should check that your Windows programs terminate properly. How? It's easy. Run any of the various memory viewer programs, and check for unexpected objects labeled "Task Database" when you think your program should have terminated. If you find such objects, you'll know that your program has not exited properly.

The Module Database

There is an entry in the TDB that points to another data object that the KERNEL uses: the module database. The module database contains an abbreviated version of the header to an .EXE file, known more simply as an EXE header. Borland C++ version 4.0 comes equipped with a utility called TDUMP.EXE that, among its other capabilities, will read the header of an executable file and tell you more about its contents.

Windows uses the module database whenever it needs to load anything from an executable file. This includes code, resources, and data. When we discuss dynamic linking in Chapter 19, you'll see that Windows sets up tiny code fragments called **thunks** to make dynamic linking work. In real mode, thunks allow code to be discarded and moved with a minimum of overhead. The module database is basically a directory of segments that can be read from an executable file.

Programs have module databases, but so do dynamic link libraries. If you run a memory viewer program, you'll notice that KERNEL, USER, and GDI each have a module database. There is even a module database for fonts, which are simply dynamic link libraries that have no code.

Win32 System Memory Management

The Win16 API—and its segmented memory architecture—represent Windows' ties to the Intel-86 architecture and to MS-DOS. The Win32 API, on the other hand, represents Windows' portable future. When it ships, CHICAGO promises to bring the Win32 API to the mainstream. While prerelease information on CHICAGO is available, unreleased products have a habit of changing—sometimes drastically—before they get shipped. Therefore, this discussion will focus on the Win32 operating system that has shipped—Windows NT.

Win32 represents freedom from the segmented memory addressing of the 16-bit Intel processors. Things really get interesting in the way this particular API is implemented. Under Win32s, for example, the memory behavior reflects that of the underlying Windows 3.1 operating system components. Windows NT, which represents a mainframe operating system running on a microprocessor system, is where the flat address space of Win32 can really shine.

Windows NT Supported Processors

While researching an article on Windows NT memory management for the *Microsoft Systems Journal*[2], I spoke with Lou Perazzoli, architect of the Windows NT virtual memory manager. In designing the memory management scheme, his group studied currently available 32-bit processors to help make Windows NT portable. They did a good job, and here is a list of the processor platforms that currently support Windows NT:

- Intel x-86 (32-bit 80386 and greater)
- MIPS R4000
- DEC Alpha
- Motorola PowerPC
- Intergraph

This list will grow over time because Windows NT—with its 5 millions lines of C / C++ code—was built to be portable to other 32-bit processor platforms.

Private, Per-Process Address Space

A key architectural component of Windows NT is support for a private, per-process address space. This represents a dramatic change from Windows 3.x, in which a single address space is shared by all Windows programs, Windows DLLs, Windows system libraries, and the Windows device drivers. Since this represents a change from Windows 3.x, there can be porting problems while moving Win16 code to the Win32 API.

In particular, if a group of Win16 applications share memory by simply sharing pointers—something that works under Windows 3.x—this practice will cause the Win32 versions of these programs to fail under Windows NT. This practice, incidentally, is one that Microsoft has continually warned against. Nevertheless, quite a few Win16 programs share memory in this nonportable manner. Since Microsoft has pledged great Win16 support in all future Windows systems, it will be difficult to grant Win16 programs their own, private address space. And in fact under Windows NT, all Win16 programs do in fact share a single, common address space.

A private, per process address space makes memory sharing more difficult. But it also makes the system more secure. Processes are more robust, since one process can't easily

---

[2] "An Introduction to Windows NT Memory Management Fundamentals", *Microsoft Systems Journal*, July/Aug, 1992.

write over the memory of another process. A private address space also enhances system security, since one process cannot read the memory belonging to another process.

The 32-bit addresses under Windows NT translate into a 4-gigabyte address space. Within this address space, the top 2 gigabytes are reserved for the system use. The bottom two gigabytes are the per-process address space for normal application programs and dynamic link libraries.

Under traditional operating systems, "memory management" means the allocation of memory. This is true under Windows NT. An additional meaning to this term is that applications can manage another system resource, namely the **virtual address space**. For example, managing the allocation of memory might mean giving a program access to some random chunk, say 2 megabytes. Managing the virtual address space means that an application might ask that a contiguous range of memory addresses be reserved. For example, a program that wanted to read in various pages from a 100 megabyte file could set aside a range of contiguous addresses without asking the system to commit any RAM or page file space. Then, as specific pages are needed in this range, the application can request the commitment of actual system memory. Setting aside a range of addresses is performed through a Windows NT specific feature known as **virtual address descriptors**.

Virtual Address Descriptors

When memory is allocated, the allocation granularity is one page—which might mean 4K on an Intel or MIPS platform, and 8K on the DEC Alpha. Because different processors use different page sizes, one challenge to the implementors of the virtual memory manager was handling this difference. The mechanism that hides these differences is the **VAD database**, which consists of a collection of virtual address descriptors for each process address space.

A virtual address descriptor (VAD) describes the attributes for a range of virtual addresses. For example, a range of addresses might be marked read-only, read/write, copy-on-write, or no access. Virtual addresses are clumped together in units called a **region**, which has arbitrarily been defined to be 64K bytes. This number allows an even mapping from the 4K, 8K and 16K page size on different 32-bit processors.

The application's address space is bound by two 64K areas—both no man's land—to help trap out of range pointers. At the bottom of the address space, it helps catch null pointers. Any access to either region results in a processor exception, thus helping detect invalid pointers.

Paged Virtual Memory

While the granularity of the address space is 64K, the granularity of actual allocation is one page. While always a power of 2, the page size varies from one processor to another. On the Intel x-86, for example, a 4K page is used. The MIPS R4000 allows an operating system to select the page size—so that a page could be 4K, 16K, 64K on up to 16 megabytes. For compatibility with Intel processors, Windows NT uses a 4K page when running on

MIPS processors. The DEC Alpha, by contrast, has an 8K page that Windows NT—because of its 64K region granularity—is able to honor with a minimum of overhead.

When a page of physical memory gets allocated, it is either a **private page** or a **shareable page**. Private pages can only be accessed from within a process, and are typically used for read/write data. Shareable pages, on the other hand, are used for interprocess memory sharing. One common use of shareable pages is for code. As you might expect, when two copies of a program are running at the same time, they share the same set of physical pages for the program's code. Each would then have its own private pages for read/write data.

Two processes can share a common data area by allocating a shareable data page. By itself, this is not a terribly exciting proposition. An interesting twist added by Windows NT, however, is that *the address of the page might be different in the two processes.* For example, one process might map a shared page into its address space at the five-megabyte line. A second process sharing the same page could map the same page at the six-megabyte line. A third process could map it at yet another address. This is all perfectly normal, and allows the address space of each process to be completely flexible for the use of that process.

From the point of view of data sharing, this means that you should not expect to be able to share memory between processes by sharing memory addresses. Any address within a data block must be a relative reference—perhaps to the start of the shared block—and *not* an absolute reference within any process's address space. If you are sharing data in a Win16 program today, make sure you follow this guideline to avoid porting problems when you go to Win32.

In spite of all these differences, a 32-bit pointer under Windows NT looks just like a Win16 `far` pointer. The key difference lies in what happens when you start doing pointer arithmetic. Under Win16, for example, adding 64K to a `far` pointer causes it to wrap around to the beginning of the segment. A similar Win32 pointer, on the other hand, doesn't experience this kind of deja-vu with pointer arithmetic.

In this chapter, I have looked at the way that Windows 3.x takes advantages of the memory capabilities of the entire Intel-86 family of processors. Also, I've touched on some of the wonders that Windows NT brings to a wide range of 32-bit processors. In the next chapter, I'm going to look at application-specific memory use issues. In particular, I'm going to describe all the types of memory available in both APIs.

18

Memory, Part II: Application Memory Use

The amount of time and effort you put into thinking about memory use depends on your memory budget. If your target system is a fully loaded Windows NT system, you probably don't think about it much. You'll use local variables within function, maybe a few global variables where you can't avoid them, and rely on the C++ `new` operator to dynamically allocate memory. But if your memory use budget is a 4 megabyte Windows 3.x or Chicago system—the target for which Microsoft is building Chicago itself—you'll want to know about every trick in this book for making optimal use of system memory.

Windows was born when memory was very scarce. As I discussed in the last chapter, its Real Mode roots meant that it had a one-megabyte address space for all the things it needed. While poor in available memory, Windows provides a rich set of choices to application developers. To the Win16 programmer trying to shoehorn two megabytes of code into a 300K working set of Windows 1.x, this was an absolute necessity. For the sake of compatibility, as you might expect, these choices are also available to Win32 programmers developing for Windows NT and Chicago. As memory becomes less and less scarce, this rich set of tools may be less and less necessary.

In designing the approach that your programs will take in using memory, there are a number of basic issues to deal with. These include allocation, visibility, lifetime, and overhead. As we look at the different types of memory available to an OWL Windows program, we'll consider each of these issues and weigh its importance. Table 18.1 summarizes these issues for the many types of memory available to a Windows application.

The issue of **allocation** involves *who* allocates a given piece of memory. The compiler allocates some memory for you, which is the case with static and automatic variables. In other cases, you must explicitly allocate memory. For example, to allocate memory using

Table 18.1 A Summary of Application Memory Use

Memory Type	*Allocation*	*Visibility*	*Lifetime*	*Overhead*
Local variable	Compiler	A function	A function	None
Global variable	Compiler	A program	A program	None
Local Heap[a]	**LocalAlloc()**	A program	A program	4 or 6 bytes
Global Heap[b]	**GlobalAlloc()**	Program/System	Program/System	24 bytes
Private pages[c]	**VirtualAlloc()**	Win32 process	Win32 process	80 bytes
Shared pages[d]	**MapViewOfFile()**	Multi-process	Multi-process	80 bytes
Private Heap[e]	**HeapAlloc()**	Win32 process	Win32 process	32 bytes
Resource Data	Resource Manager	Program/System	Owner	24 bytes
GDI Objects	GDI routines	System in Win16, Process in Win32	System in Win16, Process in Win32	Varies
USER Objects	USER routines	System	Owner	Varies
Thread Local Storage	**TlsAlloc()**	Thread	Thread	The TEB, 64 bytes

[a] This is the Win16 subsegment allocator. Under Win32, it's implemented with calls to the Win32 heap allocation routine, HeapAlloc.

[b] This is the Win16 segment allocator. Under Win32, it's implemented with calls to the Win32 heap allocation routine, HeapAlloc.

[c] This Win32 allocator allocates private pages when used with the MEM_COMMIT flag, and allocates address space when used with the MEM_RESERVE flag.

[d] This Win32 allocator provides two capabilities: It creates a connection between a memory mapped file and a range of addresses. When mapping to an invalid file handle (-1), it maps to the system page file, and is the mechanism for interprocess shared pages.

[e] This is the primary Win32 heap allocator.

one of Windows' dynamic memory allocation packages, you make explicit calls to either **`LocalAlloc`** or **`GlobalAlloc`**. In some cases, memory allocation is a side effect of creating certain types of system objects. For example, when you create a device context (DC) in GDI, objects are allocated in GDI's local heap space.

The issue of **visibility** has to do with who can see the memory. Some objects have a very limited visibility, like automatic variables declared inside a function. Others have a visibility that is system wide, like GDI drawing objects and certain objects allocated from the global heap. Such objects can be shared between programs, but be careful to clean up such objects when you are done. Windows doesn't automatically clean them up for you.

The issue of **lifetime** describes how memory is reclaimed. With some objects, memory is reclaimed automatically when a program terminates. This is the case with static and automatic variables, as well as objects allocated from the local heap. Other objects must be explicitly deallocated to free up this memory for other uses. In general, it is a good programming practice to free memory when it is no longer needed, whether or not that memory will be automatically freed.

And finally, the issue of **overhead** describes what extra costs are associated with allocating a piece of memory beyond the actual bytes that are used. This issue is especially important when deciding how to use dynamic memory allocation—allocation from the local and global heaps. For example, every global memory object has an overhead of 24 bytes *minimum*. If you are in the habit of allocating hundreds of tiny (12-byte) objects, you'll want to think again before putting them into a global memory object.

Let's begin by looking at each of the different types of memory available. We'll then discuss issues relating to the allocation of memory from the global heap—the most flexible and useful type of dynamic memory allocation. We'll look at how code structure affects memory use, then look at allocation from the local heap, the use of custom resources, and some tricks that will allow you to perform local heap allocation in a dynamically allocated segment. We'll provide you with a lot of sample code, so you can examine in detail all of the pieces that are necessary to make each type of memory work properly.

Overview of Application Memory Use

In the last chapter, we described how the Intel-86 family of processors uses a segmented addressing scheme. Since Windows is built on top of this architecture, Windows programmers should keep in mind that the segment is the fundamental unit of memory. This being the case, our discussion of memory is organized in terms of segments. We'll start with the default data segment, which holds three types of data objects: static variables, automatic variables, and the local heap.

The Win16 Default Data Segment

Windows works best with programs that have a *single* data segment. With the Microsoft compiler, this means using the small or medium memory models. The reason is that the other memory models automatically create two (or more) data segments. With the Borland C++ compiler, you can use any of the memory models. You can even use the large memory model (which we have done throughout this book), as long as you avoid creating too much static data. Doing so will require the compiler and the linker to allocate additional data segments. A single data segment is best because of the way that Windows' dynamic linking works. As we'll describe in Chapter 19, when we describe the dynamic link mechanism, Windows tries to fix up the data segment register when a Windows library routine calls a function in your program. This call-back mechanism is used for window procedures, and therefore is fundamental to the way that Windows works. For each program, Windows internally stores only *one* data segment value.

Programs that *must* have more than one default data segment can do so. But such programs are subject to certain restrictions. For one thing, Windows will only allow one instance of your program to run at a time. While a single data segment might seem to be too small for real-world applications, you have a few alternatives (which are covered in detail in this chapter): First, you can store read-only data objects in a custom resource. Second, you can use dynamically allocated memory to handle most of your program's memory needs.

Every Windows application will have a default data segment. In some respects, a program's default data segment is just another segment in the global heap: The Windows loader allocates the segment from the global heap using the global heap allocation routine, `GlobalAlloc`. The segment can move and it can grow, just like any other segment.

In other respects, a default data segment is unique. Windows sets up the correct value in the DS (data segment) register when a message is delivered to a program. This means that applications can assume they will always have access to their most important data. We'll discuss the setup of the DS register in Chapter 19, when we delve into the code-related aspects of dynamic linking. The default data segment also contains an application's stack and a local heap that can be used for dynamic memory allocation.

A program's data segment is divided into four or five parts: a header, static data area, stack, local heap, and an optional atom table. Figure 18.1 shows a typical program's data segment, with each part labeled. For the sake of comparison, it's interesting to note that a dynamic link library's data segment may contain all of these same elements, except DLLs ordinarily do not have a stack. Instead, DLLs use the stack of the programs that call the library routines. Figure 18.2 shows a typical DLL data segment. Let's look at each element in a typical program's data segment, one at a time starting with the segment header.

Default Data Segment Header

The header is a 16-byte area that contains pointers used by the KERNEL to manage the local data segment. A Windows program should leave this area alone, since it is automat-

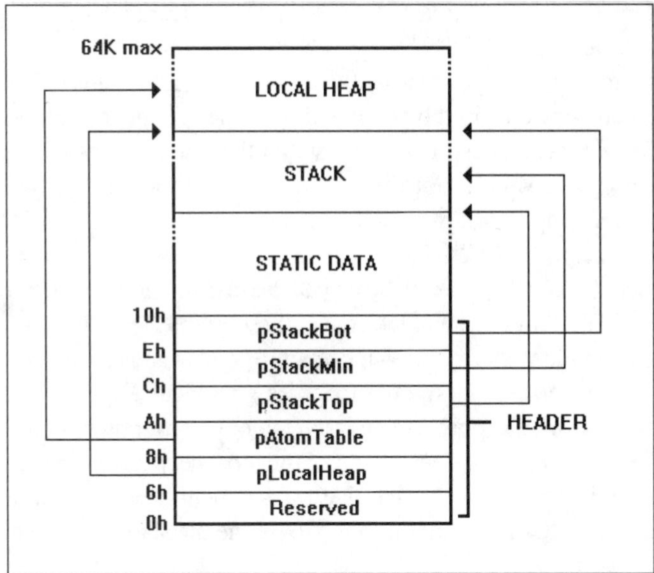

Figure 18.1 A typical program's local data segment

ically allocated at compile/link time and managed by the KERNEL at runtime. When allocating a local heap on a dynamically allocated segment, however, you'll need to set aside the first 16 bytes for use by the KERNEL. We'll show how this is done later in this chapter.

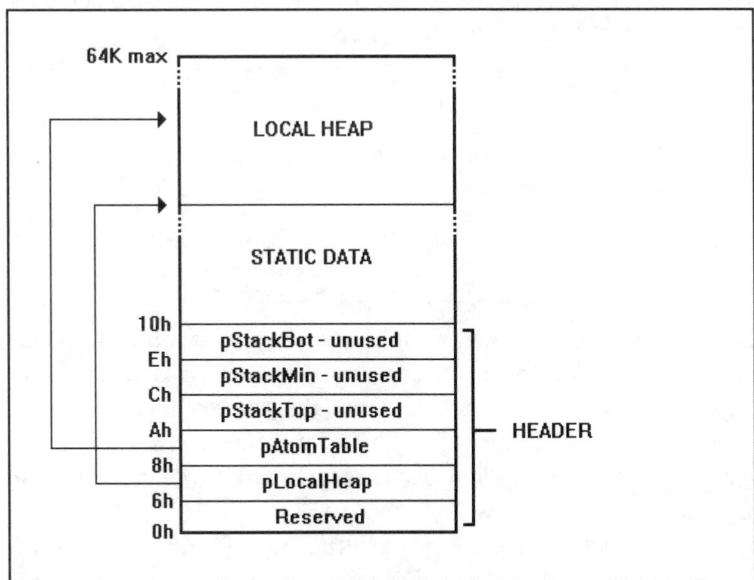

Figure 18.2 A typical dynamic link library's data segment

Other than that, our primary interest in this data area rests in what we can learn about Windows' management of a local data segment.

Of the five pointers in the segment header, by far and away the most important is the pointer to the local heap, **`pLocalHeap`**. It is used by the local heap management routines to find the local heap so that the local heap doesn't interfere with other data objects in the data segment. Your Windows program should not directly modify the local heap, but should instead call the various local heap routines—another subject we'll discuss later in this chapter.

Three of the pointers reference the stack: **`pStackBot`**, **`pStackMin`**, and **`pStackTop`**. When the debug version of Windows is installed, these three pointers are used to check for stack overflows. It's a good idea to test your Windows programs against this special version, since it will help you find errors that might otherwise go undetected.

The fifth and final pointer, **`pAtomTable`**, points to an atom table if a program has created one. Atom tables are created from memory allocated out of the local heap and are managed by the various atom management routines. Notice that the segment header doesn't have any pointer to the static data area. It's the compiler's job to define the static data area and generate the correct code to use it.

The Static Data Area

The static data area holds a program's "global" data. This includes all variables declared outside of functions, all variables declared with the **`static`** keyword, all static strings, and the static data allocated for use by the various runtime library routines.

In the following code fragment, four different objects are allocated in the static data area, and five are not. Can you identify the static data objects?

```
char *pch = "String of Characters";
int  i;

int PASCAL WinMain (HINSTANCE hInstance, HINSTANCE hPrevInstance,
                    LPSTR lpszCmdLine, int nCmdShow)
    {
    static int iCount;
    long       lValue;
    ...
```

As you might expect, the two variables defined outside any function—**`pch`** and **`i`**—are allocated in the static data area. So is **`iCount`**, which uses the **`static`** keyword. This declaration, since it's inside the bounds of a function, limits the **scope** of this variable to the `WndProc` function. In other words, **`iCount`** is only visible to code *inside* this function. But, as a static object, it has a lifetime as long as the program itself, which means that it resides in the static data area.

The fourth object placed in the static area is the string: "**`String of Characters`**." Because strings can take up quite a bit of space, you can reduce the size of the static data area by putting all strings into a string resource. When a string is needed, it can be loaded and used. When it is not needed, string resources can be discarded from memory to reduce the overall demand for system memory.

The static data area is also used to hold statically allocated **instances**. In the same way that we can define normal C data types as static data objects, you can define an instance of a C++ class. The instance is initialized at program initialization, by calling its constructor. To define such an instance, you define it outside the bounds of any function. For example, here's an example of allocating an instance of **TWindow** as a static instance:

```
TWindow SomeWindow;

int PASCAL WinMain (HINSTANCE hInstance, HINSTANCE hPrevInstance,
                    LPSTR lpszCmdLine, int nCmdShow)
    {
    SomeWindow.Attr.X = 10;
    ...
```

This may not make sense in terms of this specific class, but it shows how a C++ instance can be allocated in the static data area.

The Stack

The stack is a dynamic data area that is managed for you through a high-level language like C or C++. Stacks are so central to software that the Intel processors have a set of registers that are dedicated to the use and maintenance of the stack area. These include the SS (stack segment) register, and the BP (base pointer) and SP (stack pointer) offset registers. Stack use is even built into the processor's hardware. When it makes a function call, the processor automatically pushes a return address on the stack. When returning from a function, a return address is automatically popped off the stack as the location of the next instruction to be executed.

The compiler stores three things on the stack: local variables, arguments passed to called functions, and return addresses. As you may recall, the `STACKSIZE` statement in the module definition (.DEF) file defines the amount of space reserved for the stack, with a minimum stack size of 5K. You'll want to understand how your program uses this stack, so that you can allocate the proper amount of stack space.

Variables declared inside a function that don't use the **static** keyword are local variables, such as the **lValue** variable in the code fragment we looked at a moment ago. Space on the stack for local variables is allocated when a function is called, and freed when returning from a function. If you are writing a program that allocates a lot of local variables, you may wish to use a higher STACKSIZE value to reflect the additional memory that is needed. A higher stack size should also be requested for programs that do a lot of recursive calling, since local variables are allocated for *each* call made into functions. The following boxed discussion provides some additional details on the use of the stack for the three basic stack objects.

The accompanying figure shows the relationship of the three main types of stack objects: arguments, return address, and local variables.

Also shown is the C call and the resulting assembly language instructions that support this stack structure. The **`push`** *instruction puts arguments on the stack for called functions. The* `call` *instruction places a return address on the stack, and passes control to the called function. Inside the called function, the compiler creates the code to adjust the base pointer, BP, and the stack pointer, SP, to access both the passed arguments and the local variables on the* ***stack frame****. Notice that the variable defined with the* ***static*** *keyword, j, is not allocated on the stack. Instead, as a static data object, it is allocated in the static data area.*

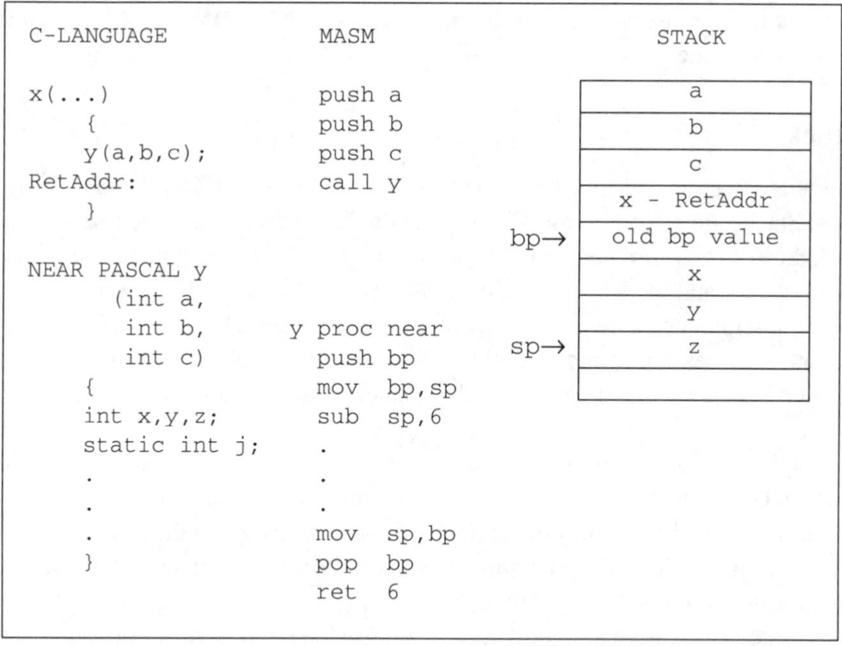

The BP, or base pointer, register is set up to allow arguments and the local variables to be referenced from a fixed location. If you run a debugger like the Turbo Debugger, you can see the machine language references to arguments as positive offsets from BP. Here is an assembly language instruction that references the third passed argument in our example:

```
MOV    AX, [BP+04]
```

Local variables are referenced as negative offsets from BP. For example, here is how the third local variable might be accessed:

```
MOV   AX, [BP-06]
```

Because the Pascal calling convention has been selected, the called function cleans up the stack. This is actually built into the return instruction, which is one reason that this calling convention creates smaller, faster code:

```
RET   6
```

If this seems somewhat esoteric and complex to you, don't worry too much. Fortunately, the details of stack management are mostly the concern of assembly language programmers and compiler writers. The compiler takes care of everything, so that you don't have to think about it. The important things to keep in mind are the three uses of the stack, so that you can be sure to adjust your stack size when you write a Windows program that uses either a lot of local variables or deeply nested recursive calls.

C++ class instances can also be allocated on the stack. In fact, every OWL program in this book has a **`WinMain`** function like this one:

```
int PASCAL WinMain (HINSTANCE hInstance, HINSTANCE hPrevInstance,
                    LPSTR  lpszCmdLine, int nCmdShow)
    {
    TMinApplication Min ("MIN", hInstance, hPrevInstance,
                         lpszCmdLine, nCmdShow);
    Min.Run();
    return Min.Status;
    }
```

In this example, **`Min`** refers to an instance of **`TMinApplication`** which is stored on the stack. The primary value of such stack data objects is their great convenience: Their life is the same as the life of the function. When we leave the function, the instance—along with any other stack data—gets cleaned up.

The Debug Version of Win16 Windows and Stack Checking

Under ordinary circumstances, a stack overflow will go unnoticed. Or, it will result in mysterious and untraceable problems with your program. To prevent this problem, you must test your programs under very special circumstances, since the normal stack checking is disabled under Windows. Here's what you need. First, you must compile your programs with stack checking *enabled*, which means compile *with* the `-N` switch. Next, you must have a special version of Windows installed on your system that is known as the **debug**

version. The debug version of Windows is created by copying a set of dynamic link library files from the Windows software development kit into the system subdirectory (\windows\system). The set of DLLs performs extra error checking. And finally, you need to have an extra monitor hooked up to your system. This allows you to receive debugging information (and to communicate with debuggers like Turbo Debugger) without disturbing the graphic display screen.

The Win16 Local Heap

Local heaps are one of two places from which programs can perform dynamic memory allocation (the other is the global heap). Local heaps are always set up inside a single data segment. A local heap is automatically set up for a program's use in the default data segment. In addition, a program can allocate other segments in which a local heap can be created. We'll describe how this is done later in this chapter.

Without requiring any special effort on your part, every program has one local heap, which resides at the end of the default data segment. The initial size of the heap depends on the value defined in the module definition (.DEF) file with the `HEAPSIZE` statement. The heap can grow beyond this size, though. And when it does, the segment that contains the local heap will grow as well. A local heap can continue to grow until its segment reaches a maximum size of 64K.

Programs allocate memory from a local heap using one of the 12 local heap management routines. You can easily tell one of these routines, since the name of each routine starts with the word "Local." For example, **`LocalAlloc`** is the name of the routine that allocates memory from a local heap. **`LocalFree`** releases memory that has been allocated in a local heap. Table 18.2 provides a complete list of the local heap management routines. Later in this chapter, we'll take a closer look at local heap management, and provide some more detail on the routines marked with `*`.

Table 18.2 Windows Local Heap Management Routines

Routine	Description
LocalAlloc *	Allocates memory from a local heap.
LocalCompact	Reorganizes a local heap.
LocalDiscard	Discards an unlocked, discardable object.
LocalFlags	Provides information about a specific memory object.
LocalFree *	Frees a local memory object.
LocalHandle	Provides the handle of a local memory object associated with a given memory address.
LocalInit *	Initializes a local heap.

Table 18.2 Windows Local Heap Management Routines *(Continued)*

LocalLock *	Increments the lock count on a local memory object, and returns its address.
LocalReAlloc *	Changes the size of a local memory object.
LocalShrink	Reorganizes a local heap and reduces the size of the heap (if possible) to the initial, starting size. If this routine is successful, it reduces the size of the data segment that contains the heap, so that the memory can be reclaimed by the global heap.
LocalSize	Returns the current size of a local memory object.
LocalUnlock *	Decrements the lock count on a local memory object.

In the preceding chapter, we described how three types of segments can be allocated on the global heap: moveable, discardable, and fixed. The local heap also supports these three types. Moveable objects can be allocated to help minimize memory fragmentation, and discardable objects can be allocated to give the local memory manager the freedom to purge unneeded objects when memory is low. By comparison, the standard runtime library routines only allocate fixed objects and do not support moveable or discardable objects. In this way, the local memory manager provides quite a bit more sophistication than the runtime library's **`malloc`** routine in allocating and managing a heap space.

To support moveable and discardable memory objects, the local heap manager provides a **memory handle** when it allocates a local memory object. Like the handles that we encountered in the context of GDI objects, a memory handle is simply an identifier that can be traded in to access the real object. When a memory handle is passed to the **`LocalLock`** routine, a memory pointer is provided. As we'll see later, this means that code like the following is required to access a local memory object:

```
HANDLE hMem;
PSTR   pstr;

/*  Allocate a 15 byte moveable object.   */
hMem = LocalAlloc (LMEM_MOVEABLE, 15);

/*  Lock the object, getting a pointer.   */
pstr = LocalLock (hMem);

lstrcpy (pstr, "Hello World");

/*  Unlock the object.  */
LocalUnlock (hMem);
```

In addition, when you create an OWL program in a small or medium model, dynamic instances are created on the local heap. In particular, when you create an instance with the `new` keyword, the small and medium model OWL libraries call the `malloc` routine. This call gets converted to a set of calls to the various local heap allocation routines. In compact and large models, on the other hand, dynamic instances are created as part of a subsegment allocation scheme built into OWL.

Later in this chapter, we'll provide you a full-blown example of a program that uses local heap allocation. Let's continue our tour of program memory management by looking at the last item in the default data segment, the atom table.

Atom Tables

Optionally, a program can create an atom table in its local data segment. An atom table provides a way to store and retrieve variable-length character strings. When an atom is created, a handle is issued that uniquely identifies the string. At two bytes, a handle is a small, fixed-size value that can easily and conveniently be placed into fixed-length data structures with a minimum of overhead. And atom tables are efficient, since duplicate requests create the same atom value. The USER module uses atoms to store the names of window classes, clipboard formats, and application-defined messages. You may wish to use them to help you deal efficiently with variable-length strings.

In addition to the private atom table that resides in the local data segment, Windows provides a global atom table. Windows' Dynamic Data Exchange (DDE) protocol relies on the global atom table to pass the ASCII names of data topics between programs. Since DDE uses messages to relay requests for data, an atom provides a compact way to store the name of a desired data element in a very small space.

Dynamically Allocated Win16 Segments

Dynamically allocated segments provide the most flexible type of read/write memory for an application to use. Up to the limit of available system memory, you can have as many as you want, and each segment you allocate can be as large as 64K. In fact, you can allocate segments larger than 64K, although the methods required to support this are beyond the scope of this book.

How many dynamically allocated segments *can* a program create? There are three factors: available system memory, the size of a handle table, and whether Windows is running in real mode, standard mode, or 386-Enhanced Mode. Real mode has a maximum address space of one megabyte, standard mode has a maximum of 16 megabytes, and 386-Enhanced Mode has a maximum of 64 megabytes. In all three modes, the maximum size of a handle table is 8,192 entries, which means that a maximum of 8,192 segments can be created. However, standard mode uses *two* table entries for each segment, so the system-wide maximum for standard mode is 4,096 segments. Future versions of Windows will probably fix standard mode, so that 8,192 segments can be allocated. In addition, in future versions of Windows these protected mode limits will most likely become a *per task* limit. In Windows 3.0, however, these limits apply on a system-wide basis.

Programs allocate and manage dynamic segments using Windows' global heap management routines. This is a set of 21 routines that start with the word "Global." **GlobaAlloc**, for example, allocates a dynamic segment and **GlobalFree** deallocates a segment. Incidentally, the Windows KERNEL itself uses these allocation routines for managing system-level objects like code segments. These routines provide the "lowest-level" of memory allocation in the Windows API.

There are three basic types of segments: fixed, moveable, and discardable. The use of fixed segments tends to be limited to device drivers, which require that a memory object always stays in one place. The reason is that fixed segments prevent the memory manager from compacting memory when it needs to, so that most programs use moveable segments to store data. From the Memory Manager's point of view, the most "friendly" kind of object is a discardable one. It can be moved or discarded, as the Memory Manager sees fit, when system memory starts to get a little cramped. Code and resource segments are usually discardable segments, although a program could store data in a discardable segment to implement a type of virtual memory system under real and standard mode Windows.

Just like the local memory manager, the global memory manager provides a handle when it allocates a block of memory. The use of a handle instead of a pointer allows moveable and discardable objects to be moved or discarded. When a program wishes to access the memory, it calls a special routine which locks the object in place and provides a pointer: **GlobalLock**. When a program has finished using a block of memory, it releases the object by calling **GlobalUnlock**. Here is a sample code fragment that shows how a segment from the global heap can be allocated so that a string can be copied into the segment:

```
HANDLE hMem;
LPSTR   lpstr;

/*  Allocate a 15 byte moveable object.  */
hMem = GlobalAlloc (GMEM_MOVEABLE, 15L);

/*  Lock the object, getting a pointer.  */
lpstr = GlobalLock (hMem);

lstrcpy (lpstr, "Hello World");

/*  Unlock the object.  */
GlobalUnlock (hMem);
```

If you compare this code fragment to the one we looked at during our discussion of the local heap routines, you'll find that the two sets of dynamic memory allocation routines look very similar. This is no accident. The two subroutine packages were developed at the same time, to provide similar services but at two different levels: One manages the system-wide global heap and the other manages the private local heap that each program is given by default.

Later in this chapter, we'll provide a complete program to demonstrate the use of the global heap management routines. For now, let's move on to discuss another place that C++ programs use to store data: resources.

Windows 3.1 Application Note

The locking/unlocking described here is required for a program to work in real mode. Starting with Windows 3.1, real mode support is being discontinued in Windows. For this reason, the dynamic segment allocation process is greatly simplified. In particular, you can lock a segment right after it is allocated, and avoid unlocking it until you free the segment. The `SEGALLOC` sample, which is included later in this chapter, provides an example of this type of allocation.

Resources

An important type of memory object often overlooked for their memory management qualities are resources. A resource is a read-only data object that has been merged into a program's .EXE file by the resource compiler. When the data is needed, the resource manager reads it from disk and places it into a discardable memory object. And when the memory manager needs to reclaim the memory for another use, a resource can typically be discarded or purged from system memory. As allocated segments, resources can be allocated as fixed, moveable, or discardable segments. Since discardable resources are the most flexible, they are the most common.

Table 18.3 provides a list of the different types of resources that Windows supports, along with the chapter in this book that discusses the use of each type. As you can see, resources play a key role in how certain data objects are packaged for use. Resources are used for user-interface objects, GDI objects, and space-saving objects like string tables and custom resources.

Table 18.3 Window's Predefined Resources

Resource Type	*Covered In Depth*
Accelerator table	Chapter 11
Bitmaps	
Cursors	Chapter 17
Custom resources	Chapter 18
Dialog box templates	Chapter 14
Fonts	Chapter 10
Icons	
Menu templates	Chapter 11
String tables	Chapter 18

From a memory use point of view, each resource resides in a separate segment. In other words, a program with one accelerator table, two menu templates, and four dialog box templates has a total of seven different segments worth of resources. The advantage of having each resource packed in its own segment is that each can be loaded and discarded in a manner that is completely independent of other resources.

GDI Win16 Data Segment

Whenever a program creates a GDI object, space is allocated out of GDI's data segment. Or more specifically, space is allocated from GDI's local heap. While there's no doubt that programs will need to use such objects, care should be taken to avoid creating too many of these types of objects. In addition, programs that create GDI drawing objects should be careful to destroy the objects when they are not needed. Otherwise, if GDI's heap gets full, it will prevent other programs from being able to run properly. In a future version, Windows will delete GDI objects when the owning application terminates. In the meantime, allocate only a minimum number of objects, and be sure to destroy objects when you are done using them.

Table 18.4 provides a list of GDI objects and the size that each takes from GDI's data segment. These sizes are subject to change; they are provided to help you get a sense for the demands that each object places on system memory. Two GDI objects reside in their own segment: fonts and bitmaps. The local heap object contains a pointer to the larger object.

Table 18.4 Space Taken in GDI's Local Heap by Various GDI Drawing Objects

Object	*Size*
Brush	32 bytes
Bitmap	28–32 bytes
Font	40–44 bytes
Pen	28 bytes
Region	28 bytes to several Kbytes
Palette	28 bytes

One other data area can get filled by the actions that programs take, and should be monitored carefully: the USER library's data segment.

USER Win16 Data Segment

Windows' USER module provides the support for Windows' user-interface objects. This includes windows, menus, dialog boxes, and accelerator tables. Unlike GDI objects, USER objects in general are not shared between programs. For this reason, when a Windows program terminates, USER can free the data objects that were created. Nonetheless, the wise Windows programmer makes frugal use of memory and will destroy objects when done using them.

Quite a few user-interface objects are stored as resources, and therefore reside in their own segments. Included in this group are cursors, icons, dialog box templates, and menu templates. Other objects take up USER heap space, including those shown in Table 18.5. The exact size of individual objects is less important (since it can change from version to version) than the fact that your use of these objects takes up space which, at least for now, is in short supply. For example, if you define 10 window classes and create 100 windows of each class, you consume about 7,500 bytes of USER heap space. Since USER's heap is also used by other programs, including the Program Manager, File Manager, etc., you need to be careful not to create too many objects that may cause this heap space to be overrun.

Table 18.5 Appropriate size of various USER data objects

Object	*Size*
Menus	20 bytes/ menu plus 20 bytes/ menu item
Window class	40–50 bytes
Window	60–70 bytes

Assuming you don't create too many objects and overload USER's heap space, there are two often overlooked types of memory areas: class extra bytes and window extra bytes. These are small data areas that reside in USER's data segment, but which are attached to a specific window or window class. A program might put flags, or even a memory handle, into these extra bytes. Then they can be accessed by simply providing the window handle. Here is a list of the routines that access window and class extra bytes:

Class Extra Bytes	*Window Extra Bytes*
`SetClassWord`	`SetWindowWord`
`SetClassLong`	`SetWindowLong`
`GetClassWord`	`GetWindowWord`
`GetClassLong`	`GetWindowLong`

The advantage of these extra bytes is that they allow you, for example, to store the head of a linked list in an area that is directly related to a window. Or, you can store a memory handle, to give each window—n effect—its own private data area. The most obvious use of this type of memory is in implementing custom dialog box controls. But it is equally useful in implementing applications that support the Multiple Document Interface (MDI).

GDI and USER Objects under Win32

Windows 3.0 solved many of Windows' memory problems: With megabytes of memory, a program could be entirely RAM-resident and provide great performance. One problem that didn't get solved, however, was the strict limitation on GDI and USER objects. Under the various Win16 systems, these are allocated from a single segment for each library.

Starting with Windows NT, this system bottleneck has been removed. With the removal of the segmented architecture, the Win32 system creates its own heap—using the **`HeapCreate`** and **`HeapAlloc`** functions. Now the limit is no longer 64K total data for each heap; instead, up to 64K different objects can be allocated in each heap. Win32 programmers won't have to worry about this limitation any more. As an added bonus, the Win32 subsystem tags process ownership to each object that it allocates, allowing proper cleanup on process termination.

With this brief introduction to the different types of memory available to Windows applications, you have a reasonably complete picture of the choices you can make. Now it's time to roll up our sleeves and look at the implementation details for using different types of memory. The rest of this chapter provides five complete code examples to answer any further questions you might have regarding an application's use of memory. Here is a list of the code examples and the topics that each focuses on:

- **SEGALLOC.** This sample program demonstrates how to use memory allocated out of the global heap. The accompanying discussion provides more details on the various global heap management routines.
- **MIN2.** We're going to take a second look at the minimum Windows program to support a discussion of code structure and memory use. This program demonstrates how a Windows program can be divided into multiple code segments to improve memory use.
- **LOCALMEM.** This program provides an example of using the local heap management routines to allocate objects from a program's default data segment. This program also demonstrates the use of string tables.
- **SUBSEG.** This program shows how the local heap management routines can be used with a segment that is dynamically allocated from the global heap. This program combines global heap management routines and local heap management routines.
- **CIRCLE.** This program demonstrates the creation of a custom resource. A sine table is stored as a resource and used to calculate sine and cosine values, which are used to draw a circle.

Let's get started, then, with a look at using the global heap management routines.

Win16 Global Heap Allocation

When a program allocates memory from Windows' global heap, it is allocating a segment. Segments can be allocated that are fixed, moveable, or discardable, depending upon what a program needs. In general, though, programmers should keep in mind the words of John Pollock, who worked on Windows' first KERNEL and was the first Windows instructor for many Windows programmers. He urged programmers to keep dynamically allocated segments "as *few* as possible, as *small* as possible, and as *discardable* as possible."

As Few As Possible

You'll want to keep your segments as *few* as possible because of the overhead of a segment. Segments are expensive. Each incurs 24 bytes of overhead: a 16-byte invisible header that links all segments together and an 8-byte entry in a master segment table. In real mode, this segment table is called the Burgermaster. In protected mode, the segment table is the local descriptor table (LDT). See Chapter 17 for more details.

Because of this high overhead, you'll probably want to minimize the number of segments you allocate. For example, with an overhead of 24 bytes, if you allocate a segment to hold a 24-byte data object, it really costs you 48 bytes. That's a lot like having a sales tax of 100% on everything you buy. But since this is a fixed cost, you can effectively lower your "memory-use tax" by putting many objects into a single segment. For example, if you put 2,400 bytes of data into a single object, you have effectively lowered your taxes to a mere 1%. When you start to think about how to make the best use of dynamically allocated segments, think about using arrays of records instead of working with a linked list of segments. It will help you get your money's worth from the Memory Manager.

A second issue that relates to segment overhead involves **granularity**. This refers to the actual pieces of memory that Windows carves out when you allocate a segment. Dynamically allocated segments have a granularity of 32 bytes—or, in real mode memory terms, two paragraphs. (Recall that in real mode the smallest segment is 16 bytes, which is called a paragraph. Even though protected mode allows for smaller segments, Windows doesn't.) In real and standard modes, 16 bytes of every object is used as a header. In either of these modes, if you ask for a segment that is between one and 16 bytes long, it costs you 32 bytes. This table shows how a 32-byte granularity affects the size of the *actual* versus the *requested* memory:

Requested Size	*Actual Size*	*Header*	*Actual Data Area*
1–16 bytes	32 bytes	16 bytes	16 bytes
17–48 bytes	64 bytes	16 bytes	48 bytes

Requested Size	*Actual Size*	*Header*	*Actual Data Area*
49–80 bytes	96 bytes	16 bytes	80 bytes
81–112bytes	128bytes	16 bytes	112bytes

Notice that the size of the actual data area jumps in odd-paragraph increments, so that every segment request is an odd multiple of 16 bytes (1, 3, 5, 7, etc.).

In 386-Enhanced Mode, a 32-byte granularity is also used. However, the implementation is a little different since this mode is able to take advantage of features of the Intel 80386. The granularity is in terms of even paragraphs. Here is a table that demonstrates this:

Requested Size	*Actual Size*	*Header*	*Actual Data Area*
1–32 bytes	32 bytes	16 bytes (hidden)	32 bytes
33–64 bytes	64 bytes	16 bytes (hidden)	64 bytes
65–96 bytes	96 bytes	16 bytes (hidden)	96 bytes
97–128 bytes	128 bytes	16 bytes (hidden)	128 bytes

Since the 386-Enhanced Mode runs in protected mode, just like standard mode, a reference beyond the limit of a segment causes a program to terminate with a UAE error. However, since this mode has a different alignment from standard mode, it is possible that a bug that causes a UAE error in one of the protected modes might not cause the same error in the other protected mode. You should advise the people who test your programs to be sure to run a full set of tests in both modes. A small difference like this can cause a stable program in one environment to crash in the other.

As Small As Possible

Keep your segments as small as possible, because Windows is a multitasking system, and memory that you allocate is not available for other Windows programs. This is particularly an issue in real mode, with its tiny, one-megabyte address space. But even in other modes, only allocate the amount of memory you need and no more.

One reason that John Pollock made this recommendation has to do with the way some DOS programs behave. Since DOS is a single-tasking operating system, the first thing that many DOS programs do is to allocate all of system memory. If a Windows program tried to do this, it would effectively lock out other programs from being able to run.

So, whether you are moving to Windows from DOS or from some other programming environment, keep in mind that memory is a shared, and in some cases, a scarce resource. Allocate only what you need, when you need it. And, when you are done using a block of memory, free it so that other Windows programs can use it.

As Discardable As Possible

In the last chapter, we talked about the three types of memory objects: fixed, moveable, and discardable. To the Windows Memory Manager, fixed is the least flexible and therefore least desirable type of memory object, and discardable is the most desirable. But programmers new to Windows tend to see things just the opposite way: Fixed memory seems the most comfortable, discardable seems the most disastrous, and moveable only slightly less so. After all, what programmer in his right mind wants to deal with data that keeps wiggling away, or disappears completely?

John Pollock's recommendation to make memory as discardable as possible reflects the fact that memory should be treated as a scarce resource. Programs with moderate requirements for memory usually keep data in moveable data segments. After all, a moveable segment gives the memory manager the freedom to shuffle memory so it can minimize fragmentation.

Programs with a large or unlimited need for memory, like word processing programs or spreadsheet programs, require their own mechanism to transfer data between main system memory and disk. After all, even a virtual memory system can run out of memory. And when Windows is without virtual memory in the standard and real modes, such programs will run out of "real memory" sooner. Discardable memory provides a way for such programs to volunteer objects to be purged. When memory is plentiful, discardable objects don't have to be purged. But when memory is scarce, the memory manager can exercise its option to remove discardable objects.

Global Heap API

Table 18.6 shows all of Windows' global heap management routines. This table is set up to show how 12 of these routines must be paired together to create a sandwich construction that we first introduced in Chapter 7. The other nine routines act either on a specific global memory object or on the global heap as a whole.

For the most common uses, programs can get by with just five of these routines: **GlobalAlloc**, **GlobalReAlloc**, **GlobalLock**, **GlobalUnlock**, and **GlobalFree**. We're going to take a close look at these routines, to provide you with enough information so you can start using them in your Windows programming.

Table 18.6 All of Windows' Global Heap Management Routines

Top Slice	*Bottom Slice*	*Description*
GlobalAlloc	GlobalFree	Allocates a segment from the global heap.
GlobalCompact	na	Reorganizes the global heap to determine the largest block of available free memory.

Table 18.6 All of Windows' Global Heap Management Routines *(Continued)*

Top Slice	*Bottom Slice*	*Description*
GlobalDiscard	na	Purges an unlocked, discardable segment from memory.
GlobalDosAlloc	GlobalDosFree	Allocates a block of memory in the DOS address space, that is, below the one-megabyte line, so that a Windows program can share a data area with a DOS program or a DOS device driver.
GlobalFix	GlobalUnfix	Prevents an object from moving in the linear address space. Notice that this doesn't keep an object from being swapped to disk≈only the GlobalPageLock routine can do that.
GlobalFlags	na	Retrieves the flags associated with a global memory object.
GlobalHandle	na	Provides the global handle associated with a specific segment address
GlobalLock	GlobalUnlock	Retrieves the address of a global memory object. In real mode, it also increments the lock count to prevent it from moving in physical memory. In all modes, it prevents a discardable object from being discarded
GlobalLRUNewest	na	Changes a segment's priority in the LRU discarding table to make it *least* likely to be discarded.
GlobalLRUOldest	na	Changes a segment's priority in the LRU discarding table to make it the *most* likely to be discarded.
GlobalNotify	na	Sets up a call-back procedure through which the global heap manager notifies a program *before* a segment is discarded. A program can implement a virtual memory management scheme using this routine, that will work in all Windows' different operating modes.

(continued)

Table 18.6 All of Windows' Global Heap Management Routines *(Continued)*

Top Slice	*Bottom Slice*	*Description*
GlobalPageLock	GlobalPageUnlock	Fixes a segment's location in the linear address space, and also prevents the virtual memory pages from being swapped out to disk. This provides the maximum protection against any movement of a segment, which is required for certain types of device drivers. However, programs should avoid using this since overuse of page locking can be severely detrimental to overall system performance.
GlobalReAlloc	na	Changes the size of a segment on the global heap. Both locked and unlocked segments can be resized, although a special flag must be set if you want to allow a locked segment to move if it is necessary to satisfy the allocation request.
GlobalSize	na	Returns the size of a segment on the global heap.
GlobalWire	GlobalUnwire	In real mode Windows, moves a segment to a very low memory position for segments that are going to be locked for an unusually long period of time. This measure helps avoid serious fragmentation that otherwise occurs when moveable or discardable memory objects are left locked for longer periods of time than to process a single message.

GlobalAlloc

The **GlobalAlloc** routine allocates memory from the global heap. It is defined as

```
HANDLE GlobalAlloc (wFlags, dwBytes)
```

- **wFlags** is a combination of one or more global memory allocation flags, discussed below.
- **dwBytes** is an unsigned long value for the number of bytes to allocate.

GlobalAlloc returns the handle that identifies the segment you've allocated. Be sure to *always* check the return value from this function, since there is no guarantee that your request can be satisfied. When an allocation request cannot be met, **GlobalAlloc** lets you know by returning a NULL handle.

The value of `wFlags` can be a combination of nine different flags, depending on the type of memory you wish to allocate (fixed, moveable, or discardable), whether the memory is going to be shared or not, and other considerations. Here are the nine flags:

Description	*Flag*
Fixed memory object	`GMEM_FIXED`
Moveable memory object	`GMEM_MOVEABLE`
Discardable memory object	`GMEM_DISCARDABLE | GMEM_MOVEABLE`
Initialize with zeros	`GMEM_ZEROINIT`
Segment will be shared	`GMEM_DDESHARE`
Do not compact	`GMEM_NOCOMPACT`
Do not discard	`GMEM_NODISCARD`
Tag a discardable segment so that a notification routine is called *before* the segment is discarded	`GMEM_NOTIFY`
Do not put in EMS memory	`GMEM_NOT_BANKED`

The first four sets of flags are the most important and most useful. Most of the time, you'll start by deciding the disposition of your memory object: fixed, moveable, or discardable. Next, you'll decide whether to initialize the data area with zeros or not, and your job is done. The other flags have more specialized uses, which we'll review briefly to help you decide when one might be useful to you.

The second parameter, **`dwBytes`**, is the number of bytes to allocate. Since this is an unsigned long value, you'll often have to supply a type-cast if you have calculated the size of an object using regular integer values. For example, here is how to allocate a 200-byte, moveable segment:

```
hMem = GlobalAlloc (GMEM_MOVEABLE, (DWORD)200);
```

This routine accepts an unsigned long value for the size of a memory object because it supports memory objects that are larger than 64K. Since this is the limit on the size of a segment, Windows allocates objects larger than 64K by setting aside multiple segments to satisfy your memory request. If you wish to allocate objects larger than 64K, you'll have to do some special **segment arithmetic** to allow segment boundaries to be crossed correctly.

One approach to handling the segment arithmetic that is required for objects larger than 64K is to rely on the built-in support that some compilers provide. Pointers to such objects are referred to as **huge** pointers. However, this approach involves taking on quite a bit of overhead for even the simplest pointer operations. A more efficient approach is to use the **__AHINCR** symbol that Windows provides, which you can add to a segment address yourself if a segment boundary has been crossed. A simpler approach involves avoiding the allocation of memory objects that are larger than 64K.

The remaining flags are used for special circumstances. For example, the **GMEM_DDESHARE** flag marks a segment as one that may be shared between different programs. The "DDE" in the flag name is the acronym for the **dynamic data exchange (DDE)**, a data sharing protocol built on top of Windows' message passing system. This flag should be used when sharing data using either DDE or the clipboard. In general, programs should use one of these two mechanisms to share data, and not simply share memory handles. The reason is that certain configurations of Windows are built around the idea of private address spaces. As time goes on, this will be the case for all protected mode implementations of Windows, but for now, it is limited to Windows running with EMS memory. All data sharing *must* be based on a client-server model. That is, one program *writes* the data, and a second one *reads* the data and makes a copy for its own use. Two programs can never share the same dynamically allocated segment with both having read/write privileges.

The **GMEM_NOCOMPACT** flag tells the Memory Manager not to move memory to satisfy the memory request. The **GMEM_NODISCARD** flag says the same thing, and adds an additional condition: No segments should be discarded to satisfy the allocation request. These are useful for programs that want to avoid disturbing the global heap. For a program that is very sensitive to performance issues, memory movement is expensive. These flags tell the Memory Manager that memory should be allocated *only* if it can be done quickly from an existing free block.

The **GMEM_NOTIFY** flag is used for discardable segments to request the Memory Manager to notify you before it discards your segments. When the time comes to discard a segment, the Memory Manager calls a function that you have defined as a notification callback function. The notification routine is assigned using the **GlobalNotify** routine. It is useful for implementing a virtual memory system that works in all of Windows' operating modes.

The final flag, **GMEM_NOT_BANKED**, is primarily for the use of optimizing device drivers for real mode when EMS memory is present. EMS was a very important addition to Windows 2.x. But since Windows 3.1 will drop support for Real Mode, this flag can be safely ignored.

GlobalLock

The **GlobalLock** routine provides the address of a global segment, and increments the lock count for certain types of segments. It is defined as

```
LPSTR GlobalLock (hMem)
```

- **hMem** is a memory handle of a segment allocated with **GlobalAlloc**.

Programs make calls to **GlobalLock** to get the address of a moveable or discardable segment. In addition, this routine increments the lock count for discardable objects, to prevent them from being discarded. Using moveable or discardable segments requires a two-step process. The first step is to allocate the memory itself. The second step involves calling **GlobalLock** to retrieve a far pointer that can be used to access the memory. For example, here is how to allocate a moveable segment that can accommodate a 274-byte object, and lock it for use:

```
HGLOBAL hMem;
LPSTR lp;

hMem = GlobalAlloc (GMEM_MOVEABLE, (DWORD)274));
if (!hMem)
    goto ErrorExit1;

lp = (LPSTR) GlobalLock (hMem);
if (!lp)
    goto ErrorExit2;
```

Notice the two sets of error checking in this code fragment. The first check makes sure that the allocation was successful. Most programmers agree that this is reasonable. The second check is to make sure that the lock is successful. Many programmers are hesitant to check every time they lock an object. It's a little extra effort, but it prevents a program from unpleasant surprises. For one thing, a program that tries to use a null pointer will cause a general protection error—sometimes known as a GP fault. Then, Windows will terminate the program with an "Unexpected Application Error" message.

To help you understand the necessity for this message, here is a list of the things that cause a call to **GlobalLock** to fail:

- A discardable object that has been discarded.
- Inability to copy a clipboard or DDE object to the local address space. At present, this is only a concern in real mode Windows when running with EMS. But this will likely be an issue in protected mode in a future version of Windows.
- Invalid memory handle. This can happen if an object has already been freed, or if the memory location that the program has been using to store the memory handle has been overwritten.

At first glance, it may appear as if **GlobalLock** only fails in the most extreme circumstances. You might wonder whether you can avoid checking for a failed return for moveable objects that are not being used in the context of the clipboard and DDE. Unfortunately, the third set of causes is the "catch-all" that makes it necessary to always check the return value of **GlobalLock**. A memory handle can get overwritten, which will likely cause **GlobalLock** to fail.

When a program allocates a fixed object, there is no need to call **GlobalLock**. The reason is that the handle of fixed objects is always the segment address of the allocated memory. Here is how to allocate a fixed block of memory and convert the memory handle into a pointer:

```
HGLOBAL hMem;
LPSTR lp;

hMem = GlobalAlloc (GMEM_FIXED, (DWORD)200);
lp = (LPSTR)MAKELONG (0, hMem);
```

The MAKELONG macro packs two-word (two-byte) values into a long (four-byte) value, which can be cast to a far pointer. Of course, to work well in all of Windows' operating modes, you should probably avoid allocating fixed memory objects. But we are showing you this to give you a peek at something that you *can* do quite freely in the context of local heaps. But more on that later on.

GlobalReAlloc

The **GlobalReAlloc** routine changes the size of a memory object on the global heap, and is defined as

```
HGLOBAL GlobalReAlloc (hMem, dwBytes, wFlags)
```

- **hMem** is a memory handle, obtained by calling **GlobalAlloc**.
- **dwBytes** is an unsigned long value for the number of bytes to allocate, or zero if the **GMEM_MODIFY** flag is being used to change the memory disposition of a memory object.
- **wFlags** is one or more flags, or zero if the object is just changing sizes.

The **GlobalReAlloc** routine can be used to do two different things: change the size of a global memory object, and change the memory disposition of a memory object. It takes all the same flags as the **GlobalAlloc** routine plus one new one: **GMEM_MODIFY**. This flag indicates when the memory disposition is being changed—for example, when a moveable object is being made discardable, or when a discardable object is being made moveable. Aside from this, the **GlobalReAlloc** routine can pretty much be treated as an extension of the **GlobalAlloc** routine. Here are some examples of its usage:

```
/*  Make an object moveable.  */
GlobalReAlloc (hMem, 0, GMEM_MODIFY | GMEM_MOVEABLE);

/*  Resize an object.  */
GlobalReAlloc (hMem, (DWORD)1843, 0);

/*  Resize an object, filling new area with zeroes. */
GlobalReAlloc (hMem, (DWORD)dwSize, GMEM_ZEROINIT);
```

GlobalUnlock

The **GlobalUnlock** routine decrements the lock count for certain types of segments, and is defined as

```
BOOL GlobalUnlock (hMem)
```

- **hMem** is a memory handle allocated with the **GlobalAlloc** routine.

In general, you'll call **GlobalUnlock** as the second part of a sandwich construction whenever you call **GlobalLock**. For example, here is a typical usage in response to a **WM_LBUTTONDOWN** message, to retrieve the mouse location from the **LParam**:

```
long far PASCAL WndProc (...)
    {
    LPPOINT lp;

    switch (msg)
        {
        case WM_LBUTTONDOWN:
            lp = (LPPOINT)GlobalLock (hmem);
            *lp[cp] = MAKEPOINT(lParam);
            GlobalUnlock(hmem);
            ...
```

The key issue that this code fragment demonstrates is the need to keep a memory segment locked for only a very brief period of time. Otherwise, you risk fragmenting the global heap and wasting memory. This will affect the performance of your program, as well as all other programs currently running in the system. In short, locks should be very short term.

GlobalFree

The **GlobalFree** routine frees an unlocked global memory object that was allocated with the **GlobalAlloc** routine. It is defined as

```
HGLOBAL GlobalFree (hMem)
```

- **hMem** is a global memory handle that was allocated by calling **GlobalAlloc**.

GlobalFree releases the segment and all internally created data structures that are associated with a given memory handle. Even though Windows frees all memory segments when a program terminates, it's a good practice to explicitly free every object when you are done using it.

This in-depth introduction to Windows' global heap management routines has almost gotten us ready to look at some sample programs. But first, we're going to look at an issue that should give you another perspective on the way that memory is managed in Windows. Even if you never use any of these routines in any of your Windows programs, understanding where they might be useful will help you better understand Windows' memory management. What we're referring to is the various sets of routines that lock, wire, fix, and otherwise coerce a global segment to reside in a fixed location.

Locked, Wired, Fixed, and Page Locked

In our discussion of Windows global heap management routines, we identified **`GlobalLock`** as the routine that programs use to **dereference** a handle to get a pointer. By dereference, we simply mean to convert into a pointer. **`GlobalLock`** has a second role: When needed, it keeps objects from moving. Because of the difference in real and protected modes, the exact meaning of this depends on the current operating mode. For example, in protected mode, **`GlobalLock`** doesn't prevent a moveable object from being relocated, or even from being swapped to disk. In real mode, however, which doesn't have special hardware memory management support, **`GlobalLock`** *does* prevent such objects from moving. And in all modes, it prevents discardable objects from being purged. Windows supports three other ways to influence the movement of a memory segment besides locking. A segment can also be wired, fixed, or page locked. Let's explore the meaning of each of these.

Wired Segments

When a program asks Windows to allocate a segment from the global heap, Windows searches through its free list. The free list is a set of doubly linked lists that can be walked from either end. When allocating a fixed or moveable object, the Memory Manager always starts at the low-memory end of the free list. When allocating a discardable object, the search starts at the high-memory end. As depicted in Figure 18.3, this tends to group fixed and moveable objects at the bottom of memory, and discardable objects at the top of memory.

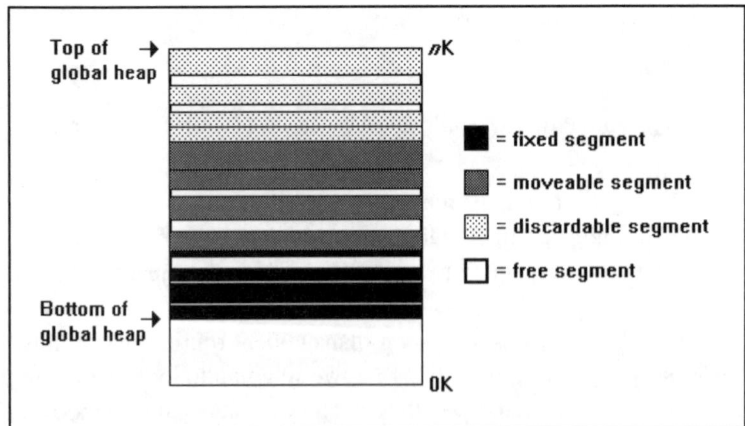

Figure 18.3 The layout of the global heap

In addition, when allocating a fixed object, the global memory manager works quite hard to move moveable objects so that fixed objects can be as low as possible. This accentuates the layering of the global heap even more, so that—ideally at least—all fixed objects will be allocated lower than any moveable object. With fixed objects at the bottom of memory, moveable objects in the middle, and discardable objects at the top, fragmentation among moveable objects can be minimized. In a low-memory situation, Windows can purge several discardable objects at once, freeing up space for other uses.

For the most part, programs will allocate moveable or discardable objects. However, it is easy to change the disposition of a moveable object to be discardable and vice versa. On the other hand, it is not possible to change either of these objects into a fixed memory object. In fact, from the point of view of the global heap manager, this would not be a good thing. If a program were able to change a moveable or discardable segment into a fixed segment, it would create a memory sandbar. In other words, it would create a block in the middle of memory that would prevent the global heap manager from being able to freely move objects around.

However, there are times when an application may wish to lock a piece of memory down over a longer period of time than is normal. The **`GlobalWire`**/ **`GlobalUnwire`** pair of routines provides the necessary support for this kind of operation. The **`GlobalWire`** routine first *moves* a moveable or discardable object to a very low memory location. This allows such objects to be fixed, without the fragmentation that would otherwise occur if the **`GlobalLock`** routine were to be used, for example. When a wired object does not have to be fixed any more, the **`GlobalUnwire`** routine can be used to let it rejoin the ranks of moveable and discardable objects.

Fixed Segments

In the two protected modes, a global memory object might be "locked," but may still be able to move. In fact, it can even be swapped to disk (although it will not be discarded). As described in the preceding chapter, this movement is possible because of the hardware memory management that is built into protected mode. The LDT table, for example, allows a memory segment to move in physical memory without a change in its logical address.

Certain device drivers, however, don't operate on the logical address. Instead, they use the physical address. For their use, the global heap management routines include the **`GlobalFix`**/ **`GlobalUnfix`** pair. The **`GlobalFix`** routine forces a segment to remain at the same physical address. In the same way that programs shouldn't lock down segments for lengthy periods of time, segments should not be fixed for lengthy periods of time. This can cause fragmentation of the physical address space, which makes overall system memory management less efficient. But for device drivers and other uses that require a fixed physical addresss, the **`GlobalFix`** routine can be used. To counter the effect of the **`GlobalFix`** routine, a call to **`GlobalUnfix`** is required.

Page Locked Segments

Even though **GlobalFix** can prevent an object from moving in the physical address space, it can still be swapped to disk. The reason is that there are two memory managers at work: one that manages the linear, "virtual" address space, and another one that supports this address space by moving blocks of memory—also known as "pages"—to disk. When a page is referenced that is not present, a page fault is created that causes the virtual memory manager to bring the required page into memory.

While **GlobalFix** prevents an object from moving in the virtual address space, there are times when even more control is needed. In particular, for time-critical device drivers, it may be necessary to select certain segments and designate them as **page locked**. A page locked segment is the most securely attached segment that Windows 3.0 can provide. Such segments cannot move in the virtual address space, so their "physical" address stays the same. But also, such segments cannot be swapped to disk—so that response time to access that memory is always the best it can be. Even if you never write a device driver that requires page locking, it's nice to know that Windows has this capability to allow time-critical operations—like keyboard and mouse driver code, for example—to be serviced as quickly as possible.

From earlier versions of Windows, some programmers have gotten into the habit of using a segment's lock count to determine whether it needed to be unlocked or not. However, in Windows 3.0, with its sophisticated memory management, certain things have changed. If you are new to Windows programming, or if you are starting a new programming project, you may not need to worry about this practice. But if you are planning to work on some older Windows code, be on the lookout for code that relies on the lock count.

Hint Avoid depending on using the lock count to determine whether **GlobalLock** has locked a segment. In both protected modes, **GlobalLock** does not affect the lock count of a moveable segment.

With this under our belt, it's time to take a look at a sample Windows program that allocates memory from the global heap.

A Sample Program: SEGALLOC

This sample program allocates three different segments from the global heap and displays information about each segment. Figure 18.4 shows the output from our program, SEGALLOC. As you can see, SEGALLOC allocates one fixed, one moveable, and one discardable segment. Also displayed are the bytes requested, the actual size of the allocated object, the handle, and the address of the segment.

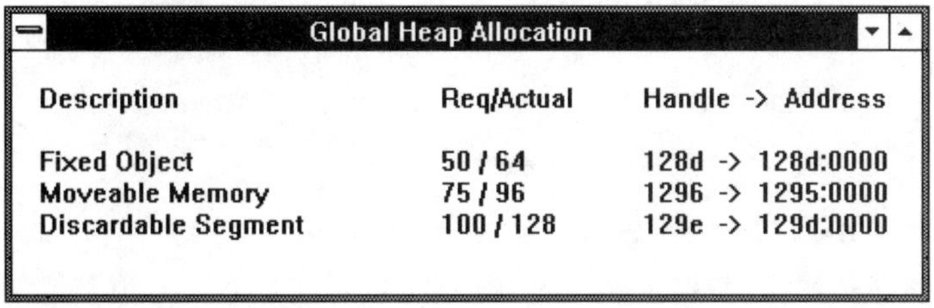

Description	Req/Actual	Handle -> Address
Fixed Object	50 / 64	128d -> 128d:0000
Moveable Memory	75 / 96	1296 -> 1295:0000
Discardable Segment	100 / 128	129e -> 129d:0000

Figure 18.4 SEGALLOC displays information about the segments it allocates

If you compare the handle and the address for the fixed memory object, you'll notice that the handle *is* the segment address. This is true for all fixed segments, in all of Windows' operating modes. Notice that the offset portion of every address is zero. When you allocate a segment from the global heap, you get to start writing your own data at the beginning of the segment, which is what this address tells you. This will be the case for all types of segments in all operating modes.

If you compare the handle and the address for the moveable and discardable objects, you'll notice some similarity. It seems that this formula can be used to find a segment address:

```
segment_address = handle - 1; /* Don't do this! */
```

This formula works in protected mode for Windows 3.0; but don't do this, and don't depend on this working in future versions of Windows. Microsoft plans to continue enhancing Windows. If you rely on this particular quirk, your programs may stop working in a future version of Windows.

SEGALLOC.CPP

```
// SEGALLOC.CPP  - Global heap allocation in Windows.
//
#include <owl\owlpch.h>
#include "segalloc.h"

DEFINE_RESPONSE_TABLE1 (DFrame, TFrameWindow)
  EV_COMMAND(CM_FILEEXIT, CmFileExit),
  EV_COMMAND(CM_HELPABOUT, CmHelpAbout),
END_RESPONSE_TABLE;

DFrame::DFrame(char * title) : TFrameWindow(0, title)
    {
    Label1 = "Description";
    Label2 = "Req/Actual";
    Label3 = "Handle  ->  Address";

    cb1 = lstrlen(Label1);
    cb2 = lstrlen(Label2);
    cb3 = lstrlen(Label3);
```

```
    lstrcpy (sdInit[0].achDesc, "Fixed Object");
    sdInit[0].dwAlloc  = 50;
    sdInit[0].wFlags   = GMEM_FIXED;

    lstrcpy (sdInit[1].achDesc, "Moveable Memory");
    sdInit[1].dwAlloc  = 75;
    sdInit[1].wFlags   = GMEM_MOVEABLE | GMEM_ZEROINIT;

    lstrcpy (sdInit[2].achDesc, "Discardable Segment");
    sdInit[2].dwAlloc  = 100;
    sdInit[2].wFlags   = GMEM_DISCARDABLE | GMEM_MOVEABLE;
    }

void DFrame::CmFileExit()
    {
    CloseWindow(0); // Cause application to terminate
    }

void DFrame::CmHelpAbout()
    {
    MessageBox(" Global Heap Allocation Demo\n\n"
               "'Borland C++ 4.0 Programming\n"
               "  for Windows', by Paul Yao", Title);
    }

void DFrame::SetupWindow()
    {
    HDC  hdc;
    int  i;

    TFrameWindow::SetupWindow();

    for (i=0;i<COUNT;i++)
        {
        hSegment[i] = GlobalAlloc(sdInit[i].wFlags,
                                  sdInit[i].dwAlloc);

        lpSegData[i] = (LPSEGDATA)GlobalLock (hSegment[i]);
        if (!lpSegData[i])
            {
            MessageBox ("Not enough memory", Title);
            continue;
            }

        lstrcpy (lpSegData[i]->achDesc, sdInit[i].achDesc);
        lpSegData[i]->dwAlloc = sdInit[i].dwAlloc;
        lpSegData[i]->dwActual = GlobalSize (hSegment[i]);
        lpSegData[i]->wFlags = sdInit[i].wFlags;
        } /* [for] */

    // Fetch font measurement values for later drawing.
    TClientDC dc(HWindow);
    dc.GetTextMetrics (tmSys);

    return;
    }

void DFrame::CleanupWindow()
    {
    // Unlock & free all segments.
    for (int i=0;i<COUNT;i++)
        {
```

```
        GlobalUnlock (hSegment[i]);
        GlobalFree (hSegment[i]);
        }
    }

void DFrame::Paint (TDC& dc, BOOL, TRect&)
    {
    //  Calculate text positioning variables.
    int xText1 = tmSys.tmAveCharWidth * 2;
    int xText2 = xText1 + (STRSIZE * tmSys.tmAveCharWidth);
    int xText3 = xText2 + ((cb2+5) * tmSys.tmAveCharWidth);
    int yText = tmSys.tmHeight;

    //  Print titles.
    dc.TextOut (xText1, yText, Label1, cb1);
    dc.TextOut (xText2, yText, Label2, cb2);
    dc.TextOut (xText3, yText, Label3, cb3);

    yText += tmSys.tmHeight * 2;

    // Loop through displaying segment info.
    char buff[30];
    int  cb;
    for (int i=0;i<COUNT;i++)
        {
        //  Print description.
        dc.TextOut (xText1, yText, lpSegData[i]->achDesc,
                 lstrlen(lpSegData[i]->achDesc));

        //  Print allocated vs actual size.
        cb = wsprintf (buff, "%ld / %ld", lpSegData[i]->dwAlloc,
                                  lpSegData[i]->dwActual);
        dc.TextOut (xText2, yText, buff, cb);

        //  Print handle and actual address.
        cb = wsprintf (buff, "%04x  ->  %04x:%04x", hSegment[i],
                 HIWORD(lpSegData[i]), LOWORD(lpSegData[i]));
        dc.TextOut (xText3, yText, buff, cb);

        //  Advance to next line.
        yText += tmSys.tmHeight + tmSys.tmExternalLeading;
        }
    }

DApp::DApp() : TApplication()
    {
    }

void DApp::InitMainWindow()
    {
    SetMainWindow (new DFrame("Segment Allocation"));

    MainWindow->AssignMenu("MAIN");
    MainWindow->SetIcon(this, "SNAPSHOT");
    }

// Application main entry point.
OwlMain(int, char **)
    {
    return DApp().Run();
    }
```

SEGALLOC.H

```
#define CM_FILEEXIT 100
#define CM_HELPABOUT 200

/*------------------------------------------------------------*\
 |                        Constants.                           |
\*------------------------------------------------------------*/
const int STRSIZE = 30;
const int COUNT   = 3;

/*------------------------------------------------------------*\
 |                        TypeDefs.                            |
\*------------------------------------------------------------*/
typedef struct tagSEGDATA
    {
    char  achDesc[STRSIZE];  /*  Description of data.  */
    DWORD dwAlloc;           /*  Amount asked for.     */
    DWORD dwActual;          /*  Actually allocated.   */
    WORD  wFlags;            /*  Allocation flags.     */
    } SEGDATA;

typedef SEGDATA FAR *LPSEGDATA;

// Main window
class DFrame : public TFrameWindow
    {
  public:
    DFrame(char * title);
    void CmFileExit();
    void CmHelpAbout();
    void SetupWindow();
    void CleanupWindow();
    void Paint (TDC& dc, BOOL, TRect&);
  private:
    PSTR Label1;
    PSTR Label2;
    PSTR Label3;

    int cb1;  // Label lengths.
    int cb2;
    int cb3;

    HGLOBAL hSegment[COUNT];
    SEGDATA sdInit[COUNT];

    TEXTMETRIC tmSys;
    LPSEGDATA lpSegData[COUNT];

  DECLARE_RESPONSE_TABLE (DFrame);
    };

// Application object
class DApp : public TApplication
    {
  public:
    DApp();
    void InitMainWindow();
    };
```

SEGALLOC.RC

```
#include "segalloc.h"

snapshot icon segalloc.ico

main menu
    BEGIN
    POPUP "&File"
        {
        MENUITEM "E&xit", CM_FILEEXIT
        }
    POPUP "&Help"
        {
        MENUITEM "&About...", CM_HELPABOUT
        }
    END
```

SEGALLOC.DEF

```
EXETYPE WINDOWS

CODE MOVEABLE DISCARDABLE
DATA MULTIPLE MOVEABLE

HEAPSIZE   512
STACKSIZE 8192
```

DYNA16.MAK

```
#  MAKE file for Win16 API using dynamic BIDS,
#  OWL and C-runtime libraries.
#
#    C> make -fstatic16.mak
#

.AUTODEPEND
CC = -c -H -H"owl\owlpch.h" -ml -R -vi -WS -X-
CD = -D_RTLDLL;_BIDSDLL;_OWLDLL;_OWLPCH;
INC = -I\BC4\INCLUDE
LIB = -L\BC4\LIB

segalloc.exe :  segalloc.obj segalloc.res
  tlink -c -C -Twe $(LIB) @dyna16.lnk
  brc segalloc.res segalloc.exe

segalloc.obj :  segalloc.cpp
  bcc $(CC) $(CD) segalloc.cpp

segalloc.res :  segalloc.rc segalloc.ico segalloc.h
  brc $(INC) -31 -R segalloc.rc
```

DYNA16.LNK

```
\bc4\lib\c0wl.obj+
segalloc.obj
segalloc,segalloc
\bc4\lib\bidsi.lib+
\bc4\lib\owlwi.lib+
\bc4\lib\import.lib+
\bc4\lib\crtldll.lib
segalloc.def
```

DYNA32.MAK

```
#  MAKE file for Win32 API using dynamic BIDS,
#  OWL and C-runtime libraries.
#
#    C> make -fdyna32.mak
#

.AUTODEPEND
CC = -c -H -H\""owl\owlpch.h\"" -p- -R -vi -W -X-
CD = -D_RTLDLL;_BIDSDLL;_OWLDLL;_OWLPCH;
INC = -I\BC4\INCLUDE
LIB = -L\BC4\LIB

segalloc.exe :  segalloc.obj segalloc.res
  tlink32 -aa -c -Tpe $(LIB) @dyna32.lnk
  brc32 segalloc.res segalloc.exe

segalloc.obj :  segalloc.cpp
  bcc32 $(CC) $(CD) segalloc.cpp

segalloc.res :  segalloc.rc segalloc.ico segalloc.h
  brc32 $(INC) -w32 -R segalloc.rc
```

DYNA32.LNK

```
\bc4\lib\c0w32.obj+
segalloc.obj
segalloc,segalloc
\bc4\lib\bidsfi.lib+
\bc4\lib\owlwfi.lib+
\bc4\lib\import32.lib+
\bc4\lib\cw32i.lib
segalloc.def
```

Perhaps the most important aspect of this code involves the error checking that is performed when a global memory object is allocated and locked. It is important to check the return value from the various allocation and locking routines, because there is no guarantee that you will get the memory you have asked for. And even if you get the memory you ask for, you must guard against the possibility that a memory handle will become invalid. In a large program, with many different pieces, it's always possible that a memory handle can get overwritten, or inadvertently freed.

Another important aspect of global heap allocation has to do with locking. To run well in real mode, Windows programs keep all dynamic memory objects unlocked. The reason is simple: Without hardware support for memory management, memory must be managed in software. Windows programmers who worked with versions 1.x and 2.x created a "Windows sandwich" whenever they wished to access a global memory object.

Starting with Windows 3.1, however, Windows will no longer support real mode. Instead, Windows will rely on the protected modes of the host CPU. This means that Windows will rely on *hardware* memory management. Because of this, you can lock global memory objects when you allocate them, and keep them locked until you need to free the object. When you free a global memory object, you must first unlock it.

Our next sample program looks at the relationship between the structure of a program's code and good memory usage. The recommendation that a program be divided into multiple, small code segments goes against the grain of many DOS programmers. But since DOS is a single-tasking system, with no built-in support for dynamic overlays, DOS programmers can get away with creating monolithic programs with large code segments. Efficient operation under Windows, on the other hand, requires a different approach.

Code Structure and Memory Use

Most of the material in this chapter deals with the data used by a program. But an equally important issue is the memory used by a program's code. Because of the magic of dynamic linking, Windows can run with only part of a program loaded into memory at any given time. Dynamic linking gives you all the benefits of a sophisticated overlay manager, without requiring you to carefully design each overlay.

While care is not *required* in putting together the different overlay working sets that make up a program, some effort is required to get the best performance in a low-memory situation. Even in protected mode, when there are megabytes and megabytes of memory, a program can encounter a low-memory situation when there are lots of other programs running. To help you create programs that run well in low-memory situations, we're going to provide two basic recommendations: one easy and one requiring a little more effort. The approach you take will depend on the size of your program, and the need to perform well in low-memory situations.

The simple approach involves dividing your program into multiple, small (4K or so) code segments. You accomplish this by dividing your code between multiple source files. But beyond that, you must make entries into your program's module definition (.DEF) file. This is necessary because the linker (TLINK.EXE) will try to pack smaller code segments into larger code segments. But hopefully, by restructuring your application, you'll be able to define your own **PRELOAD** segments, so that the Windows loader can be sure to load the minimum required set of segments to make your program's startup perform quickly.

The second approach that you can take to improve your program's performance in low-memory situations involves running a swap-tuning utility. There are a number of these available, including one from MicroQuill of Seattle. These utilities let you determine your program's actual **working sets**. A working set is the group of code segments required to perform a specific task or set of tasks. A swap-tuning utility helps you see the actual memory activity of your program, so that you can adjust the code that each code segment contains to minimize thrashing—the need to reread many different segments from disk in order to accomplish a specific task.

A Sample Segmented Program

We're going to start by showing a simple example of a segmented program. This is hardly going to be a "realistic example," since we're just going to divide our minimum Windows program, MIN, into three segments. However, our experience shows that some of the trouble with segmenting an application involves using the development tools properly. Therefore, this example will show you how to overcome these quirks to successfully divide a program into multiple code segments.

We're going to call this program MIN2, although you can call it "Son of Min," if you'd like. MIN2 has two source files: MIN.CPP and DFRAME.CPP. Here is the source code:

MIN.CPP

```
// MIN.CPP      A Minimum OWL 2.0 Program which demonstrates the
//              principle of code segmentation.
//
#include <owl\owlpch.h>
#include "min.h"

DApp::DApp() : TApplication()
    {
    }

void DApp::InitMainWindow()
    {
    SetMainWindow (new DFrame("Segmented Minimum OWL Program"));

    MainWindow->AssignMenu("MAIN");
    MainWindow->SetIcon(this, "SNAPSHOT");
    }

//
// Application main entry point.
OwlMain(int, char **)
    {
    return DApp().Run();
    }
```

MIN.H

```
#define CM_FILEEXIT 100
#define CM_HELPABOUT 200

// Main window
class DFrame : public TFrameWindow
    {
  public:
    DFrame(char * title);
    void CmFileExit();
    void CmHelpAbout();

  DECLARE_RESPONSE_TABLE (DFrame);
    };

// Application object
class DApp : public TApplication
    {
  public:
    DApp();
    void InitMainWindow();
    };
```

DFRAME.CPP

```
// DFRAME.CPP  Class functions for DFrame, MIN's frame
//             window class derived from OWL's
//             TFrameWindow class.
//

#include <owl\owlpch.h>
#include "min.h"

DEFINE_RESPONSE_TABLE1 (DFrame, TFrameWindow)
  EV_COMMAND(CM_FILEEXIT, CmFileExit),
  EV_COMMAND(CM_HELPABOUT, CmHelpAbout),
END_RESPONSE_TABLE;

DFrame::DFrame(char * title) : TFrameWindow(0, title)
    {
    }

void DFrame::CmFileExit()
    {
    CloseWindow(0); // Cause application to terminate
    }

void DFrame::CmHelpAbout()
    {
    MessageBox("Segmented Minimum OWL 2.0 Program\n\n"
               "     'Borland C++ 4.0 Programming\n"
               "      for Windows', by Paul Yao", Title);
    }
```

MIN.RC

```
#include "min.h"

snapshot icon min.ico

main menu
    BEGIN
    POPUP "&File"
        {
        MENUITEM "E&xit", CM_FILEEXIT
        }
    POPUP "&Help"
        {
        MENUITEM "&About...", CM_HELPABOUT
        }
    END
```

MIN.DEF

```
EXETYPE WINDOWS

CODE MOVEABLE DISCARDABLE
DATA MULTIPLE MOVEABLE

HEAPSIZE   512
STACKSIZE 8192

SEGMENTS
   _TEXT        PRELOAD MOVEABLE DISCARDABLE
   MIN_TEXT     LOADONCALL MOVEABLE DISCARDABLE
   DFRAME_TEXT  LOADONCALL DISCARDABLE
```

DYNA16.MAK

```
#  MAKE file for Win16 API using dynamic BIDS,
#  OWL and C-runtime libraries.
#
#    C> make -fstatic16.mak
#

.AUTODEPEND
CC = -c -H -H"owl\owlpch.h" -ml -R -vi -WS -X-
CD = -D_RTLDLL;_BIDSDLL;_OWLDLL;_OWLPCH;
INC = -I\BC4\INCLUDE
LIB = -L\BC4\LIB

min.exe :  min.obj dframe.obj min.res
  tlink -c -C -Twe $(LIB) @dyna16.lnk
  brc min.res min.exe

min.obj :  min.cpp
  bcc $(CC) $(CD) min.cpp

dframe.obj :  dframe.cpp
```

```
  bcc $(CC) $(CD) dframe.cpp

min.res :  min.rc min.ico min.h
  brc $(INC) -31 -R min.rc
```

DYNA16.LNK

```
\bc4\lib\c0wl.obj+
min.obj+dframe.obj
min,min
\bc4\lib\bidsi.lib+
\bc4\lib\owlwi.lib+
\bc4\lib\import.lib+
\bc4\lib\crtldll.lib
min.def
```

DYNA32.MAK

```
#  MAKE file for Win32 API using dynamic BIDS,
#  OWL and C-runtime libraries.
#
#     C> make -fdyna32.mak
#

.AUTODEPEND
CC = -c -H -H\""owl\owlpch.h\"" -p- -R -vi -W -X-
CD = -D_RTLDLL;_BIDSDLL;_OWLDLL;_OWLPCH;
INC = -I\BC4\INCLUDE
LIB = -L\BC4\LIB

min.exe :  min.obj dframe.obj min.res
  tlink32 -aa -c -Tpe $(LIB) @dyna32.lnk
  brc32 min.res min.exe

min.obj :  min.cpp
  bcc32 $(CC) $(CD) min.cpp

dframe.obj :  dframe.cpp
  bcc32 $(CC) $(CD) dframe.cpp

min.res :  min.rc min.ico min.h
  brc32 $(INC) -w32 -R min.rc
```

DYNA32.LNK

```
\bc4\lib\c0w32.obj+
min.obj+dframe.obj
min,min
\bc4\lib\bidsfi.lib+
\bc4\lib\owlwfi.lib+
\bc4\lib\import32.lib+
\bc4\lib\cw32i.lib
min.def
```

Even though this program has only two source files, there are actually three code segments. The first two code segments, **MIN_TEXT** and **DFRAME_TEXT**, are created from the code in the files, respectively, MIN.CPP and DFRAME.CPP. The third code segment, **_TEXT**, contains MIN's startup code and other support routines that are automatically linked in at program creation time.

Each segment is listed under the SEGMENTS keyword in the module definition file. This mechanism allows you to set different memory attributes for different segments. You use the following keywords to request different attributes: **PRELOAD**, **MOVEABLE**, **DISCARDABLE**, **FIXED**, and **LOADONCALL**.

Each keyword gives a memory attribute to a segment. Note that you should avoid using the **FIXED** keyword. There is a bug in version 3.0 of Windows that makes such segments fixed and page locked. While this will be corrected in a future version, you should avoid this keyword for now. While the use of this keyword is suitable for device drivers, it is not suitable for application programs because of the constraints its use puts on the global heap manager.

The next step to tuning MIN2, of course, involves running it through the swap tuner. This would allow us to see when segments are loaded and discarded. Of course, there are only a few routines in the two segments that make up MIN2. In a larger program, the swap tuner would help to restructure a program to improve the performance in a low-memory situation.

The results of swap tuning can seem paradoxical at times. For example, to make the best use of memory, it may be necessary to duplicate certain routines that are used in several different places. Instead of centralizing the "helper" routines in a program, it may make sense to create multiple copies of each, with a local copy in the code segments where the service is needed. Another alternative involves proving each function with its own code segment. Of course, the trade-off here is that far calls are quite a bit more expensive than near calls.

We hope this introduction to the effect of code structure on memory use will help you start thinking about code in a different way. Code structure *can* affect the performance of a Windows program, just as surely as the structure of a program's data will affect its performance. It's time to look at our next sample program, which provides an example of using the local heap that is automatically provided as part of every program's default data segment.

Local Heap Allocation

Let's take a look at Windows' local heap allocation routines. Table 18.7 lists all of the routines that are provided for local heap management. We're going to focus our attention on six of them: **LocalInit**, **LocalAlloc**, **LocalReAlloc**, **LocalLock**, **LocalUnlock**, and **LocalFree**.

Table 18.7 All Windows' Local Heap Allocation Routines

LocalAlloc	Allocates memory from a local heap.
LocalCompact	Reorganizes a local heap.
LocalDiscard	Discards an unlocked, discardable object.
LocalFlags	Provides information about a specific memory object.
LocalFree	Frees a local memory object.
LocalHandle	Provides the handle of a local memory object associated with a given memory address.
LocalInit	Initializes a local heap.
LocalLock	Increments the lock count on a local memory object, and returns its address.
LocalReAlloc	Changes the size of a local memory object.
LocalShrink	Reorganizes a local heap and reduces the size of the heap (if possible) to the initial, starting size. If this routine is successful, it reduces the size of the data segment that contains the heap, so that the memory can be reclaimed by the global heap.
LocalSize	Returns the current size of a local memory object.
LocalUnlock	Decrements the lock count on a local memory object.

LocalInit

The **LocalInit** routine initializes a local heap. **LocalInit** takes three parameters:

```
BOOL LocalInit (wSegment, pStart, pEnd)
```

- **wSegment** is the segment address of the heap to be initialized. Or, if it is zero, the data segment referenced by the DS register is initialized.
- **pStart** is the beginning offset of the heap in the segment.
- **pEnd** is the offset of the end of the heap in the segment. Or, if **pStart** is zero, then **pEnd** is the size of the heap, and a heap is created at the *end* of the designated segment.

LocalInit installs the necessary data structures that are required to support local heap allocation in a segment. Windows programs do not need to initialize their default data segment, since **LocalInit** is called automatically for you. However, **LocalInit** *can* be called to set up a local heap in another segment. As we'll detail later in this chapter, this allows you to have access to as many local heaps as you need.

Unlike application programs, Windows dynamic link libraries must explicitly call **LocalInit** in order to have a local heap. We'll discuss how this is done in Chapter 19, when we describe how to write dynamic link libraries.

LocalAlloc

The **LocalAlloc** routine allocates memory from a local heap. It is defined as

```
HLOCAL LocalAlloc (wFlags, wBytes)
```

- **wFlags** is a combination of one or more local memory allocation flags, discussed below.
- **wBytes** is an unsigned integer value of the size of the object to allocate.

LocalAlloc returns a handle that identifies the object you've allocated. Be sure that you *always* check the return value, since there is never a guarantee that you'll get the memory you requested. A NULL handle is returned when a memory allocation request fails.

The value of **wFlags** can be a combination of five flags, depending on the type of memory object you wish to allocate (fixed, moveable, or discardable), whether you wish to avoid disturbing the heap, and whether you wish to initialize with zeros. This table lists your choices:

Description	*Flags*
Fixed memory object	LMEM_FIXED
Moveable memory object	LMEM_MOVEABLE
Discardable memory object	LMEM_MOVEABLE | LMEM_DISCARDABLE
Do not compact or discard	LMEM_NOCOMPACT
Initialize with zeros	LMEM_ZEROINIT

As this table suggests, if you wish to allocate a discardable object, you use *both* the moveable and the discardable flag. This makes sense, since a discardable object must also be moveable. The **LMEM_NOCOMPACT** flag tells the local memory manager that your need for memory can be satisfied some other way, and that if there isn't an available free block, no moving or discarding should be done to satisfy the memory allocation. When you wish to use more than one flag, you combine them using the OR operator "|." For example, to allocate a five-byte moveable object that is initialized with zeros, you say

```
hMem = LocalAlloc (LMEM_MOVEABLE | LMEM_ZEROINIT, 5);
```

Be careful to avoid the **LMEM_NODISCARD** flag, which is mentioned in the Microsoft documentation but doesn't seem to have the effect that the documentation says it should. The documentation says that it should prevent discarding, but it seems to have no effect at all.

LocalAlloc returns a memory handle. For moveable and discardable memory objects, you obtain a pointer by calling the **LocalLock** routine, which we'll discuss shortly. For fixed objects, the handle itself is a pointer. In this way, **LocalAlloc** can be used in exactly the same manner as the runtime library's **malloc**. In other words, here is how to allocate and use a fixed memory object:

```
char * pch;
pch =(char *)LocalAlloc (LMEM_FIXED|LMEM_ZEROINIT, 15);
lstrcpy (pch, "Hello World");
```

For the sake of clarity, this code uses the normal C++ type, `char *`, instead of the more precise Windows type, **PSTR**. You may have already noticed that this code casts the return value from **LocalAlloc**. This prevents the compiler from complaining about assigning a `HANDLE` value (unsigned int) to a pointer. We know it's correct. The cast tells the compiler to save its error messages for real problems.

LocalLock

The **LocalLock** routine increments the lock count on a local memory object and returns its address:

```
PSTR LocalLock (hMem)
```

- **hMem** is a handle to a memory object, returned by a call to **LocalAlloc**.

Programs call **LocalLock** to get the address of a moveable or discardable object. At the same time, this routine makes sure that the object won't get moved or discarded so that the address will be valid until a call is made to **LocalUnlock**. In general, it's a good idea to keep all objects unlocked until the precise time that they are needed. This gives the local heap manager the freedom to move memory as it needs to so that it can optimize the use of the local heap.

According to the prototype in WINDOWS.H, **LocalLock** returns a near pointer to a character string. However, this doesn't mean that only character values can be placed into a memory object. You put the return value from **LocalLock** into any type of pointer, to provide you with a convenient way to access any type of dynamically allocated data. The following example makes it easy to store an array of integers into a local memory object:

```
int * pi;

pi = (int near * )LocalLock (hmem);
if (pi)
    {
    pi[0] = 1;
    pi[1] = 2;
```

```
        LocalUnlock (hmem);
        }
    else
        {
        /* Error.  */
        }
```

It's very important to check the return value from **LocalLock**, as we've done in this example. A null pointer indicates that the lock has failed. There are several things that could make this happen. If we are trying to lock a discardable object, it's possible that the object has been discarded. Or, perhaps the memory handle has been accidentally overwritten. Whatever the cause, you don't want to write using a null pointer. You will overwrite the memory locations at the bottom of your data segment, which means the data area that is used to maintain your data segment.

LocalReAlloc

The **LocalReAlloc** routine changes the size of a local memory object. **LocalReAlloc** is defined as

```
HLOCAL LocalReAlloc (hMem, wBytes, wFlags)
```

- **hMem** is a memory handle returned by the **LocalAlloc** routine.
- **wBytes** is the new size. When you make an object smaller, it truncates (and loses) the data from the end of the object. When you make an object larger, it preserves the previous contents of the object.
- **wFlags** is a combination of one or more local allocation flags.

LocalReAlloc returns a HANDLE, which is one of three values. If the reallocation fails, the return value is NULL. For moveable and discardable objects, if the allocation is successful, the return value is the same handle value that was passed into the routine. For fixed objects, the handle may be the same or may be different, depending on whether the object must be moved to satisfy the allocation request.

To understand why, recall from our earlier discussion that the handle to a fixed memory object is actually a pointer to the object itself. If the object must be moved to satisfy a memory allocation request, it follows that the pointer must change as well. To prevent the local memory manager from mysteriously moving a fixed object, a fixed object will only be moved by the **LocalReAlloc** call if the **LMEM_MOVEABLE** flag is specified. For example, here is how to reallocate a fixed memory object, allowing it to move:

```
/*  Enlarge a fixed object, and let it move.          */
hNew = LocalReAlloc (hOld,
                     cbSize,         /* New size.     */
                     LMEM_MOVEABLE);/* Ok to move.    */
if (!hNew)
```

```
        {
        /*  Error.  */
        }
    else
        hOld = hNew;
```

The **LMEM_MOVEABLE** flag has another use. This flag allows a moveable or discardable memory object that is *locked* to be moved if needed to satisfy an allocation request. In most cases, you'll only change the size of a moveable or discardable memory object when it is unlocked. At such times, the memory manager is free to relocate the object. But, if you wish to make a locked object larger, you'll need to include the **LMEM_MOVEABLE** flag in case the object must be moved.

If you want to change the *size* of a local memory object and *not* its memory disposition (fixed, moveable, discardable), you can set **wFlags** to zero. Or, use the **LMEM_ZEROINIT** flag to ask for a larger object with the newly allocated space zero initialized. For example, even though the **wFlags** field is set to zero in this example, it doesn't change the memory disposition—only the size:

```
    h = LocalReAlloc (hMem,
                      28,          /*  New size.        */
                      0);          /*  Ignore flags.    */
```

To change the memory disposition of a memory object, use the **LMEM_MODIFY** flag. You can't change the disposition of a fixed memory object. However, you *can* make a moveable object discardable, or make a discardable object into a moveable object. To make a moveable object discardable, you say

```
    LocalReAlloc (hMem,
                  0,                  /* Ignore the size.   */
                  LMEM_MODIFY    |    /* Just change flags. */
                  LMEM_MOVEABLE  |
                  LMEM_DISCARDABLE);
```

and to make a discardable object moveable, you say

```
    LocalReAlloc (hMem,
                  0,                  /* Ignore the size.   */
                  LMEM_MODIFY |       /* Just change flags. */
                  LMEM_MOVEABLE);
```

When you change the memory disposition like this, the reallocation size is ignored. In these examples, even though we request a reallocation size of zero, the **LMEM_MODIFY** flag has precedence. So we can safely use a value of zero, to avoid having to figure out the current size of the object and pass it in to **LocalReAlloc**.

LocalUnlock

The **LocalUnlock** routine decrements the lock count on a local memory object;

```
BOOL LocalUnlock (hMem)
```

- **hMem** is a local memory handle, as provided by the **LocalAlloc** routine.

The **LocalUnlock** routine is the second slice to a Windows sandwich. To give the local memory manager the greatest freedom to manage the local heap, you should lock memory objects for only the briefest period of time. For example, to store character values that a program receives from a **WM_CHAR** message, you would say

```
WndProc (...)
    {
    switch (msg)
        {
        case WM_CHAR:
            pch = LocalLock(hmem);
            pch[iNextChar] = (unsigned char) wParam;
            LocalUnlock (hmem);
            break;
            ...
```

In this case, the memory object identified by the handle **hmem** is only kept locked for as long as it takes to copy a character into the memory object.

LocalFree

The **LocalFree** routine frees a local memory object:

```
HLOCAL LocalFree (hMem)
```

- **hMem** is a memory handle returned by **LocalAlloc**.

Any time a dynamic memory object is allocated, it consumes memory that cannot be used for other purposes. Therefore, care should be taken to free memory that is not needed. The **LocalFree** routine is provided for this purpose.

Of course, Windows has *some* safeguards to keep memory from going away permanently. For example, when a program terminates, all of the dynamic memory that it allocated is automatically freed. This helps prevent the global heap from becoming congested with unnecessary blocks of memory that programs forgot to free. In spite of this, Windows programmers should be careful to always free memory that is no longer needed.

LOCALMEM: A Sample Heap Allocation Program

Let's take a look at a sample Windows program that shows some basic techniques in dealing with local memory. This program actually shows how to use two different types of

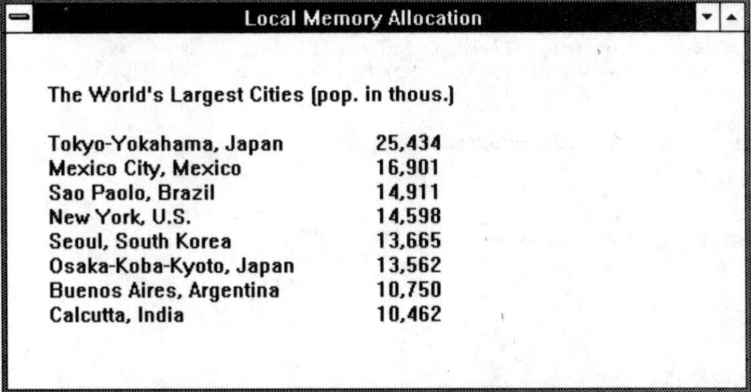

Figure 18.5 Sample program showing local heap allocation

application memory: the local heap and string resources. This program reads in a list of cities that are saved as string resources. These are stored in moveable memory objects that have been allocated from the local heap. Figure 18.5 shows the program running.

LOCALMEM.CPP

```
// LOCALMEM.CPP  Demonstrates use of local heap
//               and of string table.
#include <owl\owlpch.h>
#include "localmem.h"

//
// Main window
class DFrame : public TFrameWindow
    {
  public:
    DFrame(char * title);
    void CmFileExit();
    void CmHelpAbout();
    void SetupWindow();
    void Paint (TDC& dc, BOOL, TRect&);
  private:
    HINSTANCE  hInst;
    HLOCAL     ahCities;
    PSTR       pchNoMem;
    TEXTMETRIC tmSys;
  DECLARE_RESPONSE_TABLE (DFrame);
    };

DEFINE_RESPONSE_TABLE1 (DFrame, TFrameWindow)
  EV_COMMAND(CM_FILEEXIT, CmFileExit),
  EV_COMMAND(CM_HELPABOUT, CmHelpAbout),
END_RESPONSE_TABLE;

DFrame::DFrame(char * title) : TFrameWindow(0, title)
    {
    // Make a copy of the instance handle.
    hInst = GetApplication()->GetInstance();
```

```
    //  Load 'out of memory' message from string table.
    pchNoMem = (PSTR)LocalAlloc (LMEM_FIXED, MAXSTRLEN);
    if (!pchNoMem)
        {
        Status = 1;  // Fail?  Exit program.
        return;
        }

    int ccSize = GetApplication()->LoadString (IDS_NOMEM,
                                               pchNoMem,
                                               MAXSTRLEN);
    LocalReAlloc ((HLOCAL)pchNoMem, ccSize+1, 0);
    }

void DFrame::CmFileExit()
    {
    CloseWindow(0); // Cause application to terminate
    }

void DFrame::CmHelpAbout()
    {
    MessageBox("       Local Heap Allocation\n\n"
               "'Borland C++ 4.0 Programming\n"
               "  for Windows', by Paul Yao", Title);
    }

void DFrame::SetupWindow()
    {
    int     cbSize;
    int     i;
    PHANDLE pah;
    PSTR    pstr;

    TWindow::SetupWindow();

    // Fetch text metric info.
    TClientDC dc(HWindow);
    dc.GetTextMetrics (tmSys);    //  Save for later.

    //  Allocate and lock memory for array of handles.
    ahCities = LocalAlloc (LHND, sizeof(HLOCAL) * CITYCOUNT);
    pah = (PHANDLE)LocalLock (ahCities);

    //  Error checking:  if lock fails, exit.
    if (!pah)
        {
        goto ErrExit1;
        }

    // Loop to read city names.
    for (i=0;i<CITYCOUNT ;i++)
        {
        //  Allocate and lock memory.
        pah[i] = LocalAlloc (LMEM_MOVEABLE, MAXSTRLEN);
        pstr = (PSTR)LocalLock (pah[i]);

        //  If lock fails, exit.
        if (!pstr)
            {
            goto ErrExit2;
            }
```

```
        //  Copy string into dynamic memory object.
        cbSize = GetApplication()->LoadString (i+IDS_CITY,
                                               pstr, MAXSTRLEN);

        //  Unlock and resize memory to exact string size.
        LocalUnlock (pah[i]);
        LocalReAlloc (pah[i], cbSize+1, 0);

        } /* [for i] */

    LocalUnlock (ahCities);

    //  All went well.
    return;

ErrExit2:
    //  Out of memory.  Free everything.
    for (i--;i>=0;i--)
        LocalFree (pah[i]);
    LocalUnlock (ahCities);
    LocalFree(ahCities);

ErrExit1:
    return;  //  Unable to complete.
    }

void DFrame::Paint (TDC& dc, BOOL, TRect&)
    {
    PSTR    pstr;
    int     i;

    //  Initialize values for writing lines of text.
    int xText = tmSys.tmAveCharWidth * 4;
    int yText = tmSys.tmHeight * 2;
    TRect rClient = GetClientRect ();
    int xTabPosition = rClient.right/2;

    //  Lock array of handles.  If fail, exit.
    PHANDLE pah = (PHANDLE)LocalLock (ahCities);
    if (!pah)
        goto ErrExit;

    // Loop through each item in the list.
    for (i=0;i<CITYCOUNT;i++)
        {
        pstr = (PSTR)LocalLock (pah[i]);
        if (pstr)
            {
            TPoint pt(xText, yText);
            dc.TabbedTextOut ( pt,
                               pstr,
                               lstrlen(pstr),
                               1,
                               &xTabPosition,
                               0);
            LocalUnlock (pah[i]);
            }

        //  Increment for next line.
        yText += tmSys.tmHeight + tmSys.tmExternalLeading;
        }
```

```
    LocalUnlock (ahCities);

ErrExit:
    return;
    }

//
// Application object
class DApp : public TApplication
    {
  public:
    DApp();
    void InitMainWindow();
  private:
    PSTR  pchTitle;
    };

DApp::DApp() : TApplication()
    {
    //  Load application title from string table.
    pchTitle = (PSTR)LocalAlloc (LMEM_FIXED, MAXSTRLEN);
    if (!pchTitle)
        {
        Status = 1;  // Fail?  Exit program.
        return;
        }

    int ccSize = LoadString (IDS_TITLE, pchTitle, MAXSTRLEN);
    LocalReAlloc ((HLOCAL)pchTitle, ccSize+1, 0);
    }

void DApp::InitMainWindow()
    {
    SetMainWindow (new DFrame("OWL Minimum"));

    MainWindow->AssignMenu("MAIN");
    MainWindow->SetIcon(this, "SNAPSHOT");
    }

//
// Application main entry point.
OwlMain(int, char **)
    {
    return DApp().Run();
    }
```

LOCALMEM.H

```
#define CM_FILEEXIT 100
#define CM_HELPABOUT 200

#define IDS_TITLE  0
#define IDS_NOMEM  1
#define IDS_CITY  16
#define MAXSTRLEN 80
#define CITYCOUNT 10
```

LOCALMEM.RC

```
#include "localmem.h"

snapshot icon localmem.ico

main menu
    BEGIN
    POPUP "&File"
        {
        MENUITEM "E&xit", CM_FILEEXIT
        }
    POPUP "&Help"
        {
        MENUITEM "&About...", CM_HELPABOUT
        }
    END

stringtable
  {
  IDS_TITLE, "Local Memory Allocation"
  IDS_NOMEM, "Unable to Initialize Program - Out of Memory"
  IDS_CITY    "The World's Largest Cities (pop. in thous.)"
  IDS_CITY+1, " ";
  IDS_CITY+2, "Tokyo-Yokahama, Japan\t25,434"
  IDS_CITY+3, "Mexico City, Mexico\t16,901"
  IDS_CITY+4, "Sao Paolo, Brazil\t14,911"
  IDS_CITY+5, "New York, U.S.\t14,598"
  IDS_CITY+6, "Seoul, South Korea\t13,665"
  IDS_CITY+7, "Osaka-Koba-Kyoto, Japan\t13,562"
  IDS_CITY+8, "Buenos Aires, Argentina\t10,750"
  IDS_CITY+9, "Calcutta, India\t10,462"
  }
```

LOCALMEM.DEF

```
EXETYPE WINDOWS

CODE MOVEABLE DISCARDABLE
DATA MULTIPLE MOVEABLE

HEAPSIZE   512
STACKSIZE 8192
```

DYNA16.MAK

```
#  MAKE file for Win16 API using dynamic BIDS,
#  OWL and C-runtime libraries.
#
#    C> make -fstatic16.mak
#

.AUTODEPEND
CC = -c -H -H"owl\owlpch.h" -ml -R -vi -WS -X-
CD = -D_RTLDLL;_BIDSDLL;_OWLDLL;_OWLPCH;
```

```
INC = -I\BC4\INCLUDE
LIB = -L\BC4\LIB

localmem.exe :  localmem.obj localmem.res
  tlink -c -C -Twe $(LIB) @dyna16.lnk
  brc localmem.res localmem.exe

localmem.obj :  localmem.cpp
  bcc $(CC) $(CD) localmem.cpp

localmem.res :  localmem.rc localmem.ico localmem.h
  brc $(INC) -31 -R localmem.rc
```

DYNA16.LNK

```
\bc4\lib\c0wl.obj+
localmem.obj
localmem,localmem
\bc4\lib\bidsi.lib+
\bc4\lib\owlwi.lib+
\bc4\lib\import.lib+
\bc4\lib\crtldll.lib
localmem.def
```

DYNA32.MAK

```
#  MAKE file for Win32 API using dynamic BIDS,
#  OWL and C-runtime libraries.
#
#    C> make -fdyna32.mak
#

.AUTODEPEND
CC = -c -H -H\""owl\owlpch.h\"" -p- -R -vi -W -X-
CD = -D_RTLDLL;_BIDSDLL;_OWLDLL;_OWLPCH;
INC = -I\BC4\INCLUDE
LIB = -L\BC4\LIB

localmem.exe :  localmem.obj localmem.res
  tlink32 -aa -c -Tpe $(LIB) @dyna32.lnk
  brc32 localmem.res localmem.exe

localmem.obj :  localmem.cpp
  bcc32 $(CC) $(CD) localmem.cpp

localmem.res :  localmem.rc localmem.ico localmem.h
  brc32 $(INC) -w32 -R localmem.rc
```

DYNA32.LNK

```
\bc4\lib\c0w32.obj+
localmem.obj
localmem,localmem
\bc4\lib\bidsfi.lib+
\bc4\lib\owlwfi.lib+
\bc4\lib\import32.lib+
\bc4\lib\cw32i.lib
localmem.def
```

Most of the action in LOCALMEM occurs in response to two messages: **WM_CREATE** and **WM_PAINT**. Memory is allocated and string tables read in response to **WM_CREATE**. All of this is displayed when the **WM_PAINT** message is received.

If there is any one issue in local memory management that is more critical than any other, it involves error checking. In order for a Windows program to be robust and error free, it must respond properly to failed memory allocation requests. The point is simple: Not every allocation request can be satisfied. When an allocation fails, a program must be ready to take corrective action to avoid losing data.

For this reason, every dynamic allocation request in LOCALMEM is followed by a check for a valid memory handle. For example:

```
/*  Load application title from string table.        */
pchTitle = (PSTR)LocalAlloc (LMEM_FIXED, MAXSTRLEN);
if (!pchTitle)
    {
    Status = 1;  // Fail?  Exit program.
    return;
    }
```

Since a fixed memory object is being allocated, the handle is a pointer to a character string. In the terms of WINDOWS.H definitions, **PSTR** is the same as **char near ***. If **LocalAlloc** fails, it returns a null value. On receipt of a null, this code sets the application object's error status flag and returns.

If the above lines of code are successful, the **LoadString** routine is called to copy a string from a string table resource into the memory that is allocated. The object is then shrunk so that it is just large enough to hold the number of characters that **LoadString** reports as having been copied.

```
ccSize = LoadString (hInst, IDS_TITLE, pchTitle,
                     MAXSTRLEN);
LocalReAlloc ((HANDLE)pchTitle, ccSize+1, 0);
```

The **LoadString** routine is defined as follows:

```
LoadString (hInstance, wID, lpBuffer, nBufferMax)
```

- **hInstance** is an instance handle.

- **wID** is an integer identifier of the string to be retrieved.
- **lpBuffer** is a long pointer to a character string buffer.
- **nBufferMax** is the maximum number of characters to copy to `lpBuffer`.

Later in this chapter, we're going to discuss some of the memory implications of using resources. In brief, it provides a great deal of flexibility in moving read-only data out of a program's data segment and onto disk. Like the strings from the string table resource, resources are read into memory when they are needed and discarded from memory when they aren't needed. Resources provide another type of data container that should be considered as part of a Windows program's total memory management picture. For now, let's get back to LOCALMEM.

Another approach that you can take to error checking involves testing only the return value of **LocalLock** and *not* **LocalAlloc** when the two are paired together. Here is an example:

```
/*  Allocate and lock memory.                                    */
pah[i] = LocalAlloc (LMEM_MOVEABLE, MAXSTRLEN);
pstr = (PSTR) LocalLock (pah[i]);

/*  If lock fails, exit.                                         */
if (!pstr)
    {
    bRetVal = FALSE;
    goto ErrExit2;
    }
```

In this case, a single test validates the calls to *both* routines. Programmers are often eager to omit error checking, but this is unwise. After all, an "invalid" pointer is still usable from the point of view of the C++ programming language: It points to the bottom of the data segment, which is where the segment header lives. A single write to the right byte in this area can cause otherwise robust programs to come crashing down.

A program can have more than one local heap. This capability is often overlooked by Windows programmers. The primary reason is probably the lack of a well-documented approach, plus the need to write some assembly language code. The Borland C++ compiler supports embedded assembly language, which we're going to take advantage of to show how a program can create many different local heaps. Each heap resides in a separate, dynamically allocated segment, and can grow to fill an entire segment.

Local Heap Allocation in a Dynamically Allocated Segment

As you know, there are two dynamic memory allocation packages in Windows: local heap allocation and global memory allocation. By default, every Windows program has a local heap. The heap is created by a routine called **InitApp**, which is not documented anywhere but is part of the standard (but hidden) startup sequence of every program. The advantage of the local heap is that the overhead for objects is fairly low and, with an alignment of four bytes, wastage is at a minimum. The only problem with the default local heap, however, is that it is too small for many uses. At most, depending on the size of your stack and static data, a default local heap might be 30–50K.

The problem of size can be solved by using the global heap. The global heap, after all, is the sum total of the address space in the system. On systems with an 80386, this means disk space in addition to physical RAM. The problem with the global heap, however, is that the overhead per object is very high. And, at 32 bytes, the granularity of segments is too high to be used for very small objects. Only large objects, or arrays of small objects, are suitable for storage in objects allocated from the global heap.

To get the benefits of both local and global heap management routines, it's possible to create a local heap in a dynamically allocated global segment. From this heap, small objects can be allocated which can efficiently share the segment with the other objects, all managed by the local heap manager. Doing this requires a little sleight of hand and a little assembly language programming, but the results can be well worth the effort.

The first thing to think about is the fact that the first 16 bytes of the segment are reserved. The local heap manager uses various bytes in this area for its own purposes. If you use this space for something else, you risk overwriting the pointers into your local heap. So, whatever you do, make sure the first 16 bytes are initialized to zero.

The second issue is the initialization of the local heap. This is easily done with the **LocalInit** routine. Here is one way to initialize a local heap in a dynamically allocated segment:

```
HGLOBAL hMem;
int    pStart, pEnd;
LPSTR lp;
WORD  wSeg;

hMem = GlobalAlloc (GMEM_MOVEABLE|GMEM_ZEROINIT, 4096L);
if (!hMem)
    goto ErrorOut;

lp = (LPSTR) GlobalLock (hMem);
wSeg = HIWORD (lp);

pStart = 16;
pEnd   = (int)GlobalSize (hMem)-1;
LocalInit (wSeg, pStart, pEnd);
GlobalUnlock(hMem);
GlobalUnlock (hMem);
```

Notice that two calls to **GlobalUnlock** are required. The first is to counteract the lock of our own call to **GlobalLock**—it's the second slice in a code sandwich. The second call to **GlobalUnlock** is required because **LocalInit** leaves a segment locked. Without this second call, the data segment would be locked in memory. This would prevent the segment from growing, and would create a memory sandbar in the global heap.

As always, **GlobalAlloc**'s return value should always be checked to make sure that the requested memory is available. Even though we asked for a 4,096-byte segment, because different operating modes align on different segment boundaries, we call **GlobalSize** to make sure we know the exact size of the segment. pStart is set to 16 to make room for the header. pEnd is set to the offset of the last byte in the segment, which is the segment size minus 1.

Incidentally, a slightly shorter way to do the same thing involves setting pStart to zero and setting pEnd to the actual *size* of the local heap. Here's the code that does that:

```
pEnd  = (int)GlobalSize (hMem)-16;
LocalInit (wSeg, 0, pEnd);
```

In this case, notice that we're subtracting 16 from the size of the segment rather than just 1. The reason is simple: We must set aside the first 16 bytes for the segment header.

Accessing the local heap requires a little assembly language programming. We're going to cheat a little, and embed assembler into C code. If your compiler doesn't support this, you will have to write stand-alone assembly language subroutines. We can call any local heap management routine. The only difference is that before and after each call, we must change the value in the DS register to hold the address of our local heap. Here's how to do it:

```
LPSTR lp;
HGLOBAL hmem;
WORD  wHeapDS;  /*  Must be a stack variable!  */

lp = (LPSTR) GlobalLock (hmem);  /* Where local heap lives. */
wHeapDS = HIWORD (lp);

_asm{
    push  DS

    mov   AX, wHeapDS
    mov   DS, AX

    }

hmem = LocalAlloc (LMEM_MOVEABLE, 16);

_asm{
    pop   DS
    }

GlobalUnlock (hmem);
```

While this may look rather complex and bizarre, this approach allows a Windows program to derive the benefits of both memory management packages, and to surmount some of the drawbacks of each.

Of course, to use a memory object, you must call two lock routines: one for the segment and one for the local heap object. And, to keep either of these data areas from becoming too fragmented, you will probably want to unlock at both levels. There are compromises, of course. For example, a program might make all local heap objects *fixed*, which removes the need to do the second lock. And, for the most effective use, it probably makes sense to build a small subroutine library to manage the two-level allocation scheme. This might be as simple as creating 32-bit handles, with half for the local handle and half for the global handle. That, in fact, is the approach taken by our sample program. Or, a subroutine package could issue its own, private 16-bit handles that it would then use to find the right segment and the right local memory object. There are several approaches to take, and we hope this brief introduction has provided you with enough information to find one that will work for you.

If you're like many programmers, all this theoretical discussion and bits of code are not as interesting as a full-blown working program that demonstrates how to put the theory into practice. So, without further ado, here is our sample program: SUBSEG.

SUBSEG: A Combined Local/Global Heap Allocation Program

SUBSEG demonstrates how to perform subsegment allocation in a dynamically allocated segment. We borrow the term "subsegment allocation" from the world of OS/2, since it seems to be more suggestive of what we are doing than the term "local allocation." To help you get the most from this example, we have written a set of subsegment allocation routines that mirrors the format of the routines in Windows' standard memory allocation routines. In other words, we've written a routine called **`SubAlloc`** which takes all the same parameters as the **`LocalAlloc`** routine. Four other routines provide the basic allocation services to get you started in writing a complete suballocation library. There is one additional function, **`SubInitialize`**, which allocates a segment from the global heap and initializes the segment to hold a local heap.

SUBSEG is adapted from SEGALLOC, which is the segment allocation sample we presented earlier in this chapter. SUBSEG displays information about the allocated data objects. To convince you that it works as advertised, it reads this information from the data object itself. Figure 18.6 shows SUBSEG running. If you compare this program to the SEGALLOC program, one thing you may notice is that the overhead of objects is much lower in this program. That is because segments allocated from the global heap are aligned on 32-byte boundaries, whereas objects allocated from a local heap are allocated on four-byte boundaries. The wastage due to "rounding" is much less in local heaps.

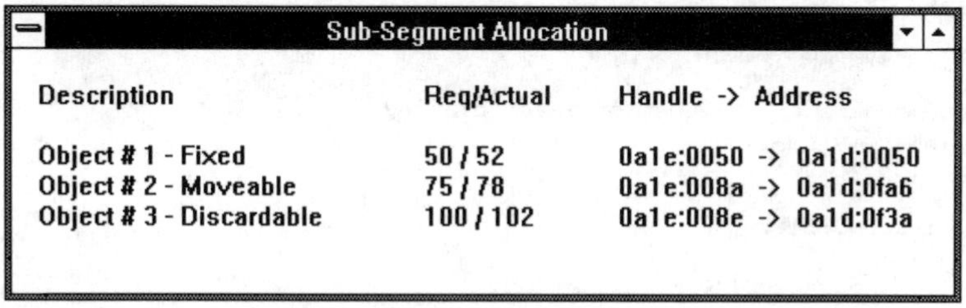

Sub-Segment Allocation

Description	Req/Actual	Handle -> Address
Object # 1 - Fixed	50 / 52	0a1e:0050 -> 0a1d:0050
Object # 2 - Moveable	75 / 78	0a1e:008a -> 0a1d:0fa6
Object # 3 - Discardable	100 / 102	0a1e:008e -> 0a1d:0f3a

Figure 18.6 SUBSEG shows information about the objects it allocates

SUBSEG.CPP

```
// SUBSEG.CPP   Demo of sub-segment allocation in Win16.
//
#include <owl\owlpch.h>
#include "submem.h"
#include "subseg.h"

DEFINE_RESPONSE_TABLE1 (DFrame, TFrameWindow)
  EV_COMMAND(CM_FILEEXIT, CmFileExit),
  EV_COMMAND(CM_HELPABOUT, CmHelpAbout),
END_RESPONSE_TABLE;

DFrame::DFrame(char * title) : TFrameWindow(0, title)
    {
    Label1 = "Description";
    Label2 = "Req/Actual";
    Label3 = "Handle  ->  Address";

    cb1 = lstrlen(Label1);
    cb2 = lstrlen(Label2);
    cb3 = lstrlen(Label3);

    lstrcpy (sdInit[0].achDesc, "Fixed Object");
    sdInit[0].dwAlloc  = 50;
    sdInit[0].wFlags   = GMEM_FIXED;

    lstrcpy (sdInit[1].achDesc, "Moveable Memory");
    sdInit[1].dwAlloc  = 75;
    sdInit[1].wFlags   = GMEM_MOVEABLE | GMEM_ZEROINIT;

    lstrcpy (sdInit[2].achDesc, "Discardable Segment");
    sdInit[2].dwAlloc  = 100;
    sdInit[2].wFlags   = GMEM_DISCARDABLE | GMEM_MOVEABLE;
    }

void DFrame::CmFileExit()
    {
    CloseWindow(0); // Cause application to terminate
    }

void DFrame::CmHelpAbout()
    {
    MessageBox(" SubSegment Heap Allocation Demo\n\n"
               "   'Borland C++ 4.0 Programming\n"
               "      for Windows', by Paul Yao", Title);
    }

void DFrame::SetupWindow()
    {
    TFrameWindow::SetupWindow();

    // Fetch font measurement values for later drawing.
    TClientDC dc(HWindow);
    dc.GetTextMetrics (tmSys);

    for (int i=0;i<COUNT;i++)
        {
        hSegment[i] = SubAlloc(sdInit[i].wFlags,
                               (WORD)sdInit[i].dwAlloc);

        lpSegData[i] = (LPSEGDATA)SubLock (hSegment[i]);
```

```
        if (!lpSegData[i])
            {
            MessageBox ("Not enough memory", Title);
            break;
            }

        lstrcpy (lpSegData[i]->achDesc, sdInit[i].achDesc);
        lpSegData[i]->dwAlloc = sdInit[i].dwAlloc;
        lpSegData[i]->dwActual = SubSize (hSegment[i]);
        lpSegData[i]->wFlags = sdInit[i].wFlags;
        } /* [for] */

    return;
    }

void DFrame::CleanupWindow()
    {
    // Unlock & free all segments.
    for (int i=0;i<COUNT;i++)
        {
        SubUnlock (hSegment[i]);
        SubFree (hSegment[i]);
        }
    }

void DFrame::Paint (TDC& dc, BOOL, TRect&)
    {
    //  Calculate text positioning variables.
    int xText1 = tmSys.tmAveCharWidth * 2;
    int xText2 = xText1 + (STRSIZE * tmSys.tmAveCharWidth);
    int xText3 = xText2 + ((cb2+5) * tmSys.tmAveCharWidth);
    int yText = tmSys.tmHeight;

    //  Print titles.
    dc.TextOut (xText1, yText, Label1, cb1);
    dc.TextOut (xText2, yText, Label2, cb2);
    dc.TextOut (xText3, yText, Label3, cb3);

    yText += tmSys.tmHeight * 2;

    // Loop through displaying segment info.
    char buff[30];
    int  cb;
    for (int i=0;i<COUNT;i++)
        {
        //  Print description.
        dc.TextOut (xText1, yText, lpSegData[i]->achDesc,
                  lstrlen(lpSegData[i]->achDesc));

        //  Print allocated vs actual size.
        cb = wsprintf (buff, "%ld / %ld", lpSegData[i]->dwAlloc,
                                      lpSegData[i]->dwActual);
        dc.TextOut (xText2, yText, buff, cb);

        //  Print handle and actual address.
        cb = wsprintf (buff, "%04x  ->  %04x:%04x", hSegment[i],
                   HIWORD(lpSegData[i]), LOWORD(lpSegData[i]));
        dc.TextOut (xText3, yText, buff, cb);

        //  Advance to next line.
        yText += tmSys.tmHeight + tmSys.tmExternalLeading;
        }
```

```
    }

DApp::DApp() : TApplication()
    {
    // Initialize sub-memory allocator.
    SubInitialize();
    }

void DApp::InitMainWindow()
    {
    SetMainWindow (new DFrame("Sub-Segment Memory Allocation"));

    MainWindow->AssignMenu("MAIN");
    MainWindow->SetIcon(this, "SNAPSHOT");
    }

// Application main entry point.
OwlMain(int, char **)
    {
    return DApp().Run();
    }
```

SUBSEG.H

```
#define CM_FILEEXIT 100
#define CM_HELPABOUT 200

/*------------------------------------------------------------*\
 |                         Constants.                          |
\*------------------------------------------------------------*/
const int STRSIZE = 30;
const int COUNT   = 3;

/*------------------------------------------------------------*\
 |                         TypeDefs.                           |
\*------------------------------------------------------------*/
typedef struct tagSEGDATA
    {
    char  achDesc[STRSIZE]; /* Description of data.  */
    DWORD dwAlloc;          /* Amount asked for.     */
    DWORD dwActual;         /* Actually allocated.   */
    WORD  wFlags;           /* Allocation flags.     */
    } SEGDATA;

typedef SEGDATA FAR *LPSEGDATA;

// Main window
class DFrame : public TFrameWindow
    {
  public:
    DFrame(char * title);
    void CmFileExit();
    void CmHelpAbout();
    void SetupWindow();
    void CleanupWindow();
    void Paint (TDC& dc, BOOL, TRect&);
  private:
    PSTR Label1;
    PSTR Label2;
```

```
    PSTR Label3;

    int cb1;  // Label lengths.
    int cb2;
    int cb3;

    HANDLE32 hSegment[COUNT];
    SEGDATA sdInit[COUNT];

    TEXTMETRIC tmSys;
    LPSEGDATA lpSegData[COUNT];

  DECLARE_RESPONSE_TABLE (DFrame);
    };

// Application object
class DApp : public TApplication
    {
  public:
    DApp();
    void InitMainWindow();
    };
```

SUBMEM.C

```
/*-----------------------------------------------------------*\
 |  SUBMEM.C  -  Sub-segment allocation routines, for creating |
 |               local heaps in dynamically allocated segments.|
\*-----------------------------------------------------------*/
#define WIN31
#define STRICT
#include <Windows.H>
#include <WindowsX.h>

typedef DWORD HANDLE32;

/*-----------------------------------------------------------*\
 |                    Static Data Definitions.                 |
\*-----------------------------------------------------------*/
HGLOBAL hSegment;

/*-----------------------------------------------------------*\
 |  SubInitialize - Call first to allocate a segment from the  |
 |                  global heap.                               |
\*-----------------------------------------------------------*/
BOOL     FAR PASCAL SubInitialize(VOID)
    {
    BOOL  bRetVal;
    LPSTR lp;
    WORD  wSeg;
    WORD  wSize;

    hSegment = GlobalAlloc (GMEM_MOVEABLE | GMEM_ZEROINIT,
                            4096);
    if (!hSegment)
        return FALSE;

    lp = GlobalLock (hSegment);
    if (!lp)
```

```
        return FALSE;

    wSeg = HIWORD (lp);
    wSize = (WORD)GlobalSize (hSegment) - 16;

    bRetVal = LocalInit (wSeg, 0, wSize);

    GlobalUnlock (hSegment);
    GlobalUnlock (hSegment);  /*  Undo LocalInit's GlobalLock. */

    return bRetVal;
    }


/*------------------------------------------------------------*\
 |  SubAlloc - Allocate a subsegment.                          |
 |                                                             |
 |  Input:  wFlags = local heap allocation flags.              |
 |          wBytes = number of bytes to allocate.              |
 |                                                             |
 |  Returns:  A 4-byte "handle", put together as:              |
 |            HIWORD = Handle to global segment.               |
 |            LOWORD = Handle to local object.                 |
\*------------------------------------------------------------*/
HANDLE32 FAR PASCAL SubAlloc(WORD wFlags, WORD wBytes)
    {
    HLOCAL hMem;
    LPSTR  lp;
    WORD   wSeg;

    lp = GlobalLock (hSegment);
    if (!lp)
        return 0L;

    wSeg = HIWORD (lp);

    _asm { push    ds
           mov     ax, wSeg
           mov     ds, ax   }

    hMem = LocalAlloc (wFlags, wBytes);

    _asm { pop     ds }

    GlobalUnlock (hSegment);

    if (!hMem)
        return 0L;
    else
        return MAKELONG (hMem, hSegment);
    }

/*------------------------------------------------------------*\
 |  SubFree - Free a subsegment.                               |
 |                                                             |
 |  Input:  A 4-byte "handle", put together as:                |
 |            HIWORD = Handle to global segment.               |
 |            LOWORD = Handle to local object.                 |
 |                                                             |
 |  Returns:  The original handle, if successful.  Otherwise,  |
 |            returns NULL.                                    |
\*------------------------------------------------------------*/
```

```
HANDLE32 FAR PASCAL SubFree(HANDLE32 hSubMem)
    {
    HGLOBAL hSeg;
    HLOCAL  hMem;
    LPSTR   lp;
    WORD    wSeg;

    hSeg = HIWORD (hSubMem);
    hMem = LOWORD (hSubMem);

    lp = GlobalLock (hSeg);
    if (!lp)
        return 0L;

    wSeg = HIWORD (lp);

    _asm { push    ds
           mov     ax, wSeg
           mov     ds, ax   }

    hMem = LocalFree (hMem);

    _asm { pop     ds }

    GlobalUnlock (hSeg);

    if (!hMem)
        return 0L;
    else
        return MAKELONG (hMem, hSeg);
    }

/*--------------------------------------------------------------*\
 |  SubLock - Lock a subsegment and the segment it lives in.    |
 |                                                              |
 |  Input:  A 4-byte "handle", put together as:                 |
 |            HIWORD = Handle to global segment.                |
 |            LOWORD = Handle to local object.                  |
 |                                                              |
 |  Returns: A far pointer to the object.                       |
\*--------------------------------------------------------------*/
LPSTR    FAR PASCAL SubLock(HANDLE32 hSubMem)
    {
    HGLOBAL hSeg;
    HLOCAL  hMem;
    LPSTR   lp;
    PSTR    p;
    WORD    wSeg;

    hSeg = HIWORD (hSubMem);
    hMem = LOWORD (hSubMem);

    lp = GlobalLock (hSeg);
    if (!lp)
        return 0L;

    wSeg = HIWORD (lp);

    _asm { push    ds
           mov     ax, wSeg
           mov     ds, ax   }
```

```
    p = LocalLock (hMem);

    _asm { pop     ds }

    /*  No Matching GlobalUnlock -- leave segment locked       */
    /*  for caller to use.  We'll unlock twice in SubUnlock.   */

    if (!p)
        return (LPSTR)0;
    else
        return (LPSTR)MAKELONG (p, wSeg);
    }

/*--------------------------------------------------------------*\
 |  SubSize - Returns the size of a subsegment.                 |
 |                                                              |
 |  Input:  A 4-byte "handle", put together as:                 |
 |            HIWORD = Handle to global segment.                |
 |            LOWORD = Handle to local object.                  |
 |                                                              |
 |  Returns: a WORD value with the subsegment size, or zero     |
 |           if the handle is invalid.                          |
\*--------------------------------------------------------------*/
WORD    FAR PASCAL SubSize(HANDLE32 hSubMem)
    {
    HGLOBAL hSeg;
    HLOCAL  hMem;
    LPSTR   lp;
    WORD    wSeg;
    WORD    wSize;

    hSeg = HIWORD (hSubMem);
    hMem = LOWORD (hSubMem);

    lp = GlobalLock (hSeg);
    if (!lp)
        return 0;

    wSeg = HIWORD (lp);

    _asm { push    ds
           mov     ax, wSeg
           mov     ds, ax   }

    wSize = LocalSize (hMem);

    _asm { pop     ds }

    GlobalUnlock (hSeg);

    return wSize;
    }

/*--------------------------------------------------------------*\
 |  SubUnlock - Unlock a subsegment, and the segment it lives   |
 |              in.                                             |
 |  Input:  A 4-byte "handle", put together as:                 |
 |            HIWORD = Handle to global segment.                |
 |            LOWORD = Handle to local object.                  |
 |                                                              |
 |  Returns: The LocalUnlock return value, which is zero if     |
 |           the block's reference count was decreased to       |
```

```
 |           zero, otherwise it is non-zero.                       |
\*-----------------------------------------------------------------*/
BOOL     FAR PASCAL SubUnlock(HANDLE32 hSubMem)
    {
    BOOL    bRetVal;
    HGLOBAL hSeg;
    HLOCAL  hMem;
    LPSTR   lp;
    WORD    wSeg;

    hSeg = HIWORD (hSubMem);
    hMem = LOWORD (hSubMem);

    lp = GlobalLock (hSeg);
    if (!lp)
        return 0L;

    wSeg = HIWORD (lp);

    _asm { push    ds
           mov     ax, wSeg
           mov     ds, ax    }

    bRetVal = LocalUnlock (hMem);

    _asm { pop     ds }

    GlobalUnlock (hSeg);
    GlobalUnlock (hSeg);

    return bRetVal;
    }
```

SUBMEM.H

```
/*-----------------------------------------------------------------*\
 | SUBMEM.H  -  Include file for SUBMEM.C                          |
\*-----------------------------------------------------------------*/

typedef DWORD HANDLE32;


/*-----------------------------------------------------------------*\
 |                      Function Prototypes.                       |
\*-----------------------------------------------------------------*/
extern "C" BOOL     FAR PASCAL SubInitialize(VOID);
extern "C" HANDLE32 FAR PASCAL SubAlloc(WORD, WORD);
extern "C" HANDLE32 FAR PASCAL SubFree(HANDLE32);
extern "C" LPSTR    FAR PASCAL SubLock(HANDLE32);
extern "C" WORD     FAR PASCAL SubSize(HANDLE32);
extern "C" BOOL     FAR PASCAL SubUnlock(HANDLE32);
```

SUBSEG.RC

```
#include "subseg.h"

snapshot icon subseg.ico

main menu
    BEGIN
    POPUP "&File"
        {
        MENUITEM "E&xit", CM_FILEEXIT
        }
    POPUP "&Help"
        {
        MENUITEM "&About...", CM_HELPABOUT
        }
    END
```

SUBSEG.DEF

```
EXETYPE WINDOWS

CODE MOVEABLE DISCARDABLE
DATA MULTIPLE MOVEABLE

HEAPSIZE   512
STACKSIZE 8192
```

DYNA16.MAK

```
#  MAKE file for Win16 API using dynamic BIDS,
#  OWL and C-runtime libraries.
#
#    C> make -fstatic16.mak
#

.AUTODEPEND
CC = -c -H -H"owl\owlpch.h" -ml -R -vi -WS -X-
CD = -D_RTLDLL;_BIDSDLL;_OWLDLL;_OWLPCH;
INC = -I\BC4\INCLUDE
LIB = -L\BC4\LIB

subseg.exe :  subseg.obj submem.obj subseg.res
  tlink -c -C -Twe $(LIB) @dyna16.lnk
  brc subseg.res subseg.exe

subseg.obj :  subseg.cpp
  bcc $(CC) $(CD) subseg.cpp

submem.obj :  submem.c
  bcc $(CC) -w-rpt $(CD) submem.c

subseg.res :  subseg.rc subseg.ico subseg.h
  brc $(INC) -31 -R subseg.rc
```

DYNA16.LNK

```
\bc4\lib\c0wl.obj+
subseg.obj+submem.obj
subseg,subseg
\bc4\lib\bidsi.lib+
\bc4\lib\owlwi.lib+
\bc4\lib\import.lib+
\bc4\lib\crtldll.lib
subseg.def
```

The first thing you may notice about this program is that very little is different from the SEGALLOC program from which it was derived. This is intentional, since the allocation routines that we have created are meant to exactly mirror both the local and global heap management routines. So, the **SubAlloc** routine takes the place of **GlobalAlloc** or **LocalAlloc**, and the **SubLock** routine takes the place of **GlobalLock** or **LocalLock**. However, when you look at the code to the subsegment routines, you'll find that calls are made to *both* local and global heap management routines.

There is also an important difference in the handle that `SubAlloc` returns. Instead of the normal 16-bit handle, it returns a 32-bit handle. This is really two handles in one: The high word contains the handle of the segment, and the low word contains the handle of the local heap object. This allows the routines to be extended to support several local heaps in several different segments. The only requirement is that `LocalInit` be called to initialize each segment. This program only uses one segment for the sake of simplicity.

Another limitation of this program is that the segment that contains the local heap is never freed. While this may be reasonable for a tiny, sample program, this is clearly a case of "do as I say, and not as I do." In other words, please be sure to free any memory you allocate, unlock any memory you lock, and in general undo whatever needs undoing to free any resource you use.

Let's move on to our next and final sample program, which creates a custom resource.

Custom Resources

Although Windows provides built-in support for several different types of resources, you may wish to create your own custom resource types. This lets you take advantage of the built-in memory management features of resources, with a minimum of effort on your part. The best candidates for custom resources are data objects that won't change. We're going to show an example of a resource that will be used to calculate sine and cosine values. This table allows a calculation of an integer sine value, which is simply a sine value multiplied by 10,000. The advantage of using a lookup table is that it is faster than calculating on the fly. In addition, since the low-end members of the Intel-86 family (80386 and earlier) do not have built-in floating-point support, you'll get faster overall performance if you limit your calculations to integer arithmetic. It may interest you to know that this factor influenced Microsoft enough to build Windows without *any* use of floating-point arithmetic.

We're going to write two routines that will provide sine and cosine values for an angle entered in degrees. Roughly speaking, then, with two functions and 360 degrees, 720 different values are required for our lookup table. But we're going to take advantage of the symmetry of this table to play a few tricks, do a little folding and rotating, and produce the same results with a single table of 90 sine values. To see how we're going to pull this off, read on!

The first thing we'll need to do is to create a table of values. There are many ways to do this, but the most straightforward involves writing a small C program that calculates our sine values and writes them as ASCII text to a data file. Why ASCII text? We're going to show you a trick that will allow you to build complex binary data objects from ASCII text files. The only tools that are required are the macro assembler (TASM), the linker, and a special converter called EXE2BIN.EXE which comes with DOS. Here are the program files that we use to create our table of sine values:

MAKEFILE.MAK

```
#
#  Make file for sine table.
#
#  Create sine table with:
#     C> make sinedata.bin
#

sine.exe: sine.c
    bcc sine.c

sinedata.asm: sine.exe
    sine

sinedata.bin: sinedata.asm
    tasm sinedata.asm
    tlink sinedata.obj
    exe2bin sinedata.exe
    copy sinedata.bin ..\custres\sinedata.bin
```

SINE.C

```
/*-------------------------------------------------------------*\
 |  SINE.C - Creates an .ASM data file containing sine values   |
 |           from 0 to 90 degrees.  This file is suitable      |
 |           for creating a custom Windows resource.           |
\*-------------------------------------------------------------*/

#include "stdio.h"
#include "math.h"

char achFileHeader[] =
     ";\n"
     "; Sine/Cosine Data Table\n"
     ";\n"
     ";\n"
```

```
        "; Table of Sine values from 0 to 90 degrees\n"
        ";\n"
        "SINDATA segment public\n";

    char achFileFooter[] =
        "\n"
        "SINDATA ends\n"
        "END\n";


    main()
        {
        double dbPI  = 3.1415926536;
        double dbRad;
        FILE   * fp;
        int    iAngle;
        int    iSin;

        if (!(fp = fopen("sinedata.asm", "w")))
            {
            printf("Can't create sinedata.asm.\n");

            exit(1);
            }

        fprintf (fp, achFileHeader);
        fprintf (fp, "DW ");

        for (iAngle = 0; iAngle <= 90; iAngle++)
            {
            dbRad = (((double)iAngle) * dbPI) / 180.0;
            iSin = sin(dbRad) * 10000.0 + 0.5;
            fprintf(fp, " %5d", iSin);

            if (iAngle % 8 == 7)
                fprintf (fp, "\nDW ");
    else if (iAngle != 90)
                fprintf (fp, ",");
            }

        fprintf(fp, achFileFooter);

        fclose(fp);

        return (0);
        }
```

The data file created by this program is essentially an MASM language file, containing the data definitions suitable for use as a data segment. But we're not going to write any MASM code to support it. Instead, we're going to let MASM convert the data definitions into binary format. Here is the MASM file that is created, SINEDATA.ASM:

```
; Sine/Cosine Data Table
;
;
; Table of Sine values from 0 to 90 degrees
;
SINDATA segment public
DW      0,   175,   349,   523,   698,   872,  1045,  1219
DW   1392,  1564,  1736,  1908,  2079,  2250,  2419,  2588
DW   2756,  2924,  3090,  3256,  3420,  3584,  3746,  3907
```

```
DW    4067,  4226,  4384,  4540,  4695,  4848,  5000,  5150
DW    5299,  5446,  5592,  5736,  5878,  6018,  6157,  6293
DW    6428,  6561,  6691,  6820,  6947,  7071,  7193,  7314
DW    7431,  7547,  7660,  7771,  7880,  7986,  8090,  8192
DW    8290,  8387,  8480,  8572,  8660,  8746,  8829,  8910
DW    8988,  9063,  9135,  9205,  9272,  9336,  9397,  9455
DW    9511,  9563,  9613,  9659,  9703,  9744,  9781,  9816
DW    9848,  9877,  9903,  9925,  9945,  9962,  9976,  9986
DW    9994,  9998, 10000
SINDATA ends
END
```

After this data file has been run through the macro assembler and the linker, the result is an .EXE file that is almost ready to run as a DOS program. Well, not really, since it doesn't have any code. It's just an executable file with a data segment. To isolate the data into a pure binary object, we run the EXE2BIN program. This program is ordinarily used to create .COM files from .EXE files. .COM files are simply memory images that can be loaded and run "as is." Since that's exactly what we want—a pure, binary image—EXE2BIN does the trick to create our sine table resource.

To test that the sine and cosine functions are providing accurate values, our sample program, CIRCLE, connects 359 points together to draw a circle with a radius of 100 pixels. The drawing appears in Figure 18.7. While this is quite a bit slower and rougher than you would expect from calling GDI's **`Ellipse`** routine, it demonstrates quite nicely that the sine and cosine values that we generate at least *look* right in the range 0 to 360 degrees.

Here is the code for our custom resource program, CIRCLE.EXE, that used the sine table information to calculate sines and cosines that were used to actually draw the circle shown in the figure.

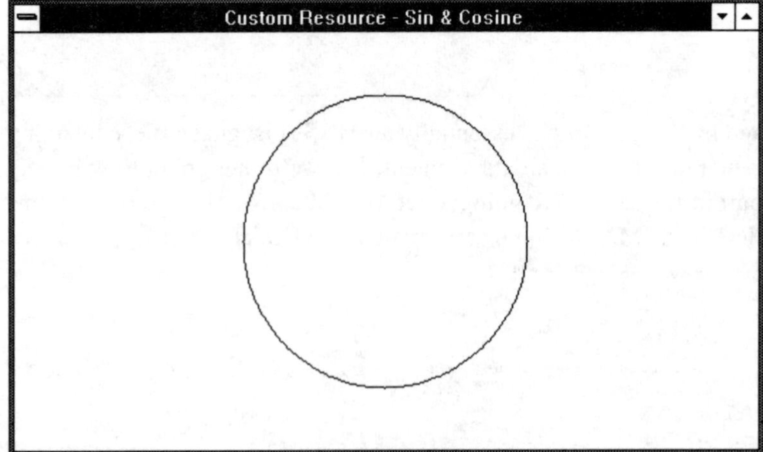

Figure 18.7 Circle drawn by CIRCLE

CIRCLE.CPP

```
// CIRCLE.CPP  Demonstrates creation and
//             use of custom resources.
//
#include <owl\owlpch.h>
#include "circle.h"

//
// Main window
class DFrame : public TFrameWindow
    {
  public:
    DFrame(char * title);
    ~DFrame();
    void CmFileExit();
    void CmHelpAbout();
    void EvSize(UINT type, TSize& size);
    void Paint (TDC& dc, BOOL, TRect&);
    int intCos (int iValue);
    int intSine (int iValue);
  private:
    HGLOBAL hresSineData;

  DECLARE_RESPONSE_TABLE (DFrame);
    };

DEFINE_RESPONSE_TABLE1 (DFrame, TFrameWindow)
  EV_WM_SIZE,
  EV_COMMAND(CM_FILEEXIT, CmFileExit),
  EV_COMMAND(CM_HELPABOUT, CmHelpAbout),
END_RESPONSE_TABLE;

DFrame::DFrame(char * title) : TFrameWindow(0, title)
    {
    // Prepare handle to custom resource.
    HINSTANCE hInst = GetApplication()->GetInstance();
    HRSRC hRes = FindResource (hInst,
                 MAKEINTRESOURCE(SINE),     // Name.
                 MAKEINTRESOURCE(TABLE));   // Type.
    hresSineData = LoadResource (hInst, hRes);
    }

DFrame::~DFrame()
    {
    FreeResource (hresSineData);
    }

void DFrame::CmFileExit()
    {
    CloseWindow(0); // Cause application to terminate
    }

void DFrame::CmHelpAbout()
    {
    MessageBox("      Custom Resource Demo\n\n"
               "'Borland C++ 4.0 Programming\n"
               "   for Windows', by Paul Yao", Title);
    }

// Force a repaint when window size changes.
void DFrame::EvSize(UINT /* type */, TSize& /* size */)
```

```
    {
    Invalidate();
    }

void DFrame::Paint (TDC& dc, BOOL, TRect&)
    {
    // Query client rectangle size.
    TRect rClient = GetClientRect();

    // Move origin (0,0) to window center.
    TPoint pt = TPoint (rClient.right/2, rClient.bottom/2);
    TPoint ptOld;
    dc.SetViewportOrg (pt, &ptOld);

    // Set Current position.
    int x = intCos (0)/100;
    int y = intSine (0)/100;
    dc.MoveTo (x, y);

    // Draw circle.
    for (int i=0;i<=360;i++)
        {
        x = intCos (i)/100;
        y = intSine (i)/100;
        dc.LineTo (x, y);
        }
    }

/*-------------------------------------------------------------*\
 |              Integer Sine Routine:  intSine.                  |
 |                                                               |
 |        Calculates an integer sine value in units equal        |
 |        to 10,000th for any degree entered, using a            |
 |        value derived from a custom Sine resource.             |
\*-------------------------------------------------------------*/
int DFrame::intSine (int iValue)
    {
    int iSign;

    int FAR * fpSine;

    fpSine = (int FAR *)LockResource (hresSineData);
    if (fpSine == NULL)
        return (0);

    while (iValue < 0)   iValue +=360;
    while (iValue > 360) iValue -=360;

    iSign = 1;

    if (iValue > 90 && iValue <=180)
        {
        iValue = 180 - iValue;
        }
    else if (iValue > 180 && iValue <= 270)
        {
        iSign = -1;
        iValue = iValue - 180;
        }
    else if (iValue > 270 && iValue <= 360)
        {
        iSign = -1;
```

```
        iValue = 360 - iValue;
        }

    /*  Adjust pointer to correct table entry.  */
    fpSine += iValue;

    iSign = *fpSine * iSign;
    UnlockResource (hresSineData);

    return (iSign);
    }

/*----------------------------------------------------------------*\
 |              Integer CoSine Routine:  intCos.                  |
 |                                                                |
 |        Calculates an integer cosine value in units             |
 |        equal to 10,000th for any degree entered, using         |
 |        a value derived from a custom sine resource.            |
\*----------------------------------------------------------------*/
int DFrame::intCos (int iValue)
    {
    return (intSine (iValue-90));
    }

//
// Application object
class DApp : public TApplication
    {
  public:
    DApp();
    void InitMainWindow();
    };

DApp::DApp() : TApplication()
    {
    }

void DApp::InitMainWindow()
    {
    SetMainWindow (new DFrame("Custom Resource Data"));

    MainWindow->AssignMenu("MAIN");
    MainWindow->SetIcon(this, "SNAPSHOT");
    }

//
// Application main entry point.
OwlMain(int, char **)
    {
    return DApp().Run();
    }
```

CIRCLE.H

```
#define CM_FILEEXIT 100
#define CM_HELPABOUT 200

#define TABLE  100   //  Custom resource type value.
#define SINE   100   //  ID of particular custom resource.
```

CIRCLE.RC

```
#include "circle.h"

snapshot icon circle.ico

SINE TABLE sinedata.bin

main menu
    BEGIN
    POPUP "&File"
        {
        MENUITEM "E&xit", CM_FILEEXIT
        }
    POPUP "&Help"
        {
        MENUITEM "&About...", CM_HELPABOUT
        }
    END
```

CIRCLE.DEF

```
EXETYPE WINDOWS

CODE MOVEABLE DISCARDABLE
DATA MULTIPLE MOVEABLE

HEAPSIZE   512
STACKSIZE 8192
```

DYNA16.MAK

```
#  MAKE file for Win16 API using dynamic BIDS,
#  OWL and C-runtime libraries.
#
#    C> make -fstatic16.mak
#

.AUTODEPEND
CC = -c -H -H"owl\owlpch.h" -ml -R -vi -WS -X-
CD = -D_RTLDLL;_BIDSDLL;_OWLDLL;_OWLPCH;
INC = -I\BC4\INCLUDE
LIB = -L\BC4\LIB

circle.exe :  circle.obj circle.res
  tlink -c -C -Twe $(LIB) @dyna16.lnk
  brc circle.res circle.exe

circle.obj :  circle.cpp
  bcc $(CC) $(CD) circle.cpp

circle.res :  circle.rc circle.ico circle.h
  brc $(INC) -31 -R circle.rc
```

DYNA16.LNK

```
\bc4\lib\c0wl.obj+
circle.obj
circle,circle
\bc4\lib\bidsi.lib+
\bc4\lib\owlwi.lib+
\bc4\lib\import.lib+
\bc4\lib\crtldll.lib
circle.def
```

DYNA32.MAK

```
#  MAKE file for Win32 API using dynamic BIDS,
#  OWL and C-runtime libraries.
#
#    C> make -fdyna32.mak
#

.AUTODEPEND
CC = -c -H -H\""owl\owlpch.h\"" -p- -R -vi -W -X-
CD = -D_RTLDLL;_BIDSDLL;_OWLDLL;_OWLPCH;
INC = -I\BC4\INCLUDE
LIB = -L\BC4\LIB

circle.exe :  circle.obj circle.res
  tlink32 -aa -c -Tpe $(LIB) @dyna32.lnk
  brc32 circle.res circle.exe

circle.obj :  circle.cpp
  bcc32 $(CC) $(CD) circle.cpp

circle.res :  circle.rc circle.ico circle.h
  brc32 $(INC) -w32 -R circle.rc
```

DYNA32.LNK

```
\bc4\lib\c0w32.obj+
circle.obj
circle,circle
\bc4\lib\bidsfi.lib+
\bc4\lib\owlwfi.lib+
\bc4\lib\import32.lib+
\bc4\lib\cw32i.lib
circle.def
```

CUSTRES does all its work in three places: in the application object's constructor, in response to **`WM_PAINT`**, and in the application object's destructor. The sine and cosine information is provided in two routines: **`intSin`** and **`intCos`**. The second function actually cheats: Since a cosine is always 90 degrees out of phase with a sine, the **`intCos`** function subtracts 90 degrees from the actual angle and calls the **intSin** function—just a little trigonometric sleight of hand to make Mom proud.

To use a custom resource, you call three routines: **FindResource**, **LoadResource**, and **LockResource**. In the application constructor, the first two are called. The result is a memory handle that is stored in **hresSinData**. **FindResource** searches for the reference to a resource in the module database, which, as we mentioned earlier, is simply an abbreviated memory image of the module's file header. **FindResource** takes three parameters:

```
FindResource (hInstance, lpName, lpType)
```

- **hInstance** is an instance handle.
- **lpName** is a long pointer to a character string with the resource name.
- **lpType** is a long pointer to a character string with the resource type.

Even though **lpName** and **lpType** are pointers to character strings, this is not the most efficient way to identify a resource. The reason is simple: A string comparison is more expensive than an integer comparison. For this reason, we use a macro, **MAKEINTRESOURCE**, which lets us define integers and use them in place of a character string. Here are the two integers we defined in CUSTRES:

```
#define  TABLE  100  /*  Custom resource type.    */
#define  SINE   100  /*  ID of sine table.        */
```

We use them in the call to **FindResource**, as follows:

```
hRes = FindResource (hInst,
           MAKEINTRESOURCE(SIN),        /* Name.  */
           MAKEINTRESOURCE(TABLE));     /* Type.  */
```

The **MAKEINTRESOURCE** macro creates a pseudopointer, with zero for a segment identifier and the integer value for the offset value. It casts this value as an **LPSTR**, which is how this routine is defined, so that the compiler doesn't complain. When the **FindResource** routine sees this value, it does not treat it as a pointer. (This would be a fatal error!) Instead, it uses the two-byte integer value to find the resource definition. It can find it, because the resource file, CUSTRES.RC, has the following line:

```
SIN   TABLE  sinedata.bin DISCARDABLE
```

This causes the data in the resource file, SINEDATA.BIN, to be copied entirely into CUSTRES.EXE at compile/link time. This means that CUSTRES is a stand-alone program and doesn't need the original resource data file to be present at runtime.

Once **FindResource** has identified the specific resource that we are interested in, it provides a resource identifier: a handle that must be provided to the **LoadResource** routine to be useful. **LoadResource** is the next routine called, and it is defined as

```
LoadResource (hInstance, hresInfo)
```

- **hInstance** is the instance handle.
- **hresInfo** is the handle returned by the `FindResource` routine.

In spite of its name, **LoadResource** does *not* cause the resource to be loaded into memory. Instead, it allocates a memory object from the global heap with a size of zero. This doesn't actually cause any memory to be allocated, but does cause a global memory handle to be assigned for our use. **LoadResource** provides this memory handle as a return value, which CUSTRES stores in `hresSinData`.

The routine that actually causes a resource to be loaded into memory is **LockResource**. But CUSTRES doesn't call this routine until it actually needs to use the data in the sine table. By postponing the loading of such a memory object, CUSTRES helps minimize the demand it makes on system memory. **LockResource** does several things: It loads the resource into memory, locks it in place, and returns a pointer to the data. **LockResource** is defined as

```
LPSTR LockResource (hResData)
```

- **hResData** is the handle returned by the **LoadResource** function.

LockResource returns a long pointer to a string. But if you're not storing characters in a resource, it's a simple matter to define the desired string and cast the results of **LockResource** to the right type.

Here is how CUSTRES handles its need for a pointer to integer data:

```
int FAR * fpSin;

fpSin = (int FAR *)LockResource (hresSinData);
if (fpSin == NULL)
    return (0);
```

As we have mentioned elsewhere, casting the return value to routines like **LockResource** keeps the compiler from complaining about an alleged type mismatch. We know there is no type mismatch, and by casting we let the compiler know. Notice also, that we check the return value from **LockResource**, in case it wasn't able to load the resource into memory.

The **LockResource** routine should never be discussed alone, but always in the context of an **UnlockResource**, with which it creates a *Windows sandwich*. We discussed this code construction earlier as a way to organize the use of a shared resource. In this case, the resource is memory. Calls to **LockResource** must be paired with calls to **UnlockResource**. The first loads the resource and ties it down in memory. The second unties the resource, allowing it to be moved in memory or even discarded, if the Memory Manager sees fit to do so. In CUSTRES, the **intSin** function uses these two routines to bracket its use of the sine data, creating a Windows sandwich that ensures that the object is locked when we need it, and unlocked when we don't. The **UnlockResource** function is defined as

```
BOOL UnlockResource (hResData)
```

- **hResData** is the handle returned by the **LoadResource** function.

The final routine that plays a role in the handling of the custom resource is **FreeResource**. This frees all the memory associated with our custom resource. **FreeResource** is defined as

```
FreeResource (hResData)
```

- **hResData** is the handle returned by the **LoadResource** function.

This routine is called in response in the application class destructor, to deallocate the sine data memory. In this program, we don't actually need to call **FreeResource**, since the resource will be freed when our program terminates. But, as mentioned elsewhere in this book, it is a good programming practice that will help your code survive future programmers who fix, update, modify, and in other ways use your code in their projects.

From our discussion, you can see that Windows provides many choices in how a program uses memory for its code and data. Understanding these choices will help you tune your program to work optimally in all of Windows operating modes, and for compatibility with future versions of Windows.

19

Dynamic Linking

In all its operating modes—real, standard, enhanced and Win32—Windows uses dynamic linking. Dynamic linking is several things rolled into one. First of all, it is a memory management technique that allows code to be loaded from disk on demand. Dynamic linking allows code to be discarded to free memory for other uses. When running in protected mode, Windows' dynamic linking depends on the built-in memory management features of the Intel-86 family of CPUs to trigger the loading process. And when running in real mode, even without the hardware support, Windows is able to provide dynamic linking that is just as efficient as its protected mode counterpart with a mechanism that is implemented entirely in software.

Second, dynamic linking provides a way to connect subroutine libraries to programs at *runtime*. This contrasts sharply with static linking, in which routines from a subroutine library are copied to a program's executable file at program *creation time*. For example, if a Windows program uses the `memset` runtime library routine, a copy of the routine is stored in the program's .EXE file. This is **static linking**. For the program to be able to access a new version of the `memset` routine (if it were made smaller, faster, more bug-free, or whatever), the program file must be recreated. Thus, a statically linked routine doesn't allow automatic upgrades when library functions are improved. But dynamic linking does, since the functions in a dynamic link library are not copied to a program's executable file at program creation time, but are linked to the program at runtime.

Third, dynamic linking provides an efficient mechanism for sharing code and data between application programs. For example, a single copy of the code for the subroutines in Windows' graphic library, GDI.EXE, is shareable between all the different Windows programs that wish to use them. When your program runs alongside Aldus PageMaker, for example, both programs use the same copy of the `TextOut` routine. The net result is a much lower demand on system memory. An example of *data* sharing occurs whenever text appears on a display screen. GDI fonts are implemented in dynamic link libraries, which means that they are shared by whichever programs wish to use them. Even with many programs accessing a font, only a single copy of the font data is present in the system.

The most obvious examples of dynamic linking occur between Windows programs and the main Windows dynamic link libraries: KERNEL.EXE (or KRNL286.EXE for standard mode, KRNL386.EXE for 386-Enhanced Mode), USER.EXE, and GDI.EXE. When a Windows program is running, it relies on dynamic linking to make the proper connections to the various Windows library routines. Dynamic links are also created between the three main Windows dynamic link libraries and Windows' device drivers. For example, when GDI accesses a printer, it dynamically links to a printer driver. Dynamic linking makes it easy to upgrade or replace different parts of Windows—fonts, device drivers, or even the main libraries themselves.

The Dynamic Linking Mechanism

Let's take a moment to look at the nuts and bolts of Windows' dynamic linking mechanism. Even though dynamic linking occurs without requiring you to know how it works, there are several reasons why it is helpful to understand the mechanism itself. First of all, you might not be convinced that you can build programs that are bigger than your address space on a microcomputer. Even if you're comfortable with this idea, you might be concerned that the mechanism isn't efficient or has unexpected side effects. You might want to know if you can build your own dynamic link libraries, and understanding the mechanism can help you decide when they are appropriate and when they are not. Or you might just be the kind of person who wants to know how things really work. Whatever your motivation, we think you'll find that—in all its operating modes—Windows' dynamic link mechanism is a fast, efficient, and very elegant approach to the problems of managing the dynamic loading and linking of code.

The architect of Windows' dynamic link mechanism is Steve Wood, who joined Microsoft in 1983. While a graduate student at Yale University, Steve had been involved with some systems programming projects on DEC-20 computers. One project involved the creation of a mechanism to share library code between different processes. This was accomplished by mapping the address space of different processes into the same physical address space. The net result was a reduction in required memory to support shared code.

This sounds a lot like dynamic linking. But the difference is that, when he started to work on building the dynamic link mechanism, Steve and the other members of the first KERNEL team were working on a machine with minimal capabilities. The target machine for the first version of Windows, after all, was to have an Intel 8088 CPU, two floppy disk drivers, and 256K of RAM. Dynamic linking could only require a minimum of overhead and had to be a software-only solution to a problem that had been solved elsewhere using dedicated hardware.

With a minimum amount of memory, the solution was to make much of the system reside in code segments that could be discarded. After all, if code resided on disk instead of in memory, there would be more room for applications to do their work. The trick was to figure out how to bring a code segment into memory. One of the things that was quickly apparent was that a whole new set of tools would have to be forged in order to get dynamic linking to work properly.

For example, a new linker had to be built to support the new .EXE file format that was required to support dynamic linking. A new program loader had to be built, to accommodate the fact that not all segments would necessarily be present when a program was running. And finally, a new compiler had to be built to generate code that would seamlessly connect programs and dynamic link libraries together in a working system. The first Windows development team discovered quite quickly that one of the challenges to working with new tools was determining when a bug was caused by the tools and when it was caused by your own code.

The program loader that was built into the first version of Windows served as the foundation on which all later loaders were built. To describe its operation, we need to look at how code segments are dynamically loaded and routines linked for discardable, moveable, and fixed code segments. We'll start with the hardest case: discardable code.

Dynamic Linking and Discardable Code Segments

When you are building a dynamic link mechanism like the one Windows uses, the hardest aspect of dealing with discardable code segments is the fact that you never know when a code segment is present in memory or not. Without the hardware memory magic of protected mode, real mode Windows creates a tiny code stub for every far routine in programs and dynamic link libraries. These code stubs are called **loader thunks** or **call thunks** and reside in the module database. Although real mode is being discontinued in Windows version 3.1, understanding the real mode dynamic linking mechanism will help clarify the operation of the protected mode hardware.

Consider the case of a program that uses GDI's `Rectangle` routine, which for this example we'll suppose is in a discardable code segment. We'll call our program DRAWRECT. Before this program starts running, Windows will already have created a module database for GDI. Inside GDI's module database, there is one call thunk for every far routine in GDI, including `Rectangle`. Figure 19.1 depicts GDI's module database in memory. In real mode, a call thunk for routines in discardable segments has one of two states: an interrupt to the loader, as depicted in Figure 19.1, or a jump to the routine in memory, depicted in Figure 19.3.

When the first instance of DRAWRECT starts running, the Windows loader starts the load process by creating a DRAWRECT's module database. The module database is used to resolve calls *into* DRAWRECT, and so is not interesting to us in the context of linking DRAWRECT to GDI's `Rectangle` routine. However, DRAWRECT's module database *is* needed to locate DRAWRECT's entry point. After loading all of DRAWRECT's preload segments, control is passed to this entry point.

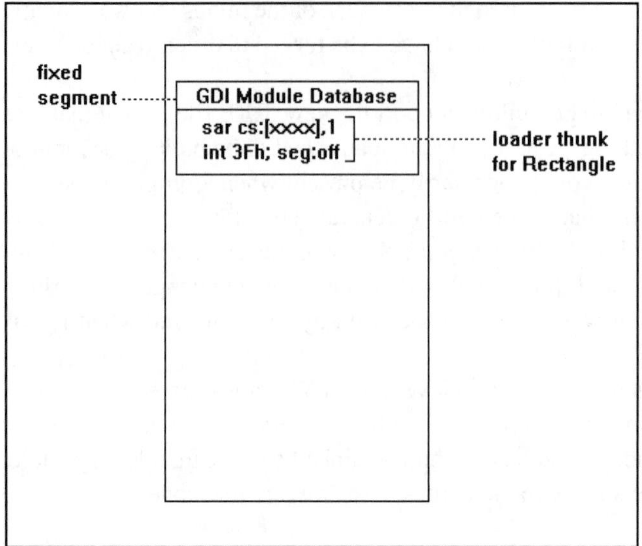

Figure 19.1 Memory before the dynamic link

The dynamic link from DRAWRECT to GDI's **`Rectangle`** routine occurs when Windows loads a code segment that actually calls **`Rectangle`**. Appended to the end of such a code segment is a **relocation table**, which contains the fix-up information needed to create the first half of a dynamic link.

There are basically two types of relocation table entries: internal references and external references. The internal references define far calls to routines inside DRAWRECT. Part of dynamic linking, then, involves creating connections between a newly loaded code segment and other code segments in the same program or dynamic link library.

The external references define calls to dynamic link library routines, such as GDI's **`Rectangle`**. When DRAWRECT's code segment is loaded into memory, the far call to the **`Rectangle`** routine is fixed up to the address of the **`Rectangle`** routine's alias—that is, to the call thunk—in GDI's module database, as depicted in Figure 19.2.

When the Windows loader has finished creating all of the fix-ups described in the segment's relocation table, it frees the memory associated with the relocation table. When the relocation information is needed again, it will be reread from disk along with the code segment.

When a code segment is loaded into memory, it is patched once for every far call in the segment, including far calls to internal as well as external routines. This means simply that the code in the newly loaded code segment has been modified so that every far call points to *something*. In the Windows programs that you write, you'll want to keep your code segments small and the number of far calls to a minimum because of the overhead incurred when a code segment is loaded into memory.

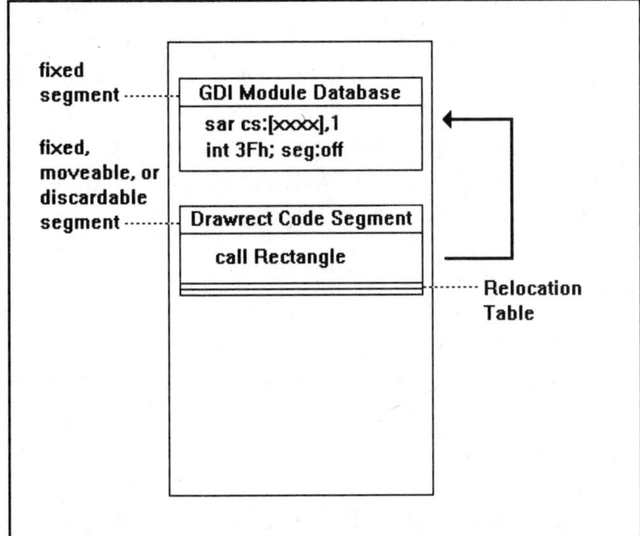

Figure 19.2 DRAWRECT fix-up to GDI's module database

Getting back to our example program, an interesting aspect of the dynamic link is that, even though DRAWRECT's code segment has been fixed up to call into GDI's module database, the code segment that actually holds the **Rectangle** routine does not have to be present in memory. As you'll see in a moment, when the code segment is not present, code in **Rectangle**'s call thunk causes the code segment containing **Rectangle** to actually be loaded into memory.

The next step in the dynamic link process occurs when DRAWRECT actually calls Rectangle. Of course, it calls into the call thunk in the module database. As we mentioned earlier, the call thunk is a tiny code stub that will have one of two states, depending on whether `Rectangle` is open for business or out to lunch. Let's assume that it is out to lunch, to see how the call thunk responds. In such cases, the call thunk will have code that looks like the following:

```
; -->> "Out-To-Lunch"
SAR  CS:[00B4h],1    ; update access flag
INT  3Fh             ; Call to the Windows' loader
DB   seg             ; Code segment number
DW   off             ; Offset to Rectangle routine
```

When DRAWRECT calls into this piece of code, it triggers a software interrupt which calls the Windows loader, interrupt `3F`. The Windows loader reads the next three bytes of information, which contain the segment number (from 1 to 255) and the offset into the code segment (0 to 65535). Since there is only a single byte for the segment number, the total number of segments that can exist in any .EXE or .DLL file is 255. (Segment zero is reserved for return thunks, to be covered later.) This limitation is intrinsic to the format of the .EXE file itself, and therefore you can't create an .EXE file with more than 255 segments. However, you can create a dynamic link library that allows a program to easily overcome this limitation.

Once the Windows loader has read the necessary code segment from disk, it modifies the module database so that the thunk associated with the **Rectangle** routine has machine instructions represented by the following assembly language:

```
; -->> "Open For Business"
SAR  CS:[00B4h],1    ; Update access flag
JMP  Rectangle
```

Not only are fix-ups performed for the **Rectangle** routine's call thunk, but also for the thunks of all *other* far routines that reside in **Rectangle**'s code segment. And if Rectangle makes far calls to other code segments, those calls are fixed up along with any other far calls *from* **Rectangle**'s code segment. That is, both inward bound and outward bound far calls are patched. Once the code segment has been loaded into memory and the module database fixed up, the dynamic link is complete. The **Rectangle** routine can retrieve its parameters off the stack and do its job. The complete dynamic link, from DRAWRECT through GDI's module database and into Rectangle, is depicted in Figure 19.3.

All calls to Rectangle are fixed up to call Rectangle's alias in the module database, which serves as a kind of switchboard operator for this routine. Notice that the Windows Memory Manager can move **Rectangle**'s segment at any time. When it does so, it does

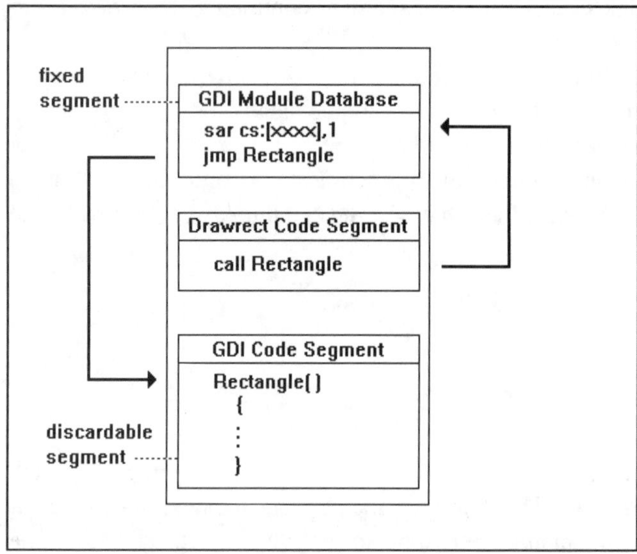

Figure 19.3 Final fix-up from GDI's module database to Rectangle's code segment

not have to patch every program's code segment that calls **`Rectangle`**. Instead, it simply patches **`Rectangle`**'s call thunk (and the call thunk of other far routines that might be in the same code segment). The code segment can also be discarded from memory at any time. When this occurs, the dynamic linker simply fixes up the call thunks with an `INT 3F` instruction to call the Windows loader to restore the code segment into memory. Of course, fix-ups are not free. But the dynamic link mechanism allows a code segment to be removed from memory, and reloaded later to give the greatest flexibility in how memory is used.

Dynamic Linking and Fixed Code Segments

Once you understand how a dynamic link to a discardable code segment is created, you'll see that dynamic links to fixed code segments are even simpler. Dynamic links to fixed code segments are not routed through a call thunk, but instead link a caller directly to the called routine. One reason for this is that fixed code segments are always treated as preload segments, so that they are always resident in memory and never move.

Consider a program that calls GDI's **`TextOut`** routine, which we'll assume for the moment is in a fixed code segment. For this example, we'll call our program DOTEXT, which calls **`TextOut`**. As before, when GDI is first brought into memory, the Windows loader creates GDI's module database. Once this is done, the loader reads all fixed code segments into memory. Figure 19.4 shows the state of two objects that are in memory after GDI has been loaded: the module database and the fixed code segment that contains **`TextOut`**.

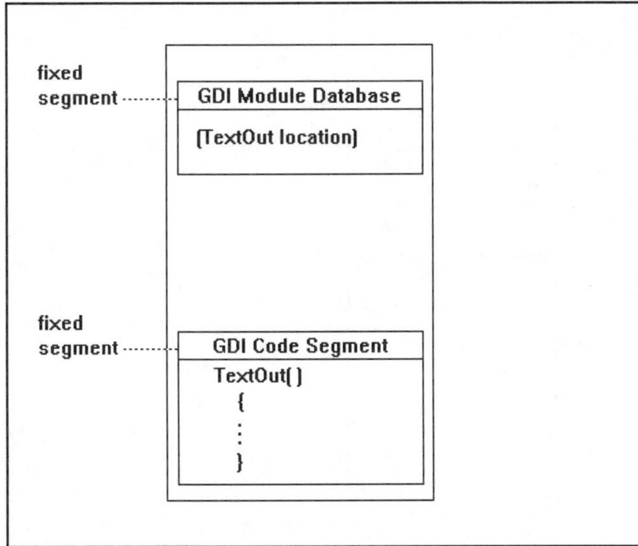

Figure 19.4 GDI immediately loading

Since the fixed code segment is loaded when GDI starts running, it will never need a loader thunk. However, to locate the routine itself, the module database lists the address of far routines. The loader will require this information when it loads DOTEXT into memory. At that time, a dynamic link is created that directly connects DOTEXT to **`TextOut`**, as depicted in Figure 19.5. Unlike the fix-up to a moveable or discardable segment, the fix-up to a *fixed* code segment always goes directly from the caller to the called routine.
In protected mode, the memory management hardware can move memory objects without changing the logical address. For this reason, all dynamic link fix-ups in protected mode are treated just like the dynamic link we just described. In other words, all fix-ups in protected mode are treated as if every code segment were fixed. Far calls are patched up by the Windows loader to directly connect a caller to the called routine. This is true for moveable segments as well as discardable segments.

Since protected mode doesn't have call thunks in the module database, you might wonder how discardable code segments get reloaded. In real mode, as you'll recall, the loader thunk in the module database triggers a code segment reload:

```
SAR  CS:[00B4h],1    ; Update access flag
INT  3Fh             ; Call to the Windows' loader
DB   seg             ; Code segment number
DW   off             ; Offset to Rectangle routine
```

In protected mode, when an absent code segment is called, a segment fault occurs. As you may recall from our discussion of protected mode operation in Chapter 17, every segment

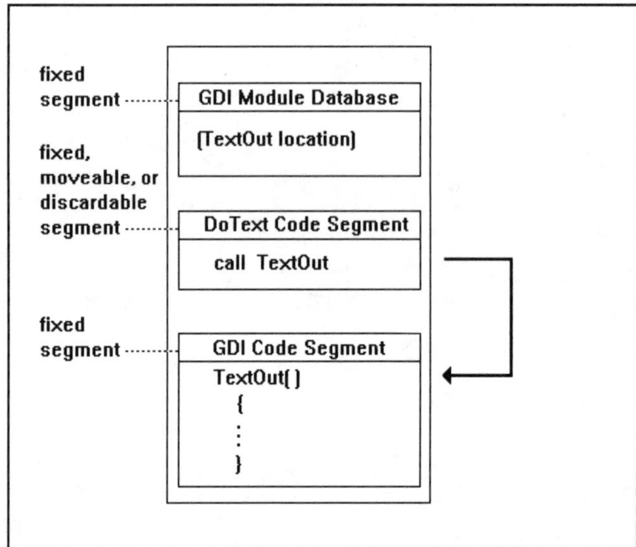

Figure 19.5 Direct fix-up from DOTEXT to TextOut

identifier contains an index into a protected mode descriptor table. Among the information that is kept in these tables is a flag that lets the system know whether a segment is actually present in memory or not. When it is not present, the segment fault—which is simply a software interrupt—notifies the Memory Manager that it must load the missing segment. Windows' Memory Manager loads the code segment into memory and then causes the instruction that triggered the segment fault to be restarted. In this way, the memory management hardware that operates in protected mode is able to operate in a manner that is transparent to application software.

Other Real Mode Dynamic Linking Considerations

In protected mode, the dynamic link mechanism is greatly simplified by the hardware memory management provided by the various Intel processors. Segments can be moved around in physical memory without invalidating the logical address that programs use. Discarded code segments can be automatically reloaded when a *segment not present* interrupt occurs.

In real mode, Windows has to play a number of tricks to achieve the same flexibility that comes for free in protected mode. Two of these tricks are **stack patching** and the use of **return thunks**. To help you appreciate the work that real mode Windows does for you, we're going to describe each of these mechanisms in a little detail.

Stack Patching

Stack patching involves walking the stack of a program and updating references that have been made to code segments that have moved. Earlier, we mentioned that the only thing that had to happen when a code segment was moved was to update the references to the routine in a module database. This is true most of the time. But if the address of a routine is referenced as a return address on the stack, that reference must also be fixed up.

Whenever a function is called—inside a dynamic link library or inside a regular program—a return address is placed on the stack. This address identifies the location of the machine instruction that is to be executed next when we return from the function. When a code segment referenced on the stack moves, Windows must walk the stack and patch the return address so that calls can correctly find their way back to the calling function. Windows patches the stack for every instance of every program running in the system.

Because Windows can patch stacks, it is free to move any code segment at any time. This gives the Windows Memory Manager the freedom to move any moveable code segment at any time. This allows real mode Windows to have the same flexibility of protected mode Windows—which is critical, given the greater memory constraints that are part of real mode operation.

Return Thunks

In the same way that stack patching allows code segments to be *moved*, return thunks allow code segments to be *discarded*. In our discussion of dynamic linking, we mentioned that a code segment could be discarded at any time, as long as the module database was updated to call the Windows loader the next time a function in the segment was called. We mentioned that the reloading of discardable code segments is done by a tiny code stub called a call thunk.

When Windows discards a code segment that is referenced as a return address on the stack, the stack is also patched. The stack patching operation involves walking the stack of all programs, looking for a reference to the discarded code segment. Since the stack cannot be patched with the address of a discarded code segment, which has no address, it is instead patched to return to a tiny code stub called a **return thunk**. A return thunk is similar to a call thunk, except that after loading the necessary code segment, it provides a bridge for a return instruction instead of a call instruction. After the segment has been loaded, execution continues at the return address that was on the stack before the segment was discarded. Here is an example of a return thunk:

```
INT  3Fh        ; Call to the Windows' loader.
DB   0          ; Zero segment = return thunk.
DW              ; seg:IP packed into 20 bits.
DB              ; Handle to data segment packed
                ; into 12 bits.
```

A return thunk looks a lot like a loader thunk, except that an invalid segment number is given: zero. This flags the `INT 3F` loader that this is a return thunk. In this case, it knows that the three bytes that follow contain all the data it needs to continue, although things are packed a little tightly. For one thing, the segment number and the code segment offset are crammed into 20 bits. This is possible since the code segment number will be a number between 0 and 255, which means it only takes one byte. That leaves 16 bits for the offset. A handle to the data segment is stored in the return thunk, since the data segment itself may have moved while memory was being jostled around. When the return thunk is run, the data segment is patched to reflect the new location of the data segment. All of this allows Windows to survive even a very low memory situation, since *any* code segment in the entire system (except the currently executing one) can be discarded if more memory is needed.

Up until now, our discussion of dynamic linking has focused on *code*. We have described the way that code can be loaded, moved, and discarded in all of Windows' operating modes. Windows takes advantage of the features of protected mode, when they are available, but also adapts to the constraints and limitation of real mode with no change in overall system capabilities. We're now going to look at the impact of dynamic linking on *data*. Windows allows every program and dynamic link library to create a default data segment, and it provides several mechanisms to make sure that every program and dynamic link library is always able to access its default data.

Dynamic Linking and Module Data Segments

When you write a stand-alone application in most operating systems, you may use functions from various static link libraries. When you do, these blend invisibly into your program so that it is almost impossible to distinguish the machine instructions created by *your* code from the machine instructions associated with library routines. If a static library routine needs to store global variables to maintain state information, the linker blends the library's global variables with your program's global variables.

When working with dynamic link libraries, the distinction between your program and the library code is more evident. For example, dynamic link libraries have their own separate executable files. GDI.EXE, for example, is the dynamic link library file where GDI routines live. The file maintains an existence that is separate from the programs that use the library routines.

Dynamic link libraries also have their own data segment that allows them to keep global variables separate from the data areas of the programs that use their routines. You can convince yourself of this by running a memory viewer utility. For example, the Microsoft SDK utility, HEAPWALK, lets you detect a dynamic link library's data segment. In Figure 19.6, HEAPWALK highlights the data segments of the USER and the WINOLDAP DLLs. (WINOLDAP provides support for DOS applications when they are running in Windows.)

A Windows library makes certain functions available to Windows programs. These functions serve as a doorway into the capabilities and features of the dynamic link libraries. Such functions are given a very special flag so that Windows can help the DLL access its proper data segment. The flag marks a function as **exported**. Windows modifies the first

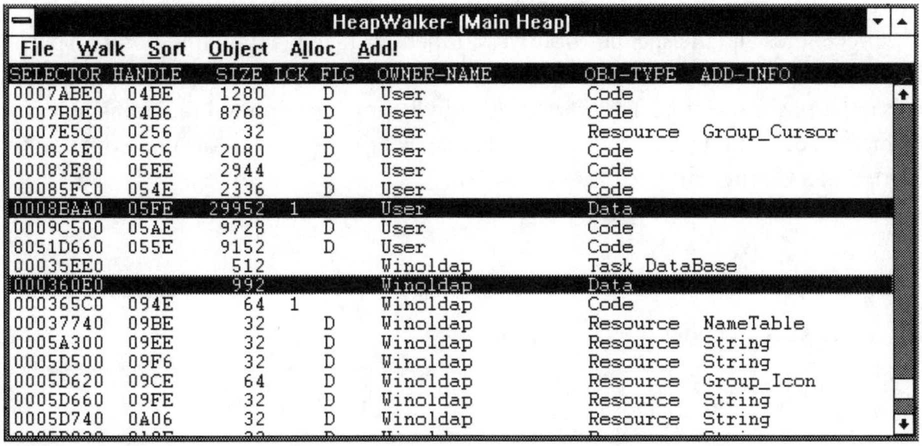

HeapWalker- (Main Heap)

File Walk Sort Object Alloc Add!

SELECTOR	HANDLE	SIZE	LCK	FLG	OWNER-NAME	OBJ-TYPE	ADD-INFO
0007ABE0	04BE	1280		D	User	Code	
0007B0E0	04B6	8768		D	User	Code	
0007E5C0	0256	32		D	User	Resource	Group_Cursor
000826E0	05C6	2080		D	User	Code	
00083E80	05EE	2944		D	User	Code	
00085FC0	054E	2336		D	User	Code	
0008BAA0	05FE	29952	1		User	Data	
0009C500	05AE	9728		D	User	Code	
8051D660	055E	9152		D	User	Code	
00035EE0		512			Winoldap	Task DataBase	
000360E0		992			Winoldap	Data	
000365C0	094E	64	1		Winoldap	Code	
00037740	09BE	32		D	Winoldap	Resource	NameTable
0005A300	09EE	32		D	Winoldap	Resource	String
0005D500	09F6	32		D	Winoldap	Resource	String
0005D620	09CE	64		D	Winoldap	Resource	Group_Icon
0005D660	09FE	32		D	Winoldap	Resource	String
0005D740	0A06	32		D	Winoldap	Resource	String

Figure 19.6 HEAPWALK with data segments of USER and WINOLDAP highlighted

three bytes of every exported library function to set up the library's data segment, using code like this:

```
MOV  AX, DGROUP      ; Get data segment address
PUSH DS              ; Save caller's DS
MOV  DS, AX          ; Install in DS register
```

When the library's data segment moves, Windows updates the value of DGROUP for all exported routines in the library. This causes the data segment register to be correctly set whenever a program calls into one of the exported "doorway" functions. Here is the complete set of assembly language instructions used to set up the data segment of an exported far routine in a dynamic link library:

```
MOV  AX, DGROUP      ; Get data segment address
INC  BP
PUSH BP
MOV  BP, SP
PUSH DS              ; Save caller's DS
MOV  DS, AX
```

Earlier, when we described some of the tricks that real mode Windows must play, we said that it must sometimes walk and patch the stack when a code segment has moved or been discarded. The **`PUSH BP`** and **`MOV BP,SP`** instructions are how the compiler ordinarily saves the old `BP` value and initializes it for the private use of the current function. This effectively creates a linked list of stack frames that make it easy for the stack walking to take place. The **`INC BP`** instruction is only used for far calls, and so helps the stack walker distinguish between near and far calls.

At certain times, a Windows library routine will call functions within a Windows program. Such routines are referred to as **call-back functions**. Up until this point in this book, we have discussed two types of call-back functions: window procedures and dialog box procedures. Other types include enumeration procedures and subclass procedures. Just like window procedures and the special "doorway" functions in a dynamic link library, special provision must be made to set up a call-back function's data segment register. One method involves exporting a function. This can be done by listing the exported functions in a program's module definition (.DEF) file. For example, here's how a window procedure might be exported in a C program:

```
EXPORTS
    MinWindowProc
```

Or, the **`_exports`** compiler directive can be used:

```
LONG FAR PASCAL _exports MinWindowProc
                         (HWND hwnd,   UINT wMsg,
                          WPARAM wParam, LPARAM lParam)
```

A third approach, which is available with the Turbo C++ compiler, is to use a **smart export**. This technique was discovered by Michael Geary, a long-time Windows programmer who was a developer of the Windows version of the Adobe Type Manager and Gupta Technology's SQL Windows. A smart export takes advantage of the fact that—at task context switch time—Windows makes sure the stack segment (SS) register contains the correct value. Since an application's stack is almost always in the application's default data segment, it's a simple matter to copy the value of the SS register into the DS register. Doing this for every far call means you never have to worry about exporting a function, nor having to use the **MakeProcInstance** routine (an issue we'll discuss later in this chapter). Here's the code associated with a smart export:

```
MOV  AX, SS     ; Copy stack to AX
INC  BP
PUSH BP
MOV  BP, SP
PUSH DS                ; Save caller's DS
MOV  DS, AX
```

Without a smart export, you must be sure to export a program's call-back functions. When you don't use a smart export, the compiler puts the following at the start of every far function:

```
PUSH DS         ; Put DS value into
POP  AX         ; the AX register.
NOP             ; Place holder
INC  BP         ; stack-walking preparation
PUSH BP         ; stack-walking preparation
MOV  BP, SP     ; set up regular stack frame
PUSH DS         ; save caller's DS
MOV  DS, AX     ; install our own DS
```

At first glance, it looks like this routine does a lot of work for nothing. But in fact this somewhat complicated piece of code makes sure that every far call saves a copy of the caller's data segment on the stack. Why? This allows Windows to patch the address of *data segments* that are moved at the same time that it patches code segment addresses. Anytime any code or segment address moves, Windows has no problem patching this up correctly.

When a code segment is loaded into memory, the prolog of exported functions is patched. Windows replaces the `PUSH DS, POP AX` with three `NOP` (no operation) instructions:

```
NOP
NOP
NOP
INC  BP         ; stack-walking preparation
PUSH BP         ; stack-walking preparation
MOV  BP, SP     ; set up regular stack frame
PUSH DS         ; save caller's DS
MOV  DS, AX     ; install our own DS
```

This allows an exported function to receive its data segment value in the `AX` register. But wait—how does the data segment value get into the `AX` register? That depends on the type of call-back function: Window procedures use one mechanism, and all other call-back functions use another.

A window procedure receives its data segment fix-up value as part of Windows' message delivery mechanism. When you call **`CreateWindow`** (or **`CreateWindowEx`**) to create a window, you pass an instance handle that identifies the data segment that is to be associated with the window. The message delivery mechanism uses this value to set up the proper `AX` value for window procedures.

All other call-back functions must use another mechanism that requires a little work on your part, but ensures that the `AX` register will be set up properly with the address of the data segment. The mechanism is called an **instance thunk**.

The Instance Thunk

The dynamic link mechanism allows the code from different **modules**—executable programs and dynamic link libraries—to be linked together efficiently at runtime. Every module can have its own data segment, which allows programs and dynamic link libraries to store global variables that they need to do their work. The rule about data fix-ups is that *a data segment* (DS) fix-up is required every time a module boundary is crossed. We have already described how this is done for dynamic link libraries, and for window procedures in applications. The third type of data segment fix-up must be set up and managed by a Windows program.

Here is a list of the different call-back procedures that can be created in Windows. As you can see, call-backs play many different roles in Windows. A call-back provides a way for Windows to deliver information to a Windows program in a fairly efficient manner.

Call-Back Function	*Description*
Dialog box procedure	Used to initialize and maintain a dialog box.
Enumeration procedure	When a program wants to query Windows about certain types of objects, an enumeration procedure is used. Windows calls the enumeration procedure once for each object. Objects that are enumerated include windows, fonts, GDI drawing objects, clipboard formats.
Hook	Allows a program to eavesdrop and change message traffic in the system. A keyboard hook, for example, lets a program respond to any "hot-key," even if the program isn't currently active.

Call-Back Function	*Description*
Memory discarding notification procedure	**GlobalNotify** lets a program set up a call-back procedure that is called before the Windows Memory Manager discards a memory object.
Subclass procedure	Provides a means of eavesdropping in and modifying the message traffic for a particular window.
Timer	A timer procedure allows a program to specify an alternative method for receiving timer notifications other than by a **WM_TIMER** message.

An instance thunk is only required if a call-back procedure resides in a Windows program. When these call-back procedures are implemented in a dynamic link library, an instance thunk is not needed. Nor is it required when you are using smart exports.

An instance thunk is a very small piece of code. Here is an example of one:

```
MOV   AX, DSvalue
JMP   DialogBoxProc
```

If the routine, **DialogBoxProc**, resided in a fixed code segment, this fix-up would jump directly to the code itself. Figure 19.7 shows the relationship of the different pieces to one another, and shows the flow of control through an instance thunk for all protected mode and for fixed code segments in real mode.

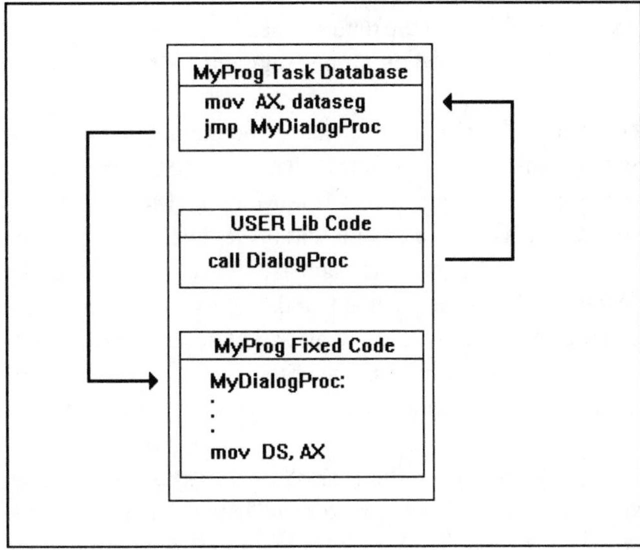

Figure 19.7 An Instance Thunk and a fixed code segment

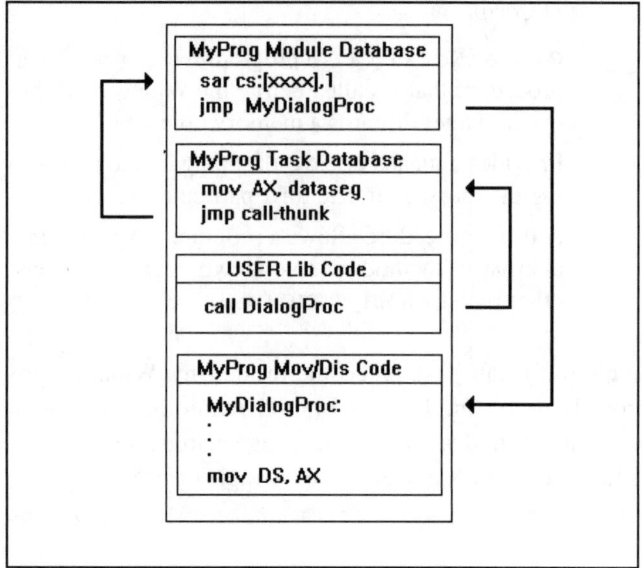

Figure 19.8 An Instance Thunk and a movable or discardable code segment

There is another case worth looking at briefly, since it helps to bring the complexity of real mode operation into perspective. Earlier, we mentioned that in real mode, calls into moveable and discardable code segments are always routed through a module database call thunk. When you add an instance thunk, you get an arrangement like that depicted in Figure 19.8. That is, the instance thunk is first called to put the data segment value into the `AX` register. Then, control passes to the call thunk to load an absent segment, or to jump to the segment when it's present.

Notice that the call gets routed through both the task database and the module database of the program. In the task database, the instance thunk puts the value of the program's data segment into the `AX` register. If the data segment moves, the Memory Manager walks through all the active thunks in the task database to ensure that these thunks stay current. From the task database, a jump is made into the module database. It arrives at the loader thunk that we described earlier. After all, this is the mechanism that allows a code segment to be discarded or moved in real mode. And finally, control arrives at our call-back procedure. Of course, as we saw in the earlier code fragments, one of the first instructions in the call-back procedure will establish the data segment address by copying the value in the `AX` register into the `DS` register.

A program creates an instance thunk by calling the **`MakeProcInstance`** routine, which we have seen already in our discussion of dialog boxes in Chapter 14. This routine takes as one of its parameters a procedure address—which, in real mode operation, is the address of a module database call thunk for functions that reside in moveable or discardable segments. It returns an instance thunk, which can then be provided as the address of a far procedure for those Windows library routines which require the address of call-back procedures.

Clean Up Before You Go Home

We have described three different sets of entries that can be made into far functions: exported library entries, unexported program entries, and exported program entries. The first reflects how the Windows loader sets up a dynamic link library's data segment. The second is simply what the C compiler creates to allow the other two entries to work properly. And the third is for call-back functions like window procedures and dialog box procedures.

Although there are three different entries for far functions, all far functions in Windows clean up the stack in the same way, with the following instructions:

```
MOV  SP, BP     ; restore caller's stack frame
POP  DS         ; restore caller's DS
POP  BP         ; clear off stack-walking link list
DEC  BP         ; flip even/odd far call bit
RETF 0002       ; far return
```

In other words, the caller's data segment value—the `DS` register—is restored. While it was on the stack, the Memory Manager may have modified it to reflect a new location for a data segment. The stack-walking link list value is removed by the `POP BP` instruction, and the `BP` register, which is used as a flag to help distinguish far calls from near calls when the stack is being walked, is decremented. And finally, a return instruction sends control back to the caller (or back to a return thunk, if in real mode the caller's code segment had to be discarded).

The dynamic link mechanism is a robust, flexible mechanism that helped the earliest versions of Windows run in real mode with acceptable performance. It continues to be used in the present version of Windows, in both its real and protected modes of operation. In addition, dynamic linking is a key architectural component of OS/2 and of the Windows NT operating system.

As you've seen, dynamic linking has both a code and a data aspect. The code aspect allows a program to be linked to library code at runtime instead of at link time. This has allowed programs written for previous version of Windows to run (almost) effortlessly in Windows 3, and will allow the programs that you write today to run unmodified in future versions of Windows. The data aspect of dynamic linking is almost as transparent as the code end. Before there were smart exports, Windows programmers had to export their call-back procedures and fuss with **`MakeProcInstance`**. The availability of smart exports helps make the data side of dynamic linking effortless.

A Minimum Dynamic Link Library: BEEP

The first program in this book was MIN, a minimum OWL application program. It's fitting, then, that the last program be a minimum dynamic link library. Every program in this book calls into one dynamic link library or another, including the Windows system DLLs and the various Borland DLLs provided to support OWL. You can use this DLL as a starting point for any DLL that you wish to build.

There isn't much code to this DLL, but I've gotten into the habit of keeping BEEP around because it used to be very difficult to get a DLL built from scratch. The problem wasn't actually the code, though, it was getting the compiler and linker switches set correctly. The TargetExpert in the Borland IDE certainly makes that problem go away, however. There are include files provided with BEEP, in case you prefer the command line compiler. But even if you choose this route, you're still relying on the TargetExpert, since it selected the compiler and linker switches that I used to build these make files.

A DLL is a passive server that can be used to share many things: code, data, resources, etc. This DLL shares two things: a tiny function called **`MakeBeep()`**, and a menu. The function calls the WinAPI **`MessageBeep()`** function and is not terribly complicated:

```
void _FAR _EXPFUNC MakeBeep (int iCount)
    {
    for (; iCount > 0; iCount--)
        MessageBeep (MB_OK);
    }
```

I like to use this library as a starter for other DLLs I write because I get audible evidence that my DLL was successfully created. Here is the source code to BEEP:

BEEP.CPP

```
// BEEP.CPP  A Minimum Dynamic Link Library
#include <owl\owlpch.h>
#include "beep.h"

// Library handle for everyone to share.
HMODULE hLib;

// Library entry point.
BOOL FAR PASCAL
LibMain(HMODULE    hLibrary      , // Instance handle.
        WORD    /* wDataSeg    */, // Data seg (Win16).
        WORD    /* cbHeap      */, // Initial heap (Win16).
        LPSTR   /* lpszCmdLine */) // Command line (Win16).
    {
    hLib = hLibrary;  // Save for everyone's use.

    return TRUE;      // Say "initialization Ok."
    }
```

```
// Library cleanup function.
int FAR PASCAL WEP (int /* code */)
    {
    return 0;
    }

void _FAR _EXPFUNC MakeBeep(int iCount)
    {
    for (;iCount > 0; iCount--)
        MessageBeep(MB_OK);
    }
```

BEEP.H

```
// Menu ID values.
#define CM_FILEEXIT 100
#define CM_HELPABOUT 200

// BEEP.DLL exported entry point.
void _FAR _EXPFUNC MakeBeep(int iCount);
```

BEEP.RC

```
#include "Beep.H"

main menu
    BEGIN
    POPUP "&File"
        {
        MENUITEM "E&xit", CM_FILEEXIT
        }
    POPUP "&Help"
        {
        MENUITEM "&About...", CM_HELPABOUT
        }
    END
```

BEEP.DEF

```
LIBRARY BEEP

DESCRIPTION 'A Minimum OWL 2.0 Dynamic Link Library'

DATA SINGLE PRELOAD MOVEABLE
CODE MOVEABLE DISCARDABLE

HEAPSIZE 512

EXPORTS
   @MakeBeep$qi @1
```

BEEP32.DEF

```
LIBRARY BEEP32

DESCRIPTION 'A Minimum OWL 2.0 Dynamic Link Library'

DATA SINGLE PRELOAD MOVEABLE
CODE MOVEABLE DISCARDABLE

HEAPSIZE 512

EXPORTS
   @MakeBeep$qi @1
```

DYNA16.MAK

```
#  MAKE file for Win16 API using dynamic BIDS,
#  OWL and C-runtime libraries.
#
#     C> make -fdyna16.mak
#

.AUTODEPEND
CC = -c -H -H"owl\owlpch.h" -ml -R -vi -WD -X-
CD = -D_RTLDLL;_BIDSDLL;_OWLDLL;_OWLPCH;
INC = -I\BC4\INCLUDE
LIB = -L\BC4\LIB

beep.dll :  beep.obj beep.lib beep.res
  tlink -c -C -Twd $(LIB) @dyna16.lnk
  brc beep.res beep.dll

beep.lib : beep.def
  implib beep.lib beep.def

beep.obj :  beep.cpp
  bcc $(CC) $(CD) beep.cpp

beep.res :  beep.rc beep.h
  brc $(INC) -31 -R beep.rc
```

DYNA16.LNK

```
\bc4\lib\c0dl.obj+
beep.obj
beep,beep
\bc4\lib\bidsi.lib+
\bc4\lib\owlwi.lib+
\bc4\lib\import.lib+
\bc4\lib\crtldll.lib
beep.def
```

DYNA32.MAK

```
#  MAKE file for Win32 API using dynamic BIDS,
#  OWL and C-runtime libraries.
#
#    C> make -fdyna32.mak
#

.AUTODEPEND
CC = -c -H -H\""owl\owlpch.h\"" -p- -R -vi -WD -X-
CD = -D_RTLDLL;_BIDSDLL;_OWLDLL;_OWLPCH;
INC = -I\BC4\INCLUDE
LIB = -L\BC4\LIB

beep32.dll :  beep.obj beep32.lib beep.res
  tlink32 -aa -c -Tpd $(LIB) @dyna32.lnk
  brc32 beep.res beep32.dll

beep32.lib : beep32.def
  implib beep32.lib beep32.def

beep.obj :  beep.cpp
  bcc32 $(CC) $(CD) beep.cpp

beep.res :  beep.rc beep.h
  brc32 $(INC) -w32 -R beep.rc
```

DYNA32.LNK

```
\bc4\lib\c0d32.obj+
beep.obj
beep32,beep32
\bc4\lib\bidsfi.lib+
\bc4\lib\owlwfi.lib+
\bc4\lib\import32.lib+
\bc4\lib\cw32i.lib
beep32.def
```

If you are working with DLLs, a major issue is whether to ship a Win16 DLL or a Win32 DLL. This is important because the various Windows systems don't let you call Win32 code from Win16 code, or vice versa. Available solutions are all quite painful: **Universal thunks** let you call Win16 libraries from Win32 applications under Win32s. **Generic thunks** let you call Win32 libraries from Win16 applications under Windows NT. The current rumor about Chicago is that it will have yet another thunking mechanism. Without some sort of automated tool, thunk creation is very difficult. A simple answer is to provide both—but you will want to be sure that the DLLs have different names. This is the approach taken with BEEP: BEEP.DLL is the Win16 version, and BEEP32.DLL is the Win32 version.

The entry point to a dynamic link library is **`LibMain`**. It's the first function called, just like an application's **`WinMain`** entry point. The purpose of this function is to allow you to initialize your DLL, then return **`TRUE`** if you were successful or **`FALSE`** if you weren't. A limitation of this function is that you are limited in the functions you can call. In particular, if your DLL is statically linked to an application—like CALLBEEP, my next program—you can't call any functions that require a message queue. If initialization fails, you might be tempted to call **MessageBox**—but since this requires a message queue, the call always fails and users won't know why things didn't get started correctly. If you need to explain a DLL load failure to a user, you'll want to write an application for that purpose and **WinExec** that application to start it up.

Another limitation on what you can do in a DLL's **LibMain** function has to do with calling functions in other DLLs that you have written. The problem occurs when you have two DLLs that each call functions in the other. Since this situation is sometimes unavoidable, you'll want to call **LoadLibrary** from within one of the library's **LibMain** functions to make sure that the other one has been completely loaded:

```
// Calling another DLL from LibMain.
BOOL FAR PASCAL
LibMain (HMODULE hLib, WORD, WORD, LPSTR)
    {
    HMODULE hOtherLib = LoadLibrary ("STRINGLIB.DLL");
    if (hOtherLib < 32)
        return FALSE; // They couldn't load
                      // so we can't either.

    // Calling our mythical string library.
    strcpy (buf1, buf2);
    }
```

Any time you call **LoadLibrary**, you need to make sure that you call **FreeLibrary**. Otherwise, the DLL will get stranded in system memory. We'd probably do this in our DLL's WEP function, which is the last function that gets called in our DLL:

```
int FAR PASCAL WEP (int /* code */)
    {
    FreeLibrary (hOtherLib);
    }
```

By itself, a DLL doesn't look that interesting: It's just a collection of code and data waiting for someone to call. This next program, CALLBEEP, does just that:

CALLBEEP: Calling our DLL

Here's a program that uses the functionality of BEEP.DLL (or its Win32 equivalent, BEEP32.DLL). This program was built from MIN with two differences: In response to a **WM_LBUTTONDOWN** message, it calls BEEP's **MakeBeep()** function. In addition, CALLBEEP doesn't have a menu resource, but instead uses a menu resource that it loads from BEEP.

CALLBEEP.CPP

```
// CALLBEEP.CPP  MIN calling BEEP.DLL minimum
//               dynamic link library.
//

#include <owl\owlpch.h>
#include "callbeep.h"
#include "beep.h"

//
// Main window
class DFrame : public TFrameWindow
    {
  public:
    DFrame(char * title);
    void CmFileExit();
    void CmHelpAbout();
    void EvLButtonDown (UINT, TPoint&);
    void SetupWindow();
  DECLARE_RESPONSE_TABLE (DFrame);
    };

DEFINE_RESPONSE_TABLE1 (DFrame, TFrameWindow)
  EV_WM_LBUTTONDOWN,
  EV_COMMAND(CM_FILEEXIT, CmFileExit),
  EV_COMMAND(CM_HELPABOUT, CmHelpAbout),
END_RESPONSE_TABLE;

DFrame::DFrame(char * title) : TFrameWindow(0, title)
    {
    }

void DFrame::CmFileExit()
    {
    CloseWindow(0); // Cause application to terminate
    }

void DFrame::CmHelpAbout()
    {
    MessageBox("     MIN Calling BEEP.DLL\n\n"
               "'Borland C++ 4.0 Programming\n"
               "  for Windows', by Paul Yao", Title);
    }

void DFrame::EvLButtonDown (UINT, TPoint&)
    {
    MakeBeep(3);
    }

//
// Application object
class DApp : public TApplication
    {
  public:
    DApp();
    void InitMainWindow();
    };

DApp::DApp() : TApplication()
    {
    }
```

```
void DApp::InitMainWindow()
     {
     SetMainWindow (new DFrame("MIN Calling BEEP.DLL"));

     // Connect normal icon.
     MainWindow->SetIcon(this, "SNAPSHOT");
     }

void DFrame::SetupWindow()
     {
     // Call base class member first.
     TFrameWindow::SetupWindow();

     // Fetch menu resource from BEEP.DLL
     HMODULE hmod = GetModuleHandle("BEEP");
     HMENU hmenu = ::LoadMenu(hmod, "MAIN");
     SetMenu(hmenu);
     }

//
// Application main entry point.
OwlMain(int, char **)
     {
     return DApp().Run();
     }
```

CALLBEEP.H

```
#define CM_FILEEXIT 100
#define CM_HELPABOUT 200
```

CALLBEEP.RC

```
#include "callbeep.h"

snapshot icon callbeep.ico
```

CALLBEEP.DEF

```
EXETYPE WINDOWS

CODE MOVEABLE DISCARDABLE
DATA MULTIPLE MOVEABLE

HEAPSIZE   512
STACKSIZE 8192
```

DYNA16.MAK

```
#  MAKE file for Win16 API using dynamic BIDS,
#  OWL and C-runtime libraries.
#
#    C> make -fstatic16.mak
#

.AUTODEPEND
CC = -c -H -H"owl\owlpch.h" -ml -R -vi -WS -X-
CD = -D_RTLDLL;_BIDSDLL;_OWLDLL;_OWLPCH;
INC = -I\BC4\INCLUDE
LIB = -L\BC4\LIB

callbeep.exe :  callbeep.obj callbeep.res
  tlink -c -C -Twe $(LIB) @dyna16.lnk
  brc callbeep.res callbeep.exe

callbeep.obj :  callbeep.cpp
  bcc $(CC) $(CD) callbeep.cpp

callbeep.res :  callbeep.rc callbeep.ico callbeep.h
  brc $(INC) -31 -R callbeep.rc
```

DYNA16.LNK

```
\bc4\lib\c0wl.obj+
callbeep.obj
callbeep,callbeep
..\beep\beep.lib+
\bc4\lib\bidsi.lib+
\bc4\lib\owlwi.lib+
\bc4\lib\import.lib+
\bc4\lib\crtldll.lib
callbeep.def
```

DYNA32.MAK

```
#  MAKE file for Win32 API using dynamic BIDS,
#  OWL and C-runtime libraries.
#
#    C> make -fdyna32.mak
#

.AUTODEPEND
CC = -c -H -H\""owl\owlpch.h\"" -p- -R -vi -W -X-
CD = -D_RTLDLL;_BIDSDLL;_OWLDLL;_OWLPCH;
INC = -I\BC4\INCLUDE
LIB = -L\BC4\LIB

callbeep.exe :  callbeep.obj callbeep.res
  tlink32 -aa -c -Tpe $(LIB) @dyna32.lnk
  brc32 callbeep.res callbeep.exe

callbeep.obj :  callbeep.cpp
```

```
    bcc32 $(CC) $(CD) callbeep.cpp

  callbeep.res :  callbeep.rc callbeep.ico callbeep.h
    brc32 $(INC) -w32 -R callbeep.rc
```

DYNA32.LNK

```
\bc4\lib\c0w32.obj+
callbeep.obj
callbeep,callbeep
\bc4\lib\bidsfi.lib+
\bc4\lib\owlwfi.lib+
\bc4\lib\import32.lib+
..\beep\beep32.lib+
\bc4\lib\cw32i.lib
callbeep.def
```

The call to **`MakeBeep()`** looks like every other function call in CALLBEEP. Unlike the other function calls, however, the linker has to be told how to find this function[1]. The compiler, after all, is happy to chew up all our C++ code and create independent .OBJ files. The linker has harder task: tying together all the pieces into a workable executable file.

The piece that's required is an **import library**. There are two import libraries in our example: BEEP.LIB describes the exported functions in BEEP.DLL. BEEP32.LIB describes the exported functions in BEEP32.LIB. With the command line tools, you create import libraries by calling IMPLIB.EXE. From the IDE, it's even easier: it does it for you when it links the DLL.

Whichever tool you use, the result is the same: an import library (.LIB) file that you provide to the linker so it can correctly build the application's executable file. With the command line tools, just add this library name to the list of library names already used. With the IDE, add it as a node to the application's executable target file.

To get access to the menu resource in BEEP.DLL (and BEEP32.DLL), the library's module handle is needed. One way to get the module handle is by calling **`LoadLibrary`**, which was described earlier. Since CALLBEEP calls functions within BEEP.DLL, it doesn't have to explicitly load the library—the Windows KERNEL has done this already. Since it's already loaded, a call to **`GetModuleHandle`** provides the handle needed in the call to the WinAPI **`LoadMenu`** function. Connecting the menu to the window requires calling **`TWindow::SetMenu`**.

[1] Actually, the linker must be told how to find every function. The difference is that the mechanism is already in place to find OWL and WinAPI functions. For every DLL you build, you need to let the linker know about your DLL functions by building an import library.

Appendices

Appendix A: A Taxonomy of Messages

The Eight Types of Messages

Type	*Description*
Hardware	Mouse and Keyboard Input.
Window Maintenance	Notification, Request for action, Query.
User-Interface Maintenance	Menu, mouse pointer, scroll bar, dialog boxes, MDI.
Termination	Application or system shutdown.
Private	Dialog box controls: edit, button, list box, combobox.
System Resource Notification	Color Changes, fonts, spooler, device modes.
Data Sharing	Clipboard and Dynamic Data Exchange (DDE).
Internal System	Undocumented Messages.

Hardware Messages

Mouse Messages: In a window's client area

WM_LBUTTONDBLCLK	Left button double-click.
WM_LBUTTONDOWN	Left button down.
WM_LBUTTONUP	Left button up.
WM_MBUTTONDBLCLK	Middle button double-click.
WM_MBUTTONDOWN	Middle button down.
WM_MBUTTONUP	Middle button up.

Hardware Messages (continued)

Mouse Messages: In a window's client area

WM_MOUSEMOVE	Mouse move.
WM_RBUTTONDBLCLK	Right button double-click.
WM_RBUTTONDOWN	Right button down.
WM_RBUTTONUP	Right button up.
WM_NCLBUTTONDBLCLK	Left button double-click.
WM_NCLBUTTONDOWN	Left button down.
WM_NCLBUTTONUP	Left button up.

Mouse Messages: In a window's nonclient area

WM_NCMBUTTONDBLCLK	Middle button double-click.
WM_NCMBUTTONDOWN	Middle button down.
WM_NCMBUTTONUP	Middle button up.
WM_NCMOUSEMOVE	Mouse move.
WM_NCRBUTTONDBLCLK	Right button double-click.
WM_NCRBUTTONDOWN	Right button down.
WM_NCRBUTTONUP	Right button up.

Keyboard Messages

WM_CHAR	Character input.
WM_DEADCHAR	Dead-character (umlaut, accent, etc.).
WM_KEYDOWN	Key has been depressed.
WM_KEYUP	Key has been released.
WM_SYSCHAR	System character input.
WM_SYSDEADCHAR	System dead-character.
WM_SYSKEYDOWN	System key has been depressed.
WM_SYSKEYUP	System key has been released.

Timer Messages

WM_TIMER	Timer has gone off.

Windows Maintenance Messages

Window Messages: Notification

WM_ACTIVATE	Window is active.
WM_ACTIVATEAPP	Application is active.
WM_CREATE	Window has been created.
WM_DESTROY	Window has been destroyed.
WM_ENABLE	Input to the window has been enabled.
WM_KILLFOCUS	Window has lost keyboard control.
WM_MOUSEACTIVATE	Notifies a window that it is going to become active because of a mouse click.
WM_MOVE	Window has been moved.
WM_PARENTNOTIFY	A child window has been created, destroyed, or has received a mouse button message.
WM_SETFOCUS	Window has gained keyboard control.
WM_SIZE	Window has changed size.

Window Messages: Request for Action

WM_CLOSE	Close (destroy) window.
WM_ERASEBKGND	Erase background.
WM_ICONERASEBKGND	Erase background of iconic window.
WM_NCACTIVATE	Change title bar to show active state.
WM_NCCREATE	Create nonclient area data.
WM_NCDESTROY	Destroy nonclient area data.
WM_NCPAINT	Redraw nonclient area.
WM_PAINT	Redraw client area.
WM_PAINTICON	Redraw iconic window client area.
WM_SETREDRAW	Inhibit redrawing of window.
WM_SETTEXT	Change window text.
WM_SHOWWINDOW	Change window visibility.

Window Messages: Query

WM_GETMINMAXINFO	What is min/max sizes for window?
WM_GETTEXT	What is the window text?
WM_GETTEXTLENGTH	What is the length of the window text?

Windows Maintenance Messages (continued)

Window Messages: Query

`WM_NCCALCSIZE`	How big should the client area be?
`WM_QUERYDRAGICON`	For windows that do not have a class cursor: Do you have a cursor to be used as your icon while you are being dragged around the screen?
`WM_QUERYNEWPALETTE`	Do you have a new palette?
`WM_QUERYOPEN`	Can iconic window be opened?

User Interface Messages

Menu Messages

`WM_COMMAND`	Menu item has been selected.
`WM_INITMENU`	Initialize menu bar menu.
`WM_INITMENUPOPUP`	Initialize popup menu.
`WM_MENUCHAR`	Mnemonic key used to select menu.
`WM_MENUSELECT`	User is browsing through menus.

System Commands: System Menu, Min/Max Buttons, Titlebar, etc.

`WM_SYSCOMMAND`	A system command has been selected.

Mouse Pointer Messages

`WM_NCHITTEST`	Query: Where is mouse on the window?
`WM_SETCURSOR`	Request: Change pointer to correct shape.

Scroll Bar Messages

`WM_HSCROLL`	Horizontal scrollbar has been clicked.
`WM_VSCROLL`	Vertical scrollbar has been clicked.

User Interface Messages *(continued)*

Dialog Box and Dialog Box Control Messages

WM_CHARTOITEM	Message sent from a list box to its parent window in response to a WM_CHAR message. Only list style send this message. Among other things, it allows a keyboard interface for owner-draw list boxes.
WM_COMMAND	Control communicating with Dialog Box.
WM_COMPAREITEM	Sent to the parent of an owner-draw dialog box control, asking to compare two items for the purpose of sorting.
WM_CTLCOLOR	Control asking for colors to be set.
WM_DELETEITEM	Notification to an owner-draw listbox or an owner-draw combobox that an item has been deleted.
WM_DRAWITEM	Request to the parent of an owner-draw control, or owner-draw menu, to draw.
WM_GETDLGCODE	Query control: Want keyboard input?
WM_GETFONT	Query control: What font are you using?
WM_INITDIALOG	Initialize dialog.

Dialog Box and Dialog Box Control Messages

WM_MEASUREITEM	Request to the parent of an owner-draw control or an owner-draw item to provide the dimensions of the item that is going to be drawn.
WM_NEXTDLGCTL	Message sent by a dialog box control to allow the proper handling of the Tab and Return keys for controls that process keyboard input themselves.
WM_SETFONT	Request to control: Use this font.
WM_VKEYTOITEM	Message sent from a list box to its parent window in response to a WM_KEYDOWN message. This is only sent by list boxes which have the LBS_WANTKEYBOARDINPUT style set.

User Interface Messages (continued)

Multiple Document Interface Messages

WM_CHILDACTIVATE	Notifies a parent window that a child is active.
WM_MDIACTIVATE	Notifies an MDI child window that it is either gaining or losing activation.
WM_MDICASCADE	Request to arrange the open MDI child windows in a cascading, stair-step fashion.
WM_MDICREATE	Requests an MDI client window to create an MDI child window.
WM_MDIDESTROY	Requests to an MDI client window to destroy an MDI child window.
WM_MDIGETACTIVE	Query an MDI client window for the currently active MDI child window.
WM_MDIICONARRANGE	Request to arrange the iconic MDI child windows in an orderly fashion.
WM_MDIMAXIMIZE	Request to maximize, or zoom, an MDI child window so that it occupies all of its parent's client area.
WM_MDINEXT	Request to activate the next MDI child window.

Multiple Document Interface Messages

WM_MDIRESTORE	Request to restore an MDI child window to its previous state—iconic, normal, or zoomed.
WM_MDISETMENU	Adjusts the menu on an MDI frame window.
WM_MDITILE	Request to arrange the open MDI child windows in a tiled fashion in the MDI parent's client window.

Termination Messages

Application and System Termination

WM_QUIT	Request that a program should terminate.
WM_QUERYENDSESSION	A Query: Ready for system shutdown?
WM_ENDSESSION	Notification of results of shutdown query.

Private Messages

Button Control Messages

BM_GETCHECK	Query whether a button is checked or not.
BM_GETSTATE	Query state of a button.
BM_SETCHECK	Toggles a radio button or a check box.
BM_SETSTATE	Toggles the highlighting in a radio button or check box.
BM_SETSTYLE	Changes the style of an existing button.

Combo Box Control Message

CB_ADDSTRING	Adds a string to the list box of a combo box.
CB_DELETESTRING	Removes a string from the list box of a combo box.
CB_DIR	Adds a list of files from the current directory to the list box of a combo box.
CB_FINDSTRING	Searches the list box in a combo box for a string.
CB_GETCOUNT	Queries the number of items in the list box of a combo box.
CB_GETCURSEL	Queries the index of the currently selected item in the list box of a combo box.
CB_GETEDITSEL	Queries the selected text in the edit control of a combo box.
CB_GETITEMDATA	Queries the item identifier from the list box of a combo box.
CB_GETLBTEXT	Queries a string from the list box of a combo box.
CB_GETLBTEXTLEN	Queries the length of a string in the list box of a combo box.
CB_INSERTSTRING	Inserts a string into the list box of a combo box.
CB_LIMITTEXT	Sets the maximum number of characters that may be entered into the edit control of a combo box.
CB_RESETCONTENT	Removes all items from the list box of a combo box.
CB_SELECTSTRING	Creates a selection in the list box of a combo box.

***Private Messages** (continued)*

Combo Box Control Message

CB_SETCURSEL	Sets the current selection in the list box of a combo box, and places the text into the edit or static control.
CB_SETEDITSEL	Selects a range of characters in the edit control of a combo box.
CB_SETITEMDATA	Sets the identities for an item in a combo box.
CB_SHOWDROPDOWN	Shows or hides the drop down list box of a combo box.
CB_SETCURSEL	Sets the current selection in the list box of a combo box, and places the text into the edit or static control.
CB_SETEDITSEL	Selects a range of characters in the edit control of a combo box.
CB_SETITEMDATA	Sets the identities for an item in a combo box.
CB_SHOWDROPDOWN	Shows or hides the drop down list box of a combo box.

Dialog Box Messages

DM_GETDEFID	Queries the ID of the default push button in a dialog box.
DM_SETDEFID	Sets the default push button in a dialog box.

Edit Control

EM_CANUNDO	Queries the ability of an edit control to undo a previous edit.
EM_EMPTYUNDOBUFFER	Instructs an edit control to clear its undo buffer.
EM_FMTLINES	Instructs an edit control on how to handle end of line characters.
EM_GETHANDLE	Queries an edit control created with the DS_LOCALEDIT style for the handle of the object allocated from the local heap.
EM_GETLINE	Retrieves a line of text from an edit control.
EM_GETLINECOUNT	Queries the number of lines of text in an edit control.

Private Messages (continued)

Edit Control

EM_GETMODIFY	Queries an edit control to determine if the user has entered or changed any text.
EM_GETRECT	Queries an edit control for its display rectangle, which is either its client area or a subset as set by the EM_SETRECT message.
EM_GETSEL	Queries the characters that are included in the current selection.
EM_LIMITTEXT	Sets a limit to the number of characters that may be entered.
EM_LINEFROMCHAR	Finds the first line that contains a specific character.
EM_LINEINDEX	Queries the number of lines that have been scrolled in a multiline edit control.
EM_LINELENGTH	Queries the length of a line in an edit control.
EM_LINESCROLL	Scrolls a multiline edit control.
EM_REPLACESEL	Overwrites the current selection with new text.
EM_SETHANDLE	For edit controls with the DS_LOCALEDIT style, this message instructs the edit control to use a new local memory object for its data.
EM_SETMODIFY	Sets the modify flag for an edit control.
EM_SETPASSWORDCHAR	Sets the character to be displayed when a password is entered in an ES_PASSWORD style edit control.
EM_SETRECT	Sets the display rectangle for a multi-line edit control and causes an immediate repaint to occur.
EM_SETRECTNP	Sets the display rectangle for a multi-line edit control, and postpones painting until later.
EM_SETSEL	Defines a range of characters to display as selected.
EM_SETTABSTOPS	Sets the tab-stops in a multiline edit control.
EM_SETWORDBREAK	Defines a call-back function to be used for word-break processing in a multiline edit control.
EM_UNDO	Instructs an edit control to undo the last edit.

Private Messages (continued)

List box Control

`LB_ADDSTRING`	Inserts a string into a list box.
`LB_DELETESTRING`	Removes a string for a list box.
`LB_DIR`	Adds a list of files from the current directory to a list box.
`LB_FINDSTRING`	Searches a list box for a string.
`LB_GETCOUNT`	Queries the number of items in a list box.
`LB_GETCURSEL`	Queries the index of the currently selected item in a list box.
`LB_GETHORIZONTALEXTENT`	Queries the width in pixels that can be scrolled for a list box with horizontal scroll bars.
`LB_GETITEMDATA`	Queries the item identifier from a list box.
`LB_GETITEMRECT`	Queries the dimensions of a rectangle that bounds a list box item.
`LB_GETSEL`	Queries the selection state of a specific list box item.
`LB_GETSELCOUNT`	Queries the total number of items that are selected in a list box.
`LB_GETSELITEMS`	Queries the indices of the selected items in a list box.
`LB_GETTEXT`	Query the text of a list box item.
`LB_GETTEXTLEN`	Queries the text length of a list box item.
`LB_GETTOPINDEX`	Queries the index of the item currently displayed at the top of a list box.
`LB_INSERTSTRING`	Adds a string to a list box.
`LB_RESETCONTENT`	Removes all items from a list box.
`LB_SELECTSTRING`	Selects an item in a list box.
`LB_SELITEMRANGE`	Selects a range of items in a multiselection list box.
`LB_SETCOLUMNWIDTH`	Sets the column width of multicolumn list box.
`LB_SETCURSEL`	Sets the current selection in a list box.
`LB_SETHORIZONTALEXTENT`	Sets the horizontal scrolling range of a list box.
`LB_SETITEMDATA`	Replaces an owner-draw item in a list box.
`LB_SETSEL`	Highlights a string in a multiple selection list box.

List box Control

Private Messages (continued)

LB_SETTABSTOPS	Sets the tab stop of a list box that was created with the LBS_USETABSTOPS style.
LB_SETTOPINDEX	Scrolls a list box to place a specific item at the top of the list box.

System Private Messages

WM_CANCELMODE	Request by system to cancel a mode, such as a mouse capture.
WM_ENTERIDLE	Notification that the system is in an idling state, because the user is browsing a menu or a dialog box.

System Resource Notification Messages

System Resources Notification Messages

WM_COMPACTING	Notification that system memory is low, and that the Memory Manager is trying to free up some memory.
WM_DEVMODECHANGE	Printer setup has changed.
WM_FONTCHANGE	Installed fonts in the system have changed.
WM_PALETTECHANGED	Hardware color palette has changed.
WM_SPOOLERSTATUS	Job has been removed from spooler queue.
WM_SYSCOLORCHANGE	One or more system colors has changed.
WM_TIMECHANGE	System time has changed.
WM_WININICHANGE	Initialization file, WIN.INI, changed.

Data Sharing Messages

Clipboard Messages

WM_ASKCBFORMATNAME	Asks for the name of a Clipboard format.
WM_CHANGECBCHAIN	Notification of a change in the viewing chain.
WM_DESTROYCLIPBOARD	Clipboard contents are being destroyed.

Clipboard Messages

Data Sharing Messages (continued)

WM_DRAWCLIPBOARD	Clipboard contents have changed.
WM_HSCROLLCLIPBOARD	Horizonal scrolling of owner-draw clipboard item.
WM_PAINTCLIPBOARD	Requests drawing of an owner-draw clipboard item.
WM_RENDERALLFORMATS	Request to provide the data for all clipboard formats that have been promised.
WM_RENDERFORMAT	Request to provide data for a single clipboard format that has been promised.
WM_SIZECLIPBOARD	Notification to the owner of owner-draw clipboard data that the size of the Clipboard viewer window has changed.
WM_VSCROLLCLIPBOARD	Vertical scrolling of an owner-draw clipboard item.

Dynamic Data Exchange (DDE) Messages

WM_DDE_ACK	Acknowledgment.
WM_DDE_ADVISE	Request from a DDE client to establish a permanent data link.
WM_DDE_DATA	Send a data item from a DDE server to a DDE client.
WM_DDE_EXECUTE	Request a DDE server to execute a series of commands.
WM_DDE_INITIATE	Logon to a DDE server.
WM_DDE_POKE	Request by a client for a server to update a specific data item.
WM_DDE_REQUEST	One-time request by a DDE client for a piece of information.

System Resource Notification Messages

Dynamic Data Exchange (DDE) Messages

WM_DDE_TERMINATE	Logoff from a DDE server.

Dynamic Data Exchange (DDE) Messages

System Resource Notification Messages *(continued)*

`WM_DDE_UNADVISE`	Terminate a permanent data link that was initiated with the WM_DDE_ADVISE message.

Appendix B: The Default Window Procedure

For your convenience, here is a listing of the default window procedure that Microsoft provided in the Windows software development kit. To see the latest revision of this code, please refer to the sample source diskettes which Microsoft provides as part of the SDK. And here is a list of the messages to which DefWindowProc responds:

```
WM_NCACTIVATE
WM_NCHITTEST
WM_NCCALCSIZE
WM_NCLBUTTONDOWN
WM_NCMOUSEMOVE
WM_NCLBUTTONUP
WM_NCLBUTTONDBLCLK
WM_CANCELMODE
WM_NCCREATE
WM_NCDESTROY
WM_NCPAINT
WM_SETTEXT
WM_GETTEXT
WM_GETTEXTLENGTH
WM_CLOSE
WM_PAINT
WM_PAINTICON
WM_ICONERASEBKGNE
WM_ERASEBKGND
WM_QUERYOPEN
WM_QUERYENDSESSION
WM_SYSCOMMAND
WM_SYSKEYDOWN
WM_KEYUP
WM_SYSKEYUP
WM_SYSCHAR
WM_CHARTOITEM
WM_VKEYTOITEM
WM_ACTIVATE
WM_SETREDRAW
WM_SHOWWINDOW
WM_CTLCOLOR
WM_SETCURSOR
WM_MOUSEACTIVATE
WM_DRAWITEM
```

```
/*--------------------------------------------------------*/
/*                                                        */
/*  DefWindowProc() -                                     */
/*                                                        */
/*--------------------------------------------------------*/

LONG FAR PASCAL DefWindowProc(hwnd, message, wParam, lParam)

register HWND hwnd;
         WORD message;
register WORD wParam;
         LONG lParam;

{
  int         i;
  HDC         hdc;
  PAINTSTRUCT ps;
  HICON       hIcon;
  RECT        rc;
  HANDLE      hCurs;
  HBRUSH      hbr;
  HWND        hwndT;

  if (!CheckHwnd(hwnd))
      return((DWORD)FALSE);

  switch (message)
    {
      case WM_NCACTIVATE:
        if (wParam != 0)
          SetWF(hwnd, WFFRAMEON);
        else
          ClrWF(hwnd, WFFRAMEON);

        if (TestWF(hwnd, WFVISIBLE) && !TestWF(hwnd, WFNONCPAINT))
          {
            hdc = GetWindowDC(hwnd);
            DrawCaption(hwnd, hdc, TRUE, TestWF(hwnd, WFFRAMEON));
            InternalReleaseDC(hdc);
            if (TestWF(hwnd,WFMINIMIZED))
              RedrawIconTitle(hwnd);
          }
        return(TRUE);

      case WM_NCHITTEST:
        return(FindNCHit(hwnd, lParam));

      case WM_NCCALCSIZE:
        CalcClientRect(hwnd, (LPRECT)lParam);
        break;

      case WM_NCLBUTTONDOWN:
      {
        WORD     cmd;
        RECT     rcWindow;
        RECT     rcCapt;
        RECT     rcInvert;
        RECT     rcWindowSave;

        cmd = 0;

        switch(wParam)
          {
```

```
    case HTZOOM:
    case HTREDUCE:
      GetWindowRect(hwnd, (LPRECT)&rcWindow);
      CopyRect((LPRECT)&rcWindowSave, (LPRECT)&rcWindow);

      if (TestWF(hwnd, WFSIZEBOX))
        InflateRect((LPRECT)&rcWindow,
                    -cxSzBorderPlus1, -cySzBorderPlus1);
      else
        InflateRect((LPRECT)&rcWindow,
                    -cxBorder, -cyBorder);

      rcCapt.right = rcWindow.right + cxBorder;
      rcCapt.left = rcWindow.right - oemInfo.bmReduce.cx-
                    cxBorder;

      if (wParam == HTREDUCE)
        cmd = SC_MINIMIZE;
      else if (TestWF(hwnd, WFMAXIMIZED))
        cmd = SC_RESTORE;
      else
        cmd = SC_MAXIMIZE;

      if (wParam == HTREDUCE && TestWF(hwnd, WFMAXBOX))
        OffsetRect((LPRECT)&rcCapt,
                   -oemInfo.bmReduce.cx, 0);

      rcCapt.top = rcWindow.top;
      rcCapt.bottom = rcCapt.top + cyCaption;

      CopyRect((LPRECT)&rcInvert, (LPRECT)&rcCapt);
      InflateRect((LPRECT)&rcInvert,
                  -cxBorder, -cyBorder);

      rcInvert.right += cxBorder;
      rcInvert.left += cxBorder;

      /* Converting to window coordinates. */
      OffsetRect((LPRECT)&rcInvert,
                 -(rcWindowSave.left + cxBorder),
                 -(rcWindowSave.top + cyBorder));
      /* Wait for the BUTTONUP message and see if cursor
       *  is still in the Minimize or Maximize box.
       *
       * NOTE: rcInvert is in window coords, rcCapt is
       * in screen coords
       */
      if (!DepressTitleButton(hwnd, rcCapt,
                              rcInvert, wParam))
        cmd = 0;

      break;

    default:
      if (wParam >>= HTSIZEFIRST && wParam <<= HTSIZELAST)
        /* Change HT into a MV command. */
        cmd = SC_SIZE +
              (wParam - HTSIZEFIRST + MVSIZEFIRST);
  }

if (cmd != 0)
  {
    /* For SysCommands on system menu,
     * don't do if menu item is disabled.
```

```
             */
            if (TestWF(hwnd, WFSYSMENU))
              {
              /* don't check old app child windows
               */
              if (LOWORD(GetExpWinVer(hwnd->>hInstance)) >>= VER
                  || !TestwndChild(hwnd))
                {
                  SetSysMenu(hwnd);
                  if (GetMenuState(GetSysMenuHandle(hwnd),
                                   cmd & 0xFFF0,
                                   MF_BYCOMMAND)
                      & (MF_DISABLED | MF_GRAYED))
                    break;
                }
              }
            SendMessage(hwnd, WM_SYSCOMMAND, cmd, lParam);
            break;
        }
      /*** FALL THRU ***/
    }

    case WM_NCMOUSEMOVE:
    case WM_NCLBUTTONUP:
    case WM_NCLBUTTONDBLCLK:
      HandleNCMouseGuys(hwnd, message, wParam, lParam);
      break;

    case WM_CANCELMODE:
      if (hwndCapture == hwnd && pfnSB != NULL)
        EndScroll(hwnd, TRUE);

        if (fMenu && hwndMenu == hwnd)
          EndMenu();

      /* If the capture is still set, just release at
       * this point.  Can put other End functions in later.
       */
      if (hwnd == hwndCapture)
        ReleaseCapture();
      break;

    case WM_NCCREATE:
      if (TestWF(hwnd, (WFHSCROLL | WFVSCROLL)))
        if (InitPwSB(hwnd) == NULL)
          return((LONG)FALSE);

      return((LONG)DefSetText(hwnd,
                   ((LPCREATESTRUCT)lParam)->>lpszName));

    case WM_NCDESTROY:
      if (hwnd->>hName)
          hwnd->>hName = TextFree(hwnd->>hName);
      break;

    case WM_NCPAINT:
      /* Force the drawing of the menu. */
      SetWF(hwnd, WFMENUDRAW);
      DrawWindowFrame(hwnd, (HRGN)wParam);
      ClrWF(hwnd, WFMENUDRAW);
      break;

    case WM_SETTEXT:
      DefSetText(hwnd, (LPSTR)lParam);
```

```
  if (TestWF(hwnd, WFVISIBLE))
    {
      if (TestWF(hwnd,WFMINIMIZED))
        {
          ShowIconTitle(hwnd,FALSE);
          ShowIconTitle(hwnd,TRUE);
        }
      else if (TestWF(hwnd, WFBORDERMASK) ==
                (BYTE)LOBYTE(WFCAPTION))
        {
          hdc = GetWindowDC(hwnd);
          DrawCaption(hwnd,
                      hdc,
                      FALSE,
                      TestWF(hwnd, WFFRAMEON));
          InternalReleaseDC(hdc);
        }
    }
  break;

case WM_GETTEXT:
  if (wParam)
    {
      if (hwnd->>hName)
        return (DWORD)TextCopy(hwnd->>hName,
                               (LPSTR)lParam,
                               wParam);

      /* else Null terminate the text buffer since
       * there is no text.
       */
      ((LPSTR)lParam)[0] = NULL;
      }
  return (0L);


case WM_GETTEXTLENGTH:
  if (hwnd->>hName)
      return(lstrlen(TextPointer(hwnd->>hName)));

    /* else */
    return(0L);

case WM_CLOSE:
  DestroyWindow(hwnd);
  break;

case WM_PAINT:
  BeginPaint(hwnd, (LPPAINTSTRUCT)&ps);
  EndPaint(hwnd, (LPPAINTSTRUCT)&ps);
  break;

case WM_PAINTICON:
  /* Draw the icon through the window DC if app used
   * own DC. If own DC is used the mapping mode may
   * not be MM_TEXT.
   */
  BeginPaint(hwnd, (LPPAINTSTRUCT)&ps);
  if (TestCF(hwnd, CFOWNDC) || TestCF(hwnd, CFCLASSDC))
    {
      /* If owndc, do the end paint now so that the
       * erasebackgrounds/validate regions go through
       * properly. Then we get a clean window dc to
       * draw the icon into.
```

```
          */
        InternalEndPaint(hwnd, (LPPAINTSTRUCT)&ps, TRUE);
        hdc = GetWindowDC(hwnd);
      }
    else
      {
        hdc = ps.hdc;
      }

    /* wParam is TRUE to draw icon, FALSE to ignore paint. */
    if (wParam)
      {
        hIcon = (HICON)(PCLS)(hwnd->>pcls)->>hIcon;
        GetClientRect(hwnd, (LPRECT)&rc);

        rc.left = (rc.right - rgwSysMet[SM_CXICON]) >>>> 1;
        rc.top = (rc.bottom - rgwSysMet[SM_CYICON]) >>>> 1;

        DrawIcon(hdc, rc.left, rc.top, hIcon);
      }

    /* Delete the update region. */
      if (TestCF(hwnd, CFOWNDC) || TestCF(hwnd, CFCLASSDC))
        {
          InternalReleaseDC(hdc);
          /* ValidateRect(hwnd, NULL); */
        }
      else
          InternalEndPaint(hwnd, (LPPAINTSTRUCT)&ps, TRUE);
    break;

  case WM_ICONERASEBKGND:
    /* Erase the icon through the window DC if app used
     * own DC. If own DC is used the mapping mode may not
     * be MM_TEXT.
     */
    if (TestCF(hwnd, CFOWNDC) || TestCF(hwnd, CFCLASSDC))
      hdc = GetWindowDC(hwnd);
    else
      hdc = (HDC)wParam;

    if (TestWF(hwnd, WFCHILD))     /* for MDI child icons */
      {
        if ((hbr = GetBackBrush(hwnd->>hwndParent)) == NULL)
          {
            /* No brush, punt. */
            goto AbortIconEraseBkGnd;
          }
        else
            goto ICantBelieveIUsedAGoToStatement;
      }

    if (hbmWallpaper)
      {
        /* Since desktop bitmaps are done on a wm_paint
         * message (and not erasebkgnd), we need to call
         * the paint proc with our dc.
         */
        PaintDesktop(hdc);
        /* SendMessage(hwndDesktop,WM_ERASEBKGND,hdc,0L);*/
      }
    else
      {
        hbr = sysClrObjects.hbrDesktop;
```

```
ICantBelieveIUsedAGoToStatement:
            FillWindow(hwnd->>hwndParent,hwnd,hdc,hbr);
          }

AbortIconEraseBkGnd:
        if (TestCF(hwnd, CFOWNDC) || TestCF(hwnd, CFCLASSDC))
          InternalReleaseDC(hdc);

        return((LONG)TRUE);

      case WM_ERASEBKGND:
        if ((hbr = GetBackBrush(hwnd)) != NULL)
          {
            FillWindow(hwnd, hwnd, (HDC)wParam, hbr);
            return((LONG)TRUE);
          }
        break;

      case WM_QUERYOPEN:
      case WM_QUERYENDSESSION:
        return((LONG)TRUE);

      case WM_SYSCOMMAND:
        SysCommand(hwnd, wParam, lParam);
        break;

      case WM_KEYDOWN:
        if (wParam == VK_F10)
          fF10Status = TRUE;
        break;

      case WM_SYSKEYDOWN:
        /* Is the ALT key down? */
        if (HIWORD(lParam) & SYS_ALTERNATE)
          {
            /* Toggle the fMenuStatus iff this is NOT a
             * repeat KEYDOWN message;  Only if the prev key
             * state was 0, then this is the first KEYDOWN
             * message and then we consider toggling menu
             * status.
             */
            if((HIWORD(lParam) & SYS_PREVKEYSTATE) == 0)
              {
                /* Don't have to lock hwndActive because it's
                 * processing this key.
                 */
                if ((wParam == VK_MENU) && (!fMenuStatus))
                  fMenuStatus = TRUE;
                else
                  fMenuStatus = FALSE;
            }

            fF10Status = FALSE;

            DWP_ProcessVirtKey(wParam);
          }
        else
          {
            if (wParam == VK_F10)
              fF10Status = TRUE;
            else
              {
                if (wParam == VK_ESCAPE)
                  {
```

```
                if(GetKeyState(VK_SHIFT) << 0)
                  SendMessage(hwnd,
                              WM_SYSCOMMAND,
                              SC_KEYMENU,
                              (DWORD)MENUSYSMENU);
              }
          }
      }
    break;

  case WM_KEYUP:
  case WM_SYSKEYUP:
    /* Press and release F10 or ALT.
     * Send this only to top-level windows, otherwise MDI
     * gets confused.  The fix in which DefMDIChildProc()
     * passed up the message was insufficient in case
     * a child window of the MDI child had the focus.
     */
    if ((wParam == VK_MENU && (fMenuStatus == TRUE)) ||
        (wParam == VK_F10 && fF10Status) )
      SendMessage(GetTopLevelWindow(hwnd),
                  WM_SYSCOMMAND,
                  SC_KEYMENU,
                  (DWORD)0);

    fF10Status = fMenuStatus = FALSE;
    break;

  case WM_SYSCHAR:
    /* If syskey is down and we have a char... */
    fMenuStatus = FALSE;
    if ((HIWORD(lParam) & SYS_ALTERNATE) && wParam)
      {
        if (wParam == VK_TAB || wParam == VK_ESCAPE)
          break;

        /* Send ALT-SPACE only to top-level windows. */
        if ((wParam == MENUSYSMENU) && (TestwndChild(hwnd)))
          SendMessage(hwnd->>hwndParent,
                      message,
                      wParam,
                      lParam);
        else
          SendMessage(hwnd,
                      WM_SYSCOMMAND,
                      SC_KEYMENU,
                      (DWORD)wParam);
      }
    else
      /* Ctrl-Esc produces a WM_SYSCHAR,
       * But should not beep;
       */
      if (wParam != VK_ESCAPE)
        MessageBeep(0);
    break;

  case WM_CHARTOITEM:
  case WM_VKEYTOITEM:
    /* Do default processing for keystrokes into
     * owner draw listboxes.
     */
    return(-1);
```

```
case WM_ACTIVATE:
  if (wParam)
    SetFocus(hwnd);
  break;

case WM_SETREDRAW:
  DWP_SetRedraw(hwnd, wParam);
  break;

case WM_SHOWWINDOW:
  /* Non null descriptor implies popup hide or show. */
  /* We should check whether it is a popup window
   * or Owned window
   */
  if (LOWORD(lParam) != 0 &&
     (TestwndPopup(hwnd) || hwnd ->> hwndOwner))
    {
      /* IF NOT(showing, invisible, and not set as hidden)
       * AND NOT(hiding and not visible)
       */
      if (!(wParam != 0 && !TestWF(hwnd, WFVISIBLE) &&
          !TestWF(hwnd, WFHIDDENPOPUP)) &&
          !(wParam == 0 && !TestWF(hwnd, WFVISIBLE)))
        {
          /* Are we showing? */
          if (wParam)
            /* Yes, clear the hidden popup flag. */
            ClrWF(hwnd, WFHIDDENPOPUP);
          else
            /* No, Set the hidden popup flag. */
            SetWF(hwnd, WFHIDDENPOPUP);

          ShowWindow(hwnd,
             (wParam ? SHOW_OPENNOACTIVATE : HIDE_WINDOW));
        }
    }
  break;

case WM_CTLCOLOR:
  if (HIWORD(lParam) != CTLCOLOR_SCROLLBAR)
    {
      SetBkColor((HDC)wParam, sysColors.clrWindow);
      SetTextColor((HDC)wParam, sysColors.clrWindowText);
      hbr = sysClrObjects.hbrWindow;
    }
  else
    {
      SetBkColor((HDC)wParam, 0x00ffffff);
      SetTextColor((HDC)wParam, (LONG)0x00000000);
      hbr = sysClrObjects.hbrScrollbar;
      UnrealizeObject(hbr);
    }

  return((DWORD)hbr);

case WM_SETCURSOR:
  /* wParam  == hwnd that cursor is over
   * lParamL == Hit test area code (result of WM_NCHITTEST)
   * lParamH == Mouse message number
   */
  if (HIWORD(lParam) != 0 &&
      LOWORD(lParam) >>= HTSIZEFIRST &&
      LOWORD(lParam) <<= HTSIZELAST)
    {
```

```
      SetCursor(rghCursor[LOWORD(lParam)
                - HTSIZEFIRST + MVSIZEFIRST]);
      break;
    }

  if ((hwndT = GetChildParent(hwnd)) != NULL &&
      (BOOL)SendMessage(hwndT,
                        WM_SETCURSOR,
                        wParam,
                        lParam))
    return((LONG)TRUE);

  if (HIWORD(lParam) == 0)
    {
      hCurs = hCursNormal;
      SetCursor(hCurs);
    }
  else
    {
      switch (LOWORD(lParam))
      {
        case HTCLIENT:
          if (((HWND)wParam)->>pcls->>hCursor != NULL)
            SetCursor(((HWND)wParam)->>pcls->>hCursor);
          break;

        case HTERROR:
          switch (HIWORD(lParam))
          {
            case WM_LBUTTONDOWN:
              if ((hwndT = DWP_GetEnabledPopup(hwnd)) != NULL)
                {
                  if (hwndT != hwndDesktop->>hwndChild)
                    {
                      SetWindowPos(hwnd, NULL,
                                   0, 0, 0, 0,
                                   SWP_NOMOVE |
                                   SWP_NOSIZE |
                                   SWP_NOACTIVATE);
                      SetActiveWindow(hwndT);
                      break;
                    }
                }

              /*** FALL THRU ***/

            case WM_RBUTTONDOWN:
            case WM_MBUTTONDOWN:
              MessageBeep(0);
              break;
            }
            /*** FALL THRU ***/

        default:
          SetCursor(hCursNormal);
      }
    }

  return((LONG)FALSE);

case WM_MOUSEACTIVATE:
  if ((hwndT = GetChildParent(hwnd)) != NULL &&
      (i = (int)SendMessage(hwndT,
                            WM_MOUSEACTIVATE,
```

```
                                        wParam,
                                        lParam)) !=  0)
            return((LONG)i);

        /* Moving, sizing or minimizing?
         * Activate AFTER we take action.
         */
        if (LOWORD(lParam) == HTCAPTION)
          return((LONG)MA_NOACTIVATE);
        else
          return((LONG)MA_ACTIVATE);

      case WM_DRAWITEM:
          if (((LPDRAWITEMSTRUCT)lParam)->>CtlType == ODT_LISTBOX)
            LBDefaultListboxDrawItem((LPDRAWITEMSTRUCT)lParam);
          break;

    }

  return(0L);
}
```

Appendix C: Glossary

_AHINCR

This is a global symbol that can be used by an application program to increment the segment selector to address memory objects that occupy more than a single segment.

32-Bit Addressing

This refers to the capability in the Intel 80386 and later CPUs to use 32-bit offset to address memory. This allows the creation of memory segments that are as large as one megabyte. When running in 386-Enhanced Mode, Windows uses this type of addressing internally, but does not make it directly available to application programs. However, Microsoft does provide support for 32-bit addressing in a dynamic link library that is included with the Windows software development kit called WINMEM32.

Accelerator

See Keyboard Accelerator.

Active Window

The Active window is a top-level window belonging to the active application. The active application is the application given the highest priority by the user. When a user clicks the mouse on any window owned by an application, selects one of the application's top-level windows from Windows' Task List, or selects the application using keystroke combinations, then the application becomes active. The caption and border of the active application change color to indicate their state to the user. In addition, the windows of the active application are positioned on top of the windows belonging to other applications.

ANSI

American National Standards Institute.

ANSI Character Set

A standard that defines how character glyphs, or images, are stored as numeric character codes. According to the ANSI standard, the values 0 to 31 (1Fh) are reserved for control codes, the values 32 (20h) to 127 (7Fh) are for a standard set of printed characters, and the values 128 (80h) to 255 (FFh) define a range in which vendors can define their own character sequences. The IBM family of personal computers define a set of code pages that use upper range for line-drawing character, Greek letters, and accented characters. Windows defines a more complete set of accented characters that allows Windows programs to more easily be written for support in non-English-speaking countries.

ASCII

American Standard Code for Information Interchange.

Application Message Queue

When a Windows application is running, Windows allocates a buffer that is used to store the messages that are posted (using the **PostMessage** routine) to a program. The messages wait in the queue until a program makes a call to **GetMessage** or to **PeekMessage**. By default, a message queue can hold up to 8 messages. Programs that need a larger message queue can request this by calling **SetMessageQueue**.

Aspect Ratio

The aspect ratio describes the ratio between the height of a pixel and its width. Another way to think about it is in terms of the relative "squareness" of pixels on a device. CGA displays have an aspect ratio of 2 to 1; EGA displays have a ratio of 1.33 to 1; VGA displays have an aspect ratio of 1 to 1.

Background Color

The background color is a DC attribute that is used for drawing text, styled (nonsolid) lines, and hatched brushes. It is controlled by the setting of the background mode, another DC attribute.

Background Mode

The background mode is a toggle switch controlling whether the background color is used or not. When set to OPAQUE, the background color is turned on. Setting the background mode to TRANSPARENT turns off the background color.

BitBlt

An acronym for "BIT-boundary BLock Transfer." This GDI function copies rectangular patterns of bits from one location to another. The most obvious use of BitBlt is for moving windows on the display screen. But BitBlts are also used to make menus appear and disappear quickly. Application programs commonly use the BitBlt function to move images stored in bitmaps to an output device like the display screen or a printer. A program can also copy an image from a display screen to a bitmap.

Bitmap

Bitmaps are one of two pseudodevices that GDI uses to store pictures. (The other type is a metafile.) Bitmaps use RAM to store rectangular picture images. Bitmaps are created by requesting GDI to allocate the RAM for the picture storage. Once allocated, a bitmap provides an invisible drawing surface on which a program can draw by calling any of the GDI drawing routines. Bitmaps are also a type of resource that allow a program to store a graphic image inside its executable file. The third type of bitmaps are device-independent bitmaps (DIBs), which provide a device-independent way to store color information.

Brush

A brush is a GDI drawing object used to fill areas. There are three types of brushes: solid, pattern, and hatched. Every DC contains a brush that is used for area filling when on of the filled figure routines is called (**Rectangle**, **Ellipse**, **Polygon**, etc.). Another function which makes use of the brush is the **BitBlt** routine, which can use the brush in the destination DC to alter the effect of the bit-blt operation.

Call-back Functions

A call-back function provides a way for Windows to communicate with a program by calling it directly into a program subroutine.

Call thunk

A call thunk is a tiny piece of code that is used by Windows in real mode as a bridge to far functions in a moveable or discardable code segment.

Capture

see Mouse Capture.

Caret

A caret is a user interface object that serves as a keyboard pointer, in much the same way that the cursor serves as a mouse pointer. A caret is a blinking bitmap that notifies the user of the window that has the keyboard focus, and also provides feedback on the location of the current position in a window.

Casting

Refers to the ability of the C compiler to convert one data type into another data type. In the following example, a variable of type int, i, is set equal to the value of a long variable, lValue:

```
long lValue;
 int i;

 lValue = 1245;
 i = (int)lValue
```

Casting overrides the default conversion that the compiler provides, and avoids the warning messages that compilers often generate in such situations. Nevertheless, Windows programmers can omit certains types of casting which were required for older versions of the C compiler. For example, in response to the WM_PAINT message, here is an outdated but still commonly encountered construction:

```
PAINTSTRUCT ps;

 BeginPaint (hwnd,(LPPAINTSTRUCT)&ps);
 .
 .
 EndPaint (hwnd,(LPPAINTSTRUCT)&ps);
```

While it is harmless enough in this example, explicit casting is not required and can hide certain types of problems. For example, if the programmer had omitted the "&" in the previous example, the compiler would not be able to see the error because of the casting:

```
PAINTSTRUCT ps;
 BeginPaint (hwnd,(LPPAINTSTRUCT)ps);
```

CDECL Calling Convention

The CDECL calling convention describes the way that parameters are passed on the stack to a subroutine (right to left), and also assigned the calling routine with the responsibility for clearing parameters from the stack. The CDECL calling convention allows routines to be defined with a variable number of parameters, with the disadvantage of creating slightly larger and slower code than the alternative PASCAL calling convention.

Class

see Window Class.

Class Database

Refers to the collection of window classes that have been registered in the system with **RegisterClass**.

Client Area Coordinates

Describe a coordinate system that has its origin (0,0) at the upperleft corner of a window. Client area coordinate units are equal to pixels.

Clipping Region

A clipping region defines a closed area used for clipping. Inside the clipping region, drawing is allowed. Outside the clipping region, drawing is not allowed. Clipping regions in Windows are always described in terms of rectangles or groups of rectangles.

Clipping

Clipping describes the behavior of GDI drawing routines in the way they recognize arbitrary borders that are defined. Clipping is defined in terms of closed areas: Inside the clipping region, drawing is allowed. Outside the clipping region, no drawing is allowed.

Clipboard

The Clipboard provides user-operated data sharing services between programs. Items on the Edit menu ordinarily serve as the primary user interface for the Clipboard, and provide Cut, Copy, and Paste options. In addition, a standard set of accelerator keys has been defined for Clipboard commands.

Code Page

A code page defines a character set. The code page determines the set of glyphs, or character images, that will be used to draw a particular character. For example, code page 437 is the standard character set for the United States version of the IBM-PC.

Common User Access (CUA)

Refers to the element of IBM's Systems Application Architecture (SAA) that covers the standards that have been developed for the user interfaces part of application and system software.

Compiler Memory Model

Refers to the set of defaults that the compiler sets for addressing both code and data.

Coordinate Transformation

A coordinate transformation refers to the way that drawing coordinates are interpreted in a graphics output environment. The three basic types of coordinate transformation include translation, scaling, and rotation. In Windows, GDI's coordinate transformations are limited to translation and scaling.

Cursor

A cursor is a bitmap that moves in response to the movement of a mouse.

Debug Version of Windows

Describes Windows when running with special copies of the KERNEL.EXE (KRNL286.EXE, KRNL386.EXE), USER.EXE and GDI.EXE dynamic link libraries.

Default Window Procedure

A Windows library routine that processes nonclient area messages, system commands, system keystrokes, and other messages that window procedures do not process.

Desktop Window

Refers to the window that covers the entire display screen and sits behind every other window in the system.

Device Capability Bits

Refers to a set of flags that are provided by a GDI display or printer driver to describe the native capabilities of the device. GDI uses these flags to determine whether to send a high-level drawing request directly to a device driver, or to simulate the request in software and send the device driver a series of low-level drawing requests.

Device Context (DC)
A data structure created and maintained by GDI in support of device independent drawing operations on displays, printers, metafiles, and bitmaps. A device context is three things rolled into one: It is a toolbox containing a set of drawing attributes or drawing tools, it is a connection to a specific device, and it is a permission slip that allows a program to draw on a device.
Device Independent Bitmap (DIB)
A device-independent bitmap provides a standard format for storing color bitmap information. DIBs come in four formats: one-bit per pixel (monochrome), four bits per pixel (16 color), eight bits per pixel (256 color) and 24 bits per pixel (16 million colors).

Dialog Box
A dialog box is a window, inside of which are other windows that are commonly referred to as dialog box controls. A dialog box is typically used to gather additional information from the user required to complete a command.

Dialog Box Control
A dialog box control is a window that rests inside a dialog box and provides a specific set of services. Among the window classes that have been defined for dialog box controls are button, combo box, edit, listbox, scroll bar, and static.

Dialog Box Coordinates
Dialog box coordinates provide a device-independent way to specify the layout of a dialog box. Dialog box units are relative to the system font, or to whatever font has been defined for the dialog box.

Dialog Box Editor
The dialog box editor is a graphic layout tool for designing the look of a dialog box and the style of each dialog box controls. Microsoft provides the dialog box editor as part of its Software Development Kit (SDK).

Disabled Window
A disabled window is one that is prevented from receiving mouse and keyboard input. For example, the parent window of a modal dialog box is disabled.

Discardable Memory
A discardable memory object is one that, when unlocked, can be purged from memory by the memory manager when available system memory is otherwise unavailable. Windows uses a least recently used algorithm to determine the segment to discard next.

Drawing Attribute
A drawing attribute is a setting or a drawing object inside a device context that can change the appearance of the output produced by different GDI drawing routines. Some examples of drawing attributes include pens, brushes, fonts, mapping mode, and text color.

Dynamic Data Exchange (DDE)
A data exchange mechanism that is built on top of Windows' message passing mechanism. A DDE interaction is called a conversation. There are always two participants in a DDE conversation, one called the client and the other called the server. There are several types of DDE converations: ongoing data exchange, one-

time data exchange, command execution, and poke of data back into the server's database.

Dynamic Link Library

A dynamic link library is a file containing code or data that can be shared by different application programs at run-time. For example, the core components that make up Windows itself are a collection of dynamic link libraries and include KERNEL.EXE, USER.EXE and GDI.EXE, as well as a set of device drivers. Fonts are an example of dynamic link libraries that contain no code, but only data to be shared between programs.

Dynamic Linking

Dynamic linking refers to the process by which different code and data of different modules—application programs and dynamic link libraries—are connected at run time.

Event-driven

Event-driven software is structured to process external events that do not necessarily occur in a sequential manner. Traditionally, interrupt-handling code in an operating system or in a device driver has been the primary domain of event driven software. But the development of personal computers and interactive software has made this a concern of application programmers. Graphical User Interfaces (GUIs) provide a programming environment which assists in the creation of event driven application software.

Expanded Memory Specification (EMS)

The expanded memory specification refers to a protocol that was first introduced in 1984 by Lotus, Intel, and Microsoft to ease the memory crunch that was caused by the 640K memory limitation of real-mode operation. Windows 1.x used EMS memory to cache DOS applications that were dormant; Windows 2.x provided enhanced EMS support to Windows applications that increased the address space of each application in a manner that was transparent to the application programmer. Windows 3.x continues EMS support, although Windows itself only uses EMS in real mode. In the other modes of operation, a Windows program can access EMS memory, but Windows itself does not use EMS because of the greater flexibility that is available with extended memory.

Extended Memory

Extended memory refers to the memory that is not ordinarily accessible from real mode, but requires protect-mode operation. Extended memory allows the address space of a machine to go beyond the one-megabyte boundary of real mode and to access up to 16 megabytes with an 80286 processor and up to 4 gigabytes with an 80386 processor.

Extended Memory Specification (XMS)

The extended memory specification defines an interface for using the memory areas above the 640K line. This includes the upper memory blocks (UMBs) between 640 and 1024K, the high-memory area (HMA) from 1024 to 1088K, and the extended memory blocks (EMBs) above the 1088K line.

File Manager

One of the desktop accessories that Microsoft has bundled with Windows 3.0.

Fixed Memory

A fixed memory object is one whose logical address does not change. However, in protect mode, the physical address of a fixed memory block can change unless the memory has been fixed, which is done by calling **GlobalFix**. In addtion, in 386 Enhanced Mode, a fixed memory object can also be paged to disk unless it has been page-locked, which is accomplished by calling **GlobalPageLock**.

Focus

see Keyboard Focus.

Font

also see Logical Font.

Function Prototype

Function prototypes provide a means by which the C Compiler can perform some automatic error checking, including check for proper use of the return value and the correct number and type of parameters. Here is an example of a function prototype taken from Window.h:

```
BOOL FAR PASCAL TextOut (HDC, int, int,
LPSTR, int);
```

Global Descriptor Table (GDT)

A global descriptor table is one of two data areas used by the Intel 80286 and higher CPUs in protect mode. A global descriptor table allows the CPU to convert segment identifier values (also known as segment selectors) into the physical addresses of segments. Intel designed the GDT to provide a shared data area accessible from all processes. However, Windows does not use a GDT for any of its memory management, but uses the other data area, the local descriptor table (LDT) instead.

Global Heap

The global heap refers to the total memory available to Windows itself, to Windows applications, and to other components like device drivers.

Global Memory Object

A global memory object is an object allocated from the global heap. In Intel memory architecture terms, a global memory object is a segment.

Granularity

In the context of memory allocation, granularity refers to the increments by which memory is actually allocated. The global heap manager uses a granularity of 32 bytes. The local heap manager uses a granularity of 4 bytes.

Graphic Device Interface (GDI)

GDI is Windows' device-independent graphics output library.

Graphical User Interface (GUI)

Refers to a type of operating system or operating environment that displays output on a bitmapped graphical display screen. Another characteristic of GUI systems is that they are event-driven, which means a different programming model is necessary besides the traditional, sequence oriented programming model that was originally developed for batch oriented systems. Microsoft Windows is an example of a GUI system. Other examples include the Apple Macintosh, the OS/2 Presentation Manager, which was jointly developed by IBM and Microsoft, and Digital Research Corporation's GEM. The various X-Windows systems deserve to be in this last as well, and they include the Open System Foundation's Motif, and Sun

Microsystem's Open Look and Digital Equipment Corporation's DEC-Windows.

GUI

An acronym for Graphical User Interface.

Handle

A handle is a 16-bit, unsigned integer that identifies an object. In most cases, the meaning of a handle is only known to the subroutine library that issued the handle. A program can modify an object by providing the handle to the subroutine library, which then acts on the objects on behalf of the program.

Hardware Event Queue

A buffer maintained by Windows to hold keyboard and mouse events that are waiting to be retrieved by application programs.

High Memory Area (HMA)

The high memory area refers to the 64 K-bytes located immediately above the one-megabyte address line on 80286 and 80386 processors. Intel designed this space as the first 64K of extended memory, which was not meant to be part of the real mode address space. However, an XMS (eXtended Memory Specification) driver, like HIMEM.SYS, is able to trick the 80286 and higher chips into allowing access into this data area.

Hit-Test Code

Refers to a code returned by the default window procedure in reponse to the WM_NCHITTEST message, which identifies the area of a window where the mouse is located. Hit-test codes are used to help the window manager to install the correct mouse cursor.

Hook

A hook is a subroutine that is called by Windows' message handling mechanism to allow the monitoring and modification of message traffic in the system. Hooks are installed on a system-wide basis, and therefore care should be taken when using them to avoid disrupting the normal operation of other programs, and to avoid slowing the system down.

Hungarian naming

Hungarian naming is a convention for creating variable and function names that provide a quick way to compose short but useful identifiers.

Huge Memory Object

A huge memory object is a memory object in the global heap that is larger than 64K. Windows allocates huge memory objects by allocating two or more segments. To access the second and subsequent segments, huge pointer arithmetic is required. This involves updating the segment portion of the address as well as the offset portion. The segment portion is modified by changing the segment value using the __AHINCR update value. This value is added to the segment address to access the next segment in a huge object segment chain.

Icon

An icon is a graphic symbol that serves to remind the user of the presence of a program, file, or data object that is presently closed, but available for future access.

Import Library

An import library provides the linker with information about the exported entry points of a dynamic link library. An import library allows the linker to create a relocation record in a program's .EXE file so that Windows' dynamic link mechanism can provide the required fix-up to the calling code at program execution time.

Instance

An instance of a program refers to a copy of a program in memory. Windows allows several copies of a single program to run simultaneously. Each instance has its own, private data segment, but shares code and resource segments with every other instance of the program.

Instance Thunk

An instance thunk is a tiny piece of code that is created in a program's task database (TDB) to assist in the fix-up of the data segment for an exported call-back function. An instance thunk is created by **MakeProcInstance**, and freed by **FreeProcInstance**. With the exception of window procedures, every call-back procedure requires an instance thunk. This includes dialog box procedure, enumeration procedures, notification procedures, and certain subclass procedures. No instance thunk is required for any of these procedures when they reside in the code segment of a dynamic link library.

Interrupt Descriptor Table

An interrupt descriptor table (IDT) is a lookup table used by the higher end Intel-86 chips (80286 and above) in protect mode to hold an array of interrupts.

Keyboard Accelerator

A keyboard accelerator provides a means to define key-strokes that are interpreted as commands. Keyboard accelerators mimic menu selection messages, to minimize special processing that would otherwise be required to support a program's command keys.

Keyboard Focus

The keyboard focus tells Windows the window that should receive keyboard input. When a program receives the keyboard focus, it is notified with a WM_SETFOCUS message. When it loses the focus, it is notified with a WM_KILLFOCUS message.

Keyboard Scan Code

A keyboard scan code is a numeric value sent from the keyboard hardware as a notification that a key was pressed, released, or is being held down. Application programs do not ordinarily handle scan codes, since they represent a hardware dependent key code. In Windows, scan codes undergo two translation before they appear in a program as ASCII characters. The first translation is from scan code to virtual key codes. The second translation is from virtual key codes to ASCII characters.

KERNEL

The KERNEL is one of the three core components of Windows, and is responsible for memory management, dynamic linking, resources, atom tables, module managment, interface to DOS, and other operating system services that are available to Windows programs.

Load On Call segment

A load on call segment is a code or resource segment that is loaded into memory when it is referenced.

Local Descriptor Table (LDT)

A local descriptor table is one of two data areas used by the Intel 80286 and higher CPUs in protect mode. A local descriptor table allows the CPU to convert segment identifier values (also known as segment selectors) into the physical addresses of segments. Intel designed the LDT to provide a process with a private address space. In Windows 3.0, a single LDT is used by all application programs. However, a future version of Windows will provide one LDT per application program.

Local Heap

Refers to the heap that is created in a module's default data segment. The automatic startup code automatically initializes the local heap of an application program by calling the **LocalInit** routine. Dynamic link libraries that wish to use a local heap must explicitly call **Local- Init** themselves.

Logical Drawing Object

A logical drawing object is a GDI description of a pen, brush, font, or color. It provides a device-independent way to describe the drawing attributes that are installed in a DC.

Logical Font

A logical font is a description of a font that GDI's font mapper uses to select a font for drawing text. A logical font description can be created using the LOGFONT data structure.

Logical Pen

A logical pen describes the color, width, and style of lines requested by a program.

Mapping Mode

A mapping mode is a DC drawing attribute that describes how drawing coordinates that are given to GDI drawing routines are interpreted. For example, the default mapping mode, MM_TEXT, interprets coordinates as pixels. The other mapping modes can be used to scale coordinates into fractions of an inch, fractions of a centimeter, or scale to arbitrary ratios.

Marker

A marker is a graphic primitive that is guaranteed to be centered on the specified location. Although GDI itself does not directly implement markers, it is a simple matter to build a set of marker subroutines that draw using GDI drawing routines. See Chapter 7.

Message

A message is a 16-bit, unsigned value that notifies a window procedure that an event of interest has occurred. Windows' predefined messages are identified in Windows.H with symbolic constants whose names start with a WM_ prefix. For example, the WM_CREATE message is sent to a window procedure to notify it that a window of that class has been created.

Metafile

A metafile is a pseudo-device that GDI can create for the purpose of storing graphic images. A GDI metafile is a data structure containing a list of calls to be made to GDI routines to reconstruct a picture, along with the parameters to provide those calls.

Module

A module is a specific type of entity in Windows, which reflects the way that code and data is organized on disk. Windows recognizes two types of modules:

executable application (.EXE) program files, and dynamic link libraries, which can have an extension of .EXE, .DRV, .DLL, or .FON, to name just a few.

Module Database
A module database is a memory resident image of the file header of an application program or a dynamic link library. The Windows loader uses the module database to load code and resources from disk when they are needed.

Module Definition File
An ASCII text file that contains program definition and memory use information. A module definition file normally has an extension of .DEF. At program creation time, the module definition file is given to the linker as part of the bulding of a .EXE or .DLL file.

Mouse Capture
Ordinarily, mouse messages are sent to the window lying under the mouse cursor. However, a program can restrict the flow of mouse messages to a single window by setting the mouse capture. This is done by calling **SetCapture**. To free mouse messages, a program calls **ReleaseCapture**.

Moveable Memory
Moveable memory objects are an artifact of real mode Windows. In real mode, a moveable object will only move when it is not locked by a program. In protect mode, segments can move at any time, since the physical address is hidden from application software. The protect mode memory management hardware converts logical addresses—which is how application software references memory—into physical addresses by means of a descriptor table. The Windows memory manager can move objects in physical memory without changing their logical addresses, which means that in protect mode, memory movement is transparent to application softare.

Multiple Document Interface
or MDI, describes a user-interface standard that opens a new window for each new file or document that is opened in a program.

Nonpreemptive Scheduling
Describes the way that a multitasking system schedules programs to run. In a nonpreemptively scheduled system, the operating system does not interrupt programs

OEM Character Set
Refers to the set of characters native to a machine. For IBM-compatible computers built for sale in United States, this means code page 437.

Page Locking
Page locking refers to a process by which memory in 386-Enhanced Mode is prevented from being swapped to disk. This is accomplished by calling the **GlobalPageLock** routine and is primarily intended for the use of time-critical device drivers that must stay memory resident.

Paragraph
When the Intel-86 processors operate in real mode, a paragraph is the smallest memory unit that can be allocated. A paragraph is 16 bytes. Windows' memory manager allocates segments in two-paragraph increments, which means the granularity of the global memory manager is 32 bytes.

Paintbrush

One of the desktop accessories that is included with Windows 3.0.

Palette (PAL)

A palette provides two services: It describes the colors that are stored in a device-independent bitmap (DIB), and it allows a program to request changes to the physical palette of display devices that support palettes.

PASCAL Calling Convention

The PASCAL calling convention describes the way that parameters are passed on the stack to a subroutine (left to right), and also assigns the called routine with the responsibility for cleaning the parameters from the stack. Routines that are defined as PASCAL must have a fixed number of parameters, but this results in slightly smaller and faster code than the alternative CDECL calling convention.

Pen

A pen is a DC attribute that describes the color, style, and width of lines. See Logical Pen.

Preemptive Scheduling

Describes the way that a multitasking system schedules programs to run. In a preemptively scheduled system, the operating system will interrupt one program to allow another one to run.

Preload Segments

A code or resource segment that is marked as preload is moved into memory before a program starts running.

Private Window Class

A private window class is reserved for the use of a single program. In contrast are global window classes, which are available for use by any program in the system.

Process Database (PDB)

A data structure created by Windows to maintain DOS related per-process data. Windows adds its own elements to this data structure.

Profiler

see Swap Kernel.

Program Manager

Refers to the main program window in Windows 3.0.

Program Segment Prefix (PSP)

see Process Database.

Protect Mode

Protect mode refers to an operating mode of Intel 80286 chips and later. Protect mode is characterized by an addressing scheme that prevents programs from illegal access to unowned memory areas. On the 80286, protect mode operation allows a physical address space of 16 megabytes. On the 80386 and 80486, protect mode allows access to a 4 gigabyte address space.

Pull-Model Processing

Refers to a style of interaction between the operating system and application software. Pull-model processing places the application software in the active role, in which it polls the system for available input. This is the traditional way that interactive application software has been written, and is how Windows' handles mouse and keyboard input. Also, messages that are transmitted to a window procedure using the PostMessage routine are delivered in a pull-model manner, that is, via the GetMessage or PeekMessage routines. See also push-model processing.

Push-Model Processing

Refers to a style of interaction between the operating system and application software. Push-model processing places the operating system software in the active role, in which it calls subroutines in the application software to perform the necessary tasks. Most of the non-hardware related messages in Windows are delivered in a push-model manner. For example, when a program calls the CreateWindow routine to create a window, a WM_CREATE message is pushed into the window procedure of the newly created window. Messages that are transmitted to a window procedure using the **SendMessage** routine are delivered in a push-model manner, which bypasses the pull-model **Get Message** routine, and calls a window procedure directly.

Raster Operation

A raster operation is a logical operation or combination of logical operations that describe how two or more inputs combine to produce a given output. One type of raster operation is the ROP2 codes, which are a DC attribute that describe how pixels, lines, and areas combine with a drawing surface. Another type of raster operation, sometimes known as ROP3 codes, are provided as parameters to the BitBlt and PatBlt functions, to describe how a source bitmap, a destination bitmap, and a brush are to combine.

Return Thunks

A return thunk is a tiny piece of code that real mode Windows uses to bridge a function return when the code segment containing the calling routine is discarded from memory.

Resource

A resource is a read-only data object that is bound into an executable file at program creation time. From a memory management point of view, resources can be discarded and reread when needed. From the point of view of the Windows user interface, resources define dialog boxes, menus, cursors, icons, bitmaps, to name just a few.

Real Mode

Real Mode refers to an operating mode of the Intel-86 family of processors. Real mode is characterized by a one-megabyte address space. Programs have access to the real, physical address of memory, which is how the mode gets its name.

Scan Code

see Keyboard Scan Code.

Scanner

A graphic scanner reads a graphic image on paper and converts it into a digital form suitable for creating GDI bitmaps.

Segment Selector

When the Intel-86 family of processors are running in protect mode, a segment identifier is referred to as a segment selector. Part of a segment selector is an index into a table of descriptors in either an LDT (local descriptor table) or a GDT (global descriptor table), from which is read the physical location of a memory segment.

Segmented Addressing

The Intel-86 family of CPUs address memory using a segmented addressing scheme. Segmented addressing requires two pieces in a memory address: a segment identifier and an offset.

Software Development Kit (SDK)
The Windows Software Development Kit is a product that Microsoft provides for the purpose of assisting software developers to create Windows programs.

Software Migration Kit (SMK)
The Software Migration Kit is a product that Microsoft provides to assist software developers in porting Windows programs to run in OS/2, version 1.2 and later.

Stack Patching
Stack patching refers to the process by which the real mode Windows Kernel updates stack references to code segments that have moved or been discarded.

Standard Mode
Refers to an operating mode of Windows in which protect mode addressing is enabled to allow Windows to take advantage of features of the Intel family of processors that are available on the 80286 and higher CPUs.

Swap Kernel
The swap kernel is a special version of the Windows kernel that runs in real mode only and provides information about the segment loading and discarding of a program. It can be used to fine tune the segment working sets of a program to minimize the program's required memory.
Systems Application Architecture (SAA)
A collection of standards created by IBM to provide software consistency that extends from personal computers to mini-computers on up to mainframes. Aspects of application software that will be affected include the user interface, and application programming interface (API). The user interface standards are described in a standard that is part of SAA and is called Common User Access (CUA).

Task Database (TDB)
A task database is a memory object created by the Window scheduler to keep track of the things that are owned by a task. This includes file handles, the current MS-DOS disk and directory, information about a task's private interrupts, and a pointer to the DOS program database, also known as a program segment prefix (PSP).

Text Alignment
The text alignment is a DC attribute that describes the placement of a line of text relative to a control point.

Text Color
The text color is a DC attribute that describes the color for drawing text. Only pure, undithered colors are actually used for text, which means that GDI maps the requested color into the closest available device color.

Thunk
A thunk is a tiny piece of code that serves as a dynamic code link (in real mode Windows)

Tiled Windows
Tiled windows refers to the placement of windows so that no two windows overlap. Windows 1.x had built-in support for automatic tiling. This support was removed in versions 2.0 and later.

Top-Level Window
A top-level window is an overlapping window (WS_OVERLAP) or a popup

window (WS_POPUP) which has no parent. All top-level windows are referenced in Windows' Task List that appears in response to the Ctrl + Esc key combination.

Unexpected Application Error (UAE)
An error that causes an application to terminate. Some of the causes of unexpected application errors include general protection faults, unexpected paging fault, and unexpected interrupt.

Viewport Origin
The viewport origin is a DC attribute that defines the coordinate translation to take place after the scaling for the various GDI mapping modes.

Viewport Extent
The viewport extent is a DC attribute that provides a pair of X and Y values that are used to define the ratios for GDI's isotropic and anisotropic mapping modes.

Virtual Key Code
A virtual key code is a value that represents keystroke information as raw keyboard input. Raw keyboard input does not distinguish, for example, between upper and lower-case letters, and does not take into account the state of shift keys like Ctrl, Shift, and Alt. Nor do virtual key codes take into account the state of the various keyboard toggle keys, like Num Lock, Caps Lock, or Scroll Lock. Virtual key codes represent an intermediate step between scan code information, which is hardware-dependent keyboard input, and ASCII characters, which are device-independent representations of ASCII characters.

Window Class
A window class is a template for creating a window. Window classes are created by calling RegisterClass and supplying a pointer to a WNDCLASS structure with the class definition information.

Window Extent
The window extent is a DC attribute that provides a pair of X and Y values that are used to define the ratios for GDI's isotropic and anisotropic mapping modes.

Window Origin
The window origin is a DC attribute that defines the translation that is to take place in the world coordinate space before the scaling transformation of any of GDI's mapping modes.

Window Procedure
A function associated with a window class that processes the messages associated with a given window.

Windows Sandwich
A window sandwich describes a code construction made up of three parts: two slices of bread and some filling in between. The top slice of bread borrows a system resource, the filling uses the resource, and the bottom slice of bread returns the resource to the owner.

Appendix D: Contents of a Device Context

Drawing Attribute	*Default Value*	*Lines*	*Filled Areas*	*Text*	*Raster*	*Comments*
Background Color	White	x	x	x		styled pen, hatch brush
Background Mode	OPAQUE	x	x	x		On/Off switch
Brush Handle	White Brush		x		x	Filled areas
Brush Origin	(0, 0)		x		x	hatch & dithered brushes
Clipping Region Handle	Entire Surface	x	x	x	x	
Color Palette Handle	Default Palette	x	x	x		
Current Pen Position	(0 , 0)	x				For LineTo routine
Drawing Mode	R2_COPYPEN	x	x			Boolean mixing
Font Handle	System Font			x		
Intercharacter Spacing	0			x		

(continued)

Drawing Attribute	*Default Value*	*Lines*	*Filled Areas*	*Text*	*Raster*	*Comments*
Mapping Mode	MM_TEXT	x	x	x	x	One unit = 1 pixel
Pen Handle	Black Pen	x	x			
Polygon-Filling Mode	Alternate		x			For Polygon routine
Stretching Mode	Black on White				x	For StretchBlt routine
Text Alignment	Left & Top			x		
Text Color	Black			x		
Viewport Extent	(1 , 1)	x	x	x	x	Coordinate mapping
Viewport Origin	(0 , 0)	x	x	x	x	Coordinate mapping
Window Extent	(1 , 1)	x	x	x	x	Coordinate mapping
Window Origin	(0 , 0)	x	x	x	x	Coordinate mapping

Appendix E: ANSI and OEM Character Sets

ANSI Character Set - Code Page 1004

	0-	1-	2-	3-	4-	5-	6-	7-	8-	9-	A-	B-	C-	D-	E-	F-
-0	I	I		0	@	P	`	p	I	I		°	À	Ð	à	ð
-1	I	I	!	1	A	Q	a	q	I	´	¡	±	Á	Ñ	á	ñ
-2	I	I	"	2	B	R	b	r	I	´	¢	²	Â	Ò	â	ò
-3	I	I	#	3	C	S	c	s	I	I	£	³	Ã	Ó	ã	ó
-4	I	I	$	4	D	T	d	t	I	I	¤	´	Ä	Ô	ä	ô
-5	I	I	%	5	E	U	e	u	I	I	¥	µ	Å	Õ	å	õ
-6	I	I	&	6	F	V	f	v	I	I	¦	¶	Æ	Ö	æ	ö
-7	I	I	'	7	G	W	g	w	I	I	§	·	Ç	×	ç	÷
-8	I	I	(	8	H	X	h	x	I	I	¨	¸	È	Ø	è	ø
-9	I	I	)	9	I	Y	i	y	I	I	©	¹	É	Ù	é	ù
-A	I	I	*	:	J	Z	j	z	I	I	ª	º	Ê	Ú	ê	ú
-B	I	I	+	;	K	[	k	{	I	I	«	»	Ë	Û	ë	û
-C	I	I	,	<	L	\	l	|	I	I	¬	¼	Ì	Ü	ì	ü
-D	I	I	-	=	M	]	m	}	I	I	-	½	Í	Ý	í	ý
-E	I	I	.	>	N	^	n	~	I	I	®	¾	Î	Þ	î	þ
-F	I	I	/	?	O	_	o	I	I	I	¯	¿	Ï	ß	ï	ÿ

Figure E.1 Ansi Character Set (Code Page 1004)

OEM Character Set - Code Page 437

	0-	1-	2-	3-	4-	5-	6-	7-	8-	9-	A-	B-	C-	D-	E-	F-
-0		►		0	@	P	`	p	Ç	É	á	░	└	╨	α	≡
-1	☺	◄	!	1	A	Q	a	q	ü	æ	í	▒	┴	╤	ß	±
-2	☻	↕	"	2	B	R	b	r	é	Æ	ó	▓	┬	╥	Γ	≥
-3	♥	‼	#	3	C	S	c	s	â	ô	ú	│	├	╙	π	≤
-4	♦	¶	$	4	D	T	d	t	ä	ö	ñ	┤	─	╘	Σ	⌠
-5	♣	§	%	5	E	U	e	u	à	ò	Ñ	╡	┼	╒	σ	⌡
-6	♠	▬	&	6	F	V	f	v	å	û	ª	╢	╞	╓	µ	÷
-7	•	↨	'	7	G	W	g	w	ç	ù	º	╖	╟	╫	τ	≈
-8	◘	↑	(	8	H	X	h	x	ê	ÿ	¿	╕	╚	╪	Φ	°
-9	○	↓	)	9	I	Y	i	y	ë	Ö	⌐	╣	╔	┘	Θ	∙
-A	◙	→	*	:	J	Z	j	z	è	Ü	¬	║	╩	┌	Ω	·
-B	♂	←	+	;	K	[	k	{	ï	¢	½	╗	╦	█	δ	√
-C	♀	∟	,	<	L	\	l	|	î	£	¼	╝	╠	▄	∞	ⁿ
-D	♪	↔	-	=	M	]	m	}	ì	¥	¡	╜	═	▌	φ	²
-E	♫	▲	.	>	N	^	n	~	Ä	₧	«	╛	╬	▐	ε	■
-F	☼	▼	/	?	O	_	o	⌂	Å	ƒ	»	┐	╧	▀	∩	

Figure E.2 OEM Character Set (Code Page 437)

Appendix F: The Windows Virtual Key Codes

(hex)	*(dec)*	*Symbolic Name*	*Key Pressed (US English 101/102 Kbd)*
1	1	VK_LBUTTON	
2	2	VK_RBUTTON	
3	3	VK_CANCEL	Ctrl-Break
4	4	VK_MBUTTON	
8	8	VK_BACK	Backspace
9	9	VK_TAB	Tab
C	12	VK_CLEAR	5 on Numeric keypad w/Num Lock OFF
D	13	VK_RETURN	Enter
10	16	VK_SHIFT	Shift
11	17	VK_CONTROL	Ctrl
12	18	VK_MENU	Alt
13	19	VK_PAUSE	Pause (or Ctrl-Num Lock)
14	20	VK_CAPITAL	Caps Lock
1B	27	VK_ESCAPE	Esc
20	32	VK_SPACE	Spacebar
21	33	VK_PRIOR	Page Up

(hex)	*(dec)*	*Symbolic Name*	*Key Pressed (US English 101/102 Kbd)*
22	34	VK_NEXT	Page Down
23	35	VK_END	End
24	36	VK_HOME	Home
25	37	VK_LEFT	Left Arrow
26	38	VK_UP	Up Arrow
27	39	VK_RIGHT	Right Arrow
28	40	VK_DOWN	Down Arrow
29	41	VK_SELECT	<unused>
2A	42	VK_PRINT	<unused>
2B	43	VK_EXECUTE	<unused>
2C	44	VK_SNAPSHOT	Print Screen
2D	45	VK_INSERT	Ins
2E	46	VK_DELETE	Del
2F	47	VK_HELP	<unused>
30-39	48-57	VK_0 to VK_9	0 to 9 above letter keys
41-5A	65-90	VK_A to VK_Z	A to Z
60	96	VK_NUMPAD0	0 on Numeric keypad w/Num Lock ON
61	97	VK_NUMPAD1	1 on Numeric keypad w/Num Lock ON
62	98	VK_NUMPAD2	2 on Numeric keypad w/Num Lock ON
63	99	VK_NUMPAD3	3 on Numeric keypad w/Num Lock ON
64	100	VK_NUMPAD4	4 on Numeric keypad w/Num Lock ON
65	101	VK_NUMPAD5	5 on Numeric keypad w/Num Lock ON
66	102	VK_NUMPAD6	6 on Numeric keypad w/Num Lock ON
67	103	VK_NUMPAD7	7 on Numeric keypad w/Num Lock ON
68	104	VK_NUMPAD8	8 on Numeric keypad w/Num Lock ON
69	105	VK_NUMPAD9	9 on Numeric keypad w/Num Lock ON

(hex)	*(dec)*	*Symbolic Name*	*Key Pressed (US English 101/102 Kbd)*
6A	106	VK_MULTIPLY	* on Numeric keypad
6B	107	VK_ADD	+ on Numeric keypad
6C	108	VK_SEPARATOR	<unused>
6D	109	VK_SUBTRACT	- on Numeric keypad
6E	110	VK_DECIMAL	. on Numeric keypad w/Num Lock ON
6F	111	VK_DIVIDE	/ on Numeric keypad
70	112	VK_F1	F1 function key
71	113	VK_F2	F2 function key
72	114	VK_F3	F3 function key
73	115	VK_F4	F4 function key
74	116	VK_F5	F5 function key
75	117	VK_F6	F6 function key
76	118	VK_F7	F7 function key
77	119	VK_F8	F8 function key
78	120	VK_F9	F9 function key
79	121	VK_F10	F10 function key
7A	122	VK_F11	F11 function key
7B	123	VK_F12	F12 function key
7C	124	VK_F13	
7D	125	VK_F14	
7E	126	VK_F15	
7F	127	VK_F16	
90	144	VK_NUMLOCK	Num Lock
91	145		Scroll Lock
		—The following codes apply to US keyboards only—	
BA	186		colon/semi-colon

(hex)	*(dec)*	*Symbolic Name*	*Key Pressed (US English 101/102 Kbd)*
BB	187		plus/equal
BC	188		less than/comma
BD	189		underscore/hyphen
BE	190		greater than/period
BF	191		question/slash
C0	192		tilde/back accent
DB	219		left squiggle brace/left square brace
DC	220		horizontal bar/backslash
DD	221		right squiggle brace/right square brace
DE	222		double quote/single quote

Appendix G: Windows 3.1 Allocation and Cleanup Routines

Resource	*Allocation Routine*	*Cleanup Routine*	*Deletion Required?*
Accelerators	LoadAccelerators	n/a	No
Atoms	GlobalAddAtom	GlobalFreeAtom	Yes
Bitmap	CreateBitmap	DeleteObject	Yes **
	CreateBitmapIndirect	DeleteObject	Yes **
	CreateCompatibleBitmap	DeleteObject	Yes **
	CreateDIBitmap	DeleteObject	Yes **
	CreateDiscardableBitmap	DeleteObject	Yes **
	LoadBitmap	DeleteObject	Yes **
Brush	CreateBrushIndirect	DeleteObject	Yes
	CreateDIBPatternBrush	DeleteObject	Yes
	CreateHatchBrush	DeleteObject	Yes
	CreatePatternBrush	DeleteObject	Yes
	CreateSolidBrush	DeleteObject	Yes
Caret	CreateCaret	DestroyCaret	No +
Clipboard	OpenClipboard	CloseClipboard	Yes
Comm Port	OpenComm	CloseComm	Yes

Note: Reprinted by permission of the publisher from Paul Yao,"Careful Windows Resource Allocation and Cleanup Improves Application Hygiene," Microsoft Systems Journal Sep/Oct. 1991.

Resource	*Allocation Routine*	*Cleanup Routine*	*Deletion Required?*
Cursor	CopyCursor	DestroyCursor	Yes
	CreateCursor	DestroyCursor	Yes
	LoadCursor	n/a	No
DC	CreateDC	DeleteDC	Yes
	CreateCompatibleDC	DeleteDC	Yes ***
	GetDC	ReleaseDC	Yes
	GetWindowDC	ReleaseDC	Yes
	BeginPaint	EndPaint	Yes
Dialog Box	CreateDialog	DestroyWindow	No
	CreateDialogIndirect	DestroyWindow	No
	CreateDialogIndirectParam	DestroyWindow	No
	CreateDialogParam	DestroyWindow	No
File	OpenFile	_lclose	No
Fonts	CreateFont	DeleteObject	Yes
	CreateFontIndirect	DeleteObject	Yes
	AddFontResource	RemoveFontResource	Yes
GDI Stock Objects	GetStockObject	n/a	No ++
Hook	SetWindowsHook	UnhookWindowsHook	Yes
	SetWindowsHookEx	UnhookWindowsHookEx	Yes
Information Context	CreateIC	DeleteDC	Yes
Icon	CopyIcon	DestroyIcon	Yes
	CreateIcon	DestroyIcon	Yes
	LoadIcon	n/a	No
Library	LoadLibrary	FreeLibrary	Yes
Memory	AllocDStoCSAlias	FreeSelector	Yes
	AllocSelector	FreeSelector	Yes
	GlobalAlloc	GlobalFree	No
	GlobalFix	GlobalUnfix	No
	GlobalLock	GlobalUnlock	No
	GlobalPageLock	GlobalPageUnlock	No
	GlobalWire	GlobalUnwire	No

Resource	*Allocation Routine*	*Cleanup Routine*	*Deletion Required?*
	LocalAlloc	LocalFree	No
	LocalLock	LocalUnlock	No
Menu	CreateMenu	DestroyMenu	No *
	CreatePopupMenu	DestroyMenu	No *
	LoadMenu	DestroyMenu	No *
	LoadMenuIndirect	DestroyMenu	No *
	GetSystemMenu	n/a	No
Metafile	CreateMetaFile	DeleteMetaFile	Yes
Palette	CreatePalette	DeleteObject	Yes
Pen	CreatePen	DeleteObject	Yes
	CreatePenIndirect	DeleteObject	Yes
Regions	CreateEllipticRgn	DeleteObject	Yes
	CreateEllipticRgnIndirect	DeleteObject	Yes
	CreatePolygonRgn	DeleteObject	Yes
	CreatePolyPolygonRgn	DeleteObject	Yes
	CreateRectRgn	DeleteObject	Yes
	CreateRectRgnIndirect	DeleteObject	Yes
	CreateRoundRectRgn	DeleteObject	Yes
Resource	FindResource	n/a	No
	LoadResource	FreeResource	No
	LockResource	UnlockResource	No
Sound	OpenSound	CloseSound	Yes
String	LoadString	n/a	No
Thunk	MakeProcInstance	FreeProcInstance	No
Timer	SetTimer	Killtimer	No
Window	CreateWindow	DestroyWindow	No
	CreateWindowEx	DestroyWindow	No

* Menus not connected to any window must be freed before an application exits.

** Bitmaps must be disconnected from DCs before being freed.

*** DCs must be disconnected from bitmaps before being freed.

\+ If a bitmap is specified for the CARET, it must be freed.

++ Calls to `DeleteObject` do not harm stock objects.

Appendix H: Patches to OWL Include Files

In general, the OWL 2.0 class libraries do a very good job of encapsulating the Win16 and Win32 APIs. By design, the focus is on today's mainstream, Win16 API. Here are patches you can make to the OWL include files to enhance Win32-specific support, and to improve the support for Win16 functions. These patches are required for version 4.0 of the compiler, which was the current compiler at the time of this writing. If you're working with a later version, check the source files first before making these changes to your include files.

SetPixelV

Use this Win32 function in place of the Win16 equivalent, **`SetPixel`**, to improve overall performance under Windows NT. In that environment, GDI drawing calls are stored in a queue and sent to the Win32 subsystem in batches. Since the Win32 subsystem runs in its own process, each call to this subsystem involves context switches—one to the Win32 subsystem and one back to the calling process. This time consuming activity slows API-bound applications. Context switches for GDI drawing calls are postponed until a batch of drawing requests have been received. (The default size of a batch is 10 calls.) Since **`SetPixel`** requires a return value for the previous value of the pixel, it flushes the batch queue and forces the context switches. **`SetPixelV`** doesn't require a return value, so it can be batched with the other GDI drawing calls. Add **`SetPixelV`** to the **`TDC`** class with the following changes to \BC4\INCLUDE\OWL\DC.H:

1. Within the curly braces for the ***TDC*** class declaration, add the following lines:

```
#if defined(__WIN32__)  // Added for Win32 support
      BOOL       SetPixelV(int x, int y, TColor color);
      BOOL       SetPixelV(const TPoint& p, TColor color);
```

```
#endif                    // Added for Win32 support
```

2. Outside the curly braces for the **TDC** class declaration, add the following inline function definitions:

```
#if defined(__WIN32__)   // Added for Win32 support
inline BOOL TDC::SetPixelV(int x, int y, TColor color) {
  return ::SetPixelV(GetHDC(), x, y, color);
}
inline BOOL TDC::SetPixelV(const TPoint& point, TColor color) {
  return ::SetPixelV(GetHDC(), point.x, point.y, color);
}
#endif                    // Added for Win32 support
```

LockResource

This Win16/Win32 function is a companion to the **FindResource/LoadResource** functions used to access custom resources. Add **LockResource** to the **TModule** class with the following changes to \BC4\INCLUDE\OWL\MODULE.H:

1. Within the curly braces for the **TModule** class declaration, add the following lines:

```
#ifdef STRICT
void far* LockResource (HGLOBAL hmem)
#else
char far* LockResource (HGLOBAL hmem)
#endif
    { return ::LockResource(hmem); }
```

SetGraphicsMode

This Win32 function sets the **graphics mode** for a device context (DC). The graphics mode is a DC attribute that enables certain Win32 enhancements to GDI drawing. When set to **GM_COMPATIBLE**, all drawing is compatible with Windows 3.1. And when set to **GM_ADVANCED**, Win32 enhancements are enabled. For example, coordinate system rotation is not supported in Windows 3.1 compatible mode but it is under Win32 compatible mode. To add this function to the **TDC** class, make the following changes to \BC4\INCLUDE\OWL\DC.H:

1. Within the curly braces for the **TDC** class declaration, add the following lines:

```
#if defined(__WIN32__)   // Added for Win32 support
    int SetGraphicsMode (int iMode);
```

```
#endif                   // Added for Win32 support
```

2. Outside the curly braces for the **TDC** class declaration, add the following inline function definitions:

```
#if defined(__WIN32__)  // Added for Win32 support
inline int TDC::SetGraphicsMode(int iMode) {
  return ::SetGraphicsMode(GetHDC(), iMode);
}
#endif                   // Added for Win32 support
```

Appendix I: OWL Sample Cross Reference

One of the best ways to solve a coding problem is to look at sample source code. This book contains 31 sample programs and the Borland C++ 4.0 compiler comes with 59 other samples. These 90 programs should give you a start in finding new and useful ways to take advantage of the OWL 2.0 class library.

There are two lists. The first list is sorted by OWL class name and provides a cross reference to each program that uses the different classes. The second list is sorted by program name and includes a brief synopsis of each program. Browse this list to get a general idea of what each program is trying to demonstrate. You'll want to use this list when you start working with a particular OWL class, or when you encounter problems working with a particular class. For example, if you can't figure out how to use the `TDialog` class, refer to the first list to get the names of the programs that use this class. Once you have the program names, the second will identify exactly where to find each sample program.

Program List by OWL Classes Used

The **UPPERCASE** program names indicate a program in this book. The **lowercase** program names are for programs supplied with the Borland C++ version 4.0 compiler.

`TApplication`	aclock, applaunc, bmpview, BRUSHES, button, calc, CALLBEEP, CARET, CARET2, CHEKMENU, CIRCLE, colordlg, combobox, commdlg, cursor, ddeml, diagxprt, dllhello, docview, dragdrop, DRAGRECT, draw, DYNACURS, edit, editsear, filebrow, FIND, GADGETS, gauge, gdidemo, GRAFMENU, groupbox, hello, help, instance, intldemo, KEYCMD, KEYCMD2, KEYINPUT, layout,

`TApplication` *(continued)*	LINES, listbox, LOCALMEM, MARKERS, mcisound, mdi, mdifile, mdistrm, MIN, MIN2, mthread, notebook, notify, OPENFILE, owlcmd, ownerdra, OWNSIZE, paint, palette, peeper, popup, printing, prntprev, progman, RECTDRAW, RECTMENU, scrnsave, scrollba, scroller, sdifile, SEGALLOC, slider, STANMENU, STARS, SUBSEG, swat, sysinfo, TEXTVIEW, transfer, truetype, tutorial, validate, vbxctl, WM_PAINT
`TArrayAsVector`	LINES, STARS, TEXTVIEW
`TBitmap`	aclock, applaunc, bmpview, BRUSHES, CHEKMENU, gdidemo, mthread, paint, swat
`TBitmapGadget`	applaunc, GADGETS
`TBrush`	bmpview, BRUSHES, DRAGRECT, DYNACURS, gauge, GRAFMENU, notebook, paint, RECTDRAW, RECTMENU, slider, WM_PAINT
`TButton`	button, diagxprt, filebrow, groupbox, intldemo, mcisound, notify, ownerdra
`TButtonGadget`	applaunc, GADGETS, mdifile, paint, peeper, tutorial
`TCheckBox`	applaunc, button, diagxprt, peeper, transfer, validate
`TChooseColorDialog`	commdlg
`TChooseFontDialog`	commdlg, TEXTVIEW
`TClientDC`	docview, draw, paint, tutorial
`TClipboardViewer`	bmpview
`TColor`	docview
`TComboBox`	applaunc, combobox, filebrow, GADGETS, layout, owlcmd
`TControl`	colordlg, docview
`TControlBar`	GADGETS, mdifile, paint, peeper, tutorial
`TControlGadget`	GADGETS
`TCursor`	swat
`TDecoratedFrame`	diagxprt, docview, GADGETS, intldemo, paint, peeper
`TDecoratedMDIFrame`	docview, mdifile, notebook
`TDialog`	applaunc, calc, colordlg, cursor, diagxprt, FIND, intldemo, layout, notify, ownerdra, paint, peeper, progman, scrnsave, swat, sysinfo, transfer, validate, vbxctl
`TDib`	applaunc, applaunc, bmpview, paint
`TDibDC`	paint
`TDocManager`	docview, tutorial
`TDocument`	docview

`TEdit`	applaunc, diagxprt, edit, filebrow, layout, owlcmd, transfer, validate
`TEditFile`	diagxprt, filebrow, mdifile
`TEditSearch`	editsear
`TFileDocument`	docview, tutorial
`TFileOpenDialog`	commdlg, OPENFILE
`TFilterValidator`	validate
`TFloatingFrame`	applaunc, owlcmd, paint
`TFont`	commdlg, diagxprt, filebrow, gdidemo, intldemo, notebook, TEXTVIEW, truetype
`TFrameWindow`	aclock, bmpview, BRUSHES, button, calc, CALLBEEP, CARET, CARET2, CHEKMENU, CIRCLE, colordlg, combobox, commdlg, cursor, ddeml, dllhello, docview, dragdrop, DRAGRECT, draw, DYNACURS, edit, editsear, filebrow, FIND, gauge, GRAFMENU, groupbox, help, instance, intldemo, KEYCMD, KEYCMD2, KEYINPUT, layout, LINES, listbox, LOCALMEM, MARKERS, mcisound, MIN, MIN2, notify, OPENFILE, ownerdra, OWNSIZE, palette, popup, printing, prntprev, progman, RECTDRAW, RECTMENU, scrnsave, scrollba, scroller, sdifile, SEGALLOC, slider, STANMENU, STARS, SUBSEG, swat, sysinfo, TEXTVIEW, transfer, truetype, tutorial, validate, vbxctl, WM_PAINT
`TGauge`	gauge
`TGroupBox`	applaunc, button, groupbox
`THSlider`	gauge, mcisound
`TICVectorImp`	applaunc
`TLayoutWindow`	filebrow, layout, prntprev
`TListBox`	applaunc, diagxprt, docview, filebrow, intldemo, intldemo, layout, listbox, peeper, progman, transfer, tutorial
`TMDIChild`	docview, gdidemo, mdi, mdifile, mdistrm, mthread, notebook, tutorial
`TMDIClient`	gdidemo, mdi, mdifile, mdistrm, mthread, notebook
`TMDIFrame`	docview, gdidemo, mdi, mdistrm, mthread
`TMemoryDC`	paint
`TMenu`	GRAFMENU, intldemo, RECTMENU
`TMessageBar`	GADGETS, peeper
`TMetaFileDC`	draw
`TModule`	dllhello, docview, intldemo

TOpenSaveDialog	tutorial
TPalette	bmpview, paint
TPen	aclock, docview, DRAGRECT, GRAFMENU, LINES, mthread, notebook, paint, RECTDRAW, RECTMENU, tutorial
TPoints	docview, tutorial, tutorial
TPopupMenu	filebrow
TPreviewPage	prntprev
TPrintDC	prntprev
TPrinter	printing, prntprev, truetype
TPrintout	printing, truetype
TPXPictureValidator	validate
TRadioButton	applaunc, button, diagxprt, groupbox, transfer
TScreenDC	gdidemo
TScrollBar	colordlg, diagxprt, scrollba, transfer
TScroller	bmpview, gdidemo, paint, scroller, TEXTVIEW
TSeparatorGadget	GADGETS, mdifile, paint, peeper, tutorial
TStatic	combobox, diagxprt, edit, filebrow, gdidemo, groupbox, listbox, mthread, peeper, scrollba, slider, sysinfo
TStatusBar	docview, intldemo, mdifile, notebook, tutorial
TTextGadget	GADGETS
TTinyCaption	diagxprt
TToolBox	applaunc, paint
TVbxControl	vbxctl
TVbxEventHandler	vbxctl
TView	docview, tutorial
TWindow	bmpview, button, dllhello, dragdrop, GADGETS, gauge, gdidemo, intldemo, layout, mthread, ownerdra, paint, palette, peeper, scrnsave, scrollba, slider, swat, tutorial
TWindowView	docview, tutorial
TXOwl	docview

Program List by Program Name

The **UPPERCASE** program names indicate a program in this book. The **lowercase** program names are for programs supplied with the Borland C++ version 4.0 compiler. For information on ordering a machine readable version of the source code to this book, please refer to ordering information on the last page of this book.

The **OWL Base Classes** lists tell which OWL 2.0 classes were used as a base class by the program. The **OWL Instanced Classes** lists tell which OWL 2.0 classes were instantiated "as is." The base classes lists were created by searching for the `class` keyword in the include (.H) files and the source (.CPP) files, so these lists are quite complete. The instanced classes lists were compiled by searching for the `new` keyword. This list, then, is somewhat incomplete because any objects created as either global or local variables are not included. I believe this shortcoming is not as bad as it sounds, however, since global variables aren't—or shouldn't be!—used very often. And while some of the local OWL 2.0 objects might show some interesting techniques, I decided that the truly interesting samples created an object for longer periods of time than just a single call to one function. Also, it was easy to tell a utility like GREP to search for a single keyword. It would have been a lot more work to GREP for each of the 120 (or so) OWL objects in all 100+ source files.

aclock — A cuckoo clock.

OWL Base Classes: TApplication, TFrameWindow

OWL Instanced Classes: TBitmap, TPen

BC4 Sample in: \bc4\examples\owl\owlapps\aclock

applaunc — A mini-application launcher. Shows how to use lots of different OWL user interface objects, including a TFloatingFrame window with its tiny caption bar. The creation of a help file is also included here.

OWL Base Classes: TApplication, TBitmap, TButtonGadget, TDialog, TDib, TFloatingFrame, TICVectorImp, TToolBox,

OWL Instanced Classes: TBitmapGadget, TCheckBox, TComboBox, TDib, TEdit, TGroupBox, TListBox, TRadioButton

BC4 Sample in: \bc4\examples\owl\owlapps\applaunc

BEEP — Dynamic link library. Shows a very simple dynamic link library that contains a function to make a sound on a computer's speaker. As a first DLL, BEEP will help you work through the details of getting a DLL up and running. When you're done, it rewards you with a sound. This DLL gets called from CALLBEEP, another sample program.

Chapter: 19

OWL Base Classes: None

OWL Instanced Classes: None

Book Sample in: \DISK\BEEP

bmpview — Bitmap view sample. Shows how to create a bitmap from a resource or from a bitmap DIB file on disk. Shows calling BitBlt to draw the bitmap at its original size, and calling StretchBlt to stretch or stretch the bitmap to the available screen space. Also shows Clipboard operation on bitmaps.

bmpview *(continued)*

OWL Base Classes: TApplication, TClipboardViewer, TWindow

OWL Instanced Classes: TBitmap, TBrush, TDib, TFrameWindow, TScroller, TPalette

BC4 Sample in: \bc4\examples\owl\owlapps\bmpview

BRUSHES

GDI sample program that shows how to create the three different types of GDI brushes, the attribute bundle used to fill areas of geometric shapes.

Chapter: 9

OWL Base Classes: TApplication, TFrameWindow

OWL Instanced Classes: TBitmap, TBrush

Book Sample In: \DISK\BRUSHES

button

Simple example showing the creation of the various types of buttons, including push button, checkbox, radio buttons and group boxes.

OWL Base Classes: TApplication, TWindow

OWL Instanced Classes: TButton, TCheckBox, TFrameWindow, TGroupBox, TRadioButton

BC4 Sample in: \bc4\examples\owl\owlapi\button

calc

A calculator implemented as a dialog box. Shows one way to create a dialog box: using OWL's `TDialog` as the framework using native WinAPI button and static controls *without* the corresponding `TButton` and `TStatic` OWL objects.

OWL Base Classes: TApplication, TDialog

OWL Instanced Classes: TFrameWindow

BC4 Sample in: \bc4\examples\owl\owlapps\calc

CALLBEEP

Sample minimum program that calls the dynamic link library sample, BEEP.DLL.

Chapter: 19

OWL Base Classes: TApplication, TFrameWindow

OWL Instanced Classes: None

Book Sample In: \DISK\CALLBEEP

CARET

Demonstrates the creation and use of a keyboard pointer, also known as a "caret" in Windows. A caret class is presented which may prove robust and efficient enough to include in your applications.

Chapter: 15

OWL Base Classes: TApplication, TFrameWindow

OWL Instanced Classes: None

Book Sample In: \DISK\CARET

CARET2

An enhancement to the CARET program in Chapter 15 that shows how the mouse can be used to position a keyboard pointer—a caret.

CARET2 *(continued)*

Chapter: 16

OWL Base Classes: TApplication, TFrameWindow

OWL Instanced Classes: None

Book Sample In: \DISK\CARET2

CHEKMENU

Shows the creation of custom check marks. These bitmaps are connected to a menu and used to replace the default system check mark bitmaps.

Chapter: 12

OWL Base Classes: TApplication, TFrameWindow

OWL Instanced Classes: TBitmap

Book Sample In: \DISK\CHEKMENU

CIRCLE

Demonstrates the creation and use of a custom resource.

Chapter: 18

OWL Base Classes: TApplication, TFrameWindow

OWL Instanced Classes: None

Book Sample In: \DISK\CIRCLE

colordlg

Demonstrates the creation of a custom dialog box control class built using OWL's `TControl` class as a base.

OWL Base Classes: TApplication, TControl, TDialog

OWL Instanced Classes: TFrameWindow, TScrollBar

BC4 Sample in: \bc4\examples\owl\owlapi\colordlg

combobox

A combobox sample app showing all the different types of comboboxes. This example shows the use of the WinAPI SendMessage call to send a `CB_SETCURSEL` message to a combobox. This is interesting, since it's how OWL ultimately communicates with a combobox. However, you will probably want to call `TComboBox::SetSelIndex` member to do the same thing.

OWL Base Classes: TApplication, TFrameWindow

OWL Instanced Classes: TComboBox, TStatic

BC4 Sample in: \bc4\examples\owl\owlapi\combobox

commdlg

Simple example showing how to call three of the common dialog boxes in COMMDLG.DLL. Shows file open dialog, color picker dialog, and font picker dialog.

OWL Base Classes: TApplication, TFrameWindow

OWL Instanced Classes: TFont, TChooseColorDialog, TChooseFontDialog, TFileOpenDialog

BC4 Sample in: \bc4\examples\owl\owlapi\commdlg

cursor

Idle-time processing demo that shows mouse location info.

OWL Base Classes: TApplication, TDialog

cursor *(continued)*

OWL Instanced Classes: TFrameWindow

BC4 Sample in: \bc4\examples\owl\owlapps\cursor

ddeml

Sample DDE client and server built to use the DDEML.DLL library.

OWL Base Classes: TApplication, TFrameWindow

OWL Instanced Classes:

BC4 Sample in: \bc4\examples\owl\winapi\ddeml

diagxprt

A ToolHelp message notification display demo. Makes extensive use of C++ templates.

OWL Base Classes: TApplication, TCheckBox, TDecoratedFrame, TDialog, TEditFile, TScrollBar, TTinyCaption

OWL Instanced Classes: TButton, TEdit, TFont, TStatic, TListBox, TRadioButton

BC4 Sample in: \bc4\examples\owl\owlapps\diagxprt

dlldemo

A sample DLL. This program doesn't use the OWL library.

OWL Base Classes:

OWL Instanced Classes:

BC4 Sample in: \bc4\examples\windows\dlldemo

dllhello

DLL demo showing how to get resources (a bitmap, a cursor, an icon and a string) from a DLL. Also shows a simple example of creating a window from a DLL.

OWL Base Classes: TApplication, TWindow

OWL Instanced Classes: TFrameWindow, TModule, TWindow

BC4 Sample in: \bc4\examples\owl\owlapi\dllhello

docview

Shows the use of the Document View classes provided by OWL 2.0. Default is to run in Multiple Document Interface (MDI) mode with a decorated frame (a status bar, in this case). Run with the '-s' switch to see the undecorated window using the Single Document Interface (SDI). Other switches are '-m' for undecorated MDI and '-d' for decorated SDI.

OWL Base Classes: TApplication, TControl, TDocument, TFileDocument, TListBox, TPoints, TView, TWindowView, TXOwl

OWL Instanced Classes: TClientDC, TColor, TDecoratedFrame, TDecoratedMDIFrame, TDocManager, TFrameWindow, TMDIChild, TMDIFrame, TModule, TPen, TStatusBar

BC4 Sample in: \bc4\examples\owl\owlapi\docview

dragdrop

Shows the creation of a Win3.1 Drag-n-Drop server using OWL's TDropInfo class. Doesn't do the OLE 2.0 Drag-n-Drop, however. This app also demonstrates use of BagAsVector container class templates.

OWL Base Classes: TApplication, TWindow

dragdrop *(continued)*

OWL Instanced Classes: TFrameWindow

BC4 Sample in: \bc4\examples\owl\winapi\dragdrop

DRAGRECT

A rectangle dragging program that shows the use of ROP2 raster operations and how mouse input can be used to draw a stretchable rubber rectangle.

Chapter: 16

OWL Base Classes: TApplication, TFrameWindow

OWL Instanced Classes: TBrush, TPen

Book Sample In: \DISK\DRAGRECT

draw

Simple demo showing how to record and playback GDI metafiles. Doesn't take coordinate mapping into account, but otherwise shows the basics of recording and playing back metafiles.

OWL Base Classes: TApplication, TFrameWindow

OWL Instanced Classes: TClientDC, TMetaFileDC

BC4 Sample in: \bc4\examples\owl\owlapps\draw

DYNACURS

Creates a dynamic mouse cursor on the fly.

Chapter: 16

OWL Base Classes: TApplication, TFrameWindow

OWL Instanced Classes: TBrush

Book Sample In: \DISK\DYNACURS

edit

Uses OWL's TEdit class to creates an edit window outside a dialog box. The NOTEPAD application does something similar. These programs show that dialog box controls are *not* limited to being inside a dialog box. Interesting details about the edit control are displayed as data is entered into the edit control.

OWL Base Classes: TApplication, TEdit, TFrameWindow

OWL Instanced Classes: TStatic

BC4 Sample in: \bc4\examples\owl\owlapi\edit

editsear

A NOTEPAD clone to show how much work OWL's `TEditSearch` class does for you.

OWL Base Classes: TApplication

OWL Instanced Classes: TEditSearch, TFrameWindow

BC4 Sample in: \bc4\examples\owl\owlapi\editsear

filebrow

A directory surfing program that shows how dialog controls can be used outside a dialog box. Traverses the disk directory and lets you use wildcards to filter the files it shows you.

OWL Base Classes: TApplication, TEditFile, TLayoutWindow

OWL Instanced Classes: TButton, TComboBox, TEdit, TFont, TFrameWindow, TListBox, TPopupMenu, TStatic

BC4 Sample in: \bc4\examples\owl\owlapps\filebrow

FIND — Shows the differences between a modal and a modeless dialog box.
Chapter: 14
OWL Base Classes: TApplication, TDialog, TFrameWindow
OWL Instanced Classes: None
Book Sample In: \DISK\FIND

GADGETS — Shows the creation and use of a toolbar and a status line using OWL's TGadgetWindow and the various TGadget-derived classes.
Chapter: 13
OWL Base Classes: TApplication, TDecoratedFrame, TWindow
OWL Instanced Classes: TBitmapGadget, TButtonGadget, TComboBox, TControlBar, TControlGadget, TMessageBar, TSeparatorGadget, TTextGadget
Book Sample In: \DISK\GADGETS

gauge — Demos two variations on the types of gauges that the `TGauge` class can create.
OWL Base Classes: TApplication, TWindow
OWL Instanced Classes: TBrush, TFrameWindow, TGauge, THSlider
BC4 Sample in: \bc4\examples\owl\owlapi\gauge

gdidemo — Shows some simple animation using line drawing and raster graphics.
OWL Base Classes: TApplication, TMDIClient, TWindow
OWL Instanced Classes: TBitmap, TFont, TMDIChild, TMDIFrame, TScreenDC, TScroller, TStatic
BC4 Sample in: \bc4\examples\owl\owlapps\gdidemo

GRAFMENU — Shows the creation and maintenance of owner-draw menu items.
Chapter: 12
OWL Base Classes: TApplication, TFrameWindow
OWL Instanced Classes: TBrush, TMenu, TPen
Book Sample In: \DISK\GRAFMENU

groupbox — Shows buttons and the role of `TGroupBox` in creating groups of radio buttons.
OWL Base Classes: TApplication, TFrameWindow, TGroupBox
OWL Instanced Classes: TButton, TRadioButton, TStatic
BC4 Sample in: \bc4\examples\owl\owlapi\groupbox

hello — The smallest possible OWL and Windows program. It displays a single window with the caption "Hello World!".
OWL Base Classes:
OWL Instanced Classes: TApplication
BC4 Sample in: \bc4\examples\owl\owlapps\hello

help — A simple help example. Don't implement context sensitive help as shown here (use a window hook instead).

OWL Base Classes: TApplication, TFrameWindow

OWL Instanced Classes:

BC4 Sample in: \bc4\examples\owl\winapi\help

instance — Shows effect of running multiple copies under Win16 (which recognizes the idea of "instances of a program") vs. Win32, which calls each new copy of a program its own process without reference to previous copies.

OWL Base Classes: TApplication

OWL Instanced Classes: TFrameWindow

BC4 Sample in: \bc4\examples\owl\owlapi\instance

intldemo — Demonstrates some useful techniques for internationalizing Windows products, including some useful APIs, supported character sets, and the use of different DLL to hold the resources for different languages.

OWL Base Classes: TApplication, TDecoratedFrame, TDialog, TFont, TFrameWindow, TListBox, TWindow

OWL Instanced Classes: TButton, TListBox, TMenu, TModule, TStatusBar

BC4 Sample in: \bc4\examples\owl\owlapps\intldemo

KEYCMD — Shows the creation of keyboard command accelerators.

Chapter: 11

OWL Base Classes: TApplication, TFrameWindow

OWL Instanced Classes: None

Book Sample In: \DISK\KEYCMD

KEYCMD2 — Enhancement to the KEYCMD program in Chapter 11. This program shows how to use a hook to make accelerators operational when a menu is visible.

Chapter: 12

OWL Base Classes: TApplication, TFrameWindow

OWL Instanced Classes: None

Book Sample In: \DISK\KEYCMD2

KEYINPUT — Shows how to receive and display raw keyboard input.

Chapter: 15

OWL Base Classes: TApplication, TFrameWindow

OWL Instanced Classes: None

Book Sample In: \DISK\KEYINPUT

layout — Lets you experiment with modifying the various layout controlling parameters of the TLayoutWindow class.

OWL Base Classes: TApplication, TDialog, TLayoutWindow, TWindow

OWL Instanced Classes: TComboBox, TEdit, TFrameWindow, TListBox

BC4 Sample in: \bc4\examples\owl\owlapi\layout

LINES — Randonly selects pens and line drawing functions to show some of the GDI line drawing capabilities. This program also shows how background processing can be done using a timer.

Chapter: 8

OWL Base Classes: TApplication, TFrameWindow

OWL Instanced Classes: TArrayAsVector (template), TPen

Book Sample In: \DISK\LINES

listbox — A test bed for seeing the different kinds of listboxes and the various ways to operate a listbox using `TListBox` member functions.

OWL Base Classes: TApplication, TFrameWindow

OWL Instanced Classes: TListBox, TStatic

BC4 Sample in: \bc4\examples\owl\owlapi\listbox

LOCALMEM — This program demonstrates the use of the local heap and of the string table resource type.

Chapter: 18

OWL Base Classes: TApplication, TFrameWindow

OWL Instanced Classes: None

Book Sample In: \DISK\LOCALMEM

MARKERS — Shows a new type of drawing object created by drawing lines.

Chapter: 7

OWL Base Classes: TApplication, TFrameWindow

OWL Instanced Classes: None

Book Sample In: \DISK\MARKERS

mcisound — An OWL application that calls the MCI multimedia sound API to control the playing of waveform (.WAV) files.

OWL Base Classes: TApplication, TFrameWindow, THSlider

OWL Instanced Classes: TButton

BC4 Sample in: \bc4\examples\owl\winapi\mcisound

mdi — Shows how to create a Multiple Document Interface (MDI) application.

OWL Base Classes: TApplication, TMDIClient

OWL Instanced Classes: TMDIChild, TMDIFrame

BC4 Sample in: \bc4\examples\owl\owlapi\mdi

mdifile

A Multiple Document Interface (MDI) text editor that shows the use of a control bar—with its associated gadgets—and a status bar.

OWL Base Classes: TApplication, TEditFile

OWL Instanced Classes: TControlBar, TButtonGadget, TDecoratedMDIFrame, TMDIChild, TMDIClient, TSeparatorGadget, TStatusBar

BC4 Sample in: \bc4\examples\owl\owlapps\mdifile

mdistrm

Shows use of C++ streams to save and restore window state in Multiple Document Interface (MDI) application.

OWL Base Classes: TApplication, TMDIClient

OWL Instanced Classes: TMDIChild, TMDIFrame

BC4 Sample in: \bc4\examples\owl\owlapi\mdistrm

MIN

A Minimum OWL 2.0 Program. MIN displays a window, has a menu, a custom icon, and a message box.

Chapter: 2

OWL Base Classes: TApplication, TFrameWindow

OWL Instanced Classes: None

Book Sample In: \DISK\MIN

MIN2

A modification to the MIN program introduced in Chapter 2. This version demonstrates the principle of code segmentation.

Chapter: 18

OWL Base Classes: TApplication, TFrameWindow

OWL Instanced Classes: None

Book Sample In: \DISK\MIN2

mthread

A multithreaded Win32 program. It provides an example of using the TThread class. While technically speaking this is not an OWL class, nevertheless it may prove useful as you start to work with multithreaded programming environments like Windows NT and CHICAGO.

OWL Base Classes: TApplication, TMDIClient, TWindow

OWL Instanced Classes: TBitmap, TMDIChild, TMDIFrame, TPen, TStatic

BC4 Sample in: \bc4\examples\owl\owlapps\mthread

notebook

An MDI application that shows how to draw and maintain a window with note-tab page selectors.

OWL Base Classes: TApplication, TMDIChild, TMDIClient, TWindow

OWL Instanced Classes: TBrush, TDecoratedMDIFrame, TFont, TPen, TStatusBar

BC4 Sample in: \bc4\examples\owl\owlapps\notebook

notify — Shows three different ways to handle a dialog box control's notification messages: (1) The default is that the parent object handles it; however (2) a control object can receive the notification itself, as was done with OWL 1.0. (3) Finally, a control object can receive the notification itself but pass it on to its parent (perhaps after first doing some processing itself).

OWL Base Classes: TApplication, TButton, TDialog

OWL Instanced Classes: TButton, TFrameWindow

BC4 Sample in: \bc4\examples\owl\owlapi\notify

OPENFILE — Demonstrates the use of Windows' built-in common dialog boxes.

Chapter: 14

OWL Base Classes: TApplication, TFrameWindow

OWL Instanced Classes: TFileOpenDialog

Book Sample In: \DISK\OPENFILE

owlcmd — This is a simple command line program. It provides an example of a `TTinyCaption` window.

OWL Base Classes: TApplication, TComboBox, TEdit, TFloatingFrame

OWL Instanced Classes:

BC4 Sample in: \bc4\examples\owl\owlapps\owlcmd

ownerdra — Demo of an owner draw push button.

OWL Base Classes: TApplication, TButton, TDialog, TWindow

OWL Instanced Classes: TFrameWindow

BC4 Sample in: \bc4\examples\owl\owlapi\ownerdra

OWNSIZE — Demonstrates window creation using system metric values and the use of a profile file.

Chapter: 13

OWL Base Classes: TApplication, TFrameWindow

OWL Instanced Classes: None

Book Sample In: \DISK\OWNSIZE

paint — A PaintBrush-style drawing program written using OWL.

OWL Base Classes: TApplication, TDialog, TFloatingFrame, TWindow

OWL Instanced Classes: TBitmap, TBrush, TButtonGadget, TClientDC, TControlBar, TDecoratedFrame, TDib, TDibDC, TMemoryDC, TPalette, TPen, TScroller, TSeparatorGadget, TToolBox

BC4 Sample in: \bc4\examples\owl\owlapps\paint

palette — Shows how OWL's TPalette object can manipulate the system's palette. No handling, however, is done of palette changing messages and issues around palette contention are ignored. Good introduction to the basics of using TPalette, however.

palette *(continued)*

OWL Base Classes: TApplication, TWindow

OWL Instanced Classes: TFrameWindow

BC4 Sample in: \bc4\examples\owl\owlapi\palette

peeper

A Win16 sample program that shows a few interapplication window interaction tricks, and also shows the use of a control bar and a status bar.

OWL Base Classes: TApplication, TDialog, TWindow

OWL Instanced Classes: TButtonGadget, TCheckBox, TControlBar, TDecoratedFrame, TListBox, TMessageBar, TSeparatorGadget, TStatic

BC4 Sample in: \bc4\examples\owl\owlapps\peeper

popup

Demonstrates the creation of the three types of WinAPI windows: (a) an overlapped window—which is the application's main window, (b) popup windows—both with and without a parent—and (c) a child window.

OWL Base Classes: TApplication, TFrameWindow

OWL Instanced Classes:

BC4 Sample in: \bc4\examples\owl\owlapi\popup

printing

Demonstrates printing using OWL 2.0 classes.

OWL Base Classes: TApplication, TFrameWindow, TPrintout

OWL Instanced Classes: TPrinter

BC4 Sample in: \bc4\examples\owl\owlapi\printing

prntprev

Shows use of OWL 2.0 print preview classes.

OWL Base Classes: TApplication, TFrameWindow, TPrintout, TWindow

OWL Instanced Classes: TFrameWindow, TLayoutWindow, TPreviewPage, TPrintDC, TPrinter

BC4 Sample in: \bc4\examples\owl\owlapi\prntprev

progman

Shows how to use DDE to add program groups and program items to the Windows 3.x Program Manager.

OWL Base Classes: TApplication, TDialog

OWL Instanced Classes: TFrameWindow, TListBox

BC4 Sample in: \bc4\examples\owl\winapi\progman

RECTDRAW

A simple rectangle drawing program that draws in response to mouse down and mouse up input.

Chapter: 9

OWL Base Classes: TApplication, TFrameWindow

OWL Instanced Classes: TBrush, TPen

Book Sample In: \DISK\RECTDRAW

RECTMENU

Enhancement of RECTDRAW program from Chapter 9. This version responds to a right mouse click by displaying an object-specific menu.

Chapter: 12

RECTMENU *(continued)*	**OWL Base Classes**: TApplication, TFrameWindow **OWL Instanced Classes**: TBrush, TMenu, TPen **Book Sample In**: \DISK\RECTMENU
scrnsave	A sample screen saver. **OWL Base Classes**: TApplication, TDialog, TFrameWindow **OWL Instanced Classes**: TWindow **BC4 Sample in:** \bc4\examples\owl\owlapps\scrnsave
scrollba	Shows creation of a horizontal scrollbar with OWL's TScrollBar class. **OWL Base Classes**: TApplication, TWindow **OWL Instanced Classes**: TFrameWindow, TScrollBar, TStatic **BC4 Sample in:** \bc4\examples\owl\owlapi\scrollba
scroller	A somewhat unusual demo of the scrolling support provided by OWL's TScroller class. **OWL Base Classes**: TApplication, TFrameWindow **OWL Instanced Classes**: TScroller **BC4 Sample in:** \bc4\examples\owl\owlapi\scroller
sdifile	A Single Document Interface (SDI) text file editor. **OWL Base Classes**: TApplication **OWL Instanced Classes**: TFrameWindow **BC4 Sample in:** \bc4\examples\owl\owlapps\sdifile
SEGALLOC	Demonstrates global heap allocation in Windows. **Chapter**: 18 **OWL Base Classes**: TApplication, TFrameWindow **OWL Instanced Classes**: None **Book Sample In**: \DISK\SEGALLOC
SINE	An MS-DOS program that builds a table of sine values for use in the custom resource demonstration program, CIRCLE. **Chapter**: 18 **OWL Base Classes**: None **OWL Instanced Classes**: None **Book Sample In**: \DISK\SINE
slider	Demos the use of the OWL slider control. **OWL Base Classes**: TApplication, TWindow **OWL Instanced Classes**: TBrush, TFrameWindow, TGauge, THSlider, TStatic, TVSlider **BC4 Sample in:** \bc4\examples\owl\owlapi\slider

STANMENU

Shows a standard File and Edit menu.

Chapter: 11

OWL Base Classes: TApplication, TFrameWindow

OWL Instanced Classes: None

Book Sample In: \DISK\STANMENU

STARS

This program shows randomly drawn stars twinkling in a night sky. It demonstrates drawing in a window for WM_PAINT to refresh a dirty window, WM_ERASEBKGND for window erasing, and non WM_PAINT drawing. It also shows idle-time processing and how to enumerate a device's colors.

Chapter: 7

OWL Base Classes: TApplication, TFrameWindow, TArrayAsVector (template)

OWL Instanced Classes: None

Book Sample In: \DISK\STARS

static

Shows some of the different styles available from `TStatic`.

OWL Base Classes: TApplication, TWindow

OWL Instanced Classes: TFrameWindow, TStatic

BC4 Sample in: \bc4\examples\owl\owlapi\static

SUBSEG

Demonstration of Win16 subsegment allocation.

Chapter: 18

OWL Base Classes: TApplication, TFrameWindow

OWL Instanced Classes: None

Book Sample In: \DISK\SUBSEG

swat

A little game that shows drawing bitmaps and text. It also shows the creation of timers.

OWL Base Classes: TApplication, TDialog, TWindow

OWL Instanced Classes: TBitmap, TCursor, TFrameWindow

BC4 Sample in: \bc4\examples\owl\owlapps\swat

sysinfo

Displays interesting system information.

OWL Base Classes: TApplication, TDialog

OWL Instanced Classes: TFrameWindow, TStatic

BC4 Sample in: \bc4\examples\owl\winapi\sysinfo

TEXTVIEW

A text file viewing program. Shows font selection and the use of an OWL TScroller to handle scrolling. Also, it shows a few subtle Win16 to Win32 programming differences.

Chapter: 10

TEXTVIEW *(continued)*

OWL Base Classes: TApplication, TFrameWindow, TArrayAsVector (template)

OWL Instanced Classes: TChooseFontDialog, TFont, TScroller

Book Sample In: \DISK\TEXTVIEW

transfer

Demos the use of the transfer buffer for moving data to and from a dialog box.

OWL Base Classes: TApplication, TDialog, TFrameWindow

OWL Instanced Classes: TCheckBox, TEdit, TListBox, TRadioButton, TScrollBar

BC4 Sample in: \bc4\examples\owl\owlapi\transfer

truetype

A fairly decent sample program that demos some interesting GDI tricks, including the rotation of TrueType fonts, use of coordinate mapping, and printing.

OWL Base Classes: TApplication, TFrameWindow, TPrintout

OWL Instanced Classes: TFont, TPrinter

BC4 Sample in: \bc4\examples\owl\winapi\truetype

tutorial

There are twelve programs in this subdirectory. They are meant to accompany the tutorial in the ObjectWindows 2.0 **Programmer's Guide**. They start with a simple 22 line program (STEP01.CPP) that just creates a window and progress to an 884 line program (STEP12.CPP) that lets the user draw lines using the mouse. The fully-featured ending program shows how to create control bars and status bars, how to use common dialog boxes, how to draw using GDI, and how to create MDI applications.

OWL Base Classes: TApplication, TFileDocument, TListBox, TPoints, TView, TWindow, TWindowView

OWL Instanced Classes: TButtonGadget, TControlBar, TClientDC, TDocManager, TFrameWindow, TMDIChild, TOpenSaveDialog, TPen, TPoints, TSeparatorGadget, TStatusBar

BC4 Sample in: \bc4\examples\owl\tutorial*.cpp

validate

Demos the use of the text input validation classes provided by OWL.

OWL Base Classes: TApplication, TDialog, TFrameWindow

OWL Instanced Classes: TCheckBox, TEdit, TFilterValidator, TPXPictureValidator

BC4 Sample in: \bc4\examples\owl\owlapi\validate

vbxctl

Shows the use of Visual Basic controls in an OWL program.

OWL Base Classes: TApplication, TDialog, TVbxEventHandler

OWL Instanced Classes: TFrameWindow, TVbxControl

BC4 Sample in: \bc4\examples\owl\owlapi\vbxctl

whello

A non-OWL, C++ program that shows one way to build classes over the Windows API. Its 275 lines will probably convince you that a class library like OWL really *does* make your life simpler.

OWL Base Classes:

OWL Instanced Classes:

BC4 Sample in: \bc4\examples\windows\whello

WM_PAINT

Demonstrates how the all-important WM_PAINT message draws in a conservative—and sometimes unexpected—way.

Chapter: 6

OWL Base Classes: TApplication, TFrameWindow

OWL Instanced Classes: TBrush

Book Sample In: \DISK\WM_PAINT

Appendix J: TWindow Message Response Function Prototypes

Message	*OWL Message Response Function Prototype*
WM_ACTIVATE	void EvActivate(UINT active, BOOL minimized, HWND hWndOther)
WM_ACTIVATEAPP (Win32)	void EvActivateApp(BOOL active, HANDLE threadId)
WM_ACTIVATEAPP (Win16)	void EvActivateApp(BOOL active, HTASK hTask)
WM_ASKCBFORMATNAME	void EvAskCBFormatName(UINT bufLen, char far* buffer)
WM_CANCELMODE	void EvCancelMode()
WM_CHANGECBCHAIN	void EvChangeCBChain(UINT bufLen, char far* buffer)
WM_CHAR	void EvChar(UINT key, UINT repeatCount, UINT flags)
WM_CHARTOITEM	int EvCharToItem(UINT key, HWND hWndListBox, UINT caretPos)
WM_CHILDACTIVATE	void EvChildActivate()
WM_CHILDINVALID	void EvChildInvalid(HWND)
WM_CLOSE	void EvClose()
WM_COMPACTING	void EvCompacting(UINT compactRatio)

Message	*OWL Message Response Function Prototype*
WM_COMPAREITEM	LRESULT EvCompareItem(UINT ctrlId, COMPAREITEMSTRUCT far& cmpInfo)
WM_CREATE	int EvCreate(CREATESTRUCT far &)
WM_CTLCOLOR	HBRUSH EvCtlColor(HDC, HWND hWndChild, UINT ctlType)
WM_DEADCHAR	void EvDeadChar(UINT deadKey, UINT repeatCount, UINT flags)
WM_DELETEITEM	void EvDeleteItem(UINT ctrlId, DELETEITEMSTRUCT far& delInfo)
WM_DESTROY	void EvDestroy()
WM_DESTROYCLIPBOARD	void EvDestroyClipboard()
WM_DEVMODECHANGE	void EvDevModeChange(char far* devMode)
WM_DRAWCLIPBOARD	void EvDrawClipboard()
WM_DRAWITEM	void EvDrawItem(UINT ctrlId, DRAWITEMSTRUCT far& drawInfo)
WM_DROPFILES	void EvDropFiles(TDropInfo dropInfo)
WM_ENABLE	void EvEnable(BOOL enabled)
WM_ENDSESSION	void EvEndSession(BOOL endSession)
WM_ENTERIDLE	void EvEnterIdle(UINT source, HWND hWndDlg)
WM_ERASEBKGND	BOOL EvEraseBkgnd(HDC)
WM_FONTCHANGE	void EvFontChange()
WM_GETDLGCODE	UINT EvGetDlgCode()
WM_GETMINMAXINFO	void EvGetMinMaxInfo(MINMAXINFO far &)
WM_GETTEXT	void EvGetText(UINT bufLen, char far* buffer)
WM_GETTEXTLENGTH	UINT EvGetTextLength()
WM_HOTKEY (Win32)	void EvHotKey(int idHotKey)
WM_HSCROLL	void EvHScroll(UINT scrollCode, UINT thumbPos, HWND hWndCtl)
WM_HSCROLLCLIPBOARD	void EvHScrollClipboard(HWND hwndView, UINT scrollCode, UINT pos)
WM_ICONERASEBKGND	void EvIconEraseBkgnd(HDC)

Message	*OWL Message Response Function Prototype*
WM_INITMENU	void EvInitMenu(HMENU)
WM_INITMENUPOPUP	void EvInitMenuPopup(HMENU hPopupMenu, UINT index, BOOL sysMenu)
WM_INPUTFOCUS (Win32)	void EvInputFocus(BOOL gainingFocus)
WM_KEYDOWN	void EvKeyDown(UINT key, UINT repeatCount, UINT flags)
WM_KEYUP	void EvKeyUp(UINT key, UINT repeatCount, UINT flags)
WM_KILLFOCUS	void EvKillFocus(HWND hWndGetFocus)
WM_LBUTTONDBLCLK	void EvLButtonDblClk(UINT modKeys, TPoint& point)
WM_LBUTTONDOWN	void EvLButtonDown(UINT modKeys, TPoint& point)
WM_LBUTTONUP	void EvLButtonUp(UINT modKeys, TPoint& point)
WM_MBUTTONDBLCLK	void EvMButtonDblClk(UINT modKeys, TPoint& point)
WM_MBUTTONDOWN	void EvMButtonDown(UINT modKeys, TPoint& point)
WM_MBUTTONUP	void EvMButtonUp(UINT modKeys, TPoint& point)
WM_MDIACTIVATE	void EvMDIActivate(HWND hWndActivated, HWND hWndDeactivated)
WM_MDICREATE	LRESULT EvMDICreate(MDICREATESTRUCT far& crs)
WM_MENUCHAR	UINT EvMenuChar(UINT nChar, UINT menuType, HMENU hMenu)
WM_MENUSELECT	void EvMenuSelect(UINT menuItemId, UINT flags, HMENU hMenu)
WM_MEASUREITEM	void EvMeasureItem(UINT ctrlId, MEASUREITEMSTRUCT far& msrInfo)
WM_MOUSEACTIVATE	UINT EvMouseActivate(HWND hWndTopLevel, UINT hitTestCode, UINT msg)
WM_MOUSEMOVE	void EvMouseMove(UINT modKeys, TPoint& point)
WM_MOVE	void EvMove(TPoint &clientOrigin)

Message	*OWL Message Response Function Prototype*
WM_NCACTIVATE	BOOL EvNCActivate(BOOL active)
WM_NCCALCSIZE	UINT EvNCCalcSize(BOOL calcValidRects, NCCALCSIZE_PARAMS far &)
WM_NCCREATE	BOOL EvNCCreate(CREATESTRUCT far &)
WM_NCDESTROY	void EvNCDestroy()
WM_NCHITTEST	UINT EvNCHitTest(TPoint& point)
WM_NCLBUTTONDBLCLK	void EvNCLButtonDblClk(UINT hitTest, TPoint& point)
WM_NCLBUTTONDOWN	void EvNCLButtonDown(UINT hitTest, TPoint& point)
WM_NCLBUTTONUP	void EvNCLButtonUp(UINT hitTest, TPoint& point)
WM_NCMBUTTONDBLCLK	void EvNCMButtonDblClk(UINT hitTest, TPoint& point)
WM_NCMBUTTONDOWN	void EvNCMButtonDown(UINT hitTest, TPoint& point)
WM_NCMBUTTONUP	void EvNCMButtonUp(UINT hitTest, TPoint& point)
WM_NCMOUSEMOVE	void EvNCMouseMove(UINT hitTest, TPoint& point)
WM_NCPAINT	void EvNCPaint()
WM_NCRBUTTONDBLCLK	void EvNCRButtonDblClk(UINT hitTest, TPoint& point)
WM_NCRBUTTONDOWN	void void EvNCRButtonDown(UINT hitTest, TPoint& point)
WM_NCRBUTTONUP	void EvNCRButtonUp(UINT hitTest, TPoint& point)
WM_OTHERWINDOWCREATED	void EvOtherWindowCreated(HWND hWnd)
WM_OTHERWINDOWDESTROYED*	void EvOtherWindowDestroyed(HWND hWnd)
WM_PAINT	void EvPaint()
WM_PAINTCLIPBOARD	void EvPaintClipboard(HWND, HANDLE hPS)
WM_PAINTICON	void EvPaintIcon()
WM_PALETTECHANGED	void EvPaletteChanged(HWND hWndPalChg)

Message	*OWL Message Response Function Prototype*
WM_PALETTEISCHANGING	void EvPaletteIsChanging(HWND hWnd)
WM_PARENTNOTIFY	void EvParentNotify(UINT event, UINT Value1, UINT Value2)
WM_POWER	int EvPower(UINT powerEvent)
WM_QUERYDRAGICON	HANDLE EvQueryDragIcon()
WM_QUERYENDSESSION	BOOL EvQueryEndSession()
WM_QUERYNEWPALETTE	BOOL EvQueryNewPalette()
WM_QUERYOPEN	BOOL EvQueryOpen()
WM_RBUTTONDBLCLK	void EvRButtonDblClk(UINT modKeys, TPoint& point)
WM_RBUTTONDOWN	void EvRButtonDown(UINT modKeys, TPoint& point)
WM_RBUTTONUP	void EvRButtonUp(UINT modKeys, TPoint& point)
WM_RENDERALLFORMATS	void EvRenderAllFormats()
WM_RENDERFORMAT	void EvRenderFormat(UINT dataFormat)
WM_SETCURSOR	BOOL EvSetCursor(HWND hWndCursor, UINT hitTest, UINT mouseMsg)
WM_SETFOCUS	void EvSetFocus(HWND hWndLostFocus)
WM_SETFONT	void EvSetFont(HFONT)
WM_SETTEXT	void EvSetText(char far* text)
WM_SHOWWINDOW	void EvShowWindow(BOOL show, UINT stat)
WM_SIZE	void EvSize(UINT sizeType, TSize& size)
WM_SIZECLIPBOARD	void EvSizeClipboard(HWND hWndViewer, HANDLE hRect)
WM_SPOOLERSTATUS	void EvSpoolerStatus(UINT jobStatus, UINT jobsLeft)
WM_SYSCHAR	void EvSysChar(UINT key, UINT Count, UINT flags)
WM_SYSCOLORCHANGE	void EvSysColorChange()
WM_SYSCOMMAND	void EvSysCommand(UINT cmdType, TPoint& point)
WM_SYSDEADCHAR	void EvSysDeadChar(UINT key, UINT Count, UINT flags)

Message	*OWL Message Response Function Prototype*
WM_SYSKEYDOWN	void EvSysKeyDown(UINT key, UINT Count, UINT flags)
WM_SYSKEYUP	void EvSysKeyUp(UINT key, UINT Count, UINT flags)
WM_SYSTEMERROR	void EvSystemError(UINT error)
WM_TIMECHANGE	void EvTimeChange()
WM_TIMER	void EvTimer(UINT timerId)
WM_VKEYTOITEM	int EvVKeyToItem(UINT key, HWND hWndList, UINT caretPos)
WM_VSCROLL	void EvVScroll(UINT scrollCode, UINT thumbPos, HWND hWndCtl)
WM_VSCROLLCLIPBOARD	void EvVScrollClipboard(HWND hWndView, UINT scrollCode, UINT pos)
WM_WINDOWPOSCHANGED	void EvWindowPosChanged(WINDOWPOS far& windowPos)
WM_WINDOWPOSCHANGING	void EvWindowPosChanging(WINDOWPOS far& windowPos)
WM_WININICHANGE	void EvWinIniChange(char far* section)

Appendix K: ObjectWindows Hierarchy Diagram

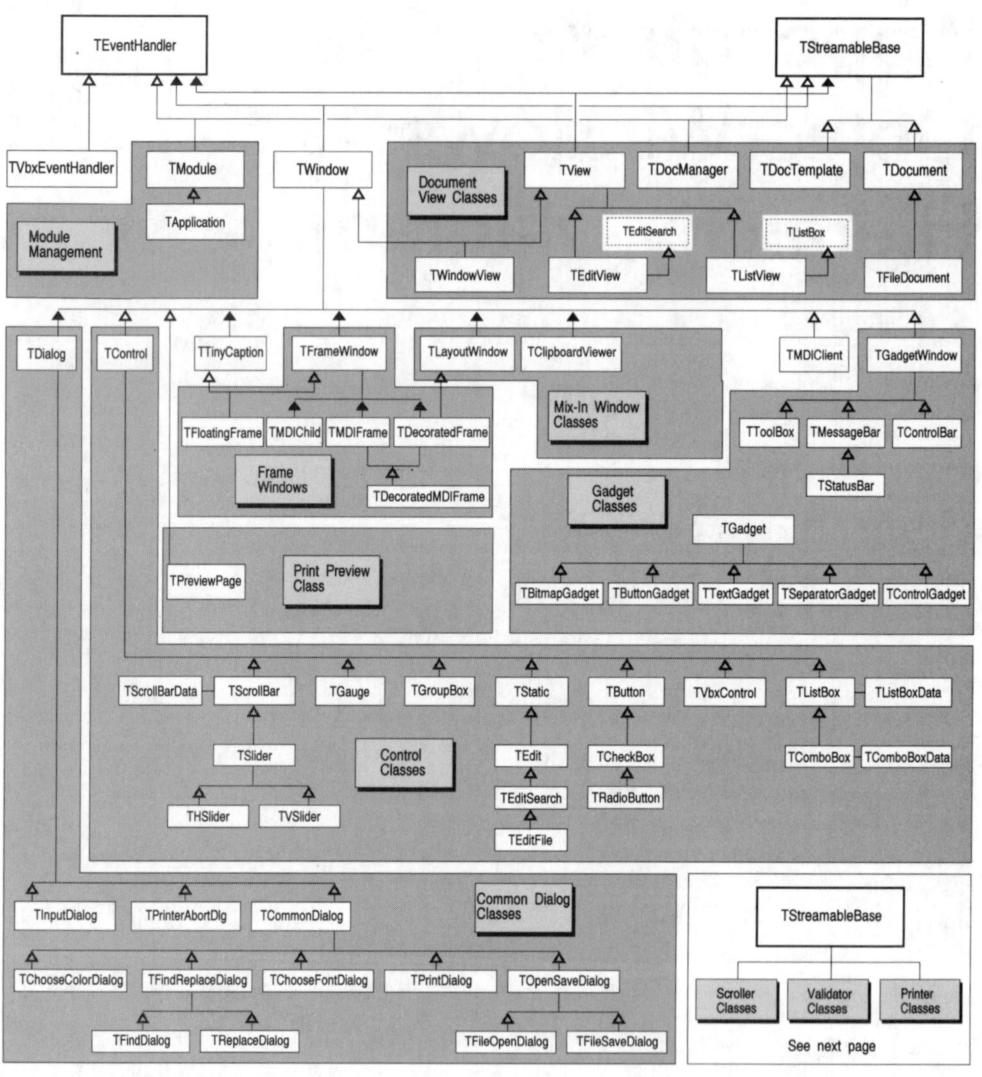
TEventHandler
TStreamableBase
TVbxEventHandler
TModule
TApplication
Module Management
TWindow
Document View Classes
TView
TDocManager
TDocTemplate
TDocument
TEditSearch
TListBox
TWindowView
TEditView
TListView
TFileDocument
TDialog
TControl
TTinyCaption
TFrameWindow
TLayoutWindow
TClipboardViewer
TMDIClient
TGadgetWindow
Mix-In Window Classes
TFloatingFrame
TMDIChild
TMDIFrame
TDecoratedFrame
Frame Windows
TDecoratedMDIFrame
TToolBox
TMessageBar
TControlBar
TStatusBar
Gadget Classes
TGadget
TPreviewPage
Print Preview Class
TBitmapGadget
TButtonGadget
TTextGadget
TSeparatorGadget
TControlGadget
TScrollBarData
TScrollBar
TGauge
TGroupBox
TStatic
TButton
TVbxControl
TListBox
TListBoxData
TSlider
Control Classes
TEdit
TCheckBox
TComboBox
TComboBoxData
THSlider
TVSlider
TEditSearch
TRadioButton
TEditFile
TInputDialog
TPrinterAbortDlg
TCommonDialog
Common Dialog Classes
TStreamableBase
TChooseColorDialog
TFindReplaceDialog
TChooseFontDialog
TPrintDialog
TOpenSaveDialog
Scroller Classes
Validator Classes
Printer Classes
TFindDialog
TReplaceDialog
TFileOpenDialog
TFileSaveDialog
See next page
Nonvirtual inheritance
Virtual inheritance

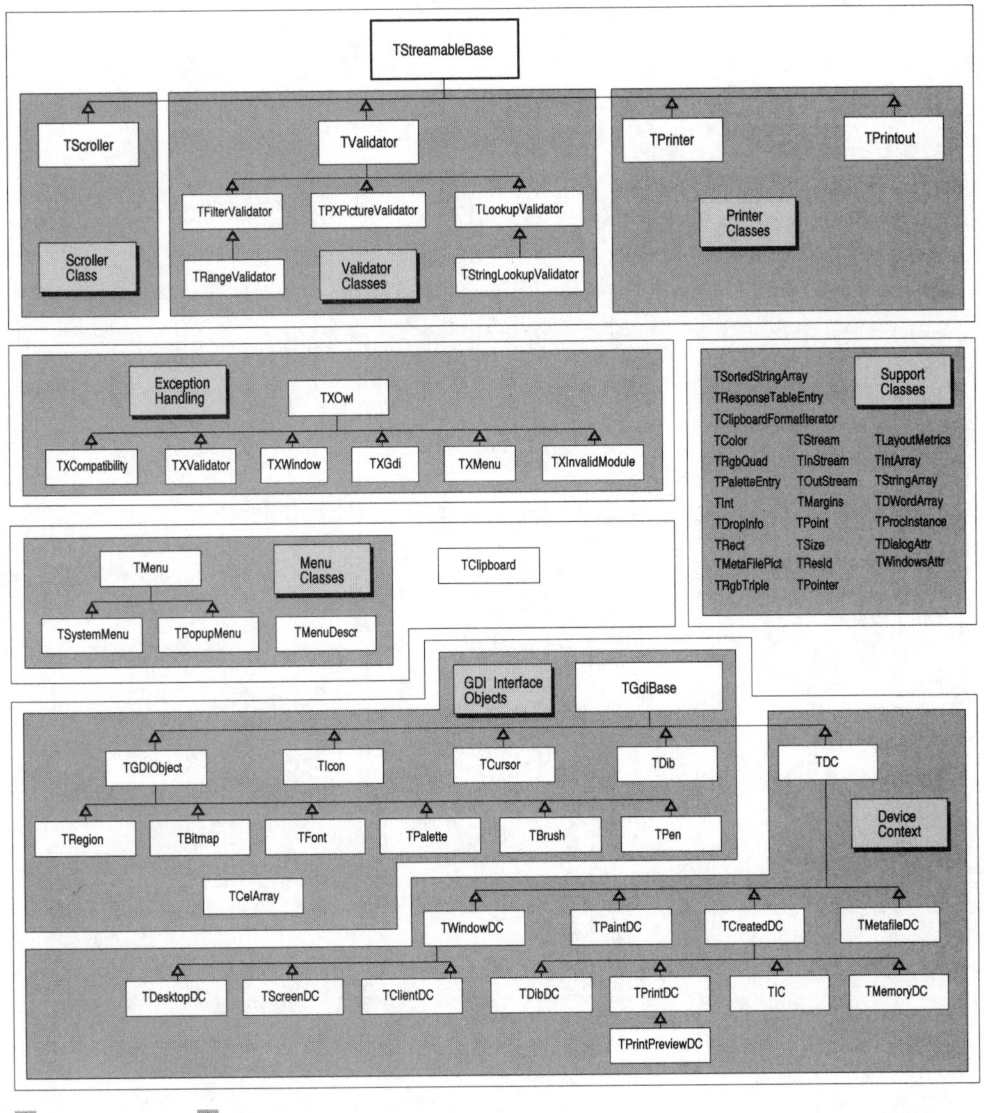

Nonvirtual inheritance   Virtual inheritance

Index

A

E

F

G

H

I

J

K

L

Q

R

S

T

U

V

X